D1423078

WORLD HISTORY FACTFINDER

WORLD HISTORY FACTFINDER

Colin McEvedy

CRESSET PRESS
London Sydney Auckland Johannesburg

Editor
ADRIAN SINGTON

Design and cartography
BRIDGEWATER ASSOCIATES

Picture research
JACKIE COOKSON

Additional material
RICHARD JONES
MALCOLM FALKUS
PETER WAY

Datechart research 1665–1984
DAVID HERMAN
GUY ARNOLD

This impression published in 1989 by
Cresset Press, an imprint of
Century Hutchinson Limited,
Brookmount House, 62–65 Chandos Place,
Covent Garden, London WC2N 4NW

Century Hutchinson Australia Pty Limited,
89–91 Albion Street, Surry Hills, Sydney,
New South Wales 2010, Australia

Century Hutchinson New Zealand Limited,
PO Box 40–086, Glenfield,
Auckland 10, New Zealand

Century Hutchinson South Africa Pty Limited,
PO Box 337, Bergvlei, 2012 South Africa

First published in Great Britain in 1984
by Century Publishing Co. Ltd

Designed and produced by Grisewood and Dempsey Ltd
Elsley House, 24–30 Great Titchfield Street
London W1P7AD

Printed in Italy by Vallardi Industrie Grafiche, Milan.

Phototypeset by Southern Positive and Negatives (SPAN),
Lingfield, Surrey

British Library Cataloguing in Publication Data
McEvedy, Colin
The Century world history factfinder.
1. Chronology, Historical
I. Title
902'.02

ISBN 0 7126 3459 2
D. L. TO: 1313–1984

CONTENTS

INTRODUCTION

In the World History Factfinder *the author has attempted to produce a logical, comprehensive and accurate record of man's achievements. In doing so, his first consideration has been to recognize that most of those who will use the book will seek information on political, military and diplomatic history. This therefore forms the primary strand of the work. At the same time, he has acknowledged the ever-growing interest in non-political aspects of history, particularly in the arts, science, technology and, most notably, in social history. These form the subsidiary strands of the work.*

There are those who would argue that such an 'in the round' presentation of historical events does not easily lend itself to a book of this scope: social, religious, intellectual and cultural currents are often hard to trace back to source and are difficult to define precisely. Nevertheless, we agreed that some attempt to give more than a passing glimpse at the side-shows of history was worth while. In the attempt we have squarely faced up to the many inherent problems – for instance, trying to reconcile variations of dating of notable artistic or social landmarks; or of attributing an invention or discovery which may have evolved as a result of the work of several people independently and in different places.

In order to put the bare factual landmarks of this chronology into some perspective, every spread is accompanied by a background essay together with maps and photographs which expand and explain particular historical highlights. This is an important feature of the work.

If we have helped to give a lively all-round perspective of our past, and provided a starting-point for further investigations then we shall have achieved our purpose.

Adrian Sington

The universe of which we form an infinitesimal part made its explosive appearance some 18 billion years ago (BYR). Our galaxy began to condense at about 14 BYR: our sun, a relative latecomer among this group of stars, not before 4.5 BYR. Earth and the other planets emerged at the same time as the sun, the accretion of new material ceasing around 3.9 BYR. There are rocks on Earth (in south-west Greenland) which have been dated to 3.8 BYR.

Life of a sort appeared soon after that. The earliest form for which we have physical evidence consists of the aggregations of bacteria known as stromatolites: specimens dating back to 3.5 BYR have been found in Australia where living versions still occur. These bacteria utilized sunlight in their vital processes but they were not plants and produced no oxygen – the earth's atmosphere at this time consisted mainly of carbon dioxide and nitrogen. The change to an oxygen-rich atmosphere took place around 1.7 BYR which suggests that this is the date at which the photosynthetic processes that are the basis of plant life evolved.

Over the next billion years the various single cell forms ancestral to present day plants and animals established their separate identities. Seven hundred million years ago (700 MYR) the emphasis shifted to multicellular forms and by 570 MYR the seas, and to a lesser extent the land, were stocked with a wide range of invertebrate life forms – worms, wood lice, squids, starfish and so on. Some species had rudimentary internal skeletons, a line of development that was to lead to the appearance of the first fishes by 500 MYR. Lobe-finned fish started to scuttle across the mudflats and beaches in search of food during the Devonian era (400–345 MYR): by its end newt-like creatures, the prototypes of the order Amphibia, had carried the vertebrate lineage firmly ashore.

If some of the animals around at this time would have seemed familiar to us, the map of the world would not. The continents were drifting towards each other, Europe colliding with North America around 400 MYR and the huge aggregate known as Gondwanaland (consisting of South America, Africa, India, Antarctica and Australia) moving up from the south to combine with the two of them by 280 MYR. By 230 MYR Asia had attached itself to the eastern edge of Europe so that the world's land mass consisted of a single supercontinent, Pangaea. This lasted until 150 MYR when the individual continents began to break off and move away – first Antarctica-Australia, then (separately) North and South America. Since then they have progressed steadily to their present positions leaving the Old World assemblage essentially intact.

For most of the time that this continental square dance was going on the dominant form of advanced life was the reptile order and the most successful form of reptile was the dinosaur. Plant-eating Sauropods like *Brontosaurus* munched their way through the Jurassic and Cretaceous, one eye cocked against the approach of predatory Therapods such as *Tyrannosaurus*. Related forms, the Pterodactyls, glided through the skies while Ichthyosaurs and Plesiosaurs chased fish not very different from today's through the Mesozoic seas. This reptilian Eden came to an abrupt end in the Great Extinction of 65 million years ago following which the Mammalia emerged as the dominant group. The Mammalia soon produced the new creatures needed to fill the gaps left by the reptiles. Dolphins and seals replaced the Ichthyosaurs and Plesiosaurs, Ungulates and elephants the Sauropods, carnivores the Theropods. Only in one element did the mammals fail to carry the day: the skies filled not with bats, but with birds which, believe it or not, represent a comeback by the dinosaur stock.

The mammals also produced an entirely new evolutionary line – the arborial, binocular primate. This animal prospered because it put brains before brawn, kept its body plan simple and concentrated on expanding its behavioural repertoire. Within 30 million years forms as advanced as present day baboons had appeared in the Old World; another 20 million years and creatures similar to today's great apes were to be seen in the forests of Africa and Asia. The last 10 million years have seen the final steps to Australopithecine apeman (4 million years ago), primitive man (Homo erectus, one million years ago) and the first versions of Homo sapiens (100,000 years ago).

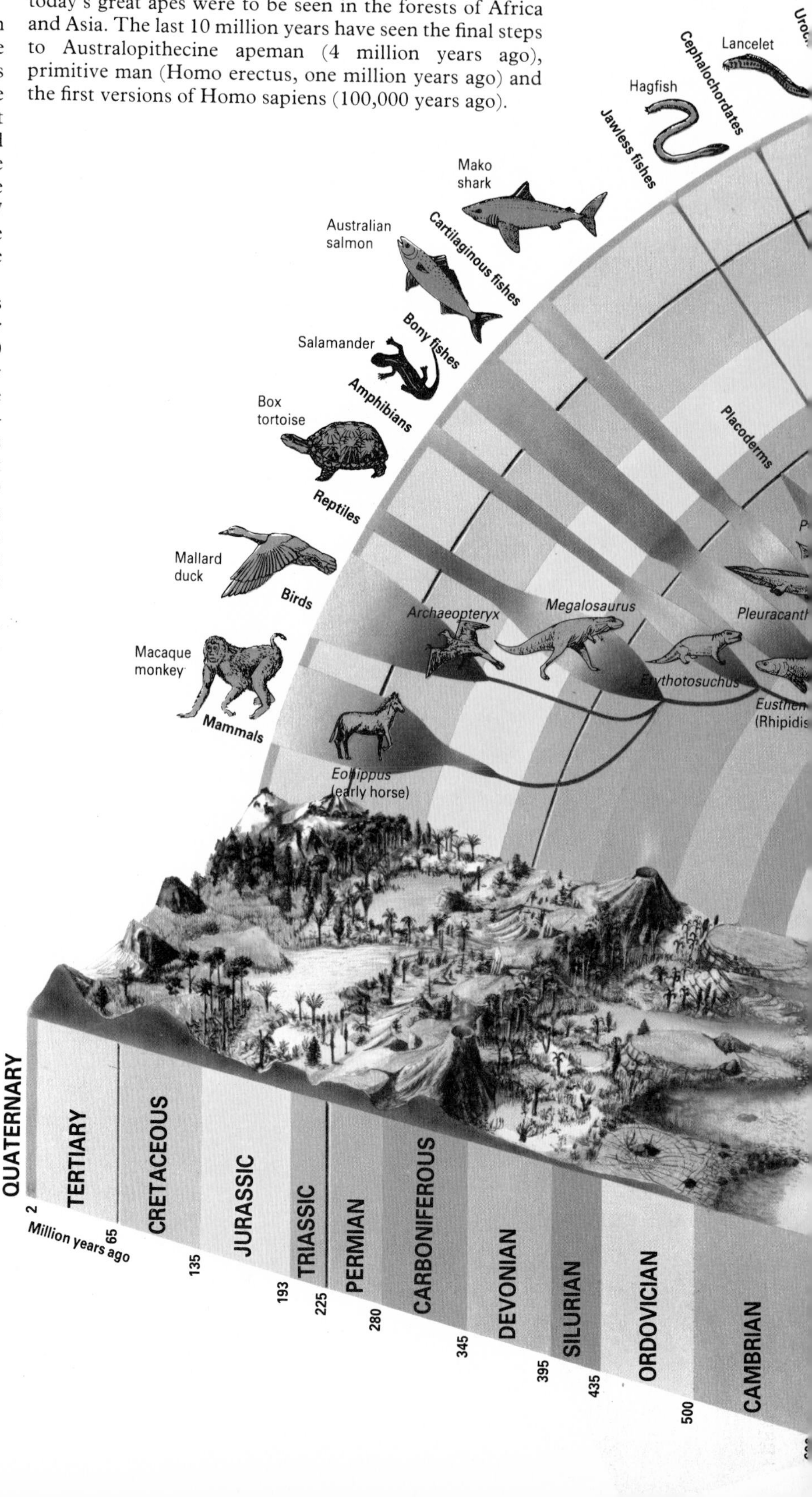

The 'Great Extinction' that put paid to the dinosaurs 65 million years ago has received a lot of attention lately because of the discovery of an iridium-rich layer in deposits of this date. This raises the possibility that an iridium-containing meteorite of kilometre size hit the earth at this time, raising a cloud of dust that totally obscured the sun. A few years of this would have caused the death of most plants and all large animals, leaving the small nocturnal mammals as the unwitting beneficiaries of the catastrophe.

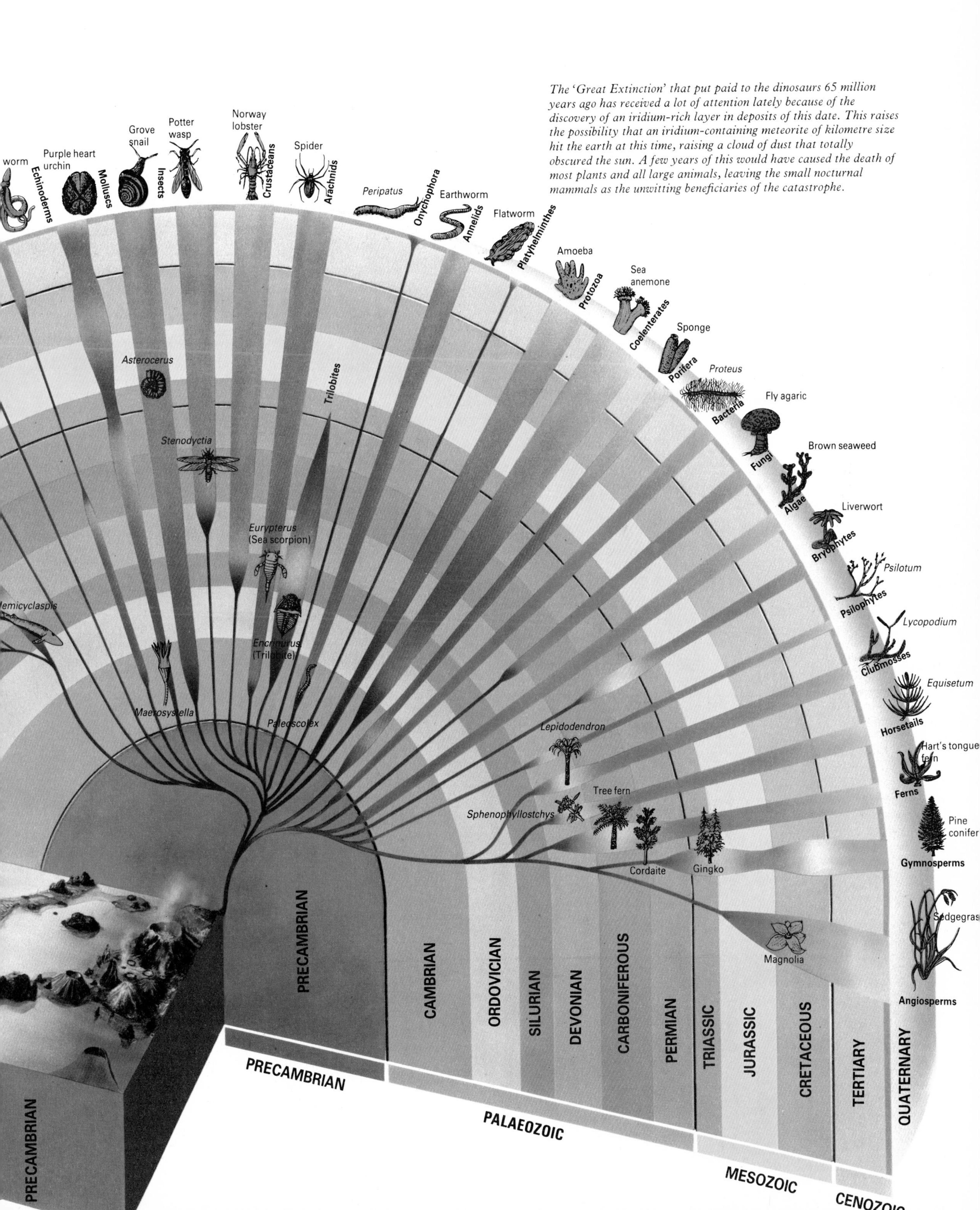

THE

ANCIENT WORLD

3000 BC - 500 BC

Human beings have undoubtedly made a success of their first million years but nearly all the success has been in the last one per cent of this time. Between 1,000,000 BP (Before the Present) and 10,000 BP human society changed very little: it consisted of family-sized groups scattered thinly across the Old World to a total of something like a million individuals. Homo sapiens evolved in a physical sense, becoming bigger and brainier, but his life style hardly altered.

The last 10,000 years have seen one revolution after another. Each has been accompanied by a quantum leap in population, by an increase in specialization and a decrease in the numbers directly engaged in the collection and production of food. There have also been important increases in the size of the community in which the typical individual lives. Of the billions of people alive today, many live in urban conglomerates counting several million each.

This process of change was initiated by the neolithic revolution and the subsequent invention of writing, events that took place in the Middle East between 7000 and 3000 BC.

Right: Apemen and Homo erectus. The Australopithecines are the 'missing link' between apes and people that Darwin visualized when he first put forward the idea of evolution. The unexpected thing about them is that whereas their skulls are primitive and their brains small – little bigger than an ape's – their bodies are similar to ours. It seems that the business of walking upright was solved first and that it was only when this had been done that the development of the brain began. This fits in with the idea that it was the use of the hand for complicated tasks that is responsible for the increase in brain size. The Australopithecines evolved in sub-Saharan Africa and never spread outside this area. The first true humans – Homo erectus as opposed to present day Homo sapiens – must have evolved there too but they soon spread to the other parts of the Old World. Their remains have been found in Europe, Asia and Indonesia as well as in both northern and southern parts of Africa.

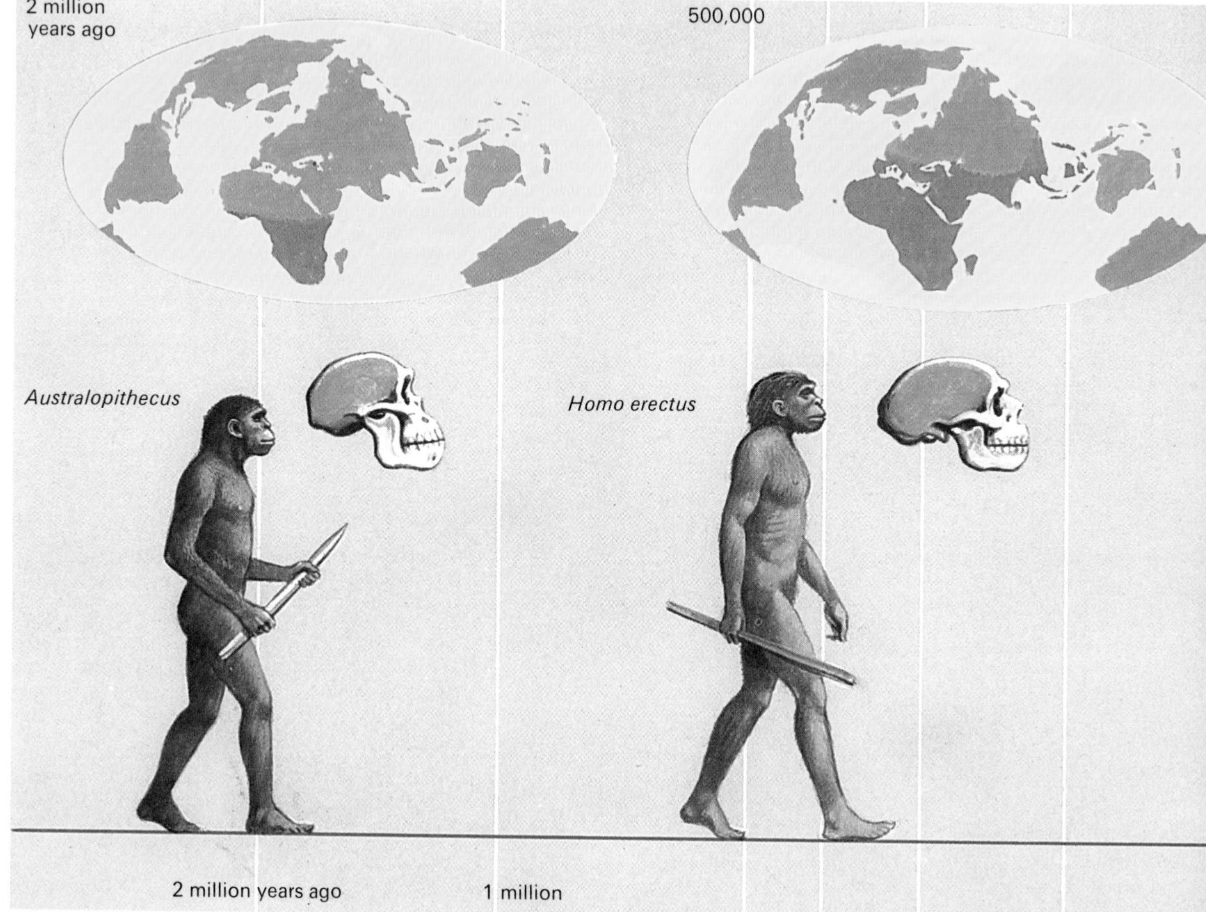

FROM PREHISTORY TO HISTORY

The first important events in man's history are the acquisition of the two traits that mark him off from the apes, tool-making and speech. Neither appeared overnight and it would be nonsense to try to put an exact date to either, but what we can say for sure is that the two developed together. The link is 'handedness' – the preferential use of one hand rather than the other hand when performing complicated manipulations. Apes show no such preference but we do and our speech centre is always built alongside the controls for the preferred hand – the right one in 90 per cent of cases. In fact, what look like two separate functions are really just the software and hardware of the same system. As we know that the earliest form of man, *Homo erectus*, was a tool maker it follows that speech and tool-making are as old as he is. On current estimates this is a million years, give or take a quarter of a million.

The next important advance came comparatively recently. As the last Ice Age drew to an end around 10,000 BC the big game animals, which were specially adapted to cold weather living, began to get scarce. Man – *Homo sapiens* by now – had to search for alternative sources of food. One of the answers he came up with was the seed of the wheat plant which he learned to harvest and bake into bread. By about 7000 BC he had also learned to plant it. This produced a revolution in his habits. From being a roving hunter and food-gatherer he became a sedentary food-producer with an interest in fields and flocks that he was reluctant to be parted from. This change from non-farming to farming society, from Paleolithic to Neolithic can be dated fairly accurately: it happened in the 8th millennium BC in the Middle East, the 6th in Europe, the 4th in East Asia and the 3rd in sub-Saharan Africa. It was achieved, quite independently, by the Amerindians (with maize as a staple) in the 2nd millennium BC.

The last in the series of discoveries that fundamentally altered human society can be placed in time with even more accuracy. Towards the end of the 4th millennium BC – around 3200 BC, give or take a hundred years or so – the Sumerians of lower Mesopotamia (the southern half of modern Iraq) began to write. They used a stylus of wood or bone to incise or impress characters on tablets of clay. At first they were simply recording the numbers and quantities of things that interest people in an agricultural community: beer and bread, sheep and cows, cloth and clothes. By the beginning of the 3rd millennium they had developed phonetic signs and were able to record proper sentences. The other peoples of the Near East, the Elamites, the Akkadians and the Egyptians copied the Sumerian system which eventually spread to India and China. Their scripts look quite different because they all invented new signs of their own but they made use of them in exactly the same way as the Sumerians and there is no doubt at all that they derive from the Sumerian prototype.

Sumerian writing was incredibly cumbersome. As is the case with its only surviving descendant, Chinese, its complexities are too great for the average person to fully master and literacy must always have been confined to a few specially trained scribes. In fact, it is arguable that writing only began to transform society when the system was simplified by the Phoenicians and Greeks in the period 1250–750 BC. Nevertheless, it is the Sumerians who led the way: they were the first to cross the divide between prehistory and history, between barbarism and civilization. Because they were literate we know who they were: because they kept records we can begin our chronology.

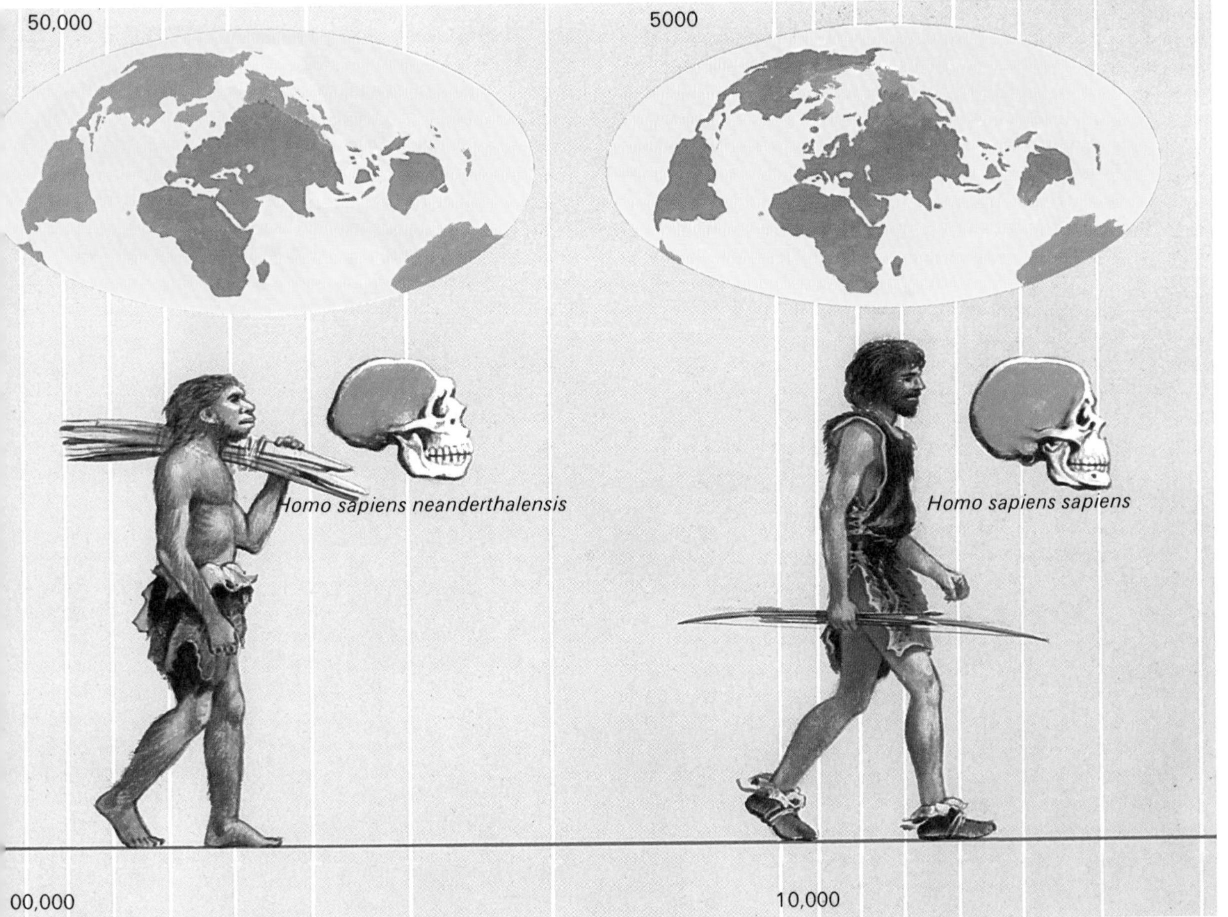

Left: Homo sapiens. The recent history of the Earth is characterized by intensely cold spells lasting a hundred thousand years or so. During these ice ages Canada and northern Europe were covered by glaciers hundreds of metres thick and because of the immense amount of water locked up in these ice-caps the sea level was anything up to 100 m lower than it is today. This made it easier for men to move through island chains such as Indonesia and it was during the last ice age, around 50,000 BC, that men first reached Australia. The colonization of the Americas via Alaska was a trickier business because although the sea receded sufficiently to expose a land bridge where the Bering Strait is now, the American end was still blocked by ice. And as the ice melted, so the sea level rose and the bridge disappeared. There was only a short period in which the bridge was there and the ice was not, perhaps no more than a hundred years. However long it was, it was enough and, by 10,000 BC one or more bands of hunters were safely across.

	3000–2800*	2800–2700	2700–2600	2600–2500
Politics & Military History	= Menes, King of Upper Egypt, conquers the Delta, unifies the country and becomes first pharaoh of the first dynasty. This makes Egypt the first nation state, for though the Mesopotamians are in most respects more advanced, they remain divided into separate 'city states' till the time of Sargon the Great 2400 BC H).	= Mesopotamia: first dynasties of Kish and Uruk. No entries for Ur in the King lists though the city certainly had a royal family by this date (see below).	= Third dynasty in Egypt, first dynasty at Ur. Ur wins supremacy of Lower Mesopotamia, then loses it as a result of Elamite incursions.	= Fourth dynasty in Egypt, supremacy of Lagash in Lower Mesopotamia.
Cities & Social Development	= Menes establishes his residence at Memphis at the junction of Upper and Lower Egypt. The biggest settlements at this time were all in Mesopotamia where there were half a dozen places – Kish, Lagash, Ur, Uruk, Nippur, and Umma – that could properly be called towns. Egypt, by contrast, was a land of villages and even Memphis would not have been more than a royal *kraal*.	= Hero-king Gilgamesh builds the city wall of Uruk enclosing an area of 450 hectares. This is an order of magnitude greater than the norm for a Mesopotamian town and suggests that Uruk was not only the leading place in Sumer but the first place where the use of the word city is appropriate. The implication is that it had a population of 10–15,000 rather than 4000.	= Imhotep builds the step pyramid of Saqqara for Pharaoh Zoser. = 'Royal tombs' at Ur show that the city's rulers had their household servants slaughtered and buried with them.	= Mortuary obsession of the Egyptian pharaohs reaches its first peak with the construction of the three pyramids of Gizeh. The sphinx, a human-headed lion carved from living rock, forms part of Chephren's mortuary complex.
Discovery & Invention	= Earliest examples of Egyptian hieroglyphic and Elamite pictographic scripts. Neither of these scripts can be classified as original inventions, they are too obviously derived from the Sumerian cuneiform system for that, but the Egyptian method of writing does involve new materials – ink, and the form of paper known as papyrus. Until the invention of true paper (AD 105 D) this was much the most convenient of the various materials (animal hides, clay tablets, pottery flakes) available to the scribe.		= Evolution of masonry techniques at Saqqara.	= Simple (outflow) water-clocks in use in Egypt.
The Arts	= Victory tablet of King Narmer (Cairo museum), usually identified with Menes. This shows that the Egyptian state had already developed some of its most characteristic emblems (for the gods, for the king, for the provinces) and that Egyptian artists had established conventional ways of representing these. The carving of low relief friezes with outsize pharaohs and obedient lines of subjects separated by hieroglyphic eulogies, was to continue as long as pharaonic civilization lasted. Much the same could be said of an alabaster vase found at Uruk (Baghdad museum) which illustrates the panoply of Mesopotamia's gods, priests and kings.	= 'Standard of Ur', a decorative panel in shell mosaic showing a king, his ass-drawn war chariots and his retinue of spearmen on one side, and the celebration of the victory won by the army on the other (British Museum). Specimens of the lyres shown in use at the celebration have been recovered.	= Reliefs and statues in the Saqqara complex show that Egyptian artists have achieved complete mastery of their idiom. Particularly notable are the limestone reliefs and seated statues of King Zoser and the wood reliefs of his courtier Hesire.	= 'Vulture stele' of Eannatum, ruler of Lagash, celebrating his defeat of Umma (Louvre). This gives a grimmer picture of a Mesopotamian army than the 'Standard of Ur'. = Examples of portrait sculpture become relatively frequent in Egypt: among the finest are a series of Mycerinus between pairs of goddesses (Cairo).

Though ancient Egyptian culture was an offshoot of Mesopotamia's, the Egyptians had one thing the Sumerians did not, good building stone. It was not used in the earliest days of the Egyptian kingdom: the pharaohs of the first two dynasties built their palaces and tombs out of mud brick, just like the Mesopotamians. But when Zoser, founding pharaoh of the 3rd dynasty, started work on his funeral complex, he let his chief minister, Imhotep, talk him into trying stone. After all, the idea was to make a structure that would last forever and brittle mud-brick could not be expected to do that.

The complex that Imhotep built consists of several dozen buildings arranged around three courts. Much of it seems to be a copy of the royal palace at Memphis, doubtless because the king hoped to keep up the same style in the next life as he had in this. But the dominating feature was a step-pyramid – the equivalent of a Mesopotamian ziggurat – built over the royal grave at Saqqara. It is partly ruined now but originally it rose in six massive stages to a height of 62 metres.

Zoser's immediate successors started step-pyramids very similar to his but for one reason or another none of them was ever completed. Probably the 3rd dynasty was just losing its grip. If so, the first pharaoh of the next dynasty, Sneferu, more than made up for the lost time. He built no less than three pyramids, one at Meidun and two at Dahshur. The one at Meidun started off as a step-pyramid but Sneferu, feeling no doubt that the design was not exploiting the possibilities of stone as a building material, decided to finish it off as a true pyramid with sloping sides. The change of plan did not work: the cladding slid off and the structure was ruined. The pyramid at south Dahshur, of which the bottom half had already been built, was hastily redesigned, the slope of the top half being reduced from 54° to 43°. And the same low angle was used from the start in Sneferu's third pyramid, north Dahshur.

Above: Reliefs from the tomb of Ti at Saqqara. Ti was the official in charge of the pyramid complex built by the pharaohs of the 5th dynasty at Abusir. His tomb contains some of the finest reliefs to survive from the age of the pyramid builders: this one shows his servants herding sheep and cattle.

This low angle does not suit a pyramid: to impress, it needs the steepness that Sneferu had tried for originally. Egypt's architects went back to their drawing boards and by the time Sneferu's son Cheops came to the throne they felt they had the answer: they would use big blocks of stone and lay the courses horizontally, rather than perpendicular to the face. Pharaoh Cheops approved the plans and the result, the first of the Gizeh pyramids, went up at a 51.5° angle – and stayed up.

*The chronology of this period has been reconstructed from the lists of kings kept by the scribes of Egypt and Mesopotamia. Given the number of years that each king reigned it is, in theory, possible to draw up a table of dates for each dynasty, but in practice the early entries are so obscure and corrupt that dates obtained in this manner could well be out by a hundred years either way. The situation gradually improves so that by the end of the millennium the error is probably down to ±50 years.

2500–2400	2400–2300	2300–2200	2200–2100	2100–2000	
= Kish ousts Lagash from the leadership of Sumer (southern Mesopotamia) and Akkad (central Mesopotamia). = Fifth dynasty in Egypt.	= Sargon the Great gains the throne of Kish and then establishes his supremacy over all Mesopotamia. = Sixth dynasty in Egypt. = Beginning of the Bell-Beaker movements in western Europe.	= Guti, tribesmen from the west of Iran, invade Mesopotamia and destroy Sargon's empire. = Death of Pepy II, last pharaoh of the 6th dynasty, is followed by a period of political fragmentation in Egypt with separate dynasties at Memphis (7th), Coptos (8th) and Heracleopolis (9th and 10th).	= Utuhegal, King of Uruk, drives out the Guti but is himself replaced as ruler of Mesopotamia by Urnammu, founder of the 3rd dynasty of Ur.	= The hegemony of Ur vanishes as its armies are defeated by the Elamites and Amorites. In the course of the century they gain control of Damascus, Aleppo, Mari, Assur and Babylon.* = Mentuhotep of Thebes, Upper Egypt, restores the unity of the country, establishing the Middle Kingdom** and the 12th dynasty.	Politics & Military History
= Spread of the Mesopotamian urban lifestyle to Upper Mesopotamia (Mari, Assur) and Syria (Aleppo, Ebla). = Era of simple henge (circular bank and ditch) monuments in England.	= Sargon establishes his capital at Agade in central Mesopotamia (exact site unknown)	= Agade destroyed by the Guti.	= Urnammu elaborates the temple-on-a-platform into the multi-storey ziggurat. He also promulgates a code of laws which includes a scale of payments in silver as fines for evil-doing.	= Triumph of Mentuhotep marks the beginning of monumental building at Thebes. = At Stonehenge the addition of a circle of bluestones to the funerary henge suggests it is acquiring a more elaborate function.	Cities & Social Development
= Cuneiform adapted for writing Akkadian: this eventually becomes the medium of diplomatic correspondence in the Middle East.	= Earliest examples of the Indus Valley script.				Discovery & Invention
= Abusir, Egypt: earliest version of Palm capital employed in the hall of pillars built by fifth dynasty Pharaoh Sahure.	= Bronze bust of an Akkadian ruler, possibly Sargon himself (Baghdad). = Copper statue of Pepi I, second pharaoh of the sixth dynasty, made by nailing worked copper plates to a wooden core (Cairo).	= Alabaster statuette of Pepy II and his mother (Brooklyn).	= Sumerian sculptural technique is shown at its finest in the series of diorite statues of Gudea, governor of Lagash (Louvre).	= Painted limestone statue of King Mentuhotep (Cairo). = Models of Egyptian life of great vivacity from the tomb of Chancellor Meker-Ra (Cairo, Metropolitan).	The Arts

Left: Step-pyramid of Zoser, Saqqara.

Right: Relief from the tomb of Ti, showing Ti hunting hippopotamus.

Below: Sections through the step-pyramid of Zoser, the pyramid of Sneferu at Meidun and the Great Pyramid of Cheops at Gizeh.

The complex set of passages within the Great Pyramid shows how the plan for the burial chamber evolved. Originally Cheops was to have been given an underground vault but the preparations for this were abandoned at an early stage in favour of a chamber deep in the heart of the pyramid. This too was abandoned when the architect decided to extend the obliquely rising section of the entrance corridor into a 'grand gallery' leading to an upper tomb chamber. This was the one in which Cheops was eventually buried.

There are a few more statistics to this pyramid. It was built to a high degree of accuracy, its sides being true to better than a tenth of one per cent. It was also built on a far bigger scale than any of its predecessors: it is reckoned that more than 2 million blocks of limestone, each averaging more than 2 tonnes in weight, went into its construction. Its height of 146.7 metres made it by far the tallest structure in the world and nothing taller went up and stayed up until modern times (see AD 1876 D). Other pharaohs built pyramids both alongside and elsewhere, but none of them tried ever to surpass Cheops: his pyramid remains, as it always will, the one and only Great Pyramid.

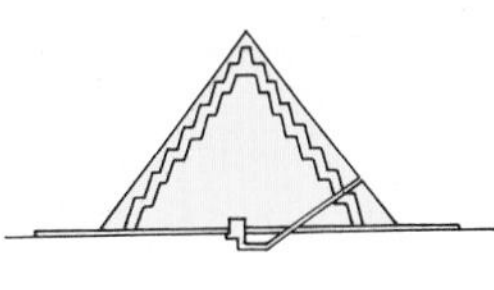

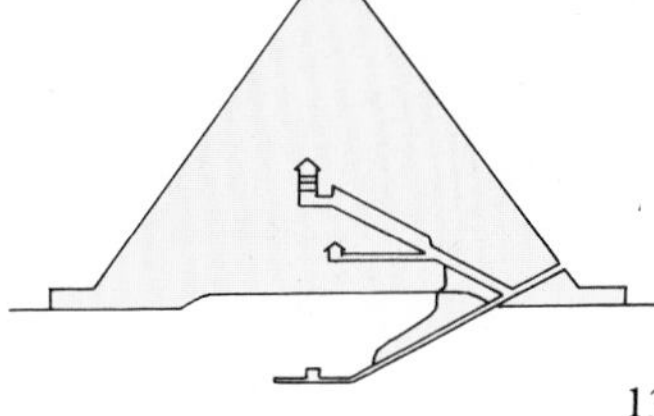

*The migration of Abraham is seen by some as a facet of the Amorite movement.
**Middle in time: it comes between the Old Kingdom founded by Menes and the New Kingdom of the post Hyksos period.

Left: Some of the near 3000 standing stones at Carnac, Brittany. The whole complex extends over 4 km, with the majority of the stones being arranged in parallel lines.

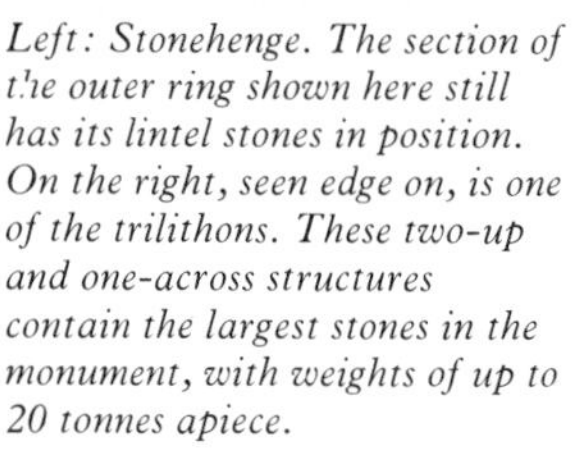

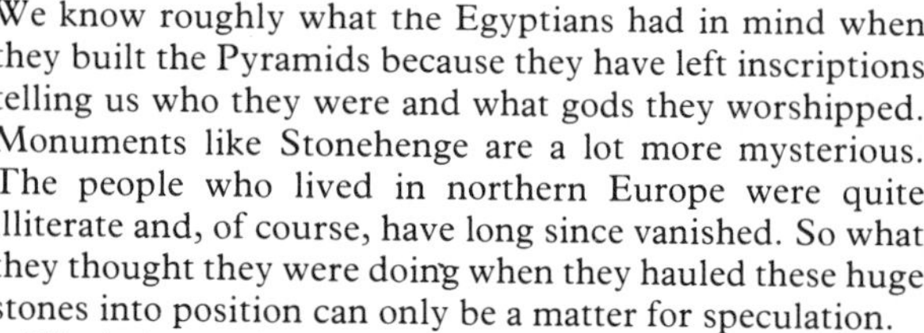

Left: Stonehenge. The section of the outer ring shown here still has its lintel stones in position. On the right, seen edge on, is one of the trilithons. These two-up and one-across structures contain the largest stones in the monument, with weights of up to 20 tonnes apiece.

Below: Circle of standing stones at Brogar, Orkney.

We know roughly what the Egyptians had in mind when they built the Pyramids because they have left inscriptions telling us who they were and what gods they worshipped. Monuments like Stonehenge are a lot more mysterious. The people who lived in northern Europe were quite illiterate and, of course, have long since vanished. So what they thought they were doing when they hauled these huge stones into position can only be a matter for speculation.

We do know that most megalithic structures – meaning buildings constructed of big, unshaped or only roughly shaped stones – are tombs, usually communal ones that remained in use for several generations. The megaliths were used to make the tomb chamber which was then buried under a mound of earth. Some of the oddest looking groups of megaliths are simply the exposed remains of these tomb chambers: over the centuries the rain has washed away the earth covering leaving the megaliths free standing. They may look like temples, especially if the capstones have remained in place, but they never had any such function and the tales told about them are just tales.

More truly enigmatic are the standing stones at Carnac in Brittany. There are literally thousands of these, many of them arranged in long columns 12 abreast. The rows are evenly spaced and there is no discernible central path-way: nevertheless, the most likely explanation for these 'alignments' is that they are ceremonial pathways of some sort. Certainly attempts to make out that they are 'Neolithic observatories' do not seem at all convincing.

Stonehenge, the most famous of all megalithic monuments, has been the subject of even more far-fetched theories. There is no doubt that its builders had the heavens in mind, for the ring faces the point on the horizon where the sun rises on Midsummer Day and it does so with an accuracy that cannot be due to chance. This orientation was preserved through many subsequent rebuildings so it is fair to deduce that it was considered an essential part of the monument's 'function'. On the other hand, there is no reason to read too much into it. The most likely function for Stonehenge is as a seasonal meeting place: the orientation indicating that hundreds of clans from far and wide gathered there on Midsummer Eve.

They must have come from far and wide. The bluestones used to mark out the ring of Stonehenge II (constructed c 2000 BC, as against c 3000 BC of Stonehenge I) were brought from a quarry 300 kilometres away in Wales. And the third and final rebuilding of the monument (c 1500 BC) was on such a massive scale that all the tribes of the south must have contributed their labour. The system of beliefs that the stones celebrate may have been lost forever, but the sense of common purpose has not.

	2000–1900	1900–1800	1800–1700	1700–1600	1600–1500
Politics & Military History	= Middle Kingdom of Egypt reaches peak of prosperity during reigns of Sesostris I and his successors of the 12th dynasty. = Sumerians gradually replaced by Semites in south Mesopotamia.	= Beginnings of movement of 'Battleaxe' peoples in northern and eastern Europe.	= Contest between Aleppo, Babylon and Larsa for supremacy of Mesopotamia won by Hammurabi of Babylon. Mari destroyed in the course of this contest. = 'Palace culture' of Crete prospering with Palace of Minos at Knossos the most important example. = Middle Kingdom of Egypt in decline.	= The Hyksos, nomads from Syria and Palestine, invade Egypt and conquer the Delta* (their kings feature in the king lists as dynasties 15 and 16): Upper Egypt independent under Princes of Thebes (Dynasty 17). = Harappan civilisation of the Indus Valley destroyed by Aryan (Indo-European) invaders.	= King Mursilis of the Hittites sacks Aleppo and Babylon but the empire he creates (which historians call the Hittite Old Kingdom) collapses on his death. = Kassites occupy Babylonia; Hurrians occupy Syria (the leading groups among both these peoples were Iranians and came from the Iranian Plateau). = Ahmose, Prince of Thebes, defeats the Hyksos and expels them from Egypt*; founds the 18th dynasty which marks the beginning of the period known as the New Kingdom or Empire.
Religion & Learning	= Earliest surviving fragments of Sumerian Epic of Creation.			= Appearance of first 'open' syllabaries (scripts with signs for the combination consonant/vowel only) which allows reduction in number of signs from several hundred to 80 or so. Examples: Hittite hieroglyphic, Minoan Linear A. Simultaneous appearance of scripts with signs for consonant/any vowel (the so-called consonantal alphabets) allowing reduction in number of symbols to 20–30. Examples: Early Canaanite, Sinai script.	
Cities & Social Development	= Sesostris I erects an obelisk at Heliopolis, the first example of this type of monument. He also builds a traditional-style pyramid at Lisht on the approach to his residence in the Fayyum.	= Urbanism spreads to the Indus valley (Harappa, Mohenjo-daro). = Construction of Sarsen circle and trilithons at Stonehenge. = Assyrians exporting lead to Kanesh, Anatolia, where it is desilvered in conjunction with local copper ores. Donkey caravans take the lead (and textiles) to Anatolia; members of the Assyrian trading community bring the silver back.	= Hammurabi publishes his 'Eye for an Eye' law code. This continues the tradition established by Urammu (see BC 2200 C) but toughens up the penalties. = Assur emerges as the main urban centre in north Mesopotamia.		= Mursilis establishes the Hittite capital at Hattusas (modern Bogazkoy).
Discovery & Invention	= By observation of the Heliacal rising of Sothis (Sirius) Egyptian astronomers become aware of the difference between their 365 day calendar and the true year of 365.24 days but feel no need to do anything about the discrepancy: the Egyptian calendar is allowed to rotate slowly through the 'Sothic cycle' of 1460 years. The Sumerians, with a 360 day calender and a more obvious problem, try inserting extra 'intercalary' months. They do so on a purely empirical basis: the earliest systematic intercalations belong to the next millennium (see BC 750 D).	= Knowledge of bronze-working reaches Europe via Greece at this time which is conventionally taken to mark the beginning of the European Bronze Age.	= Mud-brick arches and vaults built in Mesopotamia using 'pitched-brick' (no centring) technique.	= The Indo-European expansion of this era is associated with the appearance of the two-wheeled war chariot. This was never a very effective weapon but it was a great way of emphasising status and for this reason remained in use to the end of antiquity.	= Core-moulded opaque glass used to make small containers, mostly for unguents and perfumes, in Mesopotamia: technique spreads to Egypt in the next century.
The Arts	= Sesostris' kiosk for the Sacred Barge of Ammon of Thebes. = Rock-cut tombs of the Princes of Elephantine, Aswan.		= Ceremonial frescoes of the palace of Mari.		

*The fortunes of Israel and Egypt are plausibly related to the rise and fall of the Hyksos. Presumably the nuclear members of the Israelite clan arrived in Egypt with the Hyksos and were enslaved after their defeat.

	1500–1400	1400–1300	1300–1200	1200–1100	1100–1000
Politics & Military History	= Pharaohs Tutmosis I and III take Egyptian Empire to its greatest extent by conquering Palestine and Syria as far as the River Euphrates, and Nubia up to the 4th cataract of the Nile. Syria abandoned later in the century because of pressure from the Mitanni (Hurrians). = Start of Bronze Age in China and of the Shang dynasty of kings who controlled the settled parts of the country.	= Hittite Empire re-established: Hittite armies overthrow the King of the Mitanni. = Egypt's 18th dynasty peters out with the religious reformer, Akhnaton (see below) and his son, Tutankhamen (only remembered for his tomb, discovered intact in 1922): 19th dynasty founded by Ramesses I. = Minoan Kingdom of Knossos, Crete, falls to the Greeks. = Greeks of the mainland recognise the king of Mycenae as the overlord of the peninsula.	= Ramesses II, attempting reconquest of Syria, is rebuffed by Hittites at Battle of Kadesh. = Agamemnon, King of Mycenae, leads Greeks against Troy. = Exodus of the Israelites from Egypt, probably from forced labour camp at Zoan: entry to promised land later in the century. = Lausitz Urnfield culture in Poland, often taken to mark genesis of Slav peoples. = Phrygians cross from Thrace to north-west Anatolia.	= Dorians (Greeks from the northern half of the peninsula) overthrow the Mycenaean principalities of Pylos, Mycenae and Tiryns. = Phrygians and allied tribes overthrow Hittite Empire. = 'Peoples of the Sea' appear in the Levant, devastate Syria and Palestine but are beaten back from Egypt by Ramesses III, first pharaoh of the 20th dynasty: remnants settle on the coast of Palestine under the name of Philistines. Israelites who have now replaced the Canaanites in much of Palestine are forced to recognise Philistine suzerainty.	= Tiglath Pileser I of Assyria briefly masters Syria and Babylonia. = Aramaeans, nomads from the Syrian desert, spill over the settled areas of the Fertile Crescent. = Egypt divided between pharaohs of the 21st dynasty ruling from Tanis in the Delta and the High Priests of Thebes ruling Upper Egypt. Nubia independent. = Last king of the Shang dynasty overthrown by first king of the Zhou. = Era of the judges in Israel ends with the selection of Saul as king.
Religion & Learning	= Egyptian ideas about the after-life codified in the Book of the Dead. = First surviving specimens of Chinese script incised on divinatory 'oracle bones'.	= Akhnaton attempts to substitute his sun god Aton for Amon, chief god of the Theban pantheon. = Minoan script (Linear A) adapted for Greek (= Linear B).	= Sundisc on model horse-drawn cart: Trundholm, Denmark.	= Linear B script goes out of use: Greeks (apart from Cypriots) lapse into illiteracy. = Longest papyrus known, the 40m Great Harris Papyrus now in the British Museum. It records the gifts made by Ramesses III to the different temples of Egypt.	
Cities & Social Development	= First settled communities appear in the Americas: Harvesting maize. = Tutmosis I is buried in the Valley of the Kings, Thebes, starting a fashion that lasts for three dynasties. = Volcanic eruption buries Minoan village of Santorini.	= Akhnaton briefly moves capital of Egypt to modern El-Amarna. = Fortification of Mycenae includes monumental Lion Gate.	= Shang kings of China fix their capital at Anyang. = King Untash-Gal of Elam establishes his residence at Tchoga-Zanbil, where he builds a 5-stage ziggurat rising to 53 metres.	= China: Fu Hou, a consort of King Wu Ding, is buried with 16 sacrificed servants and 200 bronze vessels.	= Last burials in the Valley of the Kings. = Mesopotamia increasingly polarised between Assur and Babylon.
Discovery & Invention	= Phaistos, Crete: disc-bearing syllabic signs made with punches. This is the closest to printing the Western world got for the next 3000 years.	= During this period the Hittites develop the technique of working iron from a bloom to the point where small quantities are available for exceptional articles, e.g. the dagger found in Tutankhamen's tomb.		= Start of the Iron Age. Much of the success of the Dorians in Greece, the Phrygians in Anatolia and the 'Peoples of the Sea' in the Levant appears to have been due to the fact that they had iron swords and their enemies did not. Someone, somewhere in the Aegean region, had succeeded in simplifying the technique of iron working to the point where iron weapons could be standard issue. Subsequently the use of iron tools and weapons became general throughout the Near East.	= Phoenicians sail the length of the Mediterranean and establish contact with the King of Tarshish in southern Spain. The exchange of Near Eastern Mediterranean textiles for Spanish silver brings wealth to the Phoenician cities of Tyre and Sidon.
The Arts	= Queen Hatchepsut erects 29.5m, 371 tonne obelisk at Temple of Ammon, Thebes. Tutmosis III erects three more only slightly smaller, one at Thebes (now in Rome), two at Heliopolis (now in London and New York). = Other major Egyptian monuments of the period include the mortuary temple of Queen Hatchepsut at Deir el Bahri and the colossal seated statues of Amenophis III (the 'colossi of Memnon') in front of his even larger but now vanished mortuary temple.	= Amarna style painting and sculpture characteristic of reign of Akhnaton includes the head of his wife Nefertiti (now in Berlin) which is considered by many to be the masterwork of Egyptian art. = Tholos (meaning bee-hive shaped) tomb of king of Mycenae, the so-called 'Treasury of Atreus'.	= Ramesses II's immense building programme includes hypostyle hall at Karnak (columns 3.5m in diameter, still the biggest in the world), his mortuary temple at Thebes (the Ramesseum), his palace city at Zoan in the Delta and the temple of Abu Simbel in Nubia. Also two obelisks in front of the Temple of Luxor (one of which is now in Paris). = Chinese produce large bronze drums and bells.	= Ramesses III's funeral temple at Medinet Habu featuring bas-reliefs of his victory over the 'Peoples of the Sea'.	= Tomb of Pausennes I at Tanis. = Chinese begin producing elaborate bronze vessels for food and wine.

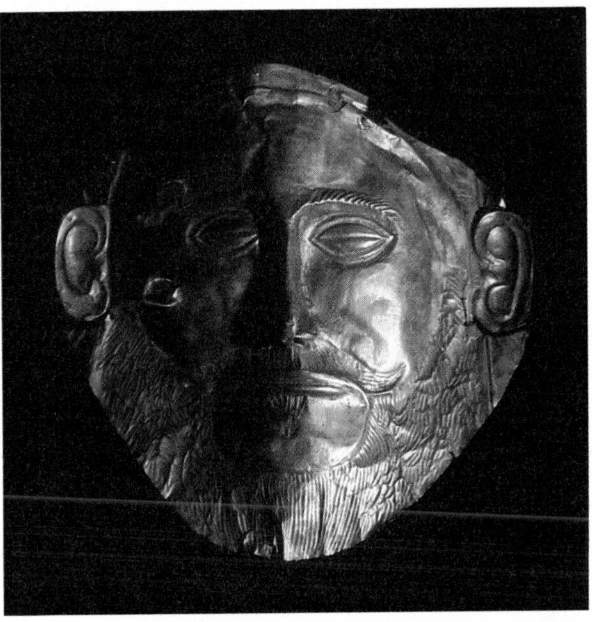

The first people we can identify in Europe are the Greeks. They were living in the same area as they do now – the Greek peninsula and associated islands – and despite being split up into several dozen different confederations and kingdoms, they recognized that they were a single people with a common destiny. Towards the end of the Bronze Age, around 1200 BC, they were even prepared to acknowledge a single overlord, Agamemnon, High King of Mycenae.

We can identify the Greeks because they were literate and archaeologists have recovered clay tablets inscribed in the script they were using at the time. This is a rather cumbersome syllabary (Linear B) that they had borrowed from their predecessors in Crete, the people archaeologists refer to as Minoans. But we do not know what sort of people the Minoans were from their version of this script (Linear A) because we cannot read it, nor are we all that much wiser from being able to read Linear B. The tablets are all storeroom accounts: there is not a single story, poem or reference to a contemporary event in any of them.

Luckily the later Greeks, the Greeks of the Classical period, preserved some stories from their Bronze Age predecessors. The most famous concerned the Trojan War in which the Greeks sailed to Troy (on the Asiatic side of the Hellespont) to take revenge for the theft of Helen by the Trojan prince, Paris. After ten long years they took Troy, killed Paris and brought Helen back to Greece again. An episode in the war formed the subject of Homer's epic poem the Iliad which every Classical Greek knew chunks of by heart: the adventures of one of the main protagonists, Odysseus, on his way home formed the subject of the companion piece, the Odyssey. Both were once considered to be more imaginative than historical but Homer gets so much of the Bronze Age detail right that most people now think the Homeric heroes were real people. For example, although Homer was writing in the Iron Age, probably about four centuries after the events he was describing, he always gives the Greeks bronze arms and armour, never iron. And he lists the places that were important in the 13th century BC, not the 8th.

Of course, some things in the Iliad are not very plausible. Ten years seems too long for the Greeks to have been on campaign: the operation sounds more like a raid than a long drawn-out war. And a lot of the tales that are told about Odysseus, including the one about the wooden horse, are clearly fables. But nowadays few doubt that Agamemnon ruled in Mycenae and Odysseus in Ithaca and that between them they brought Troy to ruin.

The sack of Troy was one of the last acts of the Mycenaeans. A generation later the northern Greeks, the Dorians, acquired iron weapons and used them to overthrow the Mycenaean hegemony. The great castle of Mycenae was stormed and left, like Troy, a silent ruin. The complicated mysteries of account-keeping in Linear B were forgotten. Greece slid back into a Dark Age that lasted till the 8th century BC. The society that emerged at that point was very different from the Mycenaean. It was more democratic (no kings at all), more prosperous (better and cheaper tools) and more literate (alphabetically instead of syllabically). It treasured Homer's stories of the Old Days all the same.

Above: Linear B tablet from Knossos, Crete. The decipherment of Linear B is one of this century's most important cryptographic coups but although it has confirmed that the Myceneans were Greek it has not told us much more than that: the surviving tablets are just storemen's lists and none carries any material of direct historical or literary value.

Above right: The Mask of Agamemnon. When Schliemann excavated the royal graves at Mycenae in 1876 and found this gold mask he sent a telegram to the king of Greece with the jubilant message 'I have gazed on the face of Agamemnon'. Alas, the mask belongs to an earlier epoch: it is now dated to the 16th century BC, 300 years or more before Agamemnon led the Greeks against Troy.

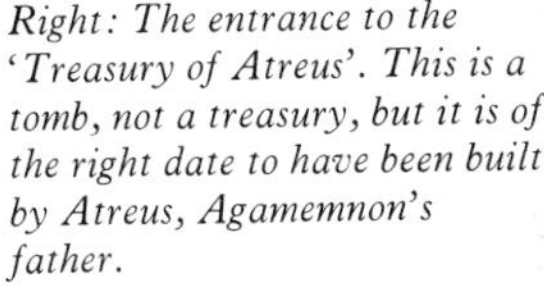

Right: The entrance to the 'Treasury of Atreus'. This is a tomb, not a treasury, but it is of the right date to have been built by Atreus, Agamemnon's father.

Left: The Assyrian King Shalmeneser III receiving the submission of King Jehu of Israel in 825 BC. An attendant holds a sun-shade over the Assyrian monarch, another stands over Jehu who kneels before the king kissing the ground. Above Jehu float the symbols of Shamash, the Assyrian Sun God (the winged disc) and Ishtar, the Assyrian Venus (the star in a circle). Scene from the black obelisk found in Shalmaneser's palace at Nimrud and now in the British Museum.

Most of the action in the Old Testament takes place between the end of the 11th century BC when Saul became King of Israel and the beginning of the 6th century BC when the Babylonian king Nebuchadnezzar all but extinguished the Jewish state. In between, the Jews had their triumphs and disasters but none of the disasters, except the final one, ever came near to cancelling out the essential achievement of the period, the creation of a national sense among the Jewish people.

The state of Israel came into being at a time when Palestine was in considerable confusion. The Empires of the Hittites and the Egyptians, which had once divided the Levant between them, had crumbled away and marauding bands – like the Peoples of the Sea and, for that matter, the Israelites themselves – were able to carve out territories at the expense of the native Canaanites. The task facing Saul, Israel's first king, was to weld the Israelite tribes that had occupied central Palestine into one nation and then free it from the overlordship of the Sea Peoples on the coast (by then going under the name of Philistines). He succeeded in the first but over-reached himself in the second: the Philistines killed him and three of his sons at the Battle of Mount Gilboa.

David of Judah (one of the southernmost of the Israelite tribes) saved the situation. He got the upper hand over the Philistines, then over Israel's other neighbours too. By the end of his reign all of them – Damascus to the north, Ammon and Moab across the Jordan, and Edom in the south – had acknowledged Israel's superiority. King David also gave the Israelite kingdom a proper capital by taking the hill town of Jerusalem from the Canaanites and making it the centre of his government.

The Israelite kingdom reached its zenith under David's son Solomon who ruled for 40 years – from 968 to 928 BC. He maintained Israel's position as the paramount state in Palestine and south Syria: he also enhanced its prestige by building a Temple in Jerusalem for Yahweh, the God of the Israelite nation. Then the split between David's patrimony and the other tribes of Israel opened up again and for the next 200 years there were two Israelite kingdoms in existence: Judah, which was really too small to make its voice heard, and Israel, which counted very much as a second rank power.

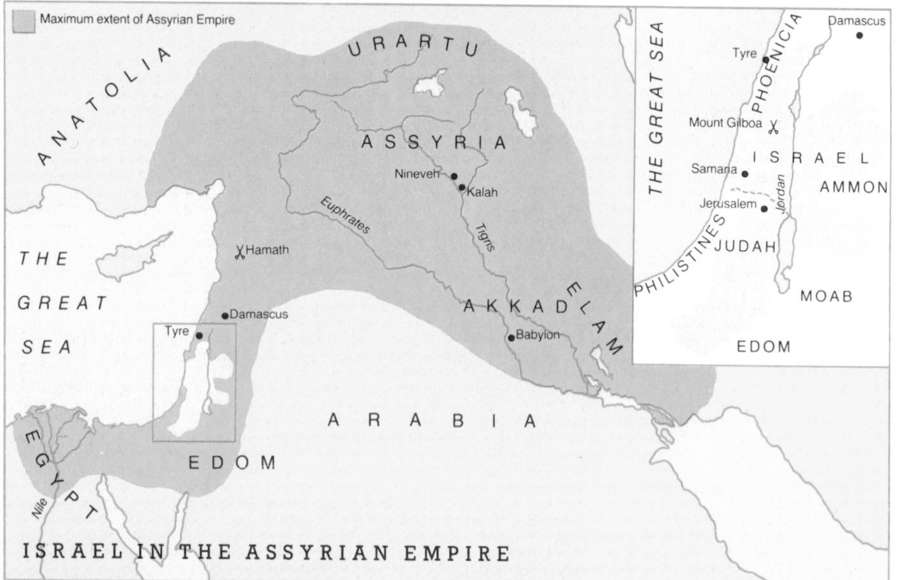

By the 8th century BC the days of second rank powers were numbered. Assyria was on the warpath and its armies were so strong, so well-led and so experienced that in the end nothing could stop them. In 732 BC King Tiglath Pileser III annexed Damascus and made Israel and Judah tributaries. Ten years later his successor, Sargon II, punished the Israelites for a revolt by putting an end to the kingdom: it became the province of Samaria. The kingdom of Judah survived till 587 when it fell foul of the next Mesopotamian empire, Babylon. Eleven years earlier the Babylonian King Nebuchadnezzar had deported 3000 leading members of the Jewish community to Iraq. Now, angered by repeated rebellions, he stormed Jerusalem, destroyed the Temple and ordered the deportation of another 1500 Jews. To judge by what had happened in Israel where similar deportations by the Assyrians had led to a near complete loss of national consciousness, there was a real danger that the Jews would soon cease to be numbered among the peoples of the Earth.

The steadfastness of the Jews in their Babylonian exile determined that this would not happen. At the end of the 6th century BC, when Babylon had gone the way of all empires, bit by bit the Jews found their way back to Jerusalem. There they rebuilt the Temple and rekindled the nation's faith.

Left: The Assyrian army assaults the gate of Lachish, a town in the south of Palestine. Behind the tank-like vehicle advancing up the ramp towards the gate tower an Assyrian archer bends his bow. A hail of stones and blazing torches greets the attackers but many of the citizens of Lachish have decided that the day is lost: they can be seen slipping out of the gate with their possessions on their shoulders.

Scene from Senacherib's palace at Nineveh excavated by Rassam in 1853 and now in the British Museum.

	1000–951	950–901	900–851	850–801	800–751
Politics & Military History	= David takes Jerusalem from the Jebusites, makes it the capital of Judah, to which he unites Israel: receives homage of Damascus, Moab, Ammon and Philistia. = Aeolian and Ionian Greeks colonise the Aegean coast of Anatolia.	= Solomon maintains supremacy of Jewish state in the Levant till his death (928), when Judah and Israel split. **924** Shishonk, first pharaoh of Egypt's 22nd dynasty, exacts tribute from Judah and Israel.	= Beginning of new Assyrian bid for supremacy in Mesopotamia: Assyrian King Shalmaneser III fights Battle of Qarqar against coalition headed by Hadad of Damascus and including Irhuleni of Hamath and Ahab of Israel. = Foundation of Kingdom of Urartu (biblical Ararat) in the mountains north of Assyria.	**841** Shalmaneser III takes tribute from all the states of the Levant including Israel. **806** Adadnirari III takes Damascus but Assyrian supremacy in the Levant lapses because of intensifying war with Urartu.	**771** China: Zhou emperor flees Wei river valley because of nomad attacks; capital re-established at Luoyang. **753** Traditional foundation date of Rome. This can be associated with the emergence of the Etruscan city-states to the north, for Rome in its early days was hardly more than an Etruscan satellite.
Religion & Learning			= Prophet Elijah.	= Prophet Elisha. = First inscriptions in south Arabia.	
Cities & Social Development		= Solomon builds First Temple of Jerusalem with the assistance of Hiram, King of Tyre.	= Omri establishes capital of Israel at Samaria. **879** Assurnasirpal II builds second capital for Assyria at Kalah (modern Nimrud) replacing Nineveh: celebrates completion with 10 day feast for 69,574 people. = Italy enters the Iron Age.	**814** Carthage founded by the Phoenicians at the mid-point of their route to Spain. = North India moves into its Iron Age. Perhaps because iron tools make forest clearance easier, the centre of gravity of the country begins to shift from the Indus to the Ganges, where the first political and cultural centres of Hinduism are soon to emerge: Indraprastha (modern Delhi), Mathura, Kosam and Benares.	**776** First games held in honour of Apollo at Olympia. Held every 4 years from this time till AD 398, the games became important as a festival attended by all Greeks (even when they were at war with each other), as a system of dating (e.g. 'at the time of the 58th Olympiad') and as the inspiration of the modern games (first held 1896). = Earliest *nuraghi* (stone castles) in Sardinia.
Discovery & Invention	= Horse-riding evolved as a way of life by the Scyths of the Russian steppe. = Camel-riding practised in Arabia.				= Greek seamen explore the routes to the mines of Etruria and Transcaucasia; found way-stations on island of Ischia and at Cumae in the west and at Sinope and Trapezus in the east.

PHOENICIANS AND GREEKS

	750–701	700–651	650–601	600–551	550–501
Politics & Military History	**750** King of Nubia conquers Egypt, becoming first pharaoh of 25th dynasty. **732** Assyrian King Tiglath Pileser III annexes Damascus, makes Israel and Judah tributary states. **729** Tiglath Pileser III annexes Babylon. **c725** Spartans conquer Messene. **724–1** King Shalmaneser V of Assyria annexes Israel: his successor, Sargon II, deports the 'ten tribes'. **710** Cimmerians from the Russian steppe invade Transcaucasia devastate Urartu and Kingdom of Phrygia in Anatolia. **705** Sargon II killed fighting Cimmerians: succeeded by Sennacherib. **701** Sennacherib's army unexpectedly withdraws from punitive campaign in Judah.	**696** Assyrians sack Tarsus. **687** Throne of Lydia (western Anatolia) usurped by Gyges. **669–663** Assyrian Empire reaches its maximum extent as Egypt is conquered by kings Esarhaddon and Assurbanipal: satellite 26th dynasty established at Sais in the Egyptian Delta. = Hegemony of state of Qi (equivalent to modern province of Shandong) recognised by other Chinese principalities. Other states succeed to this hegemony at intervals through the next 20 years. = Suzerainty of Carthage acknowledged by Phoenician colonists in the west. = Scyths invade Transcaucasia.	**646** Assurbanipal crushes Elam which is occupied by Persians on this retreat. **626** Downfall of the Assyrian Empire begins when Babylon revolts on the death of Assurbanipal. **614** Assur sacked by the Medes. **612** Nineveh sacked by Babylonians and Medes. **610** Babylonians overthrow last Assyrian army at Harran, extinguishing Assyrian state. **609** Pharaoh Necho, marching to support Assyrians at Harran, opposed by Israel: kills King Josiah at Megiddo. **605** Necho defeated by Babylonian King Nebuchadnezzar at Carchemish. = Kypselid tyranny at Corinth.	**598** Nebuchadnezzar takes Jerusalem and deports 3000 Jews to Babylonia but leaves Jewish state intact. **587** Nebuchadnezzar takes Jerusalem again and destroys first Temple: subsequent deportation of another 1500 Jews to Babylonia. = Expansion of Celtic tribes includes movement from Gaul to Spain.	**550** King Cyrus of Persia defeats Medes and becomes paramount King of Iran: defeats Croesus and takes Lydia (546); annexes Babylonia (539), establishing supremacy of Persian Empire in Near East. **546–529** Pisistratus, tyrant of Athens. **525** Cyrus' son Cambyses conquers Egypt. **521** Darius usurps the Persian throne: campaigns unsuccessfully against the Scyths (516). **510** Romans expel King Tarquin and establish a republic.
Religion & Learning	**722** First entry in the *Annals of Lu* which, under its alternative title of *Spring and Autumn Annals*, has given its name to the period of Chinese history it covers, i.e. 722–481 BC. = Invention of true alphabet (with signs for vowels as well as consonants) in Greece.		= Zoroaster, founder of the Persians' national religion.	= Aesop of Samos (brought there as a slave, later freed), traditional inventor of the moral *Fable*. How many of the tales ascribed to him are actually his is anyone's guess; the collection we have is Roman.	= Prince Gautama achieves enlightenment, so becoming the Buddha: preaches his new faith at Benares. = Confucius (Kung Fu Zi) teaches the 5 virtues of humanity, courtesy, honesty, moral wisdom and steadfastness. = Laozi *Dao Do Jing* ('The Book of the Way and its Power') prescribes masterly inactivity as the key to the good life.
Cities & Social Development	= Wave of Greek emigration to Southern Italy and Sicily: foundation of Syracuse, Catania, Reggio, Tarentum and Sybaris. **720** Sargon II builds new Assyrian capital at Dur Sharrukin (Fort Sargon, modern Khorsabad). **701** Sennacherib abandons Dur Sharrukin and makes Nineveh the capital of the empire again.	= Greek emigration to shores of Propontis (Sea of Marmara): foundation of Chalcedon, Byzantium, Abydos and Lampsacus.	= Draco codifies the laws of Athens. = Cyrene (hence Cyrenaica) founded by Greeks from Thera. = Greeks begin colonising suitable sites on the Black Sea and Adriatic coasts, founding Olbia, Tomi and Epidamnus in this period; Heraclea, Theodosia and Apollonia-in-Illyria in the first half of the next century.	= Massilia (Marseilles) founded by Greeks from Aeolia. = Solon reforms Athenian constitution. = France enters the Iron Age.	**537** Jews in Babylonian exile allowed to return to Palestine by Cyrus: second Temple completed 515. **508** Cleisthenes introduces democratic constitution at Athens. **518** Darius begins the construction of the palace complex at Persepolis which is to replace Pasargadae, residence and burial-place of Cyrus as the administrative centre of the empire.
Discovery & Invention	= Babylonians make systematic observations of lunar eclipses and the movements of the planets but fail to establish a self-regulating calendar because they set themselves the almost impossible target of keeping in step with both sun and moon.	= First 'coins' struck from electrum (gold and silver alloy) by Lydians: hall-marked for purity, not weight. True coins struck by Greek states of Aegina, Athens and Corinth shortly after.		**585** Solar eclipse, said to have been predicted by Thales of Miletus, the Greek 'Father of Physical Sciences'. The claim is discounted nowadays for the mechanism of eclipses does not appear to have been understood before the 5th century BC.	= Pythagoras discovers the ratios underlying the musical scale: founds a mystical school of numerology in Greek Italy. = Anaximander and Anaximenes of Miletus theorize, more philosophically than scientifically, about the universe.
The Arts	= At about this time the two cycles of epic poems about the Trojan War, the Iliad and the Odyssey, were put in the form in which we have them today. In this state they are traditionally ascribed to Homer though in truth no one knows whether he wrote one or both or neither.	= Hesiod *Works and Days* uses tales of the Gods to illustrate traditional Greek lifestyle.	= Bronze lurs (trumpets) in use in Denmark. **c600** Statues of Kleobis and Biton dedicated at Delphi.	**c580** Temple of Artemis, Corcyra, the first stone temple in Greece. Temple of Athena, Athens, rebuilt in stone shortly after. = Nebuchadnezzar builds the Ishtar Gate and the 'Hanging Gardens'*. = Sappho, poetess of Lesbos. = Athenians develop black-figure painted pottery.	**550** Fashion for giant temples in Greece begins with Temple of Artemis at Ephesus (108.6m long) and Temple 'G' at Selinus (109.5m): more representative are the temples of Apollo at Syracuse (47m), Corinth (48.5m), Paestum (54m). = Athenians develop red-figure pottery style.

*Later accounted one of the Seven Wonders of the Ancient World.

While the old empires of the Near East charted their spectacular courses – first Assyria, then Babylon, then the greatest of all, Persia – two relatively humble peoples made a more important sort of history. Both were seafaring nations and the achievement was essentially a maritime one: they brought the Mediterranean into the civilized world.

It was the Phoenicians, the people of present day Lebanon, who were first to cast off. Some time around 1000 BC they began sending ships through the Sicilian-Tunisian narrows into the western half of the Mediterranean. They already had the trade in the eastern half buttoned up. Maybe they would find equally rich pickings in the West.

Their enterprise was quickly rewarded: Spain turned out to be a prime source of silver, one of the few commodities worth trading over this sort of distance. The problem was to stop other people muscling in on the discovery. The Phoenicians decided to establish strong points either side of the Tunisian-Sicilian narrows and in Spain, and try to keep foreign ships out of this part of the Mediterranean. To a remarkable extent they succeeded. More important from our point of view the posts on the African side gradually developed into colonial towns. The most successful of them, Carthage, finally ended up as an imperial power in its own right.

The Greeks came into the picture about 750 BC. At first they seem to have wanted to trade, particularly for metals, just as the Phoenicians had. And they did find trading partners: the Etruscans in northern Italy (who had copper to sell) and the Caucasians at the far end of the Black Sea (who panned gold from their mountain streams: hence the legend of the Golden Fleece). But very soon the Greeks became less interested in trade than in the emptiness of the shores they were sailing past. Their homeland was overcrowded, good land at a premium. Clearly there was a lot to be said for founding new communities overseas to take the surplus citizens. The emigration programme proved a great success: during the next 150 years a near continuous string of Greek colonies was established along the coasts of Sicily and south Italy and another, more widely spaced set, along the shores of the Black Sea.

In other areas the Greeks did not do so well. The Phoenicians kept them out of Spain and the Etruscans prevented them from settling in the northern half of Italy. The Etruscans were weakening, though: in 510 BC they lost control of Rome which had emerged as the most important city in the central sector of the Italian peninsula. The Romans expelled the Etruscan king, Tarquin the Proud, and vowed to have no more kings of any sort.

That is the beginning of another story. The point of this one is that by the end of the 6th century BC a new world had been created rivalling the Near East in its level of sophistication. In some ways it has to be accounted ahead. For example, all the Mediterranean communities used a type of alphabetic script which was far superior to the syllabaries in use in the Near East. Perhaps because of this – literacy is a great leveller – they also had a strong feeling for constitutional government. Altogether an interesting development.

Below: The greatest seafarer of them all, Odysseus, the hero of Homer's epic poem, The Odyssey. This vase painting illustrates a famous episode in his travels, the passage between Scylla and Charybdis which was made especially dangerous by the song of the Sirens. This was supposed to be so seductive that Odysseus had himself bound to the mast so that he would not succumb. They must have sounded better than they looked.

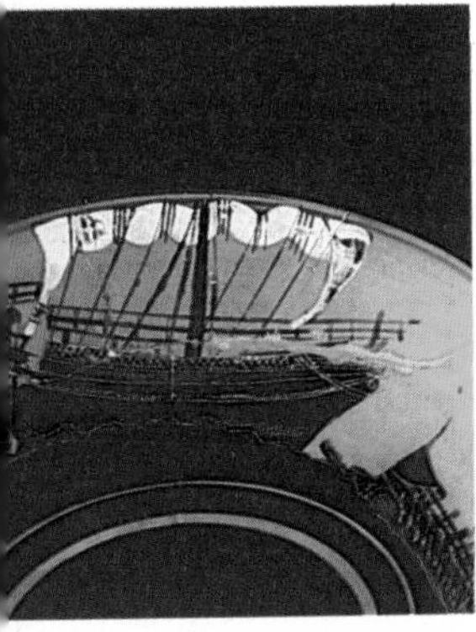

Above: Greek merchant-ship of the mid-6th century BC. Note that the only oar is the steering oar at the stern: for propulsion the vessel relied entirely on its sail. This makes a marked contrast with the warship closing in on it from the right which has two tiers of oars and a wicked looking bronze ram in the shape of a boar's head.

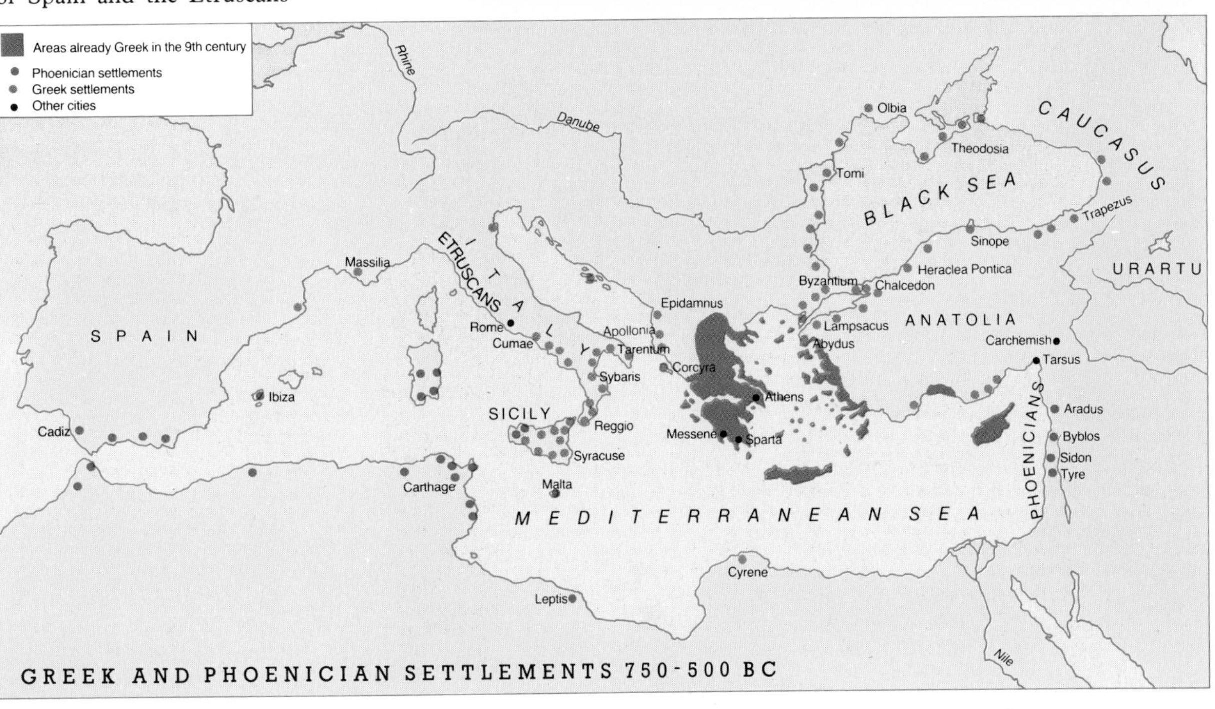

GREEK AND PHOENICIAN SETTLEMENTS 750-500 BC

THE RISE AND DECLINE OF THE

CLASSICAL WORLD

500 BC - AD 1000

The foundations of the Classical World were laid by the Greeks. They set the style of its arts and sciences and they formulated, even if they did not always achieve, the ideal of the citizen as an active contributor to the political process. In theory, at least, the Classical Greek community recognized no authority other than that of its own citizen body. We derive our ideas on the freedom and dignity of individuals from the precepts of this relatively simple Iron Age society.

The Greek city state was usually small, frequently at odds with its neighbours and almost impossible to recruit into any permanent alliance: nothing less suitable for empire building can be imagined. If its military potential was ever to be realized the Greeks had to accept some loss of autonomy: they had to be disciplined in the way they liked least. The job was done by King Philip of Macedon. With the army he created, his son Alexander was able to impose his rule on the area between Egypt and the Punjab. This triumph marks the start of the Hellenistic chapter in the Classical story.

The next chapter belongs to Rome. The Romans were disciplined from the start: their common people allowed the senatorial class to run the state; they trusted that they would do so fairly and the senators rarely abused that trust. It was a formidable combination. The Roman Empire took over the Mediterranean and ran it successfully for 600 years.

The final act followed the sack of Rome by Alaric the Goth. As the western, truly Roman half of the empire foundered, the eastern half gradually recovered its Greek roots. There is no concealing that this was a phase of decline. The empire of Constantinople guarded its Classical heritage with diminishing comprehension. The rest of the world had moved on: what had once been a vital culture was now merely curious.

To go back to the beginning. The first task facing the Greeks was to make sure that their society was not strangled at birth. And in the opening years of the 5th century BC, when Persian armies twice had Athens in their grasp, the chances of Greece preserving its liberty must have seemed very dubious. Never more so than in 490 BC, on the eve of Marathon.

MARATHON

The Persian Empire was bigger than all the empires that had preceded it; in fact it was bigger than all of them put together. It included Assyria, Babylonia and Egypt as well as Persia (modern Iran) and Anatolia (modern Turkey). King Darius, who was its ruler at the end of the 6th century BC, enlarged it further: in the east he added part of the Punjab, in the west he crossed the Hellespont and invaded Europe. This operation did not go entirely smoothly and it was not until 492 BC that his first European province, Thrace, was properly established: next was Greece.

Darius already had some experience of Greeks for there were several dozen Greek communities scattered along the seaboard of Anatolia, that is, already within the boundary of the empire. They had proved unruly subjects: in 499 BC the most important group of them, the Ionians of the Aegean coast, had rebelled against Persian rule and it had taken five years of hard fighting to bring them to heel. It would have taken even longer if the Greeks of mainland Greece had aided the rebels on a big scale: as it was, only Eritrea and Athens sent any help, and what they sent was not enough to make any difference to the outcome. Nonetheless, while Greece was free, the Ionians would never rest content: Darius knew he had to conquer Greece if he was to have peace on his western border.

In 490 BC Darius made his move. He dispatched an army by sea from Samos with orders to destroy Eritrea and Athens and collect tribute from the other Greek states. Eritrea was duly taken by storm and razed to the ground: the Persians then sailed to Attica, the peninsula on which Athens stands, and disembarked at the Bay of Marathon. The Athenian army marched across the hills to meet them.

In their previous encounters the Persians had not had much trouble beating Greeks because the Greeks had neither cavalry nor archers: on level ground this made them easy game for the Persian cavalry. The Athenians had obviously thought about this and chose, for the moment at least, to stay in the foothills overlooking Marathon. After several days in which neither side moved, the Persians decided to break the deadlock by shipping part of their army round the coast to make a direct attack on Athens: to cover the embarkation of this striking force – which seems to have included all the cavalry – they moved the rest of their army across the plain towards the Athenian position. The Athenian General Miltiades seized the opportunity the Persians had offered and ordered an attack. With only a few hundred metres to go the Greeks were on the Persians almost immediately and once the two armies had closed, the armoured Greek spearmen proved more than a match for their opponents. The battle turned into a massacre: 6400 Persian dead against 200 Greeks.

Marathon was a devastating defeat for the Great King: against all expectations David had beaten Goliath. The mighty Persian Empire, with its population of many millions, had been rebuffed by a single Greek state which could mobilize no more than 10,000 men. It was astonishing and, as far as Darius was concerned, insupportable: the verdict of Marathon had to be overturned. New invasion plans were put in hand.

In the event, Darius died before the invasion force was ready and it was his son Xerxes who led the main force of the empire against Greece in 480 BC. The huge army, maybe a hundred thousand strong, marched round the northern shore of the Aegean, annihilated a small Greek unit that tried to stop it at the pass of Thermopylae and took and burnt Athens. The Persian fleet was less successful: it went down to defeat at the hands of the Athenians at the Battle of Salamis. Nevertheless, Xerxes was by no means dissatisfied with the results of the campaign: all Greece bar the Peloponnese was now under his control. Leaving enough men behind to complete the job the next year, he departed for Persia as winter was setting in.

The embattled Greeks put forward every man they could for the campaign of 479 BC. Under the leadership of the Spartans, who had the biggest and best army in the peninsula, they fielded a force of perhaps 40,000. It was enough to put them on a near equal footing with the Persian corps that Xerxes had left behind. The two armies met near Plataea. The Persian cavalry circled round the Greeks forcing them to pull back into the foothills and the Persians were foolish enough to allow the main clash to develop there. It was Marathon all over again with the Greeks gradually turning the battle into a one-sided slaughter.

Like most epics the Greek-Persian War is easily over-idealized. A surprising number of Greeks joined the Persian side in 480 BC and fought against their countrymen at Plataea: an even larger number refused to fight at all. Nor were the numerical odds quite so overwhelming as they seemed. Greece was in the throes of a population explosion and by the early 5th century BC there were about three million Greeks in the peninsula and archipelago. The manpower was there to match any force that the Persians could keep permanently in the field. Nevertheless, the bones of the legend are sound: it was a fight of free men against despotism, it was a fight against the odds and it was won by people like the Athenians who were prepared to see their homes burnt rather than live under tyranny.

MACEDON
THRACE
THESSALY
AEGEAN SEA
Hellespont
XERXES EXPEDITION 480–479
PERSIAN EMPIRE
IONIA
Cape Artemesium 480
Thermopylae 480
EUBOEA
Eritrea
THEBES
Plataea 479
ATTICA
ATHENS
Marathon 490
DARIUS EXPEDITION 490
CORINTH
Salamis 480
SAMOS
PELOPONNESE
SPARTA
PERSIAN INVASIONS OF GREECE 490-479 BC

Above: Map showing the Marathon campaign of 490 BC and the invasion of Greece by King Xerxes of Persia.

Right: Greek youth bringing up the rear of the procession that was part of the Panathenaea, a festival held in Athens each summer. From the frieze of the Parthenon, sculpted under the direction of Phidias in the 430s.

Recently it has been pointed out that there is no mention of horsemen in contemporary descriptions of the festival and that the number on the frieze – 192 in all – is the same as the number of Athenians killed at the Battle of Marathon. This makes it likely that these are not living participants in the festival but a band of heroes held in especial honour, the young men who gave their lives to make Marathon an Athenian victory.

Far left: Greek hoplite. More heavily armoured than foot soldiers of the past, they were almost unbeatable when they stood, or charged, shoulder to shoulder.

Athens had already established itself as the most remarkable city in Greece when Xerxes captured it and burnt it to the ground in 480 BC. It became a lot more remarkable when the Athenians had got it back after the Battle of Plataea and rebuilt it. In the first place, instead of being just a bit bigger than its rivals, the new Athens quickly grew to an unprecedented size: in the later 4th century BC it had a population of at least 36,000 which would be about three times that of its nearest rival, Corinth. In the second place, it became wealthy to a degree that no other Greek city could match. Partly this was luck: a rich vein of silver was found at the mines of Laurion near Athens in 483 BC. But it was much more a matter of the people of Athens taking the right decisions – some of them very hard ones – at the right time. For example, they did not use the first year's revenue from Laurion to cut taxes but spent it instead on commissioning new warships. Then they did not try to defend the city against Xerxes as a do-or-die faction wanted: they evacuated the non-combatants to the safety of the Peloponnese, manned their ships and bided their time. And when they had got their victory and won their city back they did not relax, they launched a series of lightning campaigns around the Aegean that brought them an empire. This was where the real money came from.

The Athenians had good leaders at this time, men like Themistocles who was behind the navy-first policy and Aristides who organized the tax system on which the empire was run. But most of the credit belongs to the Athenian people themselves for Athens was a democracy and their votes were needed on every important issue.

Making their democracy work was probably the achievement of which the Athenians were proudest. They knew that unless they were careful the rich and well-connected would gradually come to dominate the state and they went to great trouble to see that this did not happen. They made the important committees very large, they chose their members by lot rather than by ballot and they paid the poor for their attendance. These measures took money but they worked well and so long as the money lasted Athenian democracy was never in serious peril.

In their heyday the Athenians had money to spare. Much of it they spent on making their city as magnificent as possible. Between 447 and 405 BC all the monuments of the Acropolis were rebuilt in marble, several of them on a colossal scale. The most important, the Parthenon, is undoubtably the supreme masterpiece of Greek architecture. But there was more to the city than its buildings: there was a quality of intellectual life that no other place could match. Playwrights and satirists, philosophers and historians wrote and argued to public applause at a time when anywhere else they would have been hard put to it to find an audience of one. Pericles, who presided over the city in its greatest days, was not boasting when he described Athens as 'an education to Greece': it has been an education to all subsequent ages.

Above: The Acropolis of Athens with its monumental gateway, the Propylaea, on the left, and the Parthenon, the temple of Athena Parthenos (Athena as Virgin) to the right. Between the two stood the colossal bronze of Athena Promachos (Athena as Warrior) the gleam from whose helmet could be seen from as far away as Piraeus. The ruins at the foot of the hill are Roman.

Left: Lower half of a kleroterion, the simple device the Athenians used to randomize their juries. Would-be jurors inserted their identity cards in the slots on the front of the marble slabs. On the left of the slab there was a bronze tube which was loaded with balls, half of which were black and half white. Each vertical column on the slab constituted a potential jury but whether or not it was allocated to a court was determined by the colour of the ball released from the tube.

Left: The final defence of Athenian democracy was the procedure known as ostracism. If anyone seemed to be getting too powerful his name could be put up for temporary banishment and if enough votes were cast against him he had to go. A vote was cast by writing the victim's name on a piece of pottery (an ostrakon – hence the name of the procedure).

	500–476	475–451	450–426	425–401	400–376
Politics & Military History	**499** Revolt of the Ionian Greeks against Persian rule. **494** Ionians suppressed. **490** Persian seaborne invasion of Greece defeated by Athenians at Marathon. **480** Second Persian invasion of Greece: Xerxes marches round the Aegean, defeats the Greek advance force at Thermopylae and takes Athens. Athenians defeat Persian fleet at Salamis. Greeks of Sicily defeat Carthaginians at Himera. **479** Spartan-led Greek army defeats Persians at Plataea, liberating Greece. Athenians defeat Persians at Mycale in Ionia. **477** Athens enrols liberated Greeks of islands and Ionia in 'League of Delos', effectively an Athenian empire.	**474** Syracusans defeat Etruscans off Cumae. **460** Athenian expedition to Egypt, ultimately ending in disaster (454). **453** Beginning of the 'Warring States' period in China, the more serious phase of the struggle for supremacy. **443** Pericles achieves first place in Athens: elected as one of the city's ten commanders every year from this date to his death (429). = Habesh (Abyssinians) migrate from Arabia to Eritrea (maritime Ethiopia). = Halstatt Celts cross from France to England.	**431** Start of Peloponnesian War between Athens and Sparta.	**421** First round of the Peloponnesian War ends in a draw. **415–13** Athenian expedition against Syracuse ends in total loss. **412–404** Second round of Peloponnesian War: Sparta defeats Athens and establishes short-lived 'Tyranny of the Thirty'. **409–406** Carthaginian successes in Sicily: Selinus, Himera and Acragas destroyed. **404** Egypt rebels against Persia. **401** Civil war in Persia: Battle of Cunaxa and subsequent retreat of Greek mercenary force to the Black Sea coast. (For Xenophon's account see under 386 R.)	**396** Romans capture Veii. **390** Gauls, now expanding from central Europe into Italy, sack Rome. **387** In the treaty known as 'the King's Peace' the Spartans agree to the Persians re-occupying Ionia. **378** Athenian revival in alliance with Thebes.
Religion & Learning	**480** Anaxagoras of Clazomenae founds the Athenian school of Philosophy. = Codification of China's 'Five Classics'. = Serpent column dedicated at Delphi by members of Greek Alliance as thanks offering for victory over Xerxes.	= Hecataeus of Miletus *Periegesis*, a geography of the known world with a map attached.	**430** Herodotus *History*. This account of the war between the Greeks and Persians is the first coherent history ever written. Earlier historical writings are no more than collections of annals – statements about the official activities of the year, usually brief and always one-sided. Herodotus combines a detailed narrative of the conflict with explanations and asides on such a lavish scale that the end product is really a history of the world as known to the Greeks.	= The first five books of the Bible (the Hebrew Torah, traditionally ascribed to Moses) given the form in which we have them today. = Hindu mythology codified in the Ramayana.	**400** Thucydides dies leaving his *Peloponnesian War* unfinished. **399** Socrates condemned to death for 'corrupting the youth of Athens'. **386** Xenophon *March of the Ten Thousand*. **385** Socrates' pupil Plato founds the Academy at Athens: the metaphysical style of his *Dialogues* becomes an important influence on Greek philosophy. = Xenophon *Anabasis*.
Cities & Social Development	= Common people of Rome (plebs) win political recognition from the ruling aristocracy (patricians). = Britain enters the Iron Age.	**458–6** Athenians build the Long Walls connecting the city with Piraeus, its port. This makes Athens impossible to blockade by land alone.	**430** Plague at Athens, due to wartime overcrowding, kills a quarter of the citizens.	**409** Founding of the city of Rhodes.	= Start of La Tène culture in the Celtic zone.
Discovery & Invention	= Athens develops the trireme (galley with three banks of oars) which becomes the standard warship design for the 5th century BC. = China enters its Iron Age. Because Chinese iron ores were high in phosphorous and therefore had a low melting point, the Chinese were able to produce cast iron from the start. The equivalent technology was not developed in the west until the 14th century AD.	= During this period the Greeks made great advances in their understanding of the heavens, working out the mechanism of eclipses and making the first measurements of the ecliptic. Clearly they had already accepted that the earth was a sphere but just when they came to this conclusion and who put forward the idea is not recorded. It is, however, safe to assume that it was a Greek of the early 5th century BC.	**427** Athenian trireme reaches Mitylene in under 24 hours (i.e. covers 350km at an average of 9 knots).	**405** Democritus publishes his atomic theory: around the same time Hippocrates of Cos elaborates his 'four humours' theory of human physiology.	= The true arch, built with wedge shaped stone voussoirs, appears in Italy. The ancients credited the Etruscans with the invention and this fits the facts we have; the earliest surviving examples all occur within the Etruscan sphere of influence (Perugia, Volterra, Rome, Velia). = Syracusans develop the quinquereme.
The Arts	**490** Athenian shrine at Delphi, first marble building in Greece. Production of Aeschylus' first play marks the beginning of the great age of Athenian drama. = First pyramid-and-plaza cult centre built at La Venta in Tabasco Province, Mexico.	**467** Aeschylus *Seven Against Thebes*. = Greek sculpture reaches a peak with the Zeus of the west pediment, Olympia, the Poseidon from Cape Artemesion, the Diskobolos (discus-thrower) by Myron.	**447** Reconstruction of the Athenian acropolis begins with building of the Parthenon: Pheidias' statue of Athena installed 438; building completed 432. **430** Pheidias'* gold and ivory cult statue of Zeus, Olympia. **430** Sophocles *Oedipus Tyrannus*.	**425** Erectheum rebuilt. **423** Aristophanes *Clouds* satirises Socrates' philosophical teaching. **417** Euripides *Electra*. **406** Deaths of Euripides and Sophocles bring the great age of Athenian drama to an end.	

*Accounted one of the Seven Wonders of the Ancient World.

ALEXANDER AND HELLENISM

	375–351	350–326	325–301	300–276	275–251
Politics & Military History	**371** Thebans defeat Spartans at Leuctra, ending Spartan hegemony. **359** Philip II becomes ruler of Macedon which he quickly makes the most powerful state in Greece. **351** Demosthenes *First Philippic* (speech to the Athenian assembly warning of Philip of Macedon's ambition).	**343** The Persians recover Egypt. **338** Philip of Macedon defeats Athenians and Thebans at Chaeronea: declares war on Persia (337); is assassinated (336). His son, Alexander the Great, conquers the Persian Empire (334–326), winning the battles of Granicus (334), Issus (333), Guagamela (331) and Hydapses (326). **338** The Romans establish their authority over the other Latin cities. **327** The Romans go to war with the Samnites, the hill tribes of the Apennines: hostilities continue on and off for the next 37 years.	**323** Alexander dies at Babylon: his generals fight for the empire till 301 BC when the Battle of Ipsus decides the issue; Ptolemy gets Egypt, Seleucus nearly all the Asiatic provinces. **321** India: Chandragupta Maurya takes the throne of Magadha and expands his rule over northern India: buys the Punjab from Seleucus for 500 elephants (303 BC). **318–316** China: King of Qin annexes Sichuan.	**290** Romans annex Samnium. **280** Pyrrhus, King of the Greek state of Epirus, tries to stop the Romans encroaching on the Greeks of south Italy: fails and withdraws from the peninsula (275). **279** Gauls invade Greece and Thrace: three tribes cross to Anatolia and settle on the central plateau (hence Galatia). = Tongans (proto-Polynesians) colonise Samoa.	**264** Romans intervene in Sicily: war with Carthage (First Punic War) begins as a result. **260** Seleucids lose control of Cappadocia. **256** China: King of Qin annexes Zhou. = India: King Ashoka conquers Orissa, bringing Mauryan Empire to its peak.
Religion & Learning	**367** Aristotle joins the Athenian Academy.	**343** Aristotle becomes tutor to the 13 year old Prince Alexander of Macedon.	**306** Epicurus founds his School of Philosophy at Athens. **301** Zeno founds the rival 'Stoic' school. **315** Foundation of Salonica (originally named Thessalonika after Alexander the Great's sister who was married to Cassander, King of Macedon at the time): it soon becomes the second city in Greece.	**c285** Zenodotus appointed Librarian of Alexandria. Rapid expansion of the library which by the next century contains 490,000 volumes. = Sayings of Mencius, follower and successor of Confucius, issued by his disciples after his death (?289 BC).	**c270** Apollonius of Rhodes, author of *The Argonauts*, succeeds Zenodotus as librarian at Alexandria. = Ashoka's rock and pillar edicts proclaim his devotion to the precepts of Buddhism. = Production of the Septuagint, Greek version of the Hebrew Old Testament.
Cities & Social Development	**356** Shang Yang begins remodelling Qin state along 'Legalist' (totalitarian) lines.	**332** Alexander founds Alexandria-in-Egypt. Over the next hundred years this becomes the largest city in the Greek world and its leading cultural centre.	**312** Construction starts on the Appian Way between Rome and Capua. = Wave of Greek emigration to the provinces of the old Persian Empire especially Anatolia, Syria and Egypt.	**300** Seleucus founds Antioch in Syria. **c300** Early version of Great Wall built to keep nomads out of northern China, states of Qin, Zhou and Yan each build a section.	**264** First public combat of gladiators in Rome: three pairs fight at the funeral games in honour of D. Brutus Pera.
Discovery & Invention	= Eudoxius of Cnidos develops geometrical approach to mathematical problems: creates the prototype of the Ptolemaic cosmos using a nest of invisible spheres to explain the movements of sun, moon, stars and 5 planets known to him.		**307** King Wu-ling of Zhao raises first cavalry units in China, copying equipment from northern nomads.	**c300** Euclid founds School of Geometry at Alexandria.	**c275** Aristarchus of Alexandria proposes a heliocentric solar system. He also calculates the moon's distance as 40 earth diameters (*v.* true figure of 30) and sun's as 764 (v. 12,000). = Ctesibius of Alexandria invents the water-organ and a more accurate version of the water-clock, the 'inflow clepsydra'.
The Arts	**353** Widow of Mausolus, governor of Caria, begins construction of his tomb, the *Mausoleum. To the same era belongs the Hellenistic *Temple of Artemis at Ephesus, built to replace an earlier building destroyed by fire in 356 BC.	= Apelles, considered the greatest painter of antiquity, working at the Macedonian court (none of his paintings survive).	**317** Menander's comedy *The Curmudgeon* marks the shift from political satire to domestic farce.	**c280** Construction of the *Pharos (Lighthouse) of Alexandria and the *Colossus of Rhodes.	

*Accounted one of the Seven Wonders of the Ancient World.

Though the Athenians and Spartans between them defeated the Persian invasion of Greece they were not strong enough, either together or separately, to mount a counter-invasion of the Persian Empire. In liberating the Aegean area the Athenian navy shot its bolt: its attempts to operate at longer range – in Cyprus, or Egypt – were all disastrous, with men and ships being lost at a rate that could not be sustained. Nor were the Spartans up to a continental campaign: they had not the organization, the will, or, for that matter, the right sort of army. They were especially hopeless at sieges which were bound to feature largely in any thrust into Asia.

So the Great King continued master of the two dozen satrapies (provinces) that made up his Persian empire. In fact, he soon stopped worrying about the Greeks altogether. They were usually quarrelling among themselves and if the quarrels ever looked like being resolved a few judicious bribes and the promise of a subsidy would soon get them going again. When the Spartans were discouraged by their defeats in the early phases of the Peloponnesian War, Persian gold helped them to a new strategy and ultimately to victory. When the Spartans showed signs of getting a bit above themselves as a result, the king switched the subsidy to Thebes: in 371 the Theban general Epaminondas, the first really innovative tactician the Greeks had produced, achieved the unthinkable and crushed the Spartan army. This desirable result was achieved without the spilling of one drop of Persian blood. No wonder the Great King said that his best troops were his archers – meaning not the archers of his bodyguard but the archers on his gold coins.

Above: Gold coin of Alexander. The portrait is posthumous and idealized: coins issued in his lifetime show him with heavier features and a more businesslike expression.

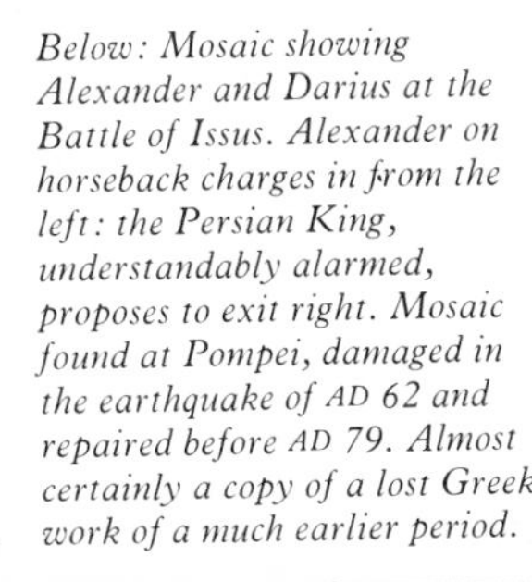

Below: Mosaic showing Alexander and Darius at the Battle of Issus. Alexander on horseback charges in from the left: the Persian King, understandably alarmed, proposes to exit right. Mosaic found at Pompei, damaged in the earthquake of AD 62 and repaired before AD 79. Almost certainly a copy of a lost Greek work of a much earlier period.

The man who changed all this – put a stop to the quarrelling and made all the Greeks march under one banner – was Philip of Macedon. First he conquered Thessaly which was the one part of Greece that produced good horsemen. Then he built up a corps of military engineers capable of taking cities by storm. Finally he and his young son Alexander defeated the Thebans and Athenians at the Battle of Chaeronea and forced them to join his coalition. He was ready to march against Persia when he fell to the knife of an assassin, perhaps put up to it by the Persian king (those archers again) or, more likely, by Alexander's mother (Philip just had a son by a new wife).

Whether he had had a hand in it or not the Persian king must have seen Philip's death as a piece of good fortune: the throne of Macedon was now occupied by a 19 year old boy. But Alexander was no ordinary 19 year old. In a whirlwind campaign through the peninsula he showed the Greeks that Macedon was still their master: two years later he crossed into Anatolia in pursuit of his father's grand design.

The Great King left the defence of Anatolia to the local satraps. They drew up their forces on the banks of the River Granicus and it was there, in the summer of 334, that the two armies came face to face. Alexander personally led the right wing of his cavalry in a charge that drove the opposing horse from the field; then, using the manoeuvre invented by Epaminondas, he brought his crack regiments down on the left flank of the enemy infantry. Victory was total: all Anatolia was under Macedonian control by the year's end.

It took Alexander seven more campaigns, two set piece battles and four major sieges before the rest of the empire was his. Then, after an adventurous if not entirely necessary excursion into the Punjab, he came back to Babylon where, in the midst of plans of which we only have rumoured versions – a circumnavigation of Arabia, a campaign against Carthage – he contracted typhoid and died within a week.

In his short span, Alexander did more than conquer the Persian Empire, he began to remodel it. In particular, he encouraged Greeks to come and settle in Asia and Egypt, a policy that was continued by his successors. As a result, Greek cities as big as or bigger than any in Greece itself grew up in the western provinces of the Empire. This expansion of the Greek world was the foundation for the achievements of the Hellenistic era that followed.

Right: When Alexander invaded Cilicia, he had his first encounter with the Great King Darius. The victory he won at this stage (at Issus in 333) showed that the empire was his for the taking; but there was still a Persian fleet operating in his rear. Alexander had no fleet of his own – and the only way he could eliminate the Persian navy was by taking its bases. Having done this he set out for Mesopotamia and his final battle with the Persian king. This time he was in a position to follow up on his victory (at Gaugamela, near Erbil, in 331) with a rapid march via Babylon and Susa to Persepolis, the ancient centre of Persian power.

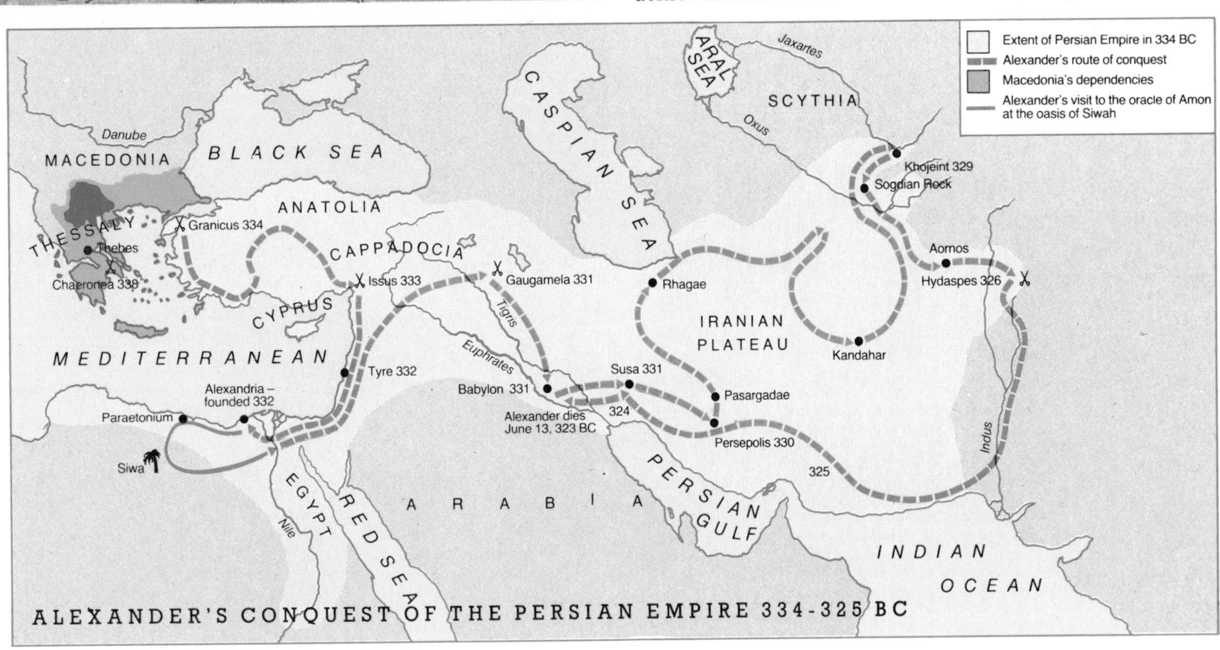

Though the Chinese have always believed that their civilization is the world's oldest, this is not really so: its first phase only dates from 1500 BC, a good thousand years later than the equivalent cultural level – that of a literate Bronze Age society – in the Fertile Crescent. Nor did the Chinese have a great deal to offer in the way of new ideas at this stage: their political organization, their script, their weapons, even their chariots, are all similar in type to their equivalents in western Asia. What the Chinese did have, then as now, was numbers. The China of this period – the era of the Shang Kings – was limited to the valley of the Yellow River but it contained a population of the same size as the entire Near East.

Around the middle of the 11th century BC the last Shang ruler was ousted by a member of a relatively uncivilized clan from the western borderlands, the Zhou. In theory the dynasty founded by the newcomers lasted something over 800 years, but the reality was different. As early as the 8th century the Zhou lost control over their vassals and thereafter China split up into a patchwork of independent fiefs. The Zhou emperors continued to reign but they were entirely ignored by the various dukes, marquises and counts who in theory owed them obedience: in time the most successful of these magnates even began to call themselves kings.

The next four centuries saw a steady reduction in the number of these competing states: the larger swallowed up the smaller until there were only a dozen or so survivors. One of the most powerful was the kingdom of Qin – it was not the biggest but it was the most ruthlessly run. Most Chinese officials followed the precepts of Confucius, adviser to the Duke of Lu in the late 5th/early 4th century BC, who taught that a ruler should be just and moderate and so, by his example, bring his subjects to a similar state of virtue. The kings of Qin would have none of this: they believed in terror. A fearful scale of punishments was enacted for every sort of wrongdoing. The laws of Qin were so complicated and demanding that it was easier to be a wrongdoer in Qin than anywhere else in China. Long lines of convicts laboured on roads, canals and fortifications, making the state ever stronger and its kings yet more powerful.

Above: A pottery soldier buried by Shih-Huangdi's tomb.

Top: Stone relief showing an attempt to assassinate Shih-Huangdi in 218 BC. The emperor is holding up a jade disc symbolizing authority: the would-be assassin, rather clumsily superimposed on a fleeting courtier, has buried his dagger in the pillar. On the floor is the head of a fugitive Qin general, the present which gained the assassin admission to the emperor's presence.

In the short run, as it so often does, this sort of totalitarianism paid off. Between 230 and 221 BC the armies of Qin conquered the last ten Chinese kingdoms and extinguished their royal houses: the King of Qin was able to take the title Shih-Huangdi, meaning 'First Emperor'. He was not forgetting about his Shang Zhou predecessors, he just did not consider that the sort of vague suzerainty they had exercised over China was worth talking about. He was going to be a real emperor.

And so he was. He standardized weights and measures throughout the empire: he built fine roads across it; he codified the law and the script; he issued a uniform currency. He also showed his intolerance of opposition by persecuting the Confucians and burning their books: and his megalomania by building the Great Wall along the frontier between China and the nomads of the north. Stretching for more than 1500 kilometres this extraordinary monument took the labour and ultimately the lives of tens of thousands of Chinese: if nothing else it demonstrated the power of the Qin state.

Almost as soon as the first emperor was dead his empire fell apart. Peasants, goaded by the repeated exactions, rose up all over the empire, converged on the capital and sacked the palaces it contained. In time a new leader emerged, the humbly born Gao Tsu, who became the founding emperor of the Han dynasty. Gao Tsu deliberately dissociated himself from the first emperor's policies. He brought back the Confucians and made quite a speciality of half measures. The Qin dynasty had lasted just 14 years (221–206 BC): the Han were to rule for more than 400.

	250–226	225–201	200–176	175–151	150–126
Politics & Military History	**c250** Seleucids lose control of Parthia and Bactria. **241** Carthage, defeated in First Punic War, cedes Sicily to Rome. **237** Romans take Corsica and Sardinia from the Carthaginians. **236–226** The Romans conquer the Po Valley and the Carthaginians conquer the Mediterranean half of Spain. **230–228** China: King of Qin conquers rival kingdoms of Han, Zhou and Qi. = Ancestors of present day Japanese move from Korea to Japan, establishing islands' first agricultural community (Yayoi culture): subsequent decline of aboriginals of Ainu ethnic type (Jomon culture).	**230–222** King of Qin unites China; takes the title Shih-Huangdi ('First Emperor') (221). **220–206** Antiochus III restores Seleucid hegemony in the east. **218** Second Punic War begins with Hannibal's march from Spain to Italy: Hannibal wins victories of Lake Trasimene (217) and Cannae (216). **210–206** Qin dynasty founders following death of Shih-Huangdi. **210–206** Scipio conquers Carthaginian Spain. **204** Scipio lands in Africa: Hannibal, recalled from Italy, is defeated by Scipio at Zama (202): Second Punic War ends with Carthaginian surrender (201). **202** Gao Tsu founds the Han dynasty.	**197** Romans defeat Philip V of Macedon at Cynoscephalae. **190** Romans defeat Antiochus III, King of the Seleucid Empire, at Magnesia. **187** Mauryan Empire, reduced to nuclear kingdom of Magadha, extinguished by Pushyamitra, founder of the Sunga dynasty.	**171–168** War between Rome and Macedon ended by Roman victory at Pydna. **166** Maccabees rebel against Seleucids: Jewish state established by Jonathan Maccabeus (152). = Migration of the Yuezhi, Iranian nomads, from the borders of China to Turkestan.	**149–6** Romans force Carthage into Third Punic War; take and destroy the city. **148–6** Romans annex Greece. **141** Parthians conquer Mesopotamia. **133** Attalos III of Pergamum bequeathes his state to Rome. **128** *Han Emperor Wu Di annexes South Manchuria, first in a series of expansionary moves.* = Bactrian Greeks conquer the Punjab which then becomes a separate kingdom under Menander: Bactria succumbs to the Yuezhi shortly after.
Religion & Learning	**c245** Eratosthenes (see below) succeeds Apollonius as Royal Librarian at Alexandria.	**211** Archimedes killed during Roman sack of Syracuse.		**164** Rededication of the temple at Jerusalem by Judas Maccabeus.	= Standardized text established for *Ramayana*.
Cities & Social Development	**220** Construction begins on the Via Flaminia from Rome to Rimini. = Han Fei Zi formalises Legalist theory of Chinese totalitarian state.	**221–210** Shih-Huaugdi burns the classics and terrorises the educated classes of China; standardises weights and measures, script and coinage; builds the Great Wall in the north. **210** Shih-Huangdi buried in a mortuary complex at Mount Li, Shaanxi, that covers two square kilometres. Guarding the approach to this is an underground 'terracotta army' consisting of more than 4500 life-sized statues of soldiers fully equipped for battle.	**194–190** New Chinese capital laid out at Changan.	= Chinese begin using written examinations to select officials.	**146** Romans destroy two of the major cities of the period, Carthage and Corinth. **144** Marcian aqueduct built to bring water to Rome from a source 37 kilometres to the east. To maintain a steady gradient takes a path of more than twice this length, most of it underground but the last part on arcades. Long arcades of this sort – 11 kilometres in the case of the Marcia – will one day characterise the approaches to many Roman cities. **142** First stone bridge over the Tiber.
Discovery & Invention	= Eratosthenes measures the circumference of the Earth to within 10% of the correct value. = Archimedes of Syracuse establishes the basic laws on mechanics and hydrostatics.		= Romans develop concrete as their standard building material.		**139–126** Zhang Qian travels from China to the Oxus (Amu Darya) and back. = Hipparchus of Nicaea, the greatest practical astronomer of antiquity, catalogues 850 stars in 6 magnitudes, measures the ecliptic to 5′, estimates the tropical year correctly at 365.24 days and discovers the precession of the equinoxes (1° in 75 years).
The Arts	= Temple of Horus, Edfu, and Temple of Isis, Philae, built by Ptolemys in traditional Egyptian style.		**191** Plautus *Pseudolus*. **190** Winged victory of Samothrace (Louvre). **179** Basilica Aemilia, Roman Forum. = Construction of the Altar of Zeus at Pergamum. Frieze of battle between Gods and Giants (now in Berlin) marks beginning of baroque phase of classical sculpture.	**174** Work begins on the Temple of Zeus at Athens (not finished till AD 131). **170** Basilica Sempronia, Roman Forum. **160** Terence *Adelphi*. = Colossal group of Laocoön and his sons sculpted by the Rhodians Hagesandros, Polydoros and Athanodoros. (see AD 1506 A).	= Stoa of Attalos at Athens, a gift from the ruler of Pergamum.

	125–101	100–76	75–51	50–26	25–1 BC
Politics & Military History	**117** Chinese expand to the north west, garrisoning Gansu, the gateway to Central Asia. **115** Teutons and Cimbri leave their homelands in Germany. **112** Rome at war with Jugurtha, King of Numidia. **111** Chinese conquer Kingdom of Nan Yue (south China plus north Vietnam). **108** Chinese conquer North Korea. **106** Jugurtha captured. **105** Teutons and Cimbri defeat the Romans at Orange. **102** Roman General Marius defeats the Teutons at Aquae Sextiae (Aix en Provence): defeats the Cimbri at Vercellae (101).	**91–89** 'Social War' in Italy between Rome and her Italian allies ends with all Italians getting Roman citizenship. **86** Sulla defeats Mithradates VI of Pontus in Anatolia; establishes dictatorship in Rome (82–79). = Bantu migration of Negro peoples from west Africa into central Africa begins.	**68** Chinese pull back behind the Great Wall. **66** Pompey finally disposes of Mithradates: campaigns in trans-Caucasia (65); deposes last Seleucid (64) and organises the whole of the eastern Mediterranean into provinces of states subordinate to Rome. **62** Pompey returns to Italy. **60** Pompey, Caesar and Crassus form the First Triumvirate. **59–51** Caesar conquers Gaul with side expeditions to Germany (55 and 53) and Britain (55 and 54). **53** Crassus killed by the Parthians at Carrhae.	**49** Civil war between Caesar and Pompey ends in Pompey's defeat at Pharsalus (48). **47–44** Dictatorship of Caesar ends with his assassination. **43** Second Triumvirate of Antony (Caesar's lieutenant), Octavian (Caesar's heir) and Lepidus (a nonentity): defeats Caesar's assassins at Philippi (42) and divides empire (40). **40** Herod recognized as King of Judea by the Romans: takes Jerusalem (37). **36** Lepidus dropped. **31** Octavian defeats Antony at Actium: suicide of Antony and Cleopatra (30). **27** Octavian takes the name Augustus.	**20** Parthians restore the standards captured at Battle of Carrhae in 53. **2** Augustus, who has refused the title of Dictator (but has been running the empire single-handed all the same), accepts the title of Pater Patriae. = Bantu peoples reach Lake Victoria, Africa.
Religion & Learning	**113** Prince Liu Sheng, half brother of Emperor Wu Di, buried at Mancheng, Hebei, in a 'jade suit'. Made of 2,690 separate jade plates sewn together with gold wire, the suit is an example of a type of burial gear exclusive to the imperial family.	= Sima Qian's *Historical Records* lays the foundations for Chinese historical writings.	**70** Cicero makes his reputation by prosecuting Verres, retiring Governor of Sicily, for corruption. **c60** Diodorus begins work on his *World History*. **c55** Lucretius *On Nature*. **51** Caesar *Gallic War*.	**48** Fire destroys the Royal Library at Alexandria. **47** Varro, Librarian of Rome, publishes his 41 volume encyclopaedia. **c40** Sallust *Jugurthine War*. **c30** Vitruvius *On Architecture*. **26** First volume of Livy's *History of Rome* published.	**4** Death of Herod the Great traditionally associated with birth of Christ and 'Massacre of the Innocents'.
Cities & Social Development	**118** Narbonne founded, the first Roman colony outside Italy. Becomes the capital of the province of Transalpine (southern) Gaul.	**87** Athens sacked by Sulla.	**73–71** Rebellion of the gladiators of Capua led by Spartacus.	= Julius Caesar plans the refounding of Carthage and Corinth as Roman colonies: Augustus implements these plans on becoming Emperor. Other important provincial colonies founded at this time include Lyons, Nimes, Trier and Seville.	**22** Herod founds Caesarea: begins rebuilding of the Temple of Jerusalem (20). = Augustan building programme at Rome includes Theatre of Marcellus (13), Altar of Peace (9) and Augustan Forum (2). = Construction of Temple (Maison Carreé) and aqueduct (Pont du Gard) of Nimes. = Aosta and Turin founded following Augustus' pacification of the Alps.
Discovery & Invention		= Cargo of Rhodian ship wrecked off Antikythera includes cogwheel device for calculating the relative motions of the sun, moon and 5 known planets (recovered 1900–2). = Opening of trans-Asian 'silk route' between China and the West.	= Invention of glass-blowing (?in the Levant) leads to glass vessels of all sizes and shapes becoming common articles throughout the Roman world.	**46** Caesar institutes the Julian calendar based purely on the solar (tropical) year. Uses value of 365.250 days as against true value of 365.242. **36** Mexico: Earliest surviving example of a dating inscription in the 'Long Count' style invented by the Olmecs. = Use of the waterwheel general in the Roman world. = Tower of the Winds, Athens, bearing a wind vane and nine sundials and containing a water-clock: this probably operated an astronomical dial of the type later used in medieval astrolabes.	
The Arts	= Venus de Milo (Louvre).		**c55** Catullus *Poems*. **55** Pompey uses the spoils of his eastern campaign to build Rome's first stone theatre.	= Construction of major Buddhist monuments in India including Great Stupa at Sanchi and rock-cut temple at Karli.	**23** Horace *Odes*. **19** Virgil dies leaving the *Aeneid* almost complete.

During the 3rd and 2nd centuries BC the Romans made themselves masters of the Mediterranean world. The hardest fought wars were the earliest, against Carthage, the so-called Punic Wars (Punic being a contracted form of Phoenician). In the first war, the Romans took Sicily, in the second Spain and in the third Carthage itself. The East fell relatively easily, the Macedonian kingdoms often collapsing after a single battle. This area was eventually organized into a complicated mix of provinces (Asia, Bithynia, Syria and so on) and client states (Cappadocia, Armenia, the Jewish principality *etcetera*) by the Roman general Pompey the Great.

When Pompey returned to Rome he expected to get a warm welcome from the senate. He had after all pacified a major bloc of territories and in doing so practically doubled Rome's revenues. But the senators were jealous: they feared successful generals and they snubbed Pompey when he asked for the usual land grants on behalf of his soldiers. This rebuff precipitated the very situation they sought to avoid. Pompey teamed up with Caesar, the leader of the Populist party and Crassus, the richest man in Rome, and the three of them elbowed the senators aside. Rome became a military dictatorship, albeit a relatively benign one.

Above: Silver denarius with the head of Julius Caesar.

Below: The map of the Roman Empire was to simplify as the client states were turned into regular provinces but this was a process that took a long time and was not completed till well into the 2nd century AD.

At this stage Pompey was undoubtedly the senior partner: he had the prestige of a dozen successful campaigns behind him. Caesar determined to do something about this and restlessness among the tribes of Gaul gave him the opportunity he was looking for. He took the army of north Italy off on a series of annual forays that extended further and further across Gaul, finally reaching as far as Germany and Britain. Ten years later he could claim to have added as many provinces to the empire as Pompey had: more important, he had won the devotion of the toughest legions in the Roman army.

The break with Pompey came in 49 BC. In the subsequent civil war, Caesar was an easy victor and he returned to Rome as dictator for life. With the Roman people as well as the Roman soldiers he was immensely popular for he ensured that the rewards of empire were enjoyed by all the citizens and not just the senatorial class. The senators found means to assassinate him in 44 BC but they proved unable to dismantle his system. Caesar's son-in-law, Octavius, re-established the dictatorship and, as the Emperor Augustus, institutionalized it.

The transformation of the Roman Republic into a Populist dictatorship was probably inevitable: what was quite unexpected was the incorporation of the northern two-thirds of Gaul in the Roman Empire. This area lay outside the Mediterranean cultural world and continued to do so for a long time after the conquest: Romans never tired of pointing out the contrast between the south where the Gauls wore togas and the north where they wore trousers. Caesar's ambition and the political and military needs of the moment had driven him into an adventure beyond the normal Roman horizon.

What Caesar wanted from Gaul was an army: what he left behind was a country and a culture that had been altered in ways that are still relevant today.

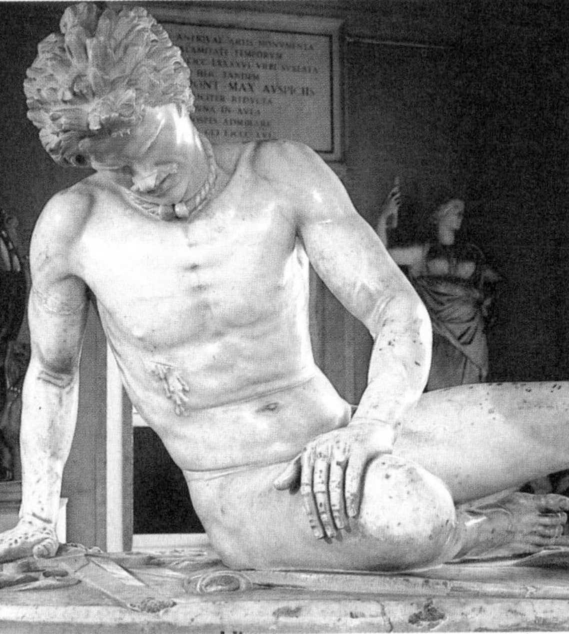

Left: The dying Gaul. A Greek sculpture celebrating the defeat of a Gallic invasion of Anatolia in the late 3rd century BC. Note the torc round the warrior's neck.

Right: Trajan prepares for the invasion of Dacia. Scene from the victory column he erected at the conclusion of his campaigns there in AD 113.

It was under Trajan that the empire reached its maximum territorial extent.

In AD 62 Pompeii was a prosperous little country town overlooking the Bay of Naples and overlooked by the irregular cone of Mount Vesuvius. This sounds a bit ominous but as there was no record of Vesuvius ever having caused any trouble it is unlikely that the Pompeians themselves thought of it that way. For them life was good. The empire was at peace, the local farmers were making money and the property market was booming.

Vesuvius had, in truth, been dormant for a long time – more than a thousand years according to present estimates. But that period was now coming to an end. In February molten rock working its way up into the cavities of the old volcano caused a sudden shift in its bulk: a violent tremor shook the mountain and rumbled out to Pompeii. It was a frightening business. One of the city gates caved in, the main temple collapsed and everywhere pavements split and walls cracked. The inhabitants fled into the countryside and waited to see what would happen next.

Nothing did. Gradually the people came back and started to put their houses in order. Subscriptions were raised, repair work started on the public buildings and gradually life returned to normal. Seventeen years after the earthquake the town was still badly scarred but it was functioning briskly enough.

In the interim the magma chamber at the heart of Vesuvius had filled to bursting point. Shortly after midday on 24th August, AD 79 the volcano made its return to active life apparent: gas began to vent from the old crater creating a plume of volcanic dust that – in the words of the younger Pliny who was watching it from Misenum across the bay – soon began to spread out like a pine tree.

The wind was blowing from the north: Pompeii on the south side of the mountain received a coating of ash that became steadily thicker as the eruption progressed. By early morning on the 25th the town was buried under two metres or more of pumice: many buildings had collapsed under the weight, and frequent tremors suggested that another earthquake was about to bring down the rest. The terrified Pompeians did not know whether to stay indoors and risk getting trapped, or go out and risk getting hit by the rocks with which the town was being bombarded.

Above: Arch at one of the entrances to the Forum of Pompeii: in the distance, Vesuvius in one of its quiet phases.

For the eruption was now changing its character: the throat of the volcano was getting choked with magma, and the smooth venting of gas was frequently interrupted. Fissures had appeared in the side of the mountain, fires were flashing out of them; Vesuvius was beginning to disintegrate. And, shortly before first light on the 25th, that is just what it did. With a colossal roar, the whole west side of the mountain blew out and a cloud of red hot gas and ash swept down over stricken Pompeii.

The advancing edge of the cloud killed everyone in the town: the lava flow that followed and the final ash falls that marked the end of the eruption buried it deep enough to preserve all but the uppermost parts of the buildings. Pompeii was sealed in pumice, awaiting its rediscovery (in the 16th century) and subsequent excavation (on and off since 1748).

Few tragedies have given so much pleasure to subsequent generations, remarked Goethe, and a visit to Pompeii is as near to a trip in a time machine as any of us are going to make. It is not the public buildings that impress, for many other sites have better ones, better preserved. The unique feature of Pompeii is the way it shows what life was like for an ordinary Roman citizen. Here are the streets as he walked them, the shops where he bought his bread, his oil and his wine, the houses where he and his friends lived, and eating places they went to and the workshops where his household goods were made. The walls still bear the slogans of the last elections, the scribbled names of girlfriends and the imprecations of unlucky gamblers. And over it all is the same blue sky and the same peaceful looking mountain.

Right: Illusionist wall painting of the type that became fashionable during the reign of the Emperor Augustus. Casa del Frutteto, Pompeii.

Left: A particularly grand Pompeian house, the 'House of the Silver Wedding'. View from the atrium, the small court round which the living rooms were arranged, into the garden.

	AD 1–24	25–49	50–74	75–99	100–124
Politics & Military History	**9** Wang Mang usurps the throne of China. Roman attempt to conquer West Germany ends with loss of three legions. **14** Death of Augustus who is succeeded by his stepson Tiberius. **23** Wang Mang overthrown and Han Dynasty reinstalled by Guang-Wudi: capital established at Luoyang (25). = Chinese control over north Korea ebbing.	**37** Caligula succeeds Tiberius as Roman Emperor; assassinated (41) and succeeded by Claudius. **43** Roman invasion of Britain.	**54** Claudius poisoned by Agrippina so that her son, Nero, can succeed. **59** Nero murders Agrippina. **61** Revolt of British Queen Boudicca. **66** First Jewish revolt begins. **68** Nero deposed. **69** Year of the Four Emperors ends with Vespasian gaining the imperial throne. **70** Capture and destruction of Jerusalem by Vespasian's son Titus: Masada falls (73).	**91** Chinese General Ban Chao establishes protectorate over central Asia.	**115** Roman Empire reaches its maximum extent under Trajan who conquers Dacia (Romania) (106) and Mesopotamia (115). **116** Second Jewish revolt. = Empire of the Kushans (Turkestan, Afghanistan and the Punjab) reaches its greatest extent in the reign of Kanishka (exact dates uncertain). = Bantu peoples of Africa reach the Indian Ocean. = Beginning of Arawak movement from Venezuela to the Lesser Antilles.
Religion & Learning	**6** Census in Syria, linked by Matthew to birth of Christ. = Strabo *Geography*.	**30** Crucifixion of Jesus of Nazareth. **46** First missionary journey of St Paul (to 48). **49** Seneca appointed tutor to the 12 year old Nero.	**53–57** Third missionary journey of St Paul. **64** Nero persecutes the Christians of Rome whom he blames for the fire in the city (see below): martyrdom of SS Peter and Paul. **65** Seneca, Lucan and Petronius Arbiter involved in conspiracy against Nero: all die. **68** Monastery of Qumran destroyed by Roman forces engaged in the supression of the Jewish revolt (see also 1947–D). **c70** Composition of the synoptic gospels.	**75–79** Josephus *Jewish War*. **77** Pliny the Elder completes his 37 volume encyclopaedia. **82** *History of the Han* by Ban Biao, his son Ban Gu and his daughter Ban Zhou.	**100** First Chinese dictionary; 9353 entries. **100–110** Tacitus *Histories*. **111–113** Pliny the younger's correspondence with Trajan. **121** Suetonius *Lives of the Caesars*. = Plutarch *Lives*.
Cities & Social Development	**2** First surviving census figure for China, 57.7 millions. **14** In his will Augustus notes that in eight sets of games he gave at Rome he employed a total of 5000 pairs of gladiators.	**49** Colchester, residence of the Belgic kings of south-east Britain, confirmed as capital of Roman Britain by Claudius.	**50** Cologne, previously just a garrison town, made into a Roman colony. **60** The three important towns of Roman Britain – Colchester, London and St Albans – all burned by Boudicca. This is the first indication that London has emerged as a substantial town. **63** Earthquake at Pompeii. **64** Fire at Rome lasting nine days: Nero uses the space created to build a palace and park, the Domus Aurea (Golden House).	**79** Eruption of Vesuvius buries Pompeii and Herculaneum. **97** Frontinius appointed Curator of Rome's aqueducts; prepares treatise *(De Aquis)* on their history and function.	**121** Emperor Hadrian, Trajan's successor, begins the first of his tours of the empire: starts construction of the Wall in Britain (122).
Discovery & Invention	= King Juba of Mauretania sends expedition to explore the recently discovered Canaries.		**57** Japanese chieftain in Kyushu sends embassy to China, the first direct contract between the two countries.		**105** Paper invented in China. = Iron-framed torsion catapult *(cheiroballista)* developed by Roman military engineers.
The Arts	**8** Ovid publishes *Art of Love* and is banished to Tomi (on the Black Sea coast of Romania) by Augustus.		**62** Lucan *Civil War*. **c65** Petronius Arbiter (probably) *Satyricon*.	**80** Inauguration of the Colosseum at Rome. **85** Arch of Titus, Rome, featuring spoils of Jerusalem.	**100–110** Juvenal *Satires*. **112** Dedication of Trajan's Forum, Basilica and Column (38 metres high) in Rome. = Kanishka constructs 13-storey pagoda at Peshawar (perhaps 100 metres high).

	125–149	150–174	175–199	200–224	225–249
Politics & Military History	**131** Third Jewish revolt against Rome led by Simon Bar Kokhba: suppressed by 135. From this time on it is easier to be a Jew outside Palestine than in, and the dispersion of the Jewish people, always considerable, steadily increases. **140** Romans move forward to Scottish lowlands: Antonine Wall built 140–3.		**180** Romans in Scotland pull back to Hadrian's Wall. **184** 'Yellow Turbans' revolt in China: Luoyang sacked (190). **192** Disorder in Rome following the assassination of Marcus Aurelius' son Commodus: empire auctioned by the Praetorian guard; three short-lived emperors before Septimius Severus takes control (193); Severus then defeats rival emperors in Syria (194) and Britain (197).	**222** Start of Three Kingdoms period in China: Han Empire replaced by Kingdom of Wei (in the Yellow River valley), Wu (in the lower Yangzi) and Shu-Han (Sichuan). = First Abyssinian kingdom established, with capital at Axum.	**226** Ardashir I founds new (Sassanid) dynasty in Iran and starts hostilities with Rome.
Religion & Learning	= Arrian *Life of Alexander*. = Asvagosha *Life of Buddha*. = Buddhism spreads into central Asia under Kushan patronage.	**174** Marcus Aurelius, the philosopher emperor, begins his *Meditations*. = Pausanias *Description of Greece*.	**197** Tertullian *Apologeticum*. = Development of Mahayana Buddhism in India: intervention of saints accepted as an aid to achieving *Nirvana*.		**c230–245** Origen produces his Hexapla bible (six parallel versions: one Hebrew, three Greek and two Latin). **240** Mani preaches new dualistic religion in Iran. = Dio Cassius *History of Rome*.
Cities & Social Development	**128–132** Hadrian's second tour of the empire. = London now the leading place in Britain.	**165–7** Plague spreads from the East across the Mediterranean to Rome.		**212** Roman citizenship conferred on all free adults in the empire.	**247** Emperor Philip celebrates the 1000th anniversary of Rome's foundation.
Discovery & Invention	= Claudius Ptolemy of Alexandria summarizes the geographical and astronomical knowledge of the Classical World in his *Almagest* which remains the standard work on these topics to the end of the Middle Ages.	= Galen of Pergamum, physician to Marcus Aurelius, proves that arteries as well as veins convey blood.	**175** Text of China's Five Classics cut on standing stones at Luoyang. Rubbings taken from this master text represent a first step towards printing, though the idea was to ensure accuracy not cut the cost.		**232** Traditional date of invention of wheelbarrow in China. 243 China: court of Yangzi Kingdom of Wu receives embassy from Cambodia.
The Arts	= Hadrian's building programme at Rome includes reconstruction of the Pantheon as a domed building with a central span of 43 metres (118–125), the Temple of Venus and Rome (135) and his mausoleum (139: now the Castel S. Angelo). Also extensive Villa at Tivoli outside the city (118–134).	**173** Equestrian statue of Marcus Aurelius, Rome (now in the Campidoglio). = Apuleius' romance *The Golden Ass*. = Lucian *Satiric Dialogues*.	= Bellows organ replaces water organ.	**203** Arch of Septimius Severus and Baths of Caracalla at Rome: extensive building programme at Leptis magna (Tripolitania), the birthplace of Severus.	= (probably) Longus' romance *Daphnis and Chloë*.

Pompeii had about 8000 inhabitants, an average number for a Roman town. In the entire Mediterranean world there were only a handful of places with populations of more than 25,000. This makes the position of Rome, which had at least 250,000, all the more remarkable.

Remarkable but not unique. A lot of small towns and a huge metropolis seems to be the characteristic urban pattern for early empires. It is true of China at this time: Luoyang, the capital of the later Han emperors, was probably about the same size as Rome, and the average Chinese county town was certainly no bigger than Pompeii. It is also true of later empires like Byzantium, the Arab caliphate and the Aztec state. These tribute-collecting organizations spent their money on their capital cities and directly or indirectly it was this government expenditure that sustained their exceptional populations.

In the Roman case the support was direct: the imperial government fed the people for free. In the 1st century BC this was on a relatively small scale and the only food supplied was bread. By Augustus' time the number of people receiving free bread had risen to 200,000 and the safe delivery of the grain to Ostia, the port of Rome, had become one of the main responsibilities of the government. Most of the grain came from Egypt in specially built freighters: it was stored in huge warehouses in the southern quarter of the city, baked under government contract and distributed to ticket holders on a rota basis. Later the authorities added free oil and pork as well.

What the government could not provide was jobs. To some extent the citizens kept themselves busy taking in each other's washing, but the basic economic truth was that having conquered the Mediterranean world there was nothing more for them to do. They needed not only feeding but entertaining.

Hence the comment of the satirist Juvenal that the Romans of his day had only two preoccupations, bread and circuses. The second was just as important as the first and the emperors gave it equal time. To this end they built immense entertainment complexes: the Circus Maximus round which the chariots raced Ben Hur-style, the Colosseum, where anything up to 50,000 spectators watched the gladiatorial shows and the vast public baths where the masses could pass the day steaming or swimming and watching, or even joining, athletic contests. Such were the rewards of empire.

Right: Mithras, god-hero of one of the new religions that came to Rome from the East.

Building these enormous structures meant that Rome did have one major industry even if this was, in economic terms, purely incestuous. The Roman construction industry was the biggest and most advanced the world had seen so far. It achieved some technically remarkable buildings, for example, the Pantheon with its dome 43 metres in diameter. It also built five and six storey tenement blocks to house the city's teeming thousands. Rome looked very different from Pompeii.

In truth Rome was too big. The narrow streets were jammed with people and carts, the sanitation and lighting in the tenements was inadequate and most of the people would have been happier and healthier if they had returned to their ancestral farms. But cities like this – and there are plenty of them in the Third World today – hold their populations despite the obvious disadvantages: the squalor and underemployment is outweighed by the free handouts and the excitements of professional sport.

Below left: The market place at Leptis magna, a town in present-day Libya.

Below right: Model of Imperial Rome. The Circus Maximus is in the centre, the Colosseum above and to the left. In between the two is the complex of buildings on the Palatine Hill that made up the imperial palace. Several sets of baths are visible, a small one just to the right of centre and two massive ones further off – the Baths of Caracalla to the upper right, and the Baths of Trajan to the upper left, behind the Colosseum.

Above: Fresco of Christ, c.5th century AD from the catacomb of St Bassilla in Rome. Catacomb paintings are the main source for Early Christian art. From these images it can be deduced that they were not meant to record historical event rather they are painted as a gesture of thanksgiving for deliverance from death and sin, which explains why so many of the paintings are so rich in contemporary inscriptions, some are prayers, some are graffiti.

Left: Sardis, Turkey – ruin of the temple of Artemis with a Christian chapel added at the east at the time of the early Byzantine empire.

By the 3rd century AD Rome's legions had been the dominant military force in the Mediterranean world for more than 500 years. During this period they had lost some of their battles but they had always won their wars and there was no reason to believe that they would not go on doing so for another 500.

The reality turned out very differently. In 251 the Emperor Decius was killed fighting the Goths on the Danube frontier: eight years later the Emperor Valerian was captured by the Persian King Shapur; in both Europe and Asia the defences of the empire collapsed. The legions had proved to be obsolete as well as unruly and expensive. It took a succession of hard working soldier-emperors to restore the situation, and doing so involved revamping not just the army but the administration and indeed the whole style of the empire. The Roman world of the 4th century AD was a very different affair from the empire of Augustus.

Most of the administrative reforms were introduced by the Emperor Diocletian. He saw that the soldiers would be less likely to rebel if they already had an emperor of their own and he set up a somewhat cumbersome system known as the tetrarchy in which two senior and two junior emperors shared responsibility for the empire. This meant that each of the four main armies (on the Rhine, the upper Danube, the lower Danube and the Euphrates) had an emperor to command it. He also squeezed the economy hard because the new armies were not only bigger and better than the legions had been but far more expensive.

For the vast majority of the population the Roman Empire had always been a harsh institution: it brought peace and a species of customary law, but it also bore down hard on the many in favour of the few. Small wonder that increasing numbers turned to the Eastern religions that promised a better life next time. The worse conditions got, the more recruits flocked to the most caring and best organized of these religions, Christianity. The church emerged as a state within a state.

In his hurry to rebuild the empire Diocletian chose to do so on the old foundations: the result was that he botched the job. He sent his best regiments back to the old frontier line, many of them to the very forts that had once been garrisoned by the legions. He attempted to stop inflation by decrees fixing the wages of everyone and the prices of everything. He tried to revive the old religions by persecuting the new ones. None of these measures worked and it was left to Constantine, the son of one of Diocletian's co-emperors, to come up with the fresh set of answers that was needed.

Constantine reversed many of Diocletian's policies immediately. He kept his crack regiments near at hand and used them for mobile warfare, a much cheaper and more effective way of defending the empire. He issued a new, gold-based coinage which remained a standard for centuries. And instead of persecuting the Christians he allied himself with them: he used their enthusiasm to bolster his new order.

Constantine cut away the dead wood. His genius for doing so and for making exactly the right new start is shown best of all in his choice of a new capital for the eastern half of the empire. Diocletian had picked Nicomedia which turned out to be nowhere: Constantine chose Byzantium, a marvellous site at the centre of the Eastern Empire's communications. There he reigned in a splendour more medieval than Roman, among people who thought in terms of counts and their retainers, bishops and their disputations. This sounds a bit down-market from the grave senators of Old Rome but is really to his credit. He anticipated, indeed partly created, an age that was still to come.

	250–274	275–299	300–324	325–349	350–374
Politics & Military History	**251** Emperor Decius killed fighting the Goths on the Danube: Goths and other German tribes plunder the empire (till 269). **259** Gaul breaks away under its own emperor, Postumus. **259** Emperor Valerian captured while fighting Persian king Shapur. **262** Persians driven out of eastern provinces by Odenathus, Prince of Palmyra. **263** China: Wei annexes Shu-Han; King of Wei takes dynastic name of Jin. **270** Aurelian becomes emperor, restores prestige and integrity of the empire by defeating the Germans (270), deposing Zenobia, widow of Odenathus (273) and reconquering Gaul (274).	**280** Jin annexes Wu, reuniting China. **285** Emperor Diocletian begins complete reorganization of the empire; makes Maximian his co-emperor. **286** Britain breaks away under rebel Emperor Carausius. **293** Diocletian makes two more co-emperors, Constantius and Galerius. **296** Britain recovered by Constantius. **298** Galerius gets the upper hand over the Persians: imposes frontier changes in Rome's favour.	**305** Diocletian and Maximian abdicate in favour of Constantius and Galerius. **306** Constantius dies at York: his son Constantine proclaimed emperor by the soldiers without waiting for Galerius' nomination. **308** Hun chieftain sets up independent state in north China: takes Luoyang (316); Jin retreat to Nanjing (317), initiating period in which China is divided into northern and southern empires with Gansu usually independent.* **312** Constantine defeats Maxentius (Maximian's son) at the Milvian Bridge outside Rome: takes Italy. **313** Chinese lose Pyong yang to native Korean kingdom of Koguryo. **320** Chandragupta founds Gupta Empire of north India. **324** Constantine defeats Licinius near Byzantium and takes the East: Constantine now sole emperor.	**337** Roman Empire divided between Constantine's three sons. = Japan: emergence of the Yamato state which gradually acquires hegemony over the regions bordering the Inland Sea. = Samoans (Polynesians) colonise Tahiti and the Marquesas.	**351** Roman Empire reunited under sole surviving son of Constantine, Constantius II: he appoints Julian co-Emperor (355); dies (361). **363** Death of Julian on campaign in the east: end of Constantinian dynasty. Empire passes to Valentinian I who takes the west and gives his brother Valens the east (364). **367** Order restored in Britain, after Picts and Scots overwhelm local defences. **372** Huns defeat Ostrogoths (East Goths) on the Russian steppe. = Two kingdoms emerge in the south of Korea, Paikche and Silla. The Japanese gain a foothold in the extreme south; the north continues under the rule of the kings of Koguryo.
Religion & Learning	**250** Emperor Decius persecutes the Christians. **c255** Plotinus' *Enneads* expounding his neo-Platonist philosophy (not published till c300). = Mithraism increasingly popular in the Roman world, especially with the military.	**c285** China: *History of the Three Kingdoms.*	**303** Armenia becomes the first Christian state. **303** Diocletian persecutes the Christians: campaign continues intermittently till 313 when Constantine issues Edict of Toleration at Milan. **314** Conference of Arles, first general council of the western Church. **321** Sunday declared a statutory holiday. = Monasticism initiated by St Anthony. = Eusebius of Caesarea *Ecclesiastical History.*	**325** Council of Nicaea establishes basic Christian dogma. Constantine bans gladiatorial combats. **337** Deathbed conversion to Christianity of Constantine the Great. **342–3** Council of Sardica fails to solve the Arian controversy but is important because it gives Papal prerogatives their first formal recognition.	**350** Bible translated into Gothic. **361–3** Julian ('the apostate') tries to revive classical paganism in the Roman Empire – unsuccessfully.
Cities & Social Development	**267** Sack of Athens by the German Heruls reduces the city to a village. **271** Aurelian orders new walls to be built around Rome.	= Towns of Gaul ordered to build defensive walls. The small areas enclosed by these show how far urban life in the West had fallen below its initial aspirations.	**301** Diocletian attempts to stop inflation by fixing the price of everything. = Trier, Salonica and Nicomedia upgraded to serve as secondary capitals.	**330** Constantinople (ex-Byzantium) becomes the capital of the eastern half of the empire: Constantine brings monuments of ancient Greece to the city including the Serpent Column from Delphi and the Zeus from Olympia.	
Discovery & Invention	**c250** Diophantus of Alexandria introduces algebraic notation.		= Pappus of Alexandria summarises and comments on many of the achievements of Classical science.		
The Arts		**298** Rome: Baths of Diocletian.	= Basilica of Maxentius at Rome, completed by Constantine: Arch of Constantine (315). Palaces built at Split (Dalmatia) and Piazza Armerina (Sicily) for Diocletian and Maximian to retire to.	= Official recognition of Christianity is followed by church-building programme that includes Church of the Holy Sepulchre in Jerusalem and Old St Peter's and the Mausoleum of Constantina (now S. Constanza) in Rome. = Era of the *Kofun* tumuli in Japan, royal tombs with *haniwa* (pottery figurine) attendants.	

*Chinese historiography puts the formal beginning of this phase more than a century later, in 440.

	375–399	400–424	425–449	450–474	475–499
Politics & Military History	**375** Huns cross the Dniester and defeat the Visigoths (West Goths) who flee into Roman territory. **378** Visigoths defeat and kill the eastern emperor Valens at Adrianople. **382** Theodosius restores order in the Balkans: he briefly – and for the last time – reunites the empire (394). **395** Empire divided between Theodosius' sons Honorius (the West) and Arcadius (the East). **398** Turkish chieftain takes imperial title in north China founding Northern Wei dynasty. = Japanese defeat Korean kingdoms of Paikche and Silla, briefly establish control over the southern half of the peninsula.	**406** Vandals and other German tribes cross the Rhine and ravage Gaul. **408** Alaric the Visigoth invades Italy. **409** Vandals move from Gaul to Spain. **410** Rome falls to Alaric. **417** Visigoths settle in Aquitaine. **420** Liu Song dynasty replaces Jin in South China. **423** Northern Wei take Luoyang. = Gupta empire of north India reaches its peak. = First kingdoms emerge in South East Asia: Pyu (Burma), Funan (Cambodia) and Champa (Central Vietnam), all under Indian cultural influence.	**429** Vandals cross from Spain to Africa (tribe numbered at 80,000). **439** Vandals capture Carthage. **441–7** Attila, King of the Huns, forces the East Roman Empire to cede territory on the Danube and pay an annual tribute.	**451** Huns turned back from Gaul by combined Roman-Gothic army at Campus Mauriacus. **453** Death of Attila: his empire disintegrates when its German tributaries revolt (Battle of the Nedao 454). **455** Vandal fleet sacks Rome. **469** Visigoths begin conquest of Spain. = Anglo Saxons begin to settle in England. = India: Gupta Empire disintegrates under the attacks of the White Huns.	**476** Romulus Augustulus, last emperor of the West, deposed by his Master of Troops, Odoacer, who takes the title of King of Italy. **486** Clovis, King of the Franks, conquers north-west Gaul. **489–493** Theodoric the Ostrogoth conquers Italy: recognised as King by East Roman Emperor. = British check Anglo-Saxon advance at siege of Mount Badon (site unknown). = Maize cultivation begins in the woodland zone of North America.
Religion & Learning	**382–5** St Jerome produces his Latin translation of the bible, the Vulgate. **391** Theodosius bans pagan rites and closes the temples of the gods. The empire changes from an institution that favours Christianity to one that requires it (though Jews are allowed to follow their faith). **398** 293rd and last Olympiad: the next year Theodosius prohibits further games. **399** Fa Xian sets out from China to study Buddhism in India.	**412** Fa Xian returns to China: publishes *Treatise on Buddhist Kingdoms* (414). **426** St Augustine *City of God.* = Japan adopts Chinese style script.	**430** *History of the Later Han.* **431** Council of Ephesus rejects the view of Nestor, Bishop of Constantinople, on the dual nature of Christ. **432** St Patrick lands in Ireland: founds see of Armagh (444). **438** Theodosius II orders new codification of Roman law.	**451** Council of Chalcedon. = Northern Wei emperors encourage spread of Buddhism in north China.	**496** Baptism of Clovis initiates conversion of the Franks. = Development of Hopewell cult, centred on Ohio, among the North American Indians.
Cities & Social Development	**376** Turks of Inner Mongolia make Datong (Shanxi) their chief centre: it becomes the northern Wei capital in 398. **381** Milan becomes the *de facto* administrative capital of the western half of the Roman Empire.	**402** Honorius, Emperor of the West, moves his court to Ravenna. **415** Constantinople: Theodosian wall begun, doubling the size of the city. = Arles made capital of the remnants of Roman Gaul.			Northern Wei move capital to Luoyang. = Rise of the city of Teotihuacan in the Mexico valley marks the beginning of urban life in Middle America. (Contemporary sites in Yucatan (Uxmal, Chichen Itza) and Guatemala (Tikal) were ceremonial centres not true towns).
Discovery & Invention				= Metal stirrup in use among the horsemen of the Asian steppe. **467** Chinese make earliest known observation of Halley's comet.	
The Arts	= Rome: S Clemente (380) and St Pauls Outside the Walls (386). = Constantinople: obelisk of Tutmosis III, first erected at Heliopolis in 1450 BC, re-erected at Constantinople by Theodosius.	= Constantinople: First church of Hagia Sophia (begun c415). = Rome: SS John and Paul (410–20), S Sabina (422–32). = Ravenna: St John the Evangelist (424–34).	= Ravenna: Mausoleum of Galla Placidia; Orthodox baptistry (both c425). = Rome: S Maria Maggiore (432–40).	= Rome: S Stefano Rotondo (468–83). = Syria: Basilica of S Simeon Stylites (489), built around the pillar on top of which the saint had lived for the last 30 years of his life. = Rock carvings of Buddha in caves of Yungang, Shanxi, begun under patronage of Northern Wei Emperors.	= Ravenna: S Apollinare Nuovo (490). **494** Work begins on Buddhist carvings in the caves of Longmen, near Luoyang: continues intermittently to the end of the Tang dynasty.

The main threat to the Roman Empire of the 4th century AD came from the Germans who, at that time, occupied not only their original homeland – much the same as the Germany of today – but the whole of eastern Europe and the southern part of European Russia. They had spilled out to the east because the Romans, starting with Julius Caesar, had stopped them moving in on the west but they never forgot that the lands Rome ruled were the ones they wanted and every generation or so they felt compelled to test the Empire's defences again.

The crucial contest blew up suddenly and unexpectedly. The easternmost of the German tribes, the Gothic confederation of south Russia, took a beating from the Huns, a Turkic tribe whose pastures stretched from central Asia to the River Volga. Like all Turks, the Huns were masters of mounted warfare and the Goths proved quite unable to cope with them. After a few years of one-sided slaughter the Goths retreated to the Danube with their tails between their legs and insisted that the Romans give them sanctuary.

The Romans were grudging, the Goths insistent: tempers flared and the two were soon at war. The East Roman Emperor, Valens, was outmanoeuvred by the Goths who had learned a thing or two about cavalry tactics from their exchanges with the Huns, and the battle that the Romans had rashly precipitated (at Adrianople in 378) ended in his defeat and death. The empire that had looked so solid the week before was immediately in dire trouble.

By a combination of blockade and bribery, by hiring Germans to fight Germans, and by letting those they could not beat settle as 'allies' in imperial territory, the Romans managed to keep the empire more or less intact for another 25 years. Then the western half started to run out of men and money. Its finances had been shaky ever since the empire had been divided, for the tribute that had previously flowed to Rome from the eastern provinces was thereafter diverted to Constantinople. Old Rome could no longer meet its commitments. The Germans, sensing this, closed in for the kill.

Stilicho, the commander of the western armies, faced an impossible task. In 406, to meet a threatened invasion of Italy, he concentrated all his forces in the Po Valley even though this meant leaving the Rhine frontier undefended. In August it looked as if his strategy had paid off: he won a remarkable victory over the horde of Goths, Vandals and other Germans that had entered the peninsula and there was no sign of trouble on the Rhine. But it was brewing: another host was moving across the south of Germany and on the last day of 406 this crossed the frozen, and totally undefended, river. Next year all Gaul was in German hands. As Stilicho desperately tried to hold his striking force together – funds were so low that he was reduced to stripping the gilded tiles off the roof of the temple of Jupiter in Rome – the politicians began baying for his blood. In 408 they won over the Emperor Honorius who ordered Stilicho's arrest.

Rejoicing was general. The Romans celebrated the overthrow of the man they were convinced was a traitor (he was, after all, a Vandal, not a Roman): the German war-bands on the loose in Gaul and Illyria (modern Yugoslavia) were equally delighted; the empire was now wide open. By the end of the year Alaric the Goth was camped outside Rome and though on this occasion the city used its accumulated wealth to buy him off, he was back again in a less conciliatory mood two years later. In the year 410, while the ignoble Honorius and his court hid away in Ravenna, Alaric and his men put Rome to the sack – looting, pillaging and burning.

Right: Although Rome was sacked by the Goths in 410 and the Vandals in 455, the western empire lingered on till 476 when a Barbarian general who could not be bothered with puppet emperors any longer, got rid of the last one. By then the various German tribes had carved out kingdoms for themselves – the Franks in Gaul, the Goths in Spain and the Vandals in North Africa.

Above: Roman soldiers fighting trousered Barbarians. Scene from a Roman sarcophagus made for one of Marcus Aurelius's generals in the 2nd century. The sarcophagus was made in advance by a workshop – the general's face (centre) has been left blank for his portrait to be carved in later.

Left: Ivory diptych with portraits of Stilicho, his wife Serena and his son Eucharius. In the late empire there was a fashion for presentation booklets commemorating official appointments. Ivory panels like these were used as covers for them. This pair, one of the finest in existence, is now in the treasury of the Cathedral of Monza, not far from Milan where Stilicho had his headquarters.

When Justinian came to the throne of the Eastern Empire in AD 527 the storm that had sunk the Western Empire had blown itself out. If the cause of the disaster had been overpopulation in Germany and underpopulation in the empire – and there is probably quite a lot to this idea – then it is easy enough to see what had happened: the movement of Germans into Gaul, Spain, Italy and north Africa, had relieved the imbalance. For the moment all was quiet.

Justinian interpreted this as the signal for a counter-attack. His advisers, very conscious of the fact that the east had come perilously close to foundering itself, were unenthusiastic to say the least, but Justinian over-ruled them. He scraped together a small army, entrusted it to a general named Belisarius who had recently distinguished himself fighting the Persians, dispatched it to north Africa and was rewarded with a remarkably quick and easy success. After a couple of battles the Vandal kingdom collapsed, north Africa was recovered for the empire and the East Roman treasury replenished from the store of plunder that the Vandals had accumulated in their heyday.

Belisarius' victory showed that the German kingdoms had serious weaknesses. The Germans had imposed themselves on the provincials but they had not won their loyalty. Maybe the Gothic kingdom of Italy could be brought down just as easily? Justinian thought so and at first it looked as though he might be right again. Belisarius liberated Sicily and south Italy without any trouble at all and he actually entered Rome before the Goths had their army assembled. But though the Goths were slow to move, when they finally arrived they did so in formidable numbers. Belisarius had not enough men to face them in the field so he sat in Rome and let his opponents try their hand at siege warfare. After 12 months, the Gothic army, at its least effective in this sort of situation, began to come apart and Belisarius inched forward again. It was all a bit touch and go but eventually the Gothic king threw his hand in, surrendered his kingdom and sailed off to Constantinople with Belisarius.

Upper left: Dome of Santa Sophia, Constantinople (present day Istanbul). 'Solomon, I have surpassed you' said Justinian when he first saw the dome of his new cathedral, and it still impresses today. The dome of the Pantheon may have a wider span (43 m as against 32 m) but the dome of Santa Sophia rises higher (56 m as against 43 m) and has a lighter and subtler architecture.

Upper right: The Emperor Justinian and his lords-in-waiting. Mosaic from the apse of San Vitale, Ravenna.

Above centre: Interior of Santa Sophia viewed from one of the arches of the apse.

Unfortuntely for Justinian this was not the end of the story. The Goths woke up to the fact that they had been tricked rather than defeated. They elected a new king and the war began again. In the end, after the tide of battle had flowed up and down the peninsula several more times, Justinian did get Italy back into the empire, but the cost turned out to be much higher than he or anyone else had expected. And not just financially, whole towns were completely destroyed: the country was so devastated that it had ceased to be worth having.

Much the same can be said of north Africa. The settled element in its population was declining, the Berbers of the desert took a bit more of the marginal land every year and the administration was always having to call on Constantinople for support. In retrospect it is easy to see that the premise on which Justinian had begun his western campaigns – that the empire would be the stronger for the recovery of Africa and Italy – had turned out to be mistaken. These countries were not capable of defending themselves: all they brought was more problems and Constantinople had enough of these already. The economic decline that was the root cause of the empire's malaise was still continuing: towns were dwindling, revenue falling and the emptiness increasing.

If Justinian's political design was misconceived, his plans for a cultural renaissance fared better. He revamped the legal system, saw that his campaigns were properly written up and launched a huge building programme. Here he showed that if there were new ideas around he could respond to them. Ever since Hadrian's Pantheon, Roman architects had been interested in the possibilities offered by domed buildings: gradually they had learned to make the domes higher and lighter. When Justinian decided to build a new cathedral for Constantinople he opted for a design of this type – and his architects responded with a masterpiece. The cathedral of Santa Sophia has been much imitated – it is the inspiration for a multitude of Christian churches and Turkish mosques – but it has rarely been equalled.

	500–524	525–549	550–574	575–599	600–624
Politics & Military History	**505** Clovis, king of the Franks, conquers the Alemanni of the upper Rhine. **507** Clovis defeats the Visigoths at Vouglé and drives them from France. **511** Death of Clovis, king of the Franks and founder of the Merovingian dynasty: division of the kingdom between his four sons, Theodoric, Chlodomir, Childebert and Chlotar. = Malagasy (from Sumatra?) colonize Madagascar.	**533** Justinian, East Roman Emperor, decides to attempt recovery of the west: his general, Belisarius, conquers the Vandal kingdom of north Africa. **534** Franks conquer Burgundy. **535–40** Belisarius takes Sicily and nearly all Italy from the Ostrogoths. **537** Franks conquer Provence and east Switzerland. **540** Ostrogoths launch successful counter-offensive against the Roman forces in Italy.	**552** Turks of Central Asia defeat rival tribes and establish control over the steppe from the Aral Sea to Outer Mongolia. **552** Roman victory at Busta Gallorum brings Italy back into the empire again. **554** Romans occupy south-east quarter of Spain. **555** Franks conquer Bavaria. **558** Chlotar, surviving son of Clovis, reunites the Frankish kingdom but this is divided again at his death in 561. **562** Japanese driven from their Korean foothold. **562** Tribes fleeing from the Turks establish the Avar Khanate in Hungary. **568** Lombards, displaced from Hungary by Avars, invade Italy and overrun interior: Romans cling on to Ravenna and Rome, various seaports, and the toe and heel. = Scots, originally an Irish tribe, establish control over Argyll.	**577** Anglo-Saxon victory at Deorham marks resumption of their advance in England. **589** Sui dynasty reunites China. = Slavs move across the Danube into modern Yugoslavia.	**603** Roman defence line in the Balkans collapses: Slavs pour into the peninsula. Start of 25 years war between Rome and Persia during which Persians break through in Mesopotamia (605–10), conquer Syria (611–13), Palestine (614) and Egypt (619). **613** Surviving grandson of Chlotar reunites the Frankish kingdom: he donates the eastern half (Austrasia, as opposed to Neustria) to his son Dagobert (623). **618** The Li family, utilising Turkish support, rebel against the Sui, occupy Changan, found the Tang dynasty. **c620** Emperor Heraclius reorganizes remaining Roman provinces.** **623** Heraclius launches counter-offensive in the Caucasus (623). = Cambodia: kingdom of Funan overthrown by Khmers.
Religion & Learning	**523** Boethius *Consolations of Philosophy*. = First inscription in the Indonesian archipelago, recording Buddhist sentiments in an Indian script. = Buddhism adopted by the three kingdoms of Korea. = St David founds monastery of Mynyw (now St David's Pembrokeshire).	**528** Justinian begins new codification of Roman law: he also closes down the Classical schools of Athens. **540** St Benedict formulates his monastic rule. = Emperor Liang Wu Di encourages spread of Buddhism through south China.	**551** Procopius *History of the Wars of Justinian*. **552** Buddhism introduced to Japan. **563** St Columba begins his mission to Scotland. **570** Supposed Abyssinian expedition against Mecca, traditionally associated with the birth of Muhammad. = Cosmas *Topographia*.	**587** Triumph of the Buddhists in Japan. **590** Pope Gregory the Great becomes the effective ruler of Rome as East Roman power in Italy decays. **597** St Augustine begins his mission to England. = Gregory of Tours *History of the Franks*.	**610** Muhammad's first sermon. **622** Hegira, Muhammad's flight from Mecca to Medina, marking the beginning of the Muslim era. = Isidore of Seville produces his encyclopedia *Origines*.
Cities & Social Development		= Tea drinking promoted by Chinese Buddhists as a substitute for alcohol.	**542** Plague in the Mediterranean.	**582** The first Sui emperor begins work on a new dynastic capital alongside the ruins of Han Changan. All Chinese capitals were large; Sui Changan was to be the largest walled city ever built, extending over 7775 ha: by comparison imperial Rome covered 1386 ha, Paris within the wall built by Philip Augustus 250 ha and within the 1860 lines 7761 ha.	= Teotihuacán abandoned by its inhabitants, as are the rest of the urban and ceremonial centres of Middle America in the course of the next two centuries. End of the Classic culture.
Discovery & Invention		= Silkworms smuggled out of China to Europe.	= Decimal notation in use in India.	= First porcelain produced in China.	**605–10** Construction of the Grand Canal connecting the Yangzi with the Yellow River.
The Arts		= Constantinople: Justinian's buildings include SS Sergius and Bacchus (527–36) S Irene (532) and second church of Hagia Sophia (532–8). = Ravenna: S Vitale (526–548); S Apollinare in Classe (536–49). These churches contain the finest surviving examples of the polychrome mosaic technique perfected by the Romans of the late Empire.		= Ephesus: Church of St John (565).	= First major Buddhist buildings in Japan include the Horyuji monastery (607) and the Kondo temple, for which Tori Bushi casts the Shaka trinity (623).

**This reorganization involved many changes including the use of Greek instead of Latin in the administration. Because of this, historians use the term Byzantine to describe the east Roman Empire from this time on, Byzantium being the old Greek name for Constantinople. It is worth noting, though, that in this sense, Byzantine is just a historian's word: as far as the emperors and their subjects were concerned they were Romans still.

	625–649	650–674	675–699	700–724	725–749
Politics & Military History	**626** Crisis of Byzantine-Persian War: Avars and Persians forced to retreat from Constantinople; Heraclius defeats Persians at Nineveh (627); Persians sue for peace (628). **630** Mecca submits to Muhammad **636** Arab armies defeat Byzantines at the River Yarmuk; take Syria and Palestine. **637** Arabs defeat Persians at Qadasiya: take Iraq by 638. **639** Chinese set up protectorate over Central Asia. **640** Arabs defeat Byzantines at Heliopolis: all Egypt conquered by 642. **642** Arabs defeat Persians at Nehavend and overrun western half of Iranian plateau.	**651** Last Sassanid king of Persia killed at Merv: Arabs complete conquest of Iranian Plateau. **651** Kingdom of Northumbria founded in north of England. **661** Umayyad dynasty founded (see below). **668** With Chinese support and under Chinese suzerainty the kingdom of Silla achieves the unification of Korea. **670** Arabs invade Maghreb (north west quarter of Africa). **673** First Arab assault on Constantinople: seaborne force lays siege to the city.	**679** Arabs abandon siege of Constantinople. **682** Chinese withdraw from Korea. **683** Arabs withdraw from the Maghreb. **685** Picts defeat Northumbrians. **687** Pepin becomes Mayor of the Franks and effective ruler of their kingdoms. **694** Second and successful Arab invasion of the Maghreb: Carthage falls (698). **c695** King of Srivijaya (modern Palembang, Sumatra) establishes authority over west half of Indonesian archipelago.	**705** Arabs invade Turkestan. **711** Arabs invade Spain, kill Roderick, last king of the Visigoths. **712** Arabs invade India. **717–18** Second Arab assault on Constantinople fails. **720** Arabs occupy Narbonne, France. = Arabs occupy Eritrea.	**732** Charles Martel, Mayor of the Franks, defeats invading Arab force at Battle of Poitiers. **741** Pepin the Short succeeds Charles Martel as Mayor. **747** Abbasid revolt against Umayyad Caliphate, successful in eastern half of Arab Empire by 749.
Religion & Learning	**625** Muhammad begins dictating the *Koran*. **632** Death of Muhammad: his father-in-law, Abu Bekr, elected Caliph ('successor'). **634** Omar succeeds Abu Bekr: unbelievers expelled from Arabia.	**661** Assassination of Ali, son-in-law of the Prophet and third Caliph, followed by foundation of Umayyad dynasty of Caliphs by Muawiyah, Governor of Damascus. **664** Synod of Whitby: Celtic church loses attempt to maintain separate identity.		**722** St Boniface begins conversion of the Germans. = First written version of the Anglo-Saxon epic poem *Beowulf* (surviving copy is much later, c1000). = Success of Islam guarantees widespread use of Arabic, the official language of administration throughout the caliphate.	**726** Byzantine Empire Leo III issues iconoclastic degree (ordering destruction of religious images) precipitating dispute with papacy: excommunicated by Pope Gregory II as a result (730). **731** Bede *History of the English Church and People.*
Cities & Social Development	= Arab armies found Kufa, Basra in Iraq (both 638) and Fustat (old Cairo; 641) in Egypt. **645** Chinese style capital laid out at Naniwa, Japan, as part of comprehensive plan to remodel government and society on Chinese lines.	**661** Damascus replaces Medina as capital of the Caliphate. **670** Foundation of Quairawan, Tunisia.		**702–12** Japan: new capital at Nara, intensification of the Sinification programme.	
Discovery & Invention		= Paper made at Samarkand. From this point its use gradually spread through the Islamic world reaching Arabia by the beginning of the next century and Egypt shortly after.	= 'Greek fire' used by the Byzantines in defence of Constantinople. Probably this 'secret weapon' was petroleum which occurs on the surface at several sites in the Caucasus.		= Desert palace of Qasr al-Hair ash-Sharqui built by Caliph Hisham. **743** Japan: Temple of Todajii, Nara, begun: completed (and Great Buddha dedicated) 752.
The Arts		**c650** Sutton Hoo ship-burial.	**c680** Japan: reconstruction of Horyuji Monastery in its present form. **688–92** Dome of the Rock, Jerusalem, the first major building of Islam. **698** Lindisfarne Gospel illuminated, Northumbria, England.		

Muhammad was born in Mecca in the year 570 or thereabouts. He married into the Quraysh, a wealthy family who were guardians of the city's famous shrine, the Kabah. Despite this connection Muhammad seems to have played no part in the religious life of the Meccans until at the age of about 40 he started to hear the voice of God. Immediately he took on the role of God's messenger. He told the pilgrims who came to the Kabah that they were wasting their time, that the images it contained were false. There was but one God and he bore no earthly face.

Few Meccans were pleased by the appearance of this home-grown prophet: the Quraysh, to whom the Kabah was in the nature of a family business, were outraged. Eventually feelings ran so high that Muhammad and his supporters felt it politic to leave the city. In 622, a year that was to be the starting date of the Muslim calendar, they moved to Medina, a town 350 kilometres to the north where Muhammad already had a following. From this time on he never looked back. The rules of the new religion were formulated, the nucleus of an army recruited, the Meccans forced to submit, the Kabah purified by the destruction of all the idols it contained and the rest of Arabia converted to the new faith. When Muhammad died in 632 the religion of Islam – meaning 'submission' (to the will of Allah) – was well founded.

If he had lived another five years Muhammad would undoubtedly have led his followers north against the East Roman Empire or the Persian Empire or both – more probably the former because he had already sent a probe in this direction in 629. These ancient empires might be thought weighty opponents for such a new and relatively untried power as Islam but both were exhausted by a long war in which they had pounded each other into the ground. Even more to the point, the ease with which provinces had fallen first to one side and then to the other in the course of the struggle suggested that neither inspired much loyalty in their subjects. And so it turned out. When the Arab armies finally set out on their great adventure they were rewarded with a series of ringing victories such as the world has rarely seen. Damascus fell in 636, the Roman army sent to relieve the city was wiped out the next year and as a result of this single defeat the Romans abandoned Syria and Palestine for ever. Iraq fell to another Arab army with equal ease: one battle lost and the Iranians retreated to the plateau.

Above left: Dome of the Rock, Jerusalem encloses the 'Sacred Rock' from which, according to legend, Muhammad ascended to heaven in AD 632.

Above right: The Kabah – the small shrine at the centre of the Great Mosque in Mecca. For Muslims it is the most sacred spot on earth and all Muslims orient themselves towards it when praying. The early history of the Kabah is not well-known, but it is certain that it was revered as a sanctuary in the pagan era before Islam, although it has been destroyed and rebuilt many times since then. During most of the year the Kabah is covered with an enormous cloth of black brocade – the kiswa *–with verses from the Koran woven into it. The* kiswa *is renewed every year, being brought from Egypt where it is made, to Mecca by a pilgrim caravan with great ceremony.*

This was just the beginning. In 640 Amr ibn Aasi led an Arab army into Egypt; seven months later, in a decisive encounter near Heliopolis, he destroyed the Roman force charged with the defence of the country and two years after that he was able to announce that the campaign had been brought to a successful conclusion. All Egypt was under his control: his lieutenants had already begun the conquest of Libya. In the East the Arab armies made equally dramatic progress. They fought their way onto the Iranian plateau, destroyed the main Persian army at Nehavend in 642 and the next year occupied both Rayy and Isfahan. Within a few more years the last Persian king had been chased to an ignominious death at the eastern extremity of his kingdom, and the empire of the Sassanids was no more. Arab forces stood garrison in Merv (now part of Russian Turkestan) and Herat (now part of Afghanistan).

The final stage in this breathtaking expansion came in the early 8th century. In the west the Arabs swept through north Africa to Spain and southern France, while the eastern armies occupied Sind (southern Pakistan) and Transoxiana (Russian Turkestan). Within a hundred years of the prophet's death his successors, the Caliphs, were ruling an empire that extended across half the Old World and counted 30 million subjects. Not all of these had accepted Islam as yet but most of their descendants would do so. The vision of the prophet had been amply fulfilled.

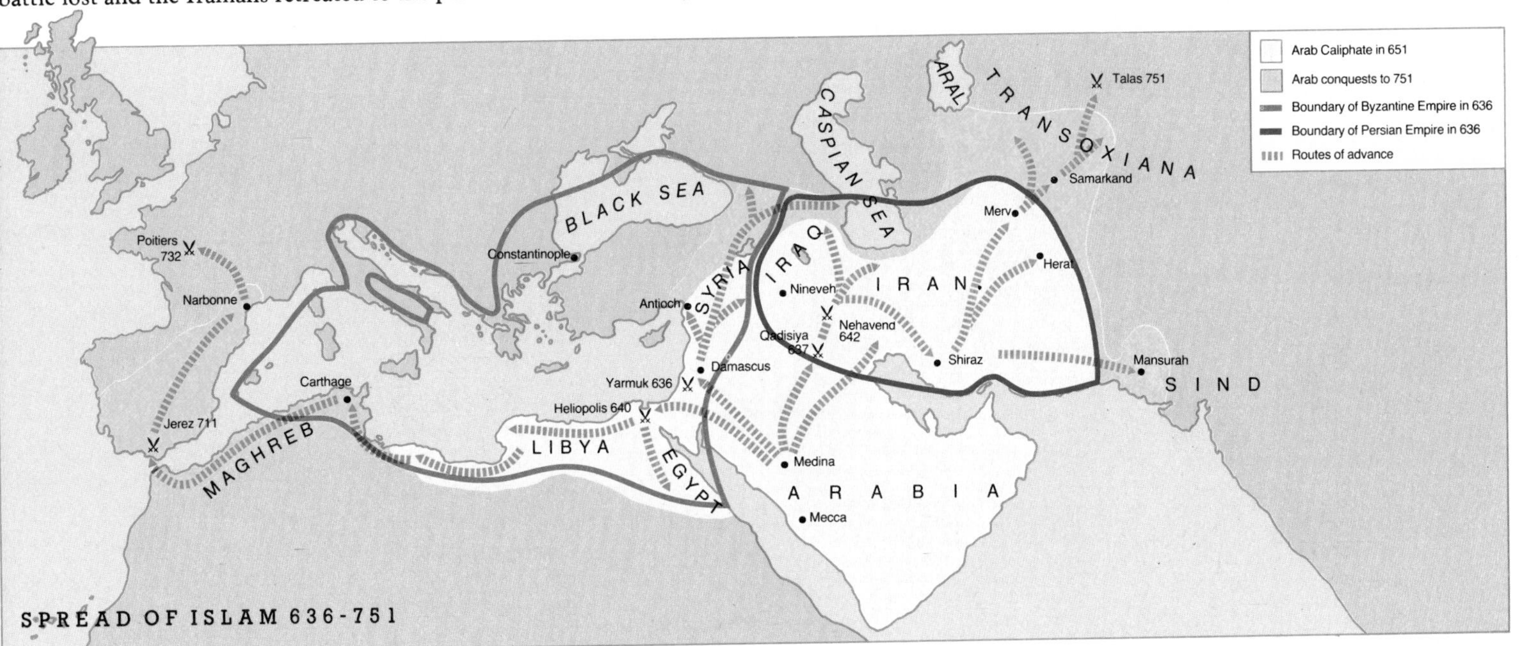

The Arab army that conquered Spain was probing deep into France by 720. In 725 one raiding party got as far as Autun, in 732 another sacked Bordeaux and then struck north for Tours. According to the historian of Rome's decline the defences of the West were at such a low ebb that 'the Arabian fleet might have sailed without a naval combat into the mouth of the Thames. Perhaps (he speculated) the interpretation of the Koran would now be taught in the schools of Oxford, and her pulpits might demonstrate to a circumcised people the sanctity and truth of the revelation of Mahomet'. Not so. The army of the Franks led by Charles Martel caught the Arabs on the road from Tours to Poitiers and cut them to pieces. Christendom, the kingdom of the Franks and the as yet unborn University of Oxford were saved.

Historians of the present generation play down Charles Martel's victory: the battle was a small one, the Arab attacks were clearly losing momentum. Spain was to prove too much for them, let alone France. Nevertheless, the encounter at Poitiers had important consequences: it gave Charles the prestige he needed to restructure the Frankish kingdom. In particular, as saviour of Christendom, the opportunity to shake down the church, confiscate the estates it had acquired over the centuries and give them to his followers. This was a momentous transaction. In return for these grants of land the Frankish nobility pledged themselves to answer Charles' call and to do so not just with sword and shield, the traditional equipment of the Frankish soldier, but with horse and lance. Charles created the social and economic basis for an army of heavy cavalry.

There was a technical innovation at the bottom of this. Some time around the year 700 the stirrup, which had been developed at the eastern end of the Eurasian steppe some hundreds of years earlier, reached Europe. It made riding easier and it made fighting on horseback more effective. A mounted spearman using stirrups could charge his enemy, confident that the shock of spear against shield would not throw him from his saddle. Cavalry equipped in this way could ride down all but the most determined infantry.

Above: Fragment of Byzantine silk, probably from the tomb of Charlemagne, now in the Musée de Cluny, Paris.

Above right: Aachen Cathedral, begun by Charlemagne at the end of the 8th century. Only the central domed structure, a free copy of San Vitale, Ravenna, goes back to Charlemagne's time.

Thus began one of history's great love affairs, the relationship between the European aristocrat and his horse. Centuries later, when all but the most boneheaded could see that the armoured horseman was a tactical anachronism, the image of the knight still dominated the social scene. The horse was the proudest possession, the hallmark, the essential product of the nobleman's estate.

In its early days the new way of fighting brought great reward. Under Charles Martel, his son Pepin and his grandson Charles the Great (Charlemagne), the Arabs were swept back over the Pyrenees and the whole of France, west Germany and northern Italy were brought into the Frankish empire. The Pope went so far as to crown Charlemagne emperor which showed that even that most conservative of institutions, the Church, had given up hoping for a revival of Roman power. True, Frankish society was not much by the high standards of Rome: it had no administrative machinery, no architecture, no towns, no trade, nothing to hold it together except the loyalty of the Franks to their chief. But at least the break with the past was complete: there was the chance to make a new beginning.

Below: Charlemagne as he was seen in the High Middle Ages. The idea of him as an armoured knight directing his peers in battle is essentially correct but the details are anachronistic: he would, for example, have worn mail, not plate. From the 14th century Venetian codice: 'Entrée d'Espagne'.

	750–774	775–799	800–824	825–849	850–874
Politics & Military History	**750** Abbasids overthrow the Umayyads and seize the caliphate. **751** Election of Pepin the Short as king of the Franks marks the official beginning of the Carolingian dynasty. = Lombard king Aistulph conquers Ravenna. = Central Asia: Chinese defeated by Arabs at the Battle of the Talas. **755–57** Rebellion of An Lushan in China brings Tang dynasty to brink of collapse. **756** Fugitive Umayyad prince founds independent Emirate of Cordoba, Spain. **768** Charlemagne succeeds his father Pepin the Short: conquers Saxony (771–2) and Lombard Kingdom (773–4). = First Polynesians reach New Zealand.	**779** Offa, king of Mercia, becomes overlord of the Anglo-Saxons: digs dyke to mark the frontier between England and Wales. **788** Charlemagne conquers Bavaria. = Moroccans establish independent Caliphate. 793–4 First Viking raids: Norse sack Lindisfarne and Jarrow. **795–6** Charlemagne destroys the Avar Kingdom. = Tang abandon attempt to control Central Asia.	**800** Charlemagne crowned Emperor of the West by Pope Leo III. **801** Charlemagne takes Barcelona and establishes the Spanish March. **821** Tang recognize the independence of Tibet. = Reign of Jayarvarman II marks emergence of Khmer king of Cambodia.	**825** Muslims from Spain conquer Crete. **827** Muslims from North Africa begin conquest of Sicily. **828** Egbert of Wessex becomes overlord of the Anglo-Saxons. **838** Norse establish permanent base at Dublin, raid as far as France and Spain (838–44). **843** Treaty of Verdun marks disintegration of Carolingian Empire. **844** Union of Picts and Scots by Kenneth McAlpine. **846** Muslim pirates sack St Peters, Rome. **849** Pyu, kingdom of Burma, collapses as modern Burmese take over north of country and found kingdom of Pagan. = Kings of Srivijaya lose much of Java to the Saivite (Siva-worshipping) Sanjaya dynasty.	**850** Viking raids reach a peak as Danes join Norse: raiders establish permanent bases at the mouths of the Scheldt, Somme, Seine and Thames. **857–8** Ascendency of the Fujiwara clan at the Japanese court: Yoshifusa becomes Grand Minister, then Regent. **859–62** Bjorn Ironside leads Viking raid into Mediterranean. **865–874** Danish army conquers north-eastern third of England. **874** Caliphate loses control over the Samanid Emir of Bukhara.
Religion & Learning	**c750** 'Donation of Constantine' forged to support papal claim to temporal supremacy. = Arab conquest of the Maghreb is followed by the rapid demise of the Christian church there. By contrast the Coptic church of Egypt proves much more resilient (even today one in ten Egyptians is a Christian).	**781** Nestorian Christian community recorded at Changan. **c786** Paul the Deacon *History of the Lombards*. = Reaction against Buddhist influence leads Japanese court to abandon Nara (784) which by then had 48 Buddhist temples. New capital built at Kyoto (794) to which monks are forbidden to transfer.	**805–6** Two new Buddhist sects founded in Japan, the Tendai sect by Dengyo Daishi and the Shingon sect by Kobo Daishi. **821** Einhard *Life of Charlemagne*	**841–5** Persecution of Buddhists in China. **842** Oath taken by Charles the Bald at Strasbourg is the first documented use of the French language.	**863** SS Cyril and Methodius convert the Moravians to Roman Catholicism: St Cyril devises alphabet for Slav languages. **864–5** Bulgars and Serbs converted to orthodox Christianity. **867** Final rupture between Roman Catholic (Western or Latin) and Orthodox (Eastern or Greek) Churches.
Cities & Social Development	**758** Chinese Government institutes salt monopoly. **762** Abbasid caliph al-Mansur lays out the 'round city' of Baghdad.	**793** Foundation of Fez, Morocco. = Carolingian court established at Aachen (Aix-la-Chapelle).	= Harun al Raschid, Caliph of Baghdad (and of the 1001 nights), sends Charlemagne an elephant and a water clock. = Oseburg ship-burial.	**836** Abbasid Caliph al-Mutasin moves to Samarra.	
Discovery & Invention	**751** Earliest printed book known: copy of Buddhist *Diamond Sutra* (found Korea 1966). **770** First large scale printing order: one million copies of a Buddhist prayer printed by order of the Empress of Japan.	**c790** Norse discover the Hordaland-Shetlands crossing and explore the British Isles: reach Bay of Biscay by 799 = Padded horse harness introduced in the west. This device, developed in central Asia or China, increased the load that a horse could pull by a factor of 4 or 5.		= Al Khwarizmi introduces word algebra (al-jabr), meaning transposition.	**861** Norse discover Iceland.
The Arts	= Deaths of Wang Wei (761), Li Bo (762) and Du Fu (770) bring the golden age of Tang poetry to a close. = Construction of Buddhist pyramidal Hindu temple of Borobodur, Java.	**788** Work begins on the Great Mosque of Cordoba. = Book of Kells illuminated.	= Cathedral at Aachen marks peak of Carolingian renaissance in architecture. = Manuscript plan of St Gall shows layout of contemporary monastery		

	875–899	900–924	925–949	950–974	975–999
Politics & Military History	**878** Danes fail in attempt to conquer Wessex. **879–80** Chinese rebel leader Huang Zhao sacks Canton and Luoyang. **880** Treaty of Wedmore divides England between Alfred the Great of Wessex (the south and west) and the 'Danelaw' (the north and east). **884** Temporary reunion of Carolingian Empire in the person of Charles the Fat: final dissolution of the empire on his death in 887. **885** Norse besiege Paris. **892** Korea: independent Kingdom of Koryu established in defiance of China. **895** Magyars migrate from Russian steppe to Hungary. = Iceland settled by the Norse.	**907** Russians make an unsuccessful attack on Constantinople. **912** Fatimid Caliph proclaimed at Mahdiya, Tunisia. **907** Final collapse of Tang dynasty: beginning of the Five Dynasties period in the north. **911** Dukedom of Normandy granted to Rollo the Viking. **917–921** Edward of Wessex conquers southern half of Danelaw.	**937** Athelstan of Wessex defeats Scots, north Welsh and Norse at Brunanburh, establishing his supremacy over England and Scotland. **939** Annam (North Vietnam) breaks away from China. **947** China: Khitan Mongols sack Kaifeng, Henan, the major political centre of the Yellow River basin at this time.	**960** Chinese General, Zhao Kuangyin founds Song dynasty at Kaifeng. Song armies reunite all the Chinese lands bar the northernmost strip over the next 20 years. **961** Byzantines recover Crete. **962** Otto crowned Emperor of the West, an event that marks the official beginning of the 'Holy Roman Empire of the German Nation'. Samanids of Bukhara employ Turks in conquest of Afghanistan. **963–5** Song conquer middle and upper Yangzi provinces. **965** Byzantines recover Cyprus. **969** Fatimids of Tunisia conquer Egypt. **971** Byzantines conquer eastern half of Bulgaria. Song conquer south China.	**979** Song conquer Shanxi completing reunification of China bar strip in the north held by the Khitan Mongols. **980** Vikings renew assault on England. Morocco repudiates Fatimid rule. **982** War between Viets of Annam and Chams of Champa: raids and counter-raids continue intermittently for the next 5 centuries. **986** Song defeated by Khitan Mongols. **994** Samanids of Bukhara appoint Turkish General Sebuktigin Viceroy of Afghanistan. **997** Sebuktigin's son Mahmud of Ghazni declares his independence. **999** Samanids of Bukhara overthrown by the Karakhanid Turks.
Religion & Learning	**891** Beginning of Anglo-Saxon chronicle marks revival of learning in England under Alfred the Great.	**910** Abbey of Cluny established: first church consecrated 914.	= Odo of Cluny extends his reform of the Benedictine rule to other monasteries in France. = al-Masudi *Annals*, a universal history in 30 volumes.	**961** Liutprand *History of Otto I.* **965** King of Denmark baptized. **967** *History of the Five Dynasties.* = *Greek Anthology* of 6000 Classical Greek poems assembled by Constantius Cephalas.	**981** Consecration of second church of Cluny. **989** Vladimir, Great Prince of Kiev, accepts orthodox Christianity. **997–984** Compilation of 1,000 volume Song encyclopedia.
Cities & Social Development	**880** Foundation of Kiev by Varangian leader Oleg marks first step in the creation of Russian state. **892** Abbasid caliph al-Mutadid abandons Samarra, returns to Baghdad and builds a new capital on the opposite bank to the 'round city'.	**c900** Yasovarman I founds Khmer capital Angkor, laying out irrigation system based on Eastern Baray: constructs pyramidal hindu temple of Phnom Bakheng.	**938** Khitan Mongols of north China establish their capital at Beijing (Peking).	**c950** Foundation of Novgorod. **968** Founding of Cairo by the Fatimid Caliph al Mansur who makes it the capital of his North African Empire in 972.	= Arabs trading along the East Coast of Africa establish their first permanent settlements, among them Mogadishu, Mombasa and Zanzibar.
Discovery & Invention		= Nailed horseshoes come into use throughout northern Eurasia. Originating focus unknown.	= Vertical axle windmills in use in Iran.	**969** Chinese using block-printed 'sheet-dice' meaning playing cards.	**982–5** Eric the Red explores Greenland: establishes small settlements a few years later.
The Arts					= The Catholic Church adopts bellows organ as accompaniment for divine service. Musical instrument known as the organistrum or hurdy-gurdy also in use. It consisted of a rosin wheel which sounded a pair of drone strings continually, and a keyboard which brought another pair into contact with the wheel and could be used to play a melody. The wheel was turned by a crank handle, one of the first applications of this device in the West.

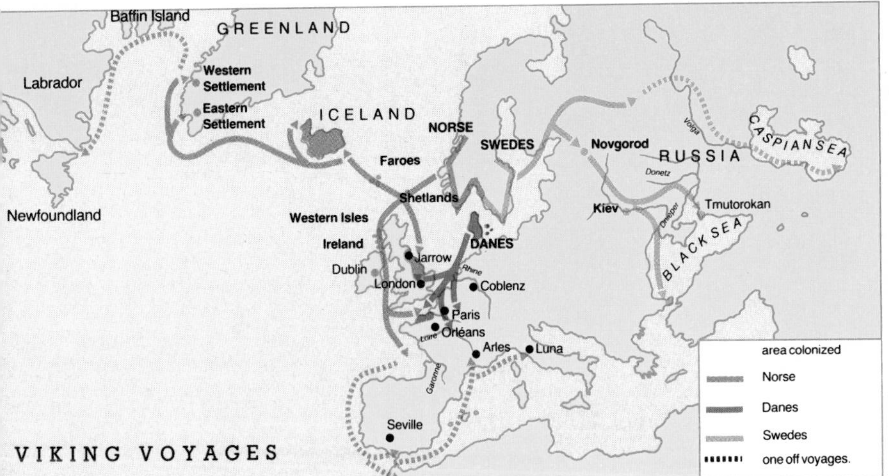

Left: Most of the Vikings who set out on plundering expeditions were headed for the British Isles or France but some bolder spirits went further. One of the boldest was Bjorn Ironside who got into the western Mediterranean in 859–60 and sacked several towns, among them one that he claimed to be Rome. Actually it was only Luna, a small place in Tuscany, but a bit of exaggeration was allowed for in sagas and no one would want to deny Bjorn his place in the Viking hall of fame. It was a remarkable bit of piracy by any standard.

Above: The Oseberg boat, found near Oslo in 1904. We owe this near perfect vessel to the Viking habit of burying important people in their boats.

The classical geographers had only the vaguest ideas about Scandinavia and no one knew much more in the 8th century when the first Vikings appeared in the west: as far as most people were concerned they were an entirely new breed of men. In a way this was correct. The Scandinavians had a long tradition of shipbuilding but they had only recently developed their sailing ships to the point where they could undertake ocean voyages. It was these ships, distinguished by their elegant clinkerbuilt hulls and square single sails, that were the engines of the Viking age.

The first sign that something unusual was going on came with the Norse (Norwegian) discovery of the route from Norway to the north of Britain via the Shetlands and Orkneys. In 793–4 the Norse used this route to plunder the monasteries of Lindisfarne and Jarrow on the north east coast of England: then they turned their attention to the Western Isles and the Irish Sea. By 800 they had a good idea of the layout – and vulnerability – of western Europe, knowledge that they put to good use over the next two centuries.

The Danes joined them in the 830s. There were more of them and it was their raids that really told. They took their boats up the Rhine, the Seine, the Loire and Garonne: they sacked cities as far inland as Clermont, Orléans and Coblenz; they conquered half England and devastated half the Continent.

The Vikings had an eye for land as well as plunder: there were too many of them for the narrow farms back home and if they could get themselves a stake abroad – as they did in Yorkshire and Normandy – then they were happy to settle down. They also followed up on stories of empty lands, such as the Irish tale of a big island to the north. This turned out to be Iceland, not everyone's idea of a welcoming place but by Norse standards perfectly acceptable. A colony, the ancestor of the present day Icelandic community, was established there in the 860s.

Exploration beyond Iceland proved disappointing. In the late 10th century Eric the Red persuaded some Icelanders to try their luck in Greenland, an island that had been discovered some fifty years earlier and where Eric had glimpsed a few patches of green between the glaciers. His son Leif led an expedition further west to Helluland, Markland and Vinland (thought to be Baffin Island, Labrador and Newfoundland): this was too far away for a colony to be a practical proposition and the first few boatloads of Europeans to explore the New World (sometime early in the 11th century) soon withdrew.

Exploration to the east of Scandinavia produced more lasting results. The Swedes who pioneered these routes are known as Varangians: they sailed up the north-flowing rivers of Russia and heard tell of even greater rivers flowing south. By the 9th century they were sailing down these to the Caspian and the Black Sea. There they traded and raided and to judge by the number of Islamic coins of this period discovered in Sweden, many of them made their fortunes doing so. They also laid the foundations of the Russian State. What began as a bit of casual bullying of the tribes they passed through on their journeys south, was gradually elaborated into a tribute-collecting network that covered the whole of agrarian Russia. The original base for this enterprise was Kiev (founded c 880): it was later supplemented by Novgorod (c 950); the two together formed the axis of a principality that by the end of the 10th century had become an important contributor to the European political scene.

Above: Reconstruction of a barracks from the Danish fort at Trelleborg. This dates from the early 11th century when the haphazard raiding of the Viking period was giving way to organized imperialism. Sixteen boats were stationed at Trelleborg: each crew had its own barracks within the circular rampart of the fort.

THE FEUDAL AGE IN WESTERN EUROPE

AD 1000 - AD 1490

The feudal forms that characterized western Europe from the 10th to the 15th century emerged first in France. They developed from the Frankish idea of knight-service and the system, roughly speaking, was that the lord of the manor extracted enough labour and produce from his villages to equip himself as a knight. His job was to turn out when his local superior, usually a count or a duke, ordered him to. Where the system did not work well was at the next stage up: the counts and dukes were reluctant to turn out for the king and he had no real way of making them do so. This made kingdoms difficult things to run and the bigger they were the more difficult they became.

As far as the individual is concerned the significant feature of the feudal system was its absolute acceptance of hereditary rights. So long as the peasant gave his lord the agreed tithe he could not be evicted: so long as the lord rendered the knight service due, he was sure of his estate and the King himself could not deprive barons of their lands for any reason other than repeated, unjustifiable and unsuccessful rebellion.

This system of two-way obligations won increasingly widespread acceptance in western Europe in the 10th century perhaps as a reaction to the prevailing political anarchy. Early on in the 10th century the West was on its knees: beset by Vikings, Magyars and Arabs and seemingly incapable of organizing any effective defence, its best bet seemed to be that Christ would, as prophesied, return to earth in the year 1000. Yet when the century ended and the world did not, no-one was too disappointed: by now the countryside was hard at work and prosperity was in the air.

The boom that followed saw England, France and Germany triple their Dark Age populations. Productivity increased too: animal husbandry, farm machinery, mills and merchant ships all showed major improvements. Europe was transformed from a backward society into a vigorous, innovative community of nations.

It is easy enough to identify an overall surge of this sort once it is under way, more difficult to put a finger on the map and say 'this is where it started'. Yet during the critical years either side of 1000 there is one institution whose name keeps cropping up as a pace-setter. A lot of what happened, happened first at Cluny.

THE ABBOTS OF CLUNY

In 909, as an act of repentance for a murder committed long before, the ageing Duke William of Aquitaine decided to found a monastery. He asked Abbot Berno of Baume, a churchman for whom he had long-standing admiration, to look around for a suitable site and though he grumbled a bit when Berno lighted on a village which contained a particularly treasured hunting lodge, he stuck to his word – after all, as Berno pointed out, where William was going he would be better served by the praying of monks than the baying of hounds. The village of Cluny, its lands and its manor were duly made over to the Church.

The Abbey of Cluny was a success from the start. Berno was a good abbot and his successor Odo a great one. Odo's reputation as a churchman, an administrator and a negotiator meant that he was in constant demand to advise kings and arbitrate their quarrels. He was also frequently called in to reform monasteries that had failed to maintain religious discipline. As a result of this, many monasteries became satellites of Cluny and within his lifetime Odo became the head of what was effectively a Cluniac Order within the Benedictine rule.

Below: The only surviving part of Cluny III, the north transept with the large Clocher de L'Eau Bénite and the smaller Clocher de L'Horloge.

By the time Cluny was into its third abbot it was clear that it had outgrown its original buildings. A plan was drawn up for an entirely new monastic complex including a much larger abbey church (known to present-day scholars as Cluny II) plus a range of living quarters for a hundred monks. All the buildings were to be in stone.

This was an ambitious project by 10th century standards. Most contemporary communities were very small, most buildings were wattle and daub and most churches little better than huts. But the Abbots of Cluny, now masters of wide estates, had the resources to operate on this relatively grand scale and by the end of the century they had their church almost complete. It was at this stage that the abbot of the day really chanced his arm. In the five centuries since the fall of Rome no-one had tried to put anything but a timber roof on this type of building. Abbot Odilo decided he wanted Cluny II vaulted in stone.

The decision was taken and the work begun in the year 1000. The vault went up over the next ten years, apparently rather shakily. Considering that no-one had experience of stone vaulting on this scale this is hardly surprising but if in engineering terms Cluny II was a rather precarious achievement it was a very remarkable one all the same. Instead of remaining content with buildings that were inferior copies of Roman models the monks of Cluny had deliberately set out to rival the best that Rome could show.

Cluny II attracted a lot of attention. Sixty metres from entrance to apse it was an imposing structure and the plainsong that was the Cluniacs' speciality resounded splendidly along its tunnel vault. Visiting churchmen went away determined to have something comparable: the result was that imitations of Cluny II started springing up all over western Europe. At the start of the century Cluny II had been unique, by its end it was commonplace.

Not that Cluny itself stood still during this period. In 1085 one of its most important patrons, King Alfonso VI of Castile, crowned a successful campaign against the Moors by capturing Toledo: in celebration of this triumph – the first step in the Christian re-conquest of the peninsula – he doubled the sum he usually gave to Cluny and promised to maintain his donation at this level in the future. With money in hand the sixth abbot, Hugh of Saumur, was able to institute a new building programme.

Abbot Hugh's church – Cluny III to archaeologists – was conceived on a quite different scale from Cluny II. It was nearly three times as long (160 metres as against 60 metres) and fully twice as high (30 metres to the top of the vault as against 15 metres). It was easily the biggest church in Christendom and remained so until the 15th century re-building of St Peter's which the popes of the time deliberately made a few metres longer.

The east end of Cluny III was finished within ten years, a remarkably short space of time for a project of this size. Pope Urban II agreed to perform the dedication ceremony. The Pope had been a monk at Cluny in his youth and here was proof visible of how the Church had come on during his lifetime. It was also a sign that the Muslim *infidel* could be flung back from the gates of Christendom. Urban had an appeal from the Eastern Emperor in his pocket: the hard-pressed Byzantines wanted the Pope's help in recruiting western mercenaries, particularly mailed knights which were getting a formidable reputation. Maybe the Pope should do more than just give his blessing to this project, maybe he ought to take the initiative himself?

One month later at the Council of Clermont, in a ceremony that was no less moving for being carefully rehearsed, Pope Urban preached the Crusade.

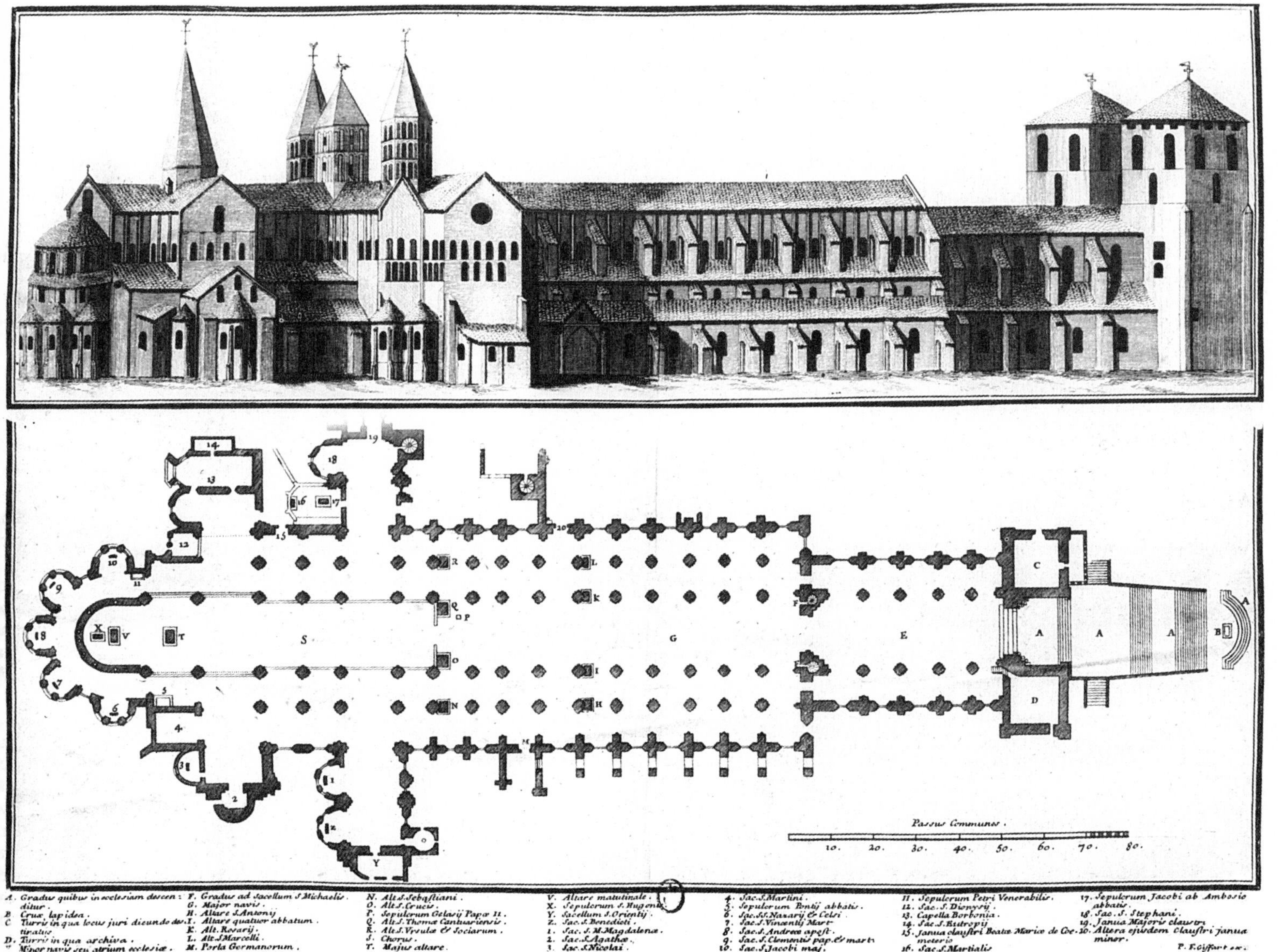

The great abbey church of Cluny (Cluny III). This drawing was made in the 18th century shortly before the French revolutionary government sold the building off. It was bought by a businessman from Macon who demolished nearly all of it between 1798 and 1823, using the stone for building work and road repairs.

THE COMING OF THE TURKS

	1000–1004	1005–1009	1010–1014	1015–1019	1020–1024
Politics & Military History	**1000** Olaf of Norway killed by Sveyn of Denmark. Venetians conquer Istria, their first step towards Empire. **1002** Muslim Corsairs sack Pisa and occupy Sardinia, but are defeated by the Venetians. Sveyn of Denmark devastates England: King Aethelred the Unready pays him 24,000 pounds of silver to stop. **1004** Song defeated in their attempt to wrest North China from the Khitan Mongols.	**1007** Aethelred pays Sveyn another 'Danegeld', this time of 36,000 pounds of silver. **1009** Khitan Mongols conquer Gansu province, NW China.	**1012** Aethelred pays a Danegeld of 48,000 pounds, but the next year Sveyn pushes him off the throne all the same. **1014** Sveyn dies: his son Cnut disputes the succession with Aethelred. **1014** Brian Boru leads the Irish to victory over the Norse at Clontarf.	**1016** Cnut makes good his claims to the English throne. **1018** Malcolm defeats the Northumbrians, adding Lothian to Scotland. **1018** Byzantines complete the conquest of Bulgaria. Cholas of South India, invade Ceylon.	**1021** Chola Empire reaches its maximum extent with expedition to Bengal.
Religion & Learning	= Foundation of Archbishoprics of Gniezno (1000) and Gran (1001) establishes Catholic hierarchies in Poland and Hungary respectively.	**1009** Jerusalem: Holy Sepulchre destroyed on the orders of al Hakim, 6th Fatimid Caliph of Egypt.		**1016** Caliph al Hakim proclaims his divinity in Cairo.	**1020** al Hakim disappears, leaving behind a small number of believers who later transmit the faith to the ancestors of the present-day holders, the Druses of Lebanon and Syria.
Cities & Social Development	= Toltecs of Tula revive meso-American tradition of the ceremonial city.				
Discovery & Invention	**1004** Pivoted-beam stone-throwers used in China. = Lief Ericson explores the North American coast from Baffin Island to Newfoundland.	= Failure of Norse attempt to found a settlement in North America (at L'Anse aux Meadow, Newfoundland?).			
The Arts	**1000** Vaulting of Cluny II begins (completed *c.*1010). **1001** Work begun on Rotunda of St Benigne, Dijon.		**1011** Firdousi completes Persia's national epic, the *Shahnama.* Dedication of Byzantine Church of *Hosios Loukas* near Delphi, Greece.	**1019** Japan: Murasaki Shikibu completes her classic novel *The Tale of Genji.*	

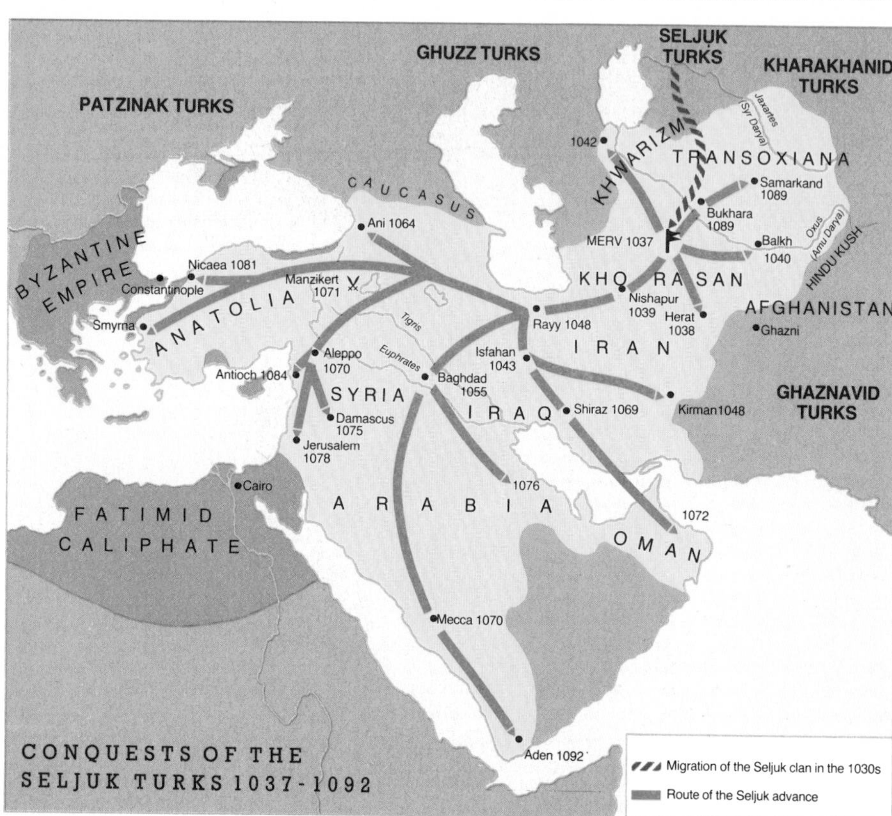

The Seljuk Empire at its peak. The speed with which the Seljuks made themselves masters was remarkable: even more so is the durability of their conquests. Turks of one sort or another were to run this area for the next 800 years.

The peoples of the central Asian steppe, the Turks and Mongols, were natural cavalrymen. As such they were often hired by their more civilized neighbours, the Arabs and Chinese, who had no difficulty conscripting infantry armies from their peasant populations but could not easily raise effective cavalry. Hiring too many Turks was dangerous, though. A successful Turkish commander could well set up on his own account, and if he did, where was the army that could turn him out?

This was an old story in China where the north had often been ruled by Turkish dynasties but in the west Turks were not very noticeable before the 9th century and did not establish any kingdoms until the end of the 10th. The first kingdom was founded by Sebuktigin, Governor-general and ultimately Sultan of Afghanistan: it was greatly expanded by his son and successor Mahmud of Ghazni (997–1030) who took over much of Iran and all of the Punjab. Mahmud's campaigns were very profitable and news of them brought more Turks into the area. Among the newcomers was the Seljuk clan which Mahmud's successor Masud settled round the oasis of Merv.

The Seljuks never really accepted Ghaznavid control. In 1037 they occupied Merv and in 1040 they defeated Masud when he tried to chase them out. After that the growth of the Seljuk power was explosive. The Ghaznavids were driven over the Hindu Kush while Seljuk-led forces swept through Iran and Iraq: by 1055 the Caliph of Baghdad was a Seljuk puppet; by 1071 the Seljuk Sultan Alp Arslan was master of the whole area between the Amu Darya (River Oxus) and the Byzantine frontier.

Perhaps master is too strong a word. Alp Arslan was riding a whirlwind: his empire was being created for him by forces over which he had very limited control. Fully

1025–1029	1030–1034	1035–1039	1040–1044	1045–1049	
1025 Chola fleet makes extended raid through Srivijaya (W Indonesia). **1027** Cnut recognized as King of Norway.	**1031** Last Caliph of Cordoba loses his throne: Muslim Spain fragments and preponderance passes to Christian kingdoms of the north. **1032** Kingdom of Burgundy absorbed into the German Empire.	**1035** The Danish Empire (England, Denmark, Norway) splits up on Cnut's death. **1037** Tughrii, leader of the Seljuk Turks, falls out with the Ghaznevid, Governor of Merv, and seizes the city. Rapidly expanding the area under his control he takes Herat in 1038 and Nishapur in 1039.	**1040** Macbeth murders Duncan and takes the throne of Scotland. **1041** Tancred d'Hauteville and his brothers, Norman soldiers of fortune, seize the castle of Melfi on the Byzantine-Lombard frontier in southern Italy. **1042** Edward the Confessor, Aethelred's son, succeeds Hardacnut, Cnut's son, on the throne of England. **1043** Seljuks expand westward, taking Isfahan.	**1048** Zirids of Tunisia revert to orthodox (Sunni) Islam, repudiating suzerainty of Fatimid caliphs of Cairo. **1048** Seljuks, now masters of Iran, raid Byzantine Armenia, sacking Erzerum.	Politics & Military History
= Avicenna of Bukhara (properly ibn-Sina) *Canon of Medicine*.	= Guido of Arezzo *Aliae regulae* introduces first practical form of musical notation, enabling melodies to be sung on sight.			= The Tokolor of Senegal adopt Islam, the first people south of the Sahara to do so.	Religion & Learning
= Mantled fireplaces developed in western Europe.			**1042** First recorded use of moveable type, in China. **1044** First description of floating compass, in Chinese military encyclopedia.		Discovery & Invention
		1036 Jumieges, Normandy; work begins on the first major church of the region. **1037** Completion of S Sophia, Kiev.			The Arts

aware of their military superiority and of the riches to be obtained by its exercise, the tribes of the steppe were pouring over the Amu Darya in search of lands and loot. Alp Arslan had his work cut out keeping up with these migrating hordes, confirming them in their conquests and placing Seljuk princes over each of them.

In 1071 the Seljuks encountered a new enemy. The Byzantine Emperor decided it was time to teach the Turks raiding his eastern frontier a lesson: Alp Arslan, who was in Syria at the time, interpreted the Byzantine move as a threat to his communications and moved north to protect them. As the Byzantines entered Armenia from the west Alp Arslan led the Seljuk army in from the south: near the fortress of Manzikert the two armies came face to face. The battle was a massacre. The Turks exhausted, enveloped and finally annihilated the entire Byzantine force.

All Anatolia now passed into Turkish hands.

Right: Minaret of the Jami Mosque, Simnan. Built about the time of the Seljuk conquest of Iran it shows the elaborate brick patterns characteristic of this period.

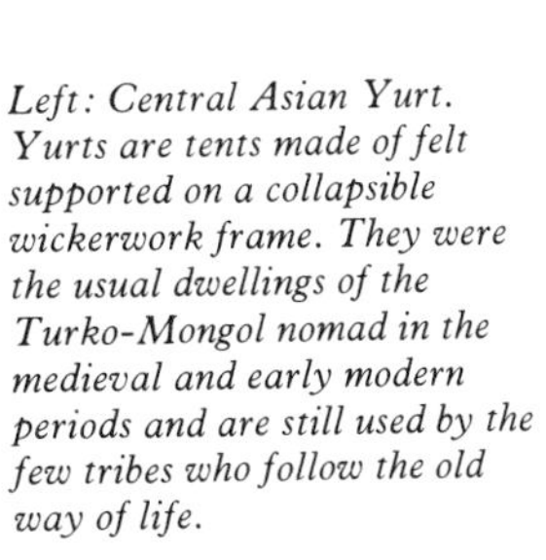

Left: Central Asian Yurt. Yurts are tents made of felt supported on a collapsible wickerwork frame. They were the usual dwellings of the Turko-Mongol nomad in the medieval and early modern periods and are still used by the few tribes who follow the old way of life.

	1050–1054	1055–1059	1060–1065	1066–1069	1070–1074
Politics & Military History	**1050** Pisans expel Muslims from Sardinia. **1052** Fatimid caliph of Egypt launches Bedouin tribes against the Zirids of Tunisia who abandon the interior to them. **1053** Concerted effort by the Pope, the Germans and the Byzantines to crush the Normans of Melfi ends with the defeat and capture of the Pope at Civitate. **1054** Audaghost in the Kingdom of Ghana (modern Mauritania) sacked by the Almoravids, a fundamentalist Muslim sect now wielding great influence among the Berbers of the Sahara.	**1057** Scotland: Macbeth killed by Malcolm Canmore. **1055** Seljuk Turks take Baghdad.	**1060** Robert Guiscard (Robert the Weasel), leader of the Normans of south Italy, conquers the toe and heel of the peninsula. **1061** Robert takes NE corner of Sicily from the Muslims.	**1066** Edward the Confessor dies: throne is taken by Harold, Earl of Wessex, who is immediately challenged, among others, by Duke William of Normandy. William kills Harold at Hastings, winning the crown and the title of Conqueror. **1069** Ibn Tashfin, leader of the Almoravids, takes Fez and becomes master of all Morocco. Sveyn, King of Denmark, makes his bid for the English throne, takes York.	**1070** William the Conqueror lays waste the north of England: rebellion there collapses. **1071** Alp Arslan, Sultan of the Seljuk Turks, destroys Byzantine army at Manzikert: Turkish clans under his suzerainty move into Anatolia (modern Turkey). Robert Guiscard takes Bari, last possession of the Byzantines in S Italy. **1072** Palermo falls to the Normans.
Religion & Learning	**1054** Schism between the eastern and western (Orthodox and Catholic, Greek and Latin) churches becomes final as the Pope blames the Byzantines for his defeat at Civitate (see above). Despite the failures of his final years the pontificate of Leo IX (1049–54) marks a turning point in the history of the church: important steps were taken to make the clergy live up to their positions rather than take advantage of them.	**1059** Pope Nicholas II decrees that Popes are henceforth to be elected by the Cardinals of the Roman Church, not by the clergy and people of Rome: he also accepts the Normans as rightful rulers of south Italy when they agree to become vassals of the papacy. Both these acts had more to them than meets the eye. The electoral reform was intended to free the papacy from the influence of the emperor as much as the Roman mob: the treaty with the Normans enabled the Pope to deploy these 'vassals' in his defence.	**1063** Michael Psellus *Chronographia*, lives of the Byzantine Emperors from Basil II to Isaac Comnenus, later extended to Michael VII.		
Cities & Social Development			**1062** Ibn Tashfin, leader of the Almoravids, founds Marrakesh as a base for the conquest of Morocco. **1063** Alp Arslan, Sultan of the Seljuk Turks, moves his capital westward from Merv to Isfahan.	**1066** William the Conqueror begins building programme in England that includes Tower of London, one of more than a score of castles to ensure his grip on the country.	
Discovery & Invention	**1056** Chinese note the appearance of a bright new star in the constellation of Taurus, now known to have been the supernova that created the Crab nebula.				
The Arts	**1052** Edward the Confessor founds Westminster Abbey.		= Work begins on St Mark's, Venice, and Speyer Cathedral.	= Great upsurge of church building in western Europe, perhaps particularly marked in the areas under Norman control. Most of the cathedrals were subsequently rebuilt in the Gothic style – for example the cathedrals of Canterbury, York and Lincoln where little remains of the buildings begun in the 1070s – but some abbeys, lacking the funds for rebuilding, survive substantially intact, e.g. Battle Abbey (commemorating Hastings) and the Abbaye aux Hommes (at Caen, Normandy).	

1075–1079	1080–1084
1076 Venetians conquer Dalmatia. Seljuks take Damascus and Jerusalem from the Fatimids. **1077** Seljuks of Anatolia (which they call Rum because it was previously part of the Roman Empire) break off from the central Seljuk sultanate.	**1081** Robert Guiscard begins abortive invasion of the Byzantine Empire via the Balkans (pursued intermittently till his death in 1085). **1084** Antioch falls to the Seljuks.
1076 Dispute between Pope Gregory VII (better known as Hildebrand) and Emperor Henry IV as to who appoints bishops. Henry declares Hildebrand deposed: Hildebrand excommunicates Henry. **1077** Henry surrenders: does penance to Hildebrand at Canossa.	**1084** Henry's counter-offensive against Hildebrand culminates in his occupation of Rome where he is crowned by a Pope of his own making (Clement III). Hildebrand holds out in the Castel S. Angelo (Vatican citadel) and is rescued by Robert Guiscard later the same year.
All feudal states relied heavily on churchmen for smooth running: the German Empire, the biggest feudal structure ever created, did so more than most. For this reason the dispute over the investiture of bishops was very damaging to the empire which already had more problems (its difficult geography, its ethnic heterogeneity) than it could readily cope with.	
1076 Robert Guiscard takes Salerno; makes it his capital and a centre of learning. The university that developed there over the next century later claimed to have been founded in Robert's day, a claim that if true would make it the oldest university in western Europe.	
= Bayeux Tapestry chronicles Norman Conquest of England (and also appearance of Halley's Comet in 1066).	

When Edward the Confessor, King of England, died childless in January 1066 there were four claimants to the throne: William Duke of Normandy who was related to Edward's mother; the kings of Norway and Denmark, representing the Viking interest, and Harold Earl of Wessex. Harold had no legal claim at all but he was English and he was on the spot. Always a man to move fast he had himself crowned king the day after Edward's death.

Harold knew that he would have to fight to keep his throne and in preparation for the struggle he mustered the entire armed force of the kingdom. This was a mistake. Both Duke William and King Harald of Norway intended to press their claims but it takes time to mount an invasion and there was no chance of their appearing on the scene so soon. Through spring and summer Harold's army and fleet stood idle until, early in September, supplies ran out and he was forced to stand down all units except his personal guard, the Housecarls.

Ten days later Harold received the news he had been expecting: Duke William had moved his fleet from its assembly point at the mouth of the Dives to its departure point, the mouth of the Somme. And the Norwegians had actually arrived: they were disembarking in Yorkshire.

Harold decided there was time to deal with the Norse before Duke William sailed. Within a week he had marched his Housecarls from London to York, collected the local levy of Northumbria and won the battle of Stamford Bridge. The remnants of the Viking army withdrew to its ships leaving Harald of Norway's body on the battlefield. Harold celebrated with a banquet at York.

The celebrations were interrupted by a messenger from London: Duke William had crossed the Channel and his army was ashore. Harold made another of his rapid marches and got to London in record time. From there he moved immediately against William.

But William had been kept well-informed of Harold's approach and on the morning of 14th October it was the Normans who moved forward and caught the English on the wrong foot. Harold managed to get his army into defensive order but he never recovered the initiative and the Battle of Hastings saw his line gradually eroded by the Normans. Defeat was already looming when Harold was killed by a stray arrow: this made the issue certain.

On Christmas Day 1066 Edward the Confessor's Abbey at Westminster saw its second coronation of the year. William the Conqueror had the crown and the Kingdom.

Above: Commoner and King in medieval England: upper picture from an 11th century manuscript in the Bodleian Library, Oxford; lower picture of a peasant reaping. Norman manuscript in the Bodleian.

Below: Norman knights charge the Saxon 'shield-wall' at the start of the Battle of Hastings. Scene from the Bayeux Tapestry, woven in the generation after the conquest.

THE FIRST CRUSADE

	1085–1089	1090–1094	1095–1099	1100–1104	1105–1109
Politics & Military History	**1085** Spain: Christians capture Toledo. Almoravids of Morocco come to the aid of the Muslims and defeat the Christians at Zalaca (1086: but they do not recover Toledo). Sicily: Normans take Syracuse.	**1091** Normans take Noto, completing their conquest of Sicily. **1092** Almoravids impose their rule on most of the Muslim part of Spain, only three Emirs retaining their independence. **1094** El Cid, Christian soldier of fortune, takes Valencia.	**1095** Pope Urban II proclaims the crusade. Henry of Burgundy created Count of Portugal by Alfonso VI of Leon. **1097** Crusaders set out from Constantinople, defeat Seljuks of Rum at Nicaea and Dorylaeum (allowing the Byzantines to recover maritime Turkey), march through to Syria and take Edessa, Antioch (1098) and Jerusalem (1099).	= Kingdom of Jerusalem, Principality of Antioch, and County of Edessa established as the three crusader states of the Levant.	**1108** Hungary takes Dalmatia from the Venetians. **1109** Crusaders capture Tripoli which becomes the fourth crusader state.
Religion & Learning		**1090** Sect of Assassins founded in Persia. The name derives from the sect's use of hashish which made its members careless of their lives and therefore good fodder for suicide missions. Hence the modern meaning of the word assassination.	**1098** St Robert founds Cistercian Order at Citeaux.	**1104** First Scandinavian archbishop consecrated (at Lund, Denmark). = William of Champeaux opens his school of Dialectic in Paris, the first step in the formation of the university.	**1107** Synod of Westminster settles England's version of the who-appoints-bishops controversy: Henry I and Anselm, Archbishop of Canterbury, agree to joint investiture.
Cities & Social Development	**1086** Domesday census of England completed.			= Rise of cities in western Europe, particularly in the northern half of Italy (Milan, Pavia, Cremona, Brescia, Verona, Padua, Venice, Bologna, Florence, Pisa, Lucca, Siena, Genoa) and either side of the English Channel (London, Rouen, Paris, Ghent, Bruges, Tournai, Louvain, Brussels). City populations at this time in the range 8–20,000.	
Discovery & Invention	**1088** Astronomical water-clock, designed by Chinese court astronomer Su Song, installed at Kaifeng. This elaborate instrument, which included a device equivalent to an escapement, represents the ultimate development of the water-clock.	**1093–6** Ribvaulting used in aisles of Durham Cathedral choir, the first instance of this technique.		**1104** Ribvaulting used in the high vault of Durham Cathedral choir.	Horizontal headle treddle looms appear in France.
The Arts	**1088** Construction of Cluny III begun.	**1092** *Eiga Monogatari* (Tale of Glory) extols the rise of Fujiwara-no-Michinaga.		= *Chanson de Roland* the first, most famous and the best of the *Chansons de Geste*, verse epics about the martial exploits of the Franks.	

The response to Pope Urban II's appeal for a Crusade was dramatic. As preachers carried his message across Europe crowds of ordinary folk, fired with enthusiasm, gathered at Cologne, took the crusading vow and set out for Jerusalem. A surprisingly large number of them made it to Constantinople where the Emperor took one look at them and shipped them across the Bosporus. There they met the Turks. The battle was a short one: by the end of the day nearly all the 20,000 Christians who had landed in Asia were dead or dying. The Turks had hardly lost a man.

But the Pope's appeal had stirred the hearts of hardened warriors as well as naive peasants and the great names – Robert of Normandy, Raymond of Toulouse, Godfrey of Lorraine, Stephen of Blois – brought with them a professional army. At Constantinople they met Bohemond, from the Norman kingdom of Sicily, who had been fighting against the Byzantines in the Balkans only a few years before. After some prickly negotiations the Emperor and the western barons agreed a plan of campaign.

The Crusaders crossed to Asia in the spring of 1097, marched to Nicaea, the capital of the Seljuk sultan of Anatolia, and laid siege to it. The sultan, who was in eastern Anatolia at the time, hurried back to find that he could make no headway against the carefully ordered and heavily armoured lines of the Crusader army. Reluctantly he withdrew, and began looking for a better battlefield.

The Crusaders came on immediately after the surrender of Nicaea, Bohemond leading the van (the advance division) into Dorylaeum at the end of June. The Turks appeared at dawn the next day. Circling round the Crusader force they would dash in, fire a volley of arrows, then pull away again – tactics guaranteed to wear down any opponent given time. Bohemond made his knights dismount and form a hollow square with the horses in the middle: this way the horses were safe and the knights were unable to make the impulsive piecemeal attacks that bring disaster. What Bohemond could not stop was the steady trickle of casualties from the Turkish arrows.

As the day wore on the Turks became bolder: they sensed the approach of the moment when the defence would start to break up. Even Bohemond was wondering how much more his men could take, how long their discipline would hold. Then came the sight he had been praying for, the second and third divisions of the Crusader army coming up behind the Turkish force. Bohemond's men were in the saddle, lances ready, before the trumpets had finished sounding. For the first time the Turks felt the impact of a charge by mailed knights as squadron after squadron tore into their ranks. The sultan's army simply disintegrated.

Top: A 15th century artist's idea of what the Siege of Jerusalem might have looked like, with weapons, armour and architecture of his own day and Jerusalem much grander than the reality.

Above: Krak des Chevaliers, the greatest of the crusader castles in the Holy Land and one of the finest surviving castles anywhere.

The Battle of Dorylaeum won the Crusaders unopposed passage across Anatolia and through the Taurus Mountains to Antioch. By October they had begun the siege of the city which was to last 18 months and bring them to the edge of disaster several times. If the Emirs of Mosul, Aleppo and Damascus had acted together they could certainly have crushed the rapidly weakening Christian force but they never made a common plan. By a hair's breadth the Christians won the victories they needed, by some timely treachery Bohemond got his men into the city and with Antioch safe in Christian hands the Crusaders were free to move against Jerusalem. They arrived there in June 1099.

The Crusading army had now been fighting for more than three years: it did not have the resources for another long siege and if it was to take Jerusalem at all it would have to be soon, by assault. After an unsuccessful attempt at rushing the walls the Crusaders put their effort into building three movable towers, which took them a month. Then they dragged them forward. By the 14th July, Raymond of Toulouse had his tower up against the south west wall and the next day Godfrey of Lorraine's tower was in position on the north side. By noon his crossbow men had cleared the parapet, the gap between tower and wall had been filled with earth and the first knight was across.

With the Crusaders already in the city, the inhabitants were left with no option but to make their surrenders individually. Few had their offers accepted, fewer still had them honoured. It was a bloodstained banner that the Crusaders broke out over Jerusalem that night.

SONG CHINA

	1110–1114	1115–1119	1120–1124	1125–1129	1130–1134
Politics & Military History	**1110** Almoravids take over Saragossa, last independent emirate in Muslim Spain.	**1115** Jurchen nomads of Manchuria found the Jin Empire. **1118** King of Aragon captures Saragossa.	**1121** Georgians expel Muslims from Tiflis. **1122** Concordat of Worms heals the breach between the Pope (in the person of Calixtus II) and the German Emperor (Henry V) over the investitutre of bishops. In appearance a compromise, the Concordat was really a defeat for the empire which needed the exclusive loyalty of its clergy.	**1125** Jin defeat the Khitan Mongols who flee west to Turkestan. **1126** Jin invade China, sack Kaifeng and capture the Song Emperor. Song dynasty continues in control of southern half of country. **1129** Roger, Count of Sicily, takes over the Norman possessions on the mainland.	
Religion & Learning		**1115** St Bernard founds Abbey of Clairvaux. **1119** Military order of Knights Templar founded.	= Omar Khayyam, scholar, mathematician and supposed author of the quatrains collected in the *Rubaiyyat*. There is no contemporary evidence for his writing poetry: the quatrains make their first appearance in a manuscript of the 14th century.		**1130** Guide for pilgrims travelling to Compostella, NW Spain, written by Aimeri Picaud. Since the construction of the cathedral there at the end of the 11th century Compostella had emerged as a centre of pilgrimage of the same order as Rome or Jerusalem.
The Arts		**1118** Completion of Cluny III marks culmination of Romanesque architecture in France.	= Song Academy of Painting at Kaifeng founded by the Emperor Huizong.	= Academy of Painting refounded at Hangzhou, capital of the southern Song: Chinese landscape painting achieves classical expression in the work of Ma Yuan. = Earliest examples of stained glass to survive *in situ*, in Augsburg Cathedral.	= Great age of abbey building in England begins with the foundation of Tintern and Rievaulx (both 1131) and Fountains (1132).

Europe's medieval population boom was mirrored in the Far East where China's population soared from 60 million to 100 million in the course of the 11th century. The Chinese economy expanded even faster. The old imperial system had fallen apart in the declining years of the Tang dynasty; a freer, cash-oriented, market-type economy brought a better life to both town and country. China even opened up a little to outsiders. Kaifeng, the imperial capital, was frequently visited by foreign embassies: Hangzhou and Canton, the great ports of the east and south became entrepôts for traders from as far away as Indonesia and south east Asia.

Presiding over this busy world was the Song Emperor whose warrior forebears had been responsible for bringing most of China under one rule again in the late 10th century. However, the one area in which the Song could not claim complete success was military. The northern border provinces remained in the hands of the Khitan Mongols who had sharply defeated several armies the Song had sent to expel them. The terms of the eventual truce included recognition of the Khitan position and a promise by the Chinese to pay an annual tribute of half a million strings of cash. This was really a bargain – the tribute amounted to less than one per cent of the Chinese budget – but it was an indignity and it rankled.

In 1114 the situation in the north appeared to change for the better. A clan of Manchurian nomads, known to Chinese history as the Jin, rebelled against Khitan rule. By 1125 the Jin had completely overcome the Khitans and the Chinese were able to reoccupy some of the lost border areas. But when the Song Emperor Hui Zong ordered the Jin out of the rest of the former Chinese area, he overdid it.

Hui Zong was a great patron of the arts. The catalogue of his collection of paintings lists 6396 works by 231 different artists. He was an accomplished artist himself, particularly admired for his studies of birds. But he was no general. The Jin marched on Kaifeng and took it by storm. Hui Zong was carted off to an ignominious captivity.

Above: A Song painting of 'birds and flowers' of the type which the Emperor Hui Zong both painted and collected.

Right: 13th century painting of Hangzhou. The lake was a famous beauty spot.

Despite the loss of north China the Song dynasty survived. Hui Zong's son was in the south when Kaifeng fell. He established his court at Hangzhou and was recognized as Emperor by the southern two-thirds of the country. Within a surprisingly short time things were back to normal. The growing trade with south east Asia and Indonesia had always been run by the south. And the population increase was largely a southern phenomenon too, being based on a high-yielding strain of rice introduced from Champa. As a result the Southern Song were soon able to relax. The Academy of Painting was re-established and court life resumed its former elegance.

1135–1139	1140–1144	1145–1149	1150–1154	1155–1159	
1135 Stephen of Blois seizes the throne of England in defiance of the legal rights of the infant Henry of Anjou. **1137** Pisans sack Amalfi. Union of Aragon and Catalonia. **1138** Polish state splits into independent principalities. **1139** Russian state breaks up into separate principalities too, with no more than formal seniority being accorded to the Great Prince of Kiev.	**1141** Decline of central Seljuk power begins with loss of Transoxiana to the Khitan Mongols. **1144** Alfonso of Portugal takes Lisbon. Geoffrey Plantagenet, Count of Anjou, pursuing the Angevin claim to the English inheritance, conquers Normandy.	**1145** Zangi, Emir of Mosul, takes Edessa: Christian counterattack, the second crusade, easily repulsed by his son, Nurredin (1147–8). Almohades take over Morocco from the Almoravids: cross to Spain (1146). **1147** Alfonso of Portugal, aided by an English fleet on its way to join the second crusade, takes Lisbon from the Muslims.	**1150** Ghurids replace Ghaznevids in Afghanistan. **1152** Marriage of Henry Plantagenet, Count of Anjou and Duke of Normandy, to Eleanor, Duchess of Aquitaine, makes him master of half France. **1153** Seljuk Sultanate of Merv destroyed by revolt of mercenaries. Henry Plantagenet inherits the throne of England, becoming Henry II and the most powerful man in Europe.	**1157** Leon secedes from Castile. **1158** Frederick Barbarossa restores imperial authority in north Italy, forcing rebel Milan to yield.	Politics & Military History
	1141 Council of Sens condemns doctrines of Abelard. = Gratian *Decretals*, a collection of canon laws			**1158** Frederick Barbarossa's recognition of student rights at Bologna marks the formal start of the University. = University of Paris emerges as a regulated body.	Religion & Learning
1135 First use of the flying buttress (at Poissy, France). **1138** First use of Arabic (really Indian) numerals in the West, on a coin of Roger II of Sicily.		**1147** First recorded use of Chinese pivoted-beam stone-thrower in the West, at the Siege of Lisbon: operated by teams of up to 100.			Discovery & Invention
	= Rebuilding of St Denis, Paris, by Abbot Suger marks the transition from Romanesque to Gothic architecture. Essential feature is freeing of walls from loadbearing function by use of pointed rib-vaults focussing weight on buttressed piers. Hence rapid increase in size of windows.		= Suryavarman II completes Angkor Wat, the largest and most impressive of all Khmer temples.	= Cathedrals of Noyon and Senlis carry Gothic architecture a stage further.	The Arts

In many ways the arts of China reached a peak in the Song period. If the Chinese have a weakness it is a tendency to over-elaboration: Song works, whatever the medium, can be counted on to combine flawless craftsmanship and the finest of aesthetic sensibilities.

Left: Porcelain wine vessel in a lotus shaped warmer. Blanc-de-chine.

Right: Monkeys in a fruit tree. Ink of silk.

	1160–1164	1165–1169	1170–1174	1175–1179	1180–1184
Politics & Military History	**1160** Ghurids drive Ghaznevids from Afghanistan. **1160–2** Henry the Lion, Duke of Saxony and Bavaria, conquers the Wends of the Lower Elbe.	**1169** Nurredin's General Saladin takes Egypt which he rules as Nurredin's viceroy for the next five years. Prince of Suzdal sacks Kiev, putting an end to its pretentions to overlordship of Russia. Anglo-Norman invasion of Ireland begins with capture of Wexford.	**1170** Anglo-Norman baron Richard Strongbow takes Dublin: King Henry II of England visits Ireland the next year and receives submission of both Anglo-Normans and Irish chieftains. **1174** Saladin declares himself sultan in Egypt. = Swedes begin to settle coast of Finland.	**1176** Battle of Myrio-cephalum, disastrous defeat of the Byzantine Emperor Manuel Comnenus by the Seljuk Turks of Iconium. This puts an end to the Byzantine revival ushered in by the First Crusade.	**1180** Japan: Outbreak oi Gempei War as Minamoto clan led by Yoritomo challenge Taira hegemony. Henry the Lion dispossessed by Frederick Barbarossa: Bavaria given to Count Otto of Wittelsbach (in whose line it remains till 1918), Saxony divided.
Religion & Learning	**1164** Swedish Archbishopric of Upsala founded. = Wends forced to accept Christianity by Henry the Lion (see above).	**1169** Averroes of Cordoba (properly ibn-Rushd) *Commentaries on Aristotle.*	**1170** Thomas Becket, Archbishop of Canterbury, murdered on the orders of Henry II: canonized by Pope Calixtus III (1173).		**1182** Jews banished from France by Philip II.
Cities & Social Development	**1160** Frederick Barbarossa razes Milan, the centre of opposition to his rule in N Italy. **1163** Verona, Padua and Vicenza form nucleus of Lombard League.	**1167** Lombard League begins rebuilding Milan in defiance of Frederick.		Battle of Legnano: Emperor Frederick Barbarossa of Germany defeated by the Lombard League of north Italian cities.	
Discovery & Invention		**1167** Alcohol distilled from wine at Salerno, Italy: first certain instance of this technique.	= Development of the western type of windmill with horizontal axle. The first examples were probably made in the Low Countries.		= Carvings of ships with what appear to be stern-post rudders on church fonts at Winchester and Zedelghem, Belgium.
The Arts	= Major cathedrals of Laon (1160) and Notre Dame, Paris (1163) mark maturity of Gothic style.	**1168** Henry the Lion commissions illuminated Gospels.	**1174** Monreale Cathedral begun by William III of Sicily: Romanesque building with Byzantine mosaic decoration. = Chrétien of Troyes *Romances*: courtly love stories.	= William of Sens introduces Gothic style to England with his design for Canterbury Cathedral.	

Within fifty years of the conquest of Jerusalem the tide turned for the Crusading states. The first to go was the County of Edessa, overrun by the Turks in 1145: next was the Kingdom of Jerusalem, all but wiped out after the Muslim leader Saladin annihilated its army at the Battle of Hattin (1187). Frantic appeals from the Pope produced a new crusade headed by the kings of France and England, no less.

Of the two the king of England, Richard Lionheart, was the more impressive figure. In the first place he was everybody's idea of what a king should be, a great big bully of a man cheerfully rewarding his many followers and decapitating his enemies. He loved fighting and was good at it, especially sieges. In the second place he owned far more of France than the French king. His inheritance included Normandy, Anjou and Aquitaine which meant that his fiefs ran all the way from the English Channel to the Pyrenees.

Philip II of France was a much more reluctant Crusader. He did not like horses, let alone fighting and he only went along because prestige demanded it. He would have been far happier building up the resources of the crown so that it could tackle its main problem, the independent behaviour of over-mighty vassals like Richard.

Richard's Crusading career was spectacular. Almost single-handed he salvaged the remnants of the Kingdom of Jerusalem and gave them a new lease of life as the Kingdom of Acre. By the time he had set off for home – and more adventures on the way – minstrels were singing of his exploits. Philip, who had gone back to France as soon as he decently could, had been burrowing away at the English king's fiefs but Richard soon turned him out of his few gains. And to stop him trying again he built a huge castle between Normandy and Philip's royal domain, the Isle de

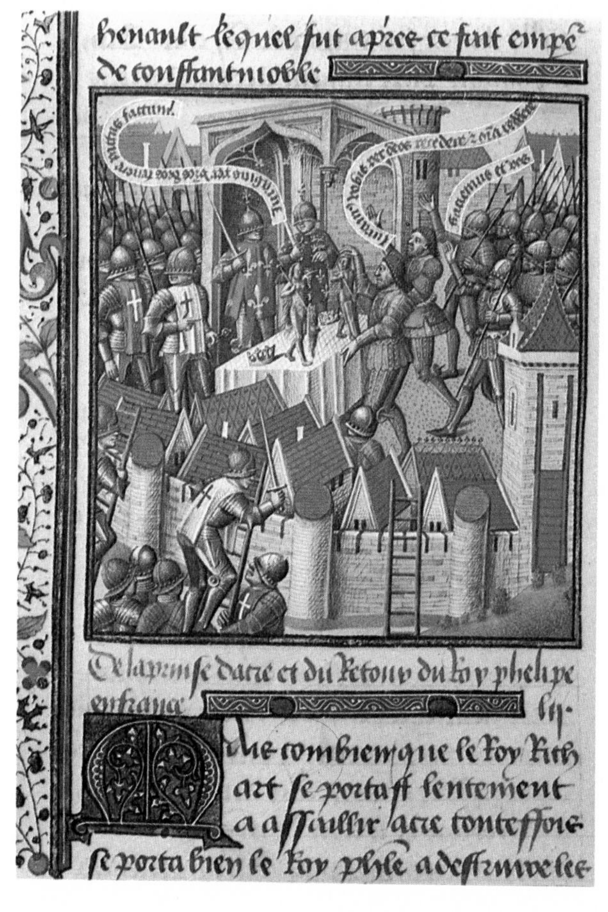

Left: Philip of France and Richard of England at the taking of Acre, from a 15th century French manuscript in the Musée Condé, Chantilly. Philip, who is about to return to France, is promising not to harass Richard's fiefs while Richard remains on crusade, a promise he has no intention of keeping.

	1185–1189	1190–1194	1195–1199	1200–1204	1205–1209
Politics & Military History	**1187** Saladin wins Battle of Hattin over King of Jerusalem. By 1189 when the kings of England and France (Richard Lionheart and Philip Augustus) and the German Emperor (Frederick Barbarossa) set out to try and retrieve the situation the Christians are reduced to the single town of Tyre.	**1190** Opening of the Third Crusade: Richard Lionheart takes Cyprus; Frederick Barbarossa drowns while bathing. **1191** Richard Lionheart beats Saladin at Arsuf and re-establishes a crusading state in Palestine, the Kingdom of Acre. **1192** Richard, on his way home, held for ransom in Germany.	**1196** Almohades win Battle of Alarcos, Spain. **1197** Richard Lionheart builds Château Gaillard to protect approaches of Normandy. **1198** Bohemia becomes a kingdom.	**1201** Fourth crusade assembles at Venice: crusaders take Zara in Dalmatia to pay off money owing to Venetians (1202): sail to and sack Constantinople (1204). **1203** Hojo clan gains control of the Kamakura Shogunate. **1204** Philip Augustus takes Château Gaillard and all Normandy from John of England.	**1206** Mongol chieftain Temujin celebrates unification of Mongolia by taking title Genghis Khan. Turkish general Aibak founds Sultanate of Delhi. **1207** Seljuks resume advance in Anatolia.
Religion & Learning		**1190** Foundation of the Military Order of Teutonic Knights.	**1198** Pope Innocent III becomes guardian for Henry VI's son Frederick II Hohenstaufen.	**1200** University of Paris obtains charter. Pope Innocent III places France under an interdict.	**1208** Pope Innocent III calls for crusade against Albigensian heretics of S France. Also excommunicates King John and lays England under an interdict because John refuses to allow Stephen Langton to take office as Archbishop of Canterbury (1209). = Oxford University in existence.
Cities & Social Development	**1190(–1209)** Construction of new wall round Paris, enclosing 250 ha.	**1192** Yoritomo takes the title of Shogun (military ruler): his residence at Kamakura becomes the effective capital of Japan.	**1196** Henry VI fails to make title to German Empire hereditary: empire dissolves into its usual turmoil on his death (1197).		
Discovery & Invention	**1185** First certain evidence of a windmill of western type, an illustration of a post-mill in an English manuscript.	**1190** First certain evidence of the use of the mariners' compass in the West, a reference in Alexander Neckam's *De Utensilibus*.		= Development of trebuchet by addition of a counterweight to the pivoted-beam stone-thrower. **1204** Water powered lumber-mill at Evreux, Normandy.	**1209** London Bridge completed (begun 1176). A masonry bridge with 20 small semi-circular arches, it took the place of a timber structure of Roman origin.
The Arts	**1185** Completion of the Pont St Benezet, Avignon (begun 1177), the first instance of the segmental arch being used in bridge building. Possibly suggested by the cathedral builder's flying butress.	**1194** Beginning of Chartres Cathedral and of great age of French Gothic architecture.	= *Nibelungenlied* (Lay of the Nibelung Men), epic poem about the hero Siegfried and his wife Kriemhild set in the 5th century AD.	= Final phase of temple building at Angkor: King Jayavarman VII builds Angkor Thom and the Bayon.	**1207** Per Abbat *Poema de Mio Cid*, epic account of the adventures of El Cid (see 1094).

KINGDOMS OF FRANCE AND ENGLAND c1200

ENGLISH CHANNEL · Calais · Château Gaillard · Paris · NORMANDY · BRITTANY · MAINE · ANJOU · TOURAINE · BLOIS · ISLE DE FRANCE · CHAMPAGNE · BURGUNDY · AQUITAINE · AUVERGNE · GASCONY · TOULOUSE · PYRENEES

France · Kingdom of England · English fiefs · English claims · Kingdom of France – inheritance of Philip II

France. Situated on a high rock overlooking the Seine this castle, which Richard named Château Gaillard, soon acquired a reputation for impregnability. Its three wards and ten massive towers represented the last word in military architecture; its builder, an acknowledged master of siegecraft, could see no fault in his magnificent fortress. 'I could hold Château Gaillard,' said King Richard 'if it were built of butter.'

Both Château Gaillard and King Richard were made of stronger stuff but Richard's heir, his brother John, was not. In fact he was widely known as John Soft-sword. When John inherited the English crown in 1199 Philip II immediately breathed more easily. Four years later, his preparations complete, he moved against Château Gaillard. It took him six months to capture it but once he had, the key to Normandy was in his hand. By the end of 1204 the whole Duchy was his, and Anjou, Maine and Touraine too. John Soft-sword had lost the lot.

Philip has gone down in history as Philip Augustus and the comparison with the founder of the Roman Empire, though based on a medieval misconception of what the word meant, is not unjust. He inherited a notoriously feeble monarchy; and without question he left it the strongest power in Europe.

Above left and above: The struggle in France; incidents in the long war to establish the power of the French crown.

GENGHIS KHAN

Right: Genghis Khan through Chinese eyes. This is not a contemporary portrait but an impression of the Mongol type to which Genghis conformed. As such it is as close to reality as we can hope to get. Ink on silk, 14th century, from the Imperial Collection, Taiwan.

In 1206, after twenty years of continuous warfare, the Mongol chieftain Temujin succeeded in imposing his authority on all of the peoples in outer Mongolia. He celebrated the achievement by taking the title of Genghis Khan which can be roughly translated as 'Lord of the Earth'. Three years later he launched his hordes on their first campaign outside Mongolia, an assault on the Tangut kingdom to the south. But this was only a prelude to the major undertaking of his middle years, the invasion of China. This began in 1211 when Genghis, at the head of 100,000 cavalry, crossed the Gobi and established forward bases on the Chinese side. In a battle near Fuzhou he inflicted a crushing defeat on the Jin rulers of north China; then he loosed his regiments on the countryside.

The campaign set the pattern for future Mongol conquests. After the defeat of the enemy's army in the field, the villages and small towns were looted. Then the native population was rounded up and used as an expendable labour force in the siege of the big cities. It was an immensely destructive process: by 1215, when Beijing (Peking) fell, north China was a wilderness.

After the capture of Beijing, Genghis withdrew to outer Mongolia leaving an army behind to keep up the pressure on the area between Beijing and the Yellow River. Over the next ten years this zone was brought under Mongol control, though the Jin emperors (ruling now from Kaifeng) never gave up and contested every Mongol advance.

The Jin owed their reprieve to the fact that Genghis had switched his attention westward. In 1218 the Shah of Iran had been foolish enough to massacre a Mongol Embassy: the next year Genghis appeared in person on the banks of the Syr Darya (River Jaxates) and let loose a hurricane of retribution. One by one the cities of Iran were reduced to smoking ruins as the Mongols swept across the plateau. Genghis himself went after the Shah's son, Ala al-Din, Viceroy of Afghanistan, who fought all the way back to the River Indus and then escaped. The Shah was hunted down by Generals Jebe and Subedei who pursued him to his deathbed by the Caspian. From there the two generals cut loose on a raid that demonstrates the quality of the army Genghis had created. In quick succession they defeated the Georgians, the Turks of the Volga steppe (Kipchaks), the Princes of Russia and the Bulgars of the upper Volga.

Back in Mongolia Genghis decided to settle accounts with the Tanguts who had refused to supply troops for his war with the Shah. He died in the course of the campaign which completed his mastery over all the lands between Russia and Iran in the west and Korea and north China in the east. In a few short years he had created an empire of unprecedented size and brought death to millions.

The Mongol Empire was far from complete: more victories were to bring more lands under its sway over the next fifty years. But, in the autumn of 1227, there was a lull in the campaigning as Subedei, perhaps the greatest of the Mongol generals, took his master's body back across the Gobi, through the Mongolian grasslands and up into the mountains. The grave has never been found.

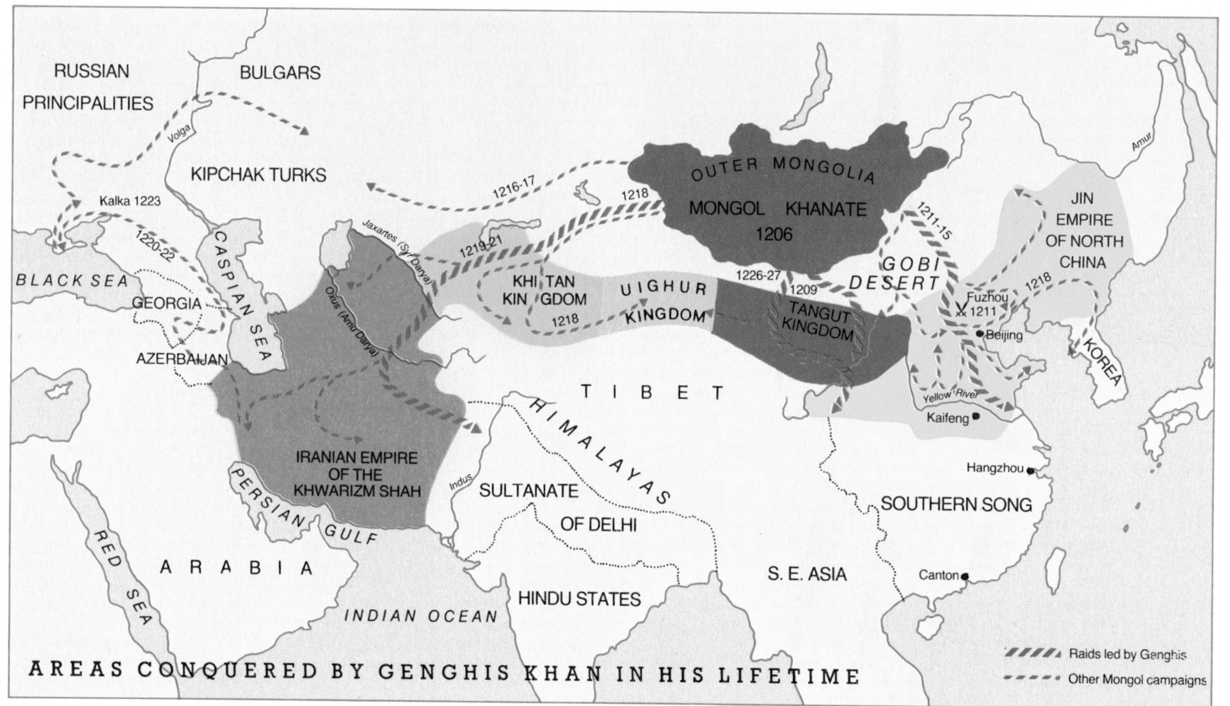

Left: Genghis Khan's empire extended over the whole Eurasian steppe from South Russia to Manchuria. It also included the lands between the Syr Darya and Amu Darya (present day Russian Turkestan) which are half pastoral, half agricultural, and North China which has a grassland zone (Inner Mongolia) but is essentially agricultural. Geographically Genghis' conquests seem equally balanced between east and west: in terms of population, though, the eastern conquests are much the more important. Of the 40-odd millions in the Mongol Empire at the time of his death at least 30 million lived in North China. This disproportion was to increase as his successors brought the 60 million Chinese of the centre and south into the empire too.

1210–1214	1215–1219	1220–1224	1225–1229	1230–1234	
1210 Genghis Khan invades N China. Shah of Khwarizm conquers Iran and Turkestan. **1211** Sultan Iltutmish of Delhi begins series of campaigns that eventually brings all N India under his control. **1212** South of Spain: Christian kings defeat Almohades at Las Navas de Tolosa. **1213** South of France: Battle of Muret. Raymond of Toulouse defeated and Peter of Aragon killed resisting Albigensian crusaders. **1214** Philip II of France defeats John of England and German Emperor Otto IV at Bouvines: after this the rival candidate for the German Empire, Frederick II, gains the upper hand in both Germany and Italy. Seljuks take Sinope.	**1215** King John of England forced to concede charter of rights (the 'Magna Carta') to Barons, Clergy and Commoners. **1218** Otto IV dies leaving Frederick II Hohenstaufen undisputed master of both the Empire and the Kingdom of Sicily. Mongols conquer Karakhitans of Turkestan. **1219** Genghis Khan begins campaign against Khwarizm Shah's Iranian Empire. Fifth Crusade takes Damietta, Egypt.	**1220** Amiens Cathedral begun, generally considered to be the perfect expression of the Gothic architectural aesthetic though it lacks the site, the sculpture and the stained glass that make Chartres its overall superior. Block printed playing cards in use in Germany and Spain. **1220–21** Genghis Khan overthrows Iranian Empire of the Khwarizm Shah. **1221** Crusaders surrender Damietta in return for safe conduct from Egypt. **1221–22** Mongol Generals Subedei and Jebe defeat Georgians, Cumans, S Russian princes and Volga Bulgars. **1223** Byzantines recover Salonika.	**1226** As part of the Albigensian Crusade Louis VII takes Avignon. **1227** Genghis Khan dies during campaign against the Tanguts. King of Denmark, defeated by Germans at Bornhovede, cedes Holstein to the Empire. **1228** Frederick II's crusade: he obtains Jerusalem for the King of Acre by negotiation (1229). **1229** Albigensian Crusade ends with French crown annexing Languedoc and the Inquisition established in Toulouse. Ogadai recognized as Great Khan in succession to Genghis.	**1230** Emperor Frederick II settles in his Kingdom of Sicily, finding this relatively small state, with its Byzantine administrative tradition, more rewarding to rule than the anarchic German Empire. Castile and Leon united by Ferdinand III. James I of Aragon captures Majorca. **1233** Teutonic Knights found Kulm and Thorn in Prussia and embark on conquest of the province. **1234** Mongols extinguish Jin Kingdom of N China. = Sundiata re-establishes the independence of the Malinke Kingdom of Mali.	Politics & Military History
1210 St Francis of Assisi founds Franciscan Order of Friars, emphasizing poverty and repentance. **1212** Children's crusade: French children offered free passage to the Holy Land end up being sold in the slave markets of N Africa. **1213** King John submits to Pope Innocent III. = Cambridge University founded by scholars from Oxford.	**1215** Dominican order of friars founded by St Dominic at Toulouse. Geoffroy de Villehardouin *The Conquest of Constantinople*.	**1222** Scholars from Bologna found University of Padua. **1224** Emperor Frederick II founds University of Naples.	**1227** Quarrel between Pope and Emperor breaks out again: Gregory IX excommunicates Frederick II for not going on crusade (1227), for going on crusade (1228) and for recovering Jerusalem without Papal permission (1229).		Religion & Learning
				1231 German princes extort formal recognition of their autonomy (*Constitutio in favorem principum*) from Frederick II's son and deputy Henry.	Cities & Social Development
				1232 China: First use of rockets in warfare. First mention of mariners' compass in an Islamic source. As by this time it has been in use in the West for a generation or more (see 1190), it seems unlikely that this Chinese invention reached the West by the sea route: it must have been either independently developed there or brought overland by the silk road.	Discovery & Invention
	= Reims Cathedral begun.	= Villard de Honnecourt *Sketchbook* containing details of contemporary cathedral architecture.	**1225** West front of Wells Cathedral. **1227** Burgos Cathedral begun. **1228** Church of Assisi begun to celebrate canonization of St Francis.		The Arts

	1235–1239	1240–1244	1245–1249	1250–1254	1255–1259
Politics & Military History	**1235** Emperor Frederick II imprisons his rebel son Henry. **1236** Ferdinand III of Castile captures Cordoba. Almohade Empire begins to disintegrate; Hafsids of Tunis declare independence. **1237** Emperor Frederick II defeats Lombard League at Cortenuova. Mongols conquer Volga Bulgars. Teutonic Knights absorb Knights of the Sword. **1238** James I of Aragon takes Valencia. Mongols conquer Principality of Vladimir. Thai kingdom of Sukhotai founded. Mongols conquer Georgians and Cumans.	**1240** Mongols destroy Kiev, conquer South Russia. Alexander Nevsky of Novgorod defeats the Swedes on the banks of the Neva. **1241** Mongols invade Poland and Hungary, defeat Duke Henry of Silesia at Liegnitz and Bela IV of Hungary at Mohi; withdraw on receiving news of death of Ogadai Khan. Alliance between Lübeck and Hamburg. **1242** Alexander Nevsky defeats the Teutonic Knights in battle on the frozen Lake Peipus. Mongols defeat Seljuks of Rum at Kuzadag. **1244** Jerusalem lost to fugitive band of Turks.	**1247–8** Emperor Frederick II fails in attempt to take Parma. **1248** Ferdinand III of Castile takes Seville from the Moors. Louis IX of France (St Louis) goes on crusade: takes Damietta, Egypt (1249).	**1250** Louis IX defeated at Mansourah, captured and then ransomed. Death of Emperor Frederick II followed by two decades in which there is no generally accepted emperor in Germany and precious little law and order of any sort. **1253** Mongols open campaign against southern Song of China. **1254** Papal invasion of Naples defeated at Foggia. Louis IX returns to France.	**1257** Mongols capture Alamut, the Assassin headquarters in the Elburz, and extirpate the sect. **1258** Mongols capture Baghdad and put an end to the Abbasid Caliphate. **1259** Mongols sack Hanoi.
Religion & Learning	= *Roman de la Rose.*		**1249** First college at Oxford (University College).	= *History of the English* by Matthew Paris of St Albans.	
Cities & Social Development	**1238** Foundation of Danzig (Gdansk).	**1244** Calibrated spherical stones produced for trebuchets in England ('the cannon ball before the cannon').		**1252** Florence strikes the first gold coins (= florins) to be issued in the West since the fall of Rome. **1254** Königsberg founded by Teutonic Knights.	**1260** First appearance of the Flagellants. = International triumph of the French Gothic style. Buildings of this type under construction include Westminster Abbey, Old St Pauls and Cologne Cathedral.
The Arts	**1235** Beauvais Cathedral, the tallest building ever attempted by Gothic architects.		**1246–8** Ste Chapelle built by Louis IX to receive the 'crown of thorns'.		

In the worst part of the Dark Ages the people of Venetia, the province in the north east corner of Italy, gave up trying to defend their homes and fled to the islands of the coast. There are literally hundreds of these because the mainland slides into the sea so gently that there is a wide zone – the famous lagoon – which is neither one thing nor the other: hillocks at the edge of it are often islands for part of the year. Conversely, some of the islands are less safe from land attack than they look. In 810 when the Franks were seeking ways of persuading the Venetians to pay tribute they were able to take three of the 12 villages that formed the 'Confederation of the Lagoon'. But try as they might they could not reach Rialto which lay right out in the middle of the lagoon. After this the Venetians had no doubt about which was the best place to live: they made Rialto their headquarters and, this being the town where most of the Venetians lived, people soon began referring to it as Venice.

Because Venice was never taken by the Franks it remained technically a part of the Byzantine Empire under the rule of a duke. In practice it was so far away from Constantinople that the Venetians were able to run their own affairs and elect their own duke – the Doge, as he was known locally. But the Byzantine connection was a useful one: after the Byzantines lost their last foothold in north Europe – which they did when Ravenna fell to the Lombards in 753 – the Venetians handled all the trade between these two parts of the world. And with the revival in Europe's fortunes in the 11th century this became big business. The Venetians undoubtedly had good luck: they were in the right place at the right time and they had good government. The stability of their republic was the envy of other Italian city-states and, if the Doge was always chosen from the rich by the rich, the position was never allowed to become hereditary. Florence might fall to the Medici, Milan to the Visconti, the Sforza and ultimately Spain, but the mistress of the Adriatic guarded her liberty.

Above: The Doge's Palace, Venice. On a column to the left of the palace is the city's emblem, the winged lion of St Mark. The domes of St Mark's Cathedral can be seen rising above the palace; its detached campanile (bell tower), then, as now, the highest building in the city, stands to the left.

The Crusaders added to Venice's prosperity: there was a constant demand for ships to take pilgrims and supplies to the Holy Land and even more money to be made carrying silks, spices and any surviving pilgrims back again. By the 14th century Venice had become the largest and richest city in Europe with a population of over 100,000 and a revenue greater than that of many kingdoms.

In the opening years of the 13th century Venice acquired an overseas empire. The story is a rather disreputable one. The Venetians contracted to ship the Fourth Crusade to the Levant for the sum of 94,000 marks but the Crusaders proved unable to pay (mostly because there were only 10,000 of them, not the 33,500 anticipated) so the Venetians suggested that the Crusaders might like to take out a rival seaport, Zara, in part payment. The Crusaders duly did so. Then the Venetians suggested the Crusaders raise further funds for their project – an attack on Egypt – by attacking Constantinople first. There was a civil war in progress there and intervention could be very profitable. Again the Crusaders complied. And that was as near to fighting the infidel as this particular crusade ever got. The Crusaders kept Constantinople where they installed their own emperor. The Venetians took three-eighths of the Byzantine Empire, mostly in the form of islands. From this time until the Turks took them away in the 16th and 17th centuries Venice had a useful string of bases around the coasts of Greece.

In the end Venice became the backwater that it is today. But in the Middle Ages and for the first century or so of the modern era it ranked as a major power.

1260–1264	1265–1269	1270–1274	1275–1279	1280–1284	
1260 Mongols defeated by Mamluks of Egypt at Ain Jalut, Palestine. **1261** Byzantine Emperor Michael Palaeologus recovers Constantinople. Pope offers crown of the Sicilies to Charles of Anjou, Louis IX's brother. **1263** Norse attempting conquest of Hebrides defeated by Scots at Largs. **1264** Mongol Khan Kublai moves capital from Karakorum to Beijing (Peking). This step marks the effective division of the Mongol Empire into four separate Khanates. Battle of Lewes: English King Henry III captured by Simon de Montfort, leader of rebel baronial faction.	**1265** Overthrow and death of Simon de Montfort at Battle of Evesham. **1266** Charles of Anjou defeats and kills Manfred of Sicily at Benevento and takes the crown. **1268** Charles of Anjou defeats, captures and executes Conradin, last of the Hohenstaufen. Mamluks take Antioch.	**1270** Louix IX dies on crusade against Tunis. **1273** Rudolf of Habsburg elected German Emperor: election disputed by King Otakar of Bohemia. **1274** Failure of Kublai Khan's first invasion of Japan.	**1276** Kublai's forces take Hangzhou: last remnants of south Song Empire mopped up over the next 3 years. **1277** Edward I of England embarks on the conquest of Wales. **1278** Rudolph of Habsburg and King Ladislas of Hungary defeat and kill Otakar of Bohemia at the Marchfeld. Mongols expelled from Annam.	**1281** Failure of Kublai's second invasion of Japan, attributed by the pious to the Kamikaze ('Divine Wind'). **1282** 'The Sicilian Vespers': successful Sicilian rebellion against the rule of Charles of Anjou; Peter III of Aragon lands on the island and accepts crown (= King of Sicily); Charles of Anjou holds mainland (= King of Naples). Rudolph of Habsburg confers Austrian duchies on his sons. **1283** Edward I completes his conquest of Wales. **1284** Genoese defeat Pisans off Meloria.	Politics & Military History
		= Thomas Aquinas *Summa Theoligica.*		**1283** Sukodaya script adopted by Thai (oldest surviving inscription 1292).	Religion & Learning
	= Construction of Great Zimbabwe, Kraal of the king of the Shona, Africa.	**1270** Use of mariners' chart recorded during St Louis' crusade: this will surely have been a '*portolano*' with a rhumb-line grid (network of compass bearings: see illustration below).	**1276** Fabriano, Italy: first paper mill in Europe, driven by seven waterwheels. **1277** Experimental mercury escapement for a weight-driven clock illustrated in MS of Alfonso X.	= Appearance of spinning wheel in the West, first device to use a cord drive outside China.	Cities & Social Development
= Nicolo Pisano sculpts pulpits for baptistery at Pisa and for Siena Cathedral.			**1277** Drawing for facade of Strasbourg Cathedral by Erwin von Steinbach, one of the few blueprints of this sort to survive.	**1283** Cimabue *Crucifix* (Santa Croce, Florence). **1284** Vault of choir of Beauvais Cathedral collapses: successfully reconstructed with intercalated columns.	The Arts

Above: View down the Grand Canal, Venice, towards the domes of Santa Maria della Salute.

Right: One of Venice's most famous sons, Marco Polo, on his way across Asia. Marco Polo spent 20 years at the court of Kublai Khan, the Mongol ruler of China, and his account of the Orient was one of the few available to western scholars. Abraham Cresques made use of it in the World Atlas from which this vignette is taken. The Atlas was presented by Cresques' patron, Peter III of Aragon, to Charles V of France in 1381.

	1285–1289	1290–1294	1295–1299	1300–1304	1305–1309
Politics & Military History	**1287** Mongols sack Pagan, Burma.	**1291** Acre, last remnant of the crusader Kingdom of Palestine, falls to the Mamluks. Nucleus of Swiss confederation formed by the three Forest Cantons: Schwyz, Uri and Unterwalden. **1292–3** Mongol expedition to Java encounters Vijaya, founder of the Kingdom of Majapahit.	**1296** Edward I annexes Scotland, takes the Scots coronation stone from Scone to London. **1297** Genoese defeat Venetians at Curzola (see below). **1298** Edward I defeats William Wallace at Falkirk. Foundation of Thai Kingdom of Chiengmai.	**1301** Mongols withdraw from Burma. **1302** Rising against French in Bruges: French army attempting its suppression defeated at Courtrai. = Ottoman clan emerges as main contender for control of NW Anatolia.	English capture and execute William Wallace: Robert Bruce, continuing struggle for Scotland's independence, crowned king (1306). **1307** Robert Bruce wins Battle of Loudon Hill. **1309** Teutonic Knights take Danzig (Gdansk): set up HQ at Marienburg. Gibraltar captured from the Moors.
Religion & Learning		**1290** Jews expelled from England.	**1296–7** Pope Boniface VIII fails in an attempt to stop Philip IV of France taxing the clergy: canonizes Louis IX as part of peace package. = Marco Polo, Venetian taken prisoner at Curzola, uses captivity to write memoirs of his stay in China in 1275–91.	**1303** Philip IV of France's men seize Pope Boniface at Anagni, outside Rome: Pope dies a month later. Mongol administration in China officially adopts Confucian doctrine.	**1305** Philip IV of France obtains election of his nominee as Pope Clement V: papal court moves to Avignon (1309) and becomes largely subservient to French interests. **1306** Jews expelled from France. **1309** Jean de Joinville *History of St Louis*.
Discovery & Invention	**1286** Mention of Bartholomew the Orologist of St Pauls is first indication that some sort of clockwork is being installed in cathedrals. Roger Bacon describes the magnifying power of lenses: spectacles come into use within the next few years (cf. 1306).	= Arabs trading with Zimbabwe discover the Comoros and Madagascar.	= Addition of compass card to mariners' compass completes western version of this instrument. Possibly first done at Amalfi which later claimed to have invented the instrument in its entirety.	**c.1300** Earliest western reference to the manufacture of gunpowder (Liber Isnium): probable date of earliest surviving Portolano marine chart (Carte Pisane).	**1306** Fra Girolamo of Pisa, preaching in Florence, says he talked to the man who invented spectacles 'not 20 years since'.
The Arts			**1296** Building of Florence Cathedral begins under direction of Arnolfo di Cambio: Palazzo Vecchio started in 1299.	**1301** Giovanni Pisano carves pulpit for Pistoia. **1304** Giotto begins his fresco cycle in the Arena chapel, Padua, which takes painting into a new, naturalistic phase.	

Because of its unique geography Venice had a head start in the medieval trading stakes and none of its contemporaries ever managed to catch it up. Nevertheless, if there was no other city that was anything like as rich and powerful, there were several in north Italy that were nearly as big and almost as prosperous – notably Genoa, which captured a fair share of the Mediterranean carrying trade, and Milan and Florence, which produced many of the goods so carried. Milan specialized in metalwork, Florence in textiles, and anything that the two did not make could be bought from one of the dozen or more towns of middling size that rounded out the urban sector of north Italy. This group of towns dominated trade throughout the Mediterranean world. The incontrovertible sign that it had achieved this position came in 1252 when first Florence and then Venice started minting gold coins. They were able to broadcast these golden seeds in the confidence that they would soon be returning with interest.

The position of northern Italy in the medieval economy makes an interesting contrast with the role of Rome in the classical world. Rome had drawn in the surplus of the Mediterranean in the guise of tribute: northern Italy sucked it in by capitalist guile. Whereas the other cities of the Mediterranean seaboard served much the same function as they had in antiquity – you can balance Tunis off against Carthage, Cairo against Hellenistic Alexandria – the structure of Renaissance Italy is something quite new: the people there lived on their intelligence, their inventions and their expertise.

North of the Alps the situation was, at first sight, less impressive. The cities were fewer, smaller and more scattered. On the other hand every one was a new growth, for in the Roman period there had been nothing in this area

14th century gold florin from Florence. The lily was the civic type together with the standing figure of St John the Baptist. Regular weight (3.5 g) and fineness (54 gr) won the fiorino *universal fame and the compliment of wide imitation.*

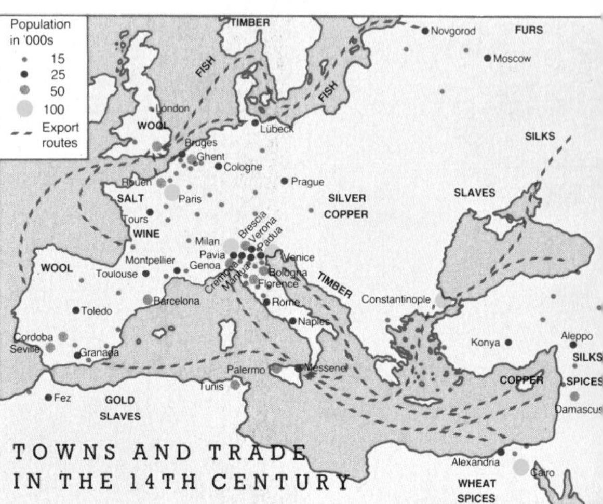

except a few token towns kept alive by imperial subsidy. Now there was a pair of major capital cities in Paris and London and a genuine cluster of manufacturing centres in the southern Netherlands (modern Belgium).

The cities of the Netherlands were essentially textile towns: they bought in wool (mostly from England but also from Spain and France); they wove it, finished it, dyed it and traded it. The commercial network they served extended far beyond anything that the Romans had conceived of: German merchants carried Flemish cloth round all the Scandinavian lands and they regularly visited Novgorod where they exchanged this and other manufactures for furs. This Baltic extension of the North Sea traffic eventually led to the creation of a bloc of

1310–1314	1315–1319	1320–1324	1325–1329	1330–1334	
1310 Knights of St John take Rhodes. **1312** Lyon incorporated in France. **1314** Robert Bruce defeats Edward II at Bannockburn, confirming independence of Kingdom of Scotland.	**1315** Leopold of Austria defeated by the Swiss at Morgarten. **1319** Accession of Magnus VII as King of Norway and Sweden. = Solomonid Kings of Ethiopia check Muslims and restabilize the kingdom.	**1320** Lithuanians take Kiev from the Golden Horde. **1324** Aragon takes Sardinia from Pisa. = Juhayna Arabs begin movement from Upper Egypt to the Sudan: Madai and Kalanjin begin movement from Sudan to Uganda and Kenya.	**1326** Ottomans take Bursa which becomes their capital. **1328** English recognize Robert Bruce as King of Scotland. Mongols recognize Ivan I of Moscow as Great Prince of Vladimir (meaning NE Russia). Gonzagas established in Mantua. = Aztecs found Tenochtitlan.	**1330** Gibraltar reconquered by Moors of Granada. **1332** Lucerne joins Swiss Confederation. = Sultanate of Delhi reaches its greatest extent under Muhammad ibn Tughluq.	Politics & Military History
1312 Pope Clement V, under pressure from Philip IV of France, abolishes Order of Knights Templar: Grand Master burnt at the stake in Paris (1314). **1314** Absolutely useless Hereford map of the world shows how monkish scholarship was failing to take account of new discoveries (cf 1311 below).	= Two Mongol Khanates, the Golden Horde of south Russia and the Ilkanate of Persia, adopt Islam.				Religion & Learning
1311 Earliest dated marine chart, signed by Pietrus Vesconte.	= *Two major technical advances in western Europe* ■ Invention of the verge and pallet escapement, the essential element in the mechanical clock. Clocks subsequently installed in many cathedrals to (a) strike the hours, (b) show the movements of the heavenly bodies. ■ Development of the first practical guns.		**1326** First documentary evidence for guns.		Discovery & Invention
1310 Lorenzo Maitani begins work on the facade of Orvieto Cathedral. **1311** Duccio completes Great Altarpiece of Siena Cathedral (the Maestà).	**1315** Wooden spire added to Old St Pauls reaches height of 142 m, marginally more than the Great Pyramid's eroded 140 m though less than its original 146.7 m.		**1328** Simone Martini *Giudoriccio de Fogliano*, fresco in the Palazzo Pubblico, Siena.	**1330** Andrea Pisano begins work on the south doors of the baptistery, Florence. **1334** Giotto begins work on the Campanile of Florence Cathedral. Pope begins work on the Palace of Avignon.	The Arts

Right: Fair of Lendit, Paris. Fairs were an important element in the medieval trading system, giving ordinary folk a chance to buy goods that they never saw the rest of the year. High class textiles formed the bulk of the goods bought and sold, and the fairs of France were much frequented by merchants from the major textile exporting regions, especially the Low Countries and North Italy. From a 15th century French manuscript.

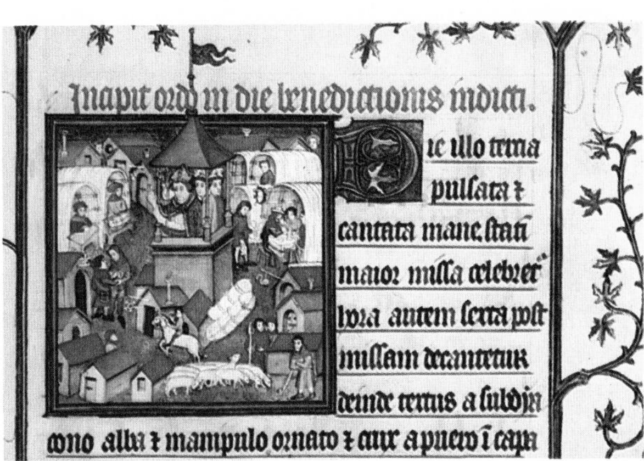

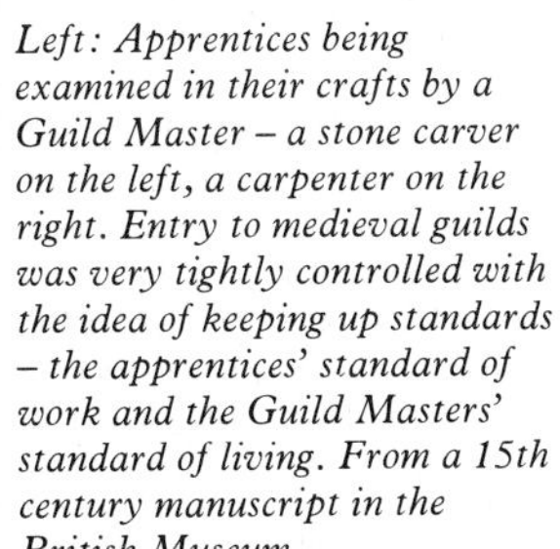

Left: Apprentices being examined in their crafts by a Guild Master – a stone carver on the left, a carpenter on the right. Entry to medieval guilds was very tightly controlled with the idea of keeping up standards – the apprentices' standard of work and the Guild Masters' standard of living. From a 15th century manuscript in the British Museum.

interested towns – the famous Hanse – which played an important part in the development of the north east sector of Europe. The scale though is tiny: Lübeck, the leader of the Hanse, never had more than 25,000 citizens and none of the other Baltic towns even rates a place on our map.

Of course it could be said that all medieval towns were small, as indeed they were by our standards. But that does not mean that they were not important. A bag of cash was worth a cartload of feudal obligations and the value of a town to the medieval economy far exceeded its equivalent weight of peasants. The same is true in social terms. The town provided an alternative model in a world obsessed with hereditary rights. It would be a nonsense to pretend any medieval institution was democratic and towns are no exception to this rule; they were rigidly and unashamedly oligarchic. But they thought themselves free and their pride in this freedom was a step on the road to better things.

	1335–1339	1340–1344	1345–1349	1350–1354	1355–1359
Politics & Military History	**1336** Ottomans take Bergama. **1337** Edward III of England asserts his claim to the French crown (via his mother Isabelle, daughter of Philip IV) against that of reigning French King Philip VI (son of Philip IV's brother Charles of Valois) despite French law of 1317 barring inheritance via a female. Start of the Hundred Years' War. **1338** Ottomans take Nicomedia.	**1340** English naval victory over the French at Sluys. **1344** Alfonso XI of Castile takes Algeciras.	**1346** Edward III wins Battle of Crecy. Scots invasion of England ends with capture of Scots king at Neville's Cross. Stephen Dushan, King of Serbia emphasizes his growing power by taking title of Emperor. Danes sell Estonia to the Teutonic Knights. **1347** Edward III takes Calais. Cola di Rienzi leads popular revolt in Rome. **1349** French King Philip VI buys the Dauphiné for his grandson: subsequently Dauphin becomes title of French king's eldest son.	**1350** Thai Kingdom of Ayutia founded. **1351** Zurich joins Swiss Confederation, followed shortly after by Glarus and Zug (1352) and Bern (1353). **1354** Ottomans take Ankara.	**1356** Ottoman Turks cross to Europe Golden Bull of the Emperor Charles IV which fixes number and powers of the Electors. Edward III's son, the Black Prince, defeats and captures the French King John the Good at Poitiers. **1358** France: peasant rising known as the Jacquerie. Venetians cede Dalmatia to Hungary. = Mongols begin to lose control in China to various factions including that of Zhu Yuanzhang who captures Nanjing (1359). = Cardinal Albornoz re-establishes papal rule in the Romagna.
Religion & Learning		**1344** Publication of the official histories of the Song, Liao (Khitan) and Jin dynasties.	**1348** Emperor Charles IV founds University of Prague.	**1353** Ibn Battuta begins dictating his *Travels* which, since 1325, had taken him through all the lands of Islam.	
Cities & Social Development	**1337** Ghent, Bruges and Ypres, the three major textile towns of Flanders, first declare their neutrality in the Hundred Years' War, then opt for the English side. French suzerainty, as exercised by the Count of Flanders, becomes nominal, though never abolished.	**1340** Edward III agrees that new taxation requires parliament's consent: also founds Order of the Garter.	**1346** The Black Death enters Europe: mortality reaches its peak in 1348–9. **1348** Widespread persecution of the Jews of Germany in the wake of the Black Death: subsequently many of the survivors migrate to Poland.		
Discovery & Invention	**1335** Earliest certain reference to a striking clock: St Gothard's, Milan.			**1352** Earliest certain reference to a striking clock north of the Alps, at Strasbourg Cathedral. One of the associated automata, a cock that stretches its neck and flaps its wings, still survives.	
The Arts	**1338** Ambrogio Lorenzetti *Good and Bad Government*, fresco in the Palazzo Pubblico, Siena.		**1349** Great East Window, Gloucester, first structure in the English 'perpendicular' style.	Boccaccio *Decameron.* = *Sir Gawain and the Green Knight.*	**1359** Orcagna completes tabernacle of Orsanmichele, Florence.

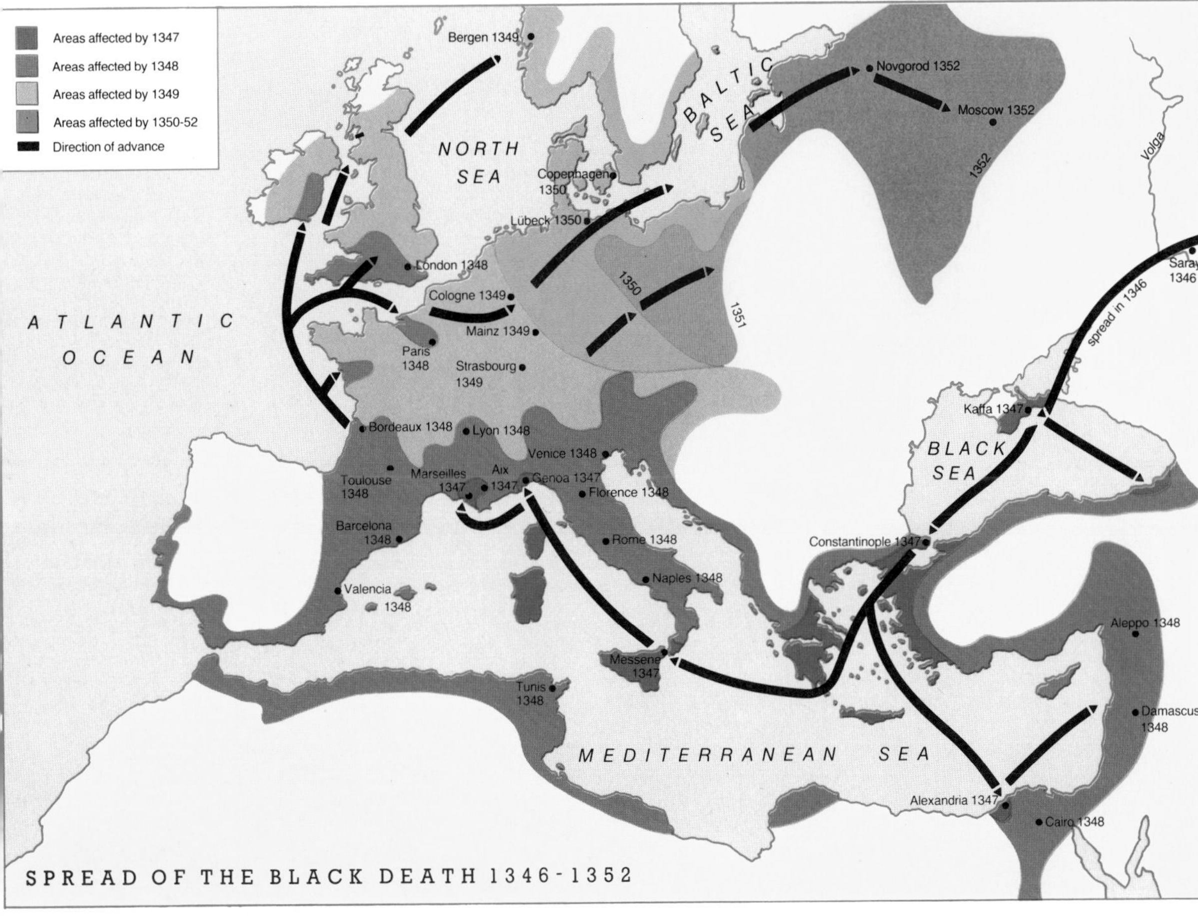

SPREAD OF THE BLACK DEATH 1346-1352

Above: French troops die of the plague.

Above: Burning contaminated clothes. The idea that clothes could spread plague was one of medieval man's better hypotheses; it may even have had some foundation in fact. However, the main agent of spread is the rat flea and essentially the Black Death was only contracted by people who were in contact with rats. That is why the mortality was so much heavier among the poor than the rich. There is a form of person to person spread via droplet infection ('pneumonic plague' as opposed to the usual 'bubonic') but it probably only operated within individual households. As it is a general rule with plague outbreaks that families are struck down as a whole (because it is the house that has the rats, not the individual) the pneumonic mode cannot have added greatly to the overall morbidity (sickness rate) of the Black Death though it may have marginally increased the mortality (pneumonic plague is 99% lethal as against bubonic's 70%). Illustration from a 14th century manuscript in the Bodleian library.

In 1346 Europe had been free of the plague for 400 years. There had been terrible outbreaks in earlier times, notably in the reigns of the Roman emperors Marcus Aurelius and Justinian, and millions of people had perished. But that was long ago and quite forgotten: no living doctor had seen a case and there was no description of the disease in any medical manual of the day.

Plague is primarily a disease of rodents and their fleas: outbreaks occur from time to time among the rodents of central Asia and when the rodents die the fleas which carry the bacillus start looking for alternative hosts. Any trapper unwise enough to pick up a sick marmot, for example, is asking for trouble. What looks like a free piece of fur could well be a death sentence.

The epidemic of plague known as the Black Death began with outbreaks at Astrakhan and Saray on the lower Volga: most likely the immediate source was a bale of infected marmot skins from a Central Asian dealer. From Saray the disease spread to Kaffa, the trading post maintained by the Genoese in the Crimean peninsula.

An outbreak of plague can only be sustained if rats and men are living in close proximity. This they most certainly did in medieval ships whose holds were full of every sort of vermin. In the last few months of 1347 Genoese ships fleeing Kaffa spread the epidemic to many of the major ports of the Mediterranean: the Black Death began to exert its fearsome toll.

Just how severe the mortality was has been the subject of much argument. It is beyond dispute that in towns that were affected – and nearly every town in Europe and the Near East was sooner or later – anything up to two-thirds of the population got the disease and of this two thirds about 70% died. What is less certain is how the countryside fared. The mortality was certainly less severe and some have claimed that the overall loss was not that inordinate. But the general run of opinion, then and now, is that the Black Death made its way from village to village much as it did from town to town and with much the same results – a swathe of death in its wake.

What is undoubtedly true is that it went fastest by boat. It reached the Atlantic-North Sea-Baltic trading network by crossing the relatively narrow neck of land north of the Pyrenees. From there it made its final progress into Poland and eventually Russia, claiming its last victim in some nameless Russian hovel a few hundred kilometres away from its starting point. By then the total count had risen to something like 25 million out of a population of a hundred million in the Europe-Near East area.

How did society cope with this staggering mortality? The answer is, amazingly well. In most places the panic only lasted a few months and the authorities were soon back in control. There were some hysterical reactions of the sort medieval man was prone to – processions of flagellants and, especially in the Rhineland, massacres of Jews – but by and large the business of the day – the Hundred Years' War, for example – continued as normal.

The long term effects were more important. Because labour was scarcer, wages rose: because marginal land went out of use, productivity increased. The result was that the standards of living for the poor showed a considerable improvement. This lasted throughout the 15th century and though during the 16th the recovery in numbers, combined with a lot of arm-twisting from the upper classes, brought wages back to the 1346 level, in the interim ordinary folk had their best time ever. In fact, provided you did not actually get it, the Black Death was good for you.

	1360–1364	1365–1369	1370–1374	1375–1379	1380–1384
Politics & Military History	**1360** Edward III of England and John of France (still in captivity) make peace: Edward abandons his claim to the French crown but gets Aquitaine, Calais and Ponthieu. Wisby sacked by Waldemar IV of Denmark. **1361** Ottomans capture Adrianople which becomes their capital in Europe (v. Bursa in Asia). **1362** John of France bestows Duchy of Burgundy on his youngest son Philip the Bold. **1363** Ottomans defeat Bosnians, Serbs and Hungarians at Marizza, take Serres and Philippopolis. **1364** China's rebel leader Zhu Yuanzhang proclaims himself king of Wu (the lower Yangzi region). Burma: Kingdom of Ava founded. Zug joins Swiss Confederation.	**1365** Alexandria sacked by Peter of Cyprus. **1366** War in Castile: France backs Henry of Trastamare, England backs Peter the Cruel: Black Prince invades Castile, defeats Henry and captures his ally du Guesclin at Battle of Najera (1367). **1368** Zhu Yuanzhang drives main body of Mongols from Beijing, becomes (under the name Hung Wu) the first emperor of the Ming Dynasty. **1369** Peter the Cruel killed by Henry who ascends throne of Castile. Hundred Years' War renewed. Thai sack Angkor: Mon kingdom of Pegu founded in Lower Burma. Timur the Lame establishes control over Transoxiana.	**1370** Black Prince sacks Limoges. **1372** Castilians defeat the English fleet off La Rochelle: tide begins to turn against the English in Aquitaine – French capture Poitiers, La Rochelle and Angoulême. **1373** du Guesclin defeats English in Brittany.	**1375** Truce in Hundred Years' War. All English possessions in France now lost bar Calais, Cherbourg, Brest, Bayonne and Bordeaux. Mamluks extinguish Kingdom of Lesser Armenia. **1379** Genoese defeat Venetians off Pola, capture Chioggia at the SE corner of the lagoon.	**1380** Venetians defeat Genoese, recapture Chioggia. Byzantine Emperor John Palaeologus acknowledges suzerainty of Ottoman sultan. Union of Norway and Denmark in person of Olaf IV. **1381** Venetians cede Dalmatia to Hungary Revolt of Ghent and Bruges against the Count of Flanders: rebels defeated at Roosebeke by Charles VI of France and revolt suppressed (1382). Timur overruns north Iran. **1382** Ming troops eliminate last Mongol garrison in Yunnan. Ottomans capture Sofia. **1384** Philip of Burgundy acquires the county of Flanders through his marriage: beginning of the Burgundian Dominion.
Religion & Learning	**1364** University of Cracow founded by Casimir III.	**1365** University of Vienna founded by Rudolf IV. **1367** Pope Urban V decides to quit Avignon for Rome.	**1370** Pope Urban V returns to Avignon. Publication of official history of the Yuan (Mongol) dynasty.	**1377** Papacy, in person of Pope Gregory XI, finally returns to Rome. **1378** Pope Gregory XI dies: split in conclave leads to election of two Popes, Urban VI ruling from Rome and acknowledged by England, Italy and Germany, and Clement VII ruling from Avignon and acknowledged by France, Scotland, Spain and Sicily. This division – the Great Schism – reflects the political line-up of the time, itself largely a product of the Hundred Years' War and the existence of the two Kingdoms of Sicily.	**1380** Wyclif translates the bible into English.
Cities & Social Development	**1362** English used for opening speech of parliament: use of English made mandatory in law courts.				**1381** Peasants' Revolt in England, anti-tax riots in Paris: both events can be seen as reactions to the economic changes caused by the Black Death.
Discovery & Invention	**1364** Giovanni de Dondi completes clock with 7 faces showing the movements of the sun, moon and 5 known planets: installed in Palazzo Capitana, Padua.			**1375** Catalan World Map combines information from Portolan Marine charts (for the West) with Ptolemy (for the East). **1377** Thirty-day quarantine imposed by Venetian authorities at Ragusa in attempt to stop spread of plague from the East: first instance of the use of a specific quarantine period.	**1384** Water-powered blast furnace in operation at Liège, Belgium.
The Arts	**1362** William Langland *Vision of Piers Ploughman.* Sultan Hasan Mosque, Cairo, masterpiece of the Mamluk style.	**1366** Petrarch *Sonnets.* **1368** Hafiz *The Diwan.*		**1377** Court of Lions, Alhambra, palace of Moorish rulers of Granada. **1382** Loggia dei Lanzi, Florence.	

1385–1389	1390–1394
1385 Portuguese defeat the Castilians at Aljubarrota. Gian Galeazzo Visconti establishes his rule in Milan and over much of Lombardy. **1386** Swiss defeat and kill Leopold III of Austria at Battle of Sempach. **1387** Ming Emperor Hung Wu finally completes his conquest of China. **1388** Leopold's brother Albert defeated by the Swiss at Battle of Naifels. **1389** Ottoman sultan defeats serbs at Kossovo: Serbia annexed to the Ottoman Empire.	**1390** Ottoman Sultan Beyazit annexes five of the seven Turkish emirates of Anatolia. **1391** Timur overruns Transcaucasia. **1392** Timur sacks Baghdad. Beyazit conquers Karaman in Central Anatolia. **1393** Ottoman Turks annex Bulgaria and emirate of Kizil Ahmadli, last independent emirate of Anatolia.
1385 University of Heidelburg founded. **1388** Cologne University founded.	
1387 Major census in China.	
1386 Salisbury clock, the earliest mechanism of this type to survive.	**1392** Wells Cathedral clock. = Ulugh Beg, Timur's grandson, establishes observatory at Samarkand.
1387–1400 Geoffrey Chaucer *Canterbury Tales.*	= Nō plays become popular in Japan. = John Gower *Confessio Amantis.*

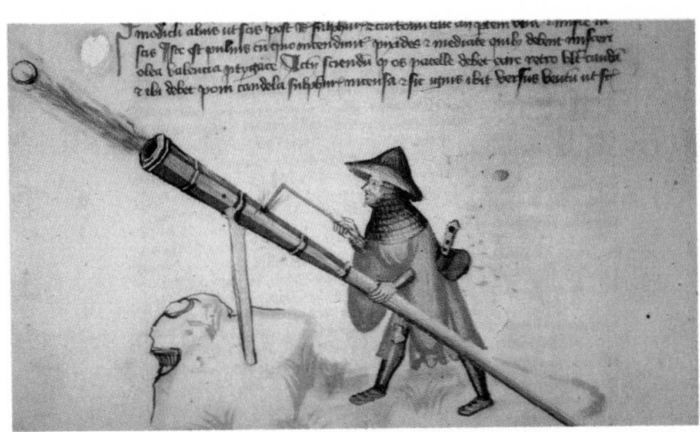

Above: Late 14th century gun weighing over 45 kg with a calibre of 5cm. The mounting allows the gun to be depressed below the horizontal making it ideal for defending castle walls. Wadding was placed down the barrel to prevent the shot rolling out.

Above right: A longer barrelled and hence more accurate weapon of the 15th century. From an Italian manuscript.

Gunpowder is first mentioned in a Chinese alchemical treatise of the 9th century AD. The reader is advised to treat it cautiously because it is a substance that can easily flare up, singeing eyebrows and burning hands. It turned out to be just the stuff for fireworks, something the Chinese were aways fond of, and it soon found other applications too: in 919 it was being used to ignite the jet of a pump-action flame-thrower.

This was only the start of a very long list of military applications. In 1126 the Chinese defending Kaifeng against the Jin launched bombs full of gunpowder from catapults mounted on the walls of the city. According to the Chinese the bombs ignited among the advancing Jin and caused a satisfactory amount of panic and confusion but they cannot have done all that much damage because the Jin went on to take Kaifeng. Nor does another Chinese gunpowder device, the 'firelance' sound much more effective. The firelance was like a child's rocket with the combustion chamber attached to the stick head down, not head up: the idea was for the user to hold the stick and let the rocket discharge its contents in the enemy's face. Conceivably it was of some value against scaling parties. The ultimate Chinese weapon of this type was a big firelance with stones and broken glass mixed into the propellant. In effect this was a sort of shotgun, although as there was no attempt to separate shot from propellant it cannot really be classed as a gun.

Chinese gunpowder was low in nitrate and deflagrant rather than explosive: it went off with a whoosh, not a bang. This suited Chinese ideas on how it was best used but it led them up a blind alley developmentally: it was fully explosive, high nitrate mixtures that repaid attention. The formula for these was known in western Europe by the 13th century and it was there, in the opening decades of the 14th century, that the first practical guns were made.

The requirements for a useable gun are (1) a metal barrel (2) an explosive charge (3) a missile (4) a wad of some sort separating 2 from 3, and (5) a way of igniting the charge which in all early guns was done via a touch hole. The earliest missiles were probably crossbow bolts: certainly such is the case in the first picture we have of a gun, the illustration to a manuscript book of 1326. But by this time other gunners were using shot – a Florentine order for the manufacture of 'metal cannon and iron bullets' is dated the same year – and it was not long before the shot was heavy enough to bring down walls.

The social consequences of artillery were enormous. Until the 14th century a single rebellious lord could defy the king and all the forces of the kingdom: all he had to do was retreat behind his castle walls. Now the king could take a castle in a week. This made the feudal lords a lot more obedient. In fact, in many ways it spelt the end of the old order. For the first time the royal writ ran to every corner of the kingdom.

	1395–1399	1400–1404	1405–1409	1410–1414	1415–1419
Politics & Military History	**1395** Timur the Lame defeats the Golden Horde. Gian Galeazzo Visconti purchases title of Duke of Milan from the emperor. **1396** Battle of Nicopolis: Sultan Beyazit annihilates crusader army led by King Sigismund of Hungary. Genoa becomes a French protectorate. **1397** Union of Kalmar brings the three Scandinavian Kingdoms of Norway, Sweden and Denmark under one rule. Beyazit takes Athens. **1398** Timur the Lame invades India, sacks Delhi. **1399** Richard II deposed and killed by Henry Bolingbroke who ascends the throne as King Henry IV. Golden Horde defeats Lithuanians.	**1400** Rebellion of Owen Glendower of Wales against Henry IV. **1401** Timur invades Syria, sacks Damascus. **1402** Timur invades Anatolia, totally defeats Ottoman army and captures Sultan Beyazit at Battle of Ankara. Scots defeated at Homildon Hill by Percys of Northumberland. **1403** Timur reinstates Anatolian emirs displaced by Beyazit: takes Smyrna from the Knights of St John. Percys join rebellion against Henry IV who defeats them at Battle of Shrewsbury. **1404** Beyazit's four sons fight for the succession to the Ottoman Empire. Venice acquires Verona and Vicenza.	**1405** Timur sets out for China but dies at Otrar. Venice conquers Padua. **1406** Florence conquers Pisa. English capture Prince James of Scotland. Chinese occupy Annam. **1407** Murder of Duke of Orléans by partisans of the Duke of Burgundy. **1408** Venetians recover Dalmatia. Final defeat of Percys at Bramham Moor.	**1410** Poles defeat Teutonic Knights at Battle of Tannenberg. **1411** Sigismund of Hungary elected German Emperor. Feud between Orléanist and Burgundian factions in France breaks out into civil war. **1414** Orléanists triumph over Burgundians.	**1415** Henry V of England lays claim to the French throne, invades France, wins Battle of Agincourt. Portuguese conquer Ceuta, Morocco. **1417** Henry V conquers Normandy (bar Rouen). **1419** Anglo-Burgundian alliance: Henry V takes Rouen. Emperor Sigismund claims crown of Bohemia; rejected by Hussites.
Religion & Learning	**1396** Florence appoints a teacher of Greek.	**1402** John Huss begins to preach in Prague. = Chinese compile a manuscript encyclopedia in 22,937 volumes. = Ibn Khaldun *Muquaddimah.*	**1409** General Council of Pisa attempts to end schism by deposing both existing Popes and electing a third: fails to make its rulings effective. Germans secede from Prague University where Huss, representing the Czech nationalist faction, is made Rector.	**1412** John Huss excommunicated for preaching against sale of indulgences. University of St Andrews founded in Scotland.	**1415–17** Papal schism finally ended by Council of Constance which elects Martin V Pope, burns Huss.
Cities & Social Development					
Discovery & Invention		**1402–3** European adventurers begin conquest of the Canary Islands. **1403** Koreans produce complete fount of metal type.	**1405–7** First in series of official maritime expeditions despatched by the Ming authorities: visits Indonesia and S India.	**1413** Fourth Ming expedition despatched: visits Mogadishu, Somalia and Aden, Yemen.	
The Arts	= Wilton Diptych: votive portrait of Richard II of England.	**1402** Ghiberti wins competition for North doors of the Baptistery, Florence.	**1405–6** Quercia's *Tomb of Ilaria del Carretto*, Lucca Cathedral. **1408–9** Donatello's *David* (Uffizi, Florence).	= *Icon of the Old Trinity* by Andrei Rublev, most famous of the Russian Icon painters.	**1418** Brunelleschi wins competition for design of dome of Florence Cathedral: builds Foundling Hospital (1419). = *Très Riches Heures* illustrated for the Duc de Berri by Paul de Limbourg. = Charles of Orléans writes the best of his poems during his capitivity in England. **1418** Block printed picture of the Virgin and Child in a Flemish manuscript.

1420–1424	1425–1429
1420 Henry V recognized as present Regent and future heir to the throne of France by French King Charles VI. Sigismund fails to take Prague. **1422** Henry V and Charles VI both die leaving France divided between Duke of Bedford (ruling from Paris on behalf of Henry VI) and Charles VII (at Poitiers). Hussites defeat Sigismund at Deutschbrod. Unsuccessful Ottoman attempt on Constantinople. **1424** Bedford defeats French at Verneuil. English release James I of Scotland after an 18-year captivity.	**1425** Florence and Venice form alliance against Filippo Maria Visconti of Milan. **1426–7** Sigismund again defeated by the Bohemians. **1427–8** Annam recovers its independence. **1428** English lay siege to Orléans. **1429** Joan of Arc inspires French to relief of Orléans: Charles VII crowned at Reims; English fortunes begin to ebb.
	= Thomas à Kempis *Imitation of Christ*, an immensely popular devotional work.
1421 Second Ming Emperor, Yong Le, transfers capital from Nanjing to Beijing.	
1420 Portuguese discover Madeira. = Bit and brace in use in Flanders: first instance of the compound crank in the West.	
1423 Gentile da Fabriano *The Adoration of the Magi* (Uffizi). = Robin Campin *Merode Annunciation* (Metropolitan). = Green Mosque, Bursa.	**1425** Ghiberti starts work on the East doors of the Baptistery. Brunelleschi demonstrates the rules of vanishing point perspective in a painting of the Baptistery. **1426–8** Masaccio frescoes the Brancacci Chapel in the Carmine, Florence.

Above: Adoration of the Magi. Bronze panel from Ghiberti's first set of doors for the Baptistery, Florence. It follows the rules laid down for the competition pieces, the figures being confined within a quatrefoil frame. Executed 1404–7.

Above right: The east door of the Baptistery, 'la Porta di Paradiso'. Ghiberti's masterwork, commissioned in 1424, finally completed in 1452.

In 1401 the Calimale guild of Florentine merchants announced that it was planning to commission the second pair of bronze doors for the Baptistery, a building that had long been the object of its patronage. The first pair of doors, designed and cast by Andrea Pisano 70 years previously, was generally reckoned to be one of the sights of the city: everything would be done to make the second pair their equal, starting off with a competition for the best design.

Each panel in a bronze door of this type was like a manuscript illustration. Inside an elaborate Gothic frame there was a group of figures in a story from the bible, the figures being rendered in high relief. The overall look was formal, even stiff. The seven competitors were asked to submit a panel in this traditional style depicting the sacrifice of Isaac. Viewing the results the next year the jury soon narrowed the field down to Brunelleschi and Ghiberti, before making a final decision in favour of Ghiberti.

Over the next 20 years Ghiberti's workshop produced the designs for the door's 28 panels, cast and chased them and finally, in 1424, installed them. The result was so obviously magnificent that the Calimale decided to go straight ahead with the commission for the third and final set of doors without bothering about a competition. Ghiberti got the contract and a free hand in every sense.

Ghiberti scrapped the traditional layout and substituted a simple division into 10 rectangular panels. He filled each with a single composition treated in an illusionist manner, varying the size of the figures and the degree of relief to create a feeling of depth. The final effect was stunning. The Calimale was pleased to pay up.

Over the next 100 years the idea of the artist as an innovator became commonplace: the High Renaissance is strewn with the names of superstars like Leonardo and Michelangelo. How far they realized that this role began with Ghiberti is debatable but there is no doubt what they felt about his work. When a passer-by saw Michelangelo standing in front of the last set of doors and asked him what he thought of them, the old man said simply 'They are fit to be Doors of Paradise'. And that is what they have been called ever since.

	1430–1434	1435–1439	1440–1444	1445–1449	1450–1454
Politics & Military History	**1430** Joan of Arc captured by the Burgundians who sell her to the English: they burn her at Rouen (1431). Ottomans take Salonica. **1431** Venetian Captain Carmagnola defeated by the Milanese: Venetians execute him (1432). **1434** Cosimo di Medici becomes *de facto* ruler of Florence, establishing a dynasty that lasts till 1737. = Africa: emergence of first Hausa states in the north of present day Nigeria: beginning of eastward movement by Fulani pastoralists in the western Sahel.	**1435** Burgundians abandon English alliance. **1436** Treaty between Sigismund and the Bohemians brings Hussite war to an end: Sigismund recognized as king after guaranteeing Bohemia's liberties. English evacuate Paris. **1437** Sigismund dies leaving Hungary and Bohemia to Albert of Austria. Portuguese attempt on Tangier fails.	**1442** Alfonso V of Aragon makes good his claim to the Kingdom of Naples: thereafter reigns as 'King of the Two Sicilies' (because King of Naples had gone on calling itself the King of Sicily after the island had broken away in 1282). **1442** Ottomans conquer Epirus. **1444** English lose Maine. Ottoman Turks defeat and kill King Ladislas of Poland and Hungary at Varna. = Khmer abandon Angkor in face of Thai pressure.	**1447** Filippo Maria Visconti, Duke of Milân, dies without heirs. **1448** Hunyadi, Regent of Hungary, defeated by Turks at second Battle of Kossovo. **1449** French invade Normandy: British resistance collapses, Rouen falls. Mongols invade China, capture Ming Emperor, then withdraw.	**1450** Sforza seizes Milan and takes title of Duke. English lose Cherbourg. **1451** English lose Gascony. **1453** Ottoman Turks take Constantinople. Fall of Bordeaux means that the English have lost all their possessions in France (bar Calais). End of the Hundred Years' War.
Religion & Learning			**1440** Lorenzo Valla proves donation of Constantine a forgery.		
Cities & Social Development		**1439** French Estates General agree to fund a standing army.	**1443** House of Jacques Coeur, Bourges. Grandiose town-house of Charles VII's banker.	**1448** Elector of Brandenburg makes Berlin his capital.	
Discovery & Invention	**1431** Portuguese discover the Azores. **1434** Portuguese Captain Gil Eannes doubles Cape Bojador, till then the limit of western navigation on the Atlantic coast of Africa. **1431–33** Seventh and last in the series of Ming maritime expeditions: reaches Jeddah, the port of Mecca.		**1443** Portuguese reach Arguin Island off the coast of present day Mauritania. **c1445** Dinis Diaz reaches the mouth of the Senegal.		**1453** Eammes de Aurara *Chronicle of the Discovery and Conquest of Guinea* dedicated to Prince Henry the Navigator, architect of the Portuguese exploration of Africa. **1454** Gutenberg uses movable type to print 31-line Indulgence, the first time this technique had been used commercially in the West.
The Arts	**1432** Jan and Hubert van Eyck, *The Adoration of the Lamb*, altarpiece for Ghent Cathedral. = Donatello's and Lucca della Robbia's *Cantoria* for Florence Cathedral. = Pisanello *St George and the Princess*, Verona Cathedral.	**1439** Strasbourg Cathedral's stone spire, at 142 m the equal of Old St Pauls' and the tallest medieval spire standing today. = Paolo Uccello: Fresco of mercenary leader Sir John Hawkwood, Florence Cathedral.	**1443** Rogier van der Weyden *Last Judgement*, chapel of the Hotel-Dieu Hospital, Beaune. Donatello's equestrian statue of Gattamelata, the first equestrian bronze cast in the West since the fall of Rome. = Fra Angelico begins fresco cycle in convent of San Marco, Florence.	**1446** Alberti's *Temple* of the Classical arts for Sigismondo Malatesta of Rimini. **1446** Kings College Chapel, Cambridge begun.	**1450–53** K. Binnyakyan of Pegu raises height of Shwe Dagon pagoda to 90.6 m. **1452** Piero della Francesca begins fresco cycle in church of San Francesco, Arezzo. **1453** Enguerrard de Charenton *Coronation of the Virgin*, Villeneuve-les-Avignon.

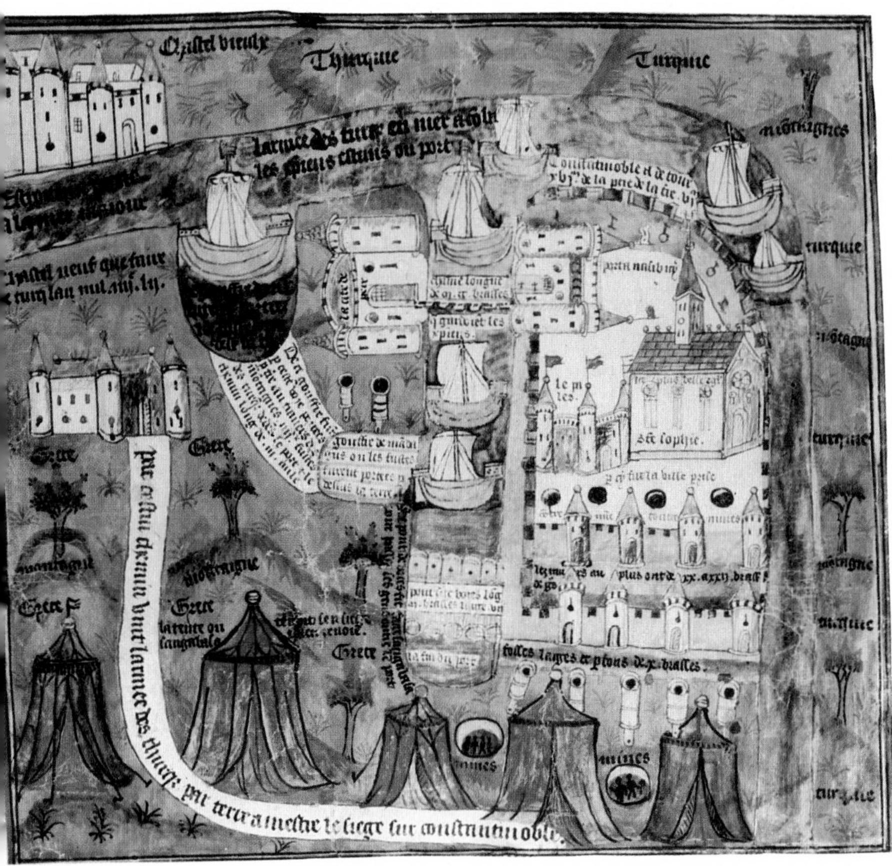

The year 1453 saw the end of two empires: one was the English dominion in France which had waxed and waned since the days of William the Conqueror but was now ended for ever; the other was the empire of Constantinople which by this time consisted of little more than the city itself. Surrounded on all sides by the Ottoman Turks its fall was long overdue but for various reasons – most notably the terrible defeat suffered by the Ottomans at the hands of Timur in 1402 – the assault had been postponed. Now a new sultan, the 21 year old Muhammad II, decided to finish off this ancient Christian bulwark.

Constantinople was no longer the city it had been. Streets that had once run between busy markets and crowded tenements now had the appearance of country lanes. The cisterns were empty, the Hippodrome was deserted, the imperial palace in ruins. The number of citizens of military age was 5000. Muhammad II, with an army 20 times this size, can have had few worries about the outcome.

Nevertheless, taking Constantinople was not to be as easy as all that. The land and sea walls were intact. And Byzantium's Italian trading partners, particularly Venice and Genoa, had a stake in the city that they would try and protect. Officially the Genoese, who had taken over Galata, the town just across the Golden Horn, counted as neutral. But in practice many of them slipped over to Constantinople to fight on the Byzantine side. And from Genoa itself came 700 mercenaries under the command of a professional soldier, Giustiniani. Altogether his Italian connections provided the Byzantine emperor with 2000 men, a sizeable navy and the hope of substantial relief when the news of the attack reached Europe.

Muhammad's plan was to keep the defenders spread out by using his navy to attack the sea walls on the north while his army probed the land defences. Unfortunately his navy proved unable to force its way into the Golden Horn – the Byzantines, fighting from behind a chain they had stretched across the entrance, repelled all attempts to break through. Muhammad had to detach two divisions of his army to help his seamen drag the ships over the hills behind Pera and launching them into the Golden Horn from its northern shore. From then on the defence got no rest.

By the eighth week of the siege the Turkish artillery had done its work. A whole section of the land walls south of the fifth gate had been knocked down and though the defenders had built a stockade across the gap this too was crumbling under the fire of the sultan's guns. In the early hours of May 29th Turkish light troops began the assault; the main attack was made by the Janissaries as the sun was coming up. Giustiniani was mortally wounded shortly after and when his men saw him being borne away they fell back too. The Emperor Constantine, seeing that the city was lost, flung himself at the Turks and disappeared in the melée.

Muhammad rode into the city in the late afternoon. He prayed to Allah in the Cathedral of St Sophia, then walked through the wreck of the imperial palace, musing on mortality. The next day he halted the pillage and the work of reconstruction began. Constantinople was to be reborn as Istanbul, capital of the Ottoman Empire.

Above: Although it looks muddled this is, by medieval standards, a relatively straightforward map of the siege. The blue band running from top left to bottom right is the Bosporus, separating Turkey-in-Asia (above and to the right) from Europe. Constantinople occupies the European peninsula formed by the arm of the Bosporus – the Golden Horn – that runs down the middle of the picture. The city is protected by a single wall on the three sides facing the sea and by an elaborate double wall across the base of the peninsula. The Turkish artillery is shown drawn up opposite these 'land walls' which had never been breached in the thousand years since their construction.

Top right: 18th century engraving of the Siege of Constantinople at the moment when the troop of Turkish Janissaries make their final assault.

Above right: Muhammad II, the Turkish sultan, painted by Sinan Bey. Muhammad, known as the Conqueror, was a patron of the arts as well as being a great statesman, his law code Qanun-name *defined some of the basic institutions and usages of the Ottoman state.*

	1455–1459	1460–1464	1465–1469	1470–1474	1475–1479
Politics & Military History	**1454** Milan, Venice, Florence and Naples make peace at Lodi. Turks conquer the Morea. **1455** Civil War known as the Wars of the Roses begins in England: Richard Duke of York (heraldic device the white rose of York) challenges King Henry VI (heraldic device the red rose of the House of Lancaster). **1456** Hungarians successfully defend Belgrade against the Turks. **1457** Poles take Marienburg from the Teutonic Knights.	**1460** Yorkists win Battle of Northampton and capture King Henry VI but later the same year the Duke of York is killed at Wakefield. James II of Scotland killed by the explosion of one of his own cannon at the siege of Roxburgh Castle. **1461** Edward Duke of York recovers the initiative, wins battles of Mortimer's Cross, St Albans and Taunton: Henry VI flees to Scotland; Edward crowned as Edward IV. Scanderbeg recognized as Lord of Albania by the Ottomans. Turks conquer Trebizond. **1463** Louis XI ransoms the Somme towns from the Duke of Burgundy.	**1465** Henry VI captured by Edward IV and imprisoned in the tower. **1466** Teutonic Knights restore western Prussia to Poland at definitive treaty of Thorn. **1467** Charles the Bold of Burgundy takes Liège. **1469** James III of Scotland marries Margaret of Norway who brings him the Orkneys and Shetlands as a dowry. Ali of Songhay conquers Timbuctoo.	**1470** Earl of Warwick defeats Edward IV who flees to Flanders: Henry VI restored to English throne. Turks take Negropont from the Venetians. **1471** Edward IV returns to England, defeats and kills Warwick at Tewkesbury, sends Henry VI back to the tower where he dies. Portuguese take Tangier. Chams finally reduced by Viets. **1474** Peace between Swtizerland and Austria.	**1475** War between Charles the Bold of Burgundy and the Swiss instigated by Louis XI of France: Charles conquers Lorraine. **1476** Charles the Bold twice defeated by the Swiss at Grandson and Morat. **1477** Swiss defeat and kill Charles the Bold at Nancy: Louis XI declares Burgundy annexed to the French crown. Matthias King of Hungary invades Austria and drives out Habsburg Emperor Frederick III. **1478** Matthias of Hungary obtains Lusatia, Moravia and Silesia for his lifetime by treaty with the Bohemians. Ivan III of Moscow conquers Novgorod. **1479** Union of the crowns of Aragon and Castile becomes effective when Queen Isabella of Castile's husband Ferdinand inherits the throne of Aragon. Ludovico Sforza ('il Moro') takes government of Milan from his infant nephew Gian Galeazzo. Maximilian Habsburg, husband of Charles the Bold's daughter Mary, defeats Louis XI at Guinegate and saves much of her inheritance.
Religion & Learning	**1455** Pope grants the Portuguese exclusive jurisdiction over Guinea 'all the way to the Indians'. **1456** Conviction of Joan of Arc annulled.	**1460** Foundation of the University of Basle.			**1477** Foundation of the universities of Uppsala and Tübingen. **1478** Ferdinand and Isabella establish the Spanish Inquisition with the aim of rooting out their Muslim and Jewish minorities. Foundation of Copenhagen University.
Discovery & Invention	**1455** Gutenberg press produces the 42-line or Mazarin Bible, the first book printed in the West and the progenitor of all subsequent printed works. **1456** Alvise da Cadamosto explores the Cape Verde Islands and the Bijagos archipelago.	**1461** Pedro de Sintra reaches Sierra Leone.	**1465** First printing press in Italy set up at Subiaco. **1469** Portuguese crown grants Fenão Gomes a 5-year monopoly of the Guinea trade on condition that he advance the exploration of the coast by 100 leagues a year.	**1470** First printing press in France set up at the Sorbonne. **1471–2** Portuguese penetrate the Gulf of Guinea reaching the Akan (Gold) Coast in 1471 and the island of Fernando Po (named after one of Gomes' captains) in 1472. **1474** Caxton's press in Bruges prints the first book in English *Histories of Troy*. = Regiomontanus (John Muller of Konigsberg) settles at Nuremberg (1471). Makes first scientific observation of Halley's comet (1472) and publishes *Ephemerides*, the first astronomical almanac (1474).	**1477** Caxton opens the first printing press in England, in the cloisters of Westminster Abbey.
The Arts	**1459** Benozzo Gozzoli *Procession of the Magi*, Palazzo Medici, Florence.	**1461** Francois Villon *Le Grand Testament*. = Fra Filippo Lippi *Virgin and Child* (Uffizi). = *Avignon Pietà* (Louvre).	= Thomas Malory *Morte Darthur*, the classical English version of the Arthurian legend.	**1470** Antonella da Messina *Ecce Homo* (Metropolitan). **1474** Andrea Mantegna frescoes the Camera degli Sposi in the Palazzo Ducale, Mantua.	**c.1475** Van der Goes *The Portinari Altarpiece* (Uffizi). **1477** Sandro Botticelli *Primavera* (Uffizi). **1479** Gentile Bellini (brother of Giovanni) *Portrait of Muhammad II, Conqueror of Constantinople* (London).

1480–1484	1485–1489
1480 Ivan III of Moscow defeats Golden Horde at Battle of the Oka. Louis XI of France acquires Anjou. Turks take Otranto (till 1481), fail to take Rhodes. **1481** Louis XI of France acquires Provence. Freiburg and Solothurn join Swiss Confederation. **1482** Ivan III acquires Rostov and Yaroslavl. **1483** Edward IV dies: his brother Richard of Gloucester deposes his nephew Edward V and has himself crowned as Richard III; Edward V, confined to the Tower with his brother the Duke of York, is murdered on Richard's orders.	**1485** Henry Tudor defeats and kills Richard III at Bosworth Field, takes crown as Henry VII. Matthias of Hungary captures Vienna. **1486** Henry VII marries Elizabeth of York and heals breach between Lancastrian and Yorkish factions. End of the Wars of the Roses. **1487** Ferdinand of Aragon captures Malaga. Venice acquires Cyprus. **1488** Genoa subdued by Milan. **1489** Ivan III annexes Viatka.
1482 Torquemada appointed Inquisitor-General of Aragon and Castile.	**1487** *Malleus Maleficarum* gives the Church's seal of approval on the popular ideas about witchcraft.
1482 Portuguese establish the fort of Elmina on the Gold Coast of West Africa. **1483** Portuguese captain Diogo Cao commissioned to continue the exploration of the Atlantic coast of Africa, reaches the Congo and Cape Santa Maria.	**1486** Diogo Cão dies at Cape Cross, the furthest point reached on his second voyage of African exploration. **1487–88** Bartholomew Diaz reaches the Cape of Good Hope and sails past it as far as the Great Fish River before returning safely to Portugal.
1480–85 Giuliano de Sangallo, Medici Villa, Poggio a Caiano. = Perugino begins the decoration of the walls of the Sistine Chapel. = Verocchio begins work on the equestrian statue of Bartolomeo Colleoni for the city of Venice.	**1485** Hieronymus Bosch *Garden of Earthly Delights* (Prado). **1489** John Skelton appointed court poet to King Henry VII.

Right: Section of a page of the 42-line Bible printed between 1454 and 1455 by Johann Gutenberg and his partners Johann Fust and Peter Schöffer. The initial was added by hand not printed. Gutenberg adapted a wine press to press the frame of type onto the paper with even pressure.

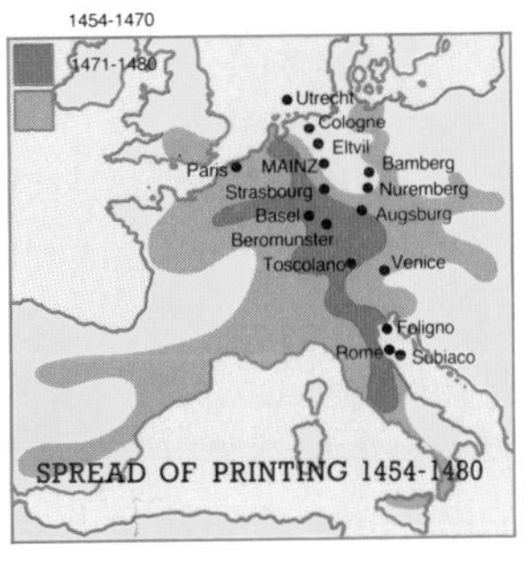

The fall of Constantinople shocked Europe. There was talk of a new Crusade and though the cynical said nothing would come of it (and events proved them right) the more idealistic tried hard to get some sort of expedition off the ground. Among these was the Pope who promised to raise some of the funds needed by selling 'indulgences'. These were a sort of spiritual pardon which guaranteed that the purchaser would go straight to heaven when he died. Plans were drawn up for a major sales drive covering every important city in Europe.

Mainz was one of these and a papal representative duly arrived there in 1454. His first job was to find someone who could copy documents for a reasonable fee: among the offers he got was a cut price one from a man named Johann Gutenberg. The papal officer accepted the bid and was soon congratulating himself on having done so: the indulgences were clearly and accurately written, far better than the usual copyists' work. Gutenberg obviously had something.

What he had was Europe's first printing press.

There is nothing very difficult about printing, the Chinese had been doing it for years. The Chinese method was to cut one woodblock for each page. What Gutenberg did was smarter. He made small single-letter blocks which could be assembled to form a page of print, then broken up and rearranged for the next job.

The Chinese had, in fact, had the same idea but never pushed it very far, partly because it has little advantage if your script contains thousands of different characters. The Koreans, who used a Western style alphabet, did take the idea further: the royal printing house in Seoul cast some sets of single letter type in 1403. But the sand-casting process used was tricky, the shallow type proved difficult to get straight and level and the experiment was not repeated.

Gutenberg is definitely the first person to have made printing by 'movable type' practical. He was a goldsmith by profession. His basic idea was to produce a set of type in a form rather like a set of goldsmith's punches. Each letter was mounted on what appeared to be an unnecessarily long shank. These long-shank type fitted snugly against one another, their shape keeping the lines of type straight and the whole page of type level.

It was a very simple idea and like all simple ideas needed twenty years' work to perfect. Gutenberg had to invent a way of casting cheap replicas of the expensive steel punches, he had to develop an adjustable mould to allow for the fact that some letters, like *m*, are wider than others, like *i*, he had to make a press that would work quickly and firmly yet damage neither paper nor type.

By 1454 he was ready to take his first small commission – the Papal indulgences. The next year he began his first big project, the printing of 180 copies of the Bible. Before a single copy of the Bible was sold Gutenberg found himself hauled to court and declared bankrupt. His financial backers took over the printing shop.

They also took the credit. It is only in the last hundred years that the story has been sorted out and Johann Gutenberg has been given his due.

THE AGE OF DISCOVERY

AD 1490 - AD 1664

Few eras have got off to such a dramatic start as the Age of Discovery: the voyages of Columbus, of Vasco da Gama and Magellan set Europe by the ears and fuelled the imagination of a generation. Yet these discoveries were only the first in a rapidly expanding series that put an end to the medieval concept of the world and replaced it with a view that was essentially modern. At the start of the period no one doubted that the Earth lay motionless at the centre of a universe which God could comfortably cup in his hands: by the late 17th century an educated man knew that the sun that warmed him was only one of millions in an apparently endless cosmos. The certainties of the Christian religion which had defined Western civilization for more than a thousand years had been replaced by a dozen conflicting interpretations of the Christian message: the traditional order of society had been challenged by new concepts that allowed the people to try a king for treason, find him guilty and cut off his head. This was an age that remade not just the maps that men held in their hands but the ones that they carried in their heads.

This said, it remains true that the most cogent image of the Age of Discovery is the ship, the three-master of 75 to 100 tonnes in which the great navigators of the period spanned the oceans and ushered in the new era. And, standing at the head of this illustrious band, is the man who sailed over the horizon that no-one else had dared to cross and found the way to the New World.

Above: Using a cross-staff to measure the height of the sun. Columbus, like most sailors venturing into unknown waters, picked a line of latitude and did his best to keep to it: he will have used the cross-staff to check if he was on course or not.

COLUMBUS

Columbus' first venture into the Atlantic ended in disaster. Signing on as a foremast hand in his native Genoa, he was shipwrecked off the coast of Portugal and finally arrived at his destination, Lisbon, alone, penniless and on foot. Nevertheless, he got there and, whether he knew it or not, it was exactly the right place to be for an aspiring young navigator.

What Lisbon had to offer was an experience of deep-water sailing that no other place could match. Since the beginning of the century the Portuguese had been probing the Atlantic looking for islands (finding Madeira and the Azores) and testing the commercial prospects in West Africa. In all they had explored something like 5000 kilometres of previously uncharted African coastline – the whole of the west African bulge and most of the Gulf of Guinea. Without doubt they were the most enterprising and skilful navigators in Europe.

Columbus took full advantage of the opportunity fate had contrived for him. In Portuguese service he sailed the Atlantic routes from Iceland in the north to Guinea in the south: he qualified as a captain and married the daughter of a master mariner. By 1484 he had acquired sufficient experience, sufficient learning and sufficient standing to put a proposal to the Portuguese king and have it taken seriously. Drop the African exploration, said Columbus, and strike out instead across the Atlantic.

The original aim of the African programme, contact with the gold-producing region of Ghana, had already been achieved. In 1481 the Portuguese had established the fort of St George of the Mine – usually referred to simply as El Mina – on the Gold Coast of west Africa and as a result had an effective monopoly of this lucrative traffic. But a second goal beckoned, the spice trade of the Indian Ocean. If the Portuguese could round Africa and cut themselves in on this, their southern venture would be doubly rewarded. Columbus was offering a quicker and cheaper way of reaching this objective.

The underlying concept was neither original nor controversial. Everyone accepted that the Earth was a globe and that it was theoretically possible to reach the East by sailing west. What was novel about Columbus' presentation was his arithmetic. By taking the largest in the range of figures available for the extent of Asia, and the smallest current estimate of the size of the Earth, he demonstrated, to his own satisfaction at least, that the distance between Europe and Asia westward was not the 10,000 miles (16,000 kilometres) that everyone thought, but less than 2500. This brought the eastern extremity of Asia safely within the range of a well-found ship which should be able to cover this distance in about three weeks. This in turn made it perfectly feasible to think of crossing the Atlantic, seizing an island off the coast of China and establishing a trading post there.

For the next four years the Portuguese king blew hot and cold on Columbus' plan. When the African explorations were going well he did not pay it much attention, but when they went badly he took it up again. The issue was finally decided at the end of 1488 when Bartholomew Diaz sailed into Lisbon harbour with the news that he had found and rounded the southernmost point of Africa. The eastern

Left: Fifteenth century sailing ship from a drawing used to illustrate the printed edition of Christopher Columbus' 'Letter'. The 'Letter' was his official report of the discoveries made on his first voyage and was addressed to the Spanish court but it aroused so much interest that it soon found its way into print. The first edition was run off by an enterprising publisher in Basle in 1493 who threw in this drawing, one he had used before in some of his earlier books. Though it does not represent the Santa Maria *it shows a ship of the class to which the* Santa Maria *belonged, a 3-masted vessel with square sails on the foremast (hidden in this picture) and main mast. Columbus' other two ships were caravels, smaller boats which normally had lateen (triangular) sails on all three masts. Lateen sails make ships handier but square sails are the best for ocean voyages and Columbus had the* Nina *rerigged with square sails in the Canaries: the* Pinta, *for some reason, already had them.*

oute to the Indies lay open: Columbus' western approach vas formally rejected.

Columbus was too sure of himself and his ideas to onsider giving up: instead he put his family and his fortune o work searching for a new backer. His brother put the plan o the king of England, who turned it down, and the king of rance, who did not reply at all: Columbus himself pproached Queen Isabella of Castile who said no, well, naybe. If Columbus liked to come back when the war with he Moors of Granada had been won she would think again. Two years later, when Granada finally fell to the forces of sabella and her husband Ferdinand of Aragon, Columbus vas on hand. He immediately presented himself to the queen, who this time said maybe, then no, and finally yes. With her commission in his pocket Columbus hurried off to he little port of Palos. It was May 1492.

The people of Palos had been ordered to provide Columbus with two 50 tonne caravels of the type favoured by the Portuguese in their explorations. Columbus made his flotilla up to three by hiring a 100 tonne Galician merchantman, the *Santa Maria,* which happened to be in Palos at the time. Ten weeks later, his provisioning completed, he led the *Santa Maria* and the two caravels, the *Pinta* and the *Nina*, out of the harbour and set course for the Canaries, his jumping off point. From there he set sail on 6th September. On the 9th, the last of the islands in the Spanish Canaries dropped below the horizon and the long voyage that would make or break him could be said to have truly begun.

Columbus knew the way the winds blew in the Atlantic and he made a splendid start to his voyage, reaching what he calculated to be the halfway point after only ten days. The crew were disappointed to see no sign of the island of Antilia which rumour held lay hereabouts but their only real worry was that the winds had been so consistently favourable that they might have difficulty beating back against them.

The next stage went more slowly. It also saw the crew get perceptibly more anxious, especially after the fourth week came and went without a landfall: after all, if Asia was where Columbus said it was, they should have sighted it by now. Columbus did not agree: according to him they still had a few hundred kilometres to go and he gave out that they were on schedule for a landfall in Asia (probably Japan) within three days. On the third day there was still no sight of land but, almost as welcome, flocks of birds were seen passing overhead west by south west. Columbus altered course to conform, a trick he had learned from the Portuguese, and after another three days of empty sea and sky all hands were vastly relieved by the sight of some fresh looking driftwood. That night Columbus ordered a special watch and sure enough, at 2 o'clock on the morning of 12th October, the lookout high up in the rigging of the *Pinta* spied land dead ahead.

Dawn confirmed the lookout's sighting: they were lying to windward of a small island. They passed its southern point, then through the reef off its western shore where Columbus made his landing from the *Santa Maria*'s longboat. He raised the royal standard of Castile while to either side of him the captains of his caravels raised banners bearing the expedition's emblem, a green cross with the letters F (for Ferdinand of Aragon) and Y (for Ysabela of Castile). Then they fell to their knees and thanked God for their safe arrival.

The next three months passed in wonder and delight. Guided by friendly natives the *Santa Maria, Pinta* and *Nina* threaded their way through the islands of the Bahamas from Watling where they had made their landfall to Ragged Island just north of Cuba. Thence to Cuba and Hispaniola. They were clearly nowhere near Japan but Columbus had no doubt at all that the essential elements in his theory had been triumphantly confirmed: these islands must be outliers of the East Indies (which is why he dubbed the natives Indians); further exploration would undoubtedly bring them to the Spice Islands proper. Even the loss of the *Santa Maria* was no great tragedy. She went gently aground off Hispaniola early on the morning of Christmas day without loss of life or stores. Columbus used her timbers to build a scaled down version of El Mina, a little fort manned by 20-odd volunteers and christened, somewhat ambitiously, Villa de la Navidad. The men were eager to stay because the Indians of Hispaniola were perfectly happy to swap their gold ornaments for bits of mirror and tin bells. Columbus was eager to get home because he had a tale to tell.

Both the *Nina*, captained by Columbus, and the *Pinta* made it back to Spain though they had to fight their way through one of the worst storms in living memory to do so. Once home Columbus, of course, was treated like a hero: his titles and offices were confirmed by the crown and he had no difficulty raising funds and volunteers for his next voyage. But from then on his fortunes began to ebb. His reports of gold and spices turned out to be unrealistic, to say the least; his geographical pronouncements increasingly difficult to believe. As an administrator he was such a hopeless disaster that he had to be forcibly removed from office.

Understandably bitter, increasingly cranky, he spent his last years pursuing impossible claims for compensation. Few outside his immediate family attended his deathbed or his funeral in May 1506: there was no official representative at either.

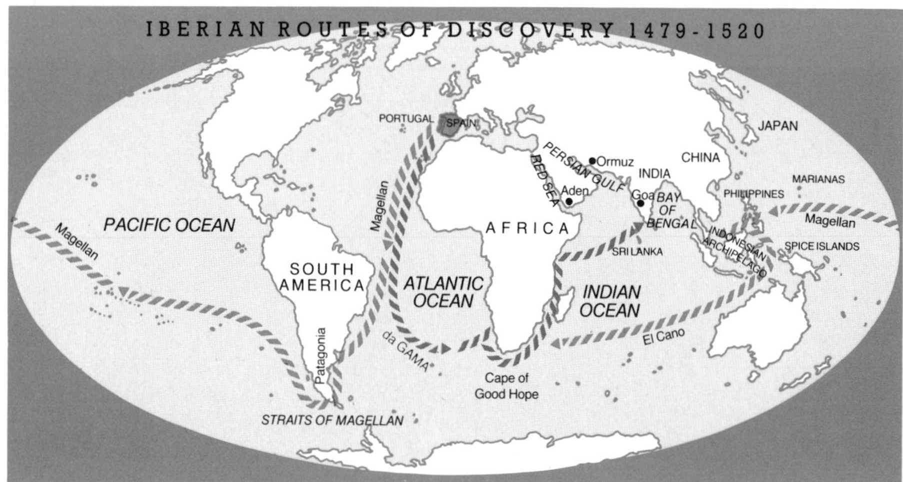

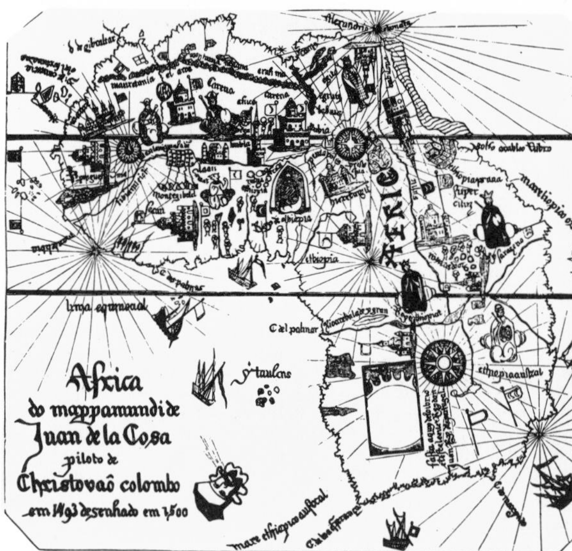

Upper right: Malacca as it looked in 1663.

Lower right: Africa from the map of the world drawn by Juan de la Cosa in 1500. This is one of the earliest maps to record the voyages of discovery and is all the more interesting for the fact that Juan de la Cosa had sailed with Columbus on his second voyage.

The Portuguese were not at all pleased to hear of Columbus' discoveries but they stuck to their plans to exploit the Cape route. In 1497 Vasco da Gama took four ships round the Cape and into the Indian Ocean: in 1499 he returned with a cargo of spices that more than repaid the expedition's cost. It was a magnificent feat, the result of years of careful planning and far-sighted investment. It was also a spur to further efforts.

Portuguese seamen rose to the occasion, forcing their way along the Asian sea lanes and challenging the traditional, mostly Muslim, traders at every point. They put in an appearance, usually a belligerent one, at all the important harbours in the Indian sub-continent: they probed the Red Sea, the Persian Gulf and the Bay of Bengal. Further to the East they sailed through the Straits of Malacca and the Indonesian Archipelago to reach the fabled Spice Islands. They also reached north-east to make contact with China and, a generation later, Japan.

In the Far East the Portuguese never tried to do more than establish trading posts – 'factories' in the jargon of the time. For the Indian Ocean their plans were more ambitious. The basic idea was to station a fleet there permanently and use it to gain control of the entire trading network. Goa was chosen as the main base: there were to be secondary strong points at Aden (to control the Red Sea traffic), Ormuz (for the Persian Gulf) and Malacca (for the routes to China and the East Indies) plus a dozen minor forts at various points between east Africa and Sri Lanka. To a remarkable extent these plans were realized. The only failure was at Aden which sharply rebuffed the attack force: elsewhere the Portuguese set up their strong points and customs posts as scheduled, and the native ships that plied these waters sailed with their permission or not at all.

All this cost money and though the spice trade brought in large sums (spices that cost 2 ducats in India sold for 30 in Lisbon) the bookkeeping of the time was not sufficiently sophisticated to determine whether or not the enterprise as a whole was making a profit. Probably it did not: certainly the crown was running further and further into debt. By 1549 it could not even meet the interest charges on its outstanding loans.

Shortage of funds was already a problem in 1517 when the Columbus project came up again in a new guise. This time the proposal was made by a Portuguese national, Ferdinand Magellan: he argued that, though Columbus had clearly miscalculated his distances and misinterpreted his geographical discoveries, he could not have been all wrong. Asia must lie the other side of America and, given the likely size of the globe, the ocean between the two could not be a big one; in all probability it was less than 200 kilometres across. If so, the route round or through South America and across the Southern Ocean – the Pacific as it was soon to be called – could well be shorter and easier than the long slog round the Cape to the Spice Islands.

Maybe so, but Portuguese resources were committed to the Cape route and Magellan, like Columbus, had to turn to Spain for funding. He got it (from the young Charles V) and in 1519 was able to lead a flotilla of five ships out of Seville and begin putting his ideas to the test.

Magellan's expedition found the Spice Islands and turned a neat profit but it is not remembered for these relatively mundane achievements: it stands in the history books as the greatest voyage of this or any other age. Reaching down the previously unexplored coast of Patagonia, Magellan discovered the strait that bears his name and made the first recorded passage from the Atlantic to the Pacific. He then crossed this unknown ocean, a feat which took three and a half months (compare Columbus' five weeks across the Atlantic) and made scarecrows of the crew who survived (a third did not). An initial unhappy landfall in the Marianas was followed by disaster in the Philippines where Magellan lost his life in an unnecessary demonstration against one of the local tribes. From there his lieutenant El Cano led a single ship back to Spain via the Spice Islands and the Cape of Good Hope. Altogether there were 18 survivors out of the 234 who set out on this, the first circumnavigation of the world.

	1490–1494	1495–1499	1500–1504	1505–1509	1510–1514
Politics & Military History	**1491** Marriage of Charles VIII of France and Anne of Brittany brings this province into the royal domain. **1492** Granada, the last Muslim emirate in Spain. surrenders to Ferdinand and Isabella. **1494** Charles VIII invades Italy in pursuit of a claim to the throne of Naples.	**1495** Charles VIII enters Naples, beats the army of his Italian and Spanish enemies at Fornovo on the way back to France but loses Naples to them shortly after. **1498** Louis XII who has a claim to the Duchy of Milan, inherits French throne on the accidental death of Charles VIII: makes alliance with Pope and Venice and conquers Milan (1499).	**1500** Louis XII and Ferdinand of Aragon agree to partition the kingdom of Naples (effected 1501). Aztec Empire reaches its greatest extent with Ahuizotl's expedition to Soconusco on the present day frontier between Mexico and Guatemala. **1501** French help Cesare Borgia, son of Pope Alexander VI, impose his rule on the Romagna (the trans-Apennine part of the Papal State). **1502** Hostilities break out between French and Spanish in Naples: French expelled (1503). **1503** Death of Pope Alexander VI and consequent downfall of Cesare Borgia.	**1507** French occupy Genoa. **1508** France, Spain, the Emperor and the Pope combine against Venice in the League of Cambrai. **1509** Cardinal Ximenes of Spain leads an expedition to North Africa and captures Oran.	**1510** Vasili III of Moscow annexes Pskov. Venetians, defeated at Agnadello and driven from their mainland possessions, submit to Pope Julius II and have their territories restored. **1511** Venetians and Spanish join Julius II's new coalition, a Holy League to expel French from Italy, succeed in 1512. Ferdinand of Aragon annexes Spanish Navarre. **1513** English rout Scots at Flodden; Scots king James IV among the dead. Emperor Maximillian and English king Henry VIII invade France, win the battle of Guineagate ('Battle of the Spurs').
Religion & Learning	**1490** Venice: Aldo Manuzio founds the Aldine press which becomes famous over the next decades for the low cost and high quality of its classical texts and for the clarity of its typography (as opposed to German black-letter). **1492** Jews expelled from Spain. **1493** Hartmann Schedel's illustrated world history *The Nuremberg Chronicle*.	**1497** Jews expelled from Portugal. **1498** Philippe de Commynes *Memoires* of the reigns of Louis XI and Charles VIII.	**1504** Amerigo Vespucci *Mundus Novus*. Columbus had recognized that South America was a land-mass of continental size but dismissed it as irrelevant to his thesis. Amerigo, in his account of his voyages there (of which the only important one was the Coelho expedition, see below), stressed its importance, terming it quite correctly a New World.	**1507** German geographer Waldseemüller accepts Amerigo Vespucci's New World and suggests it be named America in his honour: uses this term on his world map of this date. **1509** Erasmus *In Praise of Folly*.	**1513** Machiavelli *The Prince* suggesting that in politics success is the only yardstick.
Cities & Social Development	**1494** Florence: Lorenzo the Magnificent's son Piero flees the city as the French enter: Savonarola, a Dominican friar who has been preaching against luxury in general and the Medici in particular, takes control. Ivan III closes the Hanse factory at Novgorod.	**1497** Naples: first recorded outbreak of syphilis in the Old World. Introduced from the Caribbean where it was endemic, it soon established itself as one of Europe's major diseases. **1498** Florence: Pope Alexander VI contrives overthrow of Savonarola who is burnt at stake.	= Beginning of population decline in the Americas due to smallpox. It bottomed out in 1600. Fantastic figures have been proposed for the period of decline but there is no reason to believe that the overall fall was more than 20%, say from 14 million in 1492 to 11.5 million in 1600.	**1508** Syndicate at Antwerp agrees to buy all the spices the Portuguese can obtain in the Orient. City enters on a period of rapid growth, mainly at the expense of Bruges whose harbour is proving too small for the new generation of ocean-going vessels.	**1512** Subsequent to France's expulsion from Italy, Genoa recovers its independence, the Sforza return to Milan and the Medici to Florence.
Discovery & Invention	**1492** First voyage of Christopher Columbus: discovery of the Bahamas, Cuba and Hispaniola. **1493** Second voyage: discovery of the Leewards, Puerto Rico and Jamaica. **1494** Spanish and Portuguese reach agreement on a division of the world beyond Europe, the Spanish to have everything west of longitude 40°W (defined at the time as 370 leagues west of the Cape Verde Islands) and the Portuguese everything to the east (giving them Brazil). Luca Pacioli *Summa de Arithmatica*.	**1497** John Cabot (really Giovanni Caboto, a Genoese) sails from Bristol, discovers Newfoundland and returns. Vasco da Gama leaves Lisbon for India via Cape of Good Hope. **1498** Third voyage of Christopher Columbus: discovery of Trinidad and Orinoco delta. Cabot sets out on second voyage: never heard of again.	**1500** Pinzon sails along the coast of South America from Cape San Roque to Trinidad. Cabral leads Portugal's second expedition to India, touching Brazilian coasts on the outward leg. **1501** Portuguese captain Coelho explores the Brazilian coast from Cape San Roque to Sao Paulo. **1502** Fourth and last voyage of Christopher Columbus: exploration of the Central American coastline from Honduras to Panama.	**1505** Juan Bermudez, returning to Spain from Hispaniola, discovers Bermuda. **1505** First black slaves brought to the New World put ashore at Hispaniola. **1506** Ponce de Leon conquers Puerto Rico: Pinzon explores the coast of Yucatan. **1508** Portuguese establish factory at Mozambique. **1509** Battle of Diu. Almeida, destroys Muslim fleet. de Garay conquers Jamaica. = Peter Henle of Nuremberg produces the first watches, known at the time as 'Nuremberg eggs'.	**1510** Albuquerque, Almeida's successor as Portuguese Viceroy in the East, seizes Goa. **1511** Velasquez invades Cuba. **1512** Francisco Serrao reaches the Spice Islands. **1513** Balboa crosses the Isthmus of Panama and becomes the first European ever to have 'star'd at the Pacific'. Ponce de Leon visits Florida and Yucatan. Albuquerque fails to take Aden. **1514** Alvares reaches Canton. Velasquez founds Santiago di Cuba.
The Arts	**1492–5** Pinturicchio decorates the Borgia apartments in the Vatican. **1494** Sebastian Brant *Ship of Fools* (Das Narrenschiff). **1495** Hieronymus Bosch *The Garden of Earthly Delights* (Prado).	**1495(–8)** Leonardo da Vinci *Last Supper* S. Maria delle Grazie, Milan. Maître de Moulins *Virgin*, Moulins Cathedral. **1499** Luca Signorelli begins major fresco cycle in Orvieto Cathedral.	**1501(–05)** Michelangelo *David*, Florence. **1503(–07)** Leonardo da Vinci *Mona Lisa* (Louvre). **1503(–08)** Pinturicchio paints the Siena Cathedral library. = Giorgione *The Tempest* (Venice).	= Apogee of Renaissance Rome: Pope Julius II invites Bramante to submit designs for the new St Peter's (1506), commissions Michelangelo to fresco the ceiling of the Sistine Chapel (1508) and Raphael the *stanze* in the Vatican (1509). **1506** The Laocoön, one of the few documented sculptures of antiquity, is discovered in the ruins of Nero's 'Golden House'.	**1510** Medici Pope Leo X starts the Vatican sculpture gallery.

FOR CONVENIENCE OF REFERENCE ALL THE OVERSEAS ACTIVITIES OF THE EUROPEANS ARE GROUPED TOGETHER UNDER 'DISCOVERY AND INVENTION'.

	1515–1519	1520–1524	1525–1529	1530–1534	1535–1539
Politics & Military History	**1515** Francis I succeeds Louis XII, invades Italy, defeats the Swiss at Marignano and occupies Milan. **1516** Death of Ferdinand of Aragon: his grandson Charles proclaimed king of Spain (as Charles I). Ottoman sultan Selim the Grim beats the Mamluks outside Aleppo and conquers Syria. **1517** Selim conquers Egypt. Extinction of the Mamluk state though not of the Mamluks as a class. **1519** Charles elected German Emperor (as Charles V).	**1520** King Christian II of Denmark attempts to crush the independence movement in Sweden by a massacre of the aristocracy ('the bloodbath of Stockholm'). **1521** Ottomans take Belgrade. Charles V hives off the Habsburg lands in Germany to his brother Ferdinand. **1522** Charles V's forces drive the French from Milan and Genoa. Ottomans take Rhodes from the Knights of St John. **1523** Swedes succeed in establishing their independence, elect Gustavus Vasa as king.	**1525** Francis I's second invasion of Italy ends in disaster at the Battle of Pavia. **1526** Ottomans invade Hungary, defeat the Hungarian army and kill the Hungarian king at the Battle of Mohacs. Ferdinand Habsburg is elected king in his place (and king of Bohemia too, the crowns having been linked since 1490) a move that makes Austria the nucleus of an empire. Babur of Afghanistan invades India, defeats the Sultan of Delhi at Panipat and takes his throne. **1527** Charles V's men sack Rome. **1529** Ottomans fail to take Vienna.	**1530** Knights of St John resettled on Malta by Charles V. **1533** North Vietnam splits into Tongking and Annam.	**1535** Charles V takes Tunis. **1537** Barbarossa given command of the Ottoman fleet: defeats the combined fleets of Charles V and Venice at Prevesa. **1538** Ottomans take Aden. **1539** Burma: central kingdom of Toungoo conquers Mon kingdom of Pegu.
Religion & Learning	**1516** Thomas More *Utopia*. **1517** Martin Luther nails his 95 theses to the door of the castle church at Wittenberg: holds public debates at Augsburg (1518) and Leipzig (1519); repudiates papal supremacy.	**1520** Luther, declared a heretic, denounces the church and burns the Papal Bull of Condemnation. Put under the ban of the empire by Charles V (Diet of Worms, 1521) he accepts the protection of the Elector of Saxony. In hiding he produces his translation of the New Testament (1522)	**1525** Teutonic Knights turn Lutheran and secularize their state: Luther marries former nun Katherine von Bora. **1527** Sweden becomes Lutheran. Rapid progress of the Reformed religion in Switzerland, largely due to the preaching of Zwingli. Protest by the Lutherans at the Second Diet of Speyer leads to their being termed Protestants.	**1531** Zwingli killed when Catholic Cantons defeat Zurich at Kappel: subsequent agreement that each Canton can choose its own faith. Henry VIII forces clergy to recognize him as head of the English Church. **1534** Ignatius Loyola founds the Jesuit Order. Luther completes his translation of the Bible. Münster seized by fringe Protestant sect of Anabaptists.	**1535** Henry VIII executes Sir Thomas More. Anabaptists of Münster suppressed. **1536** Henry VIII begins the dissolution of the monasteries. Denmark becomes Lutheran. Calvin publishes *Christianae Religionis Institutio* at Basle, then moves to Geneva. **1538** Henry VIII issues English Bible. **1539** Brandenburg becomes Lutheran.
Cities & Social Development	**1518** Portuguese build fort at Colombo, Sri Lanka. **1519** Cortez founds Vera Cruz at the start of his expedition to Mexico. = Coffee introduced to Europe from Arabia.	= Knights war of 1522–23 and Peasants' Revolt of 1524 show that unrest in Germany was social as well as religious. = Chocolate introduced to Europe from Mexico.	**1527** Medici again expelled from Florence. **1528** Castiglione *The Courtier* (Il Cortigiano).	**1530** Charles V's army in Italy forces Florence to readmit the Medici.	
Discovery & Invention	**1516** De Solis killed by natives while exploring the River Plate. **1519** Cortez lands in Mexico, bluffs his way into the Aztec capital Tenochtitlan, but has to fight his way out in 1520. = During this period German gunsmiths developed the first wheel-lock rifles. These quickly became *de rigueur* with sportsmen but were too expensive for the military who had to remain content with the smooth-bore matchlock (of which the current model was the arquebus) until well into the next century.	**1520** Magellan, a Portuguese in the service of Charles V, finds the straits named after him and gains entry to the Pacific. Killed 1521, El Cano takes command. Pineda's voyage along the Gulf of Mexico proves the existence of a North American land mass. Cortez takes Tenochtitlan. Cuauhtemoc, last emperor of the Aztecs, surrenders. **1522** El Cano brings home the *Victoria*, the only one of the five ships that set sail with Magellan to complete the circumnavigation. **1524** Two voyages connect the North Atlantic and Caribbean discoveries: Verrazzano sails from North Carolina to Newfoundland, Gomez from Nova Scotia to Florida.	**1526** Louis Ayllon makes an unsuccessful attempt to found a colony in North Carolina. **1526** Paracelsus (Theophrastus von Hohenheim), Physician of Basle, publicly burns works of Galen and Avicenna as a prelude to lecturing on his own system. Important not because his system was correct but because he rejected classical authority. **1527** Francisco Pizarro returns to Panama after sailing down the Pacific coast of South America to the frontier of the Inca Empire. Narvaez fails to colonize Florida.	**1530** Copernicus permits the circulation of a manuscript (the Commentariolus) giving a synopsis of the heliocentric theory on which he had been working for 20 years. (The full version *De Revolutionibus orbium Coelestium*, was not published until he was on his deathbed in 1543). = Sugar cane introduced to Brazil from Madeira. **1532–33** Pizarro conquers Peru.	**1535** Cartier sails up the St Lawrence to the site of Montreal. Pizarro's associate Almagro sets out from Cuzco for Chile. Cortez explores the tip of the California peninsula. **1536** De Vaca and three other survivors of the Narvaez expedition (see 1527) reach Sonoro, Mexico after wandering across south west America for eight years. **1538** Conflict between Pizarro and Almagro ends with Almagro's capture and execution: Pizarro confers Chile on Valdiva. **1539** Hernan de Soto, Governor of Cuba, lands at Tampa Bay, Florida.
The Arts	**1515** Grunewald *Isenheim Altarpiece* (Colmar). **1515** Anecdotes of *Till Eulenspiegel*, German folk hero, first published. **1516** Ariosto *Orlando Furioso*. = Completion of King's College Chapel, Cambridge (1515) and the Henry VII Chapel, Westminster (1519), the two masterpieces of the English perpendicular style.	= Andrea del Sarto, Francabigio, and Pontormo decorate the Medici villa at Poggio a Caiano.	**1526(–34)** Giulio Romano builds and frescoes the Palazzo del Te for the Duke of Mantua. **1528** Francis I starts construction of Fontainebleau. **1529** Altdorfer *Battle of Alexander* (Munich).	**1532** Rabelais *Pantagruel* (*Gargantua* follows in 1534). **1533** Holbein *The Ambassadors* (London). = Sansorino begins the Library of St Marks, Venice (1532); Sangallo begins the Palazzo Farnese, Rome.	**1536** Michelangelo begins the *Last Judgement* on the altar wall of the Sistine Chapel. **1537** Serlio *On Architecture (D'Architettura)*. **1538** Henry VIII begins Nonesuch Palace. = Francis I employs Italian artists, notably Rosso, Serlio, Primaticcio and Cellini at Fontainebleau.

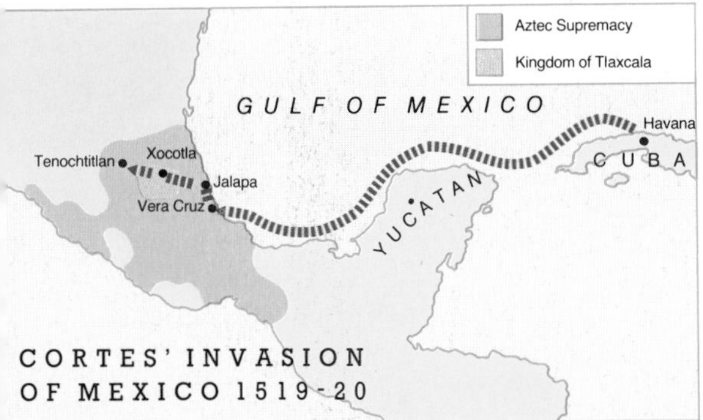

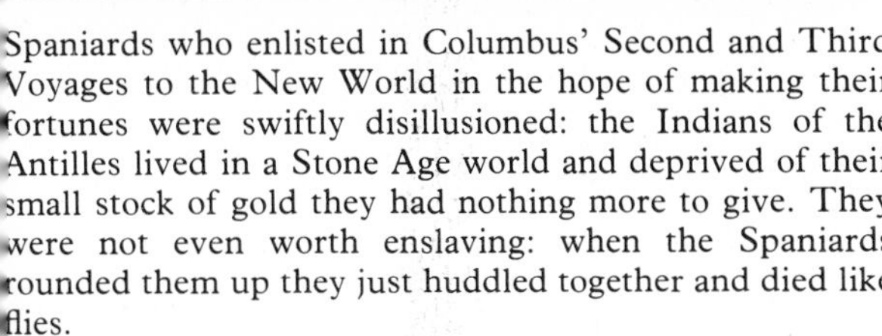

Above left: Monte Alban, Oaxaca, Mexico. Ceremonial centre of the Zapotec of South central Mexico during the classic era, AD 300–900.

Above: Gold mask of Xipe Totec, God of Spring. Zapotec work from Monte Alban.

Left: The Pyramid of the Magician', Uxmal, Yucatan. One of the monuments of the Maya civilization, built and abandoned long before the arrival of the Spaniards.

Spaniards who enlisted in Columbus' Second and Third Voyages to the New World in the hope of making their fortunes were swiftly disillusioned: the Indians of the Antilles lived in a Stone Age world and deprived of their small stock of gold they had nothing more to give. They were not even worth enslaving: when the Spaniards rounded them up they just huddled together and died like flies.

There remained the hope that the next round of exploration would bring something better. The Indians had tales of lands with gold in abundance and springs that conferred eternal youth, and the Spaniards followed up all of these, likely or not. In 1517 they got their first genuine lead. A party raiding for slaves in Yucatan caught glimpses of stone temples rising out of the jungle and though nobody could be sure exactly what these signified it was clearly something much more substantial in the way of native civilization than anything previously encountered. The governor of Cuba despatched an expedition to investigate.

The leader of the expedition, Hernan Cortez, landed on the Gulf Coast of Mexico in early 1519. Messengers reported the Spaniards' presence to the Aztec Emperor Moctezuma in his palace 300 kilometres to the west, and Moctezuma ordered them to stay out of his dominions. Cortez took no notice. Forcing aside the Aztec confederates who attempted to stand in his way he led his 500-man army through the uplands, past the smoking cone of Popacatapetl and down into the Valley of Mexico. A final march brought them to the shores of Lake Texcoco where they got their first sight of Tenochtitlan, the island capital of the Aztec Empire. Squatting like a spider at the centre of a web of causeways it seemed to them, and may well have been in fact, bigger than any city of Spain. Moctezuma, troubled in mind, undecided whether he was dealing with men or gods, allowed the Spaniards to enter unopposed.

Moctezuma's hesitations cost him his freedom and ultimately his life. Held hostage by Cortez, who intended to use him to gain control of the empire, he was stoned by his own people when he tried to assure them that all was well. The Spaniards, penned in the palace by the angry mob, ran out of water and had to fight their way out of the city, suffering grievous losses as they did so. After regrouping and reinforcement they fought their way back in again. This time there were no tricks: the city was razed to the ground, the Aztecs and their confederates forced to submit.

The Spaniards' dreams of untold wealth were as usual disappointed. When all the gold of Tenochtitlan was gathered in it turned out to be far less than was needed to repay the expenses of the expedition: at best it covered a quarter of the cost. The only way to balance the books was to enslave the surrounding Indian tribes and make them work their lands for the benefit of the conquerors. And this is what happened. The shape of the Spanish-American empire, in Mexico as elsewhere, was determined by the Amerindian population map: where the Indians were thick on the ground, as in Mexico and Peru, the Spanish erected vice royalties; where there were too few Indians to support a land-owning class, the Spaniards quickly lost interest. Land without Indians to work it was worth nothing to them.

Right: *Map of the Habsburg Empire. Shortly after Charles made over the Habsburg lands in Germany to his brother Ferdinand, a Turkish army entered Hungary and killed its king who also happened to be king of Bohemia. Ferdinand managed to establish himself as the heir to both these kingdoms and thus create the nucleus of the future Austro-Hungarian Empire. It was this that kept the Habsburg family in business into modern times; Charles V's line in Spain died out in 1700.*

Above: Charles V at the age of 32. Portrait by Titian, now in the Prado, Madrid.

The future Emperor Charles V was born in Ghent in February 1500. At the time expectations on his behalf were relatively modest: if all went well and he survived the dangerous years of infancy he would one day inherit his father's Duchy of Burgundy (meaning most of the Low Countries and part of Burgundy) plus, at the opposite corner of Europe, his grandfather Maximilian's German territories (essentially an Archduchy equivalent to modern Austria). He would not command resources on the same scale as the kings of France and Spain but he would rank among the half dozen most imporant princes in Europe. In the event Charles did much better than this for death not only spared him in his tender years but scythed away his mother's elder sibs and their offspring to such effect that their inheritance, the Spanish kingdoms of Castile, Aragon and Navarre, came to Charles instead. At the age of 20 he found himself master of Spain and of the southern half of Italy (a dependency of Aragon) as well as Burgundy and Austria. He had also been elected emperor of Germany in succession to Maximilian.

This last title gave Charles status but in other ways was more of a handicap than a help: it brought in no revenues yet carried an obligation to keep the ramshackle collection of 300 or so duchies, counties, bishoprics and free cities that constituted the German Empire in some sort of order. The task had recently become more difficult than ever because Luther had begun his challenge to the Catholic Church in Germany and if the empire had any meaning at all it was as the bulwark of a united Christendom. At least that is how Charles saw it: he was always trying to persuade the members of the various coalitions he presided over to join him in a crusade against the Turk.

The king of France, the dashing Francis I, had no such aspirations. He was for enlarging the frontiers of his kingdom and prepared to ally himself with anyone, including the Turk, who would help him in this endeavour. And standing at the head of the richest and most powerful nation in Europe he was not prepared to put up with any nonsense from Charles and his unwieldy conglomerate. While Charles was still feeling his way towards a system of government for what was, after all, an entirely new political construction, Francis was consolidating his hold on Milan, the fruit of the spectacular victory at Marignano with which he had opened his reign.

Charles had none of Francis' glamour. For much of the time he actually managed to look half-witted because his over-size Habsburg jaw was difficult to close properly and Charles sometimes forgot to try. But he was far from being a fool and many of his good qualities were exactly the ones needed for running a multinational enterprise. He was a good linguist, speaking Flemish, French, Spanish and Italian with fluency. He was a hard worker and a patient negotiator. He was a man of his word. Gradually these qualities were perceived by his subjects and increasingly he won their loyalty. The Spanish in particular, who started off mistrusting him as a foreigner, ended up giving him their complete confidence.

In 1525 things started to go Charles' way. In the ten years since Marignano, military technology had moved up another notch: German gunsmiths had developed the first practical small arm, the arquebus, and German mercenary captains in Charles' employ brought it to the north Italian theatre. At the battle of Pavia, which opened with Francis I appearing to enjoy every advantage in numbers, position and supply, they gave an awesome demonstration of the new weapon's power; the day ended with the French army destroyed, and the French king a prisoner. 'All is lost save honour' wrote Francis miserably and though he eventually cheered up enough to welsh on his ransom, he was right in thinking that France's Italian adventure was over. His son Henry II gave up the attempt to re-establish French power there, and Charles' son Philip got the Duchy of Milan. By then the whole of Italy could be classed as a Habsburg protectorate.

More good news came to Charles from the Indies, from Cortez in Mexico and Pizarro in Peru. Europe gawped at the treasures of Moctezuma and Inca Atahualpa, marvelled at the tales of the conquistadors and looked at Charles with new respect. As his New World empire spread over two continents, so his standing in the Old World grew. Charles had always been interested in geographical discovery – one of his first acts of government had been to approve the finance for Magellan's voyage – and he seems to have had a shrewd eye for potential profits – the Magellan expedition was, after all, targeted on the spice trade – but neither he nor anyone else can have expected his overseas empire to grow at such a staggering rate. Towards the end of his reign it was even promising to solve his perennial budget problems for the mines opened up in Mexico and Peru in the 1540s produced a fortune in silver.

By 1550 Charles had every reason to be pleased with himself. He was undoubtedly the most powerful monarch in Europe and the Habsburg position was not only far stronger than it had been at his accession 30 years earlier, it looked practically unassailable. But Charles did not see it that way: he was depressed by his failure to bring the Lutherans and the papacy together, to win the German princes' co-operation, to make effective war on the Turk. He did not even believe in the conglomerate idea any more: he was old, he was gouty, he wanted out.

Charles owned so much of Europe in so many complicated ways that the legal formalities of his abdication took months to complete, but the essential act was done soon enough: in 1555, in a ceremony in Brussels, he bade his Flemish subjects farewell and introduced them to his son Philip. The next year he confirmed the long standing arrangements by which his brother Ferdinand ruled the German territories, agreed to his receiving the Imperial title and resigned the Spanish kingdoms to Philip. Then he set out for the monastery of Yuste in Estremadura where, surrounded by his maps, clocks and favourite paintings (all by Titian) he spent the last two years of his life.

	1540–1544	1545–1549	1550–1554	1555–1559	1560–1564
Politics & Military History	**1540** Sher Shah drives Babur's son and successor Humayun from Delhi. Charles V gives Milan to his son Philip. **1541** Charles V fails to take Algiers. **1542** Christopher da Gama killed attempting to free Abyssinia from Muslim invaders.	**1545** Pope Paul III takes the Duchy of Parma from the Papal State and gives it to his son Pierluigi Farnese. **1547** Charles V defeats the Protestant princes of Germany at Mühlberg, captures the Elector of Saxony and gives his electoral vote (and some of his lands) to Maurice, Duke of Albertine Saxony. Ottomans occupy Massawa, completing isolation of Abyssinia. Ivan the Terrible takes the title 'Tsar of all the Russias'.	**1552** King Henry II of France annexes Metz, Toul and Verdun Maurice, the new Elector of Saxony, turns against Charles and nearly captures him at Innsbruck: Charles passes Edict of Toleration. Ivan the Terrible conquers Kazan. **1554** Death of Sher Shah opens the way for Humayun to recover Delhi the following year. Northern Burmese kingdom of Ava falls to king of Toungoo. Unified Burmese state begins to expand at expense of Thai.	**1555(–6)** Charles V abdicates. His son Philip II succeeds him in Spain, Italy, the county of Burgundy and the Low Countries: his brother Ferdinand, already king of Hungary and Bohemia and Archduke of Austria, succeeds him as German Emperor. Ivan the Terrible conquers Astrakhan. Humayun's son Akbar wins 2nd Battle of Panipat, securing Moghul power in north India. **1557** Spanish forces in the Netherlands defeat French at St Quentin. Philip II gives Siena to Florence. **1558** French take Calais, last English possession in France. **1559** France and Spain sign treaty of Câteau Cambrésis. Sweden takes Estonia.	**1560** Japan: Oda Nobunaga defeats Imagawa Yoshimoto, emerges as the leading *daimyo* (feudal baron). Ottomans defeat Spanish fleet off Jerba. **1561** Poland annexes Livonia. **1562** France: first round of the conflict between Huguenots (Protestants) and the Catholic League (headed by the Guises) begins. Ferdinand declares the crown of Bohemia, previously elective, to be hereditary in his house.
Religion & Learning	**1542** Francis Xavier arrives in Goa. **1543** Pope Paul III promulgates the Index of prohibited books	**1545** Opening of the Council of Trent which masterminds the Catholic Church's counter-attack on the Protestants, the 'counter Reformation'. Rhine Palatinate becomes Protestant. Konrad von Gesler begins publication of his *Biblioteca Universalis*, pioneering work of bibliography.	**1552** Lopez de Gomara *Historia General de las Indias*. **1553** Queen Mary brings England back into the Catholic fold. **1551** Francis Xavier leaves Japan having arrived in 1549.	**1557** Scottish reformers make their First Covenant. **1558** Elizabeth I returns England to the Protestant camp. Thomas Gresham's law 'Bad money drives out good'.	**1560** Covenanters gain the upper hand in Scotland. **1562** Akbar marries a Rajput princess, proves tolerant in religious matters. **1563** Foxe's *Book of Martyres*.
Cities & Social Development	**1540** Charles V punishes the rebellion of Ghent by depriving its citizens of their traditional liberties. **1541** Valdivas founds Santiago de Chile.		**1553** Richard Chancellor journeys from England to Moscow via the White Sea hoping to establish a new trade route.	**1559** Henry II of France killed during a joust by a lance that pierced his visor. = Tobacco introduced to Europe via Spain and Portugal (the word nicotine comes from Jean Nicot who was French Ambassador to Lisbon in 1559–61).	**1561** Spire of St Pauls, the highest in England, destroyed by fire.
Discovery & Invention	**1540** Coronado sets out on an expedition that by 1542 has covered much of the south-western USA, and includes a visit by his Lieutenant, Cardenas, to the Grand Canyon. To combat piracy, Spanish insitute a convoy system for vessels travelling to and from the New World. = Heavy arquebus or 'musket' introduced by Spanish. **1543** Andreas Vesalius *On the Structure of the Human Body (De Fabrica Corporis Humani)*. Orellano emerges at the mouth of the Amazon at the end of a transcontinental journey that had started in Quito in 1541.	**1545** Ambrose Paré *Manière de traitez les Plaies*. Anatomy demonstration hall opened at Padua University. **1548** De Irala crosses from Peru to the Rio Plata. **1549** Bogota (then Santa Fe) chosen as capital of the Audiencia of New Granada. = Major silver strikes in Spanish America at Potosi, Peru (1545) and Zacatecas, Mexico (1546).	**1550** Agricola (Georg Bauer, a Saxon) *De re metallica*, the treatise on mining which has led to his being called the Father of Metallurgy. **1552** Bartolomew Eustachio describes the Eustachian tube. **1554** Founding of Sao Paulo, Brazil.	**1557** Portuguese establish a factory at Macao which enables them to trade with China via Canton. By this time their trade with Japan (via Kagoshima) is well established.	**1560** Battista Porta invents the Camera Obscura. **1561** Gabriel Fallopius *Observationes anatomicae* on female reproductive system. Lope de Aguirre emerges from the Orinoco after crossing the Amazon basin. **1562** Ribault establishes Huguenot colony of Fort Caroline, Florida. John Hawkins begins attempt to establish a 3-sided trade in the Atlantic carrying manufactures to Africa, slaves to the Caribbean.
The Arts		**1546** Michelangelo takes over as architect of St Peters, Lescot begins the rebuilding of the Louvre. Bronzino *Portrait of Eleonora of Toledo* (Uffizi). **1549** Joachim Du Bellay *La Défense et Illustration de la Langue Française*, manifesto of the classicizing group known as the Pléiade. = Titian paints his finest portraits including *Pope Paul III and his nephews*; 1546 (Naples) and *Charles V*; 1548.	**1550** Andrea Palladio *Villa Rotonda*. Giorgio Vasari *Lives of the Artists* (of the Italian Renaissance). Goujon *Musicians' Gallery*, Louvre. **1551** Palestrina appointed Director of Music at St Peters, Rome. **1553** Hans Sachs *Tristan und Isolde*.	**1555** Ivan the Terrible starts St Basils, Moscow as a thanks offering for the capture of Kazan. **1558** Marguerite de Navarre *Heptameron*.	**1560** Tintoretto *Susannah and the Elders* (Vienna). Paolo Veronese frescoes the Villa Maser. **1561** François Clouet *Charles IX* (Vienna). **1562** Benvenuto Cellini *Autobiography* (not published till 1728). **1563** Byrd appointed organist of Lincoln Cathedral Philip II begins the Escorial Palace.

	1565–1569	1570–1574	1575–1579	1580–1584	1585–1589
Politics & Military History	**1565** Ottoman invasion of Malta repulsed by Knights of St John. **1566** Rebellion breaks out in the Netherlands as a result of Philip II's increasingly arbitary rule. **1567** War between the Catholics and Huguenots begins again in France. Mary Queen of Scots forced to abdicate because of her Catholicism and her disorderly private life: her infant son James VI declared king of Scotland. **1568.** Alva, Philip II's Governor in the Netherlands, institutes policy of repression, executes protesting nobles Egmont and Horn. William of Orange flees the country. Mary Queen of Scots escapes to England where Elizabeth imprisons her. Japan: Nobunaga seizes Kyoto. **1569** Diet of Lublin carries unification of Poland and Lithuania a stage further.	**1570** Ottomans invade Cyprus: Spanish-Venetian naval victory at Lepanto the next year is too late to prevent the conquest of the island (completed 1572). **1571** Japan: Nobunaga deposes the last Ashikaga Shogun. **1572** Revolt breaks out again in the Netherlands: Holland and three other provinces in the north declare for William of Orange. Slaughter of Huguenots in Paris with connivance of Charles IX (massacre of St Bartholomew). **1573** Alva takes Haarlem but fails to take Alkmaar: Philip II recalls him to Spain. Akbar conquers Gujerat. **1574** The Dutch open their dykes, forcing the Spanish to abandon the siege of Leiden. Ottomans conquer Tunisia. Spanish conquer Manila.	**1575** Philip II forced to declare a moratorium on Spain's debts. **1576** Spanish troops in the Netherlands, unpaid for months, seize and sack Antwerp, seat of the Spanish Governor (see below). Akbar conquers Bihar and Bengal. **1578** King Sebastian of Portugal invades Morocco: he is killed and his army annihilated at the Battle of Alcazar el-Kebir. **1579** Union of Utrecht binds the northern provinces of the Netherlands together in the rebel cause.	**1580** Philip II of Spain makes good his claim to the throne of Portugal. **1582** Nobunaga assassinated: his General Hideyoshi soon succeeds to his position as Japan's leading *daimyo*. **1583** Cossack leader Yermak defeats Kuchum, Khan of Siberia, a victory that lays the basis for future Russian expansion east of the Urals. **1584** William of Orange, father of the Dutch republic, assassinated.	**1585** Parma, Philip II's new viceroy in the Netherlands, recovers Antwerp, re-establishes Spanish rule over southern provinces (modern Belgium). **1586** Elizabeth of England sends troops to fight alongside the Dutch: Philip orders work to begin on the Armada. **1587** Elizabeth executes Mary Queen of Scots. **1588** Defeat of the Armada. **1589** Murder of King Henry III of France ends Valois line. Henry of Navarre, in line to inherit the throne, is opposed by the Catholic League because of his Protestant faith.
Religion & Learning	**1568** Brunswick becomes Protestant. **1569** Mercator (Gerhard Kremer of Louvain) publishes a map of the world using the projection named after him. Also begins part publication of his Atlas, the first collection of maps so called.	**1570** Ortelius (Abraham Wortels of Antwerp) *Theatrum Orbis Terrarum*, the first complete atlas ever published. Blaise de Montluc *Commentaires*.	**1575** Leiden University founded to commemorate the siege. **1576** Warsaw University founded. **1577** Holinshed *Chronicles* (of England, Scotland and Ireland), the source Shakespeare used for his historical plays. **1579** Christopher Saxton *Atlas of England and Wales*.	**1581** Founding of Universities of Edinburgh and Wurzburg. **1583** Jesuit missionaries Ricci and Ruggieri given permission to settle in Zhao Qing, near Canton, China.	**1586** Camden *Britannia*, first topographical survey of England. **1587** Hideyoshi bans Christian missionaries from Japan. **1589** Richard Hakluyt *The Principall Navigations, Voyages and discoveries of the English Nation* beats the drum for an English overseas empire.
Cities & Social Development	**1565** Akbar chooses Agra as his capital.	**1570** Japan: Nagasaki nominated as the port for overseas trade. **1571** Akbar moves his capital to Fatehpur Sikri. Mongols pillage Moscow, the last time they do so.	**1576** Fourteen day sack of Antwerp by mutinous Spanish soldiers ('the Spanish Fury') marks end of city's commercial dominance and provides Amsterdam with the opportunity of taking its place.	**1581** English Levant Company founded. **1584** Archangel, first port on the White Sea, founded. = Potato introduced to Europe.	= Expansion of Russia; many new towns founded, notably Samara and Tsaritsyn (1586 and 1588) to serve the lower Volga, and Tyumen and Tobolsk (1586 and 1587) to serve the valley of the Ob.
Discovery & Invention	**1568** Hawkins' 3rd Voyage ends with his defeat by the Spanish at San Juan di Ulloa. Alvaro de Mendana discovers the Solomons. 153m spire added to Beauvais Cathedral making it temporarily the world's tallest structure. Falls 1573.	**1572** Danish astronomer Tycho Brahe begins work on a new star catalogue at his purpose-built observatory, Uraniborg on the island of Hveen. Appearance of a Nova in Cassiopeia shows that the firmament of 'fixed stars' is not totally unchanging.	**1576(–8)** Martin Frobisher explores the tip of Baffin Island. **1577** Francis Drake sets out on his circumnavigation of the world: reaches Vancouver 1578.	**1580** Drake completes his circumnavigation. **1581** Galileo observes the periodicity of the pendulum. **1582** Gregorian reform of the calendar. **1583** Gilbert claims Newfoundland for England.	**1585(–7)** John Davis explores the Davis Strait. **1585(–8)** Failure of Sir Walter Raleigh's Colonies on Roanoke Island, Virginia.* Wagheraen *Spiegel der Zeevaart* (Mariner's Mirror). Simon Stevin *De Thiende* argues for decimal notation. **1586(–8)** Cavendish circum-navigates the globe.
The Arts	**1565** Pieter Bruegel *Hunters in the Snow* (Vienna). Pierre de Ronsard *Elegies, Mascarades et Bergeries*. **1568** Vignola and della Porta *Il Jesu*, Rome: the prototype counter Reformation church. **1569** Sinan begins the *Selimiye Mosque*, Edirne (finished 1578).	**1570** Palladio *On Architecture (I Quattro Libri del Architettura)*. **1572** Camoëns *The Luisiads*: Virgilian epic on the Portuguese discovery of the Cape route. **1574** Tasso *Gerusalemme Liberata* romantic epic set against a crusading background.	**1576** J. du Cerceau *Les Plus Excellents Bâtiments de France*. **1577** James Burbage opens his Theatre in Shoreditch, London's first. Nicholas Hilliard *Self-portrait* (V and A, London). **1579** Giambologna *Rape of the Sabines*, Florence.	**1580** Montaigne *Essays* (Vols I and II). **1581** Two events that mark the beginning of Classical Ballet: the performance of the *Balet de la Reyne* at the French court, the earliest ballet of which the music (by Batasar de Beaujoyeux) survives; the publication of Caroso's *Il Ballarino*, a manual of dance technique.	**1585** Edward Alleyn forms his acting company, the Lord Chamberlain's men. **1586** El Greco *Burial of Count Orgaz*, S. Tomé, Toledo. **1587** Antonio da Ponte *Rialto Bridge*, Venice.

*Within present day North Carolina

n the second half of the 16th century the conflict between :atholic and Protestant intensified: war between the two ame to be considered part of the natural order of things nd it was war of the most savage sort, war *à l'outrance*. In any ways this development was to the advantage of Philip f Spain: pro-Catholic sentiment reinforced the existing oyalties of his Spanish and Italian subjects while his olitical opponent, France, was so riven by the conflict etween reformed and established faiths that her influence ell to an all time low. The religious issue even looked like elping Philip with one of his most ambitious schemes, the reation of a Habsburg bloc in the north. His marriage to he devoutly Catholic Mary of England offered the hope hat this country would be pulled back from the Protestant rink and, together with the Netherlands, become a Iabsburg appanage ranking with Spain, Italy and Austria.

Unfortunately for Philip, Mary died childless in 1558 nd the queen who succeeded her, Elizabeth, was as taunchly Protestant as Mary had been Catholic. Gradually England drifted out of the Spanish camp, a process that ccelerated when Philip's repressive policies in the Netherlands provoked a Protestant-led rebellion there. English sea captains started raiding Spain's supply lines in he Channel, in the Atlantic and in the Indies: Englishmen egan wondering whether their future might not lie in :hallenging Spain's monopoly of the Americas rather than ining for long lost territories in France. By 1585 Philip had ad enough of this. He ordered the preparation of an normous fleet, a veritable Armada, which would clear the Channel, transport his soldiers from Flanders to England nd conquer that insolent kingdom.

Elizabeth made preparations too. She brought her fleet up to war strength, she deprived the Catholic faction in England of its best candidate for the throne by executing Mary Queen of Scots and she let Drake make a spoiling attack on the Armada as it was assembling in Cadiz. Drake did well in this raid but the next year, 1588, the Armada set sail all the same. Its 75 first line fighting ships, 30 sloops and 25 big merchantmen carried 10,000 sailors and 20,000 soldiers: its course was set for Flanders and a reinforcement of soldiers that would at least double its strength. If it could land this army in England the Protestant cause was as good as lost.

The Armada was sighted in the mouth of the Channel on 19th July. Two days later its galleons were in action as the English fleet tried to break up the Spanish formation so that it could pick off individual ships. Neither then nor in subsequent days did the English succeed: the Armada continued its slow progress up the Channel and anchored off Calais on the 28th. A couple of ships had been lost in accidents but the Armada had taken everything the English could throw at it without any significant damage.

Even so, no one on the Spanish side was happy about the next stage of the operation. The Armada was running low in powder and shot and badly needed a week in port. What was in prospect was a week, maybe a fortnight, in the open sea while the Flanders army embarked on its barges and nosed out to meet them. Whether this rendezvous was practical at all was never tested. The second night off Calais the English put in half a dozen fire ships and the Armada broke. The battle that followed gave the English the chance to run the Spanish further away from Flanders and used up the rest of the Spanish shot. The Armada could not go back, it could only go on.

'God blew with his wind and they were scattered' said the medal that Elizabeth struck to commemorate the defeat of the Armada. In truth the weather was not particularly unkind to the Spaniards, it was average for the time of year, but the way home was longer than many of the ships could manage. By the time they had rounded Scotland several were coming apart and off the coast of Ireland anything up to a couple of dozen of them did just that. Nobody knows exactly how much of the Armada finally got back to Spain, for the odd ship struggled in after the official count had been made: a third lost and a third so damaged that they would never put to sea again is a fair estimate for the ships; as for the men it is reckoned that barely one in three survived.

The war went on. Philip put together a new fleet and, by and large, held his own till hostilities petered out ten years later. But the Armada year is the one that mattered: it marked the rise of England's star, and the beginning of Spain's long decline.

Top: Silver medal of Queen Elizabeth commemorating the defeat of the Spanish Armada.

Above: Philip II of Spain. Detail of portrait by Antonio Moro, now in the Prado, Madrid.

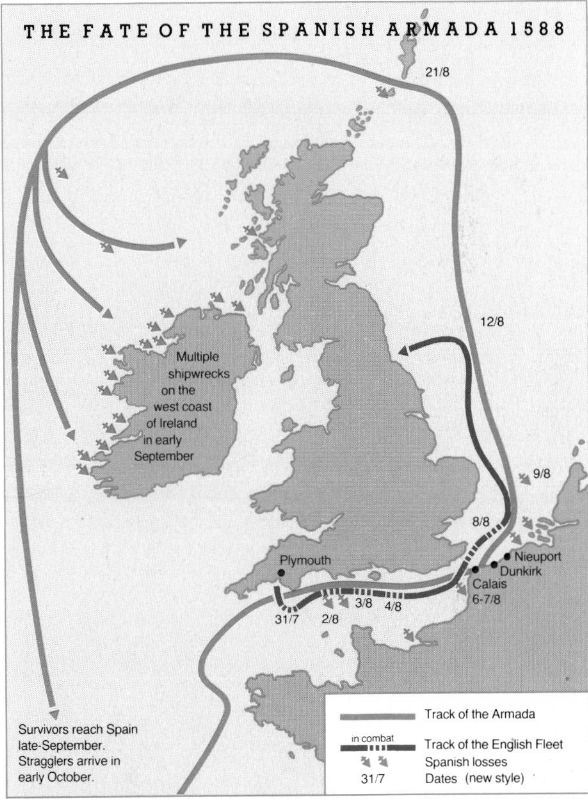

Below: The Armada in crescent formation enters the English Channel. English ships leave Plymouth harbour and try to pick off stragglers.

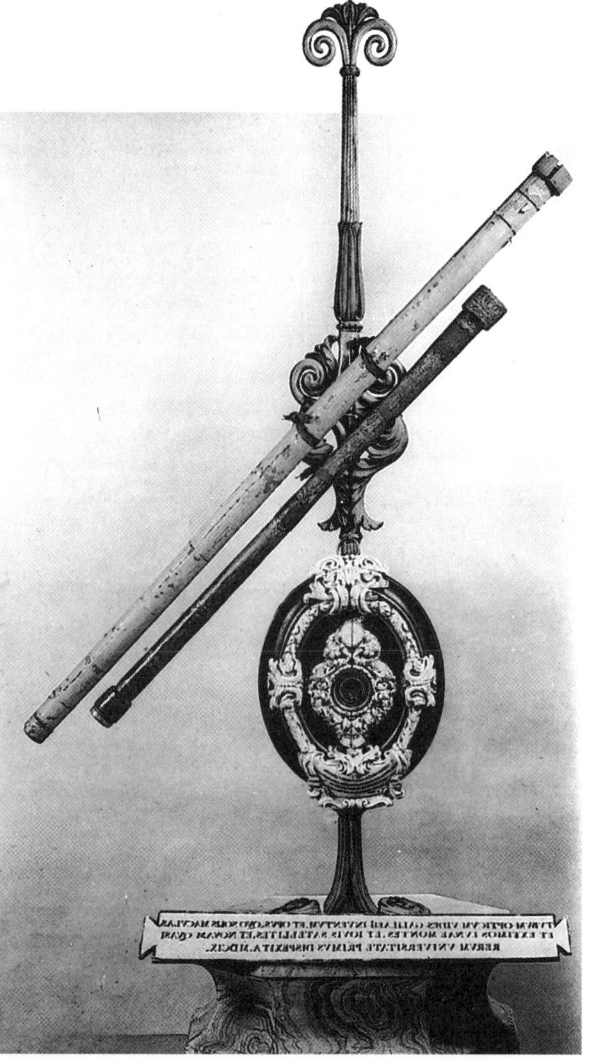

Above: Frontispiece of Regiomontanus' edition of Ptolemy's Almagest *(1496). Above the figures of Ptolemy (left) and Regiomontanus (right) is an armillary sphere (cut-away celestial globe) showing the traditional view of the heavens: a central earth with the track of the sun across the sphere of the stars represented by a band bearing the signs of the zodiac.*

Left: Two of Galileo's telescopes as they are exhibited in the Science Museum in Florence, the city where he was professor of mathematics for life at the university. Unhappily for Galileo the Church bitterly opposed his theory that it was the earth that moved round the sun and he was ordered to recant. The story goes that having done this, Galileo added under his breath, 'E pur si muove' *(Yet it* does *move').*

It is typical of the transition from medieval to early modern times that fact and fiction, sense and nonsense, scepticism and credulity were muddled up together not only in the minds of ordinary folk but in the minds of men of the greatest intelligence and originality. The chemists were all alchemists, the astronomers all astrologers; the business of sorting out the real from the bogus had scarcely begun.

Nowhere is this more apparent than in astronomy. The king of Denmark funded the astronomer Tycho Brahe's life work, the construction of a new map of the heavens, largely because it held out the promise of more accurate horoscopes. As Tycho pointed out, you could not expect horoscopes to be of any predictive value when they were constructed from tables that had been of dubious accuracy when Ptolemy drew them up in the 2nd century AD and were certainly quite inappropriate to the celestial situation existing in the 16th century.

While Tycho charted the positions of the stars and planets at his observatory on the island of Hveen, the learned men of Europe argued about the structure of the universe. The majority favoured the Ptolemaic model which had the earth motionless at the centre of a nest of revolving spheres, the outer one of which bore the stars on its inner surface. A minority preferred the heliocentric theory first advanced by Aristarchus in the 3rd century BC and recently revived by Copernicus: in this a spinning earth circled a central sun within a motionless sphere of stars. This second model was, of course, deeply offensive to many churchmen (including Luther) but the debate did not attract that much attention for it was, in every sense of the word, entirely academic. Neither theory came anywhere near explaining the actual movements of the planets.

In 1588 a new king of Denmark came to the throne and he and Tycho, who was a heavy drinker and easy to quarrel with, soon fell out. Tycho took himself, his instruments and his observations off to the court of the German emperor Rudolph where, in 1601, he died. His observations were put in order and published by the assistant who had joined him in his last years, Johann Kepler of Wurttemberg. Kepler also worked on the orbits of the planets, trying to see if any combination of circular movements could bring the various models of the universe into closer correspondence with reality. In 1609 he found the answer: it could not be done with circles, but it could with elipses. The universe was Copernican.

This was an entirely correct conclusion but as the mathematics were abstruse – the planets did not orbit at a constant speed but at a rate that gave a constant value for the area of the elipse swept out in unit time – it did not have much impact on the man in the street. But in the same year that Kepler published his *New Astronomy* Galileo, the leading man of science in Italy, made himself a telescope, a newly invented instrument for bringing distant objects closer. He turned it to the skies and saw marvellous things: the craters of the moon, the satellites of Jupiter, the spots on the face of the sun. And everywhere there were stars, more than anyone had ever dreamed of: the Milky Way resolved into stars by the thousand. The universe was clearly the universe of Copernicus and Kepler, the only one that needed no boundary.

This was all too much for the Catholic Church. It was one thing to argue about the Cosmos in scholarly publications, another to tell the faithful that the astronomy of the Old Testament, of Joshua and the Psalms, could not be taken literally. Galileo must be silenced. And so, by threat of torture, he was. But if the Church won the opening round it was in the end to lose the fight. The march of science had begun.

Left: Tycho Brahe at Uraniborg, his observatory on the island of Hveen. Tycho is directing his assistants in the use of the great quadrant with which he took the measurements for his star catalogue.

	1590–1594	1595–1599	1600–1604	1605–1609	1610–1614
Politics & Military History	**1590** Henry IV defeats Catholic League at Ivry but Parma, moving down from the Netherlands on Philip's orders, stops him taking Paris. Hideyoshi forces capitulation of the Hojo, completing his control over Japan. **1591** Moroccan expedition reaches the Niger and takes Timbuctoo. **1592** Hideyoshi invades Korea but, under pressure from Chinese, withdraws next year. **1592** Annamese take Hanoi, restoring unity of N. Vietnam. **1593** Henry IV decides 'Paris is worth a mass', converts to Catholicism. **1594** Henry IV enters Paris. Hugh O'Neill, Earl of Tyrone, leads Irish rebellion against English rule. Moghul empire reaches its peak with Akbar's conquest of Kandahar.	**1596** English sack Cadiz, disrupting Philip's preparations for a second Armada. **1597** Storms prevent Philip's second Armada from entering the English Channel. Dutch defeat his army in the Netherlands at Turnhout. Hideyoshi invades Korea again. **1598** Japanese forces in Korea withdrawn on Hideyoshi's death. Russia's 'time of troubles' begins with the death of Ivan's idiot son Fedor. **1599** Earl of Essex fails to subdue Irish rebels.	**1600** Tokugawa Ieyasu defeats rival *daimyo* at Battle of Sekigahara, establishes his supremacy throughout Japan. France attacks Savoy. Duke Charles Emmanuel forced to cede Bresse (1601): his attempt to compensate for this by a coup against Geneva fails (1602). **1602** Tyrone submits to Mountjoy, English Governor of Ireland. **1603** James VI of Scotland succeeds the childless Elizabeth, becoming James I of England and uniting the two crowns (though the two countries retain their separate identities). Ieyasu assumes the title of Shogun. **1604** Spain's General Spinola captures Ostend after a three year siege. Persians recover Tabriz from the Ottomans.	**1605** Tokugawa Ieyasu retires: his son Hidetada becomes Shogun. **1607** Dutch destroy a Spanish fleet off Gibraltar. **1609** Spain agrees to a nine year truce in the Netherlands.	**1610** Henry IV assassinated on the eve of launching a new offensive against Spain. Marie de Medici becomes Regent for the infant Louis XIII. Plantation of Ulster with Scots (about 50,000 over the next ten years). **1611** Poles take Smolensk and occupy Moscow: Swedes occupy Novgorod. **1612** Danes take Elfsborg from the Swedes. **1613** Swedes agree to pay a million dollars to get Elfsborg back.
Religion & Learning	**1590** Giordano Bruno *De Immenso et Innumerabilibus*, argues for an infinite universe: gets him arrested by the Inquisition in 1593. **1591** Founding of Trinity College, Dublin	**1593** Hideyoshi begins persecution of Christians. **1598** Henry IV issues the Edict of Nantes granting the Huguenots freedom to practise their religion within the current limits.	**1600** Rome: Giordano Bruno burnt for heresy and Copernicism. = By this time Islam has triumphed in Java and many of the other islands of the Indonesian archipelago.	**1605** Catholics Robert Catesby and Guy Fawkes plot to kill king, lords and commons at the opening of Parliament, place 2 tons of gunpowder below the House of Lords but are discovered. Subsequent increase of anti-Catholic legislation in England.	**1611** Publication of the Authorized version of the English Bible, the King James Bible.
Cities & Social Development	**1590** Hideyoshi prohibits peasants from bearing arms and Samurai from changing masters. Rigid division of Japanese society into peasants, artisans, merchants and Samurai. **1592** Pompeii discovered.	**1598** John Stow *A Survey of London*. = Because the other states fear the dominance of Amsterdam the Hague is chosen as capital of the Dutch Republic.	**1600** English East India Company incorporated. **1602** Dutch Chartered East-India Company (Vereenigde Ost-Indische Compagnie – hence VOC) founded.	**1607** Dutch West India Company (WIC) founded. = Tea introduced to Europe by VOC.	= Rapid growth of towns in Japan with castles built by the leading *daimyo* often acting as nuclei: Osaka, Kanazawa, Hiroshima and, most of all, Edo (modern Tokyo), seat of the Shogun.
Discovery & Invention	**1591** Thomas Lancaster reaches East Indies, first Englishman to do so: later (1594) trades in India despite Portuguese opposition. **1594** Dutch explores Barents and Linschoten, attempting NE passage, get as far as Novaya Zemlya.	**1596** Barents discovers Spitsbergen. Mendana makes his second expedition to the Solomons, fails to find them, dies on Santa Cruz. Dutchman Cornelius Houtman reaches Sumatra. **1598** Dutch begin assault on Portuguese in the Orient. Mauritius discovered by van Warwyck.	**1600** William Gilbert *De Magnete*. **1602** Kepler publishes Tycho Brahe's star catalogue. **1603** Champlain claims Isle St Jean (now Prince Edward Island) for France: founds colony of Port Royal, Nova Scotia (1604).	**1605** Torres, sailing from Peru, passes between Australia and New Guinea – through the strait now named after him. Spanish found Santa Fé, New Mexico. **1607** English found Jamestown, Virginia. **1608** Telescope invented by Hans Lippershey, a lens maker of Middleburg, Zeeland. Champlain founds Quebec. Hudson explores the Hudson River. **1609** Kepler *Astronomica Nova* solves the problem of planetary orbits.	**1610** Galileo *Sidereus Nuncius*, an account of his observations of the heavens with a telescope of his own design. Hudson, exploring Hudson Bay, is set adrift by a mutinous crew and never seen again. Etienne Brulé discovers Lake Huron, first of the Great Lakes to be visited by a European. East India Company establishes a factory at Madras. **1612** English colonize Bermuda. **1613** English destroy French settlement at Port Royal.
The Arts	= Golden age of Elizabethan literature begins: Edmund Spenser *The Fairie Queen* (1590), Christopher Marlowe *Dr Faustus*, Thomas Kyd *The Spanish Tragedy* (1592). = William Shakespeare joins the theatrical company known as the Chamberlain's Men and writes *The Taming of the Shrew*. At this time John Donne writes his best poetry.	**1595** Annibale Carracci frescoes ceiling of gallery in the Palazzo Farnese, Rome. **1597** Beginnings of opera: Jacopo Peri's *Dafne* performed in Florence and Vecchi's *L'Amfiparnasso* in Modena. Francis Bacon *Essays*. **1599** The Chamberlain's Men move to the new Globe Theatre where *Julius Caesar* is performed the same year.	**1600** Carravaggio *Conversion of St Paul* and *Crucifixion of St Peter*, S. Maria del Popolo, Rome – two paintings which begin a fashion for *chiaroscuro* (dramatic spotlighting). **1603** Shakespeare *Hamlet*.	**1605** Cervantes *Don Quixote*. **1607** Monteverdi *Orfeo*. Ben Jonson *Volpone*. **1608** Thomas Middleton *A Mad World My Masters*. **1609** Guido Reni *Aurora*, Villa Rospigliosi, Rome. Lope de Vega *Arte Nuevo*. How to write plays in 24 hours by a prolific Spanish dramatist.	**1612** Orlando Gibbons *First Set of Madrigals*. **1613** Beaumont and Fletcher *The Knight of the Burning Pestle*. The Globe burns down during a performance of *Henry VIII*: rebuilt within a year.

	1615–1619	1620–1624	1625–1629	1630–1634	1635–1639
Politics & Military History	**1615** Japan: Ieyasu takes Osaka and exterminates the Toyotomi. France: Queen Regent Marie de Medici dismisses the Estates General. **1616** English King James I dismisses Chief Justice Coke, putting an end to the attempt to limit the power of the king via the courts. **1617** Russia cedes Karelia and Ingria to Sweden. **1618** Bohemians rebel against their new ruler Ferdinand, head of the House of Habsburg and shortly to be elected German Emperor: Bohemian crown offered to and accepted by the Protestant Elector Palatine the next year. This attempt by the Bohemians to sever the Habsburg connection precipitates the infamous Thirty Years' War.	**1620 Thirty Years' War** The Habsburgs try to promote the Catholic and Imperial causes and are opposed, in the end successfully, by the Protestants, many of the Princes and, the traditional enemy of the House of Habsburg – the King of France. Emperor Ferdinand's troops defeat the Palatine Electors at the Battle of the White Mountain, near Prague, and recover Bohemia. **1621** Gustavus Adolphus of Sweden takes Riga (Polish). Nurhaci takes Shenyang from the Ming (see below). **1622** Ferdinand's General Tilly conquers the Palatinate, which the Emperor then gives (plus its electoral vote) to his ally Maximilian of Bavaria. **1624** Spanish take Breda from the Dutch.	**1625** Tilly defeats King Christian IV of Denmark at the Battle of Lutter after Christian's intervention in the Protestant interest. **1628** Despite attempts by the English to stop him Cardinal Richelieu, Louis XIII's chief minister, takes the Protestant stronghold of La Rochelle. After this the Huguenots are never again a threat to the unity of France though they remain an irritant to the government and extreme Catholics. Ferdinand's General Wallenstein occupies Pomerania on the Baltic arousing antagonism of Gustavus Adolphus who regards Baltic as his sphere of influence. **1629** France arranges a peace between Sweden and Poland by which Sweden gets Livonia, Gustavus to turn his attention to Germany.	**1630** Gustavus Adolphus lands in Pomerania, takes Stettin. **1631** Gustavus defeats Ferdinand's General Tilly at the Battle of Breitenfeld: his Saxon allies then take Prague while he moves west to Mainz. **1632** Gustavus takes Nuremberg, defeats and kills Tilly, enters Munich. Then defeats Habsburg-Bavarian army at Lutzen but is killed at the moment of victory. Dutch take Maastricht. **1634** Reinforced by a Spanish army the Habsburgs defeat the Swedes at Nordlingen. French move into the Palatinate.	**1635** France declares war on Spain. **1637** Dutch recapture Breda. **1639** Dutch Admiral van Tromp annihilates Spanish fleet off the Downs (in English territorial waters!) Scots 'Covenanters' (uncompromising Protestants) rebel against King Charles I who has been attempting to impose a new prayer book on them. Charles, lacking the support of the English Parliament, has to back down.
Religion & Learning		**1620** University of Uppsala founded. **1621** Robert Burton *Anatomy of Melancholy*. **1623** Protestant worship forbidden in Bohemia. = Persecution of Christians in Japan becomes a campaign of extermination.	**1625** Hugo Grotius *De Jure Belli et Pacis* establishes the fundamentals of international law. **1629** Emperor Ferdinand II, riding high, orders restitution of all Catholic property seized since 1555.	**1631** William Petty *Political Arithmetic*. **1633** Galileo summoned by the Inquisition for publishing a dialogue favouring the Copernican theory.	**1635** Academie Française founded: starts work on a dictionary of the French language in 1639. **1636** Harvard founded (though not so named till 1639): also University of Utrecht. **1637** René Descartes *Discours de la Méthode* (see also below).
Cities & Social Development	**1619** Oldenbarnevelt, Advocate of Holland, tried and executed at the instigation of Stadtholder Maurice of Nassau, William the Silent's son. A rare example of party politics in the Dutch Republic ending in bloodshed.	**1621** Nurhaci renames Shenyang Mukden and makes it the capital of the Jurchen (Manzhou) state. **1623** Silver strike at Kongsberg, Norway.	**1628** Parliament obtains Charles I's consent to the Petition of Right by which taxation without Parliament's agreement and arrest without cause are declared illegal.	**1631** Sack of Magdeburg by Tilly, so pitiless that it becomes the textbook example of the horrors of the Thirty Years' War.	**1637** Dutch 'tulipomania' which has led to fantastic prices being paid for rare bulbs, ends in classic market collapse.
Discovery & Invention	**1615** Dutch take Moluccas and found Batavia. **1616** Dutchmen Le Maire and Schouten round Cape Horn. William Baffin's exploration of the Davis Strait leads him to conclude that there is no practical NW passage to Asia. **1617** Napier *Rabdologia* describing the use of his 'bones' for logarithmic calculations. **1618** Kepler calculates sun's distance as 22.5 million km as against traditional estimates of 5 (Aristarchus) or 8 (Ptolemy) and 150, true.	**1620** Pilgrim Fathers land at Plymouth, Mass. **1621** Brulé explores Lake Superior. **1622** William Oughtred puts Napier's 'bones' into the more convenient slide-rule form. **1623** Piet Hien captures Bahia, Brazil for WIC. Dutch massacre English at Amboina and begin to squeeze them out of the East Indies. **1624** Edmund Gunter introduces the surveyor's chain (measurement of length). Dutch establish themselves on Taiwan.	**1625** Portuguese recapture Bahia, Brazil from the Dutch. English settle Barbados. French establish post at Cayenne, Guyana. **1626** Dutch found township of New Amsterdam on Manhattan Island. **1628** William Harvey *De Motu Cordis* establishes that the blood circulates and does so as a result of the heart's pumping action. **1629** English capture Quebec from the French, settle Bahamas. = Small arms: flintlock replaces matchlock.	**1630** John Winthrop founds Boston, Mass. Buccaneers seize Tortuga. **1631** Luke Foxe sails round Hudson Bay and Foxe basin. Vernier invents his scale. First settlers in Maryland. **1632** Cossacks reach the Lena River and found Yakutsk. English return Quebec to France. **1634** Jean Nicolet explores Lake Michigan and reaches St Lawrence/Mississippi divide in Wisconsin.	**1635** French settle Martinique and Guadeloupe. **1636** Founding of Hartford, Connecticut. **1637** René Descartes *Dioptrique, Météoris, La Géométrie*. Dutch take El Mina (West Africa) and Recife (Brazil) from the Portuguese. French establish post at mouth of Senegal. **1639** Dutch take Trincomalee (Sri Lanka) from Portugal English East India Company establishes factory at Madras. = Japan: series of decrees closes the country to foreigners.
The Arts	**1619** Inigo Jones *Banqueting House*, Westminster Palace, London.	= The two great artists of the Baroque in full flood: Rubens painting the *Life of Marie de' Medici* (now in the Louvre) for the Luxembourg Palace, and Bernini, sculpting his *David* and *Apollo and Daphne* (Villa Borghese) and starting work on the *Baldacchino* for St Peter's. **1623** Webster *Duchess of Malfi*. **1624** Frans Hals *The Laughing Cavalier* (Wallace Collection, London).	**1626** Carlo Maderno completes the facade of St Peters. **1627** Simon Vouet appointed court painter by Louis XIII.	**1633** Jacques Callot *The Miseries and Sufferings of War*. Pietro da Cortona *Triumph of the Barberini*, Palazzo Barberini, Rome. Jacob van Campen *The Maruitshuis*, the Hague. **1634** First performance of the Oberammergau Passion Play. = Shah Jehan begins the Taj Mahal and the Pearl Mosque, Agra, and the Red Fort and Great Mosque, Delhi.	**1635** Corneille *Médée*. Philippe de Champaigne *Portrait of Cardinal Richelieu* (London). Velasquez *Surrender of Breda* (Prado). **1636** Anthony van Dyck *Equestrian Portrait of Charles I* (London). **1637** Opening of Teatro di San Cossiano, Venice, the first opera house open to the public.

Aore than a hundred years elapsed between the European iscovery of North America and the first successful settle-ıent there. People went to fish along the Newfoundland ɪanks and to trade furs with the Indians but few tried to tay for more than a season and of the few who did none ıade a go of it. The 17th century opened with the continent ssentially unbroached.

To the English the eastern seaboard was known as /irginia after Elizabeth, the 'Virgin Queen', who had anctioned an attempt by Sir Walter Raleigh to establish a olony there in 1585–7. This had failed miserably and if here was an excuse in that the sailing of the Armada had isrupted the supply programme it was also clear that the esources available had never been adequate for the task. The England of the next generation was considerably icher, and the Virginia Company that was chartered in 606 was confident that it could succeed where Raleigh had ailed: it had the funds necessary to sustain a colony hrough its early vulnerable years. With the need for doing o well-understood, arrangements were made to land an nitial batch of 100 colonists on the Virginia coast in 1607.

The site picked for the settlement was on the north bank of the James River at a place that later became known as amestown. The initial steps – the landing and the onstruction of the stockaded village – went smoothly nough but the first winter took a fearsome toll: less than ıalf the settlers were still alive when the first supply ship rrived in 1608. And the mortality continued at the same evel over the next two years: by 1610 some 600 people had been brought to Jamestown but what with 'the famine and pestilence within and the Indians killing as fast without' the population had never risen above sixty for long.

If this was disappointing for the stockholders of the Virginia Company it was terrifying for the colonists. By June 1610 their morale had broken and they had only one dea, to get back to England as fast as possible. They were actually packed aboard one of the relief boats when Lord de a Warr arrived with another 150 settlers and ordered everyone ashore again. The experiment was to continue.

Ten years passed and the James River settlement began to show signs of independent life. Historians usually link this progress to specific developments such as the cultivation of tobacco (first exported in 1613) and the growth of private ownership (as the colonists worked off their seven year contract with the company) but the truth is probably simpler: the continuing flow of new arrivals had created a substantial population of veterans. Though it remained true that only one person in four survived the first few years there were, by 1620, some 1000 people who had acclimatized themselves to Virginia, who knew the streams with the safest water and the seasons when they held the most fish, who had learned to live in America instead of trying to impose themselves on it.

The accolade came in 1622 when the Indians made a concerted attempt to wipe out the colony. In the early days the two had co-existed, with the Indians probably more of a help than a hindrance: undoubtedly they murdered a good many settlers but they also sold them food at times when they faced starvation. Now it was the Indians who were coming under pressure and they reacted with a carefully-planned and well-executed surprise attack. Numerically this was a success. About a quarter of the settlers succumbed before the rest rallied and drove the Indians off. But with a thousand new colonists arriving each year the massacre of 1622 proved only a temporary setback for the new Virginians. For the Indians it was a disaster for they had exposed themselves to the most ruthless form of counterattack, dispossession of their lands.

Above: American Indian woman and child, the child holding an English doll.

Left: American Indian showing 'the manner of their attire and painting themselves'.

Below: Sir Walter Raleigh's attempt to plant a colony in Virginia.

The first two are watercolours by one of the leaders of the colonists, John White. The third is a worked up version of some John White drawings by the Dutch engraver De Bry.

KING CHARLES STICKS HIS NECK OUT

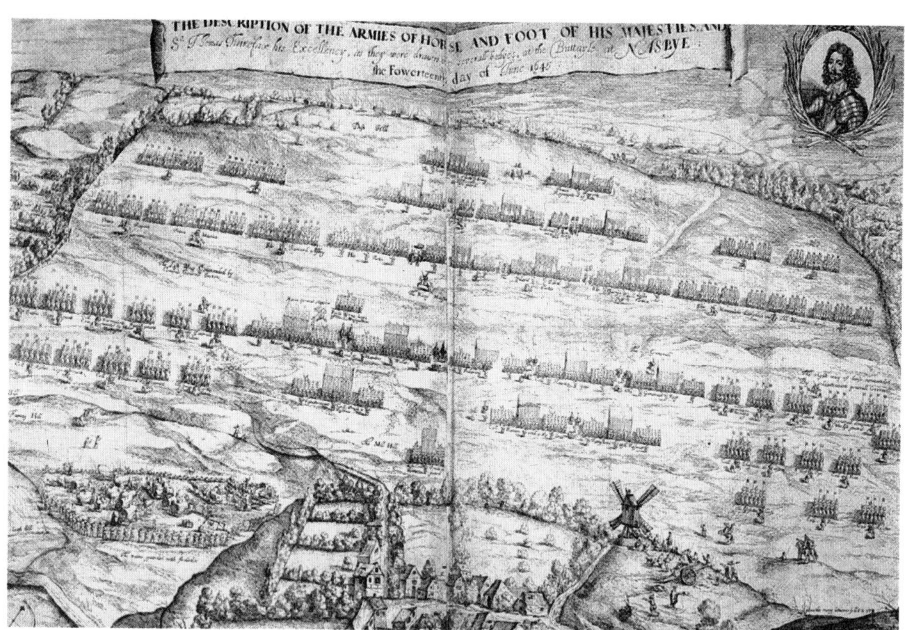

Above left: The Battle of Naseby. The parliamentary army is in the foreground: infantry – alternate companies of musketeers and pikemen – in the centre, cavalry on the wings. Cromwell was in command of the right wing.

Above right: Oliver Cromwell.

Right: Contemporary woodcut of Charles I's execution.

During the Middle Ages the king of England governed with the advice of the great barons of the realm. If he consistently flouted their collective opinions the barons could, and on several occasions did, depose him and in an entirely practical sense it could be said that sovereignty resided not with the king but with the aristocracy. By the 17th century this class was less powerful and the theory had been modified: the king governed with the advice of the Houses of Parliament, Lords and Commons both. Whether Parliament had the power to depose a king who ignored its advice was as yet undetermined, that is, no-one was sure which of the two was sovereign, but one thing was clear; a king governing without Parliament could raise no taxes.

The king had his own sources of income, specifically he had his estates and the customary duties on imports and exports (hence "customs"). These brought in just about enough cash to keep the machinery of government turning. In 1629 King Charles I, who believed that sovereignty and the sovereign were synonymous and who was greatly irked by the way Parliament gave him advice whether he asked for it or not, decided to go it alone: he dismissed both Houses and began running the country himself.

Ten years later Charles, who was foolish in several different ways, found himself in more trouble than he could cope with and willy-nilly he had to call a new Parliament. But he still would not agree to share power and the two sides finally came to open war. The king raised his standard at Nottingham: Parliament mobilized its legal arguments and the resources of the City of London (1642).

At first Parliament was handicapped by a feeling that it would not do to beat the king too badly, and two years of civil war passed with nothing much achieved by either side. This could not be allowed to go on and at the end of 1644 Parliament dismissed its generals, restructured its army and gave it new leaders. Thus was born the famous New Model Army with which Fairfax and Cromwell crushed the king's forces at Naseby in 1645. The king became a captive.

Unfortunately the king still would not give in: he and Parliament carried on the old arguments while the arbiter that the quarrel had raised, the New Model Army, watched with increasing impatience. Eventually Cromwell led the soldiers to power, expelling the MPs who favoured compromise and permitting only a rump of 90 or so members to continue sitting. Next year, 1649, he bullied a court of commission into putting the king on trial. Charles was duly found guilty and executed as 'a public enemy of the good people of this land'.

For the next nine years Cromwell ruled the country as Lord Protector. He kept the peace at home and made the name of England respected abroad but he proved just as unable to get on with Parliament as Charles ever had. And his increasingly arbitary and puritanical rule eventually made him unpopular with most levels of society. When he died in 1658 the country breathed more easily and within two years it had accepted a restoration of the monarchy in the person of Charles II.

Charles II was a success for several reasons. He had known the rootless life of the exile and had, as he put it, no mind to go on his travels again. Nor was he very interested in political questions: he liked the girls, the horses and the good life and was quite content to let his ministers quarrel with Parliament and, if they quarrelled too much, dismiss them. For he knew, as the country now knew, that it was Parliament that was sovereign.

	1640–1644	1645–1649	1650–1654	1655–1659	1660–1664
Politics & Military History	**1640** King Charles forced to call Parliament because of Scots invasion. Catalans and Portuguese rebel against Spanish rule. Japan formally adopts policy of seclusion. **1642** Civil War between King and Parliament: the king flees London and raises his standard at Nottingham. Mazarin succeeds Richelieu as chief minister of France. **1643** French beat Spaniards at Rocroi. **1644** Ming call on Manzhou for help against rebel General Li Zicheng. The Manzhou enter Beijing too late to save the Ming but in sufficient force to drive out Li Zicheng and establish their own dynasty, the Qing. Parliament begins to get the upper hand in the English Civil War when Cromwell beats Prince Rupert at Marston Moor.	**1645** Parliament's New Model Army crushes the king's forces at Naseby. Danes cede Gotland and lease Halland to Swedes. **1646** King Charles flees to the Scots. French take Courtrai. Swedes take Prague, the two together invade Bavaria. **1647** Scots sell Charles to Parliament for £400,000. Qing take Canton. **1648** Treaty of Westphalia brings the Thirty Years' War to an end, peace of Münster ends hostilities between Spanish and Dutch, but hostilities continue between France and Spain. Enghien, victor of Rocroi, defeats the Spanish again at Lens. Riot in Paris marks the beginning of the prolonged period of civil disorder known as the Fronde. **1649** Charles I executed, England declared a Commonwealth. Cromwell crushes the Irish rebels at Drogheda.	**1650** Charles II lands in Scotland: Cromwell defeats Scots at Dunbar. Cossacks build a fort on the upper Amur and come into conflict with the Qing. **1651** Cromwell defeats Charles II at Worcester; Charles flees to France. **1652** First Anglo-Dutch sea war opens with English victories. As Fronde paralyses French, Spaniards take Dunkirk. **1653** Cromwell emasculates Parliament, becomes Lord Protector of the Commonwealth. **1654** First Anglo-Dutch sea war ends with Dutch recognizing England's protectionist Navigation Acts. Queen Christina of Sweden abdicates.	**1655** Swedes beat the Poles and the Elector of Brandenburg. **1657** Elector of Brandenburg obtains the sovereignty of Prussia. **1658** French and English beat the Spanish at the Battle of the Dunes: English get Dunkirk. Aurangzeb defeats and deposes his father Akbar: becomes Emperor himself in 1659. Danes agree to relinquish all southern Sweden. **1659** France and Spain make peace on terms wholly in France's favour. Richard Cromwell abandons attempt to succeed his father (died 1658).	**1660** Charles II is accepted as King of England after promising an amnesty and a policy of religious toleration. **1661** Louis XIV takes over the government of France, dismissing Fouquet and replacing him with Colbert. Qing eliminate last Ming resistance. **1662** Charles II sells Dunkirk to Louis XIV. **1664** Second Anglo-Dutch naval war: see below for consequences in North America.
Religion & Learning	**1640** John Eliot's *Bay Psalm Book* North America's first printed book. **1643** Sir Thomas Browne *Religio Medici*.	**1648** Society of Friends founded by George Fox (term Quaker first used in 1650).	**1650** Gilles Ménage *Dictionnaire Étymologique*. **1651** Thomas Hobbes *Leviathan*. **1653** Jansenists declared heretical.	**1656** Pascal *Lettres Provinciales*. Jews readmitted to England.	**1662** Charles II charters the Royal Society. **1663** Colbert founds *Académie des Inscriptions et Belles Lettres*. **1664** Trappist Order of monks founded at La Trappe, Normandy.
Cities & Social Development	**1641** John Evelyn begins his diary. **1644** Swedish attempt to establish a copper-based currency ends when the copper price falls so low that a 10 daler coin weighs 20 lbs!	**1645** Qing force Chinese to wear the pigtail.	**1652** Foundation of Irkutsk.	**1658** First bank notes issued in the West, by the Stockholm Riksbank.	**1660** Samuel Pepys begins the Diary which he is to keep for the rest of the decade.
Discovery & Invention	**1641** Dutch take Malacca from the Portuguese. **1642** Tasman discovers Tasmania and New Zealand. Toricelli invents the barometer; Ludwig von Siegen invents the mezzotint. **1644** René Descartes *Principiae Philosophicae* develops vortex theory of the universe. Tasman explores north and west coasts of Australia. Dutch settle Mauritius.	**1647** First atlas of the moon in Hevelius *Selenographia*. **1648** Possibility of a land bridge between Asia and America excluded by Cossack explorer Dezhnev who sails through the Bering Strait. Arabs recapture Muscat from the Portuguese. = First practical thermometers made under the direction of Duke Ferdinand II of Tuscany.	**1650** Otto van Guericke invents the air pump. The famous experiment in which teams of horses fail to pull apart an evacuated globe formed of two separate hemispheres took place in 1654. **1651** English occupy St Helena. **1652** Dutch occupy Cape of Good Hope.	**1655** English capture Jamaica, Dutch annex New Sweden. **1656(–58)** Dutch displace Portuguese in Sri Lanka. **1658** C. Huygens shows that attaching a pendulum to a clock improves its accuracy by a factor of 10. **1658** Glauber prepares sodium sulphate.	**1661** Malpighi observes capillaries in the lungs of a frog establishing the anatomical link between arteries and veins called for by Harvey's theory. Guo Xingye ('Coxinga') drives Dutch from Taiwan. Robert Boyle *The Sceptical Chemist* pours scorn on Aristotle's 'elements' and Paracelsus' 'principles'. **1664** English annex New Netherland: New Amsterdam renamed New York, Fort Orange renamed Albany. = Invention of the bayonet (at Bayonne).
The Arts	**1641** Claude Lorrain *Embarkation of St Ursula* (London). **1642** Rembrandt *The Night Watch* (Amsterdam) Monteverdi *The Coronation of Poppea*. Mansart *Maisons-Lafitte* the classic French chateau. English theatres closed by order of Parliament. **1644** Claude Lorrain begins his *liber veritatis*. The Globe is pulled down.	**1645** Waller *Poems*. **1648** Poussin *Holy Family* (Washington). **1648** Cyrano de Bergerac *Histoire Comique des Etats de le Livre*. **1649** Lovelace *Lucasta*. = Georges de la Tour *Christ and St Joseph* (Louvre).	**1653** Lully composes music for *La Nuit* masque in which the role of *le roi soleil* is taken by the young Louis XIV. Tomb of Childeric I, father of Clovis discovered at Tournai. Izaak Walton *The Compleat Angler*. Borromini designs facade of Santa Agnese, Piazza Navona, Rome. Thomas Middleton *The Changeling*.	**1656** Velasquez *Las Meninas* (the Maids of Honour) Prado. **1656** Le Notre begins laying out the gardens of Vaux-le-Vicomte (finished 1661). **1656–7** Pietro da Cortona *S. Maria della Pace*. **1657** Bernini begins work on the double colonnade round the piazza of St Peters (finished 1670). **1658** Molière founds the *Theatre du Petit-Bourbon* of which the Comedie-Francaise is said to be a descendant.	**1660** London theatres reopen, this time using female actresses (previously female parts had been played by boys). **1662** Jan Vermeer *View of Delft* (The Hague). Louis XIV begins building at Versailles, takes over the Gobelins Tapestry Works. **1664** Wren *Sheldonian Theatre*, first architectural essay by the Oxford Professor of Astronomy. Sir George Etherege *The Comical Revenge* the prototype restoration comedy.

THE ENLIGHTENMENT

AD 1665 - AD 1774

During the Medieval and Early Modern periods man had been ruled by God and Brute Force. With the Enlightenment these two had to make room for a newcomer, Reason. They were far from being elbowed aside – this was not, though it is often called so, the Age of Reason – but it was an age in which Reason could make its voice heard.

The change in style is evident in many ways. One is a decline in superstition. Witch-hunting gradually died out; medicine became more coherent and less magical. In the Middle Ages it had been widely believed that skin diseases could be healed by a king's touch: it is characteristic of the new attitudes that when asked to perform this function King William III said to the lady in question 'May God give you better health, and more sense'. By the end of the period touching for the 'King's Evil' had ceased entirely.

A lot of this sounds more like reasonableness than Reason and it is true that moderation was adopted as a principle by many of the most typical figures of the Enlightenment. But the respect accorded to Reason was genuine enough. The confidence that was such a feature of the era was rooted in the success of its Natural Philosophers, the men who showed that a combination of careful thought and practical experiment could unlock the secrets of the physical world. In the arts one might still argue for the superiority of Antiquity: in the sciences there could be no doubt that the Moderns had totally eclipsed the Ancients. If the age had a single hero it was Isaac Newton.

NEWTON

In 1665 the plague struck England for the last time. Its toll was heaviest in London but some county towns were hit proportionately just as badly, among them Cambridge, where 1200 people died out of a population of 4000. The university closed its doors and did not open them again for two years.

Among the refugees from Cambridge was Isaac Newton, a young scholar of Trinity College who spent his enforced vacation on the family farm at Woolsthorpe, in neighbouring Lincolnshire. His head was abuzz with ideas, for he had just discovered the delights of mathematics as displayed in the work of the leading practitioner of the day, René Descartes. But the more he thought about Descartes' model of the world, the more Newton came to the conclusion that, for all its cleverness, it could not be right. The cosmic vortices which Descartes suggested could be responsible for the motions of the planets were fine as an image but unquantifiable as a mechanism. And surely white light was not the pristine and homogeneous element Descartes believed it to be: if it were, it was going to be extremely difficult to construct any workable theory of colour.

This was the point where Newton the scientist took over. As many others had done before, he used a glass prism to break a beam of sunlight into a spectrum. According to contemporary theory the different colours were produced by the differential weakening of the white light as it passed through the glass: the rays that took the short path through the top of the prism were merely reduced from white to red (a strong colour), those that passed nearer to the base were further weakened to blue, indigo and violet (faint colours, getting progressively closer to black). Newton could not agree. He noted that the spectrum was not circular like the incident beam of sunlight but spread out into an ovoid. It looked as if the blue rays were being bent (refracted) more than the red, an observation he made sure of by projecting the image the length of the room. Then, using a second prism, he performed his *experimentum crucis*: taking the red rays through a path no different from the first he demonstrated that this did not change them in any way: red remained red of the same strength and, for that matter, blue remained blue. The prism, it was clear, was analysing a heterogeneous beam into its component parts, not, as had previously been thought, modifying a homogeneous beam to a varying extent.

Newton at the age of 46. Portrait by Sir Godfrey Kneller, 1689.

Newton made absolutely sure he was right about this by half a dozen further experiments of which the clincher was the use of the second prism to turn the spectrum back into white light. He also showed how his theory could account for the appearance of colour in solid objects by selective reflection. But clearing up this age-old mystery was only one of the achievements of his 18-month stay at Woolsthorpe. In a staggering outburst of creativity, he gave mathematics its most powerful tool yet, the calculus, without which most of the subsequent progress in modern science would have been impossible, and replaced Descartes' model of the universe with a new theory of gravitational attraction which he checked out not just qualitatively but quantitatively.

Curiously, Newton made no move to publish anything on any of these topics when he returned to Cambridge. His mathematical genius, though, was quickly recognized and at the age of 27 he was appointed Professor. In this role he gave a series of lectures on his experiments with colour: more to the point as far as his contemporaries were concerned, he also built a telescope which, because it used a mirror as its light-collecting source, did not suffer from the coloured fringes that blurred the image in conventional instruments. News of the telescope reached the Royal Society in London which was so impressed by the originality of the design that it elected Newton to membership on the spot. But a few rowdy meetings and some vexatious correspondence convinced Newton that open advocacy of his ideas was not for him: he promptly retired into isolation again.

For the next ten years Newton lived the life of a recluse. Already famous despite the fact that only an unrepresentative fraction of his work had been published, he rebuffed the advances of the greatest names of the day when they wrote to him soliciting his opinions. He refused to see visitors: he rarely spoke to the other fellows of his college. His hours were eccentric and long and spent almost exclusively in his study pursuing experiments and writing voluminously. Was this another burst of creativity like the plague years at Woolsthorpe? Alas no, it was an aberration. Newton had taken up alchemy, that blend of chemistry, cosmology and theology which not even the greatest scientific talent of the age could reduce to useful order. Not till 1680–81 did the heavens come to the rescue of the man who had discovered, and then hidden, the key to their workings.

The re-awakening of Newton's scientific genius started with the appearance of the comet of November 1680. After a spectacular display it vanished into the sun within the month. Two weeks later another, even larger and more splendid comet appeared travelling in the opposite direction. Newton built a telescope and followed it to its final disappearance the following March. He also brought himself to reply to a letter from Flamsteed, the Astronomer Royal, who thought the two comets were really one, which had reversed direction somewhere in the vicinity of the sun. Newton was dubious and was just about to let the matter drop when a third comet appeared, the comet of 1682. This time it was another astronomer, Edmond Halley, who spurred Newton's interest. In 1684 Halley received a draft of a 9-page paper on celestial mechanics which Newton was prepared to see published. A year later this had been expanded into a 90-page book and a year after that, the Royal Society was undertaking to print a full three-book version of Newton's analysis of the universe, the work known to posterity as the *Principia*. A hundred years after its publication, the great French scientist Pierre Simon de Laplace wrote: 'The *Principia* is pre-eminent above any other production of human genius.'

The *Principia* used the concept of gravity to explain the motions of the sun and the moon, and the planets and their satellites. The comets that had brought Newton back to useful work again provided an eccentric confirmation of his rules: the tides were another example of the heavens moving the Earth. The physical world, which had been accepted as a mystery too great for man's imaginings, turned out to be a mechanism that could be understood, quantified and predicted. Others had thought that it might be so, but had never glimpsed more than a few uncertain outlines. Now Newton presented the world with a complete architecture. It was a design that was to stand essentially unaltered for the next 200 years.

In 1696 Newton left Cambridge for London where he was gradually transformed into a national monument: Master of the Mint, President of the Royal Society, consulted by the government, knighted by the Queen. When he died his pall was borne to the Abbey by two Dukes, three Earls and the Lord Chancellor. His epitaph by Pope amounted to something near deification:

> Nature and Nature's Laws lay hid in night:
> God said, *Let Newton be!* and all was light.

This is trumpeting too loud. Newton was a man of his age and much of his life was lived within customary limits. As Master of the Mint he had no scruples about sending coiners to the gallows; as a theologian he was as pedantic as any 17th century divine. His concentration on his work made him insensitive to the arts (he described poetry as "ingenious nonsense" and the classical sculptures collected by the Earl of Pembroke as "stone dolls"): less easy to excuse is the bitterness with which he pursued real or fancied enemies in scientific controversy. Yet the quality of greatness is in his life as well as his work. Who else but Newton could have said, as he did in his old age,

> I do not know what I may seem to the world, but, as to myself, I seem to have been only like a boy playing on the sea shore, and diverting myself in now and then finding a smoother pebble or a prettier shell than ordinary, whilst the great ocean of truth lay all undiscovered before me.

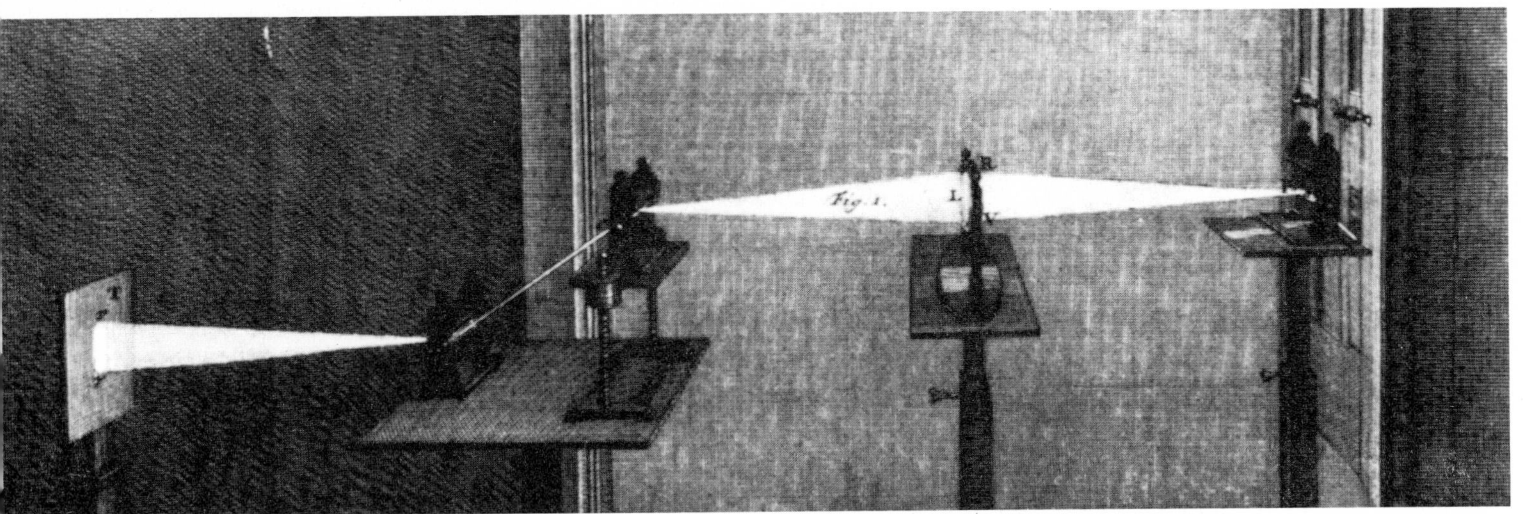

One of Newton's optical experiments: the decomposition, recomposition and second decomposition of white light. The light enters through the shutters on the right, is split into a spectrum by the first prism and is then focused onto a second prism from which it emerges as a thin ray of pure white light. This is passed through a third prism which splits it up into a spectrum again. From W J's Gravenande, Physices Elementa Mathematica Experimentis Confirmato, *Leyden (1742), table cxviii.*

	1665	1666	1667	1668	1669
Politics & Military History	British and Portuguese defeat the Spanish at Montes Claros and Villa Viciosa securing Portuguese independence. Colbert appointed Controller-General in France: founds French company with monopoly of African trade.	Anglo-Dutch War continues: De Ruyter defeats Monk in Battle of Downs; later Monk destroys the Dutch fleet in Terschelling Roads. France declares war on England in support of the Dutch. Puritans from Connecticut settle in Newark, New Jersey. Louis XIV issues edict weakening Huguenots.	End of 13 year war (Truce of Andrusovo) between Russia and Poland: Kiev ceded to Russia. Peace of Breda ends 2nd Anglo-Dutch War. Colbert increases tariffs in commercial war with Dutch: increases tensions with England.	English and Dutch sign Treaty of the Hague – leads to Triple Alliance between England, United Provinces and Sweden to protect Spanish monarchy against France. Treaty of Lisbon: Spain recognizes independence of Portugal. British East India Company obtains control of Bombay from Charles II.	Venetians lose Crete to the Turks: this is end of their colonial empire. Aurungzeb bans the Hindu religion in India and orders the destruction of all non-Islamic temples and schools: his religious intolerance hastens end of Moghul Empire (1707). Colbert is made Secretary of the French Navy. James, Duke of York, admits his conversion to Rome.
Religion & Learning	5-mile Act restricts Non-Conformist Ministers in Britain.	Publication of the first Armenian Bible. Great Schism in Russian Church.	John Locke *Essay concerning Toleration.* Leibniz *Nova methodus discendique juris.*	Sir Josiah Child *Brief Observations concerning Trade and the interest of Money.*	Protestant worship is further restricted in France.
Cities & Social Development	The Great Plague of London (July–October) kills over 60,000.	Great Fire of London (February 2–9) destroys much of the old city.	French army uses hand grenades. 6500 candle-lanterns are used in the Paris streets.	The first French trading station is set up in India. Bank of Sweden is founded.	Cholera epidemic in China.
Discovery & Invention	Isaac Newton experiments on gravitation and invents differential calculus. In *Physico-mathesis de lumine* (posthum.) Francis Grimaldi explains diffraction of light. Robert Hooke *Micrographia,* discovers with microscope that plants need to breathe and finds living cells in plants.	Newton measures the moon's orbit, and develops theory of colours, separating them with prism. Foundation of the Académie Royal des Sciences, Paris.	Hooke proposes systematic weather reading: the beginnings of meteorology. National Observatory in Paris.	Newton constructs a highly efficient reflecting telescope using mirror. Hevelius *Cometographia*: systematic record of all known comets.	Hennig Brand of Hamburg isolates phosphorus. Nicholaus Steno gives the first accurate exposition of fossil origins.
The Arts		Molière *Le Misanthrope* and *Le Médecin malgré lui.* Stradivari labels his first violin.	Racine *Andromaque.* Milton *Paradise Lost.* Rembrandt *Family Group.*	La Fontaine *Fables.* Molière *L'Avare.*	Racine *Britannicus.*

In a geographical sense the revolt of the Netherlands against Spanish rule ended in a draw: Spain kept its grip on the southern half (modern Belgium), the Dutch Republic was confined to the area north of the Rhine. The result was nonetheless a defeat for Spain, which had made the reconquest of the northern provinces its main aim for the better part of a century, and a victory for the Dutch Republic, which not only established its political and religious liberty, but emerged from the struggle with many of the trappings of a major power. Though short on numbers (less than 2 million inhabitants as against France's 20 and Britain's 9) it was rich in human resources: it had the most urbanized, best educated and most economically sophisticated population in Europe. It also had the highest standard of living.

The roots of this situation go back a long way. Under the dukes of Burgundy in the 15th century the Netherlands had been the craft centre for northern Europe and there was a long-standing tradition of independence among its many townsfolk. No wonder the region had proved a fertile field for the Reformed Faith. The effect of the war with Spain was to drive this independent spirit from the south, which had been the dominant element in the Burgundian Netherlands, to the north, of promoting the growth of Amsterdam, Leiden, Haarlem and Rotterdam at the expense of Antwerp, Ghent, Bruges and Tournai. The south was absorbed into the European order: its one glory, the painter Peter Paul Rubens, was an exponent of the international High Baroque: the north went its own way, confident in its bourgeois values and the solid success that they had brought.

In art this confidence expressed itself in the creation of a new style of painting which can be best described as Naturalism. The Dutch were the first people to produce pictures that could be taken for colour photographs, to use the arts of colour and perspective to create, not the imaginary world of the Baroque or Classical ideals, but faithful renderings of familiar scenes. The impulse to do so clearly relates to the north European Protestant ethic in general – it was after all Cromwell who made one of the clearest statements of the new aesthetic when he told Lely to paint him 'warts and all' – but the Netherlanders, with their traditional respect for craft values, took the style to its logical conclusion. Nor can anyone who has stood in front of Jan Vermeer's *View of Delft* have any doubt about the

Family Group in a Landscape *by Frans Hals. Hals' style of painting differed significantly from Rembrandt's, his most famous contemporary. Where Rembrandt used care and realism, Hals favoured speed and optimism. Nevertheless his technical ability and sureness of touch as an artist are beyond question. Painted in the late 1640s, now in the National Gallery, London.*

1670	1671	1672	1673	1674	
Secret Treaty of Dover between Charles II and Louis XIV, the French King supplying Charles with funds to fight the Dutch and restore Catholicism in England. France occupies Lorraine. Rebellion of Ukrainian Cossacks and peasants subject to Poland is crushed by Jan Sobieski. William of Orange is made Captain-General of the United Provinces.	Turks declare war on Poland for coming to the aid of the Cossacks. Charles II appoints Sir Henry Morgan, the former buccaneer, as deputy-governor of Jamaica. Spain and United Provinces ally against France but Louis XIV secures the neutrality of the Empire.	Outbreak of the third Anglo-Dutch War (to 1674). France declares war on Dutch – French forces cross the Rhine: the Dutch open the sluices to save Amsterdam. William III (of Orange) becomes hereditary *stadholder* of Netherlands. Turks and Cossacks invade Poland and the Poles surrender Podolia and Ukraine. Holy Roman Empire and Brandenburg join the Dutch in war against France.	New alliance is formed against France by Emperor Leopold, Lorraine, Spain and the United Provinces. Louis XIV moves towards absolutism by removing from the parliament the 'droit de remonstrance' so as to weaken the nobility. Poles defeat Turks at battle of Khorzim. Dutch fleet defeats French and English fleets.	Holy Roman Empire goes to war with France in defence of the Dutch. Treaty of Westminster ends the Third Anglo-Dutch War. Jan Sobieski is elected King of Poland. Sivaji Bhonsla makes himself independent of the Moghul Emperor Aurungzeb and founds the Mahratta state.	Politics & Military History
Posthumous publication of Pascal's *Pensées*.	First edition of the Bible in Arabic is printed in Rome.	Newton is made Fellow of the Royal Society.		With *L'Art Poétique* Boileau establishes literary principles of French classicism.	Religion & Learning
The founding of the Hudson Bay Company to trade in North America the basis of a huge fur trading empire, later to be part of Canada.	Founding of the French Senegal Company signals the beginning of France's West African empire. Royal Exchange, London, is built by Edward Jerman.	Baltic trade is thrown open to English merchants: end of the monopoly of the Eastland Trading Co. which dated back to Henry IV.	The last of England's Navigation Laws to restrict trade with the colonies to English and colonial ships.	Tobacco is made a state monopoly in France. French plantations in New France (Quebec) become Royal colonies.	Cities & Social Development
Borelli describes the symptoms of diabetes for the first time. First minute hands are put on watches.	Leibniz defines existence and the nature of ether. Malpighi *Anatome Plantarum*, a study of plant tissues.	Cassini estimates the distance of the sun at 87 million mi (139 million km) from the earth; it is actually 92,960,000 mi (149 million km) from the Earth.	The French explorers, Jacques Marquette and Louis Joliet, reach headwaters of the Mississippi River and descend to Arkansas.	Boyle establishes that metals increase in weight when oxidized.	Discovery & Invention
Dryden is appointed historiographer royal and poet laureate.	L'Opéra is founded in Paris. Milton *Samson Agonistes*. Wren, redesigning London, begins The Monument (completed 1677) to commemorate the Great Fire.	Kao Ts'en *Autumn landscape*. First public concert for which people paid for admission held at an inn at Whitefriars in London.		Theatre Royal, Drury Lane, is rebuilt after the Fire. Murillo *St Francis*. Lully *Alceste* (opera). Wycherley *The Plain Dealer*.	The Arts

riumphant success of the Dutch approach to art in this, heir golden century.

Of the various subjects that Dutch artists favoured – and hey developed a whole new range of landscapes, seascapes nd domestic scenes – the one with the most obvious social elevance is the group portrait as pioneered by Frans Hals. Here are the solid citizens who formed the backbone of the epublic gathered together in formal garb as officers of the nilitia, of the guilds, of learned societies or charitable nstitutions. Rembrandt made his name with paintings of his sort and it is arguable that some of his achievements in he genre – for example, the Rijksmuseum's *Syndics of the Cloth Hall* – rank among the best of his works. From an historical point of view one of the most remarkable things bout this painting is the membership of the group: of the ive syndics two are Calvinists, two Catholics and one a Mennonite (a sort of non-violent Anabaptist). It is a noving tribute to the tolerance of Dutch society, a olerance all the more remarkable in that the state had its origins in one of the most bitterly contested of all the Wars of Religion.

Rembrandt's 'Night Watch', an example of the group portrait which was one of the most profitable commissions a Dutch artist could get. Rembrandt received 100 guilders each from the sixteen members of the Company of Captain Frans Banning Cocq (in the red sash) and Lieutenant Willem van Ruytenburch (in yellow).

Group portraits were normally carefully posed affairs with symmetrical compositions. Rembrandt made the 'Night Watch' a dramatic painting with his use of deep shadows and his irregular grouping of the figures.

Painted in 1638–42: now in the Rijksmuseum, Amsterdam.

	1675	1676	1677	1678	1679
Politics & Military History	Year of war in Europe. Battle of Fehrbellin: Frederick William, the Great Elector of Brandenburg, defeats Swedes. War between Sweden and Denmark. Turenne of France defeats Great Elector at Turkheim but is killed at Sassbach. French are routed at Saarbruck by Duke of Lorraine. American Indians attack settlers in New England.	Peace of Zuravno concludes the war between Poland and Turkey which receives the Polish Ukraine. Swedes defeat Danes at Battle of Lund. Sikh uprisings occur in India. Defeat of Indians in New England gives the settlers undisputed control of North American seaboard.	Battle of Cassel: the Duke of Orléans defeats the Dutch, the French capture Freiburg. Swedish fleet defeats the Danes at the Battle of Rostock. Charles XI of Sweden defeats Danes at Landstrom. Russia and Turkey go to war. William III of the Netherlands marries Mary, daughter of Duke of York, heir to English throne.	Treaty of Nijmegen ends war between France and Netherlands (and Spain). 'Popish Plot' in England: Titus Oates falsely alleges a Catholic plot against the King and wave of anti-Catholicism follows. Louis XIV reveals the 1676 secret treaty with Charles II: as a result public opinion forces Charles to enter alliance with the Dutch against France. War between Russia and Sweden.	Act of Habeas Corpus passed in England: no imprisonment without trial. Exclusion Crisis in England: Parliament's Bill to prevent the Roman Catholic Duke of York from succeeding his brother as King of England; Charles II dismisses Parliament. Peace of Nijmegen ends war between France and the Empire. Peace between Sweden and Brandenburg. New Hampshire separates from Massachusetts.
Religion & Learning	Spinoza completes his *Ethics*, begun in 1662.	Legal protection is given to observance of sabbath in England. Western trading with Amoy: the beginning of growing trade with China.	Bossuet begins his *Politique* on absolutism. John Houghton *England's Great Happiness*.	Bunyan *The Pilgrim's Progress* (part one).	Gilbert Burnet *History of the Reformation of the Church of England* (volume one). Ashmole founds the Ashmolean Museum at Oxford.
Cities & Social Development	Population of Paris reaches half a million: city becomes the acknowledged centre of European culture, taste and power.		Ice cream becomes a popular dessert in Paris.	First chrysanthemums arrive in Holland from Japan. Plague in Hungary.	Colbert orders that French merchants be examined in book-keeping and commercial law. Edict forbids duelling in France.
Discovery & Invention	Roemer measures the velocity of light. Leeuwenhoek, using microscopic observations, discovers protozoa (one-celled organism).	Halley catalogues the southern stars. Barlow invents a repeating clock.	Halley observes the transit of Venus. Leeuwenhoek observes spermatozoon in dogs and other animals.	The Italian mathematician, Giovanni Ceva, states geometrical theorem of the nature of concurrency. De la Salle explores the Great Lakes in North America (1679).	Louis Hannepin discovers the Niagara Falls.
The Arts	Wren rebuilds St Paul's Cathedral (completed 1710).	Wren starts work on Trinity College Library, Dublin (not completed until 1684). Godfrey Kneller *Mr Banks*.	Racine *Phèdre*. Lully *Isis* (opera).		Charles Lebrun begins the Hall of Mirrors at Versailles. Scarlatti's first opera *Gli Equivoci nell' amore*.

The Ottoman State was designed for war: all its energies were channelled into its army and if more than a few years passed without any fighting the army began to get restless. This was a sign no Ottoman ruler could ignore. Even if there was no political or strategic reason for it, war had to be declared on someone, somewhere. A town might be too far away to be held, but it could be plundered: a battle on a distant steppe might be barren, but if it kept the troops out of mischief it served its purpose.

It was in this spirit that the Grand Vizier Kara Mustafa drew up the plan of campaign for 1683. The army would assemble on the European side of the Bosporus. The Austrian capital Vienna, one of the major towns of Europe, lay only 150 kilometres from the frontier: its sack would yield a satisfactory amount of plunder and confer appropriate prestige on the government of Kara Mustafa.

If the Ottomans were perennially belligerent the identifying characteristic of the Austrian Habsburgs was perpetual insolvency. They never had the money to complete any of their projects and there was not the slightest hope of their raising an army capable of facing the Ottomans in the field. When Kara Mustafa moved against Vienna all they could do was place a garrison of 5000 men in the city and send an anguished appeal for help to every Christian prince they could think of. The Turkish army – at least 80,000 fighting men plus an equal number of auxiliaries – pitched its tents opposite the Habsburg palace.

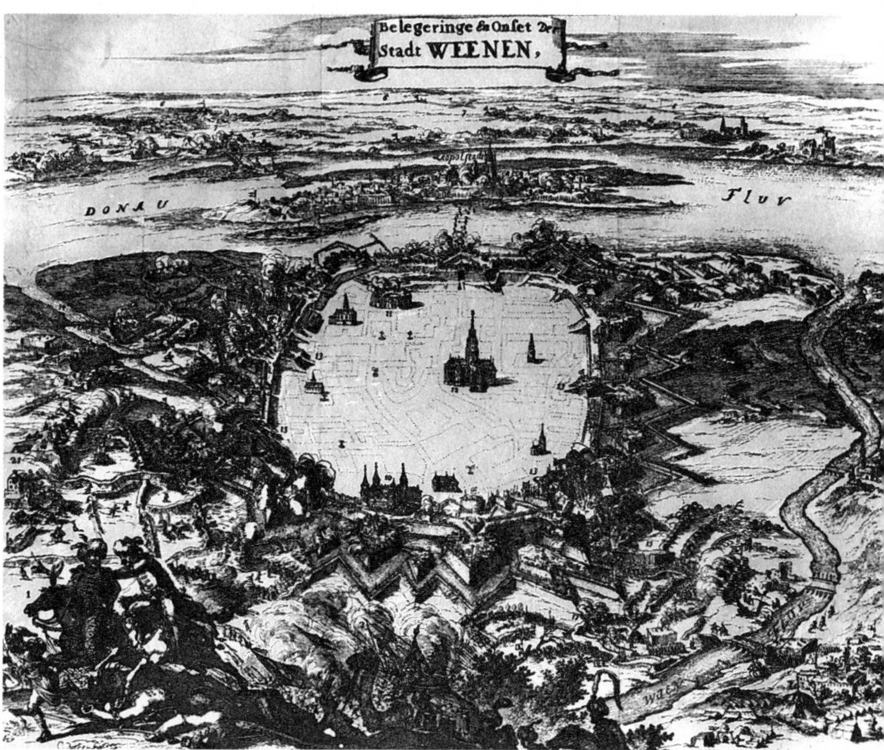

Siege warfare had changed a great deal in the two centuries since the walls of Constantinople had been breached by Sultan Muhammad's guns. Cities had learned to put their trust not in walls but in walled ditches – wide ones, cunningly laced with bastions that could pour out a withering crossfire on any attacker. Kara Mustafa's task was to gain control of a section of Vienna's walled ditch. Once this was done, it was relatively easy to make a breach in the inner face of the ditch, which in the new scheme of things corresponded to the city wall proper. Guns or mines

1680	1681	1682	1683	1684	
Charles XI makes the monarchy absolute in Sweden. Charles II rejects petitions calling for a new Parliament: the petitioners become known as the Whigs and supporters of the King as Tories. French empire in North America is organized from Quebec to the mouth of the Mississippi. Buccaneers in Caribbean cross the Isthmus of Darien to sack Panama. Dutch consolidate their East Indian Empire (Indonesia).	Charles II rejects another Exclusion Bill and dissolves Parliament as the Commons withhold supplies. Tsar Feodor of Russia reduces prestige of Boyars and institutes century long struggle with the nobility. Akbar in rebellion against his father, the Moghul Emperor Aurungzeb, flees to the Deccan which Aurungzeb then conquers. By Treaty of Radzin Russia gains most of Ukraine from Turkey.	The Empire and Spain enter into a Defensive League against France. La Salle claims the Louisiana Territory for France and takes possession of the Mississippi Valley. Following the granting of the Charter of Pennsylvania in 1681 William Penn arrives in the colony and Philadelphia is laid out.	Turks besige Vienna, their farthest push into Europe, before the city is relieved by German and Polish forces. Death of Colbert in France brings to an end the period of sound finances: the court is to become increasingly extravagant. Manchus conquer Formosa. William Penn concludes treaty with the Indians which keeps colony of Pennsylvania free of Indian wars.	Holy League is formed by Pope Innocent XI, consisting of the Empire, Poland and Venice against Turkey. The Bermudas become a Crown Colony. Huguenots revolt in Cevennes and the Great Elector offers French Huguenots refuge in Brandenburg. France invades the Spanish Netherlands.	Politics & Military History
Rechelet *Dictionnaire Français*. Sir William Temple *An Essay on Government*.	James Dalrymple *Institutes of the Law of Scotland*. Academy of Sciences is established in Moscow.	58,000 French Huguenots are forced to convert to Catholicism. Universities are established at Brest and Toulon.	William Penn *A General Description of Pennsylvania*. Sir William Petty *The Growth of the City of London*.	Pepys is made President of the Royal Society. Nearly 600 Huguenot churches are closed in France.	Religion & Learning
Penny post is established in London. Beginnings of fire insurance.	First cheques are used in England. First (oil) street lamps are used in London.	Versailles becomes the official royal residence of the King of France. A weaving mill with 100 looms is established in Amsterdam.	Dutch traders are admitted to Canton. First German immigrants arrive in North America. Wild boars become extinct in Britain.	Dutch establish control over the island of Java.	Cities & Social Development
Dodo in Mauritius becomes extinct through over-hunting. Hunckwitz produces first phosphorus matches.	In North America La Salle explores the Mississippi from south to north.	Halley observes the comet which bears his name. The 'Machine of Marly', a great water wheel to supply fountains, is one of the wonders of Versailles.	Newton explains his mathematical theory on tides under gravitational attraction of the sun, moon and earth.	Hooke invents the heliograph. Kampfer, the German explorer, travels to the Persian Gulf, Java and Japan.	Discovery & Invention
Emperor K'ang-Hsi founds factories in China for the development of art industries.	Paris Opera employs professional women dancers for the first time.	**1682** Aphra Behn, the first English woman professional writer, writes *False Count*.	Charles Lebrun is made director of the Académie Royale. Henry Purcell is made court composer to Charles II.	Part two of *Pilgrim's Progress* by John Bunyan is published. Takemoto Gidayu begins puppet theatre in Tokyo.	The Arts

Left: Vienna under siege by the Turks. Contemporary engraving by C. Decker.
The bastions which were the essential element in the city's defence are clearly visible as pointed projections from the inner wall. In between each pair is a ravelin, a small triangular structure rising out of the floor of the dry moat: its function was to give extra fire support to the troops manning the 'covered way' – the zigzag trace that marks the outer limit of the city's fortifications.

The Turks chose to attack the sector in front of the palace (the building marked 10) because the ground there was dry and easy to trench. By the time the siege was over the covered way in this area was no longer to be seen: it had been replaced by a mesh of Turkish trenches. The palace bastion and its neighbour to the left had lost most of their brick casing and were beginning to slump into the ditch. The ravelin in between the two had been reduced to a mound of rubble.

could do the job in a couple of days.

Kara Mustafa had a plan of Vienna's defences and had already picked out the sector in front of the palace as the one to attack. He ordered his sappers to run a zig-zag set of trenches up to the outer lip of the ditch (known for self-explanatory reasons as the covered way) so that his assault teams could jump the defenders and drive them first from the covered way, then from the detached bastion (the 'ravelin') that provided fire support for it, and finally from the two major bastions – the Lobl bastion on the left and the palace bastion on the right – that enfiladed the ditch. This done, the city was as good as his.

It only took Kara Mustafa's men a couple of days to get their trenches up to the covered way, but the fight for possession of this line proved much tougher than expected. Once they saw the Turks had committed themselves to this sector, the Austrians brought every available man and gun to bear on it. The Turks, despite their proverbial bravery, found themselves unable to carry the last few yards. Eventually they won by tunnelling their way forward and setting off mines big enough to blow the covered way into the ditch: then they used the same technique to wreck the ravelin and the outer faces of the Lobl and palace bastions.

This was slow work and the siege was in its fifth week before the Turks had a firm footing in the ditch. And it proved not firm enough. The Austrian commander, Starhemberg, put every man he could find into a counter-attack that swept the Turks out of their gains. But then they were back and this time they held on to every metre they gained. In the ninth week of the siege they finally succeeded in clearing the entire stretch of the ditch between the Lobl and palace bastions: work could at last begin on the mines that would bring down the inner wall. Starhemberg, with only 2000 men fit for duty, could not afford another sally. All he could do was barricade the streets behind the threatened sector and pray for relief. For a week now he had been firing distress signals: if the city was to be saved he needed an answering signal this very night.

Starhemberg got his signal, a rocket bursting over the hills to the west of the city. Better than that it became clear the next day that this rocket announced the beginning of a really serious attempt at relief. Somehow the Habsburgs had managed to beg or borrow an army.

The relieving force was in truth an extraordinary, one-off combination. If one man could take credit for it, it was the Pope whose mixture of exhortation and subsidy had worked wonders among the German princes. Better still: from beyond the imperial frontier came John Sobieski, King of Poland and one of the few men to have defeated an Ottoman army in the field. Altogether the allied force drawn up on the Wiener Wald comfortably outnumbered the wing of the Turkish army facing it.

This superiority became apparent when the allies launched their attack. Everywhere Turkish resistance proved weaker than expected and as the day wore on it became weaker still. The second round of attacks went in during the late afternoon, a full day ahead of schedule: they were rewarded by collapse all along the line. Kara Mustafa had come too far and stayed too long: now his weakened forces broke, fleeing eastward for the safety of the Hungarian frontier. The citizens of Vienna had the satisfaction of massacring the Turkish sappers as they emerged, blinking, from their mines: the Habsburgs were able to follow up the relief of their capital by taking the offensive in Hungary. They had not only averted disaster, they had gained a great victory.

	1685	1686	1687	1688	1689
Politics & Military History	Revolts in Britain on death of Charles II and accession of his Catholic brother, James II: the Duke of Monmouth's Rebellion is defeated at Sedgemoor, Monmouth executed and Judge Jeffreys carries out Bloody Assizes. James II appoints Catholics as army officers despite the Test Act which Parliament refuses to repeal; James prorogues Parliament.	League of Augsburg is formed between Empire, Spain, Sweden, Saxony, Bavaria and the Palatinate against France. Charles, Duke of Lorraine, takes Buda from the Turks who have held it for 145 years. French annex Madagascar. James II claims the power to dispense with Parliamentary laws.	James II issues Declaration of Liberty of Conscience to extend toleration to all religions. Battle of Mohacs: Turks are defeated and the throne of Hungary becomes the hereditary possession of the Habsburgs. Venetians capture Corinth and Athens: the Parthenon is badly damaged by Venetian bombardment.	'Glorious Revolution': William III of Orange invited by English Lords to save England from Roman Catholicism; he accepts the invitation and lands at Torbay to enter London in December. James flees to France and a decade of conflict between Kings and Parliament comes to an end. France and the Empire at War: Louis XIV invades Palatinate to take Heidelberg.	Convention Parliament confirms the abdication of James II and issues the Bill of Rights; establishes a constitutional monarchy in Britain; bars Roman Catholics from the throne. James II lands in Ireland: siege of Londonderry. Massacre of French settlers at Lachine, Quebec. In India Aurungzeb defeats Sambhuji, leader of the Marathas.
Religion & Learning	Louis XIV revokes the Edict of Nantes (which had guaranteed the Huguenots freedom of worship); Protestant churches are closed and all religions except Roman Catholicism are banned in France and 50,000 Huguenot families leave France.	James II disregards Test Act and appoints Roman Catholics to public offices: a Roman Catholic is made Dean of Christ Church, Oxford. Leibniz *System Theologicum.*	Fénelon *Traité de l'éducation des filles.* Pufendorf *The relation of Religious liberty to civilian life.*	An age of religious intolerance: Louis XIV is excommunicated by the Pope as part of a power conflict between them. Bossuet *Histoires des variations des églises protestantes* is a polemic against Protestantism.	Locke *On Civil Government.*
Cities & Social Development	All Chinese ports are opened to foreign trade. First French settlers move into Texas. French Huguenots take up silk manufacture in Britain.	Maison St Cyr is founded by Louis XIV and Mme de Maintenon as convent school for daughters of poor gentlefolk.	East India Company transfers its headquarters from Surat to Bombay. Huguenots settle at the Cape of Good Hope.	London underwriters begin to meet regularly at Lloyd's coffee house.	William III establishes Devonport naval dockyard. The foundation of the English factory at Calcutta.
Discovery & Invention	Newton discovers gravitational attraction theory associated with inverse square law.	Halley draws the first meteorological map and explains trade winds, monsoons and sea saltiness.	In his *Philosophiae Naturalis Principia Mathematica* Newton expounds laws of motion and theory of gravitation: it is the basis for modern mathematics and dynamics and a major influence on the 18th Century Enlightenment.	Dampier explores Australia.	Baron de la Houtan, the French explorer, visits the Great Salt Lake, Utah.
The Arts	Fourth folio of Shakespeare's works.	*Shusse Kagekiyo*, puppet play by Chikamatsu Monzaemon, is performed in Tokyo.		Thomas Shadwell *The Squire of Alsatia.* Gardens at Versailles are completed.	Henry Purcell *Dido & Aeneas* (opera). Opera is introduced to Munich.

For most of the reign of Louis XIII the government of France was conducted by his First Minister, Cardinal Richelieu: during the minority of Louis XIV it was run by Richelieu's successor in this office, Cardinal Mazarin. Given that a king could hardly be expected to spend 12 hours a day on affairs of state, the prime ministerial system was accepted as an inevitable feature of contemporary monarchy. It came as a shock therefore when, on Cardinal Mazarin's death in 1661, Louis XIV announced that there would be no more First Ministers. 'And, who do I address myself to on matters of business?' asked an ambassador. 'Me' said Louis.

The explanation was not long in coming. The man tipped to succeed Mazarin, Nicholas Fouquet, Minister of Finance, had banked too openly on his promotion and been too flamboyant in his display of power: the king was determined on his destruction. But even when Fouquet had been arrested and disgraced, Louis did not relax: he continued to be, as he had said he would, his own First Minister. And for the rest of his long reign he worked the 12 hour day that the job called for.

No one can claim that Louis governed France well or deny that the period of his personal rule saw France's position in Europe weakened. What Louis did do was give the concept of monarchy the most imposing expression it has ever received. On this task he laboured with all the patience of a dedicated actor-manager. He built the theatre, wrote the script and led the cast in every performance.

Colbert, who succeeded Fouquet as Minister of Finance and was the most important of Louis' advisers in the early part of his reign, did his best to persuade his king to keep court in Paris. With 400,000 inhabitants, Paris was the biggest city in Europe: Colbert promised to make it the grandest. He even sent to Rome for Bernini who submitted designs for the Louvre in both Baroque and Classical styles. But Louis did not like Bernini's exuberance any more than he liked the Parisians' irreverence: he had already seen what he wanted and had a team to hand. The model was the chateau Fouquet had built in his heyday at Vaux-le-Vicomte: the team consisted of Le Vau, Le Brun and Le Nôtre, respectively architect, painter-decorator and landscape gardener of Fouquet's palatial domain. As for the site, Louis had picked Versailles 23 kilometres to the west

Late 17th century view of Versailles by Langlois after Perelle.

1690	1691	1692	1693	1694	
Battle of the Boyne in Ireland at which William III defeats James. Battle of Beachy Head: French defeat English and Dutch fleets. Spain joins Great Alliance against France. The Turks retake Belgrade in major counter-offensive against the Empire. Moghul conquests in India reach widest extent.	Austro-Turkish war continues: Turks are defeated at Zelankemen; Habsburgs conquer Transylvania which is brought under Vienna's control. Siege of Limerick ends: Treaty of Limerick brings an end to Irish Revolt. Massachusetts absorbs Plymouth Colony and receives a new charter.	Massacre of Glencoe: Campbells slaughter Macdonalds on pretext of disloyalty to William III. Battle of La Hogue: French fleet is destroyed by Anglo-Dutch fleet – ends French invasion threat to England. French capture Namur and defeat William III at Steinkirk. Spanish Crown declares bankruptcy.	Battle of Lagos: French defeat English merchant fleet. Carolina is divided into North and South. Beginning of the English national debt. African risings lead to the expulsion of the Portuguese from their East African holdings.	English fleet bombards Dieppe, Le Havre and Dunkirk; fleet saves Barcelona from French attack. Death of Queen Mary leaves William III as sole ruler of England and Scotland. Triennial Act provides for new Parliamentary elections every three years.	Politics & Military History
Locke *Essay Concerning Human Understanding*. Foundation of a mathematical academy at Bologna.	Christian Faith Society for West Indies is founded in London. First directory of addresses is published in Paris.	Edict of Toleration for Christians in China. William and Mary College is founded in Virginia. Salem witchcraft trials are held in New England.	Secret Society, Knights of the Apocalypse, is established in Italy to defend the Church against Antichrist.	First edition of the *Dictionnaire de l'Académie Française* is published.	Religion & Learning
Calico printing is introduced to England from France. *Worcester Postman*: the first weekly English provincial paper (the oldest in world in continuous production). Turnips begin to be cultivated in England.		Amman *Der redende Stumme*, a manual of language for deaf-mutes. Bank, later to be known as Coutts & Co, opens in London. Queen Mary II founds Greenwich Hospital for wounded soldiers and sailors.	Foundation of Kingston in Jamaica. East India Company obtains new Charter.	Founding of the Bank of England (with government support). Bribery scandal surrounds new East India Company Charter and Indian trade is thrown open to all English subjects.	Cities & Social Development
The French engineer Papin devises a pump with piston which is raised by steam.	John Clayton demonstrates the lighting-power of coal gas.		Wallis *Algebra*, uses Newton's notation of fluxions.		Discovery & Invention
Dryden *Amphitryon*. Hobbema *The Mill* (London).	Racine *Athalie*. Purcell *King Arthur* (opera), libretto by Dryden.	William Congreve *Incognita*, a novel.	La Fontaine *Fables* (volume III). Alessandro Scarlatti *Teodora* (opera). Purcell *The Faerie Queen*.	William Congreve *The Double Dealer*.	The Arts

Above: Portrait of Louis XIV by H. Rigaud.

Left: The Hall of Mirrors at Versailles.

of Paris where his father had built first a hunting lodge, then a small chateau.

Over the next 15 years Versailles was transformed. Le Brun loaded the interior of the palace with paintings and sculptures, tapestries and mirrors; Le Nôtre laid out gardens that stretched as far as the eye could see. Everyone agreed that Louis had created the perfect backdrop for his performance as Louis le Grand, le Roi Soleil.

Not so Louis. If Versailles was truly to be the capital of France it had to be big enough to house the whole court and the entire machinery of government. In 1678 Le Vau's successor, J. Hardouin-Mansart, was given a quarter of the French budget and told to complete the set as soon as was physically possible. The additions during the next 30 years were of staggering dimensions. Each of the two wings Hardouin-Mansart built was as big as Le Vau's original palace: the garden front was extended to fully two-thirds of a kilometre. The extras included a series of fountains powered by the most complex set of water-wheels ever built, plus a couple of normal-sized chateaux for Louis to get away to when the pressures of life at the top proved too much. When Louis got the final bill even he, who prided himself on his self-control, blenched and stuffed it into his pocket: to this day no one knows for certain what it all cost.

Louis wanted to make the monarchy the sole effective source of power and at the same time place it above criticism. There is no way of doing both, but Versailles represents the most serious attempt to do so, this side of oriental despotism. To play any part in the governmental process, or indeed in the arts or sciences, aspirants had to be prepared to make the pilgrimage to Versailles and join in the ceremonial minuet conducted by the Sun King. '*L'Etat c'est moi* (I am the state),' said Louis, and he meant it.

	1695	1696	1697	1698	1699
Politics & Military History	William III, serving with his army in Holland, retakes Namur. Russo-Turkish War: Peter the Great fails to take Azov and returns to Moscow. Capitation tax in France is the first universal direct tax.	Peter the Great takes Azov from the Turks; Russia conquers Kamchatka. Suspension of Habeas Corpus in England, new act regulates treason trials and improves the conditions for the accused. Treaty of Turin: between France and Savoy, gives France possession of Nice.	Treaty of Ryswick: ends European War between France, Spain, England and the Netherlands; France recognizes William III as King of England and the Protestant succession of Anne. Battle of Zenta: Eugène of Savoy defeats the Turks following their attack upon Transylvania. China conquers west Mongolia.	Question of the Spanish succession: England, France, the United Provinces and the Empire agree on Spanish succession and the partition of the Spanish Empire. Charles II of Spain makes his first will leaving his territories to the Infant Elector Prince of Bavaria.	Treaty of Karlowitz: Austria receives Hungary from Turkey, Venice gains Morea and much of Dalmatia, Poland receives Podolia and Turkish Ukraine. Death of Prince Elector of Bavaria reopens the question of the Spanish succession. Treaty of Preobrazhenskoe: Denmark, Russia, Poland and Saxony agree to partition Swedish Empire.
Religion & Learning	Foundation of University of Berlin. Leibniz *New System of Nature.* Academy of Sciences is established at Naples.	Nicolaus Antonio *Bibliotheca Hispana vetus*, a Spanish bibliography. Kunstakademie is established in Berlin. John Aubrey *Miscellanies.*	French mathematician Demoivre is elected Fellow of the Royal Society.	Society for Promoting Christian Knowledge is established in London to promote literary and scriptural knowledge in children.	Gilbert Burnet *Exposition of the 39 Articles.*
Cities & Social Development	Government press censorship in England is abolished. First public census is carried out in Habsburg Empire. Window tax is introduced in England.	Board of Trade and Plantations is set up in England. Peter the Great sends 50 young Russians to England, Holland and Venice to study shipbuilding and fortifications.	Sedan chair becomes a popular means of transport. Spitalfields Riots: these are against the imports of Indian silks; East India House is attacked.	Tax on beards is introduced in Russia. Mrs White's Chocolate House opens in London; it soon becomes the meeting place of Tories.	Pierre Lemoyne founds first European settlement in Louisiana. Peter the Great reforms Russian calendar.
Discovery & Invention	John Morley makes brown glaze stoneware at Nottingham.	English naturalist, John Ray, describes the aromatic herb peppermint.		Thomas Savery invents the first steam pump. Newton calculates the speed of sound.	Dampier explores the north coast of Australia.
The Arts	Nikolaus Heinsius *Den Vermakelijkten Avonturier*, Dutch picaresque novel.	Reuter *Schelmuffsky*, a German adventure novel. Sir John Vanbrugh *The Relapse.*	Dryden's verse translation of Virgil. Spanish destroy the remains of Mayan civilization in Yucatan.	Fénelon *Télémaque.*	Feuillet *Choréographie*, manual of dance notation.

When Louis XIV began his period of personal rule France's situation in Europe could hardly have been better. Most of her enemies had been laid low in the course of the Thirty Years' War and it was apparent that the most important, Habsburg Spain, was never going to recover. That put all the territories between the French frontier and the Rhine within Louis' grasp: all he had to do was bribe, threaten and dissemble and he could collect up the bits of Burgundy, Lorraine and Alsace that were not his already.

The opening phase of the advance went smoothly. French armies occupied Burgundy and Alsace; all protests were brushed aside. But that was the trouble, Louis could never bring himself to be subtle about his aggressions. Gradually the list of his enemies lengthened until it was long enough and strong enough to bring his armies to a halt.

With all Europe arrayed against him even Louis saw that he had to ease up, and the 17th century closed with France less far forward than had seemed likely twenty years earlier. However, in the opening year of the new century Louis was dealt a hand of cards that he just could not resist playing. The King of Spain was childless and though the European powers had agreed not to fight over his estate but divide it up peaceably, they forgot to get Spain's agreement to the distribution. In fact, the Spanish never liked the idea at all and, when the king finally did die, in November 1701, he was found to have left everything – Spain, Belgium, Italy and the Indies – to Philip Duke of Anjou, Louis XIV's grandson. It was an invitation to Louis to help himself to Belgium and he promptly did so.

The Grand Alliance that formed against Louis for the War of Spanish Succession was essentially the same as the one that had fought him to a halt before: the bones of it were the English, the Dutch and the Austrian Habsburgs. The

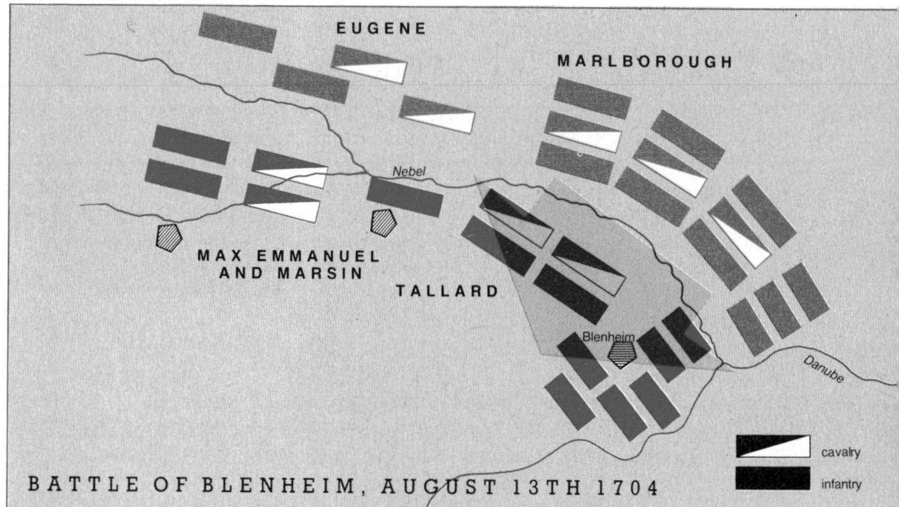

BATTLE OF BLENHEIM, AUGUST 13TH 1704

difference this time was that Louis already had what he wanted and only needed to fight defensively.

The war got off to a slow start with nothing much happening until the end of 1702 when Max Emmanuel of Bavaria, one of the most important of the German princes, suddenly declared for Louis. This opened the way for a French march on Vienna and the next year Marshal Villars fought his way forward to rendezvous with the Bavarians at Ulm. The threat to the Austrians – in continental terms the lynchpin of the Alliance – was so serious that the English Commander-in-Chief, the Duke of Marlborough, decided that he must march to the upper Danube and bring the French and Bavarians to battle. It was 1704 before

1700	1701	1702	1703	1704	
Charles II of Spain names Philip of Anjou, grandson of Louis XIV of France, as his heir (he is to reign as Philip V to 1746). Great Northern War breaks out as a result of Russo-Swedish rivalry for supremacy in the Baltic. Charles XII defeats the Russians at Narva.	War of the Spanish Succession begins (to 1713): a Grand Alliance formed by England, Netherlands, Austria and the German States against France. Act of Settlement establishes the Protestant Succession in England of House of Hanover. Charles XII of Sweden invades Poland and prevents Polish attack on Sweden's Baltic possessions.	Duke of Marlborough becomes Captain-General of the English armed forces: takes Liège. Charles XII takes Warsaw and Cracow. Combined French and Spanish fleet is routed at Vigo Bay.	Methuen Agreement: trade treaty between England and Portugal. Swedes defeat the Russians at Pultusk: capture Thorn. Marlborough takes Bonn. Delaware separates from Pennsylvania and becomes a colony. Hungarian revolt against Austria begins (continues to 1711).	Battle of Blenheim: Marlborough and Eugène defeat the French and Bavarians. British fleet captures Gibraltar from Spain. French and American Indians massacre inhabitants of Deerfield, Connecticut.	Politics & Military History
Leibniz founds the Berlin Royal Academy of Science and becomes its first President. Dominicans at the Sorbonne and the Papacy condemn the morality and religion of Confucius.	Yale College is founded in New Haven, Connecticut. Father Ximenes translates the sacred national book of the Quiche Indians of Guatemala (to 1721).	Cambridge begins to establish a number of Chairs for the sciences: anatomy, astronomy, botany, chemistry, geology, geometry, experimental philosophy (to 1750).	Lahontan introduces the idea of the 'noble savage' inspired by nature to lead a moral life – an important concept for the period of the Enlightenment.	University of Mantua is established. John Harris *Lexicon Technicum*, first alphabetical encyclopaedia.	Religion & Learning
Europe's population figures at the beginning of the Eighteenth Century: France 19m; England and Scotland 7½m; Habsburg Empire 7½m; Spain 6m. By 1700 there is a rapid and growing expansion of trade between Europe and its settlements.	Royal charters are granted to the weavers of Axminster and Wilton for making carpets. French establish a settlement at Detroit to control Illinois trade.	Asiento Guinea Co. founded to supply slaves to Spanish America. Queen Anne gives royal approval to horse racing, a habit followed by the British Royal Family ever since.	Peter the Great founds the city of St Petersburg. The first Russian newspaper *Moskovskya Vyedomosti*.	Beau Nash becomes Master of Ceremonies and leader of fashion at Bath. *Boston News-Letter*, the first newspaper in America. *Vossische Zeitung* is started in Berlin (to 1933).	Cities & Social Development
Earliest accurate metalworking lathes in use.	Jethro Tull, agricultural reformer, invents horse-drawn drill to plant seeds in rows.			Newton *Optics*: his theories of light and colour.	Discovery & Invention
Establishment of string orchestras. Horn begins to be used, perfected in France (French Horn).	The music publisher, Henry Playford, starts a series of weekly concerts in Oxford.	Ogota Korin, the Japanese painter, unites two imperial schools of Japanese painting. Earliest English pantomime is performed at Drury Lane and Haymarket Theatre is opened.	Chikamatsu Monzaemon (Japanese Shakespeare) *The Death of Sonezaki*. Richard Steele *The Lying Lover*.	Swift *The Battle of the Books* and *A Tale of a Tub*. J. S. Bach composes his first cantata *Dean du wirst meine Seele*. Handel *St John Passion*.	The Arts

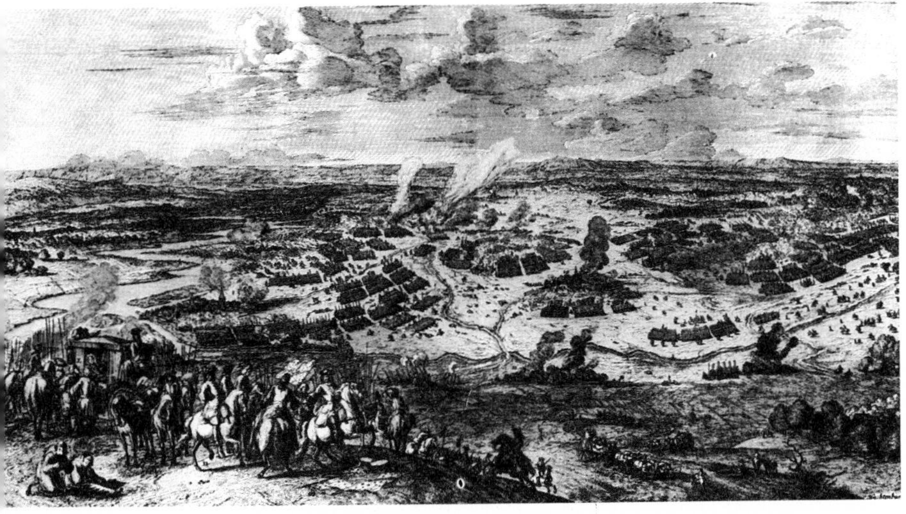

Engraving of the Battle of Blenheim by Ivan Huchtenberg. From left to right the Danube, the village of Blenheim, the English breakthrough in the centre and, on the far right, the continuing contest between the Austrian army under Prince Eugene and the Franco-Bavarian forces defending this sector.

Marlborough and his Austrian opposite number, Prince Eugène, were able to force the battle they wanted.

Considering that the English had hardly been seen on the continent since the days of Agincourt and the longbow, they came on with remarkable confidence. The Franco-Bavarian forces were drawn up in a strong defensive position, their right resting on the Danube and the village of Blenheim, their left on the foothills north of the river and their front protected by a small stream, the Nebel. Yet the British attacked as soon as they could get their troops formed up and they hit first and hardest at Blenheim, the strongest point in the whole French line. The lead British brigade pressed forward through a murderous French fire and reached the village but was there repulsed, losing a third of its men. Reinforced it came forward again only to be flung back a second time. The fury of the fighting drew in the French infantry reserve, seven battalions after the first assault, another 11 after the second. Seeing this, Marlborough called off a planned third attack.

Meanwhile another British thrust was building up in the centre. Here too the French fire extracted a heavy price from the advancing columns and even when they were over the Nebel the British faced an uphill struggle. But Marlborough knew his craft. The attack on Blenheim and the equally ferocious assaults by Prince Eugène on the Franco-Bavarian forces in his sector had fatally thinned the centre of the French army: there were only nine battalions left there to face Marlborough's 23. It had cost the English and Austrians 10,000 casualties to create this advantage: but now nothing could stop them.

Marlbrough spent the better part of an hour readying his men for the final attack, then he drew his sword and the long line surged forward. The French centre disintegrated. The English rounded on Blenheim and after a heroic defence the French laid down their arms. The final toll was 34,000 French killed, wounded or prisoners as against 13,000 British and Austrians.

Marlborough was to show the same mastery on other battlefields – his victory at Ramillies, which liberated Belgium, was just as deft and decisive as Blenheim. Nonetheless, few letters can have given him as much pleasure to write as the one he penned to Sarah his wife, that evening '. . . give my duty to the Queen and let her know that her army has had a glorious victory. Marshal Tallard and two other generals are in my coach.' Austria was saved, Bavaria conquered, the schemes of Louis XIV scotched.

	1705	1706	1707	1708	1709
Politics & Military History	Peter the Great's policy of westernization meets opposition: rebellion in Astrakhan. English navy takes Barcelona.	Charles XII defeats the Russians and Saxons at Fraustadt and forces the Saxons to abandon their alliance with Russia. Battle of Ramillies: Marlborough routs the French and conquers the Spanish Netherlands. Battle of Turin: Eugène defeats the French in Italy. Treaty of Altranstadt: Augustus II renounces the Polish throne in favour of Stanislas I.	Act of Union unites England and Scotland as Great Britain: the largest free trade area in Europe. Battle of Almanza: Allied forces are defeated by Spanish. Death of Moghul Emperor, Aurungzeb, sets off collapse of Empire. Sikh rising in Punjab.	Battle of Oudenarde: Marlborough and Eugène defeat the French. Charles XII of Sweden invades Russia. Following a Cossack uprising Peter the Great divides Russia into 8 government districts so as to centralize administration. British capture Minorca and Sardinia.	Battle of Malplaquet: Marlborough and Eugène defeat the French but the allies suffer 20,000 killed. Battle of Poltava: Russians defeat Charles XII of Sweden. Denmark, Russia and Saxony form a new coalition against Sweden.
Religion & Learning	Isaac Newton who did more than any other man to advance scientific knowledge during 17th Century is knighted.		Mapping of China begins (to continue to 1717).	Professorship of Poetry is established at Oxford. Semler founds the first German secondary school – for mechanical and mathematical subjects – at Halle.	Bishop Berkeley *Essay Towards a new Theory of Vision.*
Cities & Social Development		First modern insurance is issued in London. First evening paper *The Evening Post* is issued in London.	Last eruption of Mount Fujiyama in Japan. Billiards are introduced in Berlin coffee houses.	Canal is constructed to link the Volga and Neva rivers: it is part of Peter the Great's improvement of communications.	First Russian prisoners are sent to Siberia. Bad harvests throughout Europe: bread riots in Britain, famine in France. Magnolias are brought to Britain from Japan.
Discovery & Invention	Halley predicts the return in 1758 of the comet seen in 1682. Wheels now begin to replace tillers for steering ships.	The English inventor, Henry Mill, constructs carriage springs.	Sir John Floyer introduces the counting of pulse beats as a means of gauging health. Frenchman, Papin, invents high pressure boiler.	Well compares lightning with electric spark.	Abraham Darby (at Coalbrookdale) produces coke and uses it to smelt iron ore.
The Arts	Handel's first opera is performed in Hamburg. Vanbrugh begins to build Blenheim Palace for the Duke of Marlborough.	Farquhar *The Recruiting Officer.* Hardouin-Mansart completes the Hôtel des Invalides in Paris (commenced in 1675).	German organ builder, Silbermann, constructs his first organ at Frauenstein. Sir James Thornhill begins the Painted Hall at Greenwich.	First German theatre opens in Vienna.	Invention of the pianoforte: the Italian harpsichord maker Cristofori produces the first examples.

The weight of the atmosphere and the force it is capable of exerting are not things of which we are normally aware: they become apparent only when acting against a vacuum. Otto von Guericke, the inventor of the air pump, was the first person to make them obvious. In a series of dramatic experiments in the 1650s he showed that the atmosphere's weight was sufficient to crush copper vessels when the air was removed from them, and sufficient to press two thick-walled copper hemispheres together so firmly once the chamber they formed had been evacuated that two teams of horses, eight each side, could not pull them apart. But perhaps the most significant of his experiments was one in which 20 men – some accounts say 50 – tried to hold a piston against a partial vacuum. The pressure of the atmosphere drove the piston into the cylinder so hard that the men were pulled off their feet.

Von Guericke's experiments took place in a world which had few engines of any sort and none that was not powered by wind, water or the muscles of man or beast. Over the next 50 years several people saw the possibility of making a new sort of engine, one in which steam was used to create a vacuum and the pressure consequently exerted by the atmosphere used to do useful work – for example pumping. Mine owners were spending vast sums of money on pumping stations worked by teams of horses: they would be eager customers for an effective "atmospheric engine".

Among the mines worst affected by flooding were the tin mines of Cornwall in south west England. Their problems attracted the attention of a local ironmonger, Thomas Newcomen, who, in the opening years of the 18th century, constructed a prototype atmospheric engine consisting of a vertical piston alternately pushed up by steam and then driven back down again by the atmosphere when the steam

A Newcomen engine of 1747. The boiler (B) provides steam for the upright cylinder (C). The small tank (g) on the top floor of the engine house provides the cold water needed for injection into the cylinder. When the water is injected, the steam inside the cylinder condenses and the piston pulls the left end of the cross-beam down. The rise of the right-hand end works the pump attached to the linkage seen disappearing down the mine-shaft on the extreme right.

1710	1711	1712	1713	1714	
Whig ascendancy in Britain comes to an end: the Tories under Harley and St John (Bolingbroke) come to power. Russia conquers Swedish Baltic Provinces. French take control of Mauritius which had been part of Dutch Empire.	In war with Turkey, the Russians are defeated at the River Pruth. Peter the Great is forced to return Azov to the Turks and withdraw from Poland. Peter the Great proceeds with administrative reforms and establishes a Senate. Dean Swift's *The Conduct of the Allies* attacks Marlborough who is dismissed as C-in-C.	Peace of Szatmar: Emperor re-establishes his authority in Hungary and recognizes a Hungarian Constitution. Denmark seizes Bremen and Verden from Sweden. Disintegration of the Moghul Empire continues in India: war of succession is fought between Shah Bahadur's four sons: from 1712 to 1719 five puppet emperors rule at Delhi.	Pragmatic Sanction is issued by Emperor Charles VI to guarantee the successsion to his daughter Maria Theresa. Treaty of Utrecht: ends the War of Spanish Succession: France recognizes the Protestant succession in Britain and cedes Newfoundland, Nova Scotia and Hudson Bay claims to Britain; Britain gains Asiento contract to supply slaves to Spanish America and gains Gibraltar and Minorca.	On death of Queen Anne, George the Elector of Hanover becomes George I of Great Britain leading to a close British involvement in German affairs. Treaty of Rastatt and Baden between Austria and France. Battle of Storkyro leads to Russian domination of Finland. Tripoli becomes independent of Turkey.	Politics & Military History
Jansenist centre at Porte Royale is attacked and the nuns expelled: conflict between the Jansenists who emphasized inner regeneration and the Jesuits had long been sapping the strength of the Catholic Church.		Biblioteca National is established in Madrid; also the University of Madrid.	The Papal Bull *Unigentus* condemns the Jansenists: it is enforced by Louis XIV but leads to major Church-State conflict.	The Schism Act prevents Dissenters from being schoolmasters in England.	Religion & Learning
Meissen porcelain industry is established in Saxony. English South Sea Company is established.	Beginning of coffee production in the Dutch East Indies: by 1723 the harvest of coffee reached 6m kg.	Petersburg becomes the capital of Russia (until 1922). Last execution for witchcraft takes place in England. Slave revolts take place in New York.	By this year there are about 3000 coffee houses in London. Emigration to North America is stimulated in the Palatinate as a result of war devastation.	Last witchtrial is held in Russia; witchtrials are abolished in Prussia. East India Company wins trade concessions from the Moghul Court.	Cities & Social Development
Jakob le Blon, the German engraver, invents 3-colour printing. Chinese style hard-paste porcelain is made successfully for first time in England.	English inventor, Thomas Newcomen, constructs a successful steam engine for pumping water which remains in wide use for the next 60 years (until Watt).			Henry Mill patents a writing machine for the blind. Gabriel Fahrenheit, the German inventor, produces a mercury thermometer with temperature scale.	Discovery & Invention
Collected works of William Congreve are published. Completion of Wren's masterpiece, St Paul's Cathedral.		Twelve of Corelli's concerti grossi establish the concerto as a musical form. Handel comes to live in London: his operas *Teseo* and *Il Pastorfido.*	Watteau *L'Indifferent.* School of Dance is established at the Paris Opera. Major new buildings this year include: the Clarendon Building at Oxford and the Palais Belvedere for Prince Eugène in Vienna.	Handel *The Water Music.*	The Arts

A Boulton and Watt engine erected in 1777 for the Birmingham Canal Navigations at Smethwick. Watt made many improvements to the Newcomen engine but the first and most important was the addition of a separate condenser. This doubled the efficiency of the engine because it cut down the waste of heat caused by alternately heating and cooling the cylinder.

condensed. The condensation was initiated by admitting cold water to a jacket round the cylinder: the trouble was this process was so sluggish that the engine barely worked.

Several years of patient experimenting did little to improve the engine's performance: it remained too slow and too feeble to have any practical use. Then one memorable day the cold water in the jacket burst through a flaw in the cylinder, condensing the steam inside instantly and bringing the piston down with such force that it snapped its chain, smashed through the bottom of the cylinder and broke the boiler below. This was the sort of power Newcomen had been looking for. He rebuilt his engine so that a jet of water could be admitted to the cylinder when the upstroke was completed: the downstroke now came with satisfying force.

Progress after that was amazingly rapid. The first full scale engine seems to have been installed in 1710 at the Wheal Vor tin mine in Cornwall: it worked, but because of the high cost of coal at the minehead it proved to be uneconomic. The answer to this was obvious: set up the machine at a coal mine. In 1712 this was done and the Dudley Castle steam engine became the wonder of the south Staffordshire coal field. Burning low-cost slack it pumped away steadily at 12 strokes a minute raising 40 litres of water with every stroke. This was just the machine the mine owners needed and over the next 20 years more than a hundred of them were installed up and down the country: a dozen more were set up on the continent. By 1775 when Boulton and Watt came out with their improved design Britain had 600 Newcomen engines and by the end of the century, despite the greater efficiency of the Boulton-Watt machines, Newcomens still out-numbered them – by about 1500 to 500 on the best available estimates. On the coalfields for which they were so well-suited some of these venerable monsters remained in use until 1900.

Though in strict terminology an atmospheric engine, Newcomen's machine was referred to as a steam engine right from the start. This is not inappropriate for it pioneered the technology for all the later engines in which steam power did propel the pistons. What is surprising is that Newcomen never became a household name in the way that Watt did. Perhaps it is difficult for people to believe that coal, iron and steam – the bread, bones and breath of the Industrial Revolution – had been so effectively harnessed in the rural landscape of early Georgian England.

	1715	1716	1717	1718	1719
Politics & Military History	First Jacobite uprising in Scotland – 'The 15' in support of the Old Pretender, James Edward: the Jacobites are defeated at Sheriffmuir and Preston. Prussia and Sweden go to war: a third coalition is formed against Sweden. First Parliament of George I opens in Britain: it is the beginning of the long Whig Ascendancy.	Following the unsuccessful Jacobite revolt of 1715 a purge of Jacobites and Tories takes place in England: leaders of the revolt are executed. War between the Empire and Turkey: Temesvar, the last Turkish possession in Hungary, falls. Septennial Act of Britain extends the life of Parliament to 7 years (until 1911).	Turks are defeated at Belgrade by Prince Eugène. Separate Afghan state is established free of Persian rule. Mongols occupy Lhasa, Tibet. Spanish seize Sardinia from Austria. Spain begins a radical re-organization of her South American Empire.	Peter the Great has his son Alexis murdered in prison: Alexis had become the focus of opposition to his reforms. The Treaty of Passarowitz ends war between Turkey and Austria: this represents the height of Habsburg expansion Quadruple Alliance is formed by Austria, Britain, France and the Netherlands against renascent power of Spain.	France declares war on Spain. Spanish invasion of Scotland in support of the Jacobites is defeated at Glenshiel. Statute is passed by the English Parliament to allow it to legislate for Ireland. Russia invades Sweden and a coalition of Denmark, Sweden, Prussia and Britain is formed to oppose Russia.
Religion & Learning		Emperor K'ang Hsi prohibits the teaching of Christianity in China. Reign of K'ang Hsi was one of great cultural achievement: the K'ang Hsi dictionary of 40,000 characters was one of a number of books compiled on his orders.	The Jansenist controversy continues to divide the French clergy: four bishops appeal against the Papal Bull *Unigenitus*.	Academy of Science, Letters and Arts is formed at Palermo. First bank notes are issued in England.	Jesuits are expelled from Russia.
Cities & Social Development	First British factory at Canton is established by the East India Company. First Liverpool docks are built: Liverpool is destined to overtake Bristol as the main British west coast port.	John Law, the Scottish economist, establishes the Banque Generale in France. French construct a naval base at Louisburg which they turn into one of the strongest fortresses in the New World.	Value of the golden guinea is fixed at twenty-one shillings. Prussia make school attendance compulsory.		First English cricket match is held: Londoners v Kentish Men. Smallpox plague in Paris kills 14,000.
Discovery & Invention	George Graham designs a compensating pendulum for clocks.			Halley discovers the true motion of fixed stars. Leopold of Dessau invents iron ramrod which leads to increased efficiency of infantry fire.	
The Arts	*Architecture* (1750), the work of the Italian Andrea Palladio, is translated into English: it is to become very influential.	Hakuseki *Ori-Taku-Shiba*, a Japanese autobiography. Japan relaxes her interdict upon western culture.	Pope *Poems*. Italian opera is introduced to Dresden at this time. Watteau *Embarquement pour Cythère* (Louvre).	Young Voltaire (now aged 24) is sent to the Bastille: as writer, philosopher and critic, he is to have a profound impact on 18th century thought.	Daniel Defoe *Robinson Crusoe*. Handel is made director of the Royal Academy of Music in London.

In 1696 at the age of 24, Peter I became absolute ruler of Russia. A huge, incessantly active, highly intelligent and very violent man, he appreciated that his country had fallen far behind the West and was determined to do something about it. He wanted a modern state with efficient armed forces, a vigorous commercial life and the trappings of government that had become the norm in western Europe.

Before embarking on this programme Peter allowed himself a year off: he travelled to Germany, Holland, England and Austria and would have gone on to Italy if he had not been called home by rumours of revolt. The extraordinary thing about this grand tour is the use Peter made of his time. Instead of hobnobbing with other crowned heads he travelled incognito when he could (which was not often) and saw every mill and workshop he could get into (which was a great many). He wanted to know how everything worked: in later life he boasted that he had mastered 17 crafts, including dentistry.

Peter's curiosity was certainly all-embracing. In Holland he went to Boehoeve's anatomy demonstrations and looked down Leeuwenhoek's microscopes: in England he went to the Mint to meet Newton and to Greenwich Observatory to see the Astronomer Royal. But his real passion was for ships: he worked for four months in the Dutch East India Company shipyard in Amsterdam, humping timbers and sawing frames and getting his shipwright's certificate; he took trips on every sort of boat that was going, from warships to whalers, and he sailed them himself when he was allowed to. All this at a time when Russia's only port of any consequence was Archangel which was icebound six months in every twelve.

Back in Russia, Peter found there was nothing much to the rebellion that had cut short his tour of Europe but he

Right: Peter the Great cutting off a nobleman's beard. This is a satirical woodcut but it is difficult to be satirical where Peter is concerned. He considered the long Russian beard a sign of backwardness and, given his practical bent, it is not at all unlikely that when he saw a beard that offended him he wielded the shears himself. A second offence and the head would come off too, no doubt.

1720	1721	1722	1723	1724	
Treaty of The Hague ends hostilities between the Quadruple Alliance and Spain. Collapse of John Law's Mississippi Company in France leads to French national bankruptcy. Failure of the South Sea Company in England – the South Sea Bubble – causes financial panic: government assumes control of the national debt.	Beginning of the long administration of Sir Robert Walpole, Britain's first Prime Minister: he restores public credit after the South Sea Bubble of 1720. Peter I is proclaimed Emperor of all the Russias: the Treaty of Nystadt between Russia and Sweden sees the emergence of Russia as a great power and ends the Great Northern War. China suppresses a revolt in Formosa.	Administrative reforms in Prussia are designed to centralize government in a General Directory under the control of the King. In Russia Peter I develops a Table of Ranks to create service nobility. Shih Tsung becomes Emperor of China and establishes Yung Cheng dynasty. Policy of Russification is carried out in the Ukraine which is governed directly from St Petersburg until 1750.	Prussia establishes a Ministry of War, Finance and Domains.	Treaty of Stockholm between Russia and Sweden. Russian-Turkish Alliance against Persia. State of Hyderabad in India becomes independent of the Moghul Empire.	Politics & Military History
University of Lisbon is established.	Montesquieu *Lettres Persanes.* Peter I abolishes the Russian Patriarchate: the Church is administered by a Synod.	Protestants are expelled from Salzburg.	Protestants are expelled from Corinthia, Styria and Upper Austria (to 1725).	Professorships of modern history and languages are established at Oxford and Cambridge. Scientific Academy is set up at St Petersburg.	Religion & Learning
Wallpaper becomes fashionable in England. Further controls are applied in England on silks imported from Asia to assist the domestic industry. Plague in Marseilles is the last bout of plague in western Europe.	Regular postal services are established between England and New England and between London and the North. Dutch purchase the last Prussian trading factories in Africa. Russian factory owners are allowed to buy peasants.	The London bookseller, Thomas Guy, gives £300,000 to found Guy's Hospital.	Pedro de Ribière builds the Toledo bridge in Spain.	Longman's (Britain's oldest publishing house, still in existence) is founded. Rapid growth of gin drinking in England: consumption grows from half a million gallons in 1700 to 5 million in 1735. Paris Bourse opens.	Cities & Social Development
Lady Mary Wortley Montagu introduces innoculation against smallpox.		De Reaumur *L'Art de convertir le fer forgé en acier* on making steel.			Discovery & Invention
Pope, verse translation of the *Iliad.*	Swift *Gulliver's Travels*(1721–1725). J. S. Bach *Brandenburg Concertos.*	James Gibbs builds St Martin-in-the-Fields Church, London.	J. S. Bach *St John Passion.*	The Three Choir Festival, England's oldest musical festival, begins.	The Arts

Above: St Petersburg in the 1760s. This shows the city looking considerably more elegant than it had in Peter's day. On the left is the Winter Palace as enlarged by the Italian architect Rastrelli for Peter's daughter, the Empress Elizabeth (1741–62). Beyond is the Admiralty, the apple of Peter's eye, with two men-of-war in its dock: the fine steeple that rises above it is an addition of the 1730s.

The opposite bank is part of Vassili Ostrov, the island formed by the division of the Neva into the Bolshaya Neva (Great Neva, the one in the picture) and the Maya Neva (Little Neva). The range of buildings here includes the Academy of Sciences for which Peter was drawing up plans at the time of his death.

suppressed it with vigour all the same. His admirers in the West were alarmed by stories of how he had personally supervised the torture and execution of the ringleaders: it did not seem to fit the picture of the ruler seeking to introduce western ways. But the stories were true. Peter, an autocrat in every sense, was going to flog the Russians forward: if they resisted he was going to flay them alive.

Peter's achievement during the next 25 years provides some sort of justification for the ill-use to which he put his subjects. He turned the rag-tag Russian army, with its history of defeat at the hands of Swedes, Poles and Turks, into an up-to-date fighting force and personally led it to victory over one of the greatest soldiers of the day, Sweden's Charles XII. He created a Russian navy out of nothing at all. And he built up an iron industry in the Urals that could stand comparison with any in Europe. He also had his failures: none of his various administrative reforms really took root and the trading companies he set up never acquired independent life. But he did most of what he set out to do and in the course of it made Russia a great power.

The crowning achievement was the new capital, St Petersburg, built on territory won from the Swedes. The site was a bog near the mouth of the Neva and just laying the foundations cost the lives of so many thousands that the city was said to be built on bones. But as usual Peter had his way and the city rose to plan. With its elegant classical architecture, its long perspectives and its handsome quays, it is one of the most striking achievements of the Enlightenment and in essence it is Peter's. The little house where he lived when the city was first under construction is still in existence: so is the nearby Peter and Paul fortress where his son Alexis, who had turned out disappointingly, was flogged to death on his orders and in his presence.

	1725	1726	1727	1728	1729
Politics & Military History	In France there is resistance to the cinquantième – a 2% tax on all incomes. Treaty of Vienna: Spain accepts the Pragmatic Sanction which guarantees the Austrian succession to Maria Thérèsa; this unites the Spanish Bourbons and Austrian Habsburgs. Death of Peter I (he is succeeded by his widow Catherine I) weakens the Russian Crown in its struggle with the nobility.	Cardinal Fleury becomes Chief Minister in France (to 1743): his policies similar to those of Walpole in Britain. Russia and Austria in alliance against Turkey: Russia agrees to the Pragmatic Sanction. Treaty of Wusterhausen: Prussia accepts the Pragmatic Sanction.	War between Spain and Britain and France: the Spanish besiege Gibraltar. Death of Catherine I of Russia leads to further erosion of royal power by the Noble Privy Council. Treaty of K'achta: the frontier between Russia and China is fixed on the Amur. First annual act is passed by the British Parliament to remove the disabilities of Protestant Dissenters.	Convention of Prado: ends the war between Britain and Spain which raises the siege of Gibraltar after 14 months. Treaty of Berlin between Austria and Prussia.	Treaty of Seville: ends the war between Spain, France and Britain. Portugal loses Mombasa to the Arabs: it had been the capital of Portuguese East Africa since 1593. North and South Carolina become Crown colonies.
Religion & Learning	There is a growing revival of Christianity in North America.		American Philosophical Society is established in Philadelphia. Göttsched founds German Society at Leipzig.	Appearance of Chambers' *Cyclopaedia.* University of Havana is established: refounded in 1900.	Thomas Sherlock *A Tryal of the Witnesses of the Resurrection of Jesus*, a critical examination of evidence for miracles – during the 18th Century there were to be many critical and sceptical examinations of previously held beliefs.
Cities & Social Development	The publication of the *New York Gazette.*	Japan introduces a money economy. Spanish establish their first settlement on the site of Montevideo: this leads to the occupation of the Banda Oriental (Uruguay).	By this time there are 25 newspapers printed in the English provinces. Coffee is planted in Brazil for the first time. Quakers demand the abolition of slavery.	Widespread reform of the coinage of the Spanish South American Empire: the Spanish government to purchase the output of all colonial mines.	Opium smoking in China is prohibited by the Emperor Yung Cheng. Benjamin and James Franklin establish *The Pennsylvania Gazette.*
Discovery & Invention		Stephen Hales measures blood pressure.			Stephen Gray discovers that some bodies conduct electricity while others do not.
The Arts	Canaletto *Four Views of Venice.* Prague Opera House is established. Pope, translation of the *Odyssey.*	Voltaire is banished from the French Court and comes to live in England whose freedoms deeply impress him.	Sonata form in music is now developed with two motifs.	John Gay *The Beggar's Opera.*	J. S. Bach *St Matthew Passion.*

Japan, when Europeans first made contact with it in the mid-16th century, was a divided country. There was an emperor who held court at Kyoto but his rule was purely nominal: real power resided with the feudal barons – *daimyo* – of whom the top dozen or so kept such impressive state that western accounts usually refer to them as kings.

The Europeans came to trade and to preach. In both activities they had considerable success, at least initially: they made a large number of converts to the Christian faith and the manufactures they had for sale attracted a lot of attention. What particularly interested the *daimyo* were European firearms. They soon learned how to use these and, more remarkably, their swordsmiths soon learned how to make them. This was something that did not happen anywhere else in Asia and says a lot about Japanese craftsmen: not only were they superb technicians but they were willing to put tradition aside and try new ideas.

Firearms changed the character of warfare among the *daimyo*. Although they were always fighting among themselves these conflicts did not usually result in any change in the overall pattern. Now the big battalions started to come out on top. In the 1570s Oda Nobunaga built up a corps of 3000 musketeers and made himself master of a large part of the country: his successor, Hideyoshi, conquered the rest in the 1580s. On his death the hegemony Hideyoshi had created passed to a new leader, Ieyasu of the Tokugawa clan, who founded the dynasty of *shoguns* (military rulers – the Emperor was retained as formal head of state) that was to run Japan for the next 150 years.

Unlike their craftsmen, the Tokugawa shoguns were determined to preserve traditional Japanese society. The reaction against western ideas was already under way when Ieyasu took over: he placed further restrictions on European visitors and excluded missionaries altogether. The Spanish and Portuguese failed to toe the line properly and were expelled: the British withdrew, and by 1641 the only foreigners permitted in Japan were the Dutch. Even they were only allowed to bring in a single vessel a year and were scarcely ever given permission to leave Deshima, the tiny island in Nagasaki harbour where they had their factory.

The conservative programme was now carried to its logical conclusion. The four orders of society – warriors, merchants, artisans and peasants – were given rigid

Above: A Samurai arming himself for combat. A typical example of the Japanese habit of making an elaborate ritual out of a practical necessity.

1730	1731	1732	1733	1734	
Maratha government gains ascendancy in India (to 1735). Dupleix is appointed governor of Chandernagore: in 11 years he made it the richest European settlement in Bengal; he rapidly extended French influence with a view to expelling the English.	Treaty of Vienna: Britain, Holland and Spain guarantee the Pragmatic Sanction of Austria. French fortify Crown Point on Lake Champlain to check British North American expansion.	Frederick William I allows 12,000 Protestants expelled from the Salzburg Bishopric to settle in East Prussia; military and administrative reforms are carried out in Prussia. James Oglethorpe obtains a Charter to establish a colony in Georgia: colonists left England to settle the area in the autumn of 1732.	First family pact between the Bourbons of France and Spain is seen as a threat by Britain. Following the death of Augustus II, the War of Polish Succession between France and Spain and Austria and Russia (to 1735). Military conscription is introduced in Prussia.	War between Turkey and Persia. War of Polish Succession: Russians occupy Danzig, French occupy Lorraine.	Politics & Military History
John and Charles Wesley found the Methodist Sect at Oxford: John travelled many thousand miles preaching all over England; Charles wrote more than 6000 hymns; Methodism had special appeal for the poorer classes.	Protestant persecutions in Austria: Protestants are expelled from the Archbishopric of Salzburg. Roman Catholicism is established as the state religion in Hungary.	Pope *An Essay on Man.* Conrad Beissel founds Seventh Day Baptists in Pennsylvania.	Voltaire *Lettres sur les Anglais*: his admiration for British liberalism led to a storm which forced him to leave Paris.	University of Gottingen is established. Koran is translated into English. In *Avis d'une Mère á sa Fille* Mme de Lambert recommends university education for women.	Religion & Learning
Lord Townshend in Norfolk introduced system of four crop rotation, improved land by better drainage and manure, began the use of turnips for winter feed for cattle (nicknamed 'Turnip Townshend') and was a leader in the 'Agrarian Revolution'.	Benjamin Franklin founds a subscription library in Philadelphia; the earliest references to concerts in America – at Boston and Charleston. English factory workers are not allowed to emigrate to America.	Game of ninepins is played for the first time in New York. Guilds in Prussia are brought under strict state control with legislation from 1732–35.	The Corvée, a compulsory road, bridge and public works service, is introduced in France by Fleury.	8000 Protestants expelled from Salzburg go to Georgia as settlers. First horse race is recorded in America.	Cities & Social Development
Zinc smelting is first practised in England.	John Hadley invents the quadrant for use at sea.	Swedish botanist, Carolus Linnaeus, forms Linnaean College in Sweden.	John Kay invents his Flying Shuttle which revolutionizes the weaving industry: cloth can now be produced more quickly and in greater widths.		Discovery & Invention
The Rococo style of architecture – a lighter version of the Baroque style – now reaches its highpoint.	Abbé Prévost *Manon Lescaut.* Hogarth *The Harlot's Progress.*	Covent Garden Opera House is opened in London. London theatrical company performs for the first time in New York.	Pergolesi *La Serva Padrona,* opera buffa (Naples). Rameau *Hippolyte et Aricie,* opera (Paris).	Handel *6 concerti grossi,* Op 3. J. S. Bach *Christmas Oratorio.*	The Arts

definition. No Japanese could ever think of changing his status; the warriors – *samurai* – could not even change their masters. Of course, there was no question of travelling abroad: if anyone did he would surely be executed on his return. The same fate awaited anyone suspected of Christianity.

A good example of the lengths to which the Tokugawa were prepared to go to maintain the medieval purity of Japanese society is the gradual replacement of the gun by the sword. Once they were securely in control the Tokugawa granted few licences to gunsmiths and few of those that they did grant were renewed. Eventually the existing guns were all neatly piled away in government armouries and the *samurai* were once again exclusively armed with swords.

All this sounds, and indeed is, extremely reactionary. Nonetheless, Tokugawa Japan was not as static a society as it appeared and of the changes that did occur, some were to prove of considerable significance when the country was finally opened up to the Westernization process in the 19th century. For example, once the new order had been established there was nothing much for the *samurai* to do, but although many of them did no more than that, the more intelligent turned to administration. The state acquired a bureaucratic cadre that was capable of expansion when needed. And because the method by which the Shogun controlled his subordinate *daimyo* included residence at Tokyo (Edo as it was known at the time) for six months of the year, and the same residential requirement was imposed by the *daimyo* on their *samurai*, there was a huge increase in the size of the towns. It is not surprising then that of the ten biggest cities in the world in the mid-18th century six were Asian – Asia had, after all, 60% of the world's population: what is surprising is that three of these cities were Japanese and that Tokyo, with half a million inhabitants, was the world's fourth largest city. Far from being the total backwater it looked at first sight, Tokugawa Japan had a vigorous intellectual and artistic life.

Above: The extirpation of Christianity in Japan. Given the ferocity of the Japanese penal code, scenes like this can be taken at face value.

	1735	1736	1737	1738	1739
Politics & Military History	Treaty of Vienna ends the War of Polish Succession. Peace between Turkey and Persia. William Pitt (the Elder) becomes MP for Old Sarum.	Ch'ien Lung becomes Emperor of China and presides over a great advance of population and prosperity (to 1795). Nadir Shah becomes ruler of Persia: he attempts to make the Persians renounce the Shia heresy and become orthodox Sunnis. Russia and Austria to war with Turkey (to 1739).	In war with Turkey the Russians capture Ochakov, occupy Moldavia and ravage the Crimea. In northern India the Marathas defeat an Imperial Army at Delhi and continue their expansion; they launch a campaign against the Portuguese on the west coast. Nadir Shah of Persia reduces Baluchistan and Balkh.	In their war with Russia and Austria the Turks take Orsova and drive Austrian forces back to Belgrade. Treaty of Vienna resolves the War of Polish Succession: Lorraine is to go to France on the death of Stanislaus I, the defeated claimant to the Polish throne. Nadir Shah of Persia overruns Afghanistan and then invades the Punjab to take Peshawur and Lahore.	Britain and Spain at war: War of Jenkins' Ear – Admiral Vernon captures Porto Bello. Treaty of Belgrade ends the Austro-Russian War against Turkey with the Emperor Charles VI losing almost all the gains Austria had made since 1718. Nadir Shah defeats the Moghul Emperor at the battle of Karnal and then sacks Delhi, massacring many thousands; he levies a huge indemnity. Anglo-Maratha Treaty allows the English to trade duty free in the Deccan. Nadir Shah takes the Peacock Throne of Shah Jehan to Persia.
Religion & Learning	Benjamin Franklin *Essay on Human Vanity*. Bible is translated into Lithuanian.		Lady Mary Wortley Montagu *The Nonsense of Common Sense*. *Psalms and Hymns* of John Wesley are published in Georgia.	Papal Bull *In Eminenti*, is issued against Freemasonry. Anglican-Moravian-Methodist society is established; George Whitefield becomes a principal Methodist and follows John Wesley to Georgia.	David Hume *Treatise of Human Nature*: an 18th century sceptic of great influence. Foundation of the Swedish Scientific Academy.
Cities & Social Development	French East India Company establishes a sugar industry in the Indian Ocean islands of Mauritius and Reunion.	Porteous Riots in Edinburgh: Porteous had ordered the town guard to fire on the crowd, killing some; the mob took him from prison and hanged him. It was really a symptom of opposition to the Act of Union between England and Scotland.	William Byrd founds Richmond, Virginia.	The first cuckoo clocks appear in the Black Forest region.	American colonies are allowed to export sugar direct to the Mediterranean: flexibility of the Old Colonial System at this period puts off the coming clash between Britain and her North American colonies.
Discovery & Invention		Aymand performs the first operation for appendicitis. French mathematician, Clairaut, calculates the length of meridian degree. French expedition under Anders Celsius sponsored by the Académie Francaise visits Lapland.	Measurements taken in Lapland and Peru demonstrate the flattening of the earth towards the poles. Publication of Linnaeus' two works *Flora Lapponica* and *Genera Plantarum* marks the beginning of modern botany.	Jean Bernouilli *Hydrodynamics*, develops the science of hydrodynamics and states Bernouilli's principle – the higher the velocity of fluid, the lower its pressure.	
The Arts	Hogarth *A Rake's Progress* (London). First four volumes of Swift's *Collected Works* are published in Dublin: the total works (20 vols) will take until 1772 to appear.	Hogarth *The Good Samaritan*.	Licensing Act restricts the number of London theatres: all plays to be subject to the censorship of the Lord Chamberlain, a condition which lasts to 1950s.	Hogarth, *The 4 Stages of Cruelty*.	

Politically and economically the 17th century had been a bad time for Germany. The Thirty Years' War showed that it was impossible to make anything of the German Empire: it was just a ragbag of separate sovereignties ranging from the third rate down to the laughable. And as Europe's economic focus shifted to the Atlantic, Germany became a bit of a backwater anyway. Cities like Nuremberg, which had once set the technological pace for the continent, dwindled into sleepy country towns: ports like Lübeck, the once bustling metropolis of the Hanseatic League, saw their wharfs fall silent and their harbours silt up.

The opening years of the 18th century ushered in better times for Germany. In particular there was a marked upturn in the fortunes of the Austrian Habsburgs during the War of the Spanish Succession. Austria seemed finally to have made good its claim to great power status.

The state that held second place in Germany at this time was Prussia, previously known as Brandenburg. It was poor but it had fortified its economy by welcoming in the Protestants expelled by intolerant Catholic regimes: its way of life was harsh but this made its young men good soldiers. Its ruler, King Frederick William I, was a hard-working, bureaucratically minded, absolute monarch who, it, was generally agreed, had built up one of the best armies in Europe. However, none of his fellow sovereigns took him very seriously because he loved his army as a child loves toy soldiers: he liked taking the men out and marching them up and down but he was not going to risk getting them damaged. His particular delight was a regiment of extra-tall grenadiers. He had scouts out all over Europe looking for suitable recruits and if they could not be persuaded to volunteer he was not above kidnapping them.

If Frederick William's heart filled with joy when he thought of the Potsdam Grenadiers, it sank every time he remembered his son, the future Frederick II. This young man seemed to have developed all the qualities that his father abhorred. He was polite, sceptical, interested primarily in French literature and apt to be condescending about military matters. The irate father tried to beat virtue into his independent-minded son but without much success: relations between the two of them became so bad that after one escapade Frederick was sure he was going to be executed. It was a false alarm. The king contented himself with the execution of the prince's best friend.

PRUSSIA UNDER FREDERICK THE GREAT 1740–86

Frederick William's death in 1740 was a liberation for both Frederick II and Prussia. The new ruler immediately set about enlightening his subjects, somewhat after the

1740	1741	1742	1743	1744	
Death of Charles VI of Austria, ends the male line of the Habsburgs. His daughter, Maria Thérèsa, succeeds to the thrones of Austria, Bohemia and Hungary. The Pragmatic Sanction had been designed to persuade the rulers of Europe to accept a female succession but Frederick the Great seizes Silesia and so sets off the War of Austrian Succession which is to continue to 1748 with Bavaria, Spain and Saxony claiming the throne of Austria. As a result of this war Prussia under Frederick II will emerge as a major European power.	Alliance of Nymphenbourg between France, Bavaria, Spain, Saxony and Prussia: Maria Thérèsa accepts the Crown of Hungary (the nobles are exempted from tax in return for their support); French, Bavarian and Saxon troops occupy Prague and Charles Albert of Bavaria is recognized as King of Bohemia. Frederick II conquers Silesia and defeats the Austrians at Mollwitz. In France the battle between the Crown and the nobles continues with the aristocracy resisting attempts to make them pay direct taxes – the dixième.	Prussians evacuate Olmutz; they defeat the Austrians at Chotusitz; Peace of Berlin between Prussia and Austria ends the first Silesian War. Walpole resigns as First Minister in England, partly because of reverses in the war with Spain. Venezuela is made a separate province within the Spanish Empire. Marathas invade Bengal in the first of a series of wars aimed at Hindu supremacy in India.	Battle of Dettingen: the British leading a 'Pragmatic' army defeat the French; George II in command – the last time a British King commanded his troops in battle. Alliance is concluded between Austria and Saxony. Treaty of Worms: Austria cedes Parma and Piacenza to Sardinia. Peace of Abo: ends war between Russia and Sweden. In their far eastern empire the Dutch have achieved control of all coastal Java.	Frederick II invades Bohemia but his forces are repelled by the Austrians and Saxons. Britain and France go to war in North America – 'King George's War' for colonial mastery – till 1748 – French troops occupy Annapolis, Nova Scotia, then withdraw. Robert Clive goes to India as a clerk in the East India Company.	Politics & Military History
Hindu Marathas become more powerful in India; their authority spreads across central India and begins to threaten the British and French in Bengal and the south-east.			Franklin *A Proposal for Promoting useful Knowledge.* Voltaire visits Frederick II (The Great) of Prussia.	Ruling Sa-udi family in Arabia adopt the teachings of Abd-al-Wahhab, the founder of the Wahhabi Sect which seeks a return to pure Islamic practice.	Religion & Learning
			Yarns from East India are now imported to Lancashire for the manufacture of finer goods. First colonial settlements are established in South Dakota.		Cities & Social Development
Nadir Shah takes Bokhara and Khwarezm (Khiva): this was the greatest extent of his dominions and the year marked a turning point in his fortunes: in his efforts to stamp out Shi'ism he became more despotic.	Russian navigator, Tchivikov, lands in California. Andry, the French physician, invents the word orthopaedics. Wrought iron is used in bridge construction in England for the first time.	Celsius invents the centigrade thermometer. Bolsover discovers how to plate silver on copper: the beginning of Sheffield plate. Jean Malouin, French chemist, discovers the way to galvanize iron.	De Lyons produces the centigrade scale: Celsius had proposed the 100 divisions the previous year. French explorers reach the foothills of the Rocky Mountains.	Anson returns to England from his epic journey round the world started in 1740.	Discovery & Invention
	David Garrick, the actor, makes his debut in London as Richard III.	Handel *Messiah*, first performed in Dublin.	Henry Fielding *Jonathan Wild.*	Gluck *Iphigénie en Aulide.* opera. Tune of 'God Save the King' makes its appearance.	The Arts

Right: Voltaire receives Frederick in the apartment the king has provided for him at the Palace of Sans Souci, Potsdam.

manner of Peter the Great, but showing a better grasp of the principles involved. He abolished torture and press censorship and decreed complete freedom of religion. He also re-opened the Berlin Academy founded by his grandfather but closed down for economic reasons by the parsimonious Frederick William. Voltaire, with whom Frederick had been corresponding for several years past, started addressing him as "Your Humanity" and though the style of the time was inclined to exaggeration and no-one, not even Voltaire, reined back too hard when addressing royalty, there is no reason to believe that his praise was anything but sincere. Frederick underscored the generally favourable impression he had created by publishing a tract against cynicism in political life, the Anti-Machiavel: he gave the Italian a roasting for his defence of Cesare Borgia and denounced his maxims as self-evidently evil. Not till the last chapter did he admit that in exceptional circumstances a ruler might have to break a treaty and go to war 'for the good of the state'.

In real life it took Frederick less than a year to reach this extremity. Hearing of the death of the Austrian Emperor Charles VI, he immediately invaded, conquered and annexed the Habsburg province nearest to Prussia, Silesia. By deftly manipulating the European situation he then forced Charles' successor, the Empress Maria Theresa, to recognize the theft. It was the first step in the long road that was to make Prussia the leading power in Germany and earn its king the title of Frederick the Great.

It was not all plain sailing. In the Seven Years' War Frederick was to find his enemies almost too much for him. In battle after battle his father's much loved regiments were sent forward, slaughtered, reformed and slaughtered again. Famous victories were followed by shattering defeats. Most of Prussia was overrun, Berlin itself occupied by enemy forces. But Frederick survived, the tide turned and he was able to weld his state together again. It would be interesting to know how Machiavelli would have rated his performance. Voltaire, who spent some famously uneasy years at Frederick's court, ended with a very ambivalent attitude towards the man he called 'Mon Patron, mon disciple, et mon persécuteur'.

London became the biggest city in Europe towards the end of the 17th century when its population of 550,000 probably exceeded that of Paris by about 10%: by 1750 the margin had increased to 25%, London having around 675,000 people as against Paris, 525,000. Relative to the two countries' populations the difference between the two capitals is even more striking: London contained a tenth of England's population, Paris barely a fiftieth of France's.

London's growth reflects the emergence of England as a major trading nation. The mercantile and banking communities were bringing great wealth into the city and the money brought in great numbers of people. The immigrants came from all parts of the kingdom, hoping that the capital would provide them with something better than the ill-rewarded drudgery that was their normal lot. For some the hope was fulfilled and they became artisans or domestic servants. For others the dream soon faded and they became part of the wretched masses who inhabited the city's slums. Either way, the input was essential to the growth of the city for the death rate far exceeded the number of births. Barely one in four of the children born in London survived to its fifth year.

The government did what it could to make matters worse. The land-owning classes were producing more corn than the people could eat but had found a solution to the problem of over-production in turning the surplus into gin. Gin was both cheap and profitable; by the early 18th century every tenth house in the city was a gin-shop and gin had become the everyday drink of the labouring classes. For many of London's poor, life became a short and squalid journey through alcoholism to destitution and a pauper's grave. Parliament, dominated by the landed interest, steadfastly refused to intervene.

Eventually public order deteriorated to the point where the government had to act. In 1751 a stiff tax was placed on spirits and as a result sales of gin began a slow decline. From an annual level equivalent to three gallons for every man, woman and child in the capital, consumption fell away to less than one gallon by the end of the century. Infant mortality showed a parallel decline from over 50% to under 20%. For all the continuing harshness of life in the nation's capital it is worth remembering that by comparison with Hogarth's, Dickens' London was a salubrious, law-abiding and prosperous place.

None the less, despite its horrors the Londoner of the mid-18th century loved his city. He was proud of its size. He was proud of its fine shops and skilled craftsmen, its theatres and pleasure gardens, its elegant squares and fashionable promenades. He was even proud of its underworld, the roster of pickpockets and cut-throats, highwaymen and whores who journeyed to Tyburn pelted or fêted according to the whim of the mob. Johnson, who experienced the darker side of the city when he arrived penniless in 1737, never let his early privations dampen his enthusiasm for it. 'A man who is tired of London' he said 'is tired of life, for there is in London all that life can afford'.

Top left: London from Somerset Gardens. Painted in 1748.

Top right: Supper at Vauxhall Gardens. Fanny Burney, and William Thackeray described them as fashionable in the late 18th century. By the 1850s the gardens were the haunt of prostitutes and roués which led to their closure in 1859.

Above: A mad dog in a London coffee house by Thomas Rowlandson.

	1745	1746	1747	1748	1749
Politics & Military History	Austria, Saxony, Britain and the Netherlands ally against Prussia; following defeat Bavaria renounces its claims to the throne of Austria. Battle of Fontenoy: French defeat British who withdraw; France takes the Austrian Netherlands. Austrians are defeated at Hohenfriedburg and Soor by the Prussians. Treaty of Dresden: Prussia recognizes the Pragmatic Sanction but keeps Silesia. 'The Forty-Five': the second Jacobite rebellion led by Charles Edward Stuart, 'the Young Pretender' is at first successful. In Canada the British capture the French stronghold of Louisburg. In the complex power struggle in India the Nawab of Carnatic refuses to allow the British to bombard the French at Pondicherry.	Beginning of a series of judicial reforms in Prussia which establish a centralized judicial system. Austria and Russia conclude an alliance against Prussia: Austrians take Genoa but are then driven out by a popular uprising. Following French victory at Raucoux Austria loses the Netherlands. Battle of Culloden: the defeat of the Jacobite forces; 'the Young Pretender' flees to France; the Scottish Highlands are brutally subjugated by 'Butcher' Cumberland.	Alliance between Prussia and Sweden is matched by a Treaty between Britain and Russia. In Holland William IV of Orange is proclaimed *stadtholder*, a title which now becomes hereditary to his family. Scottish Lords who supported the 'Young Pretender' in the '45 Rebellion are executed. Nadir Shah of Persia is assassinated. Ahmad Khan Durani established himself at Kandahar: he takes Meshed and Herat and annexes Sind, Kashmir and parts of the Punjab to found a powerful Afghan state.	Treaty of Aix-La-Chapelle: ends the War of Austrian Succession; a general recognition of the Pragmatic Sanction; Prussia keeps Silesia. Maria Thérèsa institutes reforms in the Austrian Empire. British and French colonial rivalries continue. Ahmad Shah of Afghanistan invades the Punjab. Dupleix repulses a British naval attack on Pondicherry. As a result of the European peace the French returned Madras to the English in India and the British returned Louisburg to the French in Canada.	French nobility is required to pay direct taxes. Consolidation Act: a reorganization of the British Navy. Prince Kaunitz in charge of Austria's foreign policy which he reformulates; other reforms in Austria include the separation of state and judiciary. Spanish Crown introduces the office of intendant as tax collector and ends the practice of farming out revenue collecting. British turn Halifax in Nova Scotia into a fortress.
Religion & Learning		Denis Diderot *Pensées Philosophiques*: a philosopher who was to have considerable influence in the years leading to the French Revolution. College of New Jersey (to become Princeton in 1896) is established. Christians in China are persecuted (until 1780s). Gianfresco Privati produces 10 volume Venetian encyclopaedia.	Biblioteca Nazionale is established in Florence. National Library is founded in Warsaw. University of St Petersburg is founded. Dr Samuel Johnson *Plan of a dictionary of the English Language*.	Montesquieu *L'Esprit des lois*, one of the most important works of the 18th century which had an important influence upon the French Revolution. Hume *Philosophical Essays concerning Human Understanding*.	Comte de Buffon begins his monumental *Histoire Naturelle* (not completed until 1767) in which evolution in the animal world is first suggested. Diderot is imprisoned by the French government for his *Lettres sur les Aveugles*. Rousseau visits Diderot in prison: this was a turning point in his work: writes *Discours sur les Sciences et les Arts*. David Hartley, English philosopher, writes *Observations on Man*; he can claim to have founded the school of thought based upon the theory of the association of ideas.
Cities & Social Development	Middlesex Hospital is established in London. Quadrille becomes the fashionable dance in France. Robert Bakewell of Leicester begins his breeding experiments to improve sheep strains.	Wearing of Tartans is prohibited in Britain. French under Dupleix capture the British factory at Madras and defeat the Nawab of the Carnatic.	Carriage tax is levied in England.	Platinum brought from South America to Europe. Sweden becomes the first country to compile reliable reports on its population: the beginnings of modern demography.	Georgia becomes a crown colony. First settlements are made by the Ohio Company.
Discovery & Invention	Von Kleist invents the 'Leyden Jar', a fundamental electrical circuit element.	First geological map of France is drawn by Guettard. Hamburger describes the duodenal ulcer. Plant for producing sulphuric acid is opened at Birmingham by Roebuck to be followed by a second plant in Scotland in 1749.	The German chemist, Margraff, discovers the presence of sugar in beet.	John Fothergill, physician *Account of the Sore Throat Attended with Ulcers* is the first authoritative account of diphtheria. Chair of astronomy founded at Cambridge by Lowndes. The first machines for carding wool which use a revolving cylinder are created by Lewis Paul.	François Philidor, composer and chess player, writes *Analyse du jeu des Echecs*, a study of chess.
The Arts	Swift *Directions to Servants in General*. Tiepolo *Antony & Cleopatra*: frescoes for the Labia Palace, Venice.	Joshua Reynolds *The Eliot Family*.	Rousseau *Les Muses Galantes*, opera. Handel *Judas Maccabaeus*.	Tobias Smollet *Roderick Random*, his first novel; his style was to exercise considerable influence upon later writers. Thomas Gainsborough *Cornard Wood* and *View of the Charterhouse*: he was to make his greatest mark as a portrait painter.	Henry Fielding *Tom Jones*. Tiepolo *Giovanni Querini*, Italian portrait.

	1750	1751	1752	1753	1754
Politics & Military History	Britain joins the Austro-Russian alliance against Prussia. British-French commission fails to settle boundaries in North America. Treaty between Spain and Portugal fixes boundaries between their South American possessions. Jansenist controversy flares up again in France.	Robert Clive seizes Arcot from the French: this is the turning point in the struggle between the British and French in India. China invades Tibet.	Clive captures Trichinopolv from the French in India. Duquesne appointed Governor of Quebec. Ahmad Shah conquers the Punjab and annexes Kashmir to Afghanistan.	In its *Grandes Remonstrances* the French Parlement asserts its role as the guardian of the fundamental laws of France in the continuing Jansenist controversy: Parlement is exiled and there is a strike of the Judiciary. Marquis Duquesne sends an expedition from Quebec to seize the Ohio Valley: the young Washington is sent on an embassy to require the French to withdraw. France faces national bankruptcy for the second time in the century. Kaunitz becomes Chancellor of Austria.	Death of Henry Pelham in England leads to a ministerial crisis: the Duke of Newcastle becomes Prime Minister. Albany Congress of New England colonies reject a plan of union put forward by Franklin. Troops were dispatched from Virginia to Ohio (Washington as second in command) to expel the French who, meanwhile, had built Fort Duquesne; Washington at Fort Necessity was attacked by the French and forced to surrender. Recall of Dupleix from India left the English firmly in the ascendant.
Religion & Learning	Maupertuis *Essai de Criminologie*. Rapid growth of scientific interest: between 1750 and 1800 69 new scientific journals appear in Europe.	The *Encyclopédistes* in France, led by Diderot and d'Alembert, begin to produce the *Encyclopédie* which appeared in 28 volumes: it embodied the prevailing philosophical, religious and political ideas of the time. Hume *Enquiry Concerning the Principles of Morals*. University of Genoa is established. Scientific Academy at Göttingen is established. Prussian Minister of Justice, von Cocceji, produces the *Code Frederic*.	The first two volumes of the French *Encyclopédie* are suppressed for attacks upon the clergy. William Law *The way to divine knowledge*; his earlier works were his most popular with their influence from the Evangelical Revival.	Parliament makes a grant to establish the British Museum: the private collection of Sir Hans Sloane forms the basis of the collection. Archbishop of Paris makes confession and absolution conditional upon rejecting Jansenism.	Diderot *De l'interprétation de la nature*. Hume *History of England* (to 1762). George II founds King's College, New York; later to become Columbia University. Spanish Concordat with the Vatican: the Church becomes independent of the Vatican and under the government of Spain.
Cities & Social Development	Afrikaans develops its modern form as the spoken language in South Africa. Colonization of Labrador begins. Dramatic increase in Britain's trade with Africa begins based upon the shipment of slaves from West Africa to the Americas at the rate of 50,000 a year.	Royal Worcester porcelain works begin production. First mental asylum is set up in London.	Britain adopts the Gregorian Calendar: eleven days between September 2 and 14 were omitted leading to riots with the cry 'Give us back our eleven days'.	Vienna Stock Exchange is established. Naturalization of Jews is permitted in Britain. Pressure of merchants leads to the ending of internal tariffs in Russia.	American Quaker, John Woolman, had begun in 1746 to speak out against slavery: publishes *Some Considerations on the keeping of Negroes*.
Discovery & Invention	Johann Tobias Mayer, the German astronomer, produces his *Map of the Moon*. *Carte de Cassini*: between 1750 and 1789 the first map of the whole of France based upon triangulation and topographical surveys is produced by Cesar François Cassini and completed by his son.	Linnaeus *Philosophia botanica*. Chaumette designs a breech-loading gun.	Benjamin Franklin invents a lightning conductor: he demonstrates the identity of lightning and electricity.	Linnaeus *Species Plantorum*.	Henry Cort invents iron-rolling process: sets up a mill at Fareham.
The Arts	Samuel Johnson launches *The Rambler*: published twice weekly and similar to *The Spectator*, it lasts to 1752. Horace Walpole designs his Gothic residence *Strawberry Hill* which becomes the centre of fashionable learning. 'Capability' Brown designs the garden of Warwick Castle.	Hogarth *Gin Lane*. Smollett *Peregrine Pickle*. Boucher *Toilet of Venus*. The minuet becomes a fashionable dance in Europe.	La Guerre des Bouffons: Paris opera-goers are divided between pro-Italian and pro-French opera supporters. Rousseau *Le devin du village*, opera.	Carlo Goldoni *La Locondiera*; he created a new school of comedy, based upon character and domestic life. Reynolds *Commodore Keppel*. Last funeral monument of the Moghuls for Nawab Safdar Jang is constructed in Delhi.	Thomas Chippendale produces his famous work on furniture design *The Gentleman & Cabinet Master's Design*. Boucher *Judgement of Paris*, series for Mme de Pompadour (Louvre).

People who had not experienced the social round of the *Ancien Régime*, said Talleyrand, had no idea what was meant by the pleasures of life. Never before or since was so much effort and resource, so much talent, skill and taste put into giving the rich a good time. Surrounded by beautiful things and cosseted by armies of servants, they were guests at a lifelong party: their clothes, their carriages, their silver and their plate were as elegant as they were sumptuous; their houses were opulent and their gardens perfectly landscaped.

It is usually said that it was Louis XIV who set the style for this society and that his reason for doing so was as much to emasculate the nobility as to indulge his own taste for magnificence. In his youth he had seen how destructive an aristocracy that maintained its warrior traditions could be: by forcing the nobles of the sword to spend their substance on soft living, he sapped their strength. The court became their playground and their prison.

Maybe so, but the warrior caste was on the way out anyway: the Fronde, the aristocratic free-for-all that had so alarmed the young king, was the last kick of an obsolescent breed; by the 18th century it was the middle classes that mattered.

Which is why life was so good for the upper classes: they had nothing to do but amuse themselves. They also had the means to do so on an epic scale. Versailles is not really relevant to this phenomenon: it was a place of government, a rather boring pile where business was transacted, power offered and bid for. The real pleasure domes were erected by princes who reigned but did not rule.

It would be hard to think of a better example than the Residenz at Würzburg. Who today has heard of the Prince-Bishop Karl Philipp von Greiffenclau? For that matter, how many people had heard of him then? Yet mount the stairs of the Residenz – as grand a staircase as Louis ever trod – and there above you, in Tiepolo's amazing ceiling, are Europe, Asia, America and Africa paying homage to the Prince-Bishop. Leave this aery pantomime, move on through the White Salon with its exquisite stuccoes, to the Kaisersaal, Tiepolo's masterpiece. This is no dreary talking up of royal power such as the Sun King commissioned, it is a joyous celebration of a power that never existed. Water nymphs sit at the feet of ecclesiastical dignitaries, court beauties curtsey before them. Frederick Barbarossa, who invested the Bishop of Würzburg with Ducal power back in 1168 and who must have been a fearsome medieval thug, appears in silks and satins, and Apollo's chariot scatters plump *putti* gently over the whole scene. No doubt Karl Philipp enjoyed it all as much as if he had been there himself.

The vision was to fade all too soon: the middle classes were set to take over the Arts as well as the Sciences and the state. Sir Joshua Reynolds, the most important figure in British painting who became President of England's Royal Academy on its foundation in 1768, left Tiepolo out of his *Discourses* on the grounds that he was 'not wholly serious'. Men of sober habit had no use for candyfloss on their ceilings.

Top: Fresco on the ceiling of the staircase at the Wurzburg Residenz by G-B Tiepolo. In the centre Fame bears aloft the portrait of the Prince Bishop.

Above: Joseph Haydn, Kapellmeister to the Esterhazys, a family of Austrian princes who maintained a private orchestra and expected something new from it every month. Haydn never failed to oblige.

	1755	1756	1757	1758	1759
Politics & Military History	French and Indian War against Britain in North America: boundary disputes the cause, though war is not declared; French defeat the British near Fort Duquesne. French navy is reorganized by d'Armenonville. Admiralty establishes Royal Marines in Gibraltar.	Treaty of Westminster: alliance between Britain and Prussia. Treaty of Versailles: alliance between France and Austria. These two alliances constitute a diplomatic revolution in Europe. Opening of the Seven Years' War: it resulted from colonial rivalry between Britain and France and European rivalry between Prussia and Austria. 'Black hole of Calcutta': the Nawab of Bengal, Suraj-ud-Daulah, captures Calcutta and imprisons 146 British in a small room; most die. In North America the French drive the British from the Great Lakes. The Prussians defeat the Saxon army at Pirna.	Pitt becomes Minister with responsibility for the war. Russia allies herself with France and Austria against Prussia and Britain and invades east Prussia. French force the British out of Hanover and Brunswick. Sweden joins in the war against Britain and Prussia. In a series of battles Frederick II of Prussia is first defeated by the Austrians at Kolin; then he defeats the Austrians at Prague and Leuthen and the French and Germans at Rossbach. In India the British retake Calcutta and then Clive defeats the Nawab of Bengal at the Battle of Plassey: this battle establishes British ascendancy in India.	By the Treaty of London, Britain gurantees Prussia an annual subsidy of £670,000. Russia invades Prussia; repulsed at the Battle of Zorndorf. Austrians besiege Neisse; defeat the Prussians at Hochkirch. Britain establishes naval supremacy with victories at Cartagena, Basque Roads, Cherbourg.	Spain joins France in the war against Britain. France revives plans to invade Britain but the French fleets are defeated at Lagos and Quiberon Bay. Battle of Minden: the Prussians are defeated by the Austrians and Russians. British under Wolfe capture Quebec: both commanders – Wolfe and Montcalm – are killed.
Religion & Learning	Samuel Johnson's *Dictionary of the English Language*. Earthquake destroys Lisbon: 30,000 dead; the event was seen as a challenge to the optimistic outlook of the 'Enlightenment' that saw a natural harmony.			Claude Helvétius has his philosophical *De L'esprit* burned publicly by the hangman for its 'pernicious doctrines' – his key assertion was that public ethics have a utilitarian basis. Quesnay *Tableau Economique*, his most important work.	Voltaire *Candide*. Johnson *Rasselas*. Jesuits are expelled from Portugal. British Museum opens at Montague Place.
Cities & Social Development	Lisbon is rebuilt in the so-called Pombeline style of architecture after the chief minister, Pombal.	The porcelain factory at Sèvres is established.	Chinese Empire restricts all foreign ships to Canton.		Smeaton's Eddystone Lighthouse (the third) is opened officially. Carron Ironworks (the oldest extant in Britain) are opened. Wedgwood's Burslem factory is built.
Discovery & Invention			Sankey Navigation (Lancashire): the first modern British canal is constructed.	Dollond, optician, makes the first achromatic telescope. Halley's Comet returns as predicted.	Sir William Chambers *Treatise on Civil Architecture* becomes a standard work; Chambers laid out Kew Gardens.
The Arts	Gainsborough *Joseph Gibbs*, Canaletto *The Vegetable Market*. Lessing *Miss Sara Sampson*, German tragedy.	Salomon Gessner *Idylls*: the Swiss painter and poet has great vogue and his works are translated into many languages.	Smollett *History of England*. Gainsborough *The Artist's Daughter with a cat*.	Diderot *Père de Famille*, drama. Boucher *Mme de Pompadour*. John and Robert Adam begin Harewood House.	

By the middle of the 18th century North America had been divided into British, French and Spanish spheres. There were a million people of European descent in British North America but only 50,000 in the French sector and less than 5000 in the Spanish. In fact Spanish North America amounted to no more than a handful of outposts; Louisiana was hardly more substantial and though New France was a genuine enough settlement it was, in continental terms, little more than a foothold. The British, on the other hand, had created a new nation. The French decided to rectify this uneven split. Their intention was to take everything west of the Alleghenies.

One of the first people to discover this was Major George Washington who led a four man expedition over the Alleghenies to warn the French off in 1753. At 6ft 2in. (1.90m) Washington was an imposing figure and he was acting on the orders of the Governor of Virginia but it is unlikely that the French officers he made contact with took him very seriously: he was only 21 and the commission he held was in the Virginia militia, a part time organization better known for drinking than fighting.

Whatever the French thought of him Washington did not lack confidence in himself. Back in Virginia he persuaded the Governor to entrust him with the few soldiers the state disposed of and in 1754 set off back across the mountains at the head of 159 of them. Moving down into the valley of the Ohio he attacked and captured a French detachment manning what he assumed was an outpost: it was, in fact, an embassy returning his call of the year before. But if this made him feel foolish worse was to come: a superior French force arrived on the scene and he had to surrender to it.

Round two went to the French as well. The British Government, deciding that the time had come to show Colonials how to do this sort of job, sent General Braddock with two regiments to drive the French from the Upper Ohio. Braddock led his men down the valley, flags flying and drums beating, straight into an ambush. With every officer wounded – Braddock mortally – the little army was completely crushed: if Washington had not been there (serving as an aide-de-camp) few of the British would have made it back across the mountains.

All this was going on during what was officially peace time. The real war – the Seven Years' War – began the next year. Two years later Washington – a colonel by this time – found himself marching across the Alleghenies for the fourth time. Understandably enough he was far from optimistic about the new expedition's chances: the French had had plenty of time to prepare their strong point at the forks of the Ohio, Fort Duquesne, against the attack. He was both surprised and nonplussed when the French abandoned Ford Duquesne without a fight. But then this was a victory for grand strategy, not tactical planning, and Washington's view had of necessity been a local one.

The French had been brought to their knees by a naval blockade instituted by the British Prime Minister William Pitt. Louisbourg, the key to the St Lawrence, had already fallen to a British expeditionary force; Quebec, the heart of French Canada, was taken the next year. It was entirely fitting that Fort Duquesne should be re-named Pittsburg.

Washington resigned his commission at the end of the 1758 campaign sure of only one thing, that his military career was over. Though a hero in Virginia he had not impressed the British generals as he had hoped to and there was no chance of converting his militia rank to its professional equivalent. Settling in at Mount Vernon he took up the life of a planter.

Above: The British take Quebec. General Wolfe outwitted his opponent, General Montcalm, by sailing past Quebec and landing on the Heights of Abraham overlooking the town. In the subsequent battle both Generals were mortally wounded but the day was Wolfe's: Quebec fell and French Canada with it.

1760	1761	1762	1763	1764	
Britain establishes control of the St Lawrence River in Canada and gains Montreal. Denmark joins with Russia and Sweden in Baltic Alliance. Battle of Wandewash: Eyre Coote defeats French and Indian forces to gain the Carnatic for Britain. The Marathas defeat the Nizam of Hyderabad in India: this is the climax of Maratha power in the Deccan.	In India Pondicherry falls to the British. British dominate the West Indies. Pitt resigns because George III opposes his war policy with Spain. Portugal refuses to close her ports to British shipping and is invaded by Spain; Pombal carries out administrative and judicial reforms. Battle of Panipat: the Afghan leader, Ahmad Shah Duranix, defeats the Marathas but then withdraws to Afghanistan.	Changes of Russian policy follow the accession of Catherine II (The Great): nobles are freed from service obligations and given important economic and social rights; Russia changes sides in the war, allying herself with Prussia against Austria. Britain declares war on Spain: captures Martinique, Grenada, Havana, Manilla. Treaty of Hamburg between Prussia and Sweden.	Peace of Paris: between Britain, France and Spain this ends the Seven Years' War; Britain gains Canada and nearly all land east of the Mississippi; the war leaves Britain far more powerful than formerly and the leading colonial power. John Wilkes is imprisoned for attacking the government in his paper *North Briton.*	John Wilkes is expelled from the House of Commons, following his 'libel' on the King's Speech: he goes abroad for 4 years. In India the British defeat the Moghul Emperor and the Nawab of Oudh, ending the attempt to overthrow them; the British become the undisputed rulers of Bengal. Hyder Ali usurps the throne of Mysore.	Politics & Military History
University of Haarlem is established. Papal Nuncio is expelled from Portugal.	Collected works of Voltaire are translated and published in English.	Rousseau *Du Contrat Social.* John Wilkes establishes his radical newspaper, the *North Briton.* Sorbonne Library opens in Paris.	Rousseau's *Du Contrat Social* is publicly burnt in Geneva.	Voltaire *Dictionnaire Philosophique.* Foundation of The Club in London whose members include Boswell, Burke, Garrick, Goldsmith, Johnson, Reynolds.	Religion & Learning
Beginning of intense Enclosure Acts in England is to change the face of rural England over the next 30 years. From 1760 to 1785 British cotton production increases tenfold.	Influenza epidemic spreads across Europe.		Rio de Janeiro is made the capital of Portuguese territories in South America. Philadelphia becomes the first town in the colonies to pass a population of 20,000.	Practice of numbering houses is introduced in London. First permanent settlement is established at St Louis.	Cities & Social Development
From 1760 onwards with increasing industrial inventions the Industrial Revolution may be said to have begun.	Giovanni Morgagni *On the Causes of Diseases, based on Anatomical Reasons* represents the true beginning of pathological anatomy as a science. Russian scientist Mikhail Lomonosov discovers the atmosphere of Venus; he is largely responsible for the foundation of Moscow University. First French veterinary school is opened at Lyons.		John Canton, the English scientist, demonstrates the compressibility of water.	James Hargreaves invents the spinning jenny.	Discovery & Invention
		Oliver Goldsmith *The Vicar of Wakefield.* Le Petit Trianon is built by Louis XV at Versailles.	Mozart begins his grand tour as a child prodigy.	Robert Adam builds Kenwood House in London. Mozart produces his first symphony at age eight.	The Arts

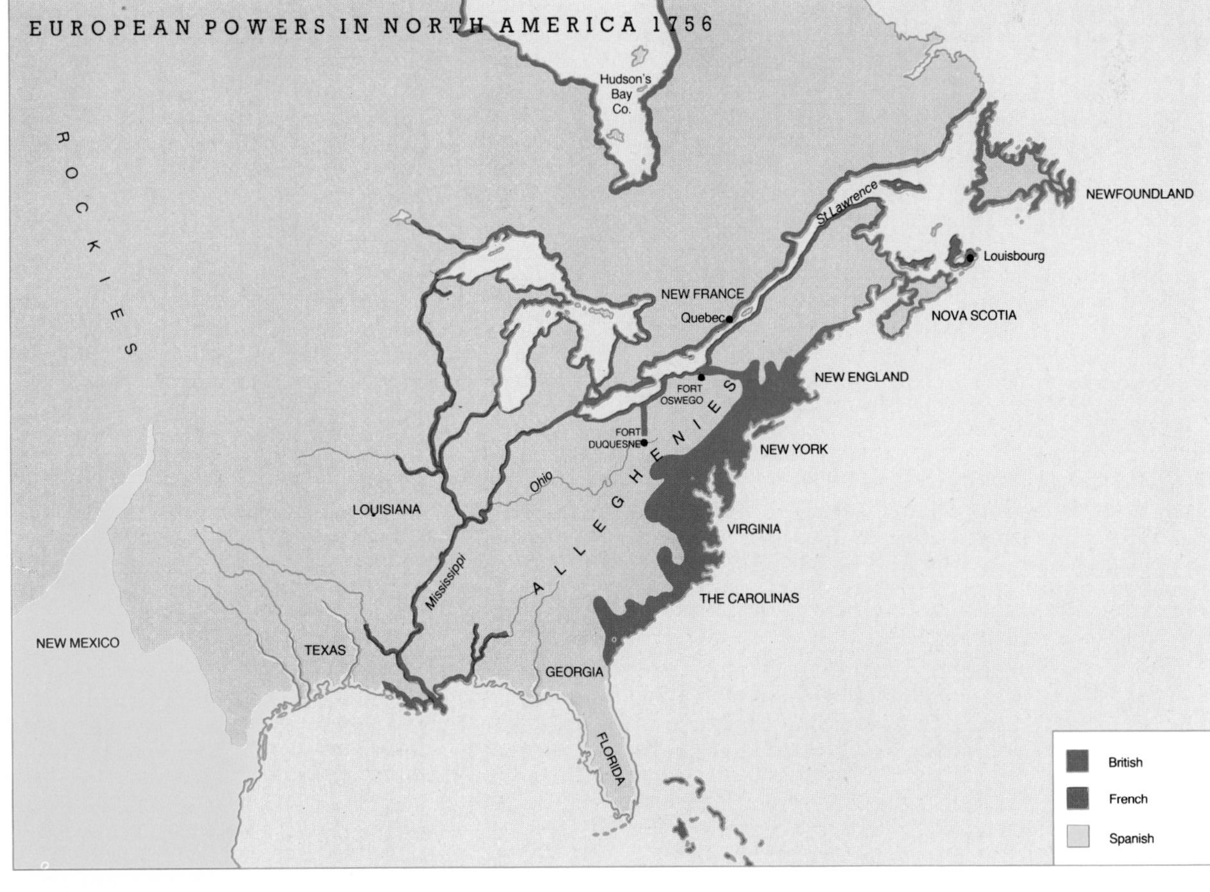

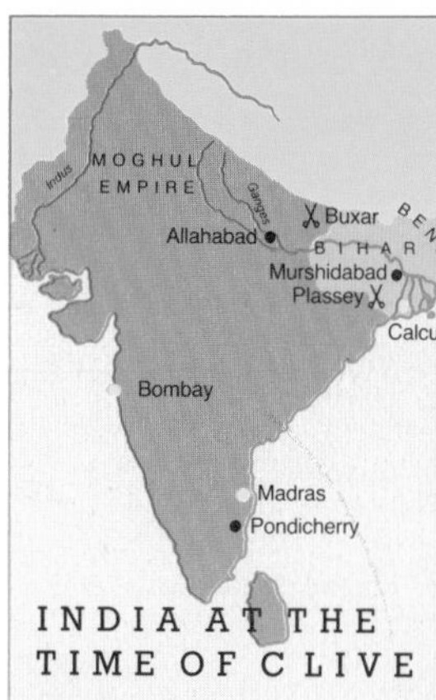

Above left: The Moghul Emperor Shah Alam hands Clive a firman *(edict) giving th British East India Company the right to collect the revenues of Bengal, Bihar and Orissa. A muslim onlooker remarked bitterly that the whole transaction 'was done and finished in less time than would have been taken up on the sale of a jackass'.*

Above: An official of the East India Company enjoying the privileges of his position.

By the middle of the 18th century the coastline of the Indian sub-continent was dotted with European trading posts – British, Dutch, French and Portuguese. But if there were more of these than ever before the style had hardly changed in 200 years: they were strictly business enterprises, under instruction from their companies not to get involved in 'country matters'. The tumultuous events in the interior, where the Moghul empire was in its death throes, largely passed them by. Anyway, even if they had wished to interfere they hardly had the means to do so, none of them disposed of more than a few hundred soldiers.

The British East India Company had three main entrepôts – Bombay, Madras and Calcutta. In 1756 a dispute arose between the Calcutta factory and the local Indian potentate, Siraj-ud-daula, Governor of Bengal. He subsequently moved on Calcutta in force, leaving the British the choice of fleeing to their ships or throwing themselves on his mercy. The less courageous chose the first option, the less wise the second and suffered a semi-accidental massacre as a result. Siraj-ud-daula retired to his capital, Murshidabad, confident that the next communication he would receive from the British would be a peace feeler.

The British reaction turned out to be more belligerent. The Madras garrison had just been reinforced by a regular infantry battalion intended for use against the French in Pondicherry. The French were quiet so its orders were amended to include the recapture of Calcutta: the Royal Navy conveyed it across the Bay of Bengal to the mouth of the Hooghly and Calcutta was recovered as easily as it had been lost. The British commander Robert Clive then took the initiative, moving north along the road to Murshidabad. Three quarters of the way there Siraj-ud-daula's army emerged to do battle. Long columns of infantry were interspersed with squadrons of gaily caparisoned cavalry, trains of bullocks pulled the artillery and lines of elephants carried the many commanders. Altogether Siraj-ud-daula had about 50,000 men and 50 guns. Clive had just over 3000 men and 7 guns.

The battle, named after the grove of Plassey which Clive chose for his initial position, never developed much beyond a cannonade. The British, who reckoned that a good gun team could get off a shot every 30 seconds, maintained a high enough rate of fire to discourage the Indian cavalry from attacking. The Indian artillerymen were satisfied with a shot every 15 minutes and so never managed to hurt the British at all. In the late afternoon Clive ordered his men forward and as they advanced the vast Indian host simply melted away.

Politically, Clive made surprisingly little use of the victory. He gave Bengal a new governor, helped himself liberally from its treasury and then sailed for home.

In 1764 the directors of the East India Company asked Clive to go back to India: the situation in Bengal had got out of hand again. The Company's men on the spot had engineered the downfall of Mir Jaffir, the man whom Clive had installed as governor, in favour of Mir Kassim who was thought to be more pliable. Far from it – Mir Kassim had broken with the Company and killed as many of its officers as he could lay hands on. Things were every bit as bad as they had been when Clive first set foot there.

Clive arrived the next year to find that the crisis was past. Mir Kassim's forces had been routed at the battle of Buxar – a more serious affair than Plassey – and Bengal was quiet again. But Clive decided to use the near-dictatorial powers the Company had granted him to create a new political order. There was still a Moghul emperor claiming control over the whole sub-continent; Clive obtained from him a *firman* (edict) granting the British direct administrative control of Bengal and Bihar. He then proceeded to put this administration on a proper footing, establishing a salary scale for officials and putting an end to the looting of provincial funds. He also faced down the mutiny this reform provoked.

Clive's high-handed actions made him many enemies. People who had been caught with their hands in the till did not relish being hauled over the coals by a man who, on his own admission, had lifted £234,000 – many millions in today's money – from the Bengal treasury after Plassey. But this time round Clive held a different commission and was doing a different job. He was laying the foundations for an empire that would one day rule everything between the Himalayas and the sea.

	1765	1766	1767	1768	1769
Politics & Military History	Stamp Act passed by English Parliament: imposes a tax on publications and legal documents in the American colonies; Virginia Assembly challenges the right of Britain to tax the Colonies; delegates from 9 colonies draw up a declaration of rights and liberties; the beginning of 10 years of conflict leading to the American War of Independence. Regency Act is passed in England. Clive introduces administrative reforms in Bengal.	Britain repeals the Stamp Act but passes the Declaratory Act asserting sovereignty over the American colonies. Following the expulsion of Wilkes, Parliament declares General Warrants to be illegal. Nizam Ali of Hyderabad cedes Madras to Britain.	Townshend Acts impose new taxes on the North American colonies including a duty on tea; the New York Assembly is suspended for refusing to support quartering of troops. Russia and Turkey at war (to 1774). Catherine II convokes Legislative Commission to discuss the re-codification of Russian laws. Chaos in India and the first Mysore War encourage British expansion.	Quarrel between Britain and her North American colonies grows. Boston citizens refuse to quarter British troops; the Massachusetts Assembly is dissolved for refusing to assist with tax collection. Wilkes is elected MP for Middlesex but is rejected by the House of Commons. Secretary of State for the Colonies is appointed in Britain. Austria renounces its claims to Silesia.	Austria seizes the Polish territory of Lvov and Zips: this is a prelude to the coming partitions of Poland; Frederick II proposes partition of Poland to Catherine of Russia. Russia invades the Turkish provinces of Moldavia and Wallachia. British Privy Council decides to retain the American tea duty.
Religion & Learning	Sir William Blackstone *Commentaries on the Laws of England* which became indispensable to lawyers and gave the first clear picture of English law as a whole. Turgot *Reflexions sur la formation et la distribution des richesses*, a reforming statesman who aimed to make taxation more equitable.	Catherine II allows freedom of worship in Russia.	Jesuits are expelled from Spain and Naples by Charles III. Rousseau flees France to England.	The first numbers of the *Encyclopaedia Britannica* appear.	*Letters of Junius* begin to appear: anonymous attacks upon men in English public life. Edmund Burke *Observations on the present state of the nation.* Austrian monasteries are dissolved to be used for charitable and educational purposes.
Cities & Social Development	Potato becomes the most popular food in Europe.	Mason-Dixon line marks the boundary between Pennsylvania and Maryland: the line later separates free and slave states. By this time there are about 200,000 Germans in the North American colonies. Under the Free Ports Act Britain attempts to make the West Indies an entrepôt for trade with the Spanish American colonies.	Arthur Young sets out on his travels through England and France. On the coast of Old Calabar English ships fire on African canoes killing hundreds of Africans to enforce slave trade.	New liberal criminal code is produced in Austria.	The domestic system of cotton spinning in England begins to disappear following Arkwright's invention of the water frame. *The Morning Chronicle* is established in London. Spain commences the colonization of California.
Discovery & Invention	James Watt improves on Newcomen's pumping engine with a separate condenser.	Henry Cavendish identifies hydrogen as an element and analyses air: this leads to balloon experiments. First dictionary of chemistry is produced in Paris.	Joseph Priestley *History and Present State of Electricity*. Carteret discovers Pitcairn Islands.	Hargreaves improves his spinning jenny and an inexpensive, hand-operated machine is produced. Captain James Cook sets off on his first voyage to the Antipodes. Linnaeus *Systema Naturae* is completed: Swedish natural history in three parts.	Arkwright's water frame: the first mechanical spinning of cotton warp. Cook explores the east coast of Australia. First lightning conductors are used on high buildings.
The Arts	Johnson's edition of Shakespeare. Fragonard *Coresus et Callirhoe*. Gabriel, architect *Place de la Concorde*.	Lessing *Laocoon* on aesthetics. Diderot *Essai sur la Peinture*.	Sterne *Sentimental Journey* and completes *Tristram Shandy*. Gluck *Alcestis*, opera.	Foundation of the Royal Academy of Arts: Sir Joshua Reynolds is first president. Thomas Augustine Arne, his Innovation: the first known explanatory concert programme. Thomas Gray *Poems*.	Joshua Reynolds begins his *Discourses* (to 1791). Goethe *Neue Liede*, early poems Fragonard *The Study*.

	1770	1771	1772	1773	1774
Politics & Military History	Boston Massacre: British troops fire on the mob in Boston killing five; this leads to the repeal of the Townshend Acts except for the tax on tea imported into North America which remains. The Parlements are abolished in France. Russia captures Bender, Ismail and Akerman in her war with Turkey.	The right to report Parliamentary debates is established in England. In war with Turkey, Russia conquers the Crimea and destroys Turkish fleet. Ali Bey, Sultan of Egypt, seizes Damascus.	First Partition of Poland between Austria, Prussia and Russia. Gustavus III of Sweden breaks the power of the Diet and imposes a new constitution after 52 years' rule by the nobles. In North America the Boston Assembly demands rights of colonies and threatens secession. Warren Hastings becomes Governor of Bengal.	The Boston 'Tea Party'. The Regulation Act: the British government brings the political activities of the East India Company under its control. In the ten years to 1773 Austrian state revenues have doubled as a result of reforms.	Intolerable Acts passed by British Parliament against colonial opposition to tea duty; Coercive Act against Massachusetts, the port of Boston is closed. Continental Congress at Philadelphia representing all the colonies except Georgia issues a Declaration of Rights. Quebec Act: guarantees Roman Catholicism to French Canadians (angers Puritan New England). Treaty of Kuchuk Kainardji: ends Russo-Turkish War; Russia gains Black Sea ports and the right to represent Greek Orthodox Church in Turkey.
Religion & Learning	Burke *Thoughts on the Present Discontents* in which he attacked the existing system of government and court patronage.	Bougainville *Voyage autour du monde*, description of a voyage of discovery he undertook following the Seven Years' War.	Mirabeau *Essai sur le déspotisme*.	Joseph II expels the Jesuits from the Empire. Pope Clement XIV dissolves Jesuit Order.	Earl of Chesterfield *Letters to his son*. Burke *On American Taxation*.
Cities & Social Development	Famine in Bengal. First public restaurant appears in Paris. European smallpox epidemic.		*The Morning Post* is first published (until 1937). Judge Wm Murray: 'a slave who sets foot on English soil becomes a free man.'	Peasant uprising in Russia is led by Cossack Pugachev – suppressed in 1775. Parliament regulates the wages of the Spitalfields silk trade.	Export of cotton making machinery from Britain is prohibited.
Discovery & Invention	Cook discovers Botany Bay in Australia. French chemist, Lavoisier, proves that water cannot be transmitted into earth so confounding a long standing theory.	John Hunter, Scottish surgeon *Treatise on the Natural History of the Human Teeth* (to 1778) which became the basis for modern dentistry. Swedish chemist Scheele discovers oxygen (independently discovered by Priestley 3 years later) and fluorine.	Cook sets off on his second voyage of discovery (to 1775). Joseph Priestley lays the foundations of modern chemistry; isolates nitrous oxide and six other new gases (1777). James Bruce, African explorer, traces the Blue Nile (1770) to its confluence with the White Nile.	Cook sights islands named after him: first person across Antarctic Circle. Samuel Crompton designs spinning mule for warp and weft producing the finest yarn ever woven. First cast-iron bridge is built (to 1792) at Coalbrookdale, Shropshire.	Franz Anton Mesmer uses hypnosis for health purposes: the founder of mesmerism. Petit successfully performs mastoid operation in France.
The Arts	Goldsmith *The Deserted Village*. Johannes Ewald, Danish poet, *Rolf Krage* (a tragedy). Gainsborough *The Blue Boy*. Mozart's first string quartets.	Smollet *Humphry Clinker*. Friedrich Gottlieb Klopstock, German poet *Odes*.	Lessing *Emilia Galotti*, a German tragedy. Haydn has a prolific year: Mass in G, Farewell Symphony, 6 Symphonies Op. 20 and Quartets 31–6.	Goethe *Urfaust*, the first version of Faust. Goldsmith *She Stoops to Conquer*. Reynolds *Lady Cockburn & her children*. Waltz fashionable in Vienna.	Goethe *The Sorrows of Young Werther*. Gluck *Iphigenia in Aulis*, German opera.

By the 1760s British naval supremacy was so firmly established that the Admiralty was free to turn its attention to the two outstanding problems of 18th century maritime geography. Was there a Southern Continent? And was there a way in which seamen could fix their longitude?

Whoever came up with the right answer on the longitude was in for a handsome reward. Back in 1714 Parliament had offered a cash prize of £20,000 for any method which would enable a ship's master to determine his longitude with an accuracy of $\frac{1}{2}°$, the equivalent of 55 kilometres at the equator. They also appointed a "Board of Longitude" to report on the various schemes that were put up by people hoping to win the prize. The betting was that the eventual winner would be an astronomer: Newton had said as much when the prize was first mooted and even sketched in a possible method, the measurement of "lunar distances". Precise tables of the moon's movements were now available: what no one had yet come up with was a way of taking sightings of matching accuracy from the deck of a rolling and pitching ship. An alternative approach was to build a better watch. If you knew Greenwich time (Greenwich being where the Royal Observatory was) and local time, working out your longitude was child's play.

But what a watch it would have to be – accurate to within a tenth of a second a day. Clockwork had come a long way since the medieval tower clocks which had been doing well if they ended the 24 hours only a quarter of an hour out of true: the addition of a pendulum to the escapement (by Christaan Huygens in 1656) had reduced the error to no more than a quarter of a minute, and the development of gear cutting machines had brought this down to a few seconds by the mid-18th century. Of course, one could not expect a pendulum to work on a rolling ship but its mechanical equivalent, the balance spring, was more tolerant and a watch of this type was a reasonable starting point for an attempt on the prize. All the same, accuracy of a tenth of a second meant an improvement of better than two orders of magnitude on existing watches, which was a lot to ask of any clockmaker.

To the Board's surprise the best instrument submitted proved to be the work, not of one of the famous London names, but of an unknown, self-taught clockmaker from the back of beyond, John Harrison of Fowleby in Yorkshire. It was an extraordinary thing to look at, a mass of cogs, springs and balances housed in a box 1m square: even weirder, most of the cogs were made of wood. Yet, testing showed that it kept time better than any previous clock. Harrison had worked out how to compensate for temperature changes (by using bi-metallic strips) and the clogging effect of lubricants (by using bearings of self-lubricating hardwood): his ingenuity was such that the Board had no alternative but to commission him to produce a watch for trial at sea. In 1761 this watch was put aboard HMS *Deptford* bound for Jamaica. There was some dispute as to the exact result but it was clear that if Harrison's watch had not met the Board's full requirement it had come closer to it than any previous entry. And a second test voyage, to Barbados and back, confirmed that Harrison had won.

The watch, which it is fair to call the world's first marine chronometer, lost no more than 15 seconds in a five month voyage: on this basis a ship's captain could determine his longitude to within 11 miles.

Rather meanly, the members of the Board refused to pay over the full £20,000. Their excuse was that they had to be sure that they had a practical instrument, not just a one-off masterpiece. If a good craftsman could copy Harrison's design successfully then he would get the entire amount, but for the moment he would have to be content with

Above: One of Kendall's versions of the Harrison Marine Chronometer. This specimen was taken by Captain Cook on his third and last voyage to the Pacific (1776–80).

Above: Hawaiian native in a feathered headdress. Captain Cook met his end on Hawaai when he took a high line over some pilfering by the natives and became involved in a lethal brawl.

£10,000. Harrison, who had spent a lifetime on the project and was now approaching his 80th year, had to hang about while another clockmaker, Larcum Kendall, copied his design and the Admiralty arranged for it to be tested by Captain Cook.

This brings us to the second of the two mysteries that the Admiralty hoped to solve, the matter of a habitable Southern Continent. In retrospect, it is extraordinary how sure everyone was that this existed, for there was little to support the idea beyond a vague feeling that the land and water areas of the globe should balance out: the only hard evidence was a coastline discovered by Tasman back in 1642 which stuck up into the Pacific as far as latitude 35°S. This could be the western edge of a land mass lying obliquely across the Southern Ocean and most atlases of the period showed it as such with the proud label *Terra Australis Incognita*.

In 1768 the Admiralty dispatched Captain Cook to chart Tasman's coastline and anything else in the same region. This he did with admirable efficiency, demonstrating that it was simply the western aspect of the pair of islands that we now know as New Zealand. He saw no sign of any other land but as vast areas of the South Pacific remained unvisited he could not say for sure that no major land mass existed. The Admiralty, deciding the time had come for definite answers, sent Captain Cook out again.

Cook's second voyage to the Pacific laid the ghost of the Southern Continent for good. His systematic survey of the latitudes between 40°S and the Arctic Circle revealed that they contained nothing but empty sea: *Terra Australis Incognita* had no existence outside the mapmakers' imagination. At the same time he subjected the Harrison chronometer (in the form of Kendall's copy) to its most stringent test yet. And it passed trimphantly, losing scarcely more than two minutes a year. Cook returned home determined to help Harrison get the rest of the prize money.

He need not have worried, for Harrison had obtained an even more powerful ally. King George III was interested in clocks and admired clockmakers and when he heard the story of the Board's penny-pinching he was outraged. 'By God, Harrison, I'll see you righted' he said, and he put on the pressure to such good effect that the money was paid over in 1773, two years before Cook's return. By then the two of them – Harrison, the foremost instrument maker of the age, and Cook, incomparably the best seaman – had done their work: they had turned the art of navigation into a science.

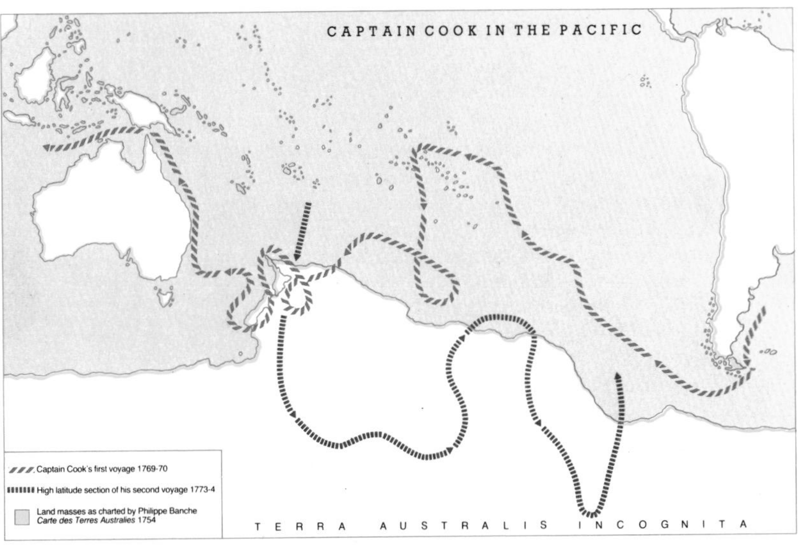

THE AGE OF REVOLUTION

AD 1775 - AD 1814

The last 25 years of the 18th century saw a series of social, political and economic upheavals that permanently altered the character of the western world. In Europe and North America old sovereignties were overthrown and new political structures – the American Republic, revolutionary France – erected in their place. And in England the rise of industry began to reshape the practices by which man had lived since the dawn of history.

All of which sounds dramatic and indeed the political and military events of the era were often dramatic in the extreme. But it is important to remember that the major changes in history are usually evolutionary not revolutionary and that a lot of things that are dazzling at the time – the Napoleonic adventure, for example – do not carry a lot of long term significance. Even the French revolution was more a matter of promise than performance: it had to be repeated several times in the 19th century before its ideas were properly sorted out and the slogans that had swept away the Ancien Régime *were translated into solid political achievement. If this is true of the political scene, what of the famous industrial revolution?*

As of now, the consensus is that the industrial revolution was a real event. The output of several English industries – iron for one, cotton for another – did not just increase, it soared. But it is worth remembering that Europe's first industrial nation remained predominantly rural to the end of the revolutionary period. And even in areas where one would expect technical progress to show up early it is surprising how slow things were to change. The ships that fought at Trafalgar were little different from those of the mid-18th century. For that matter it would take an expert to distinguish the armies that fought at Austerlitz from those that had marched on Blenheim a hundred years earlier.

Nevertheless, there was a revolution that was carried through to completion within our period, the American Revolution. Curiously enough it was hardly at all revolutionary in intent: the Patriots of 1775 did not consider that they were overturning an established order so much as defending an already existing one. Their attitude was essentially conservative. Perhaps because of this they went extremely cautiously when the time came to make a new Constitution. Its main concern was to ensure that a national government could not infringe the liberties of the individual. They got it right and the Constitution serves the cause of liberty today.

Chronology has put the American Revolution at the top of our list: by any measure it deserves no less.

THE SHOT HEARD ROUND THE WORLD

The ending of the French threat to British North America caused the British Government and the American colonies to look at their relationship anew. The colonies, with their two million free citizens, had clearly come of age but that simple statement was read very differently by the two sides. To the British Government it meant the colonies should cease to be a charge on the British tax-payer. A proportion of the sum needed to keep the colony must in future be raised on the spot. With this in mind, Prime Minister Grenville decided to tighten up the American customs and impose a stamp duty on all legal transactions. Between them these two measures should raise £100,000, a not unreasonable contribution in the circumstances.

The Americans saw the matter differently. They had never been directly taxed before, they did not like the idea at all and they had good grounds for regarding the attempt to raise money by stamp duty as illegal. One of the reasons Englishmen were free and most other nations were not was that they could not be taxed, materially or socially, without the consent of their elected representatives, specifically the members of the House of Commons sitting in Parliament at Westminster. Yet clearly the American colonies had no representatives at Westminster, nor was it practical for them ever to do so. The only logical conclusion that a patriotic American could draw was that the new English ministry was attempting to establish a tyranny.

This mood of outrage built up so quickly and became so general that it was soon clear that the British Colonial Authorities woud never be able to enforce the Stamp Act. Bowing to the inevitable, the government withdrew it and concentrated instead on trying to improve the revenue from the customs. These duties were legal but almost equally npopular, and to protect the customs houses and their fficials the British had to put troops into Boston, the main entre for the collection of the customs' dues.

The British had now painted themselves into a corner. 'he one thing all Englishmen were agreed on was that the rown should not have at its disposal a standing army of ufficient size to threaten civil liberty. Yet the British were ow maintaining an army in Boston which was every bit as ffensive to American patriotism. The surprising thing is hat when a detachment of British soldiers fired into a mob ıreatening to loot the Boston Customs' House and five eople were killed, the revolution did not erupt immedi- tely. It seems that Sam and John Adams, the organisers of ne Patriot party, deliberately defused the situation because smacked of lawlessness. What they wanted was a disci- lined bit of provocation and, in 1773, in the form of the amous "Tea Party", they provided it. One hundred and fty Patriots, lightly disguised as Mohican Indians, took ver three ships in Boston harbour and tipped the tea they vere carrying, which was dutiable, overboard. The British eacted with the ill-temper that the Adamses had hoped for: Massachusetts was put under a military governor, General Gage, and the port at Boston closed pending payment of a ine.

General Gage had enough men to control Boston but owhere near enough to carry his writ through the ountryside. In normal times he could have relied on the elp of the local militia but by now the militia had to be ounted as part of the Patriot organization: they were ctively preparing for combat with the British. In April 775 General Gage, learning that the Patriots were tockpiling powder and shot at Concord, a village 32 ilometres west of Boston, ordered Lieutenant-Colonel Smith to find these stores and destroy them.

The British column, 700 strong, set out late on Tuesday 8th April 1775. Patriot leaders in Boston sent out nessengers – one of them being Paul Revere – to warn the eople along the British route, and when the British eached Lexington, two-thirds of the way to Concord, on he morning of the 19th, they found the local militia drawn p on the village green. If the militia's leader had any idea of trying to stop the British he quickly gave it up for he was outnumbered ten to one: he ordered his men to disband and both sides held their fire. But, just as the tension was easing, someone, somewhere, fired a musket. The British let go with a volley, killing eight militiamen.

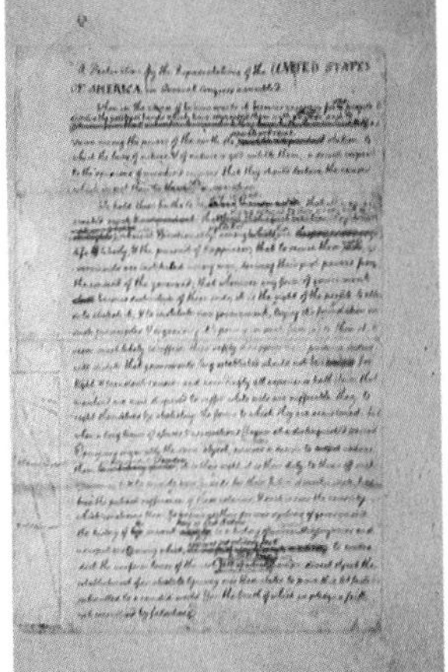

Above: Jefferson's 'rough draft' of the Declaration of Independence.

Below: The Battle of Lexington, 1775. Plate 1 of a series of four drawn by Ralph Earle and engraved by a Connecticut militiaman, Amos Doolittle, who was on the scene a few days later.

In the centre British troops let loose their fateful volley: in the foreground the Lexington militia flee or fall.

Reforming his column Lieutenant-Colonel Smith marched on to Concord: the militia there withdrew to the north, across the Concord river, as the British entered the town. A few gun carriages were discovered by British search parties and burnt: the smoke from the bonfire produced a wave of anger among the militiamen who assumed it was coming from the pillage of their homes. Crying "Will you let them burn the town down?", a militia officer led his men against the British detachment guarding the North Bridge. The British fired some warning shots, then some serious ones but the Americans, who outnumbered and outflanked them, fired to better effect. After losing three dead and nine wounded the British were forced back into Concord where Lieutenant-Colonel Smith was reassembling his men for the march back to Boston.

The return journey was a very different affair from the morning's advance. The militia began sniping at the British as soon as they left Concord and as fresh militia companies arrived from neighbouring counties and took up positions in the woods and fields flanking the road, the harassment became increasingly severe. What saved them was the reinforcing column, 1200 strong, that Lieutenant-Colonel Smith had had the foresight to send for earlier in the day. It proved sufficient to see the battered expedition safely back to Boston, though not without further serious loss.

News of the fighting at Lexington and Concord brought all New England into a state of open rebellion: only Canada, with its separate origins and interests, remained faithful to the British. In July 1775 delegates from the 13 rebel states convened at Philadelphia for the Continental Congress that in June offered command of all Patriot forces to Colonel George Washington of the Virginia delegation. In July Washington arrived in the lines before Boston and though he could not take Boston by assault nor, given British command of the sea, starve it into surrender, the means to reduce the city were already in train. Fort Ticonderoga, a British strongpoint left over from the Canadian campaigns, had yielded a handsome number of heavy guns: these were being dragged across the Green Mountains towards the beleaguered city. When they finally arrived in early March 1776 the British immediately embarked their garrison and sailed away, never to return.

The formal separation came shortly after. In June 1776 Richard Henry Lee put a resolution in favour of independence to the Continental Congress and the Congress agreed to have a committee prepare a suitable Declaration. The document, in essence the work of Virginia delegate Thomas Jefferson, catalogued the injustices under which the American people had laboured for the previous 12 years. The argument is tendentious and not always successful, and almost every item in the list could be challenged. But the preamble contains a statement of principles for the future government of America which has since become the touchstone of American political thinking.

The battle of Concord – the running fight that began with the first volley at the North Bridge – immediately captured the popular imagination in Europe as much as in America itself: the opening salvo has reasonably been apostrophized as 'the shot heard round the world'. But Jefferson's 'self-evident truths' – the equality of man and his right to life, liberty and the pursuit of happiness – though little heeded at the time, have sounded louder down the years. They were to keep America safe in crises yet to come.

Above left: The first lecture at Madame Geoffrin's salon in Paris with Rousseau and Diderot in the audience soon after Rousseau had won in 1750 a public competition writing on the theme: 'Has progress in the arts and sciences contributed to an improvement of morals?' His contribution was Discours sur les sciences et les arts *which at once made him the centre of the intellectual world of Paris and of smart society.*

Above right: Rousseau in his old age contemplating Nature.

As the 18th century drew to an end the Enlightenment was visibly running out of steam. Its achievements seemed increasingly commonplace, its failings – its tolerance of privilege, its lack of interest in the ordinary run of mortals, its assumption that it was probably better to do too little than too much – increasingly hard to bear with. A new set of ideas was needed, a demand that was met by one of the most complicated, unreasonable, original geniuses that any age can boast of: Jean Jacques Rousseau.

Rousseau stood the values of the Enlightenment on their perfectly coiffured heads. He did not think anything of civilization: he was sure that primitive man, the 'noble savage', had lived a happier, fuller, more truly moral life than any anxious, ungiving modern. Nor was he impressed by the triumphs of contemporary science: man was not the mechanical doll of the scientists' dull imaginings, he possessed a divine spark; the appetites that he shared with the beasts of the field were less important to his working than the mysterious passions and longings which emerged from his immortal soul. Rousseau could not revive the religion of the Age of Faith but he could and did create a new one, the Religion of Nature and Natural Man.

Of course all this was anathema to the Rationalists. Voltaire, the watchdog of the Age of Reason, considered Rousseau's philosophy an invitation to go down on all fours, something he declined to do on the grounds that after 60 years he had lost the habit. Dr Johnson was just as blunt: Rousseau's followers were only intellectual opportunists. 'Truth is a cow that will yield them no more milk, so they have gone to milk the bull.' And, it has to be acknowledged, Rousseau was no anthropologist, nor for that matter was he much of an historian. But for the society of his day he was a true prophet. He was passionate about equality and that passion was to change the world. Voltaire and Rousseau both died in 1778, Voltaire shortly after returning to Paris and a reception that has been justly described as an apotheosis. Rousseau, by contrast, died in obscure circumstances, possibly by his own hand, certainly in loneliness and despair. But Goethe got it right when he said that 'With Voltaire an age ended, with Rousseau a new one began'. Rousseau had put his finger on the Achilles' heel of the Enlightenment, its essential inhumanity.

Rousseau was a man of many parts. He has a small but deserved place in the history of music and a large and important one in educational theory. In the arts he is one of the founding fathers of the Romantic movement. The origins of this movement certainly go back beyond Rousseau – the vogue for gardens landscaped in the informal English style, for example, was in full swing before Rousseau ever set pen to paper – and the general trend of Rousseau's thought is far from being consistently romantic anyway: he was for Sparta as against Athens, for the stoic virtues and against the sort of emotional onanism in which the Romantic movement culminated. But he was also for Nature and against artifice, and this celebration of Nature puts him in the main stream of Romanticism.

We have still not reached the final tally. As well as making contributions of the first importance in the fields of politics and sociology Rousseau found time to be both bad and mad. His wickedness emerged in the course of one of his perennial public quarrels when it was discovered that he had unloaded the five children born to his mistress on the local foundling home. His madness took the form of suspecting that anyone who offered him help was really trying to trick or trap him. He was constantly claiming to have been misrepresented, and to prove his case he constantly misrepresented others. By the end of his life this trait had matured into a full blown paranoid illness.

From these unpromising materials Rousseau fashioned another triumph. To justify himself to the world he wrote his Confessions, in which he promised to lay bare the human soul as had never been done before. The general estimate is that he succeeded in doing so. The most famous episode, the one in which as a young man he accused a maid-servant of stealing a ribbon that he had in fact stolen himself, starts rather disappointingly. He claims, melodramatically, that he ruined the girl's life and that subsequently she could never have raised up her head in public again. He castigates himself unmercifully. But then he changes his line and puts himself back into the mind of the 17 year old boy who did the deed. He was, and is, totally innocent. The girl was the object of his fondest thoughts, her face ever in his mind. He had been deprived of the opportunity of presenting her with the ribbon. What else could he do but blurt out her name?

A hundred years were to pass before men of science – if you call psychoanalysts men of science – could bring this degree of subtlety to their introspections.

	1775	1776	1777	1778	1779
Politics & Military History	War of American Independence: Battles of Lexington and Concord; the Americans take Fort Ticonderoga and Crown Point; the second Continental Congress is held at Philadelphia; Washington is appointed C-in-C American forces. Catherine II reforms provincial government in Russia. Beginning of the First Maratha War (to 1782) in India. Battle of Bunkers Hill: British victory in America. Shah of Persia captures Basra.	Fall of Turgot in France ends his attempted reforms. British troops evacuate Boston; the colonies issue the Declaration of Independence; British forces capture New York, are repulsed at Charleston. Portuguese unify their South American empire by forming the Viceroyalty of Rio de la Plata based on Rio de Janeiro.	War in America. Lafayette's French volunteers arrive; British defeat the Americans at Brandywine and take Philadelphia; after two defeats Burgoyne surrenders to the Americans at Saratoga. Stars and Stripes is adopted as the Continental Congress flag. Perpetual Alliance between Spain and Portugal settles disputes relating to their South American colonies.	France and Holland enter the war against Britain. Battle of Monmouth, New Jersey: Washington defeats British. British take French settlements in India. Chile becomes a separate province in the Spanish Empire.	Spain joins the war against Britain: siege of Gibraltar. Anglo-French naval engagement off Flamborough Head. In West Indies French take St Vincent and Grenada. In South Africa the first clashes between the Dutch advancing north from the Cape and the Bantu peoples – Xhosa – the First Kaffir War.
Religion & Learning	Burke *Speech on Conciliation with America.*	Adam Smith *The Wealth of Nations.* Edward Gibbon *The History of the Decline and Fall of the Roman Empire* first volume (to 1788). Jeremy Bentham's first publication *Fragments on Government.* Tom Paine *Common Sense* on causes of war in America.	Priestley *Disquisition relating to Matter & Spirit.*	Buffon *Époques de la Nature.* The deaths of Rosseau and Voltaire.	Hume *Dialogues concerning Natural Religion* (posthumous).
Cities & Social Development	German lands of the Habsburg Empire form single customs area. James Watt and Matthew Boulton form a partnership to manufacture steam engines designed by Watt. England takes over from Portugal the India-China opium trade.	Somerset House in London becomes repository of records of population.	John Howard *The state of the prisons in England and Wales with an account of some foreign prisons*, the beginning of prison reform. Spain completes occupation of what today is Uruguay.	Thomas Coke of Norfolk embarks upon his agricultural experiments which play a key part in the agrarian revolution. Act of Congress prohibits the import of slaves into the US.	Royal serfs in France are liberated. Pope Pius VI begins to drain the Pontine Marshes. First children's clinic is established in London.
Discovery & Invention	Arkwright's carding patent. Thomas Jeffreys *The American Atlas.*	Cook sets out on third voyage of discovery. Watt and Boulton produce their first commercial steam engine.	Cook discovers the Sandwich Islands. Lavoisier shows that air consists of oxygen and nitrogen.	Cook discovers Hawaii; he is killed there in 1779. Smeaton, improved diving bell.	Scheele prepares glycerine: the chemistry of fats is established.
The Arts	Johnson *Journey to the Western Islands of Scotland.* Sheridan *The Rivals.* Beaumarchais *Le Barbier de Seville.* Sarah Siddons makes her first stage appearance. Reynolds *Miss Bowles & Her Dog.* Fragonard *The Washerwoman.*	Last public appearance of Garrick. Goeth *Stella*, tragedy.	Sheridan *The School for Scandal.* Chatterton *Poems* (posthumous).	Fanny Burney *Evelina* (novel). Mozart *Paris Symphony.* La Scala opera house opens in Milan.	Johnson *Lives of the Poets* (to 1781). Appearance of James Gillray's first cartoons. Mozart *Coronation Mass.*

	1780	1781	1782	1783	1784
Politics & Military History	British capture Charleston, South Carolina, but are defeated in North Carolina. Battle of Cape St Vincent: Rodney defeats the Spanish fleet. Armed Neutrality of the North: Holland, Denmark, Russia and Sweden combine to protect neutral shipping from British interference. Revolt of Peruvian Indians against Spanish rule: lasts to 1781. Henry Grattan demands Home Rule for Ireland.	Ségur Ordinance in France: commands in armed forces, high posts in Church and diplomacy are reserved for the nobility. British forces under Cornwallis surrender to the French and Americans at Yorktown. Articles of Confederation and Perpetual Union are ratified by all the American states. Austro-Russian Alliance against Turkey. Warren Hastings deposes the Rajah of Benares, plunders the treasure of the Nabob of Oudh.	Irish Parliament is made independent of that in Britain; a partial removal of Catholic disabilities. Treaty of Salbai: ends the Maratha War. Spain conquers Florida. Battle of the Saints: Rodney defeats the French to restore Britain's naval supremacy. Spanish raise the siege of Gibraltar.	Russia annexes the Crimea. German is enforced as official language of Bohemia by Joseph II. Treaty of Paris ends American War of Independence; Britain recognizes the United States; restores Minorca and Florida to Spain, retains Gibraltar. 40,000 United Empire Loyalists from the American colonies migrate to Canada.	William Pitt the younger becomes First Minister in Britain and is to dominate politics for 20 years: new finance policy and modernization of the administration. India Act: establishes government control over the East India Company. The appointment of the first Anglican colonial bishop. Convention of Constantinople: Turkey accepts Russia's annexation of the Crimea.
Religion & Learning	Lessing *On the Education of the Human Race.* Robert Raikes opens his first Sunday School in England. American Academy of Arts and Sciences is established at Boston.	Immanuel Kant *Critique of Pure Reason.* Volumes 2–3 of Gibbon's *Decline and Fall.* Edict of Toleration reduces the Pope's authority in Austria to create religious tolerance and press freedom. Pestalozzi *Leonard and Gertrude* states educational aims.	Posthumous publication of Rousseau's *Confessions.* Royal Irish Academy is established at Dublin.	Kant *Prologomena to any possible metaphysic.* Herschel *Motion of the solar system in Space.*	Wesley's *Deed of Declaration,* the charter of Wesleyan Methodism.
Cities & Social Development	Lord George Gordon leads anti-Catholic riots in London. From 1780 to 1800 British foreign trade is to treble.	Construction of Siberian highway begins. First building society is established in Birmingham. Serfdom is abolished in the Austrian Empire.	Bread riots in England. Bank of North America is established at Philadelphia.	Quakers form an association for the liberation of slaves in the West Indies.	Arthur Young begins his journal *Annals of Agriculture* concerned with the improvement of agriculture. Official London to Bristol mail coach begins operations. First school for the blind is set up in Paris. *The Boston Sentinel* is established.
Discovery & Invention	Gervinus invents circular saw. Scheller makes the first fountain pen. Watt invents letter-copying press.	Sir William Herschel discovers the planet Uranus using a 7-inch reflecting telescope. Mathurin Jacques Brisson edits the first dictionary of physics in Paris.	Montgolfier constructs a fire-balloon. Scheele discovers hydrocyanic acid. Lavoisier and Laplace identify the role of oxygen in respiration.	First working paddle-steamer on River Saône in France. Montgolfier brothers, Joseph and Jacques, make the first balloon ascent. Lavoisier establishes that water consists of hydrogen and oxygen: air and water are now resolved into their constituent elements.	Henry Cort introduces iron-puddling: conversion of pig-iron into wrought iron. Laplace *Théorie du mouvement et de la figure des planets.*
The Arts	Reynolds *Mary Robinson as Perdita.* Sebastian Erard, French musical instrument maker, produces the first modern pianoforte.	Schiller *The Robbers,* his first play. David *Belisarius,* painting gains him admission to the French Academy. Haydn *La Chasse,* symphony. Mozart *Idomeneo,* opera. Romney *Miss Willoughby.*	Cowper *Poems* and *John Gilpin.* Mozart *Haffner Symphony.* Herder *The Spirit of Hebrew Poetry.*	Blake *Poetical Sketches.* David *Grief of Andromache.* Beethoven's first works are printed.	Beaumarchais *Le Mariage de Figaro,* banned for 6 years for its attacks upon the aristocracy. Reynolds *Mrs Siddons as the Tragic Muse.* First political cartoons by Rowlandson. Haydn *Paris Symphonies.*

The first iron bridge in the world was opened to the public on January 1st, 1781, the start of a decade that was to see a crucial quickening of industrial activity in Britain. Spanning the River Severn in a single arch of 30 metres, it was – and is – a triumphant expression of confidence on the part of the local ironfounder, Abraham Darby III of Coalbrookdale, who cast the members from which the ribs were assembled, supervised their erection and added the elegant lattice that carries the roadway across the river.

The founder of the Coalbrookdale works, Abraham Darby I, moved to Shropshire from Bristol in 1708. In 1709 he pioneered the use of coked coal in place of charcoal to smelt iron, thus freeing iron production from its dependence on forestry. But further progress was slow. Impurities in both coal and iron ore made the new process difficult to manage, and it proved economic only for cast iron (pig iron), not for the purer, tougher and more malleable bariron used in the great majority of contemporary manufacturing processes. Until the middle of the century most of the iron made in Britain continued to be smelted with charcoal and until well past that date more than half the iron used in Britain was imported.

Nevertheless, the coal-based iron industry slowly built up its strength. The castings produced at Coalbrookdale proved suitable for steam engines which became a significant source of profit in the 1730s. In 1743 Abraham Darby II installed one of these engines at his own works: it was used to raise water so that the water-wheel driving the blast furnace bellows never had to stop for lack of a working head. In 1757 a second engine was set up to drive the bellows directly. Bigger furnaces that never stopped working brought the cost of pig iron down to the point where it became profitable to rework it into bar iron. Gradually the entire home industry began to turn over to coke smelting so that by 1788, out of a total production of 70,000 tonnes (up 3-fold since the beginning of the century), all but 15,000 tonnes came from coke-using iron works. The success of this changeover is reflected in the home producers' increasing share of the British market: during the 1780s imports fell from 60% to 40% of total consumption.

The first sign of the new era was the building of the Coalbrookdale Iron Bridge – of cast iron. Cast iron had become so cheap that it was possible to look beyond the normal uses for it – the cast iron pots from which the first Abraham Darby had drawn his profit, the boilers and other steam engine parts manufactured by Abraham Darby II – to novel applications in hitherto untapped industries. The bridge was one example: another is the use of iron rails for horse-drawn railways, an innovation that presaged even more momentous changes.

Perhaps the most forceful proponent of cast iron was John Wilkinson, an associate of the third Darby, who made his name with a machine that bored cannon barrels more accurately than ever before, adapted it to make cylinders for steam engines and produced the first examples of the Boulton and Watt steam engine design. He also made the first iron boat, gave Paris a new water supply based on 64 kilometres of iron pipe, sat at his desk in an iron chair and was buried in an iron coffin.

The new Iron Age made a great impression on contemporaries. England was still a green and pleasant land but it was clearly changing in ways which were without precedent. John Wesley, visiting the site of the Iron Bridge in 1779, measured the size of the castings being assembled on the Severn's banks and listed them in his notebook. Totting up the totals he commented 'I doubt whether the Colossus at Rhodes weighed much more'.

In fact, what he was witnessing was the birth of a new Colossus. The British iron industry was about to take off: from 70,000 tonnes in 1788, output was to rise to 100,000 tonnes in 1790 and 250,000 tonnes by 1800. This brought it to the top of the European league and was an essential factor in making Britain, for the next two generations, the workshop of the world.

Left: Women carrying coal from a mine, a task they commonly performed in the 18th century.

Below: The Coalbrookdale Ironworks painted in 1805, much as it was in the days of Abraham Darby III.

Bottom: The Iron Bridge, Coalbrookdale.

In November 1783 General George Washington entered New York on the heels of the British who had finally recognized the independence of the Thirteen States and agreed to withdraw their remaining garrisons from the eastern seaboard. Ten days later he said goodbye to his staff, took ship to Annapolis and laid his resignation before Congress. 'Having now finished the work assigned to me, I retire from the great theatre of action . . . and take my leave of all the employments of public life.' Two days later he was spending Christmas Eve at Mount Vernon, happier in mind than he had been for years, conscious that he had fully earned the right to 'move gently down the stream of life'.

It was a pleasant dream but he must have known all along that it was a false one. Americans faced a task every bit as difficult as the one that Washington had just successfully completed: they had to erect a just government in place of the unjust one they had overthrown. It was inconceivable that they would attempt this without first enlisting the services of the man who had been their Commander-in-Chief during the long struggle for independence. Nor could Washington remain at ease when duty called. In 1787 he accepted nomination as one of the Virginian delegates to the Convention that was to discuss the forms of the proposed Federal government. And at the Convention he accepted the unanimous request of all the delegations that he preside over their discussions.

To his great relief Washington discovered that the delegates were all agreed on one thing, there had to be a Federal power of some sort. This unanimity was surprising because at a grass roots level general American sentiment was the exact opposite: why have an extra level of government when the state governments satisfied all the needs perceived by ordinary folk? The loose alliance between the Thirteen States had served the nation well enough in wartime; it would surely be adequate to the less pressing demands of peace. To set up a Federal government was asking for the return of the sort of taxation and tyranny that the war had been fought about in the first place.

The answer to this was, as Washington and the other delegates knew, that the wartime coalition had not functioned well at all. The inability of the Continental Congress to impose any taxes meant that the Patriot army had been paid for by paper money (now worthless) or foreign loans (now due). Congress had got away with it because no one had realized at the time what a hollow vessel it was: it would never get away with it again. One of Washington's best moments at the Continental Convention came right at the start when the delegates agreed to scrap the existing Articles of Confederation. It was to be a real government or nothing.

For guidance on constitutional forms the delegates had two models, their own state governments and the theoretical studies of Montesquieu: both derived from British example which sought protection for individual liberties through the division of state power between distinct bodies. No single authority could corrupt the state for each of these bodies acted as a check on the autocracy of the others. Working along these lines the delegates came up with a proposal for a Federal government that would consist of an executive president, upper and lower legislative houses and an independent judiciary.

This division of the Federal authority between separate bodies helped solve one problem that threatened the consensus that otherwise characterized the Convention, the fear the small states had of the large ones. The states had been equal parties to the original Confederation but on the proposed Federal system, where every citizen's vote counted equally, states like Rhode Island (population 70,000) and Delaware (60,000) could be swamped by the more populous ones like Massachusetts (350,000) and Pennsylvania (400,000). The dilemma was resolved with the proposal that in the upper of the two legislative houses – the Senate, representation should be two Senators for each state regardless of size.

The Pennsylvania State House (now 'Independence Hall'), Philadelphia.

It was here that the Second Continental Congress met (in May 1775), appointed George Washington as Commander-in-Chief of its forces (in June of the same year) and adopted the Declaration of Independence (on 4 July 1776). Apart from the period when the British occupied Philadelphia, the State House continued to serve as the meeting place of both the Congress (on the ground floor) and the Provincial Assembly of Pennsylvania (on the upper floor) until the successful conclusion of the revolutionary war.

In May 1787 the State House once again became the scene of great events when the 55 delegates to the Constitutional Convention chose it as their venue. Over the next four months the delegates, George Washington presiding, agreed the form that the future government of America would take.

The building, originally erected between 1732 and 1753, has been subject to many alterations but still looks substantially the same as it did in the late 18th century.

Washington's role in all this had been the very difficult one of letting everyone have their say while saying little himself. For someone who was passionately committed to the idea of a strong Federal power it must have been hard to keep aloof from the debate but it was already clear that if the Convention was ratified the electors would insist on his occupying the presidency. He could not afford to be under suspicion of lobbying for a candidacy when he was lobbying for the Convention.

The delegates to the constitutional Convention had decreed – though quite where their authority to do so came from is a moot point – that the Federal government would come into existence as soon as the Constitution had been accepted by a two-thirds majority of the Thirteen States. Three states – Delaware, Pennsylvania and New Jersey – ratified before the end of 1787, and three more – Georgia, Massachusetts and Connecticut – by the end of February 1788. But Massachusetts had been a close thing (187 for, 168 against) and in neighbouring New Hampshire feeling was running so strongly against ratification that the Federalists decided to adjourn 'for more consultations' rather than risk losing the vote. It was April before another state ratified, May before the total reached eight. In June the Virginia Convention began voting in what was clearly going to be a very close call. Washington, waiting at Mount Vernon for the result, was relieved to hear that the final tally was 89 in favour to 79 against. Simultaneously news arrived that the reconvened New Hampshire delegation had ratified two days before. The Constitution was already in force.

As expected, the electoral college unanimously chose Washington as the nation's first president. In early 1789 he made the return journey from Mount Vernon to New York where 'grave almost to sadness' he took up the office that he was to bear for the next eight years. When he left it he was 65 and his powers were visibly failing: the Republic he had seen through from birth to manhood was twenty and growing stronger every day.

	1785	1786	1787	1788	1789
Politics & Military History	League of German Princes is formed by Frederick II against Joseph II of Austria. Russians settle in the Aleutian Islands of North Pacific. Pitt introduces a Bill to reform Parliament: it is defeated. Treaty of Fontainebleau: France supports the republican estates in Holland against the stadholder, William IV of Orange.	Assembly of Notables in France called by king to by-pass Parlements. Lord Cornwallis, Governor General of India (to 1793), establishes Indian Civil Service. British government purchases Penang. Stadholder suspends the Dutch Estates.	Joseph II reduces the powers of Estates in Austrian Netherlands: leads to outcry from Belgian patriots. Assembly of Notables in France is dismissed when it refuses to introduce financial reforms. Russia and Turkey at war. New Federal Constitution for the United States is drawn up and signed at Philadelphia. Famine in Japan leads to riots at Edo.	Gustavus II of Sweden goes to war with Russia without the sanction of the Estates. Regency Crisis in England at time of first illness of George III. Impeachment of Warren Hastings. Austria declares war on Turkey, in support of Russia and overruns Moldavia.	Estates General is convened at Versailles; Tennis Court Oath; Third Estate names itself National Assembly; Fall of Bastille and beginning of French Revolution. March to Versailles: King and Assembly are brought back to Paris which becomes centre of the Revolution. National Guard is formed in Paris. New French Constituent Assembly passes decrees abolishing feudal rights and privileges. George Washington (to 1797) becomes first President of the USA and the US declare themselves an economic and customs union.
Religion & Learning	Establishment of the University of New Brunswick, Canada. William Paley *Principles of Moral & Political Philosophy*. Charles II of Spain founds Prado.	Schiller *Philosophische Briefe*. Kant *Metaphysical Rudiments of Natural Philosophy*. Thomas Clarkson *Essay on the slavery and commerce of the human species*, against slavery.	Mary Wollstonecraft *Thoughts on the Education of Daughters*. John Adams *A Defence of the Constitutions of the USA*.	Gibbon completes *Decline and Fall*. Duc de St-Simon *Mémoires*, posthumous. Hannah More *Thoughts on the Importance of the Manners of the Great to General Society*. Linnaean Society for science of natural history in Britain is established in London.	Bentham *Introduction to the Principles of Morals and Legislation*. State University of Pennsylvania is created.
Cities & Social Development	Use of steam power is introduced in the cotton industry. Daily Universal Register, renamed *The Times* in 1788, is founded by Walter.	Population of Japan is reduced by 1 million by a famine (since 1780); great discontent. First attempts at using gas for lighting inside buildings in Germany and Britain. Pitt carries out financial reforms, reduces imports.	Marylebone Cricket Club (MCC) is established at Thomas Lord's ground (moves to St John's Wood in 1815). Britain establishes a colony at Sierra Leone for freed slaves. Dollar becomes the currency of the USA.	Colonization of Australia begins: the transportation of the first convicts to New South Wales. Bread riots in France; famine in Hungary.	Growth of political clubs in Paris. First steam-driven cotton factory is established in Manchester. Chrysanthemums are brought to Britain.
Discovery & Invention	Cartwright patents his power-loom. Salsano invents seismograph for measuring earthquakes. Blanchard and Jeffries make the first Channel crossing by balloon.	Herschel *Catalogue of Nebulae*: discovers theory of shape of galaxy. Buffon *Histoire naturelle des oiseaux*.	Lavoisier *Méthode de nomenclature chimique*, naming substances according to their chemical composition. Saussure climbs Mont Blanc and takes weather observations.	Lagrance, French mathematician, *Mécanique Analytique*: abstract formalization of mechanics. Laplace *Laws of the Planetary System*. Association for Promoting the Discovery of the Interior Parts of Africa is established in London.	Herschel constructs a 40-inch telescope: discovers 6th and 7th moons of Saturn. Luigi Galvani experiments on muscular contraction of dead frogs.
The Arts	Boswell *Journal of a Tour to the Hebrides*. David *The Oath of the 3 Horatii*. Gainsborough *Mrs Siddons*. Jefferson begins the State Capitol at Richmond, Va. (to 1796) – the first public building of the new American administration.	Robert Burns *Poems Chiefly in the Scottish Dialect*. Goya *The Seasons*. Mozart *The Marriage of Figaro*, Prague Symphony.	Goethe *Iphigenie auf Tauris*. Mozart *Don Giovanni*, *Eine Kleine Nachtmusik*.	Goethe *Egmont*. Hepplewhite *The Cabinet-makers' and Upholsterers' Guide* (published posthumously).	Blake *Songs of Innocence*. David *Lictors bringing to Brutus the bodies of his sons*. Gilbert White *Natural History of Selborne*.

	1790	1791	1792	1793	1794
Politics & Military History	Civil Constitution of Clergy and abolition of Nobility in France; naval mutiny at Brest. Treaty of Wereloe ends Russo-Swedish War. British alliance with Nizam of Hyderabad in India; the beginning of the Third Mysore War.	Louis XVI flees to Varennes: brought back to Paris; accepts new Constitution – Constituent Assembly is replaced by Legislative Assembly. Declaration of Pillnitz: the Emperor Leopold II and Frederick of Prussia call for a monarchical system in France compatible with welfare of French nation. Church and King riots in Birmingham: British government, fearing influence of French Revolution, begins decade of harsh repression. Canada Act: divides the country into English and French Canada. Bill of Rights: first 10 Amendments to US Constitution. Negro slave revolt against French in Haiti led by Toussaint L'Ouverture.	Coalition of Austria and Prussia against France; France declares war on the two powers. Battle of Valmy: French defeat Prussians – beginning of the Revolutionary Wars. National Convention is established and rules France to 1795; the Marseillais arrive in Paris to save Revolution; the Royal Family is imprisoned; the September Massacres of those in prison; Prussians defeated at Battle of Valmy. France becomes a Republic; the King put on trial. Treaty of Jassy ends Russo-Turkish War. Kentucky joins the USA.	The execution of Louis XVI. Britain joins the continental powers in a coalition against France. Royalist uprising in La Vendée; execution of Marie Antoinette; Committee of Public Safety is established; Levée en masse – conscription for the revolutionary armies; the Reign of Terror; execution of the Girondins; Maximilien de Robespierre the dominant figure. The Second Partition of Poland between Russia, Prussia and Austria.	The Terror reaches a climax in March–April. Battle of Fleurus: French defeat the Austrians and conquer Belgium. Execution of Robespierre and members of the Commune brings the Terror to an end; the Jacobin Clubs are closed. Jay's Treaty: commercial and shipping treaty between Britain and the USA. Agha Muhammad founds the Kajar dynasty in Persia (to 1925).
Religion & Learning	Burke *Reflections on the Revolution in France.* French Jews are given civil liberties.	Tom Paine *The Rights of Man.* Bentham *Panopticon.* Olympe de Gouges (feminist) *Declaration des Droits de la Femme et de la Citoyenne.*	Mary Wollstonecraft *Vindication of the Rights of Woman.* Paine *Rights of Man* Pt. II. Baptist Missionary Society is established in London.	Paine *The Age of Reason.* Condorcet *Esquisse d'un Tableau historique des progrès de l'esprit humain.* Compulsory education is introduced in France from the age of six.	Feast of the Supreme Being in Paris: separation of Church and State in France. Frederician Code covering civil, criminal and administrative law is adopted in Prussia.
Cities & Social Development	Beginnings of the new multi-storey factory blocks in towns: they are bigger than the country mills. Slater builds spinning frames at Providence, Rhode Island, to establish the US textile industry. Washington DC is established as the US capital.	Ordnance Survey is established in Britain. Wilberforce's motion for the abolition of the slave trade is passed through Parliament. Jews declared equal citizens in France: first European country to grant them full rights.	Illuminating gas is used in Britain for the first time. Civil marriage and divorce are made legal in France. Last year in which Britain exports surplus wheat. Slave trade is abolished in Danish colonies. French revolutionary calendar comes into force – the months are renamed.	Renewal of enclosures in Britain: 2000 Enclosure Acts from 1793 to 1815. US law compels escaped slaves to return to owners. Seditious Publications Act in Britain limits freedom of the press.	Habeas Corpus Act is suspended in Britain. Slavery is abolished in French colonies.
Discovery & Invention	Lavoisier produces first table of chemical elements (lists 31). George Vancouver explores the NW coast of America.	Metre is defined by the French Academy of Science.	Sir Alexander Mackenzie crosses Canada to the Pacific. Guillotine is erected in Paris.	American Eli Whitney revolutionizes the cotton industry with his cotton gin. *Le Jardin des Plantes* is established in Paris for the study of natural history.	Balloon is used for observation at the battle of Fleurus. John Dalton, English chemist, describes colour-blindness. First telegraph is used between Paris and Lille.
The Arts	Burns *Tam O'Shanter.* Blake *Marriage of Heaven and Hell.* Mozart *Cosi Fan Tutti.*	Boswell *Life of Johnson.* Mozart *Die Zauberflote.* Langhans' Brandenburg Gate in Berlin.	Haydn *The Creation.* De Lisle *La Marseillaise* becomes French National Anthem.	Louvre becomes national art gallery. Paganini makes his debut, aged 11, as violin virtuoso. David *Death of Marat.*	Blake *Songs of Experience.* Goya *Procession of the Flagellants.* Haydn *Clock, Military* symphonies.

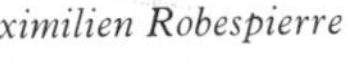

aximilien Robespierre

(1758–94)

Georges Danton

(1759–94)

Right: The execution of Louis XVI in the Place de la Revolution (originally the Place de Louis XV, now the Place de la Concorde), 21 January 1793.

The guillotine was recommended (not invented) by Dr Guillotin who was a kindly man, horrified at the way most executions were botched. It is ironical that the name of this gentle person has come to symbolize the excesses of the terror.

:ance's support of the Americans during their War of ıdependence was a success in every way but one: it cost ore than the creaking financial machinery of the *Ancien égime* could come up with. The only way to balance the oks was to tax the privileged orders, the nobles and the ergy, and as there was no way they would agree to this, the ng was reluctantly forced to turn to the people. In 1788 he greed to summon the Estates General.

The Estates General consisted of Lords and Commons ‹e the English Parliament plus a separate estate for the ergy. Few felt that this was an appropriate format in the ırrent situation; surely what was needed was a single gislature with the power to approve the measures the ng's ministers deemed necessary? And this is what the ountry got. The delegates of the Commons announced ıat they constituted a National Assembly and resisted all tempts by the king to intimidate them. When they found ıat he had locked them out of the hall they were using at ersailles they moved to a nearby tennis court.

The people of Paris showed their disapproval of the ing's opposition more forcibly. On July 14, 1789, three eeks after the tennis court oath, a mob stormed the astille, the royal fortress that seemed to Parisians to mbody all that they hated in the old order. It was the signal ›r countrywide riots against the royal authority, the ristocracy and the clergy.

The National Assembly now got down to business, bolishing feudal rights and framing the principles of a onstitution based on the sovereignty of the people. What ʼas in the delegates' minds was something in the English attern – a limited monarchy, an executive cabinet and a :gislative assembly – but the king refused to play the game y the English rules and stubbornly vetoed the bills placed efore him. This enraged the Parisians and the mass of hem – the *sans-culottes*, the *vanqueurs de la Bastille* – took ver the revolutionary process. First the king was brought rom Versailles to Paris where he was lodged, together with he Assembly, in the Tuileries. Then, after another attempt t constitutional rule had come to grief on the king's ntransigence, the mob stormed the Tuileries, overawed the Assembly and put an end to the monarchy. The Assembly ʼas replaced by the National Convention, chosen by ıniversal suffrage: the Convention decreed that this event onstituted Year One of the Revolutionary era.

The Convention, like most elected bodies, was by nstinct moderate but enemies within and without were hreatening the new Republic and extreme measures eemed both appropriate and necessary. The king was put ›n trial, found guilty and sent to the guillotine; executive ›ower was entrusted to a Committee of Public Safety, ustice to a Revolutionary Tribunal. The extreme evolutionaries, the Jacobins, howled their approval and lemanded more: the mob, now fully conscious of its role, ›acked the Jacobins all the way. The moderates lost their ıerve: their most impressive representative, Danton, went over to the Jacobins only to be elbowed off the Committee of Public Safety all the same: his place was taken by the leader of the Jacobins, the incorruptible, pitiless Maximilien Robespierre.

The storming of the Tuilleries on 10 August 1792. In this telescoped view the king and queen (on the right, labelled 1 and 2) are seeking refuge in the National Assembly while the National Guard attacks the Tuilleries Palace (on the left, labelled 9). In fact the two events were consecutive, not simultaneous, and the king was already safely ensconced in the assembly when firing broke out between his Swiss Guard, defending the palace, and the National Guard.

The Swiss Guard put up a good fight until they ran out of ammunition and had to lay down their arms. Most of them – about 600 out of the 900 – were then massacred either by the National Guard or the mob. For a while it looked as if the mob would storm the National Assembly too and though it held off from this, the day's events marked a decisive shift in power from the moderate to the extreme revolutionaries and from the Assembly to the street.

Now the rise and fall of the guillotine became a steady beat. The class enemies were destroyed first: the Queen ('the widow Capet'), the Duke of Orléans (a convention deputy under the name Philippe Egalité), the pathetic Madame Du Barry and scores of others, then the clergy – priests and nuns both, the political moderates, Danton, his supporters, their wives and families. Then any Jacobins who earned Robespierre's disfavour. To oppose the Terror was a crime, to be accused of a crime was to be found guilty, and for the guilty there was only one punishment. For a year, all France lived in the shadow of the guillotine.

Eventually the Convention's quivering deputies summoned up enough courage to order Robespierre's arrest. He fled to the real source of his power, the Paris Commune, but the National Guard refused to fight for him and he was re-arrested and guillotined the next day. Year Three of the Revolutionary era passed without the tension between the moderate Republicans and the extremists, the Convention and the Commune, being resolved, but in October 1795 a full-scale battle between the Parisian National Guard and the regular soldiers summoned by the Convention in its defence, decided the issue in favour of the Convention. Or perhaps just of Barras, the deputy who had assumed command of the Convention's forces and was soon to become the leading figure in the ruling Directory. Or perhaps just of the artillery officer who had handled his guns so well that day, young Napoleon Bonaparte.

Barras was generous in rewarding Bonaparte: a series of promotions elevated him from General of Brigade to General of Division to Army Commander. Less than six months after his 'whiff of grapeshot' had cleared the streets of Paris, he was travelling south to take over command of the Italian front where a ragged, starving force of about 55,000 men faced an equal number of Piedmontese and Austrians. 'Soldiers,' said the new General 'I am going to lead you into the most fertile plains in the world. There you will find great towns, rich provinces: there you will find honour, glory and riches. Soldiers of the Army of Italy, will you be wanting in courage?'

Bonaparte, who had served in this theatre in the opening days of the revolutionary wars, had his plan of campaign already drawn up. Knowing that, once rattled, the Piedmontese would retreat on their capital, Turin, and the Austrians on their north Italian stronghold, Milan, he struck at the junction between them and forced the Piedmontese to surrender. In 30 days he had knocked one of France's enemies out of the war. This business concluded, he chased after the retreating Austrians and caught up with their rearguard which was holding a bridgehead west of the Adda at Lodi. Under pressure from Bonaparte the Austrians pulled back across the bridge but if they thought they were going to be left undisturbed on the far side they could not have been more mistaken: Bonaparte was bringing up reinforcements as fast as he could. By 6 o'clock the same day he had 30 guns in action, a regiment of grenadiers drawn up in assault formation and an infantry division behind them. A cavalry force had been sent upstream with instructions to find a ford and make a diversion on the Austrian flank but with the sun sinking lower in the sky Bonaparte decided he could not wait for this any longer. Ordering his gunners to double their rate of fire he launched the grenadiers, six abreast, across the bridge.

The column was barely at the halfway point when Austrian volleys brought it to a bloody halt, cries filled the air and for a minute the battle hung in the balance: then from the tangled mess at the head of the column, a handful of figures emerged – Berthier, Massena, Lannes – men who would one day soon be Marshals of France. Inspired by their example, the soldiers followed, the column reformed and broke into a charge. As the French reached the Austrian positions the long awaited cavalry swept in on the flank. The grenadiers had won the bridge, their general had the making of a legend.

After Lodi, the Army of Italy went from victory to victory. Bonaparte's touch seemed infallible; he became the idol of his men, the hero of France. Barras and the other members of the ruling Directory were forced to concede him full powers to impose terms on the Austrians, and the terms he exacted were beyond anyone's imaginings: venerable institutions like the Venetian Republic disappeared forever; most of Italy passed under direct or indirect French rule.

Back in Paris the conqueror accepted the command of the 'Army of England' which was being assembled to bring the last of the Republic's enemies to heel. However, he soon lost interest in this impractical project and turned instead to one that was equally impractical but more alluring, an expedition against Egypt. This was prepared in great secrecy and with great speed, as if all concerned knew that a pause for reflection would be the end of the adventure. The best explanation for it is Bonaparte's age: he was still 28, young and impetuous when he joined the fleet at Toulon.

The legend now acquired another chapter. 'Thirty centuries are looking down on you,' Bonaparte told his soldiers on the eve of the Battle of the Pyramids and though the pyramids were nowhere to be seen – the battle was fought and won 10 kilometres to the north of Gizeh – the sentiment had the right ring to it. Eventually the English closed in and Napoleon abandoned Egypt for France. No one criticized his decision, no one questioned the worth of his Egyptian victories; everywhere he was hailed as the saviour the country needed.

His timing, indeed, could hardly have been better. The Directory had lost the confidence of the country, it had even lost confidence in itself. In a swiftly executed coup, Bonaparte seized power, emerging as First Consul and effective ruler of the French Republic.

Above: 'The plumb-pudding in danger', a cartoon by James Gillray showing the British Prime Minister Pitt and the Emperor Napoleon carving up the world. Though this was the way things worked out in the 1800s the arrangement was never the amicable one that Gillray suggests.

Right: Josephine in 1798, two years after her marriage to Napoleon. Barras encouraged the match between his mistress and his favourite General because his own fancy had turned to the dashing Therèse Tallien. Josephine was not enthusiastic about the transaction but Napoleon seems to have been genuinely in love.

Above: Defeat of the Turkish attempt to reconquer Egypt at Aboukir Bay in 1799. The Turks landed an army of more than 15,000 men on the peninsula beside the bay: ten days later Napoleon, with barely half the number, swept most of the Turks into the sea and captured the rest. Painted in 1804 by Louis-Francis Lejeune (1775–1848).

	1795	1796	1797	1798	1799
Politics & Military History	France establishes Batavian (puppet) Republic in the Netherlands. Third Partition of Poland between Russia, Prussia and Austria: Polish King abdicates. Britain takes Cape of Good Hope and Ceylon from Dutch. France ruled by Directory; end of revolt in La Vendée. Napoleon is made C-in-C of Revolutionary Army in Italy. Treaty of San Lorenzo: the USA and Spain settle boundaries of Florida and US gains right of navigation on the Mississippi.	Napoleon invades Italy and destroys the existing state system, defeating the Austrians at Lodi and Arcol. In Paris Babeuf fails to restore the 1793 Constitution. French invasion of Ireland fails. British capture Guiana. Agha Muhammad of Persia makes Teheran his capital.	Battle of Cape St Vincent: British navy defeats Franco-Spanish fleet. British navy mutinies at Spithead and Nore. British capture Trinidad from Spain. French under Napoleon invade Austria; French occupy Venice; Napoleon establishes the Ligurian Republic at Genoa and Austrian Lombardy becomes the Cisalpine Republic. Treaty of Campo Formio: Austria makes peace with France.	Formation of Second Coalition against France. Napoleon invades Egypt: Battle of the Pyramids – defeats Mamluks; Battle of the Nile (Aboukir Bay) Nelson defeats French fleet. Rebellion in Ireland: United Irishmen want separation. French invade Switzerland and establish Helvetic Republic. Tipoo Sahib of Mysore renews war against British. Britain makes Ceylon a Crown Colony.	Bonaparte invades Syria. Britain, Austria, Russia, Portugal, Naples and Ottoman Empire unite against France; French driven from Italy. Bonaparte returns to France and overthrows the Directory: he sets up a Consulate with himself as First Consul. Combination Laws (more in 1800) prohibit trade unions in Britain. Third Kaffir War: London Missionary Society begins work in South Africa. Tipoo Sahib, last ruler of Mysore, is killed and British control is extended over most of southern India.
Religion & Learning	Murray's *English Grammar* comes to be widely used in schools. French educational reforms: *écoles centrales* established in French Departments.	Vicomte de Bonard, French philosopher in exile *Théorie du Pouvoir politique et réligieux*. The basis of what becomes the Code Napoleon is worked out by Camacérès, *Projet de code civil.*	Istituto de Scienze Lettere e Arte is established at Milan.	Malthus *Essay on Population.* Joseph Lancaster, Quaker educationalist, establishes his elementary school in Borough Road, London, where he uses senior pupils or monitors to teach younger children.	Discovery in Egypt by the French of the Rosetta Stone makes possible the deciphering of Ancient Egyptian hieroglyphics. In Siberia a perfect mammoth is found preserved in ice. Pestalozzi opens school at Burgdorf in Switzerland.
Cities & Social Development	Speenhamland System to provide poor relief is adopted in England. First settlements in New Zealand.	Government in China forbids importation of opium. Freedom of press in France. Toussaint L'Ouverture becomes lieutenant governor in Haiti.	Spode organization makes modern English porcelain by adding felspar to boneash. Britain goes through a financial crisis: Bank of England suspends payments.	Hansard begins to produce Parliamentary reports. First weaving mill starts in Bradford. First great German political daily newspaper, *Allgemeine Zeitung*, is established	Pitt introduces income tax as a wartime financial measure.
Discovery & Invention	Mungo Park, Scottish explorer, traces the course of the River Niger in West Africa. France adopts the metric system. Royal Navy begins the compulsory use of limejuice as an antidote to scurvy.	Baron Cuvier, French naturalist, lays the foundations of animal palaeontology. Edward Jenner introduces immunization against smallpox.	First copper pennies are minted. De Saussure *Récherches chimiques sur la végétation.*	Bass and Flinders circumnavigate Tasmania. Adrien Legendre, French mathematician *Theory of Numbers.*	Mungo Park *Travels in the Interior of Africa.* Cuvier lays the groundwork of comparative anatomy. Tennant and Mackintosh invent bleaching powder for bleaching cloth.
The Arts	Beginning of the friendship between Wordsworth and Coleridge. Blake, print of *Newton* and *God Creating Adam.* Southey *Poems.* Beethoven Piano Concertos in B & C. Haydn *Drum-Roll* Symphony.	Wordsworth *The Borderers.* Fuseli *The Bard.* Burney *Camilla.*	Coleridge *Kubla Khan.* Goethe *Hermann und Dorothea*, pastoral poem. Cherubini *Médée*, opera	Coleridge and Wordsworth *Lyrical Ballads.* Goya *The Bewitched.*	Schiller *Wallenstein*, trilogy of plays. Beethoven, Symphony No. I and *Pathétique* Sonata. David *Rape of the Sabine Women.* Haydn *The Creation.*

	1800	1801	1802	1803	1804
Politics & Military History	Battles of Marengo and Hohenlinden: French defeat the Austrians. Russia withdraws from the coalition against France and the Tsar revives the Armed Neutrality of the north against Britain. British annexes the Straits Settlements and Malta. Napoleon appoints a committee of lawyers to draw up civil code.	Act of Union formally unites Great Britain and Ireland as the United Kingdom. Battle of Copenhagen: Nelson destroys the League of Armed Neutrality in the Baltic. US Supreme Court is recognized and given greater powers. French army in Egypt surrenders to the British. Treaty of Luneville: between France and Austria – France keeps left bank of Rhine and most of Italy. Haiti becomes republic.	Treaty of Amiens: ends war between Britain and France. Napoleon is made First Consul for life; he introduces the Legion of Honour.	War between Britain and France breaks out again. Louisiana Purchase: Napoleon sells Louisiana to the USA; this makes possible the continental expansion of the USA; Ohio becomes the 17th state of the Union. France recovers San Domingo after the revolt of Toussaint L'Ouverture had established a republic.	Bonaparte is crowned Napoleon I, Emperor of the French, by the Pope. The Code Napoleon, civil code, is adopted in France. Persia and Russia at war over Russia's annexation of Georgia. Serbians revolt against Turks – continues to 1813. Haiti achieves independence from France.
Religion & Learning	Major growth of non-Anglican religions in Britain: non-conformists and Methodists; this is paralleled by revivalism in the USA. Heeren *European Political Systems*: a German historian who pioneered the economic approach to history.	Concordat between France and the Pope; a reconstruction of the French Church. Pestalozzi *Wie Gertrud ihre Kinder Lehrt*, his methods for educating needy children.	Chateaubriand *Génie du Christianisme*. Cobbett begins his weekly *Political Register*. Bentham *Discourse on Civil and Penal Legislation*. German orientalist, Georg Friedrich Grotefend, deciphers Babylonian cuneiform script.	Lancaster *Improvements in Education*, establishes voluntary elementary schools. Jean Baptiste Say, French economist *Traite d'Économie Politique*.	Johann Gottlieb Fichte *Characteristics of the Present Age*. British and Foreign Bible Society is established.
Cities & Social Development	Robert Owen, philanthropist, begins social reforms at his New Lanark Mills. Letter post is established in Berlin. 1200 steam engines in operation in Britain producing twenty-times more coal than France. 52 private banks in London and 400 in the provinces. British trade now accounts for about 27% of world trade.	Britain holds its first census: 8 towns have more than 50,000 and there are 600,000 domestic servants. Grand Union Canal is opened in England. Surrey iron railway: horse-drawn trucks carry coal and farm produce.	Debrett's *Peerage* is first published in England. Regular mail service is started between England and India.	In England poaching is made a capital offence if capture is resisted. Thomas Telford the engineer begins constructing roads in Scotland. First settlement in Tasmania (Van Diemen's Land).	First English flower show is held at the Royal Horticultural Society. Hobart is established in Tasmania.
Discovery & Invention	Herschel discovers infra-red band of spectrum. Alessandro Volta, Italian physicist, makes the first electrical battery. Royal College of Surgeons is established in London. Eli Whitney makes muskets with interchangeable parts.	Robert Fulton invents the first submarine, *Nautilus*.	Ekeburg discovers the rare metal tantalum. Portuguese explorers begin crossing Africa from the west (Angola) to the east: they do not reach Tete on the Zambesi in Mozambique until 1811.	Henry Shrapnel's shell, which he had invented in 1784, is adopted by the British Army although it is not used until 1808. John Dalton, English chemist, begins work on atomic theory leading to systematic arrangement of chemistry. Lyceum theatre is lit experimentally with gas.	Richard Trevithick builds the first successful steam locomotive. Gay-Lussac makes balloon ascents to study weather.
The Arts	Schiller *Mary Stuart* (play). Beethoven, Piano Concerto No. 3. Maria Edgeworth *Castle Rackrent*, her first novel. Modern style Punch and Judy shows develop.	Schiller *Joan of Arc* (drama). Beethoven *Moonlight Sonata*. Haydn *The Seasons*. Elgin Marbles brought from Athens to London.	*Edinburgh Review* is launched. Scott *Minstrels of the Scottish Border* draws public attention to his talents. Beethoven Second Symphony. Mme de Staël *Delphine*, Canova, sculpture of Napoleon.	Thomas Sheraton *The Cabinet Dictionary*.	Blake *Jerusalem*. Schiller *Wilhelm Tell*. Beethoven *Eroica* symphony.

After the disastrous defeats of the Seven Years' War the French wrote off North America. Canada and the part of Louisiana between the Allegheny Mountains and the Mississippi had been taken by the British and there seemed no point in hanging on to what was left – it had never paid for itself anyway. In a fit of disillusion the whole vast area between the Mississippi and the Rockies, plus New Orleans and the Mississippi delta, was turned over to France's ally, Spain. In this guise – as a province of the Spanish American Empire – the name Louisiana remained on the map to remind Frenchmen of a dream that had gone sour.

With the Revolution, confidence returned. Spain was first asked, then pressed to give Louisiana back. In 1800 Bonaparte finally forced him to do so.

Before the French could reoccupy Louisiana they had to reconquer Santo Domingo where a slave revolt had overturned their administration. Bonaparte entrusted this task to his brother-in-law, General Leclerc and a force of 34,000 men. Leclerc landed in Santo Domingo early in 1802 and for the first few months had everything his own way: he tricked the most important of the Black leaders, Toussaint L'Ouverture, into surrendering and he got the upper hand over the rebel forces. But then things started to go wrong. The Blacks learned that the French, despite promises to the contrary, were intending to restore slavery and fought with redoubled fury: yellow fever broke out in the French ranks and carried off two-thirds of the men, including Leclerc.

Meanwhile, the Americans had learnt that the Spaniards had agreed to retrocede Louisiana. They were furious. Confident that they could lift the Western lands from Spain's feeble grasp whenever they wanted, they had not given much thought as to how and when they would so so. Suddenly there was the alarming possibility that the French would appear in force on the line of the Mississippi and thwart the natural development of the American Republic. The cry went up for war.

President Jefferson stayed calm. He made contact with the British just in case it did come to war and found that the British were eager for an alliance. But he put his main trust in an offer to buy New Orleans. He instructed his representative in Paris to offer up to $7.5 million. At first Bonaparte was not having it: then the news of the debacle on Santo Domingo and the fact that France and England were clearly drifting towards an expensive war again, made him change his mind. Conscious that he could not sustain, let alone repossess, any territory in the Gulf of Mexico in the face of British hostility, he put the whole of Louisiana up for offer. After some sharp haggling the price was eventually fixed at $12 million.

Well before the agreement was reached, Jefferson had been confident enough of the outcome to instruct his personal secretary Captain Meriwether Lewis to prepare for an expedition across upper Louisiana to the far west. In 1804–5 Captain Lewis and his fellow officer William Clark worked their way through the Rockies to the Pacific. No-one could doubt the ultimate destiny of the lands they traversed.

Top: Talleyrand, Napoleon's Foreign Minister during the Louisiana negotiations.

NORTH AMERICA IN 1802

Above: Toussaint L'Ouverture. The most important black leader to emerge from the slave revolt that destroyed French colonial rule on Santo Domingo. Tricked into surrendering by General Leclerc, he died in captivity in France in 1803.

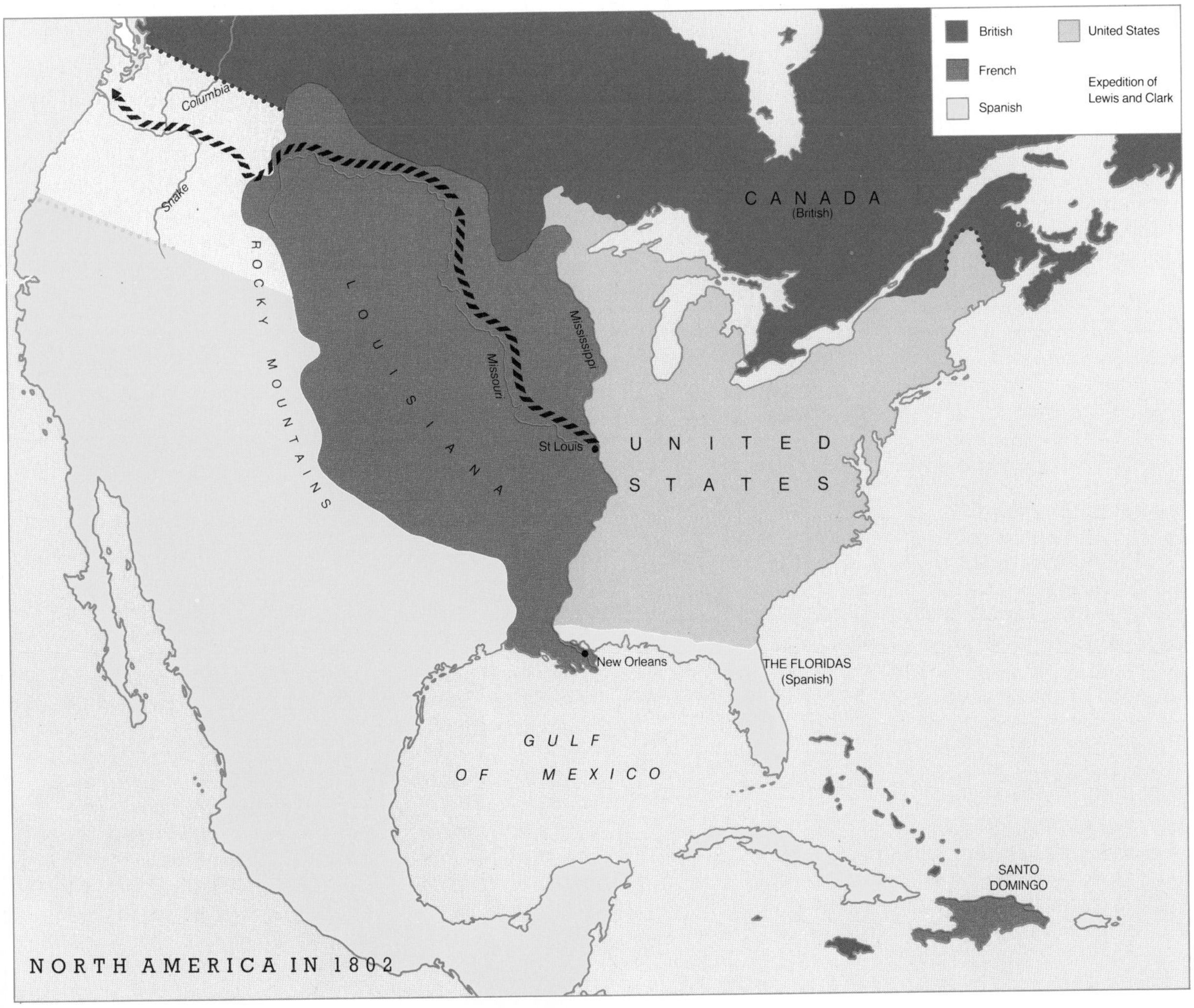

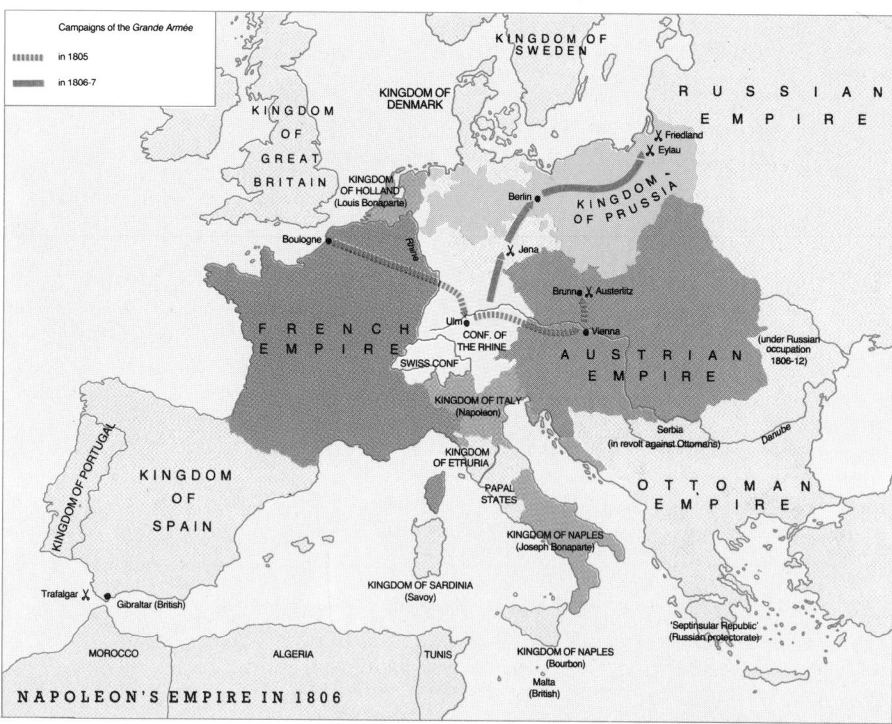

Above: Josephine receiving the imperial crown from Napoleon. Detail from the huge picture of the coronation ceremony by J-L David, now in the Louvre.

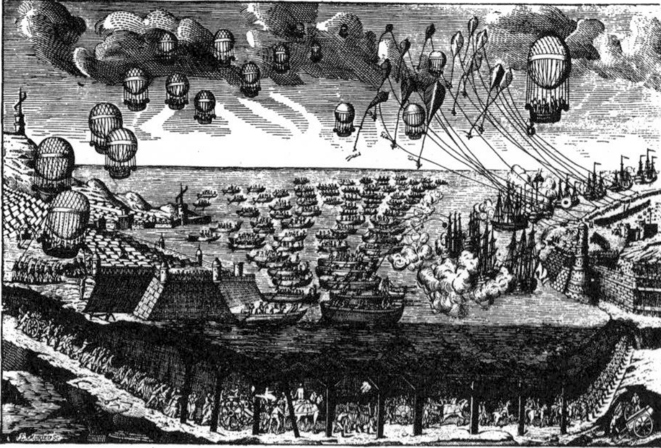

Above right: New ideas for invading England. French forces use balloons and a tunnel to get to grips with their traditional enemy. The English send snipers up by kite to attack the balloonists.

A comic French print first published in 1803.

War with England was a tantalizing business for the French: the only way to win was by invading the British Isles but with the British Navy in command of the Channel it was difficult to see how this could be done. In 1805 the Emperor Napoleon – he had had himself raised to this dignity the year before – put together the best plan he could. The scattered elements of the French and Spanish fleets, on paper the equal of the British, were to break out of their home ports, rendezvous in the West Indies and then double back to the Channel. With a bit of luck the British would be a step behind them all the way and Napoleon would have the ten days he needed to ship his Grande Armée across to England.

This was not a realistic scenario and the few moves that the French and Spanish ships were able to complete came nowhere near Napoleon's minimum requirement. And when later in the year they did achieve a useful concentration, the result was a disaster. Britain's Admiral Nelson caught up with the combined Franco-Spanish fleet off Trafalgar on October 21st, 1805. The Franco-Spanish fleet under the command of the French Admiral Pierre de Villeneuve decided to stand and fight. Nelson, attacking the enemy's centre and rear with the whole of his fleet disposed in two columns, split the Franco-Spanish fleet and picked them off one by one. Nelson, fatally wounded in the action, lived long enough to be told of a complete victory. He had taken 20 of their 33 ships of the line without losing a single one himself. It was a victory that had to be accepted as final, though as it happened Napoleon had not waited on the outcome: he had already ordered the Grande Armée to break camp and march for the Rhine. Austria and Russia were mobilizing: the Emperor could not afford to be caught facing the wrong way.

By the time the Grande Armée had reached the Rhine the Austrians had moved into Bavaria and set up their headquarters at Ulm on the upper Danube: their plan was to wait there until the Russians closed up, unless the French arrived first in which case they would conduct a fighting retreat on Vienna. Napoleon not only arrived first, he crossed the Rhine further north than expected and brought the six corps of the Grand Armée down behind the Austrians. The entire Austrian force at Ulm was trapped and forced to surrender. Hearing of this the Russians turned back and retreated into Bohemia.

By November the Russians had managed to get a respectable army together in the north eastern quarter of Bohemia and they began to move forward again. Napoleon advanced from Vienna to meet them and the two armies finally came face to face on the road between Brunn and Austerlitz. The Russians extended their left, trying to cut Napoleon's line to Vienna: Napoleon, who had anticipated this move, waited till the Russians had committed the major part of their force to this attack and then struck at their centre. The Russian army broke in two, and Napoleon was able to turn on the right half and hammer it into the ground. Two days later the campaign was over: the Russians were withdrawing and the Austrians had accepted terms.

Napoleon's next step was to redraw the map of Germany. The old German Empire was replaced by a "Confederation of the Rhine" of which the Emperor of the French was official protector. This new order was deeply offensive to the Prussians who considered the area north of the Main to be their bailiwick. Confident in the army that Frederick the Great had made the envy of Europe, they declared war on the French in October 1806.

The Prussians moved slowly; the Russians, who now took the field again, even more so: Napoleon struck like a thunderbolt. He came up on the Prussians while they were in the process of withdrawing from their initial point of concentration at Jena to a secondary position at Auerstadt. It comes as no real surprise to learn that Napoleon overwhelmed the smaller half of the Prussian army at Jena: he had more men and the advantage of surprise. What is really extraordinary is that the larger half was beaten by a single French corps. It is a telling measure of the quality of the Grande Armée in its heyday.

The pursuit after Jena-Auerstadt was conducted at the same breakneck pace as the opening of the campaign: Berlin was occupied before the end of October, Warsaw in November. At the beginning of 1807 the Russians launched a counter offensive which brought Napoleon out of winter quarters: they stood their ground and at Eylau in East Prussia the Grande Armée had to fight hard for an indecisive victory. The episode made Napoleon more cautious. His supply lines now stretched across half Europe, the number of men he could deploy was dwindling, the next encounter had to be the last. Spring brought the opportunity he needed. Playing his cards perfectly he trapped the main Russian army against a river at Friedland and methodically shot it to pieces.

Too discouraged to continue the fight, the Tsar sued for peace. Napoleon was the acknowledged master of Europe.

	1805	1806	1807	1808	1809
Politics & Military History	Battle of Ulm: French defeat Austrians. Battle of Trafalgar: Nelson defeats Franco-Spanish fleet and is killed. Battle of Austerlitz: French defeat Austro-Russian forces. Peace of Pressburg between Austria and France. Muhammad Ali becomes Pasha (governor) of Egypt.	Battles of Auerstadt and Jena: Prussia defeated by French, Napoleon enters Berlin; creates Confederation of the Rhine which destroys the old German state system. Berlin Decrees: Napoleon attempts to establish a European economic blockade of Britain; Britain retaliates with the Continental System. Napoleon abolishes the Holy Roman Empire: all Habsburg estates become part of Austrian Empire with German as the official language. Napoleon makes his brothers Joseph Bonaparte King of Naples and Louis Bonaparte King of Holland. Death of Pitt.	Battles of Eylau and Friedland; French defeat Russians leading to Treaty of Tilsit. Milan Decrees: Napoleon escalates economic warfare with Britain. British fleet bombards Copenhagen and seizes Danish fleet. French invade Portugal: France and Spain agree to divide Portugal and her Empire between them. Stein begins reforms in Prussia following defeats of previous year. Napoleon creates the Grand Duchy of Warsaw. Sierra Leone and Gambia become British colonies.	French occupy Spain and Napoleon makes his brother Joseph King of Spain; Madrid revolt against French and rising of Spanish masses; beginning of the Peninsula War. Uprisings occur in the Spanish South American Empire. France occupies Rome and annexes Papal States. Stein continues reforms but Napoleon persuades the King of Prussia to dismiss him and to limit the Prussian army to 42,000.	Battle of Corunna: British army in Portugal is defeated. Battle of Talavera: French defeat in Spain. Battle of Wagram: Austrians defeated and make peace with France. Metternich becomes Chief Minister of Austria. Britain concludes a treaty with the Sikhs at Amritsar. Treaty between the British and the Shah of Afghanistan.
Religion & Learning		Antoine Barbier, librarian to Napoleon, produces *Dictionnaire des ouvrages anonymes et pseudonymes.* First missions of the Church Missionary Society appear in Sierra Leone.	Hegel *Die Phänomenologie des Geistes.* First convention of the US Evangelical Society.	Further educational reforms in France; establishment of Imperial University. Series of teacher training colleges begin to be opened in Prussia – 17 by 1826.	Humboldt carries out educational reforms in Prussia. Ricardo *The High Price of Bullion, Proof of the Depreciation of Bank Notes.*
Cities & Social Development	London docks are opened. First factory to be lit by gaslight – in Manchester. France abandons the Revolutionary Calendar.	Gas lighting of cotton mills becomes general. Dartmoor prison, built by French prisoners, is opened. British cotton industry employs 90,000 factory workers and 184,000 handloom weavers.	Steamship *Clermont* on the Hudson River is the first commercially successful paddle-steamer. Britain passes a Bill by Wilberforce to abolish Slave Trade in British ships. Gas lighting is used for London streets. French provincial press has to take its political news exclusively from the official *Moniteur*.	Beginning of the Luddite troubles in Britain: fear of new machines in factories. Federal government of USA prohibits the import of slaves into the country. First war correspondent from *The Times* sends despatches from the Spanish War.	Law in France limits each Department to having only one political paper.
Discovery & Invention	Sartürner discovers morphine. Mungo Park sets off on his second journey of exploration of the Niger.	Sir Humphry Davy develops electrolytic method for separating potassium soda: the use of electricity in chemistry.	Air pump is developed for use in mines.	Davy isolates barium, calcium, magnesium and strontium. Laplace begins *Mécanique céleste* (to 1823, 5 volumes).	MacLure *Observations on the Geology of the US.* Gay-Lussac establishes the ratios of volumes of gases which react chemically: law of volumes of gases.
The Arts	Scott *The Lay of the Last Minstrel.* Beethoven *Fidelio*, opera. Turner *Shipwreck.*	German dramatist von Kleist produces an early realistic comedy, *Der zerbrochene Krug.* Beethoven, Symphony No. 4 and violin concerto in D. Chalgrin completes l'Arc de Triomphe in Paris.	Crabbe *The Parish Register.* Charles and Mary Lamb *Tales from Shakespeare.* Beethoven 5th Symphony.	Scott *Marmion.* Goethe *Faust* Pt. I. Beethoven 6th Symphony. Goya *Execution of the Citizens of Madrid*; his *Désastres de la Guerre* follow in years to 1815.	Scott *Lady of the Lake.*

	1810	1811	1812	1813	1814
Politics & Military History	France annexes Holland: Napoleon's Empire at its peak. Britain annexes Mauritius and the Seychelles. Napoleon marries Marie Louise, daughter of Emperor Francis I. Wellesley constructs the defence lines of Torres Vedras and holds the French in Portugal. Buenos Aires, Mexico and New Granada overthrow Spanish rule: the emergence as a nationalist leader of Simón Bolivar.	George III declared insane; Prince of Wales becomes Regent. French driven out of Portugal and Wellesley invades Spain. Muhammad Ali massacres the ruling Mamluks in Egypt. Russians fail (a second attempt) to force Japan to open trade to the West. Paraguay and then Venezuela declare independence of Spain.	Napoleon invades Russia: battle of Borodino, the burning of Moscow; French retreat. Britain's Prime Minister, Percival, is assassinated. Anglo-American War – to 1814 – over British policy towards neutral shipping. Battle of Salamanca: Wellesley advances to Madrid but is forced to retreat again.	Battle of Vittoria: French driven from Spain. US seizes West Florida from Spain. Prussia launches war of liberation against French. Napoleon defeats the Allies at Lutzen and Bautzen. Austrians join alliance against Napoleon. Battle of Leipzig (Battle of the Nations): Napoleon defeated. Bolivar becomes Dictator of Venezuela; Mexico becomes independent.	Napoleon abdicates and is exiled to Elba. Allies enter Paris and restore the Bourbons – Louis XVIII, brother of Louis XVI. Congress of Vienna: heads of state discuss post-war Europe. Treaty of Ghent ends Anglo-American War. Britain retains the Cape.
Religion & Learning	Carnot, French soldier and statesman *De la défense des places fortes*. Italian Scientific Institute is decentralized and branches are established in Venice, Padua, Verona, Milan.	Hannah More *Practical Piety*. The conflict between Napoleon and the Pope continues.	Hegel *Die Objektive Logik*. Prussia begins standard educational plan of gymnasium studies.	Robert Owen *A New View of Society*. McGill University is established in Montreal.	Pope Pius VII returns to Rome and restores the Inquisition and Society of Jesus. Chair of Sanskrit is established at Collège de France.
Cities & Social Development	Engineer John McAdam begins road construction in England and gives his name to the process of road metalling he introduced. Krupp works open in Essen. Berlin with a population of 150,000 has an estimated 3000 prostitutes. France introduces book censorship.	Agrarian distress and rioting in Britain; Luddite riots. French press is virtually muzzled by censorship. Civil code is adopted in Austria.	Steamship *Comet* operates on the River Clyde. Beginning of the Red River Settlement in Manitoba, Canada. Hardenburg reforms in Prussia emancipate the Jews. Only English famine of the Nineteenth Century.	Two British ships break into Nagasaki Harbour to dislodge a Dutch trader: growing western attempts to force Japan to open her society to the West. Francis Lowell designs the first large-scale rationalized factory to produce standardized cottons for farmwear: a major step in the growth of the American textile industry.	St Margaret's Westminster is the first district of London to be illuminated by gas.
Discovery & Invention	Dalton *New System of Chemical Philosophy* explains atomic theory. Durand discovers how to preserve food in cans.	Karl F. Gauss illustrates complex numbers. The anatomist, John Bell *New Idea of the Anatomy of the Brain*; he is the founder of surgical anatomy.	Baron Cuvier *Recherches sur les Ossements fossiles de Quadrupèdes*. Laplace *Théorie analytique des probabilités* (to 1820). Baron Larrey (Napoleon's surgeon) introduces local analgesia – he amputates limbs painlessly in retreat from Moscow by freezing them.	Davy *Elements of Agricultural Chemistry*. Evans discovers and names the Maquarie River in Australia and explores the Murray Basin.	George Stephenson's first practical steam locomotive.
The Arts	de Staël *De l'Allemagne*. San Carlo Opera House is built at Naples.	Jane Austen *Sense & Sensibility*. Establishment of the Prague Conservatory of Music. Nash begins Regent Street, London. Weber's opera *Abu Hassan*.	Byron *Childe Harold* (first cantos). Grimm Brothers *Kinder und Haus-Märchen*. Beethoven 7th Symphony. Goya *Portrait of the Duke of Wellington*. John Nash, York Gate, Regent's Park and Drury Lane Theatre.	Austen *Pride & Prejudice*. Shelley *Queen Mab*. Schubert 1st Symphony. Blake *The Day of Judgement*, a collection of mystical drawings.	Austen *Mansfield Park*. Scott *Waverley*. Byron *The Corsair*. Géricault *The Wounded Curaissier*. Ingres *L'Odalisque*.

The division of Europe between himself and Tsar Alexander of Russia did not satisfy Napoleon for long. By the summer of 1811 he was complaining to Caulaincourt, his Ambassador at St Petersburg, about the Tsar's failure to keep his engagements and listening to the Ambassador's attempts to put Alexander's point of view with ill-concealed impatience. When he spoke again it was to list the number of men, guns and horses, the quantities of powder, shot and general stores needed for a campaign in Russia, Caulaincourt, who had observed how 'enumerations of this kind always intoxicated him' sadly but correctly concluded that Napoleon was bent on war.

The invasion was, in truth, a staggering undertaking. Napoleon assembled half a million men and took most of them across the Niemen into Russia before the summer was out. The Russians intended to fight but the preparations they had made proved so inadequate that they were forced to fall back: the Grand Armée, encumbered by a necessarily elaborate supply train, moved too slowly to catch them. Napoleon, arriving at Smolensk at the head of 200,000 men, decided to press on in the hope that the Russians would at least make a stand in front of Moscow. They did, and in a murderous, head-on battle at Borodino, he gave them a drubbing: the effective strength of the Russian army was reduced at a stroke from 120,000 to 45,000. The French suffered heavily too, but Napoleon was still able to lead 95,000 men into Moscow on 14 September. From there he wrote to Alexander offering terms. There was no reply.

Napoleon seems to have realized that something was wrong early on in the campaign. He was oddly lethargic, letting his generals do most of the fighting and showing unaccustomed caution in his dispositions. This was perhaps partly age: on the eve of Austerlitz, when he was at the height of his powers, he had given himself six years more in the game of war and the six years were now up. But it was more probably a growing realization that the premise on which he had based the campaign was false: winning a battle, taking Moscow, were not going to force the Tsar to ask for terms. After a month had dragged by there was nothing for Napoleon to do but give the order for retreat.

The French filed out of Moscow laden with loot on 19th October. The weather was good but the men had to take care, for Cossacks were on their flanks picking off stragglers and cutting up isolated battalions. On 3rd November Russian regular units, recruited up to full strength again, made a dramatic reappearance, getting astride the road between the main French force and its rear corps: extracting this proved a costly business, and morale suffered. The next day the first snow fell, the temperature plummeted and movement began to get difficult. By the time the Grande Armée reached Smolensk its effective strength was down to 50,000.

Above: English print celebrating 'the Miseries of the French Grand Army in their Retreat from Moscow'. Published March 1813.

Right: Moscow ablaze, as seen from the Kremlin. The day after the French entered Moscow fires broke out in several quarters of the deserted city. No one has been able to determine how far they were started deliberately by saboteurs and how far they were caused accidentally by French or Russian looters: either way the French, whose discipline was getting increasingly unsteady, failed to put them out. By the next day it was too late: the fires were completely out of control and had engulfed large areas of the city. The conflagration lasted three days and reduced two-thirds of the city's houses – nearly all of which were still built of wood – to ashes. It provided a depressing start to what was supposed to be a triumphant occasion.

As the magnitude of the disaster became apparent Napoleon recovered some of his old form. When the army was cut in two west of Smolensk he broke back with the Guard and rescued many of the trapped men: he got a nucleus of 25,000 effectives across the Dnieper and, in a brilliant battle against all the odds, won passage for half this number across the Berezina. That was the last major obstacle on the road home and reasonably enough he left for Paris at this point: if there was to be a campaign of any sort in 1813 he needed to raise a new army. For the Grande Armée was no more. Of the 400,000 men who had taken the road to Moscow no more than 3 or 4000 returned.

When Talleyrand, Napoleon's Foreign Minister, heard the news from Russia, he remarked 'This is the beginning of the end'. And he was right. The enemies Napoleon had humbled individually now joined hands to bring him down. In two uninspired but decisive campaigns, one in Germany in 1813, one in France in 1814, they destroyed the imperial structure he had created and restored the European balance of power much as it had existed 25 years earlier, on the eve of the French Revolution. Bar the last flourish of the Hundred Days, the Napoleonic adventure was over.

THE

AGE OF IMPERIALISM

AD 1815 - AD 1913

The fall of the Napoleonic Empire was the signal for political and social reaction. The king of Prussia and the emperors of Russia and Austria were determined that nothing like the alarms and excursions of the revolutionary wars should be allowed to happen again, and they bound themselves not only to observe the new frontiers but also to enforce them. The same went for the social order: any signs of liberté, égalité *and* fraternité *would be firmly stamped on.*

One revolution escaped their scrutiny. It was taking place in England which because of its insular geography, its Atlantic orientation and its liberal parliamentary traditions, lay outside the area of concern to the continental powers. Its essence was a shift from rural to urban living: its most obvious expression was the rapid growth of London, but London had always been exceptionally large, the real boom towns were those that ranked just below the metropolis: Manchester, Liverpool and Birmingham. These three came up from nowhere in the early 18th century: Manchester, the fastest growing of all, had about half a million people by 1850.

Manchester was not just a new town, it was a new type of town. Its growth was powered by its factories with their insatiable demand for labour: its lifestyle was to become a textbook example of something that was to be experienced, some would say endured, by much of the human race in the next hundred years. The urban revolution is not the same thing as the industrial revolution but at this stage and in this instance both lay very close together.

THE KINGDOM OF COTTON

At the beginning of the 18th century the textile trade of England had two raw materials, flax and wool. Small amounts of silk and cotton were imported for the top end of the market but it was difficult to imagine either of these exotic fibres ever being of much importance to English weavers. Finished goods were another matter: printed cottons ('calicoes') from India were having such a success that the government had just decided to ban their import. This gave the infant English cotton industry based on the small northern town of Manchester a chance to justify itself.

Manchester at this time was only capable of making crude copies of Indian calicoes using as much linen as cotton. But as the 18th century progressed, the output of these 'fustian' cottons slowly increased. In fact, the demand was greater than the supply even though the quality remained less than marvellous. The trouble was at the spinning stage: the thread spun from the raw cotton was not fine enough or strong enough. And there was not enough of it.

The last two of these difficulties were overcome in the late 1760s when James Hargreaves invented the spinning jenny and Richard Arkwright the water frame. Hargreaves' 'jenny' (short for engine) was a simple hand-operated machine which spun eight threads at once: though the thread it produced was no better than the ordinary spinning wheel's the jenny put an end to the yarn shortage and the industry was finally able to catch up with the demand for fustians. The water frame was more innovative: it incorporated rollers which improved the strength of the yarn to the point where it could be used for warp as well as weft. This meant that the English weaver could make pure cotton fabrics. These could not be classed as top quality cloth – water frame thread was thick as well as strong – but they represented an important addition to the range.

Even in their prototype versions, which produced only four threads at a time, Arkwright's machines were too heavy to turn by hand: they had to be driven by a horse capstan or, as soon became normal practice, a water-wheel (hence the term 'water frame'). The contrast with the jenny could not have been more complete. On the one hand was the worker's cottage with one or at most two jennies: on the other the mill as developed by Arkwright in the 1770s with 40 machines of 24 spindles each.

The early 1780s saw two more technical advances. The first was a new machine, the Mule, which could spin cotton yarn as fine as the best oriental muslin and do so at at fraction of the cost. The second was a steam engine capable of delivering rotary power. This freed the spinners from their dependence on the waterwheel with all its locational inconveniences. Mills began to go up in Manchester alongside the warehouses that marked the city's continuing dominance of the cotton trade.

Cotton was now making its way into the national statistics. The amount of cotton imported had gone up from $2\frac{1}{4}$ million kg in the 1770s to more than 22 million kg in the early 1800s. At the same time the value of cotton goods exported had risen from less than £250,000 to over £10,000,000, more than twice the figure for woollens. The 1780s had not just been good years, they had been a turning point. A new kingdom had been created, the kingdom of cotton and Manchester was its capital.

It was difficult not to be swept away by the excitement of

ll this. Visitors trooped out to view the mills at dusk, their chimneys belching smoke, their rows of brilliant gas-lit windows contrasting with the darkness of the houses uddled round them. Everyone agreed that the sight was without parallel. Disraeli, in his guise as a novelist, has one of his characters sigh for the ruins of Athens. 'The Age of Ruins is past' says his friend 'Have you seen Manchester? Manchester is as great a human exploit as Athens'.

It certainly ruled as great an empire. As the spindles multiplied into millions the traditional sources of raw cotton – Turkey and India – proved inadequate: the merchants had to turn for their supplies from the Old World to the New. The plantation owners of the southern Jnited States rose to the challenge, pushing up their output ear by year on Manchester's demand. Gradually the slave opulation of the Deep South was transformed into a otton-producing machine, sending an unending stream of otton bales across the Atlantic to Liverpool and thence by anal to the warehouses of Manchester.

For all the wealth cotton brought Manchester the city ontained many people who were no better off than the lacks on the plantations. The wages that had attracted the abour force to the mills in the first place were good. 'Why nock yourself out for a shilling a day digging ditches for a armer when you could get five shillings a day in a cotton works?' was the cry that pulled them in and it was not ntrue in itself. But the flow of work was uncertain, for the otton trade was subject to rapid fluctuations in demand nd the millowners were ruthless about laying off hands. And of course the employers took no responsibility for the nemployed or for the conditions in which they lived. The ousing stock was in truth abysmal. It had been run up by small speculative builders and was in ruins almost as soon as it was finished. There might be a lot of money in Manchester but the place was a slum. 'Here civilization works its miracles' wrote de Tocqueville 'and civilized man is turned back almost into a savage'.

McConnel and Kennedy's Cotton Spinning Mill, Union Street, Manchester. This is an example of the fully developed factory, powered by a Boulton and Watt engine and lit by gas. It employed 1,500 hands and was one of the largest in the city. Manchester had been the centre for the cotton industry all through the 18th century but it was only in the 1780s that big mills started to be built there. The first generation of mills, of the pattern developed by Arkwright in the 1770s, relied on water power and had to be built where this was available.

This was the aspect of Manchester that most impressed young Friedrich Engels when he came to the city to work in a cotton firm part-owned by his rich German father. His position was one of privilege and many young men would have found it easy to ignore the poverty of the less fortunate millhands. Not Engels. He wrote a violent but meticulously documented denunciation of the circumstances in which the cotton oligarchs allowed the common people of Manchester to live. 'The cottages are old, dirty, and of the smallest sort, the streets uneven, fallen into ruts and in part without drains or pavement; masses of refuse, offal and sickening filth lie among standing pools in all directions; the atmosphere is poisoned by the effluvia from these, and laden and darkened by the smoke of a dozen tall factory chimneys. . . . The race that lives in these ruinous cottages, behind broken windows, mended with oilskin, sprung doors, and rotten door-posts, or in dark, wet cellars, in measureless filth and stench, in this atmosphere penned in as if with a purpose, this race must really have reached the lowest stage of humanity'.

'The Condition of the Working Class in England' was published in Leipzig in 1845 when Engels was 24. It makes Disraeli's observation look cheap and heartless. It also set many people thinking about the social consequences of laissez-faire capitalism. Engels was not against industrialization, he knew it was inevitable. But surely, he asked, there must be a better way to do it than this?

EUROPE AFTER NAPOLEON

	1815	1816	1817	1818	1819
Politics & Military History	The Hundred Days: Napoleon escapes from Elba and marches on Paris; Louis XVIII flees. Battle of Waterloo: final defeat of Napoleon who is exiled to St Helena. Congress of Vienna restores the Austrian and Prussian monarchies; the Holy Roman Empire is reconstituted as a German Confederation under Austrian Presidence. Sweden gains Norway from Denmark but loses her last foothold on the continent. New Kingdom of Poland is set up. British gains from the war include Cape Province, Mauritius, Ascension Is, Heligoland, Ceylon, Trinidad, St Lucia, Tobago: she occupies the Ionian Is (until 1864).	Constitutional Moderates gain a majority in the French Assembly. Final suppression of Barbary Pirates. Indiana joins USA. Java is restored to the Netherlands. Argentina achieves formal independence from Spain.	Mississippi joins USA. Revolt of Greeks against Turks begins; Serbs are granted partial autonomy. Bolivar establishes independent government of Venezuela.	Illinois joins USA whose westward expansion gathers pace. Congress of Aix-la-Chapelle: Allied army of occupation leaves France and Quadruple Alliance becomes Quintuple Alliance with addition of France. Chile becomes independent after defeat of Royalists. Chaka the Great founds Zulu Empire in southern Africa.	Peterloo Massacre: soldiers fi on political meeting in Manchester killing 11 and wounding 400. The Six Acts: law and orde legislation passed in Britain curbing freedoms. Britain returns to gold standard. Murder of Kotzebue, German poet, by radical student leads to the Carlsbad Decrees: tight control of universities and press censorship; constitutional reforms postponed 20 years. Alabama joins USA; Spain cedes Florida to USA. Bolivar secures independence of Greater Colombia. Singapore is founded by Sir Stamford Raffles.
Religion & Learning	Malthus *Enquiry into the Nature and Progress of Rent.* Ricardo *The Influence of a low price of corn on the profits of stock.*	Cobbett's influence at its height in Britain: his *Register* selling 40–60,000 copies a week. American Bible Society established. Papal encyclical urging clergy of rebellious South American colonies to support Spanish Crown.	Ricardo *On the Principles of Political Economy and Taxation.* Papal Bull is issued against Bible Societies. Hindu College is established in Calcutta: English is language of instruction. James Mill *History of India.*	Institution of Civil Engineers is established in Britain. Bonn University is established. Hegel becomes Professor of Philosophy at Berlin.	Schopenhauer *Die Welt als Wille und Vorstellung.* University of St Petersburg is established.
Cities & Social Development	Corn Law in Britain controls imports of cheap foreign corn so as to protect English farmers. Agrarian distress and rioting in England. Trial by jury established in Scotland. Apothecaries Act in Britain forbids unqualified doctors from practising.	The rise in wheat prices increases social distress in Britain: Spa Field Riots and agrarian riots in East Anglia. Large scale emigration to North America. Trans-Atlantic packet service begins. Britain founds Bathurst, Gambia.	March of the Manchester Blanketeers: continuing distress and unrest in Britain; Derby and Huddersfield Risings; the suspension of Habeas Corpus. Revolt against British rule in Kandy, Ceylon: suppressed.	Manchester cotton spinners' strike. Beginnings of the Prussian customs union. First iron passenger ship on the Clyde. *Savannah*, first steamship to cross the Atlantic (26 days).	British factory act for children in cotton industry: no employment for under 9's, 12 hour day for under 16's; it proves largely ineffective.
Discovery & Invention	Davy, the development of miners' safety lamps by using double wire gauze to stop flame. Lamarck *Histoire naturelle des animaux* (to 1822).	French doctor, René Laennec, invents the stethoscope.	Jons Jakob Berzelius, Swedish chemist, discovers selenium, lithium and introduces terms: halogen, allotropy, catalytic action to chemistry. Cuvier *La Regne Animal*, a classification of animals which was long to be the standard zoological work.	Ross and Parry seek North-west Passage. Jeremiah Chubb's detector lock is patented; later it is perfected by his brother.	Sir David Brewster, the refraction of light through crystals leads to development of crystallography.
The Arts	Austen *Emma.* Scott *Guy Mannering.* Schubert, 3rd Symphony. Nash rebuilds the Brighton Pavilion in neo-Oriental style. Constable *Boat building.*	Scott *The Antiquary* and *Old Mortality.* Rossini *The Barber of Seville.* Schubert 4th and 5th Symphonies. Leigh Hunt *The Story of Rimini* (volume of poems).	Hazlitt *Characters of Shakespeare's Plays.* Byron *Manfred.* Keats *Poems.* Constable *Flatford Mill.*	Austen *Northanger Abbey* and *Persuasion* published posthumously. Hazlitt, three courses of lectures *On the English Poets, On the English Comic Writers* and *On the Dramatic Literature of the Age of Queen Elizabeth* (to 1820) contain his best critical works.	Shelley *The Cenci, Prometheus Unbound.*. Keats *Ode on a Grecian Urn, Ode to a Nightingale, Hyperion* Géricault *Raft of the Medusa.* Hugo *Odes.* Pushkin *The Village.*

1820	1821
Cato Street Conspiracy: plot to assassinate British cabinet is discovered. Liberal revolutions in Spain, Portugal and Italy: the term *liberalism* comes into use. Congress of Troppau: European powers determine to oppose revolution. Assassination of Duc de Berry, sole direct heir of Bourbons, sparks off repression in France. American Colonizing Society founds the Liberian Republic in Africa for freed slaves. Missouri compromise: allows slave owning states to join Union.	Congress of Laibach authorizes Austria to put down Neapolitan revolt; Austria crushes Piedmontese Revolt at Novarra. Full-scale Greek revolt against Turkish rule begins. Peru and Mexico proclaim independence. Missouri joins USA. Gold Coast becomes a British Crown Colony.
Malthus *Principles of Political Economy*. Abolition of the Spanish Inquisition. Jacques Thièrry, historian *Lettres sur l'histoire de France*.	James Mill *Principles of Political Economy*. Robert Owen *Report to County of Lanark*. Comte de St-Simon *Du système industriel*, early socialist thinker.
Cobbett's *Rural Rides* begin to appear in the *Political Register* (to 1830). British emigrants to South Africa establish Port Elizabeth.	London co-operative society is established. *Manchester Guardian* is started as a weekly (daily from 1855). Europe's population: France 30.4m, Britain 20.8m, Italian States 18m, Austria 12m, German States 26m, the USA 9.6m.
André-Marie Ampère, electro-magnetic theory, gives name to the unit of strength of electrical current.	Faraday, principles of electric motor, fundamentals of electro-magnetic rotation. Cuvier *Researches on Fossil Bones* (to 1824).
Scott *Ivanhoe*. Washington Irving *Sketch Book*. de Lamartine *Premières Méditations poètiques*. Discovery of the *Venus de Milo* at Melos. Blake *Illustrations to the Book of Job*.	Thomas de Quincey *Confessions of an English Opium Eater*. Scott *Kenilworth*. Constable *The Hay Wain*. Weber *Der Freischutz*, opera. Heinrich Heine *Gedichte*, poems.

At the Congress of Vienna (1814–15) the Great Powers met to decide what the new, post-Napoleonic map of Europe should look like. Britain had no continental ambitions but the other three powers – Russia, Prussia and Austria – who had been pushed around and about by Napoleon for the previous decade, had extensive shopping lists. The end result of the subsequent wheeling and dealing was a westward shift in the boundaries of all three as the states that had been set up to sustain the French hegemony in the centre strip of Europe – the Duchy of Warsaw, the Kingdom of Westphalia and the Kingdom of Italy are the most important – were parcelled up and distributed among the victors.

The Congress of Vienna has to be accounted a success. It produced a settlement that went unchallenged for a generation: in fact between 1815 and 1848 there was only one boundary change of significance within the area covered by the Congress and only two in the whole of Europe. The first was simply a matter of recognizing that the Congress' attempt to unite Belgium and Holland had failed, something that became obvious when the Belgians threw out the Dutch in 1830. This event caused some alarm to the Powers because the reason for forcing the Belgians into the union in the first place was the fear that if left on their own they would be gobbled up by the French. However, it quickly became clear that the French had renounced their ambitions in this direction and, once everyone had been reassured on this point, the Belgians were allowed to establish their own kingdom. Getting the Dutch to recognize the *fait accompli* took a little longer but eventually, after lengthy and delicate negotiations in 1838, they gave it a grudging recognition.

The other alteration to the map concerned the area under Ottoman control. As the power of the Sultan waned, so the Christians of the Balkans became increasingly restive: in 1817 the Serbs succeeded in getting a substantial measure of autonomy; in 1821 the Greeks made a bid for total independence. After some victories and more defeats they were on the verge of being forced into submission again when the Powers intervened on their behalf. A combined English, French and Russian fleet under the command of the British Admiral Sir Edward Codrington destroyed the Turkish navy at Navarino on 20th October, 1827: one Russian army invaded the Balkans while another advanced in Transcaucasia. Faced with this coalition of superior forces the Sultan backed down, and agreed to recognize the sovereignity of Greece and the autonomy of the Romanian principalities of Moldavia and Wallachia.

Above: Napoleon on the Island of Elba, a contemporary caricature. The victorious Allies confined Napoleon to Elba in 1814 hoping that he would settle down there and trouble Europe no more. However, after only ten months he escaped from the island and returned to France. For a hundred days Europe watched as he tried to rebuild his empire, an attempt that came to an end on the field of Waterloo. After this the Allies chose a place of exile that was less easy to escape from – and also a lot less attractive: the dismal rock of St Helena in the middle of the South Atlantic.

Between the establishment of the USA and the post-1945 era of decolonization, there was another – scarcely remembered – period of colonial emancipation: in Latin America, in the first quarter of the 19th century, when no less than fifteen new nations were brought into being.

Up to the early 19th century, the two Spanish vice royalties of New Spain (Mexico) and Peru, established on the foundations of the pre-Colombian civilizations in the 16th century, had proved remarkably stable, their white elites successfully lording it over the Indian agricultural masses and at the same time keeping Spain well supplied with silver. Elsewhere in Central and South America, there were scattered mines and missions, ports and plantations; islands of Spanish and – in Brazil – Portuguese rule floating between the jungle and the sea.

The native-born whites, *criollos*, had their grievances; the occupation of the top rungs of public office by European-born administrators, *peninsulares*, was a particularly sore point. Yet the (North) American War of Independence had really very little impact on the rest of the Americas; only Francisco de Miranda, the unsuccessful precursor of an independent Venezuela, is remembered now for bringing the founding ideals of the USA to the southern hemisphere. Far from seeking its own independence, Latin America was cast adrift by Europe, its liberty an unintended consequence of Bonapartism.

Napoleon's occupation of the Iberian peninsula began with the 1807 campaign against Portugal which caused the Portuguese regent Dom John to flee to Brazil and set up a government in exile there. The next year Napoleon deposed the king of Spain and his heir apparent, declared the Bourbon dynasty at an end and gave the throne of Spain to his own brother Joseph. Joseph's title was not recognized in the Americas. The *peninsulares* who ran the vice-royalties of Mexico and Peru remained loyal to the Bourbons: elsewhere power devolved on the local *criollos* who became effectively independent. When Napoleon was overthrown and the Bourbons recovered Spain, Spanish authority was briefly reimposed on Ecuador, Colombia, Venezuela and Chile but the reactionary tide was already ebbing when a liberal coup in Madrid in 1820 proved one upheaval too many for the bemused colonial authorities. In

Above: Simon Bolivar.

Mexico conservatives and radicals joined forces and took the country out of the Spanish Empire in 1821. Central America went along with the Mexicans. The loyalist army struggling against the *criollo* leader Simon Bolivar of Venezuela lost heart and he was able to advance from Colombia to liberate Ecuador (1822) and finally Peru (1824). Brazil and Portugal had already parted company after a bloodless coup in 1822.

What all this adds up to is something considerably less stirring than the events at Concord and Lexington because it has little relevance to anything outside South America. In truth it amounts to little more than the expulsion of one clique, the *peninsulares*, by another, the *criollos*. There was no tradition of local self-government on which to base a representative administration and attempts to dress up authoritarian regimes as democracies of even the most limited sort were never more than claptrap. In Latin America, it was often said, 'Conservatives are always conservative, Liberals are seldom liberal and Radicals are never radical'. But then cynics have said that of other places too and Spain in the 19th century hardly set an example to anyone. The 19th century Latin Americans were not the only people to discover that democracy does not easily put down roots in a poor country.

Still it was disappointing. '(Latin) America is ungovernable' was the final dictum of Bolivar, dying in 1830 amidst the wreck of his plans for a union of Ecuador, Colombia and Venezuela. Central America was to undergo a similar disintegration eight years later. In many states the only force holding the nation together seemed to be the army and this led to the pattern of military intervention in politics which makes the evolution of democratic forms even more difficult. It is a cycle which has not been broken yet. *(R.J.*

Left: Devotional representation of Simon Bolivar in action.

	1822	1823	1824	1825	1826
Politics & Military History	Civil war in Spain: Liberals against Royalists. Death of Castlereagh leads to more enlightened British government, leading figure is George Canning, Foreign Secretary. Congress of Verona: breaks down over Britain's refusal to intervene in Spain; the end of Congress System of diplomatic alliances which had controlled Europe since 1814. Britain secures limitation of Arab slave ships to East Africa and Arabia. Brazil becomes independent of Portugal. Turks massacre 30,000 Greeks at Chios.	Huskisson and Goderich begin reforms of British fiscal policy (to 1827). Formation of Catholic Association in Ireland. Mexico becomes republic. First Ashanti War in the Gold Coast. Monroe Doctrine: President James Monroe warns European powers not to interfere in the American continent. French troops intervene in Spain and defeat Liberals.	First Anglo-Burmese War: Britain captures Rangoon and begins annexation of Burma. Bolivar becomes Emperor of Peru. Egyptians capture Crete; struggle in Greece against the Turks continues.	Britain recognizes new independent states of South America. Decembrist rising in Russia: result is years of repression under new Tsar, Nicholas I. Portugal recognizes the independence of Brazil under Dom Pedro. Ibrahim, son of Muhammad Ali, invades Greece and devastates Morea. Bolivar at peak of his power: Liberator of Colombia, Dictator of Peru, President of Bolivia.	Turks capture Missolonghi; final revolt of Janissaries in Turkey is suppressed. Treaty of Yandabu ends first Anglo-Burmese War. Russia and Persia at war. Dissension and divisions in Bolivia, Colombia and Peru end Great Colombia.
Religion & Learning	Colebrooke establishes the Royal Asiatic Society for study of eastern languages.	Jeremy Bentham starts the *Westminster Review*, journal of utilitarianism. St-Simon *Catéchisme des Industriels.* Thiers begins *Histoire de la Révolution française*, completed in 1827.	Establishment of the Berlin Polytechnic. French primary education is placed under control of the bishops.	Hazlitt *The Spirit of the Age.* Thièrry *Histoire de la Conquète d l'Angleterre* (1066).	University of Munich and University College, London, are established.
Cities & Social Development	First iron paddle steamer on the Seine. Streets of Boston, Mass., are gas-lit. *Sunday Times* begins in London.	Sir Robert Peel as Britain's Home Secretary begins penal reforms: the death penalty is abolished for over 100 crimes. Rugby football is 'invented' at Rugby School. Muhammad Ali who had conquered Sudan for Egypt between 1820 and 1822 founds Khartoum.	*Le Globe* is published in Paris; there are two daily newspapers in Berlin. The repeal of the Combination Acts in Britain gives an impetus to trade union movement. Imperial Gallon comes into use. Durban becomes port for Natal. RSPCA is established.	US government moves remaining Native American tribes west of Mississippi to establish permanent Indian Frontier. Horse drawn buses are first used in London. Stockton-Darlington Railway line (43 km), first passenger railway, built by Stephenson. New Zealand Colonization Company is established.	Telford's Menai Bridge completed. Royal Zoological Society established in London. First railway tunnel built on the Liverpool-Manchester line.
Discovery & Invention	Jean Fourier *Théorie analytique de la chaleur*, study of heat. Augustin Fresnel perfects lenses for lighthouses.	First iron railway bridge for the Stockton-Darlington railway is designed by Stephenson. MacIntosh produces his rubberized waterproof material.	Carnot *Puissance motrice du feu*, on the potential power of heat machines. Hume discovers the River Murray in Australia.	Oersted produces aluminium. Stephenson constructs the *Rocket*, his famous locomotive (completed 1829).	Ampère *Electrodynamics.* Justus Liebig opens his laboratory at the University of Giessen: the beginnings of German chemical ascendancy.
The Arts	de Vigny *Poèmes.* Schubert 8th Symphony *Unfinished.* Royal Academy of Music is established in London. Delacroix *Dante & Virgil crossing the Styx.* Pushkin *Eugene Onegin.*	Charles Lamb *Essays of Elia* (to 1833). de Lamartine *Nouvelles Méditations poétiques.*	National Gallery is set up in London. Beethoven 9th Symphony. Blake *Beatrice addressing Dante*, water-colour. Leopardi *Canzoni, Versi.*	Scott *The Talisman.* Publication of *Pepys Diary.* Manzoni *The Betrothed.* Pushkin *Boris Godunov.*	Cooper *The Last of the Mohicans.* Joseph Niépce, French physicist and inventor, makes his first photograph. Vigny *Cinq-Mars* and *Poèmes antiques et modernes.* Berlioz *Symphonie Fantastique.* Mendelssohn *Midsummer Night's Dream*, overture. Weber *Oberon*, opera.

	1827	1828	1829	1830	1831
Politics & Military History	Turks enter Athens and Ibrahim captures Acropolis. Combined British-French-Russian fleet destroys Turkish fleet at Battle of Navarino. Russians defeat Persia in war (since 1826) and annex Armenia. Anglo-Brazil trade treaty.	The repeal of the Test and Corporation Acts in Britain allows Nonconformists to hold public office. O'Connell is elected for County Clare but is debarred from the House of Commons as a Roman Catholic. A Liberal-Catholic Union is formed in Belgium to oppose the Dutch government. Regent of Portugal, Dom Miguel, usurps throne: civil war follows. Turks evacuate Greece and Britain, France and Russia guarantee Greek independence. Following war between Argentine and Brazil (from 1825) Uruguay becomes independent.	Catholic Emancipation Act in Britain following years of agitation by O'Connell's Catholic Association: Catholics can hold public office in Britain. Fremantle takes possession of Western Australia and begins colonization. Britain abolishes the Hindu custom of Suttee in India. Treaty of Adrianople: ends Russo-Turkish War; Russia gains free navigation of Bosporus and Dardanelles. Greater Colombia is divided into Colombia, Venezuela, Ecuador and New Granada.	July Revolution in France: fall of Charles X and Bourbons; Louis Philippe (known as the Citizen King) allows more liberal constitution. Agitation in Italian states. Uprising in Poland against Russia. Birmingham Political Union established to press for Parliamentary reform in Britain. Revolt against Dutch rule in Brussels: the beginning of the struggle which separates the Netherlands into Belgium and Holland. Mysore incorporated into British India. French conquer Algeria which becomes French colony.	Growing agitation for parliamentary reform in England: riots in Bristol, Nottingham, Derby. Nat Turner leads slave revolt in Virginia, USA. Austria puts down uprisings in Modena, Parma and the Papal States. Giuseppe Mazzini forms the Young Italy (nationalist) movement. Britain and France guarantee the independence of Belgium. Muhammad Ali sends his son Ibrahim to invade Syria.
Religion & Learning	Guizot *Histoire de la Révolution d'Angleterre*. John Keble, founder of the Oxford Movement *The Christian Year*. Hallam, *Constitutional History of England*; he was one of the first historians to use orginal documents in his research.	First appearance of *Webster's Dictionary*. London University, the first non-Anglican university, is established in Britain.	Cobbett *Advice to Young Men*. James Mill *An Analysis of the Phenomena of the Human Mind*.	Daniel Webster gives his famous speech in reply to Sen. Hayne: *Liberty and Union, now and forever, one and inseparable*. Cobbett *Rural Rides*. Comte *Cours de Philosophie Positive* – the beginnings of positivism.	J. S. Mill *The Spirit of the Age*. British Association for Advancement of Science is established.
Cities & Social Development	Baedeker's travel guides begin to appear. *Evening Standard* appears in London.	Exponents of free trade now dominate the British Board of Trade. Beginning of years of peasant revolts in Russia (averaging 23 a year to 1854). *The Spectator* is launched.	Creation of the Metropolitan Police in London, nicknamed *Bobbies* after the Home Secretary, Sir Robert Peel. First Oxford-Cambridge Boat Race. Louis Braille invents his system of finger-reading for the blind: not generally accepted in his lifetime.	British industrial ascendancy is clear: the country produces 80% of Europe's coal, 50% of its iron and nearly all its stream engines. Liverpool to Manchester railway is opened: Huskisson is killed, the first train casualty. Cholera epidemic spreads from Russia across Europe to Britain. Original Negro Minstrel, Rice, sings *Jim Crow*.	Sadler's Committee on employment looks at children in factories – *Condition of England Question*. National Union of Working Classes established in Britain.
Discovery & Invention	Sir John Herschel proposes use of contact lenses. Ohm defines current, potential and resistance: propounds Ohm's law.	Sir John Franklin, Arctic explorer, publishes second account of his explorations. Berzelius identifies thorium and silicon.	Stephenson's *Rocket* wins Rainham Trials. Niépce and Daguerre jointly perfect photographic process.	Landers explores River Niger; Sturt traces River Murray to its mouth. Royal Geographical Society established in London.	Darwin goes as naturalist on HMS *Beagle* on expedition surveying coral formations. Faraday demonstrates electro-magnetic induction: the basis for the development of the dynamo. Guthrie and Liebig independently discover chloroform.
The Arts	Appearance of Edgar Allan Poe's first poems. Nash builds Carlton House Terrace, London. Audubon *Birds of North America*, the first sections appear with their colour plates. Schubert *Die Winterreise*, song cycle.	Constable *A view of the Stour at Dedham* and *Salisbury Cathedral*. Publication of correspondence between Goethe and Schiller.	Balzac *Les Chouans* and *Le Physiologie du Marriage*. Rossini *William Tell*, opera. Chopin makes debut in Vienna.	Balzac begins *La Comédie Humaine*. Stendhal *Le Rouge et le Noir*. Donizetti *Anna Bolena*.	Hugo *Notre Dame de Paris*. Bellini *La Somnambula*. Daumier *Caricatures*.

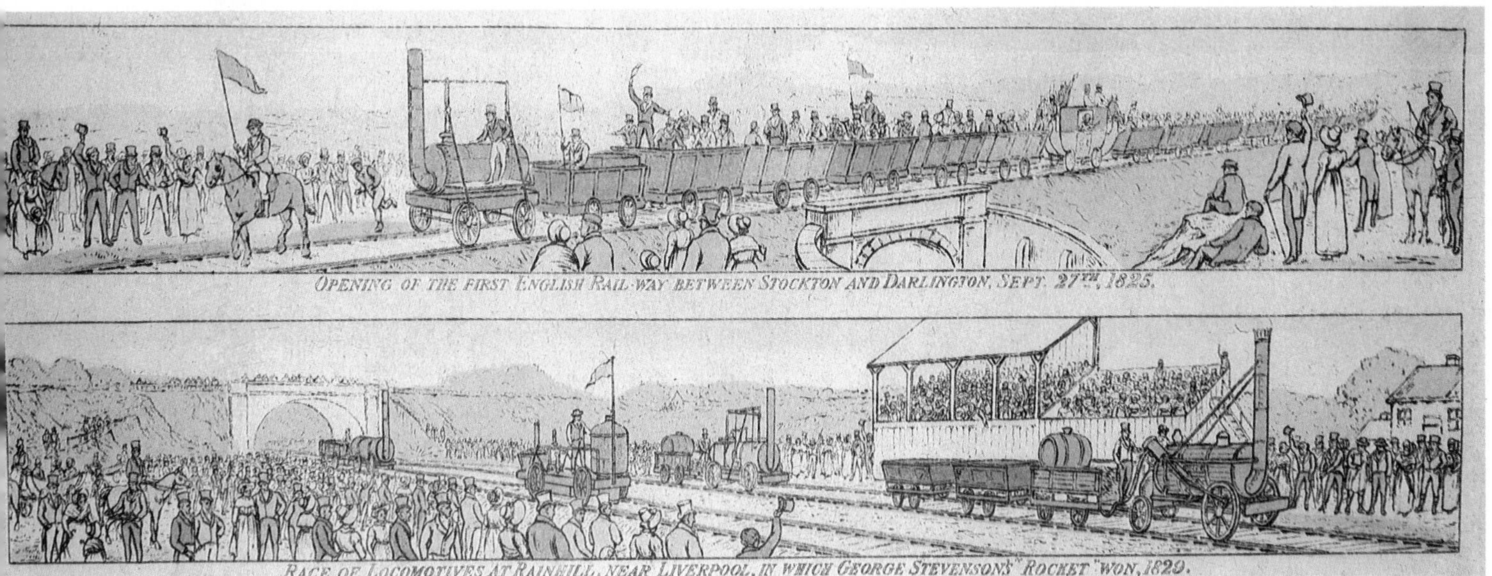

Top: Railway History. The opening of the Stockton and Darlington Railway in 1825 (upper register) and George Stephenson's Rocket *at the Rainhill trials, Liverpool, 1829 (lower register).*

The Rocket was the only one of the engines to complete the trial.

he steam railway was the most widespread symbol of the ·w industrial age. It was also the ultimate in mobile 'vertising, carrying the message of the new technology on heels, for all to see. In the course of the 19th century, it iited countries, revolutionized military strategy, and .posed uniform standards of punctuality and time-keep- ;– 'railway time' – on whole nations. The origins of the ilway, as of the Industrial Age generally, lay in Britain.

By the end of the 18th century, the major coalfields of :itain were covered with networks of horse-drawn ilways and dotted with steam engines driving all sorts of achinery, including stationary engines hauling waggons) slopes on iron rails. The coalfields, too, had a good attering of entrepreneurs and engineers who found novation and lateral thinking almost a way of life. In such atmosphere, it was only a matter of time before the steam gine was applied to the problem of transporting heavy ›ods over longer distances.

The breakthrough came right at the beginning of the th century when, in a remarkably short period, the steam gine was first successfully applied to water (1801), road 801) and rail (1804) transport. Richard Trevithick, the ɔrnish mining engineer who had built a steam-driven ›ad carriage in 1801, is credited with the first really ccessful attempt to harness a steam engine on rails to the sk of haulage. In February 1804, a locomotive designed / him hauled 10 tonnes of iron and 70 men over 15 km near erthyr Tydfil in South Wales. It was Trevithick, too, ho first displayed a steam locomotive to a wider audience, hen he ran 'Catch-me-who-can' on a circular track in ɔndon in 1808.

Over the next two decades engineers in the coalfields ade improvements in the design of both locomotives and ils. Most of the important advances came in north east ngland and it was there, in September 1825, that the first ıblic, passenger-carrying steam locomotives came into e. They plied between Stockton and Darlington, a stance of 22 km. The Stockton and Darlington Railway, ough, was still mainly used for hauling coal and relied on ɔrses and stationary engines as well as locomotives; the ·st exclusively steam railway providing general transport rived at the end of the decade, with the completion of the km railway between Liverpool and Manchester.

The Liverpool and Manchester Railway achieved fame several counts. It was the first railway to be built between two major centres of population with the deliberate intention of competing with canal and road transport for goods and passengers. At the locomotive trials for the new railway, held at Rainhill in 1829, the 'Rocket', designed by George Stephenson, the engineer of both the Stockton and the Liverpool railways, reached 50 kph and was established as the prototype of the fully-developed steam locomotive. And the publicity that accompanied the official opening of the railway in September 1830 received an unexpected fillip when the Rocket, steaming triumphantly through Parkside, ran down a leading Tory politician, William Huskisson, who died of his injuries.

With the Liverpool and Manchester the railway had arrived: in the next 12 years it conquered the country. The spine of the system, running from London via Birmingham to Liverpool and Manchester, had been completed by 1838 and the seven English cities with populations over 100,000 had all been linked by 1841. Progress abroad was equally rapid: by 1840 there were 2500 km of railway in Britain and another 5000 km in the rest of the world; by 1850 there were 10,000 km in Britain and nearly 30,000 km elsewhere.

The rapid expansion of the English system owed as much to glamour as economics. Though the trains soon took away the business of the stage-coach operators they took considerably longer to establish their superiority over inland waterways in the long distance movement of goods. Profits were often slow to materialize. But this did not deter the investors. In 1835–7 and 1844–7 two bouts of 'railway mania', of investment beyond all reason and calculation, saw fortunes made and lost and allowed full rein to every charlatan and trickster in the business. By 1850 a total of £200 million – perhaps the equivalent of £5 billion today – had been invested in railways in Great Britain, much of it not very profitably.

Nevertheless, the benefits the new technology brought to Britain were immense. British investors financed and British engineers built and ran the railways of large parts of the world. The railway's voracious consumption of iron – 200 tonnes alone for each kilometre of line – gave a massive boost to the iron and coal industries and made them leading sectors in the economy at a time when the expansion of the cotton industry was beginning to falter. Above all, the railway confirmed that a fundamental revolution had taken place in human history; humanity, of its own genius, had broken the natural barriers of time and space. *(R.J.)*

	1832	1833	1834	1835	1836
Politics & Military History	Battle of Koniah: Egyptians under Ibrahim defeat Turks in Syria. Great Reform Bill becomes law in Britain: the beginnings of the modern electoral system. 1815 Constitution of Poland is abolished and country becomes Russian province.	Britain abolishes slavery in her Empire. Factory Act forbids employment of children under nine in factories. German states form *Zollverein* (customs union). Indian Civil Service is opened to Indian subjects. Britain makes the Falkland Is a Crown Colony (occupied 1832). League of Munchengratz: Russia, Austria and Prussia form league against British-French liberalism. Death of Ferdinand VII of Spain leads to the first Carlist War (to 1838). Treaty of Unkiar Skelessi between Russia and Turkey.	Carlist Wars in Spain (to 1839) in which Pretender Don Carlos attempts to seize Spanish throne. Quadruple Alliance between Britain, France, Spain and Portugal to safeguard thrones in latter two countries. Peel issues Tamworth Manifesto: forerunner of party manifestos. Sixth Kaffir War in South Africa: Bantu people against white settlers; Dutch from Cape begin to settle north of Orange River.	Municipal Reform Act: major changes in England and Wales. War in Spain: Britain refuses to intervene and Louis Philippe refuses to occupy the Basque Provinces. Pope Gregory XVI refuses a compromise over mixed marriages with Prussia.	South Australia becomes British province. Great Trek: Boers from Cape Colony found the Orang Free State and Transvaal. Chartist Movement is launched in Britain: demands votes for all adult males. Battles of the Alamo and Sa Jacinto: Texas wins independence from Mexico. Prussian *Zollverein* become German customs union.
Religion & Learning	Harriet Martineau *Illustrations of Political Economy*. Durham University is established. Word 'socialism' comes into popular use in Britain and France. Final volume of Niebuhr's *Roman History*.	Newman *Tracts for the Times*, beginning of the Oxford Tractarian Movement. Education Grant Act: the first state grant to voluntary education societies in Britain.	Carlyle *Sartor Resartus*.	Emerson *A Historical Discourse delivered before the citizens of Concord*. de Tocqueville *Democracy in America*, volume I. Bentinck introduces western education to India.	Established Church Act is passed in Britain to reform Church of England. Schopenhauer *Uber den Willen in der Natur*.
Cities & Social Development	Operative Builders' Union set up in Britain. First French railroad St Étienne-Andrezieux begins to carry passengers.	The French Department of Highways and Bridges is charged with designing a national rail network. 10 Hour campaign in Britain.	Poor Law Amendment Act in Britain: workhouse system established. Tolpuddle Martyrs: six Dorset labourers are transported (to Australia) for attempt to set up a trade union. Owen's Grand National Consolidated Trades Union – fails. *Zollverein* widely established among German states. Hansom cabs appear in London.	First railway boom occurs in Britain: construction of Great Western Railway. Foundation of Melbourne, Australia. *New York Herald* is started. Construction of first German railway – Nuremberg-Furth.	London Working Men's Association is formed. Act is passed in Britain for the registration of births, marriages and deaths. Adelaide, South Australia, i founded.
Discovery & Invention	Adrien Legendre *Treatise on elliptic functions*, his greatest work. Beginning of geological survey in Britain.	Gauss defines magnetic field and pole strength. The invention of machine *kryptographique* in Marseilles is forerunner of typewriter.	Faraday's law of electrolysis. Lenz's law on induced current in electro-magnetic induction. McCormick patents his harvesting machine in the USA. Babbage designs his analytical engine, forerunner of the modern computer.	Colt revolver is patented in USA. Darwin studies the Galapagos Islands and notes the effects of their isolation from the world. Gas begins to be used for cooking.	Swedish naval engineer, John Ericcson, invents the screw propeller. John Gray *Elements of Botany*.
The Arts	Hiroshige, master of Japanese colour prints, publishes *53 stages of the Tokaido*. Tennyson *Lady of Shalott*. Goethe *Faust Pt II* (post.). de Musset *Le Spectacle dans un Fauteuil*, drama. George Sand *Indiana*. Donizetti *L'Elisir d'Amore*.	Turner exhibits his first Venetian paintings. Chopin *12 Etudes* (op 10). Mendelssohn *Italian Symphony*.	de Quincey *Autobiographical Sketches*. Musset *On ne badine pas avec l'amour*.	Bellini *I Puritani*. Donizetti *Lucia di Lammermoor*, his greatest success. Mendelssohn becomes conductor of the Leipzig Gewandhaus orchestra.	Musset *Lettre à Lamartine* and *Il ne faut jurer de rien*. Pushkin *Captain's Daughter*

1837	1838
Crisis develops in Canada with rebellions under Papineau and Mackenzie. Michigan joins USA. Britain introduces Hindustani as the *lingua franca* of India.	Boers defeat Dingaan at Blood River, massacring the Zulus. The first Afghan War (to 1842) between Britain and Afghanistan.
Carlyle *The French Revolution*. Fitzwilliam Museum is built at Cambridge.	Carlyle *Critical and Miscellaneous Essays*. Antoine Cournot, French Mathematician and Philosopher *Researches into the Mathematical Principles of the Theory of Wealth*.
Industrial poverty in Britain: 10,000 weavers in Leeds unemployed for three months. Pitman introduces his shorthand system. US Congress passes a 'gag' law to suppress debate on slavery issue. Financial panic in the USA: the result of inflated land values and paper speculation.	Chartists in Britain publish *People's Charter* demanding popular involvement in politics: huge demonstrations (100,000 Glasgow, 200,000 Birmingham, 300,000 West Yorkshire). Anglo-Turkish Trade Treaty gives Britain free trading rights in Turkey and Egypt. Anti-Corn Law League is established at Manchester: the beginning of Manchester Free Trade School. Regular Atlantic steamship service is inaugurated: SS *Sirius* crosses in 18 days, SS *Great Western* in $14\frac{1}{2}$ days. Beijing government bans import of opium to China. *New York Herald*, first US paper to employ European correspondents.
Morse develops the telegraph in the USA. Wheatstone and Cooke develop the first electrical railway telegraph.	Daguerre produces photographs using silver salts – Daguerreotype. Launching of SS *Archimedes*: first successful screw-driven ship.
Dickens *Pickwick Papers*. Hawthorne *Twice-told Tales*. Berlioz *Grande Messe des Morts*. Constable *Arundel Mill*.	Dickens' *Nicholas Nickleby* appears in instalments.

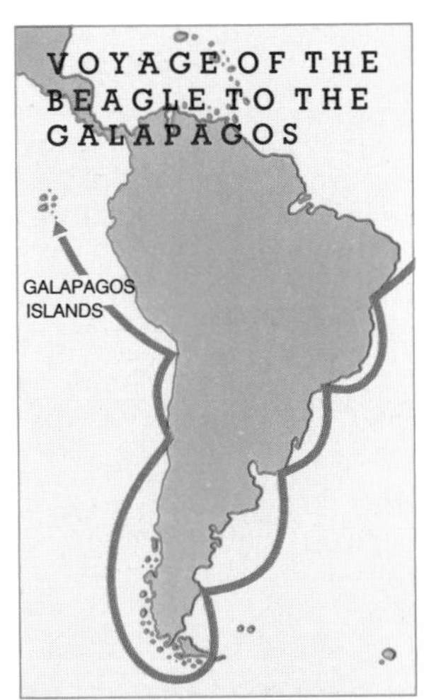

Above: Heads of finches from different islands in the Galapagos Archipelago.

Different islands, different species – the germ of Darwin's evolutionary theory lies in this simple observation. Working out all the implications was to take him more than 20 years.

On 16th September 1835 HMS *Beagle*, Captain Robert Fitzroy RN in command, entered the Galapagos Archipelago. Fitzroy and his crew had been at sea on and off for nearly four years conducting a survey of the coast of South America: now they were going the long way home via the Pacific and the Cape of Good Hope.

Captain Fitzroy was a man of firm views, most of them based on his reading of the bible. He believed that the account of the creation of the Earth given in Genesis was literally true and that the creator had at that time allocated to each part of the Earth appropriate species of animals and plants. No new species had been created since, though some had undoubtedly died out. The naturalist attached to the Beagle expedition, Charles Darwin, had found the bones of some of these unfortunate creatures in South America. Clearly they had failed to find a place in the Ark and had perished in the Great Flood.

Charles Darwin had his doubts about all this. The world seemed to him a lot older than the six or seven thousand years suggested by the biblical account. And the fossil record indicated that the plant and animal kingdom had had a much more varied history than the rather static scenario propounded by Fitzroy. The two of them had interminable, inconclusive arguments.

Arguing with Fitzroy was a tense business, not least because contradicting the capitain of a naval vessel could be construed as mutiny. And Charles Darwin was a rather hesitant young man: he had had an unsuccessful stab at medicine and an even less successful flirtation with the Church before choosing biology as a career. This did seem to suit him, the more so because he was a passionate collector. Ever since he was a child he had been collecting pebbles, shells, fossils and bones. During the voyage of the *Beagle* he filled every corner of his cabin with carefully labelled examples of the geology, flora and fauna of the lands he visited: in the Galapagos, for example, he succeeded in obtaining specimens of most of the species from most of the islands.

The Galapagos specimens set Darwin thinking. The animal species were clearly related to South American forms, which was hardly surprising: what was unexpected was that each island had its own distinct sub-species. Fitzroy suggested that as each volcanic cone emerged from the sea the Creator rewarded it with a unique fauna, but the idea that the islands had been colonized from the mainland and the special features that characterized each population were somehow produced by the subsequent isolation, seemed worth investigation. This sort of 'evolutionary' idea had been propounded before, by Darwin's grandfather Erasmus, for example: what nobody had been able to discover was a plausible mechanism for producing evolutionary changes.

Darwin opened his first notebook on the 'transmutation of species' the year after his return to England. The next year, while reading Malthus on Population, he suddenly saw how evolution might work. Given the variety of animal populations and the high mortality induced by predators, disease and competition for resources, natural forces could extract a new configuration from an existing species. That would explain the situation on the Galapagos: extend the time scale and it could account for all living things.

Alarmed by the consequences of this line of reasoning Darwin delayed publication for 20 years. Then his hand was forced by a letter from another naturalist, Alfred Wallace, who had put together the same set of ideas though not the mass of supporting evidence that Darwin had accumulated in the interval. 'On the Origin of Species by means of Natural Selection' was finally published in 1859.

	1839	1840	1841	1842	1843
Politics & Military History	Boers found independent republic of Natal. First Opium War between Britain and China (to 1842). France annexes Gabon. Treaty of London: Great powers guarantee neutrality of Belgium. Turks invade Syria but are defeated at Nesib. Britain occupies Aden.	Act of Union joins Upper and Lower Canada (following the Durham Report). Treaty of Waitangi: New Zealand becomes British Crown Colony. Quadruple Convention of London: Britain, Russia, Prussia and Austria try to settle the 'Eastern Question' of Muhammad Ali in Egypt: he is supported by France.	Straits Convention: Britain, Austria, Russia, Prussia and France agree the Dardanelles and Bosporus should be closed to foreign ships in peacetime. Convention of Alexandria between Turkey and Egypt recognizes Muhammad Ali as hereditary ruler of Egypt. British adventurer Sir James Brooke becomes White Rajah of Sarawak. Kossuth emerges as nationalist leader in Hungary.	British retreat from Afghanistan: massacre in Khyber Pass. Treaty of Nanjing ends first Opium war: Britain takes Hong Kong, Chinese ports opened to foreign trade. Webster-Ashburton Treaty: settles boundary dispute between USA and Canada. Boers establish Orange Free State. Maori War against settlers for breach of Treaty of Waitangi. French occupy Tahiti. Japan relaxes edict against foreign ships.	Britain annexes Natal in Africa and Sind in India. Irish government prohibits Clontarf meeting to support O'Connell's agitation for repeal of Act of Union. Free Church of Scotland established.
Religion & Learning	Comte gives sociology its name. American traveller, Stephens, discovers and examines antiquities of Mayan culture in Central America.	Emerson *Essays*. de Tocqueville *Democracy in America*, Vol. 2. Proudhon *Qu'est-ce que la propriété*, contains his famous maxim, Property is theft.	Carlyle *Heroes and Hero-Worship*. First university degrees are granted to women in America.	Macaulay *Lays of Ancient Rome*. Primary education is established in Belgium.	Flore Tristan *Union Ouvrière*, conceives the idea of an international workers' union. Macaulay *Essays*. Kierkegaard, Danish philosopher *Either, Or*.
Cities & Social Development	Austria recognizes Magyar as official language in Hungary. In Britain the first Royal Agricultural Show, the first Henley Regatta and the first Grand National are held. First dental school is established at Baltimore. Samuel Cunard establishes his Cunard Steamship Co.	Rowland Hill, the penny post in Britain. Britain now has 24.3% of world steam tonnage and 24% of world trade. Chimney Sweeps Act in Britain. Can-can dance becomes popular in Paris at this time. Railway boom in Europe gathers momentum.	By this year the population of Britain is 18.5m, USA 17m, Ireland 8m. Guano used as fertilizer. *New York Tribune* is started. About 135,000 slaves a year are being brought into USA.	Depression and poverty in industrial Britain: 60% of Bolton cotton mill workers and 36% of Bolton ironworkers are out of work. Chadwick *Report on the Sanitary Condition of the Labouring Population of Great Britain*. Second Chartist Petition is presented to Parliament: Chartist riots. British Mines Act forbids underground employment for women and girls and sets up inspectorate to supervise boy labour. Income Tax reintroduced in Britain.	First appearance of *News of the World* and *Economist*. First public telegraph line from Paddindgton to Slough. Modern sewage system constructed in Hamburg. World's first nightclub opened in Paris. Skiing becomes a sport.
Discovery & Invention	Steel cables are used for the first time in deep mining. American, Charles Goodyear, vulcanizes india-rubber.	Rowland Hill introduces envelopes in Britain. Liebig *Chemistry in its Application to Agriculture and Physiology*, artificial fertilizers.	Sir Joseph Whitworth proposes standard screw-threads.	Doppler states Doppler Effect: change of wavelength caused by relative motion of source and observer. Rothamsted station for agricultural research is established: Sir John Lawes implements the use of artificial fertilizer.	James Joule defines mathematical equivalent of heat in ergs per calorie.
The Arts	Poe *The Fall of the House of Usher*. Turner *The Fighting Téméraire*. Berlioz *Romeo et Juliette*. Chopin *Préludes*, Op. 28.	Dickens *The Old Curiosity Shop*. Cooper *The Pathfinder*. Delacroix *The Justice of Trajan*. Donizetti *La Favorita* and *La Fille du Regiment*.	Dickens *Barnaby Rudge*. First issue of *Punch*. Schumann *Spring Symphony*, No. 1. Poe *The Murders of the Rue Morgue*. Marryat *Masterman Ready*.	Glinka *Russlan and Ludmilla*, opera. Turner *Steamer in Snowstorm*. Wagner *Rienzi*.	Dickens *Martin Chuzzlewit*. Ruskin *Modern Painters* (vol. I to 1860). Corot *Tivoli*. Wagner *The Flying Dutchman*. Tennyson *Morte d'Arthur*.

1844	1845
O'Connell is tried and sentenced for sedition: verdict reversed by House of Lords. Anglo-Sikh War in India: Britain annexes Punjab.	Tory Cabinet of Peel divided over Repeal of Corn Laws: Peel resigns but is recalled when Russell refuses to form ministry. Maori rising against the British in New Zealand: Grey appointed first governor. Sikhs are defeated in India. War between USA and Mexico over boundaries: Florida and Texas join USA. Manufacture of breech-loading artillery with rifled barrels begins in Piedmont.
Karl Marx and Engels begin their collaboration. Emerson *The Young America*.	Engels *The Condition of the Working Class in England*. All-Protestant Alliance against Roman Catholics formed in Britain. Sir Austen Layard, archaeologist, begins excavation of Nineveh.
Companies Act in Britain: companies must register. Bank Charter Act: to regulate money supply in relation to gold in Britain. British Factory Act: a 12 hour day and no night work for women; safety provisions laid down for textile industry. Rochdale Pioneers set up a retail co-operative movement. By this year there are 3598 km of railway line in Britain. There are an estimated (Faucher) 15,000 prostitutes in London.	The Hungry '40s: poor corn harvests and soaring prices are followed by potato harvest failure throughout Europe: famine in Ireland. Between 1845 and 1860 about 2½ million Irish emigrate. Peel's budget abolishes duties on 450 items – moving towards free trade. From 1845 to 1855 some 550,000 Germans emigrate.
Cotton and Wells use nitrous oxide (laughing gas) as anaesthetic in the USA for the first time but without success. H. Grassmann, German mathematician, devises four dimensional geometry. Morse's telegraph is used for the first time from Baltimore to Washington.	R. W. Thompson patents pneumatic tyre although it is not adopted until the 1880s. Sturt explores the central Australian desert; copper is discovered.
Disraeli *Coningsby*. Dumas *The Three Musketeers*. Thackeray *Barry Lyndon*. Polka is introduced into Britain.	Disraeli *Sybil*. Poe *Tales of Mystery and Imagination, The Raven and other Poems*. Dumas *Twenty Years After* and *The Count of Monte Cristo*. Wagner *Tannhäuser*.

The Chinese were brought up to believe that the Emperor ruled the only truly civilized state in the world and that his was the sole legitimate political authority. The Emperor thought so too and, given the millions who acknowledged his rule, the vast extent of his Empire and the seclusion in which he lived, it is difficult to see how he could have believed otherwise. But it led to problems with foreign embassies as, for example, when Lord Macartney arrived in Beijing in 1793. The British ambassador was preceded by a Chinese official carrying a placard that read 'Tribute Bearer from the Red Barbarians' and the Emperor replied to Macartney's proposal for permanent British representation at the Chinese court with a lordly dismissal. 'This request is contrary to all usage of my dynasty and cannot possibly be entertained ... Europe consists of many other nations besides your own: if each and all demanded to be represented at our Court, how could we possibly consent? The thing is utterly impracticable.' And for good measure he added 'I set no value on objects strange or ingenious, and have no use for your country's manufactures.'

The Emperor did in fact hold all the cards. The British, like everyone else, wanted Chinese silks, porcelains and above all tea, but the Chinese did not want anything that the British had to sell. Except perhaps for Indian opium.

Gradually the balance changed. More Chinese acquired the taste for opium and in the early 1830s the value of imports began to exceed exports. Alarmed by the consequent drain of silver the Chinese authorities decided to crack down on the opium trade. An official of the highest rank was sent to Canton with orders to put a stop to the traffic and, by surrounding the foreign traders' compounds refusing to allow food in or people out, Commissioner Lin forced them to hand over their opium. The haul amounted to 2 million kilos: it took 23 days to burn it all.

The British had expected Lin to hand the opium back again on payment of a suitably sized bribe. When they saw that he meant business they sent off a call to the Royal Navy and, under the protection of two frigates, began trading from their ships at the mouth of Canton's island-studded estuary. Lin decided that he would have to clear them out for good and all. He drew up his fleet of 80 vessels and was so pleased by what he saw that he wrote a poem about it that night which contained the quietly confident lines 'A vast display of Imperial might has shaken all the foreign tribes/ but if they now confess their guilt we shall not be too hard upon them'. Lin's magnanimity was never put to the test: any of his junks foolish enough to approach the British ships were quickly blown out of the water.

Desultory hostilities continued for another 18 months during which a British fleet arrived and instituted a formal blockade of the China coast. Commissioner Lin, who had been sending back colourful but entirely imaginary accounts of Chinese naval victories (his 'Six Smashing blows against the Barbarian Navy' is still widely quoted in Chinese accounts) was dismissed by the Court and a new official sent out to negotiate terms with the British. He bought them off with the offer of Hong Kong Island and a $6 million indemnity but this did not satisfy either the Emperor or, when she heard about it, Queen Victoria.

This time the British pressed harder. They fought their way up to Canton and made the city fork out a $6 million ransom. They took Ningbo in the Yangtze delta, then moved up to Shanghai and Zhenjiang. It was enough. The Emperor whose predecessor had seen no need to have much truck with foreigners, found himself opening five ports to British trade and handing over an indemnity of $21 million. 'We must' he observed sorrowfully 'make our choice between danger and safety, not between right and wrong.'

Above: Chinese opium smokers. Engraving by G. Paterson, after a drawing by T Allom, 1843.

Below: Chinese delegates at the signing of the 'unequal treaty' of Nanjing, 1842.

Between 1815 and 1848 the French got through three kings: Louis XVIII who was cautious, polite and no more stupid than kings ought to be, Charles X who was deeply stupid and had to be removed, and Louis Philippe who claimed that he wanted to be a constitutional monarch on the British pattern but could not resist playing party politics. In February 1848 his meddling caused a riot in Paris and the quelling of this by an ill-advised volley produced a rebellion. Frenchmen of all political persuasions suddenly decided that they had had enough of the restored monarchy: they wanted a republic. And that, for the moment, was what they got.

If February's events put an end to the Congress of Vienna's arrangements for France, March saw the post-Napoleonic settlement challenged at just about every point in Europe. In an extraordinary series of spontaneous demonstrations people in the Netherlands, Scandinavia, Germany, Italy and Austria repudiated their existing political leaders and demanded new forms of government. The Austrian Empire, with its Italian, Czech and Hungarian subjects in varying degrees of revolt, appeared on the brink of dissolution: a German Empire, something that had been the dream of every German patriot since the War of Liberation (against Napoleon) seemed on the point of formation.

For the conservative politicians who had ruled Europe for so long with so little trouble, the situation must have been bewildering in the extreme. And it is confusing even in retrospect for there were several different things going on at one and the same time. Easiest to understand is the demand for liberal regimes on the British model. Britain, with its booming economy, was the envy of Europe: copying its institutions seemed no more than common sense. Reluctantly the kings of Prussia, Piedmont-Sardinia, Denmark and Holland, the Emperor of Austria, even the Pope, conceded this and began liberalizing their regimes. Or at least promising to.

A second, perhaps more important, component to the March risings was Nationalism. In the German case what the demonstrators were after was a political union that would bind their various principalities and petty states together in a way that the existing Confederation – a token organization if ever there was one – did not. They won the right to call a pan-German parliament at Frankfurt. What the Italian and Hungarian nationalists wanted was much simpler: independent kingdoms of their own. As all of Hungary and much of Italy lay within the Austrian Empire these were issues that could only be solved by war.

Then finally there was the question of social equality. Everywhere in Europe the distance between rich and poor was immense: the rich had every luxury, the poor were often without essentials. Existing governments felt that this was none of their business: temporary relief in times of special hardship was allowable but the long term problem of the indigent was considered part of the natural order of things and probably their own fault. But the opposite view had its adherents, particularly in France where it had never been forgotten that the Revolutionary constitution of 1789 had called for Equality as well as Liberty. Just how far government intervention should go was a matter of debate: within the general framework of what was coming to be known as Socialism there was a whole range of possible programmes starting with minimum wage legislation and ending up with the total abolition of private property. The more extreme had few adherents but the Provisional Government of France's Second Republic was sufficiently influenced by Socialist ideas of the milder sort to set up National Workshops where jobs were guaranteed to all comers. This was no small matter considering that in Paris at this time one in three adult males was out of work.

Right: The 1848 riots in Vienna: a scene outside St Stephen's Cathedral.

The tide of early 1848 soon turned. In France the first elections resulted in the return of a conservative government which promptly cut down on the welfare programme and when their doing so provoked renewed rioting it dealt with the mob much more ruthlessly than Louis Philippe had dared to do. In Germany the Frankfurt parliament offered the title of German emperor to the king of Prussia but, when he refused it, proved unable to think of anything else to do: it subsequently dissolved in confusion. In Italy the rebel governments of Milan and Venice called on King Charles Albert of Piedmont-Sardinia to save them from the Austrians but he proved unable to do so: at Custozza and again at Novara he was trounced by the Austrians who soon had their sector of Italy under control again. Republican governments in Tuscany and Rome proved scarcely more durable and though the Austrians had to call on the Russians for help in reducing the Hungarian rebellion, eventually this was done and the outline of the Austrian Empire restored in its entirety.

This was a sad end to what had seemed like the dawn of a new era. But not everything was lost. The constitutional improvements in Holland, Denmark and Piedmont survived the reaction. And the various sorts of revolutionaries – Liberals, the Nationalists and the Socialists – had learnt a lot. In future they would be less impulsive and more calculating.

Right: The 1848 rising in Paris: revolutionaries on the barricades at the Porte St Denis.

	1846	1847	1848	1849	1850
Politics & Military History	Potato famine reaches its height in Ireland: one million die by 1851. Repeal of Corn Laws: Peel resigns, Conservative party in wilderness. Austria annexes Cracow. War between USA and Mexico, US annexes New Mexico. Oregon Treaty: the US-Canada boundary west from the Great Lakes is fixed along 49th parallel. First act of segregation in South Africa: Zulu reserves set up in Natal.	Rise of Young Ireland movement. US Mormons make Salt Lake City, Utah, their centre. Federal Diet of Switzerland declares war on reactionaries: the Sonderbund is dissolved. Americans capture Mexico city.	Year of Revolutions in Europe. Revolution in Paris: Louis Philippe abdicates, Second Republic with Louis Napoleon as President. Revolutions throughout the Italian States, mainly suppressed within the year. Revolutions in Berlin, Vienna, Prague and Budapest: at first successful. Metternich resigns, Emperor Ferdinand abdicates and Franz Joseph becomes Emperor of Austria. Frankfurt National Assembly meets (to 1849) to discuss German unification. Switzerland introduces a federal constitution. End of Mexico-USA War: US gains California and New Mexico.	The Revolutions in Italy and Hungary are crushed: French troops restore Pius IX in Rome. Austrians defeat the Sardinians at the battle of Novara. Russian troops aid Austria in regaining control of her Empire. Battle of Gujarat: the end of the Sikh State; Britain annexes the Punjab.	Don Pacifico Affair: Foreign Secretary Lord Palmerston defends rights of British citizens anywhere in the world. Taiping Rebellion in China: Hung Hiu-Tsen proclaims himself Emperor and takes Nanjing and Shanghai. California joins USA. France abolishes universal suffrage. Austro-Hungarian Customs Union is formed.
Religion & Learning	George Grote *History of Greece* (until 1856). Smithsonian Institute established at Washington. Proudhon *The Philosophy of Poverty*.	French historian, Louis Blanc, begins his 12 volume *Histoire de la Révolution Française* (till 1862). Leopold von Ranke, German historian *Neun Bücher Preussiches Geschichte*.	Marx and Engels issue *The Communist Manifesto*. J. S. Mill *Principles of Political Economy*. Macaulay *History of England*, first two volumes.	Ruskin *The Seven Lamps of Architecture*, the laws that should govern art. Bedford College for Women established.	Marx *The Class-struggles in France*. French Loi Falloux makes religious education compulsory. Sydney University established in Australia. Britain is becoming heavily urbanized: London population is 2.3m; 9 cities have more than 100,000 and 18 more than 50,000. Huge growth of railways in Europe and USA.
Cities & Social Development	A further 7,260 km of new railway are authorized in Britain: Railway Commissioners appointed. Japan repulses American warships seeking to encourage foreign trade. US *Daily News* established.	European crop failure – corn and potatoes – produces an agricultural crisis; typhus and cholera epidemics. Collapse of railway boom and mass unemployment. First Swiss Railway is opened (Zurich-Baden).	First Public Health Act in Britain establishes the Board of Health. Third Chartist Petition; mass arrests and failure of movement. Beginnings of a railway boom in France.	Repeal of British Navigation Acts: further move towards free trade by Britain. Europe now moves into a period of rapid economic growth. Krupp armaments works manufacture steel guns. A dramatic rise takes place in European emigration at a rate of 200,000 to 300,000 a year; 13m between 1841 and 1880.	Britain leading industrial and commercial nation: she has 39.5% world merchant shipping tonnage and 23% world steam tonnage. Trade unionism begins to revive in Britain.
Discovery & Invention	Warren and Morton use ether in the USA as anaesthetic during an operation. Elias Howe patents his sewing machine: an improved version is produced by Singer in 1851.	British surgeon, Simpson, successfully uses chloroform in obstetric practice: he is at first opposed by the Church. Zeiss optical works open at Jena. Western world first learns of the existence of gorillas.	California Gold Rush. Lord Kelvin determines the temperature of absolute zero as −273 degrees C.	Livingstone (to 1851) begins exploration of central and southern Africa.	Bunsen designs his gas burner. Young patents synthetic oil production: the preparation of paraffin wax by slow distillation. Beginnings of petrol refining.
The Arts	Edward Lear first *Book of Nonsense*. Balzac *La Cousine Bette*. Melville *Typee*, first novel. Dostoyevsky *Poor Folk*, first novel. Schumann 4th Symphony. Berlioz *Damnation de Faust*.	Verdi *Macbeth*. de Quincey *The Spanish Military Nun*.	Thackeray *Pendennis*. Millet *The Winnower*. Dumas fils *La Dame aux Camélias*. The formation of the Pre-Raphaelite Brotherhood, rebelling against the machine age.	Charlotte Brontë *Shirley*. Dickens *David Copperfield*. Matthew Arnold *Poems*. Liszt 3 Concert Studies for pianoforte, *Tasso*.	Tennyson *In Memoriam*. Hawthorne *The Scarlet Letter*. Wagner *Lohengrin*. Millais *Christ in the Home of his Parents*.

	1851	1852	1853	1854	1855
Politics & Military History	Coup d'etat gives Louis Napoleon control of French government: Paris rising suppressed. Russian Governor-General of East Siberia, Muraviev, raises Russian flag on mouth of the Amur.	Louis Napoleon establishes Second Empire and makes himself Napoleon III, Emperor of the French; plebiscite confirms restoration of Empire. Sand River Convention: Britain recognizes independence of Transvaal. Second Anglo-Burmese War: Britain annexes Pegu.	Gladstone's first budget: wide range of duties abolished and death duties introduced. Britain annexes Kaffraria. Cape Colony receives responsible government. Russo-Turkish War: Russians occupy Moldavia and Wallachia and destroy Turkish fleet at Sinope.	The Crimean War: Britain, France and Turkey against Russia; Battles of Balaclava and Inkerman; Siege of Sebastopol. Liberal Revolution in Spain overthrows government. Cape Parliament meets for the first time; Britain leaves territory north of Orange River to the Boers.	*The Times'* correspondent, Russell, reveals the mismanagement of British forces in the Crimea. Fall of Aberdeen government in Britain; fall of Sebastopol; Queen Victoria and Prince Albert on state visit to France. Sardinia joins Britain, France and Turkey in Crimea.
Religion & Learning	Ruskin *The Stones of Venice.* British government makes the first grant towards evening classes.	Opening of the Victoria and Albert Museum.	Mommsen *History of Rome.* Comte de Gobineau, French diplomatist *Essai sur l'inégalité des races humaines*, extolling the Nordic races.	Henry Thoreau *Walden.* Pius IX: immaculate conception of the Blessed Virgin is to be an article of faith.	Michelet *Histoire de France, les Temps modernes.* Federal Polytechnic School is established at Zurich.
Cities & Social Development	Establishment of the Amalgamated Society of Engineers: New Model Unionism. Great Exhibition is held in London.	Manchester launches its first free library. US Express Co, Wells Fargo, is established. Tasmania ceases to be convict settlement.	Trevelyan-Northcote Report on British Civil Service produces major reforms. Commodore Perry of the US Navy forces Japan to open up trade relations with western countries (to 1854).	Baron Haussmann begins the reconstruction of Paris: broad boulevards difficult for revolutionaries and easy for troops to control.	Paris Exhibition. London sewers are modernized after the fourth major outbreak of cholera. First iron Cunard steamer crosses the Atlantic in $9\frac{1}{2}$ days.
Discovery & Invention	Singer produces the first practical sewing machine in USA. Submarine cable is laid between Dover and Calais.	Livingstone continues his explorations along Zambezi. Land survey of Britain completed.	Richard Burton visits Mecca. Vaccination against smallpox made compulsory in Britain.	Berthelot, French chemist, *Sur les Combinations de la glycerine avec les acides*, paper makes him famous.	Livingstone comes upon the Victoria Falls. Florence Nightingale introduces hygiene into military hospitals in Crimea.
The Arts	Verdi *Rigoletto.* Paxton builds Crystal Palace for the Great Exhibition. H. B. Stowe *Uncle Tom's Cabin.*	Holman Hunt *The Light of the World.* Turgenev *Sportsman's Sketches.*	Dickens *Christmas Stories* include *A Christmas Carol.* Wagner begins work on his Ring Cycle.	Dickens *Hard Times.* Liszt *Preludes.* Millet *The Reaper.*	Whitman *Leaves of Grass.* Trollope *The Warden.* Longfellow *The Song of Hiawatha.*

THE UNIFICATION OF ITALY 1858-1870

The map shows the route taken by Garibaldi's main force during his extraordinary campaign in the Kingdom of the Two Sicilies. Cavour, the Prime Minister of Piedmont-Sardinia did his best to stop Garibaldi setting out because he feared that the European powers would react badly to news of the expedition. As a result Garibaldi began operations with a volunteer force numbering no more than a thousand, equipped with obsolete muskets. His initial landing efforts were regarded with indifference by the Sicilians but within a few short months he had created an army and won the kingdom. Cavour reluctantly sent Piedmontese forces down to the south – a march that involved a battle with the papal army at Castelfidardo – to collect the prize on behalf of his master, the king of Piedmont-Sardinia.

The drift to the right in France's Second Republic was tinged with nostalgia: the days when Napoleon had amazed Europe were recalled with pride; the cost to the country of doing so discounted if not entirely dismissed. Banking on this mood Louis Napoleon, the son of the emperor's youngest brother, stood for the Presidency and won: three years later,with the end of his four-year term of office in sight, he seized power in a bloodless coup. The year after that he took the title of Emperor, calling himself Napoleon III in deference to the memory of the first Napoleon's so (now dead).

Europe looked askance at the new emperor and for a yea or two he was cold-shouldered by his royal colleagues. Bu circumstances soon gave him an opportunity of winnin respectability: the Russians were making moves against th moribund Turkish Empire and this threatened the balanc of power in Europe. The British and French Cabinets, wh agreed that support for Turkey was essential, dispatched a expeditionary force to Constantinople. Then, because ther was nothing for it to do when it got there, they ordered it o to the Crimea where the French contingent, which ha started off playing second fiddle to the British, took the lea in the capture of Sebastopol. Louis Napoleon began to loo less like an adventurer, more like a statesman.

His next step was to move France to the centre of th European stage where he, like all good Frenchme believed it rightly belonged. The opportunity to do so wa not long in coming: Cavour, the Prime Minister o Piedmont-Sardinia, approached the French emperor with plan for the liberation of Italy. Cavour had learned th lesson of 1848 which was that the Italians could not get th Austrians out themselves. He offered Napoleon Nice an Savoy if the French would do the job for them.

This was war on a more serious scale. The mos Napoleon could expect from England was benevolen neutrality while the rest of Europe would probably b hostile: it would have to be a quick campaign. Initially, a least, Louis Napoleon did his bit for the Napoleonic legend Sweeping into north Italy he caught the Austrian army wit its right flank uncovered and, at the Battle of Magenta drove it from its position in front of Milan. The victory wa just what he needed, and not too costly either. But as th

1856	1857	1858	1859	1860	
Treaty of Paris: ends Crimean War; integrity of Turkey is guranteed. Second Anglo-Chinese War (to 1857). Natal becomes separate colony. Britain annexes Oudh. Counter-revolution in Spain: liberal measures annulled.	British destroy Chinese fleet and enter Guangzhou (Canton) in 2nd Opium War. Anglo-Persian Treaty: Shah recognizes independence of Afghanistan. Indian 'Mutiny': rebellion of sepoys in Bengal (British) army: massacre at Cawnpore, siege of Lucknow. France completes the conquest of Algeria.	Relief of Lucknow: end of Indian Mutiny; British Parliament takes full control of British India from East India Company. Compact of Pombières: Napoleon III and Cavour agree upon French help for Sardinia against Austria. Treaty of Tianjin: France and Britain gain concessions from China.	France and Piedmont at war with Austria: Battles of Magenta and Solferino, Austria defeated; Sardinia consolidates its power in northern Italy. France annexes three provinces in Cochin-China and establishes protectorate over Cambodia. Third Anglo-Chinese War.	Garibaldi leads the *Thousand Redshirts* to conquer Sicily and Naples. British-French forces occupy Beijing and force China to open new ports to western trade. South Carolina withdraws from Union. Second Maori War in New Zealand – to 1870.	Politics & Military History
Froude *History of England*, 12 volumes (to 1870). de Tocqueville *L'Ancien Régime et la Révolution*. Discovery of a Neanderthal skull estimated to be 100,000 years old.	Spencer *Essays Scientific, Political and Speculative*. Bombay University is established.	Carlyle *Frederick the Great*. Keble College is established at Oxford.	Mill *On Liberty*. Samuel Smiles *Self-Help*.	Lecky *The Religious Tendencies of the Age*. Charles Bradlaugh, freethinker, begins the *National Reformer*.	Religion & Learning
Russian railway building begins. First Australian inter-state cricket match is played.	End of transportation of convicts to Australia. European financial crisis follows the boom years of 1852–6.	Adoption of the Bessemer steel process in France.	Peaceful picketing during a strike is legalized in Britain. First American oil-well drilled in Pennsylvania at Titusville.	Anglo-French Commercial Treaty sparks off free trade era in Europe with seven major treaties to lower tariffs between European powers 1860–1865.	Cities & Social Development
Pasteur begins his studies leading to the establishment of bacteriology. Bessemer's converter revolutionizes the steel industry.	Livingstone *Missionary Travels in South Africa*. Pasteur proves that fermentation is caused by living organisms.	Speke and Burton discover Lake Tanganyika. Introduction of iron-clads into French Navy. Laying of first Atlantic cable.	Darwin *The Origin of Species* marks the beginning of modern evolutionary theory. American George Pullman invents his Pullman sleeping car for railways.	Speke and Grant set off on expedition which reveals source of Nile. Royal Navy adopts iron-clads.	Discovery & Invention
Hughes *Tom Brown's Schooldays*. Flaubert completes *Madame Bovary*.	Trollope *Barchester Towers*. Borrow *Romany Rye*. Hallé founds the Hallé concerts in Manchester.	Royal Opera House, Covent Garden, opens. Offenbach *Orpheus in the Underworld*.	Edward Fitzgerald's translation of *The Rubaiyat of Omar Khayyam*.	Millais begins to illustrate Tennyson's poems and Trollope's novels.	The Arts

Left: Lord Raglan, Omar Pasha and General Pelissier, the commanders of the allied expeditionary force in the Crimea.

Right: The allied fleet in Balaclava Harbour, the main forward base of the Crimean expedition.

French moved forward from Lombardy to Venetia a reinforced Austrian army met them head on. This second battle – at Solferino – was an altogether more sanguinary affair: the French had the advantage but it was clear that the way ahead was going to be a long and hard one. Louis Napoleon, horrified by the carnage, decided to call a halt, and though his uncle, who prided himself on his ability to look on any battlefield dry-eyed, would have despised him for it, Louis was right. He had broken Austria's grip on the peninsula and the unification of Italy under an Italian king was now only a matter of time.

There is a curious footnote to the story of Napoleon III and Italy. By the end of 1860 the north (bar Venetia) had been united to Piedmont-Sardinia by plebiscite, the south had been conquered by Garibaldi and the Thousand, and the Adriatic part of the papal state had been incorporated as a result of a Piedmontese victory over the papal army at Castelfidardo. But though these successes were duly followed by the proclamation of the Kingdom of Italy its king had to rule from Florence, not Rome. This was because Napoleon had troops garrisoning Rome on behalf of the Pope. He had put them there in 1849 as a gesture to the Catholic party in France and try as he might he could not think of a pretext for withdrawing them. So as long as the Second Empire lasted, the Kingdom of Italy had a hole in its midriff.

	1861	1862	1863	1864	1865
Politics & Military History	Italy is united, Rome and Venice excepted, with Victor Emmanuel of Piedmont as king. Confederate States of America (eleven) are formed by South Carolina and secede from the Union. American Civil War: first battle at Bull Run; a Confederate victory over the Union (Federal) side. Britain annexes Lagos. France, Britain and Spain send troops to Mexico to enforce payment of debts: Juarez occupies Mexico City, President to 1862.	American Civil War: Emancipation Proclamation – slaves in rebelling states declared free. France becomes involved in civil war in Mexico. Bismarck becomes first minister (Chancellor) in Prussia, a position he is to hold for 30 years. Garibaldi invades Papal States but is defeated.	Battle of Gettysburg: turning point in American Civil War. Polish revolt: Prussia closes her border to fleeing Poles; revolt is crushed. French troops enter Mexico City: the Archduke Maximilian proclaimed Emperor of Mexico. Denmark incorporates the Duchy of Schleswig-Holstein into Denmark.	Austria and Prussia combine to take Schleswig-Holstein from Denmark. Expedition of British, Dutch, French and Americans bombards Shimonoseki, Japan. American Civil War: battles of Petersburg, Cedar Creek. New democratic constitution in Greece; Greeks occupy Corfu.	American Civil War: the South (Confederates) under General Lee surrenders to General Grant; President Lincoln is assassinated. Black insurrection in Jamaica. Agreement between Napoleon and Bismarck at Biarritz: France to remain neutral in the event of an Austro-Prussian War. Britain passes Colonial Laws Validity Act: important move towards colonial self-government. Russia conquers Turkestan.
Religion & Learning	Italian National Library established.	Ruskin *Unto this last.* Bryce *The Holy Roman Empire.*	Thoreau *Excursions* (post.). Taine *Histoire de la Littérature Anglaise.* T. H. Huxley *Zoological Evidences as to Man's Place in Nature.* Renan *Vie de Jésus.*	Newman *Apologia pro vita sua.* Pope Pius IX attacks Liberals, Socialism and Rationalism in *Syllabus Errorum.*	Matthew Arnold *Essays in Criticism.* Lecky *History of the Rise and Influence of the Spirit of Rationalism in Europe.* Massachusetts Institute of Technology (MIT), Cornell and Purdue universities are established in USA.
Cities & Social Development	Populations: Russia 76m, USA 32m, Britain 23m, Italy 25m. Serfs in Russia are emancipated: Russia embarks upon a programme of modernization. Mrs Beeton *Book of Household Management.* First horse-drawn trams used in London. Telegraph line across the USA is completed.	Ironworkers' Association is established. Lincoln issues the first legal US paper money (Greenbacks). Swiss banker, Jean Henri Dunant, publishes *Souvenir de Solferino* which leads to the formation of the Red Cross.	Football league is established in England. Beginning of underground railway system in London. Opening of the state institution for criminally insane at Broadmoor, England.	Deutsche Bank established in Germany and the Société Générale in France. Karl Marx founds the *First International* in London. Red Cross established.	First concrete roads are built in Britain. John D. Rockefeller forms Standard Oil in Ohio.
Discovery & Invention	First machine-chilled cold storage unit made. Magazine rifles are used in American Civil War.	Foucault measures the speed of light. American Gatling patents his machine-gun.	Manufacture (by Wilbrand) of TNT.	Baker discovers Lake Albert. Svend Foyn makes a harpoon gun.	Pasteur cures silk-worm disease and saves French silk industry. Mendel states his law of heredity based upon the cross-fertilization of the pea; leads to rational plant cultivation and animal breeding and so greater agricultural productivity.
The Arts	Eliot *Silas Marner.* Charles Reade *The Cloister and the Hearth.* Dostoyevsky *The House of the Dead.* Bibliotheque Nationale in Paris designed by Henri Labrouste.	Morris and Rossetti work upon design and interior decoration. Elizabeth Barrett Browning *Last Poems.* Flaubert *Salammbo.* Hugo *Les Miserables.* Ingres *Bain Turque.* Julia Ward Howe *Battle Hymn of the Republic.*	Kingsley *The Water-Babies.* Manet *Déjeuner sur l'Herbe.* Bizet *Les Pêcheurs de perles.* Doré illustrations for *Don Quixote.*	Rodin *L'Homme au nez cassé.* Manet *Races at Longchamp.* Vigny *Les Destinées*, poems. Browning *Dramatis Personae.*	Carroll *Alice in Wonderland.* Whistler *Old Battersea Bridge.* Rimsky-Korsakov 1st Symphony. Wagner *Tristan und Isolde.* Tolstoy *War and Peace.*

ne founding fathers of the American Republic were as ten as not slave owners, a perplexing circumstance for em as for us. How could they formulate such ringing rrases about the rights of man and yet not only condone e institution of slavery but actively participate in it? The swer seems to be that they regarded slavery as an evil hich the American people in due course would reject and iminate. But each generation of Americans had its work to and this was not theirs: their goal, and indeed their hievement, was to forge the new nation.

The anti-slavery movement of the late 18th century set self to change this 'hands off' attitude. Its first successes ere in the northern states where slaves were few and of tle economic importance: by 1820 all the states north of e Ohio river and the Mason Dixon line (the Maryland-ennsylvania border) had outlawed slavery and, by a mpromise agreed in that year, the territory acquired by e Louisiana purchase was divided into 'slave' and 'free' alves. But that a formal compromise was necessary at all as a bad sign: it showed slavery was not going quietly.

For this Manchester's cotton empire bears much of the ame. While the plantation system had been part of the griculture of the southern states for more than a century it ad not initially been all that profitable: most of the tobacco lantations in George Washington's day were heavily in ebt which is why he tried his hand at wheat. But cotton as something that the booming mills of Lancashire could ot get enough of and by the early 19th century an normously expanded cotton-growing agri-business had ecome the mainstay of the southern economy. From lemphis to Charleston, the cotton fields stretched in most unbroken sequence: the wealth this represented was ot going to be surrendered voluntarily.

Despite intensive lobbying by the abolitionists, the ajority of people in the north accepted this and roughout the 1840s and 50s it was clear that they were repared to let the southerners sustain their 'peculiar stitution': they disapproved but they did not intend to nterfere. But the fear that the abolitionists might one day ain control in Washington drove the southern politicians an ill-advised offensive. Their aim was to make sure that ne territories that were on the verge of attaining statehood and the potential number of these was significantly ncreased in 1846–8 by the acquisition of California and the Jtah-New Mexico region from Mexico – had the option of oining the slavery side and that the option was exercised as ften as possible. In fighting this campaign the southerners howed great ruthlessness: they managed for example, to et a slave constitution adopted in Kansas by a mixture of orce and fraud, even though everyone knew that the majority of people in the territory wanted it to be free.

Victories like this can be counterproductive and the North now set its face against any extension of slavery at all. The change in attitude is marked by the emergence of a new political grouping, the Republican Party, which polled strongly throughout the North on exactly this issue in 1856. The southerners said that this was covert abolitionism and in a sense it was – the Republican candidate in the 1860 presidential election, Abraham Lincoln, was on record as saying 'This government cannot endure permanently half slave and half free' – but neither the Republican Party nor Lincoln himself had any plans to abolish slavery in the immediate future. Nevertheless, when Lincoln won the election, the hotheads in the South demanded that their states secede from the union and at the end of 1860 South Carolina formally did so. Six slave states followed South Carolina's lead but eight others, including the most important, Virginia, sat on the fence waiting to see what Lincoln would do after his inauguration. Lincoln had no intention of going beyond his election pledges but neither did he intend to allow the Confederacy, the term for the states in dispute with the federal government, to expel US army garrisons from the posts they held in the South, Fort Pickens in Florida and Fort Sumter in Charleston harbour And holding Fort Sumter meant regularly reprovisioning it. Hearing that Lincoln had given the order for this to be done goaded the Confederacy into the violation that was the immediate cause of the Civil War, the bombardment and capture of the fort.

Lincoln now had no choice but to crush the rebels. To do so he asked Congress for 75,000 men to serve for three months. But it was not going to be as easy as that. The news that it had finally come to war brought Virginia into the Confederate camp and this gave the Confederacy the strength and the standing it needed. No one was more jealous of his rights than the Virginian: his was also the heart of America, the land of Washington and Jefferson, Madison and Monroe. Moreover, Virginia brought in not just a million Virginians but the better part of 2 million more Americans in North Carolina, Tennessee and Arkansas. And Robert E. Lee.

Below left: Abraham Lincoln at Sharpsburg in October 1862. On his left Albert Pinkerton, founder of the detective agency, who ran the Federal Intelligence Service during the war and produced a constant stream of misinformation. On his right General McClernand.

The war that Lincoln hoped would be over in a few months dragged on for four years and cost the lives of half a million men. The battle of Sharpsburg in September 1862 proved the bloodiest of the conflict: 12,000 northerners and 10,500 southerners were killed to nobody's advantage.

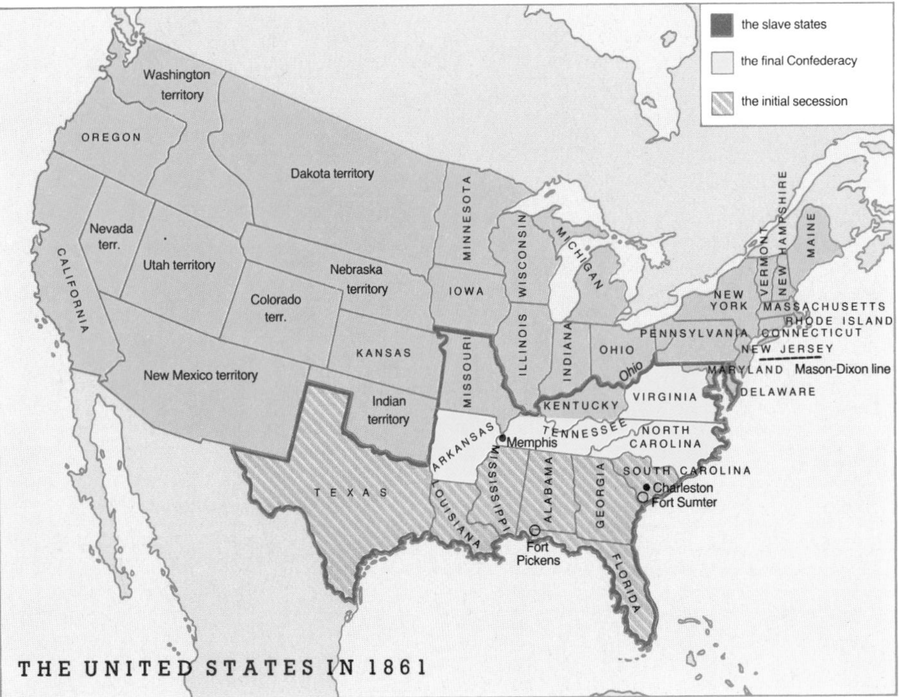

	1866	1867	1868	1869	1870
Politics & Military History	Attempt to assassinate the Tsar of Russia leads him to adopt reactionary policies. Austro-Prussian War over Schleswig-Holstein: Austria defeated at Sadowa; Italy defeated at Custozza and Lissa. Treaty of Prague: Austria forced to withdraw from German affairs; Italy gains Venice. US Senate passes the Civil Rights Bill in respect to Negroes.	Second Reform Act in Britain adds nearly one million new voters to electoral roll. British North America Act establishes Confederation of Canada. USA purchases Alaska from Russia. North German Confederation formed under Prussian leadership. Turks withdraw from Belgrade: last Turkish garrison is withdrawn from Serbia.	Liberal uprising in Spain: Queen Isabella II forced to abdicate and flees to France. Rebellion in Cuba to break away from Spain: lasts to 1878 but fails. British expedition to Magdala in Ethiopia under Napier to release captured diplomats. Britain annexes Basutoland.	Disestablishment of Irish Church passed by Gladstone government. Opening of Suez Canal. Hudson Bay Territory becomes part of Dominion of Canada. Spanish Cortes is elected by universal suffrage: Carlist rising quelled.	Franco-Prussian War: the French defeated at Sedan; Napoleon III captured; Prussian armies besiege Paris; establishment of Commune in Paris. Gladstone's Irish Land Act provides compensation for eviction but does not ease Irish problem. Italy annexes Papal States and Rome becomes capital of Italy. Turkey recognizes Bulgaria as separate religious nation.
Religion & Learning	Ruskin *Crown of Wild Olives.* Mary Baker Eddy propounds the concept of Christian Science.	Marx *Das Kapital*, vol. I. Bagehot *The English Constitution.*	Austrian schools freed from Church control.	Girton College for women is created in Britain (to Cambridge in 1873). Society of African Missionaries established.	First legislation in Britain to introduce compulsory free education. Vatican Council announces doctrine of Papal Infallibility. Schliemann begins to excavate Troy.
Cities & Social Development	Marquess of Queensberry rules are accepted for boxing. National Labour Union – craft unions – is established in USA.	Trade unions are declared illegal in Britain: a Royal Commission is set up to examine the question. Transportation of convicts to West Australia (the last place to which they were sent) ceases.	First regular meeting of Trade Union Congress in Manchester. Ku Klux Klan is launched in southern States of USA.	Inland telegraphs are *nationalized* in Britain: the first use of the word nationalized. Britain abolishes imprisonment for debt. The Union Pacific, America's first trans-continental railway, completed.	Volume of British trade is greater than that of France, Italy and Germany combined and three times that of the USA and Britain possesses 42.3% of the world's merchant shipping steam tonnage. Water closets come into wide use.
Discovery & Invention	Winchester repeating rifle comes into use in US. Atlantic Cable is first used (laying began in 1858). Propelled submarine torpedo developed by Whitehead. Pasteur *Etudes sur le vin.*	Typewriter is invented. Lister uses carbolic antiseptic: basis of aseptic surgery. Nobel produces dynamite.	Darwin *The Variation of Animals and Plants under Domestication.* Pasteur *Etudes sur le vinaigre.*	Sir Francis Galton *Hereditary Genius*, the foundation of eugenics. Reverdin carries out first skin graft.	Diamonds are discovered at Kimberley in South Africa. Huxley's theory of biogenisis; coins word 'agnostic'.
The Arts	Dostoyevsky *Crime and Punishment.* Swinburne *Poems and Ballads.*	Wagner *Die Meistersinger von Nurnberg.* Verdi *Don Carlos.* Ibsen *Peer Gynt.* Johann Strauss *The Blue Danube.* Zola *Thérèse Raquin.* Renoir *The Boat.* Monet *The Beach at Ste-Adresse.*	Collins *The Moonstone.* Louisa May Alcott *Little Women.* Dostoyevsky *The Idiot.* Impressionist movement begins to emerge: Pissarro *Streets in Pontoise*, Monet *Argenteuil-sur-Seine*, Renoir *Sisley and his wife.* Rimsky-Korsakov Symphony No. 2.	Twain *The Innocents Abroad.* Blackmore *Lorna Doone.* Verlaine *Fêtes Galantes.* Borodin 1st Symphony performed. Wagner *Rheingold.*	Dickens *The Mystery of Edwin Drood*, his last work. Rossetti *Poems.* Smetana *The Bartered Bride.* Wagner *Die Walkure.*

1871	1872
German Unification – dominated by Prussia. Wilhelm I of Prussia becomes Emperor, Bismarck becomes Chancellor. Paris surrenders; the Paris Commune opposes the peace terms but is crushed in March during La Semaine Sanglante when 20,000 Communards are killed. Alsace-Lorraine ceded to Germany and France has to pay heavy indemnity. Pope becomes the 'prisoner of the Vatican' with the loss of his temporal power.	Ballot Act introduces the secret ballot in British elections. Arbitration Tribunal in Geneva decides the *Alabama* case in favour of USA and against Britain. Three Emperor League (Dreikaiserbund) of William I of Germany, Franz-Joseph of Austria and Tsar Alexander II of Russia set up.
Jowett translates Plato's *Dialogues*. Only German is to be used in schools in Alsace-Lorraine. *Kulturkampf* begins in Germany: a state struggle with the Vatican over education.	Jesuits are expelled from Germany.
Trade Union Act secures legal status for unions in Britain but Criminal Law Amendment Act makes picketing illegal. Abolition of the practice of purchasing commissions in British armed forces.	By this year there are 32,000 friendly societies in England encompassing 4m members. Penny-farthing bicycle in general use.
Maddox, the dry photographic plate (using silver bromide). Completion of Mount Cenis Tunnel, Switzerland.	Stanley finds Livingstone: *Dr Livingstone, I presume?* Oré at Lyons gives the first anaesthetic intravenously.
Carroll *Through the Looking-Glass*. Gilbert and Sullivan begin their twenty year collaboration. Verdi *Aida*. Opening of Royal Albert Hall, London.	Samuel Butler *Erewhon*. Building of the Bayreuth Theatre commences, completed in 1876. Dostoevsky *The Possessed*. Alphonse Daudet *Tartarin de Tarascon*.

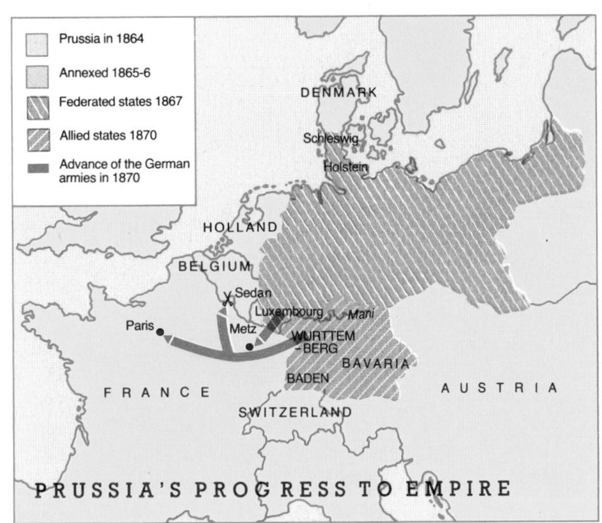

Between 1864 and 1866 Otto von Bismarck, Prime Minister of Prussia, managed to translate the idea of a united Germany into practical politics. The steps by which he achieved this are so clever, so finely calculated and so dishonest as to defy accurate précis, but in essence what he did was use the pan-German sentiment in favour of annexing the Danish held duchies of Schleswig and Holstein to fight a short, easy war with Denmark, then provoke a quarrel with his ally in this war, Austria, and bring her and her allies in the German Confederation to decisive battle in the Seven Weeks' War of 1866. Victorious in this he proceeded to incorporate all the German states north of the Main in a new Confederation of which Prussia was effective master. This left only three states of any size outside Prussian control – Baden, Württemberg and Bavaria – and they were willing to side with Prussia if for example there was a quarrel with France.

Bismarck made sure that this particular quarrel was not long in coming. To keep Napoleon III quiet during the Seven Weeks' War he had promised not to oppose the French purchase of the Duchy of Luxembourg from the king of Holland: now he reneged on the deal, saying that German public opinion was so strongly opposed that he could not let it go through. Relations between France and Prussia subsequently deteriorated and some Bismarckian fine tuning of the next diplomatic incident produced the French ultimatum that was the object of the whole exercise. With an air of injured innocence Bismarck rejected the French Note and turned the problem over to the Chief of the Prussian General Staff, General Helmuth von Moltke.

The French entered the war with great enthusiasm and the battle cry of 'to Berlin' but in sober truth there were few grounds for their optimism: the Germany army was twice as large and better led. Because both sides made their initial deployment with their main strength to the left, German superiority over the French right actually worked out at 4 to 1 which was enough to break the French line at this point and open the way to Paris. Disaster came fast on the heels of defeat: the five corps on the French left were pushed into Metz; the army that Napoleon led to their relief was headed off, encircled and then forced to surrender at Sedan. By the end of September Paris was under siege as well as Metz.

The end of the war was in sight and while Moltke waited for starvation to force the surrender of Paris, Bismarck assembled the German princes at Versailles. There, in January 1871, they formally conferred on the king of Prussia the title of Emperor of Germany. The Second Reich had been born from the ruin of the *Deuxième Empire*.

Bismarck (1815–98) in 1855.

The Germans enter Paris. One of the humiliations the Germans inflicted on the French capital after its surrender in 1871 was a victory parade through the city streets.

	1873	1874	1875	1876	1877
Politics & Military History	Britain secures effective end to export of slaves at Zanzibar. Second Ashanti War: British defeat Ashanti. France makes the final payment of war indemnity to Germany and German occupying troops are withdrawn. May Laws in Germany restrict Church powers in escalating Church-State quarrel. First Spanish Republic is proclaimed: till 1874.	Disraeli and the Tories come to power in Britain. First Trade Union MP is elected in Britain. France establishes Protectorate over Annam. Alfonso XII restores Spanish monarchy to power.	Risings against Turkey occur in Herzegovina, Macedonia and Bosnia savagely suppressed. European powers Britain, France and Germany embark upon military re-armament programmes. Third Republic is established in France bringing an end to the provisional government. Japanese are expelled from Sakhalin; they recognize the independence of Korea. Disraeli purchases Khedive Ismail's shares in Suez Canal giving Britain a 42% stake in Canal.	Liberal constitutional monarchy is established in Spain. War between Russia and Turkey. The Bulgarian Atrocities: Turkish massacres following revolts in Balkans. France and Britain establish Dual Control of Egypt's finances. Battle of Little Big Horn: Custer's 'Last Stand', the last major North American Indian victory.	Britain annexes Transvaal. Irish Nationalist MPs at Westminster begin policy of obstruction in House of Commons. Russia invades Turkey; Romania becomes independent. Satsuma Rebellion in Japan the Samurais are defeated by a conscript army. Queen Victoria is proclaimed Empress of India by Britain.
Religion & Learning	Cambridge begins its first university extension courses. Spencer *The Study of Sociology*.	J. R. Green *Short History of the English People*.	Schliemann *Troy and its Remains*. Church Missionary Society sponsors work in Uganda.	British missionary work begins in Nyasaland. Schliemann begins his excavation of Mycenae.	Belgium introduces compulsory education for those aged 6–9. Praxiteles statue of Hermes discovered at Olympus.
Cities & Social Development	Joseph Chamberlain becomes Mayor of Birmingham: municipal politics become a force in British politics. Beginnings of world depression as wheat prices fall. Germany adopts the Mark as its unit of currency.	Between 1874 and 1876 the Disraeli Government passes 11 major acts of social reform. Obligatory civil marriage established in Germany.	Britain passes legislation to permit peaceful picketing by trade unions. The Universal Postal Union established at Geneva.	Quebec and Maritime Provinces of Canada linked by railway. Geographical Congress at Brussels: International Association established to suppress slavery and develop Congo Basin.	US Railway strike: first major industrial dispute in USA. Argentina first exports frozen meat to Europe.
Discovery & Invention	American Glidden invents barbed wire. Scholes and Glidden design the first commercially successful typewriter.	Remington & Sons manufacture and sell the new Scholes and Glidden typewriter (named Remington from 1876). Stanley makes his epic journey down the Congo (to 1877).	Ernest Giles crosses Australia.	Alexander Graham Bell invents telephone. Statutory maximum loading line for ships is established, the *Plimsoll Line*. Iron spire added to Rouen Cathedral makes it, at 148m, world's tallest building.	Edison patents his phonograph. Schiaperelli observes *canals* on Mars (found not to be canals in 1969). Experiments with phosphoric ores in steel-making: the steel industry is freed from dependence upon rare phosphorus free ores. Beginning of modern steel age.
The Arts	Verne *La Tour du monde en 80 Jours*. Bruckner, 3rd Symphony.	Hardy *Far From the Madding Crowd*. Verdi *Requiem*. Cezanne *Vase of Flowers*. First Impressionist exhibition is held in Paris.	Bizet *Carmen*. Dvorak Symphony No. 5. Smetana *My Country*. Henry James *Transatlantic Sketches*.	Twain *Tom Sawyer*. Brahms Symphony No. I. The completion of the Bayreuth Theatre; opens with the first performance of Wagner's *Ring*. Degas *The Dancing Class*. Tchaikovsky *Swan Lake*.	William Morris establishes the Society for the Protection of Ancient Buildings. Henry James *The American*. Anna Sewell *Black Beauty*. Saint-Saëns *Samson et Delilah* opera. Wagner *Parsifal*.

1878	1879
Treaty of San Stefano between Russia and Turkey: Montenegro, Serbia, Bulgaria and Romania to be independent. Berlin Congress: Great Powers revise Treaty of San Stefano to reverse Russian gains; Britain gets Cyprus. Anglo-Afghan War – in 1880 Britain gains control of Afghan affairs.	Britain and France control Egypt: force abdication of Ismail. Austria and Germany enter into Dual Alliance (to 1918). Republicans win sweeping victory in French elections; end of Monarchist hopes. Zulu War: Zulus are defeated by British at Ulundi. Gladstone conducts his Midlothian Campaign: first modern style political campaign by party leader.
	Church of Christ Scientist is established at Boston. Somerville College for women is established at Oxford.
General retreat from free trade as a result of continuing fall in wheat prices. The Red Flag Act: mechanical road vehicles are limited to a speed of 4mph. CID is established at New Scotland Yard.	The British United Africa Company (trading in West Africa) established.
Stanley *Through the Dark Continent.* Mannlicher produce a repeater rifle. Karl Benz, a motorised tricycle which reaches 11kmh.	First steam tanker for transporting oil operates on Caspian Sea. Edison produces successful incandescent electric light.
Hardy *The Return of the Native.* James *The Europeans.* Gilbert & Sullivan *HMS Pinafore.* Morris *The Decorative Arts.*	Meredith *The Egoist.* Ibsen *A Doll's House.* Dostoyevsky *The Brothers Karamazov.* Tchaikovsky *Eugene Onegin*, opera.

Above: Karl Marx (1818–83) towards the end of his life.

Below: London slum. By the mid-Victorian period many people who had never heard of Marx or Engels and knew nothing of socialism or communism, were convinced that something had to be done about the monstrous cities spawned by the Industrial Revolution. The theory that poverty was due to sin no longer seemed adequate: the idea that everyone deserved a decent start in life began to take hold. And Dr Barnardo convinced many people that this approach would actually pay dividends. 'If the children of the slums can be removed from their surroundings early enough and can be kept sufficiently long under training, heredity counts for little, environment for almost everything.' This is a statement of which Marx would have approved though Barnado's remedy, the amelioration of capitalist society, would not have appealed to someone dedicated to its overthrow.

Marx saw himself as the scientific theorist of the evolution of man as a social animal; he explicitly compared himself to Darwin, who had performed the same function for natural man, identifying natural selection as the mechanism of change. For Marx, the mechanism of man's social evolution was dialectical materialism.

The dialectic had been the theory of Hegel, the early 19th century pioneer of theories of philosophical change: the process by which one idea or thesis gave rise to an opposing idea or antithesis, thesis and antithesis then coming into conflict and eventually merging to produce a new idea or synthesis. As applied by Marx to the development of human society, the dialectic worked in terms of economic groups or classes. Their conflict grew out of the development of a particular economic structure and eventually produced a new structure and society, the final synthesis arriving when those who actually did the material work in society – the proletariat – emerged victorious from the ultimate conflict.

'The history of all hitherto existing society is the history of class struggles', Marx wrote in 1848, and, to the materialist historian, it followed that all other aspects of human society – institutions, relationships, arts, religions and philosophies – were so much baggage in the trains of the opposing class armies.

However,Marx was not just a theorist writing in his ivory tower, he was a political radical passionately concerned with the inequalities of the society around him. He first offered his thesis to the world in 1848 not in an academic tome but in a revolutionary pamphlet – the Communist Manifesto. The final synthesis – the earthly paradise of the victorious proletariat, communally possessing the means of production, distribution and exchange, capitalism and its institutions and ideas withered to nothing – was not just a scientific inevitability, it was also a desirable end to be fought for.

There was a contradiction here, but not a very culpable one; Marxism was not the first philosophy to try to embrace both determinism and free will at the same time. The really major philosophical problems came – aptly – from material events or the lack of them.

The Communist Manifesto was the product of a particular moment in history. In 1848, it was still really quite reasonable for young idealists to believe that capitalist society was rapidly moving to its final and inevitable crisis. Industry was increasingly stumbling into cycles of overproduction and recession; many industrial workers were desperately poor; and the most important manifestation of all – revolution was about to shake European society for the third time in sixty years.

The moment passed. Capitalism became better at staving off its contradictions; industrial workers discovered they might gain rather than lose from its further development; the institutions of social and political control were strengthened. There was a second chance in 1871 when Moltke and Bismarck overthrew the Second Empire and the Commune of Paris was able to offer a genuinely socialist programme to the people of France. But the Commune proved no match for the elected government and by various means of coercion including force the old order was quickly restored.

The Communist Manifesto ended on a note of free will, not determinism: 'The proletarians have nothing to lose but their chains. They have a world to win. Working men of all countries, unite!' Yet they did not. It was a failure of will that was to become a major puzzle for Marxists, exercising the minds of intellectuals and activists long after Marx's death in 1883. *(R.J.)*

	1880–1881	1882–1883	1884–1885	1886–1887	1888–1889
Politics & Military History	**1880** 10,000 Irish evictions: term *Boycotting* comes into use. Afghans defeat Britain at Maiwand; Roberts' march from Kandahar to Kabul; Khan deposed and replaced by pro-British successor. Socialist Workers emerge in France. Repeal of the May Laws in Germany marks a relaxation of the state-church struggle. **1881** Nationalist revolt in Egypt under Arabi Pasha. France establishes a Protectorate over Tunis. US President James Garfield assassinated. Boers defeat the British at Battle of Majuba Hill: independence for Boer Republic of Transvaal. Beginning of Mahdi revolt against Egyptian rule in Sudan.	**1882** French capture Hanoi; Chinese assert suzeraínty over Annam. British fleet bombards Alexandria following anti-European riots: end of Anglo-French dual control and beginning of British control of Egypt. Luderitz acquires German rights in South West Africa. Phoenix Park Murders in Dublin spark off another Anglo-Irish crisis. Italy joins Germany and Austria to form the Triple Alliance. Mahdi proclaims himself the Messiah in Sudan. **1883** The French annex Madagascar (to 1885). Kruger elected President of Transvaal: dominates Afrikaaner politics to end of century. Baring (Lord Cromer) is made British Consul-General in Egypt which he 'administers' to 1907. German Protectorate is proclaimed over South West Africa.	**1884** Third Reform Act passed in Britain. Berlin Conference: the European powers lay down rules for colonizing Africa; the conference sets off the *Scramble for Africa*. Congo State personally owned by Leopold II of Belgium is recognized by the Powers. Germany occupies Togoland and Cameroons. Gordon sent to Sudan to rescue the Egyptian garrison – besieged in Khartoum. **1885** Khartoum falls to the Mahdi; General Gordon is killed. New Guinea annexed by Britain and Germany. Britain establishes protectorates over southern Nigeria and Bechuanaland in south Africa. The first meeting of the Indian National Congress.	**1886** Gladstone introduces his first Irish Home Rule Bill: it is rejected and Ministry falls. Boulanger, the French Minister of War, favours policy of confrontation with Germany to recover Alsace-Lorraine. **1887** Renewal of Russo-German Reinsurance Treaty and Triple Alliance. Bismarck refuses permission for Russia to raise loans in Berlin; France advances Russia 350m francs. Italians are defeated by Ethiopians at Dogali. Queen Victoria has her Golden Jubilee.	**1888** Imperial British East Africa Company is chartered. Mashonaland and Matabeleland become British spheres of influence: Rudd Concession granted to Rhodes' agent Rudd. Convention of Constantinople: Suez Canal to be open to ships of all nations. Sarawak and Brunei come under British protection. **1889** Panama scandal: work on the canal is halted, the company bankrupt, de Lesseps and others tried for corruption. N and S Dakota, Washington and Montana join USA. Treaty of Ucciali: Ethiopia becomes Italian protectorate. Brazil becomes republic. Rhodes founds the British South Africa Company.
Religion & Learning	**1880** Atheist Bradlaugh is elected MP in Britain but not allowed to take his seat. Mundella's Education Act makes school attendance compulsory in Britain to age 13.	**1883** Nietsche *Also Sprach Zarathustra*.	**1884** The first appearance of the Oxford English Dictionary (OED) not completed until 1928. **1885** Marx *Das Kapital*, Vol. 2 (post.).	**1886** Bradlaugh, the atheist, is finally permitted to take his seat in House of Commons. von Krafft-Ebing *Psychopathis Sexualis*. End of the Church-State quarrel (kulturkampf) in Germany. **1887** Freud uses hypnotic suggestion. John Dewey *Psychology*.	**1888** Romanes *Mental Evolution in Man* (Romanes instituted the Romanes lectures at Oxford). **1889** T. H. Huxley *Agnosticism*.
Cities & Social Development	**1880** Britain now possesses half the world's merchant shipping steam tonnage. Spires of Cologne Cathedral completed, tallest in the world at 156m. **1881** Freedom of public meetings and press established in France. Stanley founds Leopoldville in the Congo. Flogging in the Army and Royal Navy is abolished.	**1882** Standard Oil Co controls 95 per cent of US oil refining capacity. Cricket *Ashes* between Britain and Australia begin. **1883** Explosion of Mt Krakatoa, volcanic island near Java. Firth of Forth Bridge, the first all steel bridge.	**1884** Law on accident insurance in Germany and sickness insurance scheme. Washington memorial (169m) briefly becomes the world's tallest structure. William Morris establishes the Socialist League; the Fabian Society is set up. **1885** The Canadian Pacific Railway (CPR) is completed. European emigration reaches a level of 780,000 a year	**1886** German East Africa Company is established to develop Zanzibar Colony. Hydro-electric scheme is mounted to harness power from the Niagara Falls. **1887** Construction of the Kiel Canal is begun. Germany comes to dominate the new chemical industry.	**1888** Agricultural depression leads Sweden to abandon free trade. **1889** Compulsory old age and incapacity pensions introduced in Germany. Eiffel Tower is completed for the Paris Exhibition. At 300m easily the world's tallest structure, a title it holds for the next 40 years.
Discovery & Invention	**1880** Anopheles mosquito is found to be the carrier of malaria. James Finlay constructs an iron suspension bridge in Pennsylvania. **1881** Pasteur develops preventive immunization for anthrax.	**1882** Robert Koch, the German bacteriologist, discovers TB bacillus. **1883** A general acceptance of Greenwich Mean Time establishing time zones through the world. Invention of the machine gun.	**1884** Royce begins producing motor cars at Manchester. **1885** Benz produces his first car, a three wheeler. First electric tramcar is used at Blackpool. Pasteur successfully innoculates against rabies.	**1886** Gold is discovered on Witwatersrand, South Africa. **1887** Welsbach produces practical incandescent gas mantle. Daimler produces a four-wheeled motor car.	**1888** Norwegian explorer, Nansen, crosses Greenland. George Eastman patents film emulsion set on a transparent celluloid base. **1889** Brunner-Mond establish their Salt Union, a combine of 64 firms.
The Arts	**1880** Zola *Nana*. Rodin *The Thinker*, sculpture.	**1882** Conan Doyle *A Study in Scarlet* – first appearance of Sherlock Holmes. Berlin Philharmonic Orchestra established. **1883** R. L. Stevenson *Treasure Island*. Brahms 3rd Symphony. The Statue of Liberty is presented to the USA by France.	**1884** The Russian goldsmith, Fabergé, produces the first of his jewelled Easter eggs for the Tsar. **1885** Richard Burton's translation of *The Thousand Nights and a Night*. Twain *Huckleberry Finn*. Rider Haggard *King Solomon's Mines*.	**1886** Hardy *The Mayor of Casterbridge*. Stevenson *Kidnapped*. Burnett *Little Lord Fauntleroy*. Millais *Bubbles*. Rodin *The Kiss*. **1887** Kipling *Plain Tales*. Rider Haggard *She*, *Alan Quartermain*. Debussy *Le Printemps*. Verdi *Otello*.	**1888** Tchaikovsky 5th Symphony. Rimsky-Korsakov *Scheherezade*. Van Gogh *Sunflowers*. **1889** Jerome K. Jerome *Three men in a boat*. Edison laboratories develop Kinetograph strip camera using perforated film roll manufactured by Eastman.

or 300 years after Vasco da Gama's circumnavigation of frica the continent remained little more than an outline in uropean atlases. Rumour filled the interior with mounins, lakes and seas, but the simple reality was that no-one not even the people who lived there – knew where the Nile egan nor how the Niger ended. The whole vast area south the Sahara was an almost total blank.

In the course of the 19th century, explorers found the iswers to the questions that had remained unanswered for long. The Lander brothers sailed down the Niger and roved that the Oil Rivers constituted its delta in 1830–32: avid Livingstone traced the course of the Zambesi in 841–56 and John Hanning Speke discovered Lake Victoria and the Rippon Falls, the source of the White Nile in 858–62. Meanwhile the northern and southern extremies of the continent were conquered and colonized by uropeans, the French establishing their authority over lgeria in the 1830s and the Boers moving onto the grassnds north of the Orange River in the years after 1835.

European involvement in Africa took an important step rward in 1869 when the cutting of the Suez Canal was rought to a triumphant conclusion by the French engineer nd entrepreneur Ferdinand de Lesseps. This success ncouraged the ruler of Egypt, the Khedive Ismail, to seek uropean backing for an ambitious programme of odernization at home and expansion abroad. He got the oney but had little luck with his military adventures, and y 1876 his financial affairs were reduced to such chaos that he British and French would only agree to bailing him out he allowed their experts to run his exchequer. Inevitably his led to a nationalist reaction and troops had to be called n to 'restore order'. The British, who were best at this sort f thing, landed an army at Alexandria in 1882 and had the whole country under their control in a matter of weeks.

The other European powers were furious. The French nd Italians had been asked if they would like to contribute o the expeditionary force but had refused, expecting this vould make the British think again. But the British had not, hey had gone ahead and to all intents and purposes ncorporated Egypt in their empire. This was particularly ggravating to the French for ever since Napoleon's xpedition they had regarded Egypt as their protégé. Now t had been snatched from under their noses. They lemanded compensation. And so did everyone else.

So began the 'Scramble for Africa'. It started off as a aper exercise, with diplomats drawing lines across the nap, trying to agree on a reasonable share-out: it ended up vith the few people on the ground struggling to translate hese agreements into some sort of administrative reality. The diplomats did their job with surprising speed: the outines of the colonial map of Africa had nearly all been letermined by the end of the 1880s. However, it took a long ime to turn 'spheres of influence' into functioning olonies. The job was finally completed in the opening lecades of the 20th century by which time only two indeendent countries remained in the whole continent: Liberia, a state founded by an American charity as a homeand for freed slaves, and Abyssinia, which proved able to lefeat an Italian attempt to conquer it in 1896. Everywhere else was in the hands of the European elite.

The ethics and economics of this extraordinary enterorise remain unclear. There were certainly some abominations, the most often quoted example being the Congo (modern Zaire) which was run for a time as a private fief by King Leopold of the Belgians. On the other hand, leaving aside the gold and diamond-bearing areas of South Africa which were in European hands before the Scramble began, it is not very likely that anyone made much money out of the sub Saharan colonies. In most places there simply was no money to make. Perhaps the best explanation for the whole episode is that it was due to an excess of the competitive patriotism to which Europeans of this era were so prone. Certainly Bismarck, who thought the whole business of colonies was silly, was forced by public opinion to take part in the Scramble. It all comes back to the map again: a lot of it was coloured British so he had to have some bits to colour German.

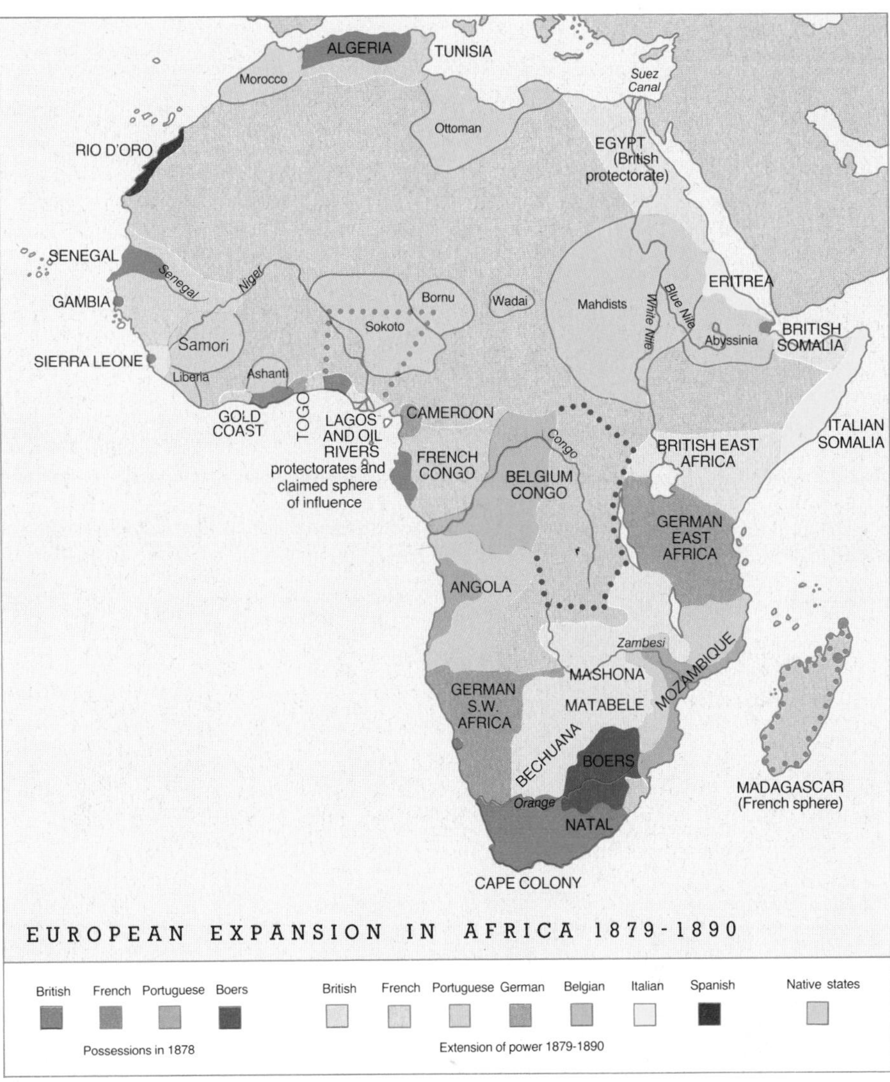

EUROPEAN EXPANSION IN AFRICA 1879-1890

Left: Dabulamanzie, brother of the Zulu King Cetewayo, the leader of the Impis *that defeated the British at Isandhlwana.*

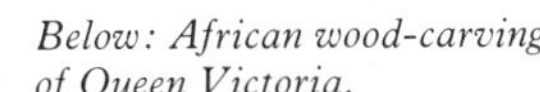

Below: African wood-carving of Queen Victoria.

	1890	1891	1892	1893	1894
Politics & Military History	Fall of Bismarck: Caprivi becomes Imperial Chancellor. Cecil Rhodes is Prime Minister of Cape Colony: his pioneers establish Rhodesia. Anglo-German Agreement: Britain gains Zanzibar and Kenya; Germany obtains Caprivi Strip and Heligoland from Britain.	Keir Hardie becomes first Independent Labour Party MP. Nyasaland made British Protectorate. France and Russia begin their entente – to last to WW1. Young Turk Movement for liberal reforms launched.	Gladstone's fourth (last) Ministry: 3 ILP MPs elected. French speaking communes of Alsace-Lorraine are ordered to conduct official business in German.	Britain establishes a Protectorate over Uganda. Keir Hardie founds the Independent Labour Party. First Matabele War in Rhodesia. France occupies Ivory Coast and Dahomey. US Marines overthrow the government of Hawaii.	War between China and Japan (to 1895): Japan captures Port Arthur. Sun Yat-sen founds the first of several revolutionary societies in China. Armenian massacres by Kurds. Dreyfus Affair: Dreyfus court-martialled for selling military secrets to Germany.
Religion & Learning	Freud begins to employ his cathartic methods. James Frazer embarks upon *The Golden Bough* (completed 1915).	Beatrice Webb *The Co-operative Movement in Great Britain*. All elementary education in England is to be free.	Freud begins the development of his concept of free association.	St Hilda's and St Anne's Colleges for Women are established at Oxford. Franchise in New Zealand extended to women.	Havelock Ellis *Man and Woman*. Beatrice and Sidney Webb *History of trade unionism*. Marx *Das Kapital*, Vol. III (post.).
Cities & Social Development	Crash of the Banca di Roma: creates financial panic in London and Paris. Opening of London-Paris telephone line.	Law for Protection of Workers regulates hours for German workers. Construction of the trans-Siberian Railway begins.	One third of French miners, engineers and foundrymen are now unionized. The Italian Benadir Co is set up to develop Italian Somaliland.	Belgian General Strike: riots suppressed by troops. Rhenish-Westphalian Coal Syndicate established; it dominates the Ruhr coal area.	Graduated death duties are introduced in Britain. Opening of the Manchester Ship Canal.
Discovery & Invention	Rubber gloves are used in surgery for the first time by Halstead.	Pithecanthropus, early human, is discovered in Java (Java Man) by Dubois.	Brunel's wide gauge is finally abandoned on British railways. Gold is discovered in Western Australia.	Henry Ford's first *gasoline buggy*. Lilienthal successfully flies a glider.	Halstead conducts an operation for breast cancer (mastectomy).
The Arts	Ibsen *Hedda Gabler*. Emily Dickinson *Poems*, published posthumously. Mascagni *Cavalleria Rusticana*.	Hardy *Tess of the D'Urbervilles*. Mahler 1st Symphony.	Leoncavallo *I Pagliacci*. Verdi *Falstaff*.	Tchaikovsky 6th Symphony and his suicide. Toulouse-Lautrec *The Clown Boum-Boum*.	George du Maurier *Trilby*. Kipling *The Jungle Book*. Shaw *Arms and the Man*. Debussy *L'Après-midi d'un Faune*.

Images and epithets capture *La Belle Époque* far better than description or analysis. For England we might choose 'Edwardian', Elgar, or Jerome K. Jerome. For Austria certainly the glitter of Vienna, Strauss, Léhar, and the Hotel Sacher, though there was also Sigmund Freud. For France, perhaps Moulin-Rouge, Proust, Toulouse-Lautrec ... but there are so many. For Germany, more serious, Thomas Mann and *Jugendstil*. And so on. All centres had their *Belles Époques*, while the new-fangled scientific achievements which were also part and parcel of the age – the motor car, wireless, portable camera – were international. Pleasure, sexual liberation, artistic exploration, intellectual challenge, technological revolution: all characterized a period which yet remained strangely secure and stable in the essentials of social caste and ultimate values.

But *La Belle Époque* belongs very much to France, and to Paris. Maxim's restaurant became a landmark for the rich and leisured, just as Montmartre became a landmark for all. Paris fashion houses, jewellery design, and expensive wines and perfumes, became emblems of *La Belle Époque* society. Phrases such as 'demi-monde' and 'Tout Paris' conjure up this world of the privileged, with its theatres, salons, clubs, and supper parties at Maxim's. Another society is portrayed in the brilliant caricatures and posters of Toulouse-Lautrec, 'the gifted and nobly born dwarf', and such followers as Chéret. 'Low life' became a cult of *La Belle Époque*, with its cafés, brothels, dance halls, and fairgrounds, Montmartre symbolized it all, with the clusters of artists' colonies and notorious nightclubs. Here was Moulin Rouge, the Folies Bergères and nightly cancan. Here people of all walks of life and all nations flocked to enjoy the decadent entertainment encapsulated by La

Above: Mlle Eglantine's troupe of can-can dancers. A poster by Toulouse Lautrec.

1895	1896	1897	1898	1899	
The Jameson Raid from Bechuanaland to Transvaal: fails, leads to Rhodes' resignation 1896. End of war between China and Japan which takes Formosa and Korea. Anglo-Venezuelan border dispute: arbitration in Britain's favour. Revolt in Cuba against Spain.	Dreyfus Affair gathers momentum in France. Beginning of Kitchener's campaign to reconquer the Sudan. France annexes Madagascar. Battle of Adowa: the Italians are defeated by the Ethiopians; this ends Italian claims to Ethiopia. Further Armenian massacres by Kurds encouraged by the Sultan.	Dingley Act in US increases moves towards Protectionism. President Faure of France visits Russia to cement their alliance. Diamond Jubilee of Queen Victoria: the high point of British Imperial grandeur. First Zionist Congress meets in Basel: the fake *Protocol of the Elders of Zion* an exercise in anti-semitism.	Battle of Omdurman: Kitchener defeats Khalifa. Fashoda Incident: Anglo-French confrontation in Sudan almost leads to war. Spanish-American War over Cuba: Treaty of Paris: Cuba becomes independent, Spain cedes Puerto Rico, Guam and Philippines to USA. USA annexes Hawaii. Social Democratic Party is founded in Russia.	Dreyfus is pardoned by new French President but not cleared. Anglo-Boer War breaks out in South Africa: Siege of Ladysmith. First Hague Peace Conference – 26 nations meet: a Permanent Court of Arbitration is set up. Geneva Convention now covers naval warfare, explosive bullets and poison gas.	Politics & Military History
London School of Economics (LSE) is established.	Term psychoanalysis first comes into use. Theodor Herzl *Der Judenstaat*, the founder of modern Zionism.	Gilbert Murray *A History of Ancient Greek Literature.* The Webbs *Industrial Democracy.*	Zola *J'Accuse*, polemic against government in Dreyfus case.	Board of Education established in Britain: Ruskin College established at Oxford.	Religion & Learning
Direct action is adopted by the French CGT (general union organization).	First modern Olympic Games held at Athens. Klondike Gold Rush in Canada's Yukon Territory.	Workmens' Compensation Act: employers' liability for insurance of workforce. British hospitals may only employ trained nurses.	Congo Railway reaches Stanley Pools.	Britain's first garden city laid out at Letchworth.	Cities & Social Development
Roentgen discovers X-rays. Gillette invents his safety razor.	Becquerel observes radiation from uranium: the discovery of radio-activity. Death of Nobel: the annual Nobel prizes instituted.	McCreary patents air-washer to purify air in buildings: the beginning of air-conditioning. Ross identifies the cause of malaria.	Marie and Pierre Curie discover radium.	First turbine ships are built by Royal Navy. First instance of wireless telegraphy from Britain to France.	Discovery & Invention
Sir Henry Wood starts Promenade Concerts in London. Wells *The Time Machine.* Chekhov *The Seagull.* First public showing of films in Paris, beginnings of cinema.	Lumière Brothers give first public performance of their films in New York. Puccini *La Bohème.* Richard Strauss *Also Sprach Zarathustra.*	First comic strip appears in the USA (by Rudolph Dirks). Conrad *The Nigger of the Narcissus.* Rostand *Cyrano de Bergerac.*	Stanislavsky establishes the Moscow Arts Theatre. Wilde *The Ballad of Reading Gaol.* James *The Turn of the Screw.*	Kipling *Stalky & Co.* Elgar *The Enigma Variations.* Sibelius *Finlandia.* Gauguin *Two Tahitian girls with mangoes.*	The Arts

Left: 'At the Moulin Rouge' by F. de Myrbach. Opened in 1889 the Moulin Rouge became the most popular of all the Paris music halls. Gentlemen came to see the jugglers, singers, acrobats and dancers who performed there, and to try their luck with the working-class girls – seamstresses, laundry maids and shop girls – who crowded the dance floors.

Goulou, so often portrayed by Toulouse-Lautrec: fat, lascivious, and luxurious. Prostitution was highly organized and little disguised; it ranged from famous houses like the Chabarnais (started by Edward VII when Prince of Wales, and still patronized by him after he became King), the great courtesans driving in their carriages along the Champs Élysées, down to the lowly disease-ridden brothels of the poorer districts.

The female image played a leading role in much of the art typical of the period, whether in an ideological and stylized form or as a voluptuous 'femme fatale'. It was an age of scandals: the death of President Faure in the arms of his mistress somehow typified *La Belle Époque*. It was, too, an age of great actresses and female opera singers. Most famous of all was Sarah Bernhardt who so enthralled the Prince of Wales and who set a fashion for costume and jewellery imitated by society ladies everywhere. Then there was Loie Fuller, whose flowing veils used in her celebrated dances became immortalized in countless posters, paintings, and sculptures.

Characteristic of the artistic ferment of the times was the succession and coincidence of diverse 'schools' and movements – the impressionists, post-impressionists, cubists, futurists, Art Nouveau, and others. The numbers involved and the distinctiveness of styles speak eloquently of the new direction art was taking and its originality, from the impressionist works of Monet and Cézanne to the cubist styles of Braque and Picasso.

Art of course, and music and literature, survived the turn of the century, but the atmosphere of *La Belle Époque* as epitomized in Paris, born of the optimism of the coming century, and sustained by a class soon to disappear, vanished quietly and completely. *(M.F.)*

	1900	1901	1902	1903	1904
Politics & Military History	Boxer Rebellion in China: Nationalist forces (Boxers) besiege foreign embassies; joint foreign intervention ends rebellion. Labour Representation Committee founded in Britain (beginning of Labour Party). German Navy Law to increase navy: starts armaments race with Britain. Russia occupies Manchuria. Boer War: British forces relieve Kimberley, Ladysmith, Mafeking and Britain annexes Orange Free State and Transvaal. Britain takes over territories of Royal Niger Company and begins conquest of Northern Nigeria.	The Australian Commonwealth is formed: self-governing Dominion. European Peace Protocol with China ends Boxer Rebellion. In South Africa Boers organize guerrilla warfare. Social Revolutionary Party established in Russia: growth of anti-government activities.	Peace of Vereeniging: end of Boer War. Secret Franco-Italian Treaty. British-Japanese Treaty for mutual defence. USA acquires perpetual control of the Panama Canal. Anglo-German fleet seizes Venezuelan fleet to recover debts.	Russian Social Democratic Party splits into Bolsheviks and Mensheviks. In Britain Joseph Chamberlain begins his programme for tariff reform. Britain sends expeditionary force to Tibet under Younghusband. The massacre of Jews at Kishinyov in Russia is climax of decades of anti-semitic persecutions.	Russo-Japanese War: Russians defeated at Liaoyang in China. Entente Cordiale between Britain and France: reach accord over Egypt and Morocco. Revolt of Hereros peoples in South West Africa against the German colonial authorities.
Religion & Learning	Freud *Interpretation of Dreams.* School leaving age in Britain is raised to 14.	Law of Associations in France allows Catholics to form associations. Rabindranath Tagore sets up his Santiniketan school in Bengal.	The beginning of *Cambridge Modern History.* J. A. Hobson *Imperialism,* classic analysis of the subject. Dewey *The Educational Situation.*	G. E. Moore *Principia Ethica.* Bertrand Russell *The Principles of Mathematics.* John Morley *Life of Gladstone.*	Leeds University established. Separation of Church and State accomplished in France.
Cities & Social Development	10-hour working day is laid down in France. By this year Britain possesses 44.5 per cent of world's merchant steam tonnage. Central Line is opened in London: underground is electrified. Europe's population has now reached 410m.	Taff Vale Judgement in Britain: union is liable for damages inflicted by its officials. Mombasa-Lake Victoria railway is completed to the Lake. Trans-Siberian Railway is opened. Oil drilling begins in Persia.	Public Health Act in France leads to better living conditions for working classes. White settlement in Kenya highlands gets under way. Turkey permits Germany to commence railway to Baghdad.	Formation of the Workers' Education Association (WEA) in Britain. Formation of the Women's Social and Political Union in Britain by Emmeline Pankhurst to demand votes for women. Henry Ford sets up his Motor Company. First coast to coast crossing of America by car takes 65 days.	General strike takes place in Italy. Construction of the Panama Canal resumed. Rapid growth of unions in Germany: numbers in unions double between 1902 and 1906. Broadway subway opens in New York. Duisberg, the German industrialist, creates IG Farben Co. *L'Humanité,* socialist newspaper, is established by Jaurès in Paris.
Discovery & Invention	Max Planck proposes quantum theory. Escalator is invented in USA and exhibited at Paris exhibition. Human speech is first transmitted by radio waves by Fessenden in the USA.	Marconi sends morse wireless signals from Cornwall to Newfoundland. Becquerel reveals dangerous effects of radioactivity on human beings. Scott takes *Discovery* on Antarctic Expedition.	English physicist, Heaviside, states the existence of an atmospheric layer which aids conduction of radio waves.	Wright Brothers make their first flight in a heavier-than-air machine.	Rutherford *Radioactivity.* Marie Curie *Recherches sur les substances radioactives.* First telegraphic transmission of photographs is carried out in Germany from Munich to Nuremberg.
The Arts	Conrad *Lord Jim.* Elgar *The Dream of Gerontius.* Puccini *Tosca.* Picasso *Le Moulin de la Galette.* Jazz: Buddy Bolden introduces improvisation into New Orleans Dance Hall music.	Kipling *Kim.* *Ragtime* is introduced into American jazz. Thomas Mann *Buddenbrooks.* Rachmaninoff Piano Concerto No. 2.	Hillaire Belloc *The Path to Rome.* Conrad *Youth* and *Heart of Darkness.* With his film *Le Voyage dans la lune* George Méliès involves cinema in storytelling. Italian tenor Caruso makes the first of 154 gramophone recordings. *The Times Literary Supplement* appears for first time.	Shaw *Man and Superman.* Chekhov *The Cherry Orchard.* Edwin S. Porter's film *The Great Train Robbery* establishes the pattern for adventure films. London *The Call of the Wild.* First recording of an opera is made: Verdi's *Ernani.* Munch *On the Bridge.*	Barrie *Peter Pan.* Puccini *Madame Butterfly.* London Symphony Orchestra gives its first concert. First radio transmission of music is made at Graz in Austria.

1905	1906
Partition of Bengal rouses nationalist opposition in India. Russo-Japanese War: Russians defeated at the battle of Mukden; their fleet is then destroyed at Tsushima; the war is ended by the Treaty of Portsmouth. Morocco Crisis between France and Germany. Bloody Sunday: Russian troops fire on workers in St Petersburg; industrial agitation leads to the formation of Soviets; in the October Manifesto Tsar Nicholas II offers limited reforms. End of the Union of Norway and Sweden: Norway becomes fully independent.	Launching of HMS *Dreadnought*, first turbine driven battleship; the naval race between Britain and Germany escalates. Powers of the Tsar are curtailed by the Duma (Parliament) in Russia. First Labour MPs are returned in the British General Election; formation of Labour Party. Alfred Dreyfus is finally cleared of treason in a retrial. Algeciras Conference: French rights in Morocco are recognized.
Freud *Three Essays on Sexuality*. Lenin *Two Tactics of Social-Democracy in the Democratic Revolution*.	Freud and Jung begin their association. Fowler *The King's English*.
Aliens Act in Britain: Home Office control of immigration. Formation of the French Socialist Party. Germany lays down the first *Dreadnought* battleship; the Cawdor Memorandum in Britain proposes that Britain constructs 4 Dreadnoughts a year.	Trades Disputes Act: unions in Britain are not liable to damages incurred by strikes. Horatio Bottomley publishes *John Bull*: rampant jingoism. San Francisco earthquake and fire: 400 dead, $400m damage to property.
Einstein begins his work on relativity and extends Planck's quantum theory. Mount Wilson Observatory established in California.	The term *allergy* is introduced into medicine by von Pirquet. Amundsen traverses the NW Passage and determines the position of the Magnetic North Pole. First radio programme of voice and music is broadcast in the US by Fessenden.
First *Nickelodeon* opens in Pittsburgh. Baroness Orczy *The Scarlet Pimpernel*. Franz Lehar *The Merry Widow*, opera. Picasso takes up residence in Paris and begins his 'Pink Period'. Debussy *La Mer*.	By this year there are more than 1,000 Nickelodeons in the USA: cinema has become mass entertainment. Cezanne *Still Life with Chair, Bottle and Apples*. Picasso *Gertrude Stein*. The beginnings of Cubism. Galsworthy *The Man of Property*, beginning of Forsyte Saga.

Above: The Flatiron building, on Broadway, Fifth Avenue and East 23rd Street, overlooking Madison Square. One of the first skyscrapers built in New York, this 20 storey structure was completed in 1902. Architect D. H. Burnham.

Until the opening years of the 19th century no city in the world had ever held a million people; by its end there were 18 of them. London reached its million shortly after 1800, Paris around 1830, New York around 1860 and then, in the final quarter of the 19th century, another 15 places burst through the barrier. The million-strong metropolis had become the norm. Really big cities had several millions: London, for example, had $6\frac{1}{2}$, New York $4\frac{1}{4}$, Paris and Berlin 3 or more each.

There were many other million-plus cities besides the capitals. Britain had Manchester, Birmingham, Glasgow and Liverpool. The United States had Chicago, Philadelphia and Boston; Germany had Hamburg and the great conurbation of the Ruhr. It was the growth of the secondary and tertiary centres that made Britain the first nation in the world to have a majority of its people living in towns: only three in every twenty lived in London but six lived in a city of a million or more and twelve in places with over 20,000 inhabitants. Most of them were first generation town-dwellers, a sizeable number came from Ireland. However, the proportion of immigrants was never so high as in America. There, nearly half the inhabitants of New York were European born while the figures for Boston and Philadelphia are of the same order of magnitude.

Coping with populations in the millions posed formidable problems: keeping this number of people fed and clothed – even if poorly – was a mammoth undertaking. Steamships and railways made it possible: the great wholesale markets stood as monuments to the fact that it was done. On a single day in 1891, 1356 tonnes of meat, poultry and other provisions passed through Smithfield and 572 tonnes of fish through Billingsgate.

These Victorian cities were constantly changing their character. The development of new forms of public transport – the horse-drawn omnibus and the train in the mid-19th century, then the electric tram in the 1880s – freed the people from the tyranny of the walk to work and created suburban man. The numbers living in the city centres started to fall, the centres themselves were rebuilt with more offices and less dwellings, ever widening belts of middle income housing spread into the countryside. Overall densities fell; the quality of life improved.

It needed to. The 19th century city was boring when it was not frightening. Most of the streets were mean and one was much like another. Outside events made little impression. 'Nations may rise, or may totter in ruin; but here the colourless day will work through its twenty-four hours just as it did yesterday, and just as it will tomorrow.' Perhaps that is why Marx got so little change out of the working class. *(R.J.)*

Right: New York, Lower Broadway from the Battery in 1904. On the left are the Washington Building and the Bowling Green Building.

	1907	1908	1909	1910	1911
Politics & Military History	Second Hague Peace Conference: Germany opposes arms limitations. Edward VII visits Russia: the Anglo-Russian Entente; the Dual Entente becomes the Triple Entente with France. New Zealand becomes a Dominion. Lenin leaves Russia: establishes his paper *The Proletarian* in exile. Sun Yat-sen announces a programme for his Chinese Democratic Republic.	Following scandals of forced labour the Belgian government takes control of the Congo Free State from Leopold; it is renamed the Belgian Congo. Austria annexes Bosnia and Herzegovina. Crete proclaims union with Greece and sparks off a revolt in Turkey by the Young Turk Movement forcing the Sultan to proclaim a liberal constitution.	Lloyd George introduces his *People's Budget*: taxing rich to pay for welfare amenities leads to constitutional crisis with House of Lords. Act of Union makes South Africa an independent Dominion within the British Empire: the act comes into force in 1910. Universal suffrage is introduced in Sweden. Liberal revolution in Persia overthrows the Shah. Young Turks depose Sultan Abdul Hamid II. Russia and Bulgaria conclude secret treaty of alliance against Austria and Germany.	Continuing constitutional crisis in Britain: two elections are held. Liberals stay in power. Botha becomes first Prime Minister of the new Dominion, the Union of South Africa. Revolution in Portugal leads to the establishment of republic. Japan annexes Korea. Mexican civil war begins: to last until 1920.	Parliament Act in Britain reduces power of House of Lords. British MPs receive a salary. Italy invades Libya: war with Turkey. Agadir Crisis: Germany sends a gunboat to Morocco to dispute France's claim; the Convention of Berlin recognizes a French Protectorate over Morocco. President Diaz of Mexico is overthrown in civil war. Revolution in China: Sun Yat-sen overthrows Manchu Dynasty, a Republic is declared in 1912.
Religion & Learning	Pope Pius X denounces *Modernism.* Imperial College is established in London.	First International Psycho-Analytic Congress is held at Salzburg.	Trevelyan *Garibaldi and the Thousand.* Universities of Bristol and Belfast and the University College of Dublin are opened.	James Frazer *Totemism and Exogamy.* Bertrand Russell and A. N. Whitehead collaborate on *Principia Mathematica.*	Fowler *Concise Oxford Dictonary.* *Cambridge Medieval History* begins to appear (to 1936).
Cities & Social Development	British government legislates to provide free meals and medical services in schools; contributory old age pensions; the beginnings of state welfare. Immigration into USA is limited by law: Japanese immigration is prohibited. Royal Dutch Shell is established.	Coal Mines Regulation Act in Britain limits men to an 8-hour day. Separate courts for juveniles are established in Britain. Lord Baden-Powell launches Boy Scout Movement. First Model T Ford motor cars are produced: known as the *Tin Lizzie*, it is to sell 15m altogether.	Russian Land Law improves conditions of the peasants. Osborne Judgement in Britain: union funds should not be used for political purposes. Anglo-Persian Oil Co (later BP) is established. Women are admitted to German universities.	British trade unions become more militant: the year sees a railway strike and coal strikes; there is a 60 per cent increase in union membership from 1907 to 1914. European migration rises to 2m a year. There is now a ratio of one car to every 44 households in the USA.	Standard Oil Trust is broken up into 33 companies although the Rockefellers retain major interests in Exxon, Mobil, Amoco, Standard Oil of California. British National Insurance Act lays foundations of health and unemployment insurance. First woman becomes a member of the Royal College of Surgeons. First British Official Secrets Act.
Discovery & Invention	First airship flies over London. Pavlov begins his studies of conditioned reflexes. Lumière develops a process for colour photography.	Landsteine and Popper isolate the virus of poliomyelitis (infantile paralysis). Shackleton gets within 160 km of the South Pole. Wilbur Wright flies an aeroplane for 48 km in 40 minutes.	US explorer Robert Peary reaches the North Pole. Blériot makes first cross-channel flight in 37 minutes. Oil refinery is established at Abadan in Persia. First commercial manufacture of bakelite signals commencement of plastic age.	Madame Curie isolates radium from chloride: *Treatise on Radiography.* Halley's Comet appears.	Lord Rutherford's theory of atomic structures. Norwegian explorer, Roald Amundsen, reaches the South Pole.
The Arts	Synge *The Playboy of the Western World.* Diaghilev begins to popularize ballet. Mahler Symphony No. 8. Picasso and Braque develop Cubism: the first Cubist exhibition in Paris. Gorky *The Mother.*	Forster *A Room with a View.* G. K. Chesterton *The Man who was Thursday.* D. W. Griffith shoots his first film and in France Pathé-Journal produces first cinema newsreel. Grahame *The Wind in the Willows.* Bennett *The Old Wives' Tale.*	Diaghilev launches *Ballet Russe* in Paris. Mahler 9th Symphony. Picasso *Harlequin.* Matisse *The Dance.*	E. M. Forster *Howards End.* Wells *The History of Mr Polly.* Stravinsky *The Fire Bird*, ballet in Paris. South American tango becomes popular in North America and Europe.	G. K. Chesterton *The Innocence of Father Brown.* Rupert Brooke *Poems.* Irving Berlin *Alexander's Rag-Time Band*, jazz tune. R. Strauss *Der Rosenkavalier.* Braque *Man with a Guitar.*

1912	1913
Home Rule for Ireland crisis grows in Britain. Anglo-French Naval Agreement: French fleet covers the Mediterranean, the British fleet the Atlantic and the Channel. Treaty of Ouchy: end of the Italian-Turkish War; Tripoli is ceded to Italy. First Balkan War: Bulgaria, Greece, Serbia and Montenegro unite against Turkey. Albania becomes independent. Sun Yat-sen founds the Chinese National Party (Kuomintang).	Third Irish Home Rule Bill is rejected by House of Lords; threat of civil war in Ireland, formation of private Protestant army (Ulster Volunteers) to oppose Home Rule. Young Turks set up a dictatorship in Turkey. Insurrection in British Somaliland (to 1920). London peace conference between Turkey and Balkan states suspended. Second Balkan War: Serbia, Greece, Romania and Turkey against Bulgaria which is defeated; further partitions result. Suffragette demonstrations in London: Mrs Pankhurst is imprisoned.
Discovery of Piltdown Man (hoax exposed in 1953). Jung *The Theory of Psychoanalysis*.	Jung-Freud partnership breaks up.
Continuing labour unrest in Britain includes coal strike, London dock strike and transport workers' strike. Britain nationalizes telephones. *Daily Herald* is founded; lasts to 1964. Liner *Titanic* sinks with loss of 1,513 lives. Royal Flying Corps (later the RAF) founded in Britain.	Trade Union Act in Britain establishes the right of unions to use funds for political purposes. Britain purchases controlling interest in Anglo-Persian Oil Co to secure naval oil supplies. Assembly line technique is fully operational in the Ford car factories. Albert Schweitzer opens his hospital at Lambaréné, French Congo (now Gabon).
Captain Scott and his team die in their attempt to be first at South Pole – beaten by Amundsen.	Bergius converts coal to oil. Geiger invents his counter to measure radioactivity.
In the USA about 5 million people a day visit the cinema. Chagall *The Cattle Dealer*. Kandinsky *Improvisation*.	Stravinsky *The Rite of Spring*. D. H. Lawrence *Sons and Lovers*. Shaw *Pygmalion*. Proust *A La Recherche du Temps Perdu*, part I; part II 1919. T. Mann *Death in Venice*. Jacob Epstein *Two Doves*, marble sculpture.

Above: A 'Model T' Ford braving the wilds of the Scottish highlands with the help of chains on the wheels. The robustness of the 'Model T' was one of the main factors in its extraordinary success.

Above left: Dropping the bodies onto the chassis in a 'Model T' Ford assembly line. Henry Ford's famous mass production assembly line really paid dividends: by 1927 when production of the 'Model T' stopped 15,007,033 of them had been made – a record which was not beaten until 1972 when the 15,007,034th Volkswagen 'Beetle' came off the production line.

The principle of internal combustion had been known since the 17th century, its crudest practical expression, the firing of a gun, considerably longer. But it was in the mid-19th century that serious attention was given to internal combustion as a source of power.

Development then was quite rapid. The first practical internal combustion engine, using gas, was developed by Lenoir in 1859, the first widely used gas engine by Otto in 1876. By the later 1870s, too, the principle had been successfully applied to vapourized oil and petrol. It took little time before the petrol-driven internal combustion engine was applied to the propulsion of a road vehicle – by Benz in 1885 and Daimler in 1886. By the end of the century, the petrol-driven road vehicle was the plaything of the industrial world.

The horseless carriage was sold at first to carriage people; it was a custom-built luxury article put together by hand in a workshop. One man alone had a vision of something different. As Henry Ford moved through a series of small-scale motor enterprises in the early 1900s, he developed the idea – the obsession – of creating a cheap, efficient, reliable automobile that could be sold to the middling groups in society, above all to the farmers, who could use it as much as a tractor as a road vehicle.

Ford's dream of a mass-consumption vehicle was his only asset. He had little formal education; others translated his ideas into plans and models until, with the Model T of 1908, Ford sensed intuitively that he had the vehicle of his vision. The price, too, had to be right. Ford persistently ignored accounting norms and, once the Model T was in full production, regularly cut its price regardless of the economics of its manufacture. The price came first; the cost of production had to be cut to fit it.

'Everytime I reduce the charge for our car by one dollar, I get a thousand new buyers.' It was a revolutionary concept – and it worked. Demand vastly outstripped supply in the early years of the Model T. Ford saw that such mass consumption demanded mass production.

The discovery of the most cost-effective way of organizing the unskilled work of putting the parts together was the culminating achievement. It took place in Ford's Highland Park factory in Detroit in the first years of the production of the Model T, under the immense pressure of his price-cutting policy. In the beginning, part after part was added to the chassis as a couple of men towed it around the factory on the end of a rope. By 1913, the world's first moving assembly line was in full flow.

The gains in productivity were massive. When the 1913 assembly line was installed, the time taken to assemble a single vehicle fell from over 12 hours to an hour and a half. And total production soared. Ford had begun by making a hundred Model T cars a day; by the end of 1913, the factory was turning out a thousand a day. That year the number of automobiles in the United States reached the million: more than half of them were Model T's. *(R.J.)*

THE TRIUMPH OF TECHNOLOGY

AD 1914 - AD 1984

Most people think of the 20th century as starting in 1900. Pedants insist that the correct date is 1901 and if you do the sums the answer has to be that they are arithmetically correct. But the real date is 1914. At the beginning of that year Europe was still a 19th century society, respectful of elders and betters, ordered by birth and occupation, ruled over by Kaisers and Tsars. And when, in June and July, the nations moved towards war, their armies were assembled and sustained by the most Victorian of all technologies, the railway. It was this instrument that put men by the million at the disposal of the generals and which, because it added nothing to their mobility on the battlefield, ordained that they be slaughtered like sheep. For as the soldiers left their trains they became simply a jostling mob of footsloggers, pitting their bayonets against the machine guns with no more prospect of success than a Zulu impi. *The vocabulary of this Armageddon belongs to the 19th century.*

We have seen equal horrors since but they have a different style. Fascism may be a regressive barbarism but it is a barbarism of the 20th century: Stalinism may be an outgrowth of Marxism but its roots are in the new Russia created by Lenin. The technology has changed out of all recognition: oil has replaced coal, the car has displaced the train, nuclear fission and fusion have spread their lengthening shadows over peace and war.

The break between the world of the first industrial societies and the world of today comes in that summer of 1914 when the armies began their march to the Marne.

German troops attacking a position under cover of a smoke screen.

BATTLE OF THE MARNE

The decline of the Ottoman Empire presented the Balkan kingdoms – Romania, Serbia, Bulgaria and Greece – with a tempting opportunity: if they could combine they could beat the Turks and the remaining Ottoman territory in Europe would be theirs for the taking. The agreement was soon made and equally quickly broken. Victory over the Ottomans in the First Balkan War (1912–13) was followed by a free-for-all in the Second (summer of 1913) which resulted in the Greeks and Serbs enlarging their territories again, this time at the expense of the Bulgars.

The Serbs had every reason to be satisfied with the outcome of those two wars which had enabled them to gather in all the lands in the south and south-east to which they could reasonably lay claim. The situation in the north was less satisfactory. There the province of Bosnia, with a basically Serb population, had been forcibly and quite illegally annexed by the Austro-Hungarian Empire in 1908. This was a standing affront to Serbian patriots. An underground movement already existed in all these provinces: now that they had secured the frontiers they wanted in the south, the Serbs decided to give it more direct support.

The Austrians did not take the Bosnian underground too seriously. They hoped that a mixture of firmness and friendliness would win over the mass of the people and as part of this programme they arranged for the heir to the throne, the Archduke Franz Ferdinand, to tour the province in the summer of 1914. Serbian intelligence had a copy of the proposed itinerary almost as soon as the Archduke: plans were put in hand to assassinate him as he drove into the Bosnian capital Sarajevo.

Of the six men in the assassination squad only one managed to do his bit when the Archduke's motorcade passed. As the car drew up opposite the fifth member of the assassination squad, a nineteen-year-old student named Gavrilo Princip, he put one bullet into the Archduke and another into the Duchess before taking cyanide himself. The cyanide did not work, but the bullets did: within twenty minutes both Archduke and Duchess were dead.

If the Serbs had intended to destabilize the European situation they could not have made a better move. The Austrians quickly found out that the assassination had been planned in Belgrade and demanded the right to interrogate suspects in the Serbian capital. This was something that no sovereign state could concede and after checking that the Russians would support them, the Serbs refused. Austria mobilized: so did Russia. So did the Germans. So did the French. The assassination of the Archduke had triggered off the confrontation between the Central Powers (Germany and Austria) and the Franco-Russian entente that diplomatists had spent sleepless nights worrying about ever since these alliances had firmed up in the late 1890s.

In early August the generals completed the assembly of their armies. These were larger and more closely packed than ever before. Because of the loss of Alsace Lorraine the French frontier was 15% shorter than it had been in 1870 yet the French had four times as many men to defend it. This posed problems for the German High Command. Faced with a

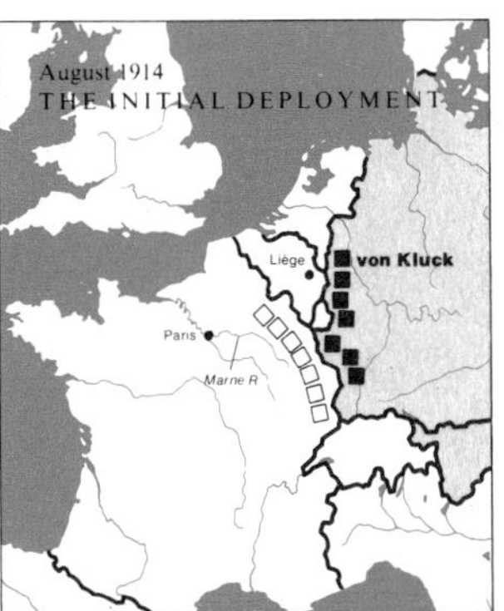

Left and right: The planning and the reality of the 1914 campaign. Note that the number of divisions in action on either side increases from 70 in August to 80 in September. The French got a reinforcement of six with the arrival of the British Expeditionary Force and found another four from their own reserves. The additional divisions were added on the left of their line and it was partly due to them that the Allies won the Battle of the Marne. The Germans were down from the 80 divisions Schlieffen envisaged because Moltke detached ten to the east. They raised an extra ten during August but were not able to deploy them where they were needed, on the right wing, because they could not get them there in time: they had to be used – and largely wasted – in a direct thrust against the French right.

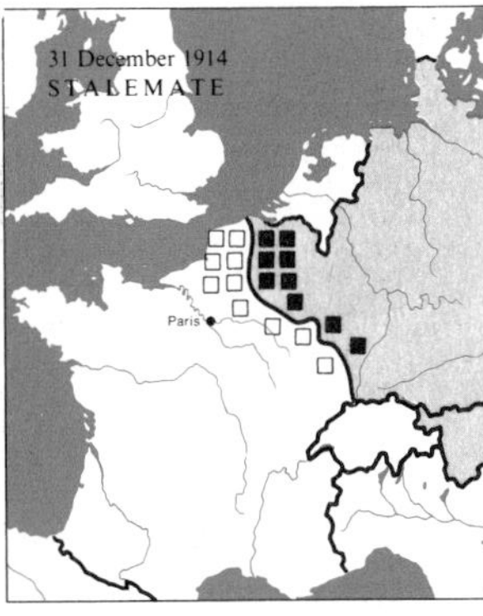

wo-front war, against France and Russia, the German Generals' instinct was to concentrate against France which ould, in theory at least, be knocked out in a single campaign. But how to get through a frontier manned by 60 or more divisions?

Count Schlieffen, who became Chief of the General Staff n 1892, worked out a solution to the problem: he would not go through, he would go round. He would place a mere 30 divisions opposite the French frontier and send 50 through Holland and Belgium. This huge force would fall on the French flank and destroy their army, bringing the war in he west to a speedy end.

Schlieffen's plan meant committing the entire German army to the western front, leaving the Russians unopposed n the east. He felt this was an acceptable risk: the Russians would not get far in the few weeks needed to bring the western campaign to a victorious conclusion and, once this had been done, they would quickly back off. And the entire German army was needed to spread the net around the French army. As Schlieffen said to his corps commanders, 'Let the last man on the right brush the Channel with his sleeve.' Not one French division must escape.

Schlieffen retired in 1906. His successor was Helmuth Moltke. He revised the marching orders of the right wing so that Holland could be left undisturbed and he decided that ten divisions must be kept back to defend the east against the Russians. Schlieffen, hearing of the changes, began to wonder if the new Chief of Staff understood the thinking behind the plan. He sent him memoranda explaining the need to deploy the strongest possible force and was far from reassured by the evasive replies he received. He was still worrying when he died (in 1913): his last words, clearly meant for Moltke, were: 'If nothing else, keep the right wing strong.'

The two weeks between the start of the war (3rd August in the West) and the beginning of the Schlieffen movement (scheduled for the 16th) were a tense time for the German High Command. Would the Belgians let the German army march through their country or would they fight? And would the British commit themselves to the anti-German entente, as they might well feel bound to do if Belgian neutrality was violated? The answers were not long in coming. The Belgians would fight, the Germans would succeed in destroying the frontier forts, and the British would declare war on Germany. On 17th August von Kluck's First Army, began its march through Belgium.

A week later von Kluck was on the Franco-Belgian frontier. He had a two to one superiority over the troops the Allies had scraped together to stop him and it took him only a day to drive them from their positions. A week after that he was still up to schedule. But the armies to his left were finding the going stiffer than he was and had had to narrow their fronts to keep up the momentum of their attacks. The German line as a whole was shortening: von Kluck would have to pass east, not west, of Paris.

On 3rd September he crossed the Marne at a point 64 km due east of Paris. It was there that he was hit on the flank by a French force debouching from the capital. It was not the attack itself that shook the Germans – von Kluck faced about and beat it off without difficulty: it was the discovery that while they had been shortening their front, the French had been lengthening theirs. By using the railways to transfer whole divisions the French had built up the forces till they outnumbered and overlapped von Kluck.

The Schlieffen Plan had failed because the new technology – specifically the vast increase in fire power – had tipped the odds in favour of the defence. For an attack to succeed, more attackers per defender were required than anyone had foreseen, which is why the Germans had had to shorten their line as they advanced and why the French had been able to lengthen theirs as they retreated. At the time, of course, it was the generalship of the two sides that came under scrutiny. Moltke's 'failure of nerve' being contrasted with the complete calm displayed by Joffre, the French Commander. In the case of Joffre the observation was correct, though whether he kept calm because he knew what he was doing (as his admirers believed) or because he never realized how bad things had got (the view taken by his detractors) is a moot point.

Either way, Joffre did what was necessary to win the battle and deserves full credit for that. Even more deserving of credit are the unsung technocrats who insisted on creating an army of sufficient size to hold and extend the French line in the critical days of early September. The French raised as large a force from their 6 million men of military age as the Germans did from their 10 million. Sometimes it is a good idea to fight the next war on the lessons of the last.

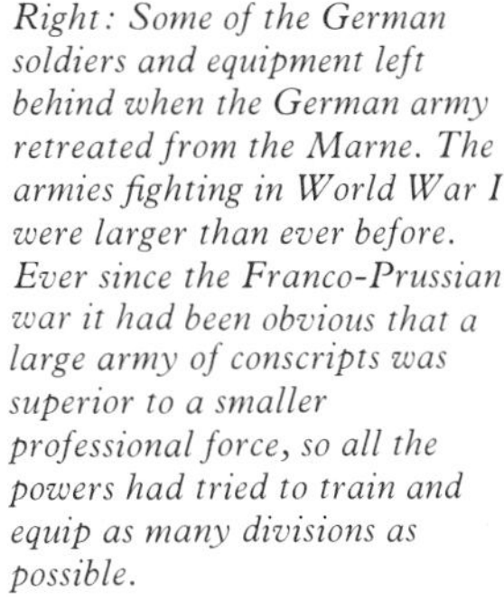

Right: Some of the German soldiers and equipment left behind when the German army retreated from the Marne. The armies fighting in World War I were larger than ever before. Ever since the Franco-Prussian war it had been obvious that a large army of conscripts was superior to a smaller professional force, so all the powers had tried to train and equip as many divisions as possible.

Above: Lenin addressing a gathering crowd from the back of a truck in 1917.

Right: Idealized painting of 'Lenin on the Rostrum' by A. Gerasimov.

Below: Peasants mobbing a train in the riots of 1917. Recreating the success of the railway strike of 1905, the interruption of traffic and communications caused big problems to the already overstretched Russian administration.

Everyone thought the war that began in 1914 would be over in a year or two. The most recent European conflicts – in 1859, 1866 and 1870–71 – had all been short and sharp affairs and the cost of the immense conscript armies that were deployed in 1914 was so horrendous that no one could envisage how to pay for them if hostilities were prolonged. But the way in which defence dominated attack meant that the war did go on and in its third year it seemed to be getting no nearer to military resolution. Paying for it was beginning to strain the banking systems of the most advanced economies: it had proved quite beyond the capacity of the less developed and less competent.

There was no doubt as to which belligerent was least competent, imperial Russia. Its archaic bureaucracy could barely cope in peacetime: its attempts to run a nation at war proved hopelessly inept. The currency had depreciated to the point where the peasantry were refusing to accept it and as a result the towns were running out of food. In the capital – renamed Petrograd in 1914 because St Petersburg sounded too German – the workers were actually starving. In late February 1917* there were serious riots.

Usually the authorities were able to break up unruly crowds easily enough: they simply turned the Cossacks loose. But when they tried it on this occasion the soldiers refused to obey orders: instead of firing on the workers they joined them. The Tsar and his minister abdicated; a western style government was installed.

This was a crucial moment in Russia's history. For all their occasional fits of reform Russian governments had always been despotic: would a liberal regime be able to establish its authority? The Allies were reassuring: if Russia stayed in the fight against Germany they would support Russia through its economic difficulties.

One man challenged their analysis. Lenin, the leader of the Russian Communist Party, saw no reason why the workers should back the new government or its policies – the right course was to end the war immediately so that the people could get on with the job of building a socialist state. Only one thing prevented Lenin expounding this view to the people themselves: he was in exile in Switzerland and had no money for a train ticket home.

Lenin's financial predicament was noted by German Intelligence who thought it well worth the price of a ticket to have him back in Russia – in fact they were prepared to give him and his associates a whole carriage. At the end of March he arrived to a warm welcome from the leaders of the Petrograd Soviet (Workers' Council) as well as from his own party members. But when they heard that the main plank in his programme was an end to the war with Germany most of them shied away from him. The February Revolution had seen an upsurge of Russian patriotism which made suing for peace unthinkable. It was only with great difficulty that Lenin was able to impose his view on his supporters.

Six months later the situation had reversed. Everyone was sick of the war, which was dragging Russia down further every day without doing any significant damage to Germany. Despite all the Allied aid the Russian war machine was falling apart: the economy had collapsed and the people were worse off than ever. The government's political credit was exhausted. Lenin's men had meanwhile gained key positions.

In October Lenin made his move. Sailors from Krondstadt brought the cruiser *Aurora* up the Neva, soldiers from the Petrograd garrison occupied the Winter Palace. Lenin took over the government in the name of the Russian people and the Communist Party. The war was over: so was Russia's brief experiment in liberal democracy.

*Early March by western reckoning. The Russian calendar was 11 days behind the western one and the two events for which 1917 is remembered, the February and October revolutions, actually took place in March and November.

	1914	1915	1916	1917	1918
Politics & Military History	Outbreak of WW1. 28 June: Archduke Ferdinand, heir to Austrian throne, assassinated at Sarajevo brings Balkan tensions to head: Austria-Hungary declares war on Serbia (28 July). 1 Aug: Germany declares war on Russia and France; invades Belgium. 4 Aug: Britain declares war on Germany invoking Belgian neutrality as reason. 5 Aug: Austria declares war on Russia. Russia, Britain and France declare war on Turkey. 26–28 Aug: Germans inflict heavy defeat on Russians at Tannenberg. Germans invade France; their advance on Paris halted at the battle of the Marne. British troops in France. Battle of Ypres (Oct–Nov). Beginning of trench warfare on western front. Irish Home Rule Act provides for separate Parliament in Ireland; the position of Ulster to be decided after the war. Panama Canal is finally opened.	Britain announces naval blockade of Germany. 18 Feb: Germany retaliates with a submarine blockade of Britain. 22 April–25 May: Second Battle of Ypres; poison gas used by Germans for first time. 25 April: Gallipoli Campaign: allied forces land on Gallipoli Peninsula but fail to gain control of the Dardanelles Straits (to 1916). Italy joins war on Allied side. Coalition government is formed in Britain under Asquith. British-French offensive fails. 6 Sept: Bulgaria joins Central Powers. Growing economic and administrative chaos in Russia as result of war.	21 Feb–16 Dec: Battle of Verdun: German offensive on western front, appalling losses on both sides, stalemate continues. 20 Mar: Secret Anglo-French (Sykes-Picot) Agreement on the partition of the Turkish Empire. 24 April: Easter Rising in Ireland is suppressed after a week. 31 May–1 June: Battle of Jutland: only major naval battle between British and German fleets. Royal Navy losses exceed German losses. Brusilov (Russian) offensive in June: fails. 5 June: Sinking of the *Hampshire* and death of Kitchener. 1 July: Battle of the Somme: first use of tanks by Britain; more than 1 million casualties. 27 Aug: Romania and Portugal join the war against Germany. 7 Dec: Lloyd George becomes British Prime Minister of Coalition. USA purchases Virgin Is; US troops land in Santo Domingo, Dominican Republic, and stay till 1924.	The February Revolution in Russia: Tsar Nicholas abdicates, provisional government established. 11 March: British capture Baghdad from Turkey. 6 April: USA declares war on Germany. 31 July–10 Nov: Battle of Passchendaele: major British offensive but little gained after German counter-offensive. 24 Oct: Battle of Caporetto: heavy defeat for the Italians. October Revolution: Bolsheviks overthrow provisional government: Lenin becomes Chief Commissar, Trotsky Commissar for Foreign Affairs. Balfour Declaration: Britain will support a Jewish State in Palestine. 9 Dec: British forces capture Jerusalem.	3 March: Treaty of Brest-Litovsk between Russia and Germany: Russia withdraws from the war. 15 July–4 Aug: The Second Battle of the Marne: last major German offensive, fails by early August. 16 July: Execution of ex-Tsar Nicholas II and family. 18 July: Allied offensive begins: Germans forced into retreat. Battle of Vittorio Veneto: Italian victory, Austria-Hungary surrenders. 9 Nov: Revolution in Germany, Wilhelm II abdicates, Republic declared. 11 Nov: Germany agrees to Armistice, end of WW1. Lenin consolidates power of the Bolshevik government: civil war until 1920. Women over 30 to get vote in Britain. Civil war in Ireland.
Religion & Learning	Clive Bell *Art*.	Toynbee *Nationality and War*.	Lenin *Imperialism*. Dewey *Democracy and Education*. Curtis *The Commonwealth of Nations*.	Lenin *State and Revolution*. Jung *Psychology of the Unconscious*.	Havelock Ellis *The Erotic Rights of Women*. Spengler *Decline of the West* (to 1922). Lytton Strachey *Eminent Victorians*. Russell *Mysticism and Logic*.
Cities & Social Development	Bank of England is authorized to issue paper money in excess of statutory limit.	Rent Restriction Act and Excess Profits Duty: they establish principle of state intervention in Britain. American workers demanding labour rights close down the Colorado Fuel & Iron Co and Rockefeller calls in private army and state militia to put down strikers: Ludlow Massacre.	Compulsory military service introduced in Britain. Food rationing introduced in Germany. 24 US States vote to prohibit alcohol.	Ministry of Labour is established in Britain. British shipping, wool, cotton, food are brought under state control and the government takes over all dollar securities.	Russia adopts metric system and Gregorian Calendar. Bolshevik government nationalizes large-scale industrial enterprises. World-wide influenza epidemic.
Discovery & Invention	Marconi sends wireless telephone messages between Italian ships which are 80 km apart. First Zeppelin air raid on England.	Einstein *General Theory of Relativity*. First automatic telephone exchange in use in Britain. Poison gas and flame-throwers on the war front. Junkers constructs first fighter airplane.	Blood for transfusion purposes is first refrigerated. Langevin constructs an underwater ultrasonic source for submarine detection.	100-inch reflecting telescope is constructed at Mount Wilson, California. Mustard gas comes into use. German twin-engined biplane, the Gotha, is the first designed specially to carry bombs.	Eddington *Gravitation and the Principle of Relativity*.
The Arts	James Joyce *Dubliners*. Paramount is established: Chaplin and de Mille make their first films. Edgar Rice Burroughs *Tarzan of the Apes*. Gide *Les Caves du Vatican*. Vaughan Williams *London Symphony*.	Buchan *The 39 Steps*. W. S. Maugham *Of Human Bondage*. D. W. Griffith *The Birth of a Nation*. Dufy *Homage to Mozart*.	Joyce *Portrait of the Artist as a Young Man*. D. W. Griffith film *Intolerance*. Kafka *Metamorphosis*, short story. Holst *The Planets*. Jazz sweeps through America.	Upton Sinclair *King Coal*. Salzburg Festival is first held in Austria. Prokofiev *Classical Symphony*. Modigliani *Crouching Female Nude*.	Arthur Waley translates two collections of poetry from the Chinese. US Post Office burns instalments of Joyce's *Ulysses* which had appeared in *The Little Review*. Chagall *The Green Violinist*.

	1919	1920	1921	1922	1923
Politics & Military History	Treaty of Versailles: Germany loses Alsace-Lorraine to France and her colonies to the allies and has to pay heavy reparations. The Rhineland is demilitarized and France occupies the Saar coalfields. Treaty of Saint-Germain: end of Habsburg Monarchy; Austria recognizes the independence of Czechoslovakia, Poland, Yugoslavia and Hungary. India: Punjab riots; the Amritsar Massacre; Government of India Act introduces limited democracy. Irish MPs meet as Dail Eirann (Irish executive) with De Valera as President of Sinn Fein. Spartacist Rising in Berlin crushed. Benito Mussolini founds Italian Fascist Movement. Bela Kun forms Soviet Government in Hungary but it is defeated in a counter-revolution. Soviet Republic established in Russia: allied intervention fails as the Red Army defeat counter-revolutionaries.	First meeting of the League of Nations: US Senate votes against American membership. Civil War in Ireland: Northern Ireland (Ulster) accepts Home Rule; British auxiliaries, the Black and Tans, fight against Sinn Fein. Poland and Russia at war: French troops support Poles who invade Ukraine but are driven out by Red Army. Widespread unrest in Italy: demonstrations and strikes lead to downfall of government. Gandhi begins civil disobedience campaign in India. American women are given vote.	Irish Free State established; IRA continue in opposition. Greece goes to war with Turkey but is defeated the following year. Turkish nationalist government is established at Ankara. Treaty of Riga: ends Russo-Polish war. Mutiny of Russian sailors at Kronstadt put down. Washington Conference (to 1922) between USA, Britain, France and Japan sets naval armament limits for the powers. First Anglo-Soviet trade agreement. Beginning of inflation in Germany: rapid fall in value of the Mark.	End of Russian civil war: the OGPU (secret police) are established; Stalin becomes Secretary-General of Communist Party. Fascists March on Rome: King Victor Emmanuel III invites Mussolini to become prime minister. Fall of Lloyd George Coalition in Britain and beginning of 22-year period of Tory ascendancy. Sultan of Turkey is deposed by Mustafa Kemal (Ataturk) who begins the modernization of Turkey. British Protectorate over Egypt is ended.	French and Belgian troops occupy the Ruhr district when Germany fails to pay reparations. Britain grants internal self-government to Southern Rhodesia. Adolf Hitler attempts to overthrow the Bavarian government in Munich but fails and is imprisoned. Mussolini begins to turn Italy into Fascist state. Sun Yat-sen establishes a Chinese Nationalist Government at Guangzhou (Canton) and reorganizes the Kuomintang. Massive inflation in Germany leads to the collapse of the currency.
Religion & Learning	Keynes *The Economic Consequences of the Peace.* Bergson *L'Energie Spirituelle.*	R. H. Tawney *The Acquisitive Society.* Oxford University admits women to degrees.	Lenin *Leftwing Communism an Infantile Disorder.* Lytton Strachey *Victoria.*	G. E. Moore *Philosophical Studies.* Tomb of Tutankhamen is discovered in the Valley of the Kings.	Freud *The Ego and the Id.* Schweitzer *Philosophy of Civilization.*
Cities & Social Development	Widespread industrial unrest on both sides of the Atlantic: steel strike in USA, New York dockworkers strike, railway strike in Britain, industrial unrest in Italy. Britain adopts 48-hour working week.	All factories in Russia employing more than 10 workers nationalized. Prohibition in effect throughout the USA.	Railway Act in Britain amalgamates companies so that only 4 remain. Safeguarding of Industries Act signals the abandonment by Britain of Free Trade. First birth control clinic is established in Britain. Ku Klux Klan becomes increasingly violent in the Southern USA.	BBC is established as a monopoly under Charter: the first regular broadcasts for entertainment go out. American 'cocktail' becomes popular in Europe.	200,000 members of the Ku Klux Klan attend a conclave in Indiana. Canberra is made Federal Capital of Australia. Nevada and Montana become the first US states to introduce old age pension. First publication of *Time* and *Radio Times.*
Discovery & Invention	Alcock and Brown fly non-stop across the Atlantic for first time. London to Paris daily air service is established.	Albert Michelson makes the first accurate measurement of a star (the diameter of Betelgeuse). Marconi in Britain and Westinghouse in the USA open broadcasting stations. Thompson patents submachine gun (Tommy gun).	Chromosome theory of heredity is postulated by T. H. Morgan. Rutherford and Chadwick disintegrate all the elements except carbon, oxygen, lithium and beryllium. A preliminary to splitting the atom.	Banting and Best isolate insulin from the pancreas: it is lifesaving in the treatment of diabetes.	Edwin Hubble, American astronomer, shows there are galaxies beyond the Milky Way. First American broadcasts are heard in Britain. Ross Institute of Tropical Medicine is established in London.
The Arts	Sassoon *War Poems.* Radio Corporation of America (RCA) is established. Jazz arrives in Europe. Walter Gropius founds the Bauhaus and revolutionizes the teaching of the arts, architecture and industrial design.	D. H. Lawrence *Women in Love.* Katherine Mansfield *Bliss and other stories.* Poems of Wilfred Owen are published posthumously. *The Cabinet of Dr Caligari* signals the beginning of the classic period of German Expressionist Cinema. T. S. Eliot *Poems.* Sinclair Lewis *Main Street.* Matisse *L'Odalisque.*	Arthur Waley translates *The Nō plays of Japan.* Chaplin *The Kid*, first full length film. Prokofiev *The Love for three Oranges*, opera.	T. S. Eliot *The Waste Land.* Joyce's *Ulysses* is published in Paris. Virginia Woolf *Jacob's Room.* F. Scott Fitzgerald *The Beautiful and the Damned.* Sinclair Lewis *Babbitt.*	Aldous Huxley *Antic Hay.* Films: Harold Lloyd *Safety Last*, von Stronheim *Greed.* P. G. Wodehouse *The Inimitable Jeeves.* Gershwin *Rhapsody in Blue.* Le Corbusier *Towards a new Architecture.* Jazz: King Oliver's Creole Jazz Band *Dippermouth Blues.* James P. Johnson *Charleston* starts new dance craze.

In March 1918 the German High Command launched the first in a series of offensives designed to win the war before the Americans could intervene in significant strength. Massing 70 specially trained 'assault divisions' opposite one of the British sectors of the Western Front, General Ludendorff smashed through the trench system that had locked the combatants together for the previous three years and reached open country. But the machine gun soon reasserted its mastery over the battlefield and as the casualty list lengthened and the advance slowed, Ludendorff was forced to admit that his attempt to put an end to the war of attrition and start a new war of movement, had failed. Rather than let the offensive degenerate into the usual slogging match he called it off and struck again at another sector of the line. Once again he won a striking tactical success but no strategic advantage. And his third blow was not only weaker, it was parried by fresh American troops. The implications for the German side were obvious: the war was now unwinnable.

This had become obvious to Germany's allies too and one by one they deserted the once mighty Reich. By early November it was clear that disorder threatened Germany itself: the sailors were mutinous, the soldiers disinclined to fight for the Kaiser any longer. There was nothing for it but to accept the armistice offered by President Wilson even though the terms of this amounted to complete surrender.

There was one mitigating circumstance. President Wilson had declared that the frontiers of post-war Europe would be decided by its people, not its politicians. Self-determination was to be the guiding principle: plebiscites would make clear the people's will. On this basis Germany would not do too badly – which, of course, is why the Germans had chosen to deal with President Wilson and not his European allies. True, the President had indicated that there were exceptions Alsace-Lorraine would have to go back to France and the new Polish state must be given access to the sea: but if he stuck to his principles, Germany should emerge from the war clipped rather than shorn.

And that, in a geographical sense, is what happened. Besides Alsace-Lorraine and the Polish provinces – the exact limits of which were determined by plebiscites in 1920–21 – the only territory the Germans lost was North Schleswig where Bismarck had long ago promised to have a plebiscite and then proceeded to forget all about it. In 1920 the people there were balloted and a majority of them chose to rejoin the Danish Kingdom. Of course, in addition to her territorial losses Germany was made to promise to pay huge reparations to the Allies – more than she could actually bear, according to some – but in a political sense her punishment was relatively light.

The fate of the Austro-Hungarian Empire was formal dismemberment. Three entirely new states emerged from this procedure: Austria, Hungary and Czechoslovakia. In the south the Slav provinces Croatia, Slovenia and Bosnia were incorporated into the greater Serbia whose proponents had engineered the war in the first place: Serbia consequently became the Kingdom of the Serbs, Croats and Slovenes before making a final change of name to Yugoslavia (South Slav Land) in 1929. Other provinces went to Poland (which got Galicia), Romania (Transylvania) and Italy (the Tyrol).

The Treaty of Versailles gave Poland a relatively modest eastern frontier which the Poles, seeing that Russia was in the throes of civil war, decided they could improve on. And so they did, occupying and holding on to a substantial amount of territory to which the Russians had, to say the least, an equal claim. The Greeks in attempting to exploit the rather similar situation that had arisen in Turkey, did less well. The army they landed at Smyrna was eventually routed by Atatürk who re-established Turkey's rule over the whole of Anatolia. The dream of a revived Greek Empire with Constantinople for its capital, vanished like summer smoke.

Above: The signing of the Treaty of Versailles in the Hall of Mirrors, with Wilson, Clemenceau and Lloyd George representing the allied powers.

At one of the less formal meetings a German delegate, speculating on what history would say about the admittedly complex causes of the war, received a memorable bit of Georges Clemenceau's mind. 'It will say many things, Monsieur,' he rasped, 'but it will never say that Belgium invaded Germany.' And that is really the size of it: it is the bully who is to blame for the fight.

Below left: The Gallic cock triumphant. A French disinfectant manufacturer combines advertising and exultation by showing Premier Georges Clemenceau using the firm's product on a captive Germany.

EXTRAIT DE JAVEL LE COQ GAULOIS
LE MEILLEUR DES PRODUITS DE BLANCHIMENT ET DE NETTOYAGE
DESINFECTANT ET ANTISEPTIQUE DE PREMIER ORDRE (en bouteilles et bonbonnes)
ESSIVE LE COQ GAULOIS
FABRIQUE DE PRODUITS CHIMIQUES
R. GUICHARD
47.48.49.50 RUE DUBOURDIEU BORDEAUX

Top: Papa Celestin's Original Tuxedo Orchestra, New Orleans 1928. The Celestin band opened at the Tuxedo Dancehall in 1910 but only got the Tuxedo suits that became their trade mark in 1917 when they found a tailor who would let them pay his bill by playing advertising spots.

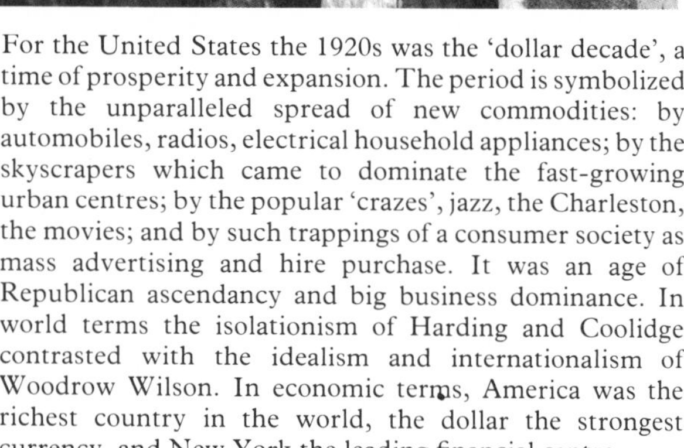

For the United States the 1920s was the 'dollar decade', a time of prosperity and expansion. The period is symbolized by the unparalleled spread of new commodities: by automobiles, radios, electrical household appliances; by the skyscrapers which came to dominate the fast-growing urban centres; by the popular 'crazes', jazz, the Charleston, the movies; and by such trappings of a consumer society as mass advertising and hire purchase. It was an age of Republican ascendancy and big business dominance. In world terms the isolationism of Harding and Coolidge contrasted with the idealism and internationalism of Woodrow Wilson. In economic terms, America was the richest country in the world, the dollar the strongest currency, and New York the leading financial centre.

All this had happened quite quickly, and the very speed of change added to the euphoria which characterized the age. The First World War had given to the Americans a period of accelerating growth and wealth at a time when the economies of Britain, France, Germany, and the other major belligerents were being bled by conflict. The contrast was noted by a European observer in 1927: 'One could feed a whole country in the Old World on what America wastes. American ideas of extravagance, comfort and frugality are entirely different from European.'

Nothing dominated the era so much as the city and the car. In 1890 America had been predominantly rural, still a frontier society; by 1930 it was urban both statistically and, more important, in psychology. Nearly half the population lived within easy access to a town of 100,000 or more, and visits by car to movie houses and supermarkets became a way of life for millions. In 1918 there were already 9 million cars in use; a decade later there were 26 million, with annual sales reaching four million. Many of these cars were Fords, and 'Fordism' became a new word, encompassing mass

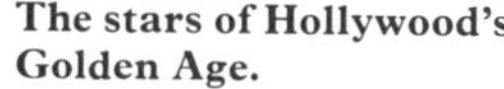

The stars of Hollywood's Golden Age.

Above left: Douglas Fairbanks Snr. as Robin Hood (1922).

Above right: Charlie Chaplin in The Gold Rush (1925).

Below: Chaplin, Mary Pickford and Fairbanks hamming it up for the benefit of photographers. The three of them had a lot to laugh about: they were the major shareholders in United Artists which made them dollar millionaires many times over.

production techniques and big business philosophy. B this time, too, there were some 13 million radios i American homes. The first broadcasting station ha opened in Pittsburgh in 1920; by 1940 there were nearl 900 radio stations and 52 million sets in use. The 1920s was too, the great era of the silent films, of Mary Pickford Charlie Chaplin, and Douglas Fairbanks. With th introduction of sound in 1927 audiences at cinema multiplied even faster until, by 1937, the movies were th fourteenth largest business in the country and Hollywoo was known the world over.

Prosperity and optimism was not for all. The rich grew richer, but there was a growing disparity of wealth. The to 5 per cent of the population received over one quarter of al incomes by 1928. Although on average American rea incomes grew by 25% per head in the 1920s, man segments of the population, the Blacks in the South and th growing numbers in the urban ghettos, for example, wer often miserably poor. Farmers, too, did not share in th general prosperity, for farm prices were falling and debt mounting. Big business, aided by a government fearful o socialist movements, set its face against organized labour The growth of the Ku Klux Klan in the South emphasize the intolerance and social divides which were part an parcel of American society in the 1920s.

Many Americans felt that they had found the secret t everlasting prosperity in the 1920s, and the many signs o impending disaster were lost in the glare of achievement which were so enthralling and seemed so permanent. In hi nomination address in March 1929, President Hoove asserted that 'We in America today are nearer to the fina triumph over poverty than ever before in the history of an land,' and he promised 'four more years of prosperity.' Si months later came the Wall Street Crash. *(M.F.)*

	1924	1925	1926	1927	1928
Politics & Military History	First Labour Government in Britain (Ramsay Macdonald) lasts from 23 Jan. to 4 Nov. Dawes Plan: an attempt to make reparations from Germany practicable; it fails to work. The death of Lenin: Stalin succeeds him. Chinese National Government recognizes the Soviet Union; Britain recognizes the USSR. Saudis conquer Arabia (to 1925). Italian elections produce Fascist majority; socialist Giacomo Matteotti murdered.	Locarno Conference: great powers agree to put disputes to arbitration and guarantee Germany's western frontiers. Italian dictatorship established and the Judiciary loses its independence, trade unions suppressed. French troops evacuate Ruhr. New dynasty is established in Persia: Reza Khan Pahlevi becomes Shah. Anti-colonial uprising in Morocco led by Abd-el-Krim crushed by France and Spain.	General Strike in Britain. Germany joins League of Nations. Trotskyists and Zinoviev are expelled from Russian Politburo. Ibn Saud becomes King of Saudi Arabia.	Labour Charter in Italy: Fascist unions to be sole representatives of the workers, strikes and lock-outs made illegal. De Valera establishes new Irish political party, Fianna Fail. Trotsky exiled. Black Friday in Germany as the economy collapses. Jiang Jieshi purges the Nationalist Party of Communists: civil war between Nationalists and Communists.	Jiang Jieshi captures Beijing; unification of Republican China. British women over 21 allowed to vote. Kellogg-Briand Pact in Paris: great powers renounce war, 65 nations sign. Outbreak of the Chaco War between Bolivia and Paraguay (lasts to 1935). Launching of the first Russian Five Year Plan.
Religion & Learning	Ivor Richards *Principles of Literary Criticism.* Primitive human remains one million years old, *Australopithecus africanus*, are discovered in South Africa.	Hebrew University is established at Jerusalem. Harold Laski *Grammar of Politics.*	Julian Huxley *Essays in Popular Science.* Tawney *Religion and the Rise of Capitalism.*	Martin Heidegger *Sein und Zeit* (Time and Being). Russell *The Analysis of Matter.*	Jung *Relationships between the Ego and the Unconscious.*
Cities & Social Development	Nina Bang is the first woman to obtain cabinet rank in a western government as Minister of Education in Denmark. Crown Colony is established in Northern Rhodesia: the end of British South Africa Co control. Ford Motor Co produces its 10 millionth car.	Britain returns to the gold standard. European industrial output reaches the level of 1913 again. *Charleston* dance becomes fashionable.	Adoption of children is legalized in Britain. Unemployment insurance introduced in Germany. British Imperial Chemical Industries (ICI) founded.	Trade Disputes Act and Trade Union Act in Britain make general strikes illegal and curb union powers. In Canada aeroplanes are first used to dust crops with insecticides.	Turkey adopts European alphabet. In the USA work begins on the Boulder Dam, Colorado River. Russia reaches level of her pre-war industrial production. Collapse of the Brazilian economy because of the over-production of coffee. Teleprinters and teletypewriters begin to come into use in the USA, Britain and Germany.
Discovery & Invention	Chrysler produces his first car; he founds the Chrysler Corporation in 1925. British Imperial Airways begin operations: taken over by BOAC in 1940. Eddington discovers that the luminosity of a star is related to its mass.	John Logie Baird transmits recognizable human features on television screen. Schoolteacher, Scopes, is tried in Tennessee for violating the law prohibiting the teaching of evolution: convicted but acquitted on a technicality.	Byrd makes the first aeroplane flight to the North Pole. Kodak produces the first 16mm movie film.	Lindbergh makes first solo flight across the Atlantic. Pavlov *Conditioned Reflexes.*	Fleming discovers penicillin which destroys bacteria: the first antibiotic.
The Arts	Melville *Billy Budd* and other prose pieces (posthumous). Forster *A Passage to India.* de Mille *The 10 Commandments*, film. Emily Dickinson *The Complete Poems*, posthumous. The Tsukiji Little Theatre opens in Tokyo: the beginning of modern Japanese theatre.	T. S. Eliot *The Hollow Men.* Alban Berg *Wozzeck*, opera. Eisenstein *Battleship Potemkin*, film, Chaplin *The Gold Rush.* T. Dreiser *An American Tragedy.* S. Fitzgerald *The Great Gatsby.* Kafka *The Trial*, posthumous. Noel Coward *Hay Fever.* Shostakovich 1st Symphony.	Kafka *The Castle*, posthumous. Colette *La fin de Chéri.* Disney arrives in Hollywood, Laurel and Hardy come together. Epstein *The Visitation.* Klee *Around the Fish.* Jazz: Jelly Roll Morton *Original Jelly Roll Blues.*	Yeats *Sailing to Byzantium.* Sinclair Lewis *Elmer Gantry.* Cocteau *Orphée* and *Oedipe-Roi.* Hesse *Steppenwolf.* Braque *Glass and Fruit.* *Jazz: Bix Beiderbecke Playin' the Blues.* Duke Ellington opens at The Cotton Club, Harlem. Meade Lux Lewis Honky Tonk Train Blues.	D. H. Lawrence *Lady Chatterley's Lover.* Waugh *Decline and Fall.* Woolf *Orlando.* Ravel *Bolero.* Brecht and Weill collaborate on *The Threepenny Opera.* Films: King Vidor *The Crowd*, Eisenstein *October* and the first Mickey Mouse film *Steamboat Willie.* Sholokov *And Quiet Flows the Don* (4 volumes to 1940). Jazz: Louis Armstrong *West End Blues.* Duke Ellington *Mood Indigo.*

	1929	1930	1931	1932	1933
Politics & Military History	Wall Street crash precipitates world depression. Lateran Treaty: Pope recognizes Mussolini's fascist government in return for the establishment of Roman Catholicism as the Italian state religion. Young Plan reassessing German reparations replaces the Dawes Plan. Anti-British riots in Palestine and the first major Jewish-Arab clashes. Strict rationing in USSR used to stimulate productivity. Salazar begins what is to be an almost 50 year dictatorship in Portugal.	Last French troops leave the Rhineland: France begins the construction of the Maginot Line of defences against Germany. 107 National Socialists (Nazis) are elected to the German Reichstag. Socialists win 143 seats and Communists 77. London Naval Treaty: the great powers fail to agree on naval limitations. Destruction of the Russian Kulaks as their property and equipment seized for collective farms. President Hoover agrees the Smoot-Hawley high trade tariff despite warnings from economists of world reprisals.	Statute of Westminster: the British Dominions become fully independent sovereign states. National (coalition) Government established in Britain which comes off gold standard. London Round Table Conference of India: Gandhi insists upon all-Indian government but is opposed by Muslims. Japanese occupy Manchuria and set up puppet state (Manchukuo) in 1932.	F. D. Roosevelt elected President of USA. Ottawa Imperial Conference: Britain gives trading preferences to Commonwealth members. Import Duties Act: Britain abandons Free Trade. Moseley founds British Union of Fascists. Falange is founded in Spain. Indian Congress is declared illegal: Gandhi arrested.	Adolf Hitler appointed Chancellor of Germany by President Hindenberg: the Reichstag fire in Berlin; the Enabling Law gives Hitler dictatorial powers; the first concentration camps; Germany becomes one party state. Germany leaves the League of Nations. Stalin carries out a purge of Communist Party in USSR. Fulham East by-election in London is won by a Pacifist. US Congress grants wide powers to President Roosevelt who launches *New Deal.*
Religion & Learning	Museum of Modern Art is established in New York. Ortega y Gasset *The revolt of the Masses.*	Keynes *A Treatise on Money.* Leavis *Mass Civilization and Minority Culture.*	Schweitzer *My Life and Thoughts.*	Trotsky *History of the Russian Revolution* (to 1933). Croce *Storia d'Europa nel secolo decimono.*	Freud's books are burnt in Berlin: Nazis attack modernism. Jung *Modern Man in search of a soul.* A. N. Whitehead *Adventures of Ideas.*
Cities & Social Development	Hunger march of unemployed Glasgow workers to London. St Valentine's Day Massacre in the USA sets style in gangsterism.	Youth Hostels Association (YHA) founded. Chrysler Building in New York reaches 319m. In USA there is one car for every 1.3 households.	Collapse of the German banking system – 3,000 banks close. Empire State Building in New York 381m high completed. Unemployment in Germany reaches 5.66m.	Slump grows worse in the USA: 5,000 banks close, unemployment rises. Great Hunger March of unemployed to London. Unemployment is estimated at 30m world-wide.	Prohibition repealed in USA. Growing famine in the USSR.
Discovery & Invention	The first regional broadcasting station is set up in Britain; the BBC begins experimental television programmes. Einstein *Unified Field Theory.* James Jeans *The Universe around us.*	Theiler produces a serum against yellow fever in USA. Crash of British airship R101 makes Britain abandon airship production. Tombaugh discovers the planet Pluto.	Radio waves from the Milky Way are detected (Jansky). Vickers-Armstrong produce amphibious tanks. Cockcroft develops a high voltage apparatus for atomic transmutations.	Cockcroft and Walton artificially accelerate particles, disintegrating a nucleus.	Eddington *The Expanding Universe.* ICI scientists discover polythene.
The Arts	Graves *Goodbye to all that.* Axel Munthe *The Story of San Michele.* Woolf *A Room of one's own.* Bunuel and Dali *Un Chien Andalou,* classic or surrealist cinema. Hemingway *A Farewell to Arms.* Braque *The round table.* Picasso *Woman in a red armchair.* Chagall *Love Idyll.* Epstein *Night and Day,* sculpture. Le Corbusier *The City of Tomorrow.* Jazz: Louis Armstrong *Knocking a Jug.* Thomas "Fats" Waller *Ain't Misbehavin'.* Bessie Smith *Nobody knows you when you're down and out.*	Robert Frost *Collected Poems.* W. H. Auden *Poems.* W. S. Maugham *Cakes and Ale.* A major year for cinema: *All Quiet on the Western Front, The Blue Angel, Sous les Toits de Paris, Little Caesar* (the first major American gangster film). Estimated 250m people a week visit the cinema worldwide (115m in the USA).	Woolf *The Waves.* Epstein *Genesis.* Films: Rene Clair, *Le Million,* Chaplin *City Lights,* Cagney in *The Public Enemy.* O'Neill *Mourning becomes Electra.* W. Walton *Belshazzar's Feast.* Utrillo *Montmartre.*	Sir Thomas Beecham establishes the London Philharmonic Orchestra. Huxley *Brave New World.* Films: *Scarface, The Music Box* with Laurel and Hardy. Faulkner *This Earth.* Hemingway *Death in the Afternoon.* Prokofiev Piano Concerto No. 5. Jazz: Sidney Bechet and Tommy Ladnier form The New Orelans Feetwarmers.	Artists and writers begin to leave Germany (about 60,000 between 1933 and 1939). Malraux *La Condition Humaine.* Films: Marx Brothers, *Duck Soup, King Kong, The Private Life of Henry VIII.* Gertrude Stein *The Autobiography of Alice B. Toklas.* Balanchine and Kirstein found School of American Ballet. Matisse *The Dance.*

Above left: Crowds gather outside the New York Stock Exchange in October 1929 as the Great Bull Market suddenly turns into the Wall Street Crash.

Above right: As the depression tightened its hold on the US economy the number of unemployed rose until by 1933 it had reached nearly 13 million – one in four of the labour force. Many of these millions had no resources at all and were dependent on handouts for their daily bread.

The depression which hit nearly every country in the world between 1929 and 1933 was the fiercest ever known. It struck first in America, and it was in that country, together with Germany, that its impact was felt most deeply.

The Wall Street crash of October 1929 did not cause the slump, though it certainly contributed. The causes of the slump lay deep in the American economy and society and in the problems which affected the world economic edifice in the aftermath of the First World War.

Briefly, we may identify three major reasons for the depression. One was the very real internal weaknesses which existed in the American economy, notwithstanding the facade of prosperity in the 1920s. Second was the level and nature of international indebtedness. Countries like Germany and Austria had borrowed far too much for their unhealthy economies to repay, many of the loans coming from America. Once anything happened to dry up the supply of further loans (like the slump) such countries immediately encountered repayment difficulties. Resulting measures such as tariff protection, currency deprivation and inconvertibility, deflationary budgets, and so on, simply added to the problems by causing declining world trade and further difficulties. Such was America's importance in the world economy that her slump was bound to have repercussions everywhere.

During 1928 and for much of 1929 the American stock market boomed in an orgy of speculative fever. Much of the buying was done on credit so that when, in the space of a few days in October 1929, millions of dollars were wiped from share values, thousands became instant bankrupts. As confidence sagged, the already flagging economy spiralled downwards still further. Unemployment mounted and output fell.

The cold statistics are eloquent enough. By the summer of 1932 – the low point of the depression – industrial production and national income were half of the average 1929 levels. Particular industries fared worse than others. Motor car production was a mere 9% of former levels, machine tools 8%. Unemployment soared, from about a million in 1929 to beyond 15 million, and at least one worker in every four had no job. Prices and wages fell too. Wholesale farm prices fell by nearly two thirds and all other prices by about one quarter. Weekly earnings for factory workers fell from about \$25 in 1929 to \$17 in 1932, while the farm labourers' wages fell by half. Many farmers were destitute, as total farm income plunged from \$7,000 million to \$2,000 million. A further twist to the depression came in February 1933 with a major banking collapse. By March 1, when Roosevelt was inaugurated as the new American President, nearly every bank in the country had closed its doors.

In the eight days before his inauguration, more than \$1,500,000,000 had been drawn from the banks. In his inaugural address Roosevelt tried to dispel the fear in people's minds. 'This great nation will endure as it has endured, will revive and will prosper. So first of all let me assert my firm belief that the only thing we have to fear is fear itself.' Remarkably this speech helped to restore confidence. On March 6 he issued a proclamation closing all the nation's banks and called Congress to meet in special session. Three days later, both House and Senate passed the Emergency Banking Relief Act, empowering the administration to strengthen sound banks and reopen them. Weaker banks were to remain closed. By March 12 three-quarters of the banks reopened, and within a month \$1,000,000,000 of hoarded money had been redeposited in them.

Attempts by the government to improve matters were hopelessly inadequate. There was no direct Federal aid for the unemployed, and some cities, faced with mounting expenditures and dwindling revenues, went bankrupt. Chicago, for example, was unable to pay its teachers and municipal workers by the middle of 1932, and still less could it help its 700,000 unemployed. A joke at the time told of a stroller on Broadway who, seeing a huge queue outside a cinema showing Chaplin's *City Lights* asked 'What's that, a breadline or a bank?' In this, the world's greatest industrial nation, breadlines and soup kitchens symbolized the age. Children grew up without fresh milk, without shoes, and reached working age without hope of work.

Roosevelt, unlike Hoover, believed in government action. His so-called 'New Deal' included spending on public works, organizing relief for the unemployed, and measures to check falling prices, like restricting farm support and encouraging industries to rationalize production. From 1933 most indices of economic activity did indeed show improvement, though how much was due to the New Deal is debatable. Certainly America's emergence from the trough of depression was slow and painful. In 1934 and 1935 more than ten millions were still unemployed. Even in the best year before the war, 1937, the figure was above 7 million. National income, prices, international trade and industrial production (except in 1937) never regained their 1929 levels before the close of the decade. As Roosevelt himself said in 1937, one third of the nation was still 'ill-nourished, ill-clad, ill-housed'. *(M.F.)*

Above right: Stage managing fanaticism. Members of the Hitler Youth salute the Fuehrer as he drives round the stadium at Nuremberg.

Above: More special effects. Albert Speer brought searchlights from all over Germany to create this spectacular backdrop for the 1936 rally.

Far right: Cover of the German satirical magazine Kladderadatsch. The Angel of Peace suggests to the members of the Nobel Committee that they award the 1935 Peace Price to her 'good friend' Adolph Hitler.

Right: Arrest of a red activist, Essen 1920. The Nazis were not the only party trying to overthrow the Republic: the communists had a great deal of support, particularly in the working class districts of the Ruhr.

For Germany, defeat in the First World War brought not just material loss but bewilderment. The army that had been held up as invincible was beaten, the Imperial government was no more, and in its place the Allies were offering democratic forms that seemed hardly strong enough to hold the state together. Particularly in view of the seductive talk of a dictatorship of the masses coming from the Comintern leaders in Moscow. Should Germans turn west, or east, or back into the past?

The militarily minded – and there were many of them in a country where the army had always had an important role – were all for a return to the good old days. Associations of ex-servicemen formed with aims that extended far beyond the usual interest of veterans: they sneered at the government, fought the communists in the streets, staged bellicose rallies and even attempted the odd local coup. One such, in Bavaria in 1923, brought Adolph Hitler, the leader of the National Socialist (Nazi) group briefly into prominence, though not to power: arrested after the coup's failure he was given a sentence of 5 years' imprisonment and actually served 9 months of it.

The antics of the Nazis and other similar outfits of uniformed bully-boys were embarrassing but not as yet alarming: the majority of Germans gave their support to the new republic and were prepared to give democratic institutions a fair try. What was alarming from the start was Germany's financial plight. The Kaiser's government, never dreaming that Germany could lose the war, made no attempt to pay for it at the time on the grounds that when it was over the Allies could be made to foot the bill. Now with the war lost the German people were being asked to find the money to meet the Allies' bills as well as their own, a truly

colossal sum which most experts agreed was beyond their capacity to pay.

There being no responsible way of solving this problem Germany's new leaders did what they had to: they borrowed abroad to meet the reparations bills and they printed money to meet the internal debt. Soon they were printing so much money that the currency became worthless. In the process the war-debt vanished but though this enabled the government to balance its budget it had its price in social terms: the middle classes who had seen their savings wiped out in the hyper-inflation, began to withdraw their trust. Worse was to come. In 1929, just as the economy was finally beginning to pick up, the shock wave from the Wall Street Crash reached Europe. Banks collapsed, factories closed, the dole queues lengthened.

The slump was the making of the Nazi party. In 1929 it held only a derisory 12 seats in the 600-seat Reichstag. In the 1930 elections, with unemployment rising past the 3 million mark, it increased its share to 107 seats: in 1932, with unemployment nearing 6 million, it emerged as easily the most powerful political force in the country, winning no less than 230 seats. On this basis Hitler was appointed Chancellor in early 1933, a position he soon transformed into the autocratic one of Fuehrer (Leader). The days of democracy in Germany were over: a reactionary nationalism was now the driving force.

It is difficult to say precisely where brass bands end and evil begins, but there were already plenty of signs that even in the half-mad world of German extremism the Nazi ideology was something special. The cult of brutality for its own sake, the tormenting of the Jews, the explicit fantasies of a future in which an Aryan master-race lorded it over all lesser breeds, were warnings of what was to come, a time of terror for any nation – and that included Germany – so unfortunate as to fall under Nazi rule.

	1934	1935	1936	1937	1938
Politics & Military History	Further purges in USSR. Death of President Hindenburg; Hitler becomes Fuehrer of Germany; Night of the Long Knives when 200 SA men, supporters of Roehm, are murdered. Nazis assassinate the Austrian Chancellor Dollfuss; von Schusnigg comes to power after a Nazi putsch fails. Civil Works Emergency Relief Act in the USA is part of New Deal. Mao Zedong leads the Chinese Communists northwards from Jiangxi on the Long March: they reach Yan'an in Shaanxi province in 1935. Allies evacuate the Rhineland and in the Saar Plebiscite there is a 90 per cent vote for reunion with Germany.	Hitler renounces Treaty of Versailles and announces a policy of rearmament; the Luftwaffe is formed. Nuremberg Laws: legitimize anti-semitism – the persecution of the Jews begins. Hoare-Laval Pact: British and French foreign ministers sanction Italy's plans to invade Abyssinia. Russia and the Comintern approve a policy of a Popular Front against Fascism. Italy invades Abyssinia; the League of Nations mounts ineffective economic sanctions. Treason Trials in Russia (to 1938): Zinoviev, Kamenev, and Radek Army Generals executed. Government of India Act: Burma separated from India and the Indian Constitution reshaped.	Abdication Crisis in Britain: Edward VIII is succeeded by George VI. Italian forces capture Addis Ababa and annex Ethiopia. Germany and Japan form Anti-Comintern Pact. Germany remilitarizes the Rhineland and Hitler denounces Locarno Pact. Spanish Civil War: the Falange led by Franco revolts against Popular Front Coalition: Germany and Italy back Franco. Hitler and Mussolini establish the Rome-Berlin Axis.	Chamberlain becomes British Prime Minister and follows policy of appeasement of Hitler. Plot to overthrow French Third Republic fails; collapse of Popular Front. Spanish Civil War: dissension splits Republicans; the Government moves to Barcelona; German planes bomb Guernica. Pact of Saadabad: sets frontiers between Turkey, Iraq, Afghanistan and Iran. Italy joins Anti-Comintern pact. Japanese forces invade China, seize Shanghai and Beijing; Jiang Jieshi and Mao Zedong collaborate against Japanese.	Japan continues the subjugation of China: installs a puppet Chinese government at Nanjing and Japanese forces take Guangzhou (Canton) and Hankou. Germany invades and annexes Austria. Further anti-Semitic legislation in Germany; Kristallnacht of anti-semitic riots – about 30,000 Jews arrested. Munich Pact: Hitler, Mussolini, Chamberlain and Daladier agree that Germany should take the German speaking Sudetenland of Czechoslovakia. Franco begins his offensive in Catalonia after his forces reach Madrid. Anti-semitic legislation is passed in Italy. Eden and Duff Cooper resign from British government over appeasement.
Religion & Learning	Toynbee embarks upon his *Study of History*.	A. J. Ayer *Language, Truth and Logic*. Haldane *Philosophy of a Biologist*.	Keynes *The General Theory of Employment, Interest and Money*. Ford Foundation established in USA.	Religious persecution takes place in Germany: Protestant and Roman Catholic priests arrested. Nuffield College established at Oxford. Trotsky *The Revolution Betrayed*.	Trevelyan *The English Revolution*. Santayana *The realm of truth*.
Cities & Social Development	Workmen's Compensation Act in Britain now covers industrial diseases. Depression shows signs of easing.	US Labour Relations Act: labour is allowed to organize freely. Hore-Belisha introduces pedestrian crossings and speed limits for built-up areas in Britain. London adopts a green belt scheme. Moscow underground train system opened.	SS *Queen Mary* makes her maiden voyage. BBC inaugurates a television service.	Billy Butlin opens his first holiday camp. Brutal anti-union measures adopted by the Ford Motor Corporation in the USA; steel strike in Chicago – 4 killed, 84 injured.	Principle of paid holidays established in Britain. Fair Labor Standards Act in USA fixes minimum and maximum wages and abolishes child labour.
Discovery & Invention	Beebe descends 800 metres under the ocean in a bathysphere.	Watson-Watt originates a plan for radio pulse-echo aircraft detection which leads to radar.	Boulder Dam completed in USA – creates Lake Mead, largest reservoir in the world.	Mitchell designs the Spitfire (to 1937). Zeppelin *Hindenburg* is destroyed by fire in USA.	Discovery of a new nickel-chrome alloy to be used in jet engines. First practical ball-point pen is produced by the Hungarian journalist, Lajos Biro. HMS *Rodney* is first ship to be equipped with radar.
The Arts	Graves *I, Claudius* and *Claudius the God*. Films: *The Scarlet Empress, Triumph of the Will, Flying Down to Rio* (the first Rogers-Astaire film). Glyndebourne Festival Theatre opens. First Soviet Writers' Congress is held in Moscow under Maxim Gorki.	Gershwin *Porgy and Bess*. T. S. Eliot *Murder in the Cathedral*. Films: *A Night at the Opera, Top Hat*. Clifford Odets *Waiting for Lefty*. Gollancz establishes the Left Book Club in London. Jazz: The Benny Goodman Trio *After You've Gone*. Swing replaces Jazz, with Benny Goodman as the King of Swing.	Huxley *Eyeless in Gaza*. Films: *Modern Times*, Chaplin *Fury*, Lang (his first after fleeing Nazi Germany) *Mr Deeds goes to Town*. Shostakovich 4th Symphony (but it is withdrawn during rehearsal for being anti-Soviet). Rachmaninoff 3rd Symphony. Prokofiev *Peter and the Wolf*. Dylan Thomas *Twenty-five Poems*.	Orwell *The Road to Wigan Pier*. *Cinecitta Studios* open in Rome. Steinbeck *Of Mice and Men*. Carl Orff *Carmina Burana*. Picasso *Guernica*. Jazz: Count Basie *One O'clock Jump*.	Orwell *Homage to Catalonia*. Films: Eisenstein *Alexander Nevsky*, Hitchcock *The Lady Vanishes*, Disney (570 artists) *Snow White and the Seven Dwarfs*. Isherwood *Goodbye to Berlin*.

	1939	1940	1941	1942	1943
Politics & Military History	Spanish Civil War: Nationalists capture Barcelona; Madrid surrenders and war ends. Britain, France and USA recognize the Franco government; Spain joins the Anti-Comintern Pact and leaves the League of Nations. Germany annexes Czechoslovakia. Germany concludes alliance with Italy and non-aggression pact with USSR. Italy invades Albania. 1 Sept: Germany invades Poland and annexes Danzig. 3 Sept: Britain and France declare war as of 5pm and British Expeditionary Force (BEF) sent to France (11 Sept). 6 Sept: First enemy air raid on Britain. 14 Oct: HMS *Royal Oak* sunk in Scapa Flow with loss of 810 lives. 8 Nov: USSR invades Finland. USA declares its neutrality. Women and children are evacuated from London. 13–17 Dec: Battle of the River Plate.	9 April: Germany invades Denmark and Norway; 10 May: Invades Belgium, the Netherlands and Luxembourg. 11 May: National Government formed under Churchill. 24 May: Germany invades France. 27 May: Belgian army capitulates on King Leopold's orders. 27 May–4 June: British army evacuated from Dunkirk, 299 British warships and 420 other vessels under constant attack evacuate 335,490 officers and men. 10 June: Italy joins the war against Britain and France. Governments in exile establish themselves in Britain. Germany, Japan and Italy sign economic and military pact. 25 June: the Fall of France. 7 Sept: Germany launches bombing blitz against Britain. 15 Sept: Battle of Britain ends with British victory. End of Russo-Finnish war; Russia re-occupies Latvia, Lithuania and Estonia. Trotsky assassinated on Stalin's orders. Japan invades French Indo-China.	Jan: North African campaign: General Wavell has initial successes. US agrees Lend Lease for Britain. 30 March: Rommel opens attack in N Africa. 6 April: Germany invades Greece and Yugoslavia. 24 May: HMS *Hood* sunk. 22 June: Germany invades USSR, besieges Leningrad, enters Ukraine. 14 Nov: HMS *Ark Royal* sunk. 6 Dec: Japan enters war – attacks US fleet at Pearl Harbor. 8 Dec: USA and Britain declare war on Japan; Germany and Italy declare war on USA. 10 Dec: Japan invades Philippines and takes Hong Kong (25 Dec). Rommel retreats in N Africa. First extermination camps for Jews are set up by the Germans and the systematic extermination of Jews in Russia and Poland begins. Romania and Bulgaria join the Axis powers.	Japan captures Manila, Singapore, Rangoon, Mandalay and the Philippines. 4–8 May: Battle of Coral Sea. USA *v.* Japan. 30 May: Over 1,000 bombers raid Cologne. 3–7 June: Midway Island: USA naval victory over Japan turns tide in the Pacific. 16 July: RAF make first daylight raid on the Ruhr. 6 Sept: Germans defeated at the Battle of Stalingrad. 23 Oct–4 Nov: Montgomery defeats Rommel at the Battle of El Alamein. 400,000 American troops land in North Africa: Anglo-American forces take Tripoli and Tunis, the Germans evacuate North Africa (May 1943). Germany takes over unoccupied (Vichy) France.	Casablanca Conference: Churchill and Roosevelt. Hitler orders scorched earth policy in Russia as Germans begin to retreat. 27 Jan: American bombers make their first attack on Germany. 31 Jan: Remnants of German army outside Stalingrad surrender to Russians. Massacre of Warsaw Ghetto. RAF bomb Ruhr dams. Mussolini is dismissed, the Allies invade Italy. USA begins to recapture the Japanese held islands in Pacific. Teheran Conference: Churchill, Roosevelt and Stalin. Allies begin round-the-clock bombing of Germany.
Religion & Learning	T. S. Eliot *The idea of a Christian Society.*	Bryan *English Saga.* Prehistoric wall paintings are discovered in Lascaux Caves, France	Marcuse *Reason and Revolution.*	Julian Huxley *Evolution up to date.* Trevelyan *English Social History.*	I. A. Richards *Basic English and its Uses.*
Cities & Social Development	Britain introduces National Identity Cards and Conscription. British Ministry of Information created. Major coal strike in the US by the United Mine Workers demonstrates the power of the union leader, John L. Lewis.	Britain leases naval and military bases to USA in the West Indies. Baghdad Railway, begun by Germany in 1902, is finally completed. 30m homes in USA now have radios.	Britain introduces severe rationing. Britain applies conscription to women.	Lord Beveridge produces his Report on *Social Security and National Insurance.* Gilbert Murray founds the British charity OXFAM.	UNRRA – the United Nations Relief and Rehabilitation Administration – established to provide supplies to liberated countries (food, clothing, etc.). President Roosevelt freezes wages, salaries and prices to prevent inflation.
Discovery & Invention	Byrd makes his third expedition to Antarctica. Sikorsky produces first serviceable helicopter. Britain has radar stations in operation round the coast able to detect enemy and friendly planes. Joliot-Curie demonstrate possibility of splitting the atom. Levine and Stetson discover the Rhesus factor in blood.	Blood plasma first used in blood transfusions. British Scientific Advisory Committee set up.	First British jet aircraft, based on the work of Whittle, flown. Bailey invents his portable military bridge. *Manhattan Project* of intense atomic (nuclear) research gets under way.	First nuclear reactor established at Chicago University. Fermi makes contribution to atomic energy research with his work on artificial radioactive resources, helps split atom. First automatic computer developed in the USA. Magnetic recording tape invented. (The atomic and electronic age may be said to have arrived.)	Antibiotic *streptomycin* isolated by Waksman. Penicillin is used successfully in the treatment of chronic disease.
The Arts	Yeats *Last Poems.* Joyce *Finnegans Wake.* Films: *Stagecoach, The Young Mr Lincoln, Ninotchka, Gone with the Wind.* T. S. Eliot *The Family Reunion.* Henry Moore *Reclining Figure.*	Greene *The Power and the Glory.* Films: *Fantasia, The Great Dictator, Rebecca.* Hemingway *For Whom the Bell Tolls.*	Films: *Citizen Kane, Suspicion.* Shostakovich 7th Symphony. Hopper *Nighthawks*, painting.	Arthur Waley *Monkey.* Films: *The Maltese Falcon, Casablanca, Mrs Miniver, Bambi.* Camus *L'Etranger.*	Films: *Shadow of a Doubt, Heaven can Wait.* Thurber *Men, Women and Dogs.* Picasso *Woman in a wicker chair.*

'rom the moment he took office Hitler was bent on war. 'he unemployment problem vanished overnight as he unched into a re-armament programme that needed men y the million for the armed services and the munitions ıctories: the provisos of the Versailles Treaty were openly outed as the German army, navy and airforce increased ıeir personnel to many times the agreed figures. In 1938 ame the first overt act of aggression, the forcible ıcorporation of Austria in Hitler's 'Third Reich'.

The world waited, hoping that Hitler would be satisfied vith the German-speaking parts of Europe. Besides ustria these included the mountainous rim of Bohemia in he west of Czechoslovakia, and the areas round Danzig and Aemel. In late 1938 Hitler demanded and got the German reas of Czechoslovakia and in early 1939 he imposed a rotectorate over the rest of the country: at the same time he orced the Lithuanians to hand over Memel. Finally in eptember 1939, he marched into Poland, precipitating the uropean conflict that developed into World War II.

One thing Hitler did not want was a repetition of the tatic slogging match battles that had characterized the 'irst World War. Shortly after coming to power he was iven a demonstration of a new sort of mobile division eveloped by General Guderian: this consisted of tanks, notorized infantry and mechanized artillery and would, ccording to Guderian, be able to punch a hole through any efence line. More important than that, it could exploit the reak-through so quickly that the enemy would never be ble to recover his balance. 'That's what I want' cried Iitler who told Guderian he could have everything he eeded to create six of the new-style Panzer (meaning rmoured) divisions.

When Hitler went to war with Poland, Guderian's six 'anzer divisions were ready for action. They sliced through he Polish defences just as he had said they would, and the ampaign was all over, with insignificant loss on the German side, in three weeks. The next year Guderian truck again, this time on the western front where France nd Britain were bracing themselves for a replay of the Schlieffen Plan. It did not work out like that. What looked ike a Schlieffen movement into the Low Countries Holland as well as Belgium this time) turned out to be a eint to draw the British and French into Belgium. Guderian fell on the right flank of this force with ten Panzer livisions, rupturing the Allies' line and splitting their ırmies into two groups. The British managed to lift off a roportion of their expeditionary force from Dunkirk but he French, with nowhere to go, were doomed. An mprovised defence line along the Somme and Aisne was ripped up by Guderian's Panzers in a few days: by 22nd une the French government had been forced to surrender.

Exactly a year later Hitler was doing what he had ntended to all along, launching the German army against Russia. Until France and Britain had been beaten he had made a point of getting on well with Stalin, letting the Russian dictator have half Poland and a free hand in the Baltic states (which meant the end of them) in return for aw materials and a guarantee of no trouble in the East. But now the time had come to overthrow Bolshevism and reduce the Russian people to what Nazi ideology had all ılong proclaimed was their proper political role – as a slave ace working for the glory of the Third Reich.

Over the next five months the Panzer divisions – 17 of hem, operating in four groups – put on a perfect display of ıow armoured warfare should be conducted. A series of pincer movements by Guderian and Hoth enveloped whole Russian armies: 30 divisions at Minsk before the end of une, as many again at Smolensk in July. In September Hitler ordered Guderian south to a junction with the Panzergruppe operating on the lower Dnieper: the haul this time was more than half a million men. Finally the three northern Panzer groups combined for an assault on Moscow. Hoth and Hoepner pinched out the main defending force of 45 divisions and, with Guderian closing in from the south, the Russian situation looked hopeless. But the Panzers were moving slower now, delayed by torrential rain, lack of essential supplies, sheer exhaustion. In early December all forward movement ceased.

Moscow, and final victory, had just eluded Hitler's grasp.

Below: Poster advertising a local SS rally in Berlin.

Left: A squadron of Ju87 dive-bombers, the famous 'Stukas'. These acted as flying artillery for the Panzer divisions.

Below left: The Pz MkIII, the main battle-tank in the Blitzkrieg ('Lightning war') campaigns of 1939–41.

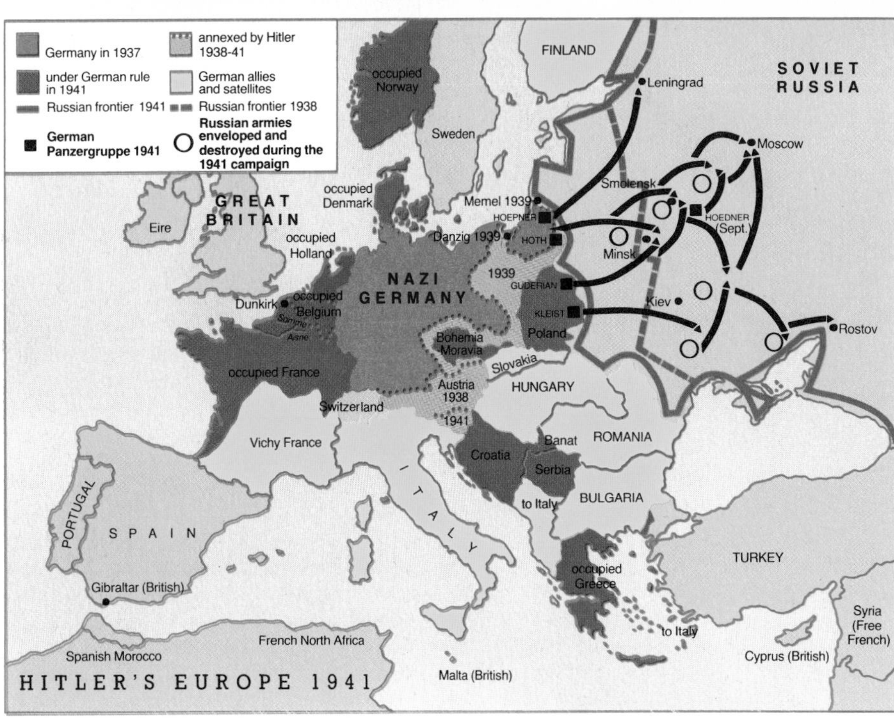

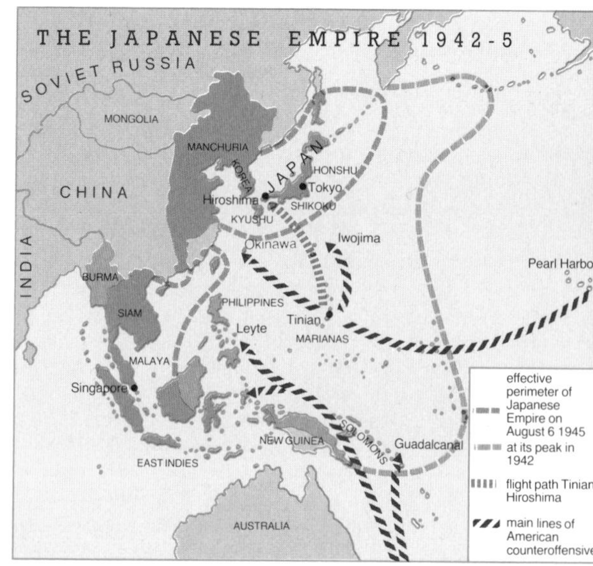

Top: Hiroshima after the Atom Bomb.

Above: A French poster lampooning the 'success' of the Japanese war machine.

Above right: The Enola Gay returns to Tinian after the Hiroshima mission.

In July 1945 the Japanese still ruled Manchuria, Korea, much of China and all of Indonesia, but theirs was an empire in ruins. The American navy ranged at will through the seas round the homeland; squadrons of B-29 bombers based on the islands to the south were methodically burning out its cities. The Imperial navy was reduced to a few battered hulks, the Army to a last ditch defence force. There was no point in continuing the fight.

This was not the way the Japanese saw it. Most of them remained serenely confident of ultimate victory; even the few who were prepared to consider a negotiated settlement felt that this was not the moment. A defensive victory – for example the repulse of an American invasion – was what was needed: then discussions could begin on the basis that Japan would give a little, keep a lot. But right now there was nothing for it but to dig in.

The Americans, who had considerable experience of how dearly the Japanese sold their lives when they were in this mood, had accepted that neither naval blockade nor conventional bombing would bring the Japanese to their senses. Grimly they set about preparing an army to invade the Japanese islands, starting with Kyushu on November 1. What it would cost was anyone's guess but if it was going to be anything like Okinawa, where 12,000 Americans and more than 100,000 Japanese had died, it would be a bloody business indeed.

There was an alternative. On August 6, with twelve weeks to go before the invasion of Japan, Colonel Paul Tibbets of the 509th Composite Group taxied his B-29 'Enola Gay' to the end of runway A on North Field, Tinian island. At 2.45am he took off and set course for Iwojima, 960km to the north. Shortly after take-off two crewmen entered the bomb-bay which contained the aircraft's load, a single 9,000lb bomb code named Little Boy. They unscrewed a plate in the bomb's side, exposing the gun barrel that ran the length of it: into the breech of this they placed four explosive charges and a detonator. Three hours later, as the B-29 passed over Iwojima and Tibbets altered course so as to pass over Shikoku, one crewmen returned to the bomb-bay and inserted the plugs that completed Little Boy's arming procedure.

Four and a quarter hours into the mission, at 7am Japanese time, Tibbets began climbing to bombing altitude. The weather over the Primary Target was fine: he confirmed this as his destination by radioing Iwojima the single word 'Primary'. Approaching from the east at 9467 metres and an indicated airspeed of exactly 320kph, he brought the Enola Gay over the aiming point, the Aioi bridge in Hiroshima harbour, a few seconds after 8.15am.

As Little Boy fell from the bomb-bay the wires connecting bomb and plane pulled out, closing an electrical switch and setting off a timing device. Twenty seconds later, when the bomb had accelerated to near sonic speed, this device closed a second switch, and at 1,500 metres above the ground a third switch, a barometric sensor, activated the bomb's trigger. This was a miniature radar set which, over the next few seconds, measured the rapidly dwindling distance to the ground. At an altitude of 576 metres it detonated the explosive charges in Little Boy's gun, sending the 5lb bullet it contained on its short journey to the 17lb target wrapped round the end of the barrel. Both bullet and target were made of the same material, uranium 235, and the two together constituted a critical, self-fissioning mass. In the micro-second of their joint existence the temperature of bullet and target rose from 18 degrees centigrade to more than 40 million degrees, many times hotter than the surface of the sun.

The crew of Enola Gay, by now more than 8km away from the aiming point, perceived Little Boy's end as a blinding flash. Seconds later the plane was rocked by a blast so fierce and so loud that even Tibbets, who had been warned what to expect, thought the B-29 had been hit by flak. As he recovered control he saw a massive cloud of smoke starting to rise up from the burning city, fed by a convection column that gave it the outline of a rapidly elongating mushroom. Within minutes the cloud had reached a height of 18,000 metres – twice the plane's atitude. By this time most of the 80,000 people the bomb was to kill were already dead.

	1944	1945	1946	1947	1948
Politics & Military History	Feb: Russian offensive in Ukraine and Crimea. 4 June: Allies enter Rome. 6 June: Allied landings in Normandy. (D-Day – over 4,000 ships in invasion fleet.) 12 June: First Flying Bombs (V1) on London. By September the Allies liberate Paris and Brussels. 8 Sept: First V2 Rockets land on London. 11 Sept: Allied forces fighting on Reich territory. Battle of Leyte Gulf: Japanese fleet decisively defeated by the Americans. Failure of Allied airborne landings at Arnhem. 16 Dec: German counter-offensive: the Battle of the Bulge in the Ardennes, France. Last German offensive in the west. Russians invade Bulgaria and Romania, then Hungary. Partisans liberate Yugoslavia. Vietnam declares independence of France under Ho Chi Minh.	Jan: British offensive in Burma. 17 Jan: Russians take Warsaw. 4 Feb: Yalta Conference between Churchill, Roosevelt and Stalin. 11 April: Russian army enters Vienna after 7-day battle. 25 April: Berlin surrounded by Russian troops. 27 April: Russians and Americans link up at Torgau, Germany. San Francisco Conference: the signing of the UN Charter. 28 April: Mussolini is killed by partisans. 30 April: Hitler kills himself. 2 May: Berlin captured by Russians. 8 May: Germany capitulates: Germany and Austria divided into 4 zones, three-power occupation of Berlin. Potsdam Conference to discuss peace terms and post-war settlements. USA drops atomic bombs on Hiroshima and Nagasaki to end Japanese war. War dead are estimated at 35m apart from 10m civilian atrocity casualties in concentration camps and elsewhere. Nuremberg Trials of Nazi war criminals.	Civil War in Greece. First session of new United Nations held. Churchill gives his *Iron Curtain* speech at Fulton, Missouri. Italy holds referendum in favour of becoming republic. Leading Nazis are executed or imprisoned following the Nuremberg trials and judgements. Chinese civil war grows in dimensions between Nationalists and Communists. Civil War in Indochina led by Ho Chi Minh against the French – lasts to 1954. USSR launches its Fourth 5 Year Plan.	UN proposes the partition of Palestine between Arabs and Jews: Arabs reject proposals. British India gains independence: partitioned to form India (Hindu) and Pakistan (Muslim); Burma becomes independent. Truman Doctrine providing funds for Greece and Turkey signals onset of Cold War. British and American troops evacuate Italy. Allies agree peace treaties in Paris with Italy, Romania, Hungary, Bulgaria and Finland. Four Powers fail to reach agreement on Germany.	Communist takeover in Czechoslovakia: People's Republic is formed. Emergency begins in Malaya. UN sanctions the State of Israel: first Israel-Arab war. Gandhi assassinated. Afrikaaners come to power in South Africa pledged to implement policy of apartheid. USSR withdraws from Allied Control Council and blockades Berlin: western powers mount Berlin Airlift. Ceylon becomes independent. Korea divided into North and South Korea. US Congress passes the Marshall Plan Act and allots $17 billion in aid for Europe. British Citizenship Act: all Commonwealth citizens qualify for British passports.
Religion & Learning	Butler Education Act: Britain to provide secondary education for all children.	Popper *The Open Society and its enemies.* Japan abolishes Shintoism.	Sartre *L'Existentialisme est un Humanisme.* Russell *History of Western Philosophy.* UNESCO created.	Dead Sea Scrolls – part of the library of the Qumran sect – found in Palestine (cf. AD 68 R). New universities are created in Nigeria, Gold Coast and Jamaica (to 1950).	Toynbee *Civilization on Trial.* The Kinsey Report in the USA: *Sexual Behaviour in the Human Male.* World Council of Churches established.
Cities & Social Development	Major nationalization carried out in France including coal, gas and electricity, deposit banks and insurance companies, Renault. Bretton Woods Conference leads to the establishment of the World Bank and the International Monetary Fund.	Black Markets for food and clothing develop all over Europe. Eastern European Church lands are confiscated and divided between public and private sectors.	Labour Government in Britain nationalizes the Bank of England, Civil Aviation, the Coal Industry. Monnet Plan for economic recovery and development is launched in France.	Christian Dior opens his salon in Paris and begins to revolutionize women's fashions. GATT (The General Agreement on Tariffs and Trades) formally launched. Marshall Plan is launched: USA provides massive aid for the economic rehabilitation of war-torn Europe; turned down by the USSR and Eastern Bloc countries.	United Nations adopts the Declaration of Human Rights.
Discovery & Invention	V1 and V2 bombs and rockets used by Germany usher in the missile age. Uranium pile is built at Clinton, Tennessee.	Two atomic bombs on Japan and the first experimental explosion in New Mexico herald the coming of the Atomic Age.	Truman sets up the US Atomic Energy Commission. Experimental rocket range established at Woomera in Australia. First US Navy atomic tests are carried out at Bikini and Eniwetok Atolls in the Pacific.	First British nuclear reactor developed. Chuck Yeager flying an American aircraft breaks the sound barrier.	A 200in. reflecting telescope is constructed at Mount Palomar, California. World Health Organization (WHO) is established as part of UN. Bondi and Gold put forward their steady state theory of the universe. Long-playing record is invented by Goldmark.
The Arts	Films: *Ivan the Terrible, Double Indemnity, Les Enfants du Paradis, Henry V.* Tennessee Williams *The Glass Menagerie.* Shostakovich 8th Symphony. Rivera *The Rug Weaver,* painting.	Orwell *Animal Farm.* Brecht *The Caucasian Chalk Circle.* Films: *Rome, Open City* (by Rossellini) heralds the beginning of Italian cinema revival; *Brief Encounter, The Lost Weekend.* Britten *Peter Grimes,* opera.	Dylan Thomas *Deaths and Entrances.* Films: *My darling Clementine, The Big Sleep, Notorious, The Best Years of our Lives*; the first Cannes Film Festival is held. O'Neill *The Iceman Cometh.*	Lowry *Under the Volcano.* Camus *La Peste.* *The Diary of Anne Frank* is published. Tennessee Williams *A Streetcar named Desire.* Matisse *Young English Girl.*	Greene *The Heart of the Matter.* Mailer *The Naked and the Dead.* Films: *The Bicycle Thief, Treasure of the Sierra Madre, Red River, Fort Apache.* Henry Moore *Family Group.*

	1949	1950	1951	1952	1953
Politics & Military History	North Atlantic Treaty Organization (NATO) is formed as a defensive alliance by the western nations. Council of Mutual Economic Assistance (COMECON) is formed by USSR and eastern Europe. Russians explode their first atomic bomb resulting in escalation of arms race with USA. Newfoundland joins Canada as tenth province. Ireland leaves Commonwealth. India becomes Republic. Germany is divided into the Federal Republic (West) and the German Democratic Republic (East). Indonesia becomes independent of Holland as a Republic. Russians lift the Berlin Blockade. Mao Zedong establishes control of the Chinese mainland as the People's Republic of China: the Nationalist forces under Jiang Jieshi escape to Formosa.	Korean War begins: North Korea supported by China, South Korea by UN Forces. Russia and China conclude a treaty of friendship. Anglo-Iranian dispute over Iranian nationalization of its oilfields and refinery. McCarthy's Senate Permanent Investigation Subcommittee begins Red Scare and witch hunt in the USA. China invades and overruns Tibet (to 1951). Cold War escalates: Klaus Fuchs arrested in Britain for alleged sale of atomic secrets to the USSR; Alger Hiss sentenced in the USA for perjury. McCarran Act in the USA: severe restrictions upon Communists in the USA.	Pacific Security Treaty (ANZUS) between the USA, Australia and New Zealand. West Germany admitted to the Council of Europe. Egypt abrogates the 1936 Treaty with Britain; British troops occupy Canal Zone. Peace Treaty signed by Japan at San Francisco with most of her opponents from World War II.	Ahmed Ben Bella forms the Algerian revolutionary committee in Cairo. Morocco revolts against France (to 1956). Cyprus Emergency begins (to 1959). Greece and Turkey join NATO. Mau Mau nationalist rebellion begins in Kenya: state of emergency to last to 1959. China accuses the US of waging germ warfare in Korea. Neguib and Nasser seize power in Egypt: King Farouk abdicates. Bonn Convention: Britain, France and the USA end their occupation of West Germany.	Death of Stalin: Malenkov becomes Premier, Beria is shot French forces occupy Dien Bien Phu in North Vietnam. Rising in East Germany suppressed by Soviet troops. Federation of Northern and Southern Rhodesia and Nyasaland formed by Britain. Treaty of Panunjon ends Korean War. Trial of Jomo Kenyatta for managing Mau Mau.
Religion & Learning	Russell *Authority and the Individual.*	Riesman *The Lonely Crowd.* Margaret Mead *Social Anthropology.*	C. Wright Mills *White Collar.* Sartre *The Psychology of Imagination.*	Niebuhr *Christ and Culture.*	De Beauvoir *The Second Sex.* Piltdown Man exposed as a fraud.
Cities & Social Development	Confederation of German Trade Unions is established in West Germany.	Establishment of the European Payments Union. Colombo Plan is launched: beginning of aid. Schumann Plan for a European Coal and Steel Community.	German companies begin to appoint workers' representatives to the boards of directors. Festival of Britain: opening of the Royal Festival Hall.	First commercial jet airline service launched. Britain abolishes identity cards. Contraceptive pills first made.	USA lifts controls on wages and prices.
Discovery & Invention	De Havilland produces the Comet jet airliner.	Danish research vessel discovers living organisms in the Pacific Ocean at depths of more than 10,000m. Einstein *General Field Theory*, expanding Theory of Relativity.	First peaceful uses of atomic energy: used for the production of electric power in Idaho and for heating at Harwell in Britain.	Britain explodes he. first atomic bomb. USA explodes its first Hydrogen Bomb. US constructs its first atomic powered submarine – the USS *Nautilus.* Radioactive carbon is used for dating prehistoric objects.	Watson, Crick and Wilkins discover structure of DNA to be a double helix. Most crucial biological discovery of the century. Hillary and Sherpa Tensing reach summit of Mt Everest. It is found there is a new scale of space outside the solar system. USSR explodes a hydrogen bomb. Piccard reaches a depth of more than 3km under the ocean in a bathysphere.
The Arts	Orwell *1984.* Arthur Miller *Death of a Salesman.* Films: *The Third Man, She Wore a yellow ribbon, On the Town, Late Spring.* Samba dance becomes fashionable. Bartok Violin Concerto. Chagall *Red Sun.* Jazz: Stan Kenton's Progressive Jazz orchestra.	Films: *Sunset Boulevard, La Ronde, Winchester 73, Rashomon.* Honneger 5th Symphony. UN Building completed in New York. Braque *Bowl of Fruit.* Roualt *Winter.*	Anthony Powell begins his series *Dance to the Music of Time.* Films: *Strangers on a Train, Ace in the Hole, Miracle in Milan, African Queen.* Salinger *Catcher in the Rye.* Britten *Billy Budd*, opera. Stravinsky *Rake's Progress*, opera.	Beckett *Waiting for Godot.* Films: *Umberto D, High Noon, Le Plaisir.* Hemingway *The old man and the sea.* Steinbeck *East of Eden.* Jazz: Formation of the Modern Jazz Quartet.	Shostakovich 10th Symphony. Films: *Limelight, Tokyo Story, I Vitelloni, M. Hulot's Holiday, The wages of fear.* Arthur Miller *The Crucible.* Moore *King and Queen*, bronze. Pop: Frankie Lane *Answer Me.*

Left: Civilians flee the Inchon battlefield, an incident in the Korean conflict of 1950–53. Originally a Russian sponsored bit of aggression by North Korea against South Korea, the war developed into a Chinese defence of North Korea against an American counter-offensive. The Americans eventually decided that the price of trying to impose themselves on the Chinese was too high and the war ended with both sides backing off and no territorial changes of any significance. What the war did demonstrate in no uncertain manner was China's return to great power status.

Above: Mao acknowledging the cheers of the crowd at the fourth anniversary celebration of the People's Republic in Beijing in 1953.

While Mao lived – and he was not to die until 1976 – he was the undisputed leader of both the Chinese Communist Party and the Chinese people. How history will assess the achievements of the last 20 years of his life it is too early to say: what is already apparent is that his philosophy of putting revolutionary purity before material wellbeing has been reversed by his successors.

If we think of the world simply as the sum total of millions upon millions of individual lives, and the history of the world as the sum total of the experiences of those lives, then whatever happens in China is the most important thing that happens in the world. In that sense, the most important date in 20th century world history – so far – is 1949, the year in which the People's Republic of China, ruled by the Chinese Communist Party, was established as the actual and legal government of mainland China, the government of 550 million people or more, just under a quarter of the population of the world at that time – a proportion that continues to rise.

Up to 1949, the 20th century history of China had been a history of disintegration. The decaying Manzhou empire had finally collapsed in 1912; the succeeding republic founded by Sun Yat-sen had rapidly become a military dictatorship under Yuan Shikai; the rule of Yuan had soon seen China disintegrate into a collection of military fiefs under rival war-lords. By the end of the 1920s, the residual legatee of the original nationalist republicans of 1912, the Guo Min Dang (Kuomingtang) under Jiang Jieshi (Chiang Kai-shek), had gained power over most of the country; then, in the 1930s, a growing Japanese advance culminated in the outbreak of war in 1937, after which Japanese forces overran the whole of lowland northern China and much of the coast to the south.

A Chinese communist party had been established in the chaos of the early 1920s. It was a typical party of the time, a group of intellectuals with a power-base among the industrial workers of the great cities of eastern China. Its early history was chequered; basically it co-operated with the Guo Min Dang – at that time a Moscow-financed leftward-leaning party – until 1927 when Jiang broke with it and massacred many of its leaders.

Following this disaster the remnants of the party leadership retreated to Jiangxi where the local bandits happened to be Communists. In this relatively inaccessible part of China the party built up a peasant state and successfully fended off attacks by Guo Min Dang forces until 1934–5, when Jiang forced it into a further retreat. This was the famous Long March in which Mao Zedong led the remaining Communist forces in a great arc across virtually the whole of China. Ninety thousand set out. A year later, after covering 10,000km, fighting 15 pitched battles, crossing 24 rivers and 18 mountain ranges, the 30,000 survivors reached a safe haven in Shaanxi.

Here a new Communist republic was established. Like the Jiangxi republic, it was essentially a rural, peasant state. The Chinese Communist Party had become the party of the peasants, its aim to establish power over China by military conquest from a rural base.

This was to throw ideological purity to the winds. In original Marxist theory, communism was the final fruition of an advanced industrial society, brought about through the conflict of industrial workers and capitalists. In revised Marxist theory, at the hands of Lenin and Stalin, communism was the result of a party representing the industrial workers bringing both industrialization and communism to a backward country. The Chinese communists under Mao were to make a new way – communism (and industrialization) imposed on a backward society by a party drawing its support from the peasants from all over China.

That support was the strength and success of the Chinese Communist Party. It was not gained to any great degree by the economic reforms of communism in the rural republics. There was land reform but it was by no means complete – not always as much as some of the peasants wished. Rich farmers survived and were essential to the working of the local economy. What Chinese communism brought was not so much economic liberation as human liberation. The poor and the oppressed of the villages, the landless, the women, were recognized as full members of society. The gleam that foreign observers saw in the eyes of the peasant volunteers to the Red Army was the gleam of human dignity and an aspiring cause. Life was austere but just; and more important it had meaning.

After 1937, the Red Army had its opportunity. The war against Japan was the turning point of Chinese communist history; in membership alone, the party grew from 40,000 in 1937 to 1.2 million in 1945 – and 90% of the new members were peasants. The Japanese invasion had changed the whole aspect of China. The Guo Min Dang government's retreat to the western city of Chongqing and the tenuous hold of the Japanese army over large areas outside the eastern cities left a great vacuum of power in between. In the vast area of the countryside outside the firm control of either the Guo Min Dang or the Japanese, the Communist Party became the party of national resistance to the Japanese; its tactics the destructive tactics of a peasant guerilla army.

With the destruction of the Japanese Empire in 1945, the temporary and uncomfortable wartime alliance of the Guo Min Dang and the Communists collapsed. The Guo Min Dang still had the larger army and was initially successful in occupying most of the areas evacuated by the Japanese. But it found itself the victim of the same guerilla tactics as the Japanese had been in the same areas. The corruption, barbarity and increasing demoralization of the Guo Min Dang army was no match in the longer term for the zeal of a peasantry in arms and the discipline and efficiency of the Red Army. By 1949, the Guo Min Dang was driven into its last retreat on Taiwan. Just under a quarter of the population of the world was about to begin a new experiment: the creation of a communist and industrial state on the foundations of a peasant revolution. *(R.J.)*

Right: The propaganda war. An electric bill board flashes the West's news into East Berlin.

Far right: Russian tanks in the streets of Budapest. Hungary's attempt to leave the Soviet bloc in 1956 was ruthlessly suppressed by the Red Army.

The wartime alliance between Communist Russia and the Western Allies had been strained even before victory. The high hopes at the Yalta Conference in 1945 that the Soviet Union and the United States would work together to ensure peace and stability were soon to be dashed, and instead east-west relations became dominated by suspicion and hostility. In 1946 Winston Churchill spoke of an 'iron curtain' which had descended across Europe 'from Stettin in the Baltic to Trieste in the Adriatic'.

The term 'Cold War' summarizes the hostility short of actual conflict which has characterized east-west relations – more particularly those of the super-powers, Russia and America – ever since the Second World War. The split has largely been couched in ideological terms, Communism versus Democracy, although military and economic factors have also been fundamental.

Manifestations of the Cold War have been countless. Nearly every international crisis for forty years has become a focus for east-west opposition, and has been seen largely in terms of the balance of power between the Communist and non-Communist world. By giving aid and backing the political factions, guerilla groups, and so on, each side has tried to undermine support for the other in countries throughout the world. International forums like the United Nations have frequently been platforms for mutual denunciation and the wooing of neutral nations. Propaganda, espionage, and infiltration are all widespread weapons of the Cold War. Overshadowing all has been the steady build-up of defence systems and armaments, nuclear and conventional, as east and west endeavour to match power with power and prevent one side from establishing a clear lead.

Hungarians burning portraits of their communist leaders during the 1956 rising.

The Cold War has not been a steady state. At times war has been imminent, during the Berlin blockade or the Cuban missile crisis, for example. Other times have seen thaw and *détente*. There have, too, been a number of conflicts involving forces from one of the superpowers (in Korea, Vietnam, and Afghanistan, for example), but so far the precarious peace between America and Russia has been preserved.

The Cold War has developed in distinct phases. The period 1945–50 was a time when Communism was expanding. Russia controlled eastern Germany, while Russian-backed revolutions set up Communist governments in Poland, Hungary, Bulgaria, Romania, and Czechoslovakia. These became satellite states of the Soviet Union. Russia threatened Turkey, Greece, and Iran, too; her troops were in occupation of Austria; in the Far East a Russian-inspired revolution installed a Communist government in North Korea, and revolutionary movements were encouraged in Indo-China, Burma, Indonesia, Malaya, and elsewhere. By 1949 China was Communist, too, as the forces of Mao Zedong drove those of Jiang Jieshi to Formosa (Taiwan) and a few off-shore islands.

The American response was a mixture of firmness and containment. Under the Marshall Plan the United States helped build up the economic strength of war-torn Europe, enabling those countries to resist the spread of Communism. President Truman gave prompt and active support to anti-Communist factions in Greece, Turkey, and Iran. In 1949 the dangerous Berlin crisis (an attempted blockade of allied-controlled West Berlin by the Russians, successfully countered by a dramatic airlift of supplies) showed further America's resolve to halt the spread of Communist influence; and in that same year the North Atlantic Treaty Organization (NATO) was formed, bringing together the USA, Canada, and ten nations of western Europe in a defensive alliance. America showed similar firmness in supporting non-Communist South Korea in the Korean War of 1950–53. In 1945 Korea had been divided into a Communist North under Russian influence, and a non-Communist South which had American support. In 1950 the Communists attacked the South and overran almost the whole country. South Korea appealed to the United Nations for help and soon an army, mainly American but provided by 15 countries, was fighting the North. It drove the Communists right back to the Chinese border which alarmed China, who sent 150,000 'volunteers' to help the North Koreans. They were successful in pushing back the UN forces to the original frontier between North and South. After three years of fighting, peace was restored. In 1954 SEATO (South-East Asian Treaty Organisation) was formed with the intention of checking Communist influence in the area. Meanwhile the Russians had caught up with America's nuclear start by exploding their first hydrogen bomb in 1953. In 1955 they responded to NATO and SEATO by forming the Warsaw Pact among the East European Communist countries.

The death of Stalin in 1953 opened the way for some improvement in the international climate, but steps towards *détente* were faltering and short-lived. Such crises as the Hungarian uprising in 1956, the Suez Canal nationalization by Nasser the same year, the building of the Berlin Wall in 1961, the siting of Russian missiles in Cuba in 1962, and the continuing conflicts in South-east Asia as America became more deeply committed in Vietnam – all these and many more threatened world peace. Many factors have occurred to shift the balance of power one way or another – the space programmes, dissension among Communist countries, America's humiliation in Vietnam – but a sort of balance still exists, as do the fundamental causes of the Cold War. *(M.F.)*

	1954	1955	1956	1957	1958
Politics & Military History	Defeat of French at Dien Bien Phu. Geneva Conference: Vietnam divided along 17th parallel into the Communist North Vietnam under Ho Chi Minh and western backed South Vietnam. South East Asia Treaty Organization (SEATO) formed to prevent the spread of Communism in SE Asia. Nasser takes full control in Egypt: Anglo-Egyptian agreement on Suez Canal. France sends 20,000 troops to Algeria: beginning of Algerian War of Independence (to 1962).	Bandung Conference: meeting of Asian and African nations declare themselves to be non-aligned in the Cold War. Warsaw Pact: USSR and East European states sign a defence treaty under Soviet command. Baghdad Pact, formed by Iran, Iraq, Turkey, Pakistan and Britain. Military occupation of Austria ends. Rebellion and general strike in Argentina force President Peron into exile.	Nikita Khruschev denounces Stalin at the 20th Party Congress. De-Stalinization policies in East Europe: Poznan riots in Poland; anti-Soviet uprising in Hungary is brutally crushed by Soviet troops. Morocco, Sudan and Tunisia achieve independence. Castro lands in Cuba: the Cuban civil war commences. Terrorism at its height in Cyprus: Archbishop Makarios is deported by the British. Suez Crisis; Nasser nationalizes the Suez Canal; Israel invades Sinai; Britain and France invade Egypt; the UN calls for cease-fire and a UN force replaces the British and French who withdraw.	Eden resigns; Suez Canal reopened to all shipping. Treaty of Rome establishes the EEC (Common Market) of the Six: France, West Germany, Italy, Belgium, Holland and Luxembourg; to become operational January 1958. Gold Coast becomes independent as Ghana under Kwame Nkrumah. Eisenhower Doctrine is proclaimed to oppose Communism in Middle East.	Fourth Republic overthrown in France and Fifth Republic under Charles de Gaulle established. Egypt and Syria form the United Arab Republic (UAR). West Indian Federation established. King Feisal of Iraq killed in revolution and a Republic is proclaimed under Abdul Kassem.
Religion & Learning	First comprehensive school opened in London. All food rationing ends in Britain.	Le Corbusier *Le Modular 2.*	William Whyte *The Organization Man.* C. Wright Mills *The Power Elite.*	Frye *Anatomy of Criticism.* Packard *The Hidden Persuaders.*	Marcuse *Soviet Marxism.* Hoggart *The uses of literacy.* Galbraith *The Affluent Society.*
Cities & Social Development	US Supreme Court rules that racial segregation in schools is violation of the 14th Amendment of the US Constitution. In USA 29m homes have television. Bannister runs the first 4 minute mile. USA has 60% of all cars, 58% of all telephones, 45% of all radio sets.	Blacks in Montgomery, Alabama, boycott the segregated city bus lines. Commercial television is introduced in Britain.	Emergence of CND as a factor in Britain: protest march to Aldermaston. Rock and Roll comes into vogue.	New city of Brasilia is established as the new capital of Brazil. Civil Rights Act is passed in the USA: race riots occur in the southern states; violence in Little Rock in Arkansas against integration of schools, Eisenhower sends in troops to maintain order. 71 cities worldwide have a population exceeding one million. Terms *Beat* and *Beatnik* come into popular usage.	Stereophonic records come into use. Race riots occur at Notting Hill Gate in London and Nottingham.
Discovery & Invention	European Atomic Energy Society established to promote industrial uses of atomic energy. First controlled flight of a vertical take-off aeroplane takes place.	Britain announces plans to construct 12 nuclear power stations. Emission of radio waves from the planet Jupiter are detected by Burk at the Carnegie Institute. Salk develops new anti-poliomyelitis vaccine. Atomically generated power is first used in the USA.	Britain constructs world's first large-scale nuclear power station in Cumberland. Extensive mineral deposits are discovered in Siberia.	Britain explodes its first H-bomb at Christmas Island. Large-scale exploration of Antarctic conducted. USSR launches its first space satellite – Sputnik I.	Electronic computers begin to be used in research, industry and commerce. US nuclear submarine, USS *Nautilus*, travels 2928 km under the Arctic ice-cap. USA begins to produce Atlas Inter-Continental Ballistic Missiles (ICBM). USA launches its first satellite: the space race with the USSR gets underway. Van Allen radiation belt round the earth detected.
The Arts	Thomas *Under Milk Wood.* Golding *Lord of the Flies.* Films: *Seven Samurai, La Strada, On the Waterfront, A Generation.* Huxley *Doors of Perception.* Tennessee Williams *Cat on a hot tin roof.* Ernst *Lonely.* British Top Twenty begins in October. *Hold my Hand* by Don Cornell is first Number 1. Jazz: Thelonius Monk *Bags' Grove.*	Greene *The Quiet American.* Films: *East of Eden, Pather Panchali.* Ehrenburg *The Thaw.* Pop: Slim Whitman *Rose Marie*, Bill Haley *Rock Around the Clock.*	Osborne *Look Back in Anger.* Wilson *The Outsider.* Emergence of the *Angry Young Men* in English literature. Films: *The Burmese Harp, The Searchers.* Jazz: Miles Davis *Round Midnight.*	Patrick White *Voss.* Lawrence Durrell *Justine.* Films: *The Seventh Seal, Twelve Angry Men.* O'Neill *Long Day's Journey into Night* (posthumous). Le Corbusier designs Tokyo Museum of Art. Pop: Elvis Presley *All Shook Up.*	Beckett *Krapp's last Tape.* Films: *Vertigo, Brink of Life, Touch of Evil.* Pasternak *Dr Zhivago.* Pinter *The Birthday Party.* Pop: Jerry Lee Lewis *Great Balls of Fire*; Everly Brothers *All I Have To Do Is Dream.*

	1959	1960	1961	1962	1963
Politics & Military History	The European Free Trade Association (EFTA) is established as alternative to EEC. Uprising in Tibet against China is crushed, Dalai Lama flees to India. Indo-Chinese border clashes. Castro overthrows the Batista regime in Cuba and institutes agrarian reforms. Hawaii becomes the fiftieth state of the Union.	US property in Cuba seized and Cuba becomes aligned with Communist powers. Seventeen African colonies become independent (the *annus mirabilis* of African independence). Cyprus becomes independent with Archbishop Makarios as President. Following independence the *Force Publique* mutinies in the Congo leading to four years of disorders; Katanga Province under Tshombe attempts to secede. Sharpeville Massacre in South Africa focuses world attention upon the brutalities of *apartheid*.	Building of the Berlin Wall. Latin America Free Trade Association (LAFTA) formed. Death of Lumumba in the Congo; the UN Secretary-General Dag Hammarskjold, is killed while travelling to talks in the Congo. South Africa becomes Republic and leaves Commonwealth. Bay of Pigs: US-backed exiles' invasion of Cuba fails. Eichmann Trial is held in Jerusalem.	Cuban Missile Crisis: a confrontation between the USA and the USSR over Russian missiles to be based in Cuba; the USSR agrees to withdraw its bases. Geneva disarmament conference on nuclear weapons. USA establishes a military command in South Vietnam. Border clashes between India and China. Algeria gains independence from France after struggle lasting for eight years.	Assassination of President Kennedy. France vetoes Britain's application to join the EEC. Organization of African Unity (OAU) is established by the Addis Ababa Conference. USA, USSR and Britain sign Nuclear Test Ban Treaty. Kenya and Zanzibar become independent; Britain dissolves the Central Africa Federation. South Vietnam government of Diem is overthrown. Martin Luther King leads the American Civil Rights Campaign. Confrontation between Malaysia and Indonesia.
Religion & Learning	C. P. Snow *The Two Cultures and the Scientific Revolution.* Leakey discovers 600,000-year-old human remains in Tanganyika. Teilhard de Chardin *The Phenomenon of Man.*	Sartre *Critique of Dialectical Reason.* Ayer *Logical Positivism.*	Beginning of a boom in higher education: universities established in Ghana, Sussex, Essex.	Universities of Keele and Singapore are established. Marshall McLuhan *The Gutenberg Galaxy.*	New universities are established at Newcastle, York and Guyana.
Cities & Social Development	Eisenhower halts steel and longshoremen's strikes in the USA by invoking the Taft-Hartley Act.	Penguin Books publish unexpurgated version of *Lady Chatterley's Lover*: obscenity trial follows.	Tanganyika Conference on the Preservation of African Wildlife. Freedom Riders, white liberals and blacks, test integration in the South; they are attacked by white racists.	Britain passes Commonwealth Immigrants Act to control immigration into country. Found that approximately 44 per cent of world's adult population is illiterate. Governor Barnett of Mississippi University denies admission to a black student: US Marshalls and 3,000 soldiers suppress riots when Meredith takes his university place.	Beeching Report leads to the rundown of the British Railway system.
Discovery & Invention	USA and the USSR begin to train astronauts: USSR launches rocket with two monkeys aboard and USSR Lunik (unmanned) reaches the moon.	International Development Association (soft aid arm of the World Bank) established. International Agreement to reserve Antarctica for scientific research: territorial claims are all waived. US X15 research aircraft reaches a speed of 3534 kmh. Galaxy 6,000 million light years away is photographed at the Mount Palomar Observatory. France explodes her first nuclear bomb. Russian Sputnik V orbits the earth carrying two live dogs.	Yuri Gagarin is the first man in space; he is followed shortly afterwards by the American Alan Shepard. Jodrell Bank team transmits radio waves which reflect back from Venus.	Drug Thalidomide causes deformities in babies and is withdrawn – long legal wrangles follow. Britain and France agree to construct Concorde, the first supersonic airliner. US Communications Satellite, Telstar, brings live TV and radio signals to Europe. USA now has 200 atomic reactors in operation, Britain and the USSR 39 each. First American in orbit, John Glenn makes 3 orbits in *Friendship 7.*	Rachel Carson *The Silent Spring*, on the effects of chemical pesticides upon the environment. Valentina Tereshkova is the first woman (Russian) in space. Quasars are discovered by Matthews and Sandage.
The Arts	Films: *Hiroshima Mon Amour, Au Bout du Souffle, Some Like it Hot, La Dolce Vita, Pickpocket*, Japan produces 493 feature films. Anouilh *Becket.* Poulenc *La Voix Humaine.* Grass *The Tin Drum.* Pop: Buddy Holly *It Doesn't Matter Anymore*, Cliff Richard *Living Doll*, Adam Faith *What Do You Want.* Jazz: Charles Mingus *Fables of Faubus.*	Pinter *The Caretaker.* Films: *Psycho, The Apartment, Don't Shoot the Piano Player, Rocco and his brother.* Pop: Eddie Cochran *Three Steps to Heaven*, Shadows *Apache.*	Heller *Catch-22.* Films: *Last Year in Marienbad, Through a glass darkly, The Misfits, The Hustler, West Side Story.* Muriel Spark *The Prime of Miss Jean Brodie.* Henry Miller *Tropic of Cancer* is first legally published in the USA (Paris 1934). Pop: Elvis Presley *Little Sister*, Helen Shapiro *Walking Back to Happiness.*	Films: *Jules et Jim, The Man Who shot Liberty Vallance.* Albee *Who's Afraid of Virginia Woolf* Solzhenitsyn *A day in the Life of Ivan Denisovich.* Philharmonic Hall of the Lincoln Centre, New York, opens. James Baldwin *Another Country.* Britten *War Requiem.* Pop: Beatles *From Me To You, She Loves You, I Want To Hold Your Hand.*	Films: *8½, The Silence, The Servant, The Birds, The Leopard.* Mary McCarthy *The Group.* The Beatles 'pop' group achieve international fame.

In the years immediately before the Second World War the colonial presence in Africa reached its fullest expression. The number of independent African states fell to one, Liberia, when the Italians finally succeeded in conquering Abyssinia. Even the hitherto untameable peoples of the Sahara succumbed to the mechanized columns that occupied their oases and poisoned their wells. Never had the rule to the European seemed more secure.

In fact, it had little more than 20 years to run. In the aftermath of the Second World War there was a reaction against the whole idea of colonial tutelage and by the early 1960s almost nothing was left of what had once been the world's most impressive imperial structure. The dismantling process began with the overthrow of the Italian Empire in Eritrea, Abyssinia and Somaliland during the war, and Britain's grudging departure from Egypt immediately after it. It accelerated during the 1950s by the end of which all the countries north of the Sahara had recovered their independence bar Algeria. Here the million strong settler community refused to face up to the altered situation, and France had, in consequence, become involved in a futile war on their behalf. South of the Sahara the decolonization process got off to a slower start with only two nations emerging from the colonial chrysalis: Ghana (previously the British Gold Coast) in 1957 and Guinea (previously part of French West Africa) in 1958.

The year 1960 was the consummation. Prime Minister Macmillan of Britain and President de Gaulle of France decided to liquidate their remaining African commitments as fast as they decently could. At the same time the Belgians determined to leave – abandon might be a better word – the Congo. The result of these decisions was the creation of a host of new nations. West and Central Africa was transformed into a mosaic of independent states: East Africa followed shortly after in the early 1960s.

Prime Minister Macmillan had prefaced the British contribution to this political transformation with a tour of Africa which took him from Ghana to Capetown. Addressing the Capetown parliament he spoke of the wind of change that was sweeping through the continent as though it was an historical force which it would be foolish to try and resist, but if he hoped that his metaphor would soften the attitude of the Boer government of South Africa towards its black population, he was to be sorely disappointed. A month later South African police shot down 67 blacks protesting against the country's repressive pass laws: at the end of the year the white community voted to make South Africa a republic and sever the connection with the British Commonwealth. Faced with the choice between apartheid and power sharing, the South African whites had opted for the existing system.

Left: Zimbabwe's first parliament in session, 1979. An experiment in multi-racial democracy following many years of white rule.

Above: Jomo Kenyatta, the father figure of independent Kenya, at the Independence Day celebrations in 1963.

In the 20 odd years since the metamorphosis – and polarization – achieved in these hectic months, surprisingly little has changed. The French gave up the struggle to retain control of Algeria in 1962, the Portuguese packed up and left their African territories in 1974–5. The British settlers in Rhodesia made more of a fight of it but in 1978 they too abandoned the attempt to sustain their colonial-style regime and the country is now under the rule of its Shona majority. This leaves South Africa isolated but not intimidated: the Boers remain unimpressed by the condemnation of the rest of the world, intransigent in the defence of their privileged position and confident that they can maintain it for the foreseeable future. It seems likely that, as far as this century goes, events will prove them right but the demographic trends must surely lead to their being overwhelmed at some stage in the next.

One of the most peculiar features of post-colonial Africa is the stability of its frontiers. Lines that were drawn on the map in haste a hundred years ago by people who knew little about African geography and less about its inhabitants, have become accepted international frontiers. Odd enclaves like the Gambia and Djibouti exist for no other reason that that colonial outposts were sited there in a bygone era. The frontiers of the nations of the Sahel – the strip of territory to the south of the Sahara – reflect not the history of these peoples but the administrative sub-divisions of French West Africa as established in the early years of this century. There have been instances where the colonial boundaries have been challenged, notably the attempt by the Ibo people of Nigeria to establish their own state ('Biafra') in 1967–70, and the campaign by which Somali hoped to wrest the Ogaden with its Somali population from Ethiopia (defeated by the Ethiopians with Russian help in 1978), but though many African states have changed their names none has changed its outline. It is the one colonial legacy that, in an age full of uncertainties, no one seems disposed to repudiate.

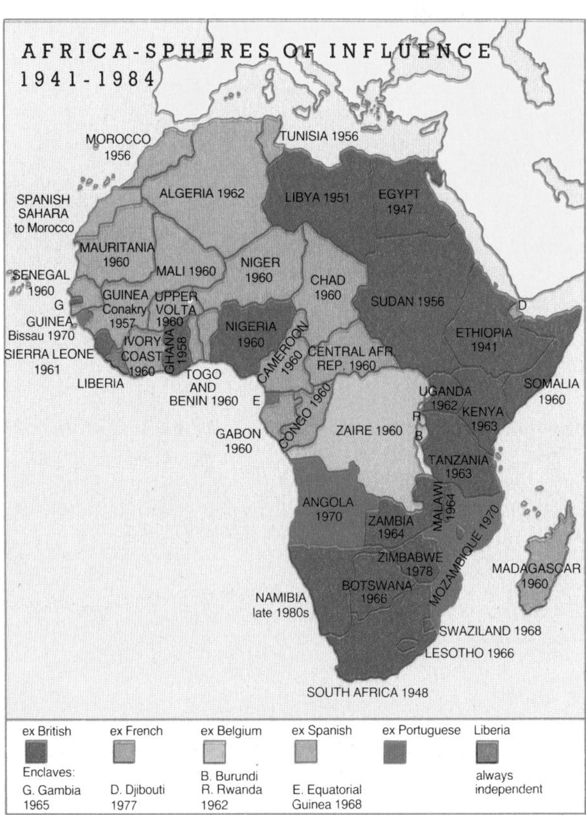

Right: This map gives a simpler picture of colonialism in Africa than the one on page 161. This is largely because the Germans were eliminated from the colonial competition in the First World War, and the Italians in the Second. However, it is also true that the map is somewhat simpler than the reality: it does not show minority interests – for example the Spanish slice of Morocco and the French slice of Libya.

All organisms walk a tightrope between reproducing too much or too little. *Homo sapiens*, one of the most successful, has managed over the millennia to walk the rope with as much balance as any. The human race has expanded at a broadly steady rate to cover more and more of the earth's surface and – with the development of agriculture – to occupy its habitat more and more intensively.

The working of the balance between births and deaths that brought about this steady expansion was complex. In many societies, social constraints on growth were added to natural ones; but the natural constraints generally dominated. Nature culled human young quite drastically; perhaps a quarter of all humans died in the first year of life, another quarter in childhood. Of the young adults, disease took many, warfare others. If these restraints were insufficient to hold growth to moderate levels, mating patterns adjusted to the levels of mortality in society, and added to the limits that ill-health and poor nutrition often set on natural fecundity.

The economic development of the world from the 18th century onwards destroyed this age-old balance by significantly reducing levels of mortality. In the heartlands of economic advance – Western Europe and the areas of European settlement overseas – dominance of the world's markets and industrialization brought substantial long-term increase in wealth and living standards and, consequently, in standards of health. In the 18th century, food supplies improved; in the 19th, society began to afford the investment in water-supplies, waste-disposal and housing which reduced epidemic disease; in the 20th, personal health services and medical advances cut into the remaining causes of premature death, particularly among children. In broad terms, in Western Europe, life expectancy at birth rose from 30 years in the mid-18th century to 40 in the mid-19th and 70 in the mid-20th.

When mortality decreases, fertility does not decline automatically and at once; as a result, the overall rate of population growth rises sharply. That is the explanation of the population explosion in the West in the 19th century and the even greater one in the rest of the world in the 20th century. Indeed, in some places – notably in 18th century Britain – one initial reaction to the increasing security of economic development is an increase in fertility, mainly

Above: A 'Pusher' at work on Tokyo commuters. The Tokyo Transport Authority employs students to pack as many people as possible into its trains.

Below left: Standing room only. Crowds on Kamakura Beach, a popular resort some 60 km from Tokyo.

Below right: Horizontal spread. A shanty town built by squatters on the outskirts of Hong Kong.

because of younger marriage and better health.

In the long-term – over two or three generations – peopl become aware that there are just too many children aroun too many to feed, clothe and find work for. The Wes though, had it easy. Europe was able to export much of i surplus exploding population to the Americas an elsewhere. Living at the centre of economic development, could offer its people the economic security and consume goods that reduced the attractions of excessive numbers children.

In the less-developed world outside the West, in the late 20th century, it is often a different story. The economi resources are not there – or not used – to transform childre from cheap economic assets into expensively educate competitors with consumer durables. Because im provements in health have generally preceded widesprea economic development rather than followed it, as in th West, the developing world is in danger of being caught u in an unpleasant vicious circle: fertility is most easil reduced by the attractions and incentives of rising livin standards but, in many countries today, rising livin standards depend on reductions in fertility – otherwis economic development, more sluggish than in the 19t century West, cannot keep pace with – let alone overtake population growth.

There are ways of side-stepping this paradox. In th absence of massive economic development, relatively chea grassroots improvements in education and health care ca produce populations receptive to the small family ideal – t the concept of quality rather than quantity – and to th means of securing it. Several densely populated islands and the state of Kerala in India – seem to be moving alon this path. In some large countries, governments hav resorted to more draconian methods. India has toye intermittently with aggressive – sometimes over-aggressiv – campaigns to encourage parents with reasonably-size families to be sterilized. China has embarked on a one child-family policy with a collectivist zeal that may ye prove successful. Since China and India together contai half of the population living in the less-developed world, i is possible that the world's population will not explode ou of all control in the next few decades. But it is going to b touch-and-go.

	1964	1965	1966	1967	1968
Politics & Military History	Indonesia invades Malaysia in continuing Confrontation. China explodes A-bomb. Fighting between Greeks and Turks in Cyprus: UN Peace Mission is sent. USA escalates its support for South Vietnam against the Communist North. Nyasaland becomes independent as Malawi. Northern Rhodesia becomes independent as Zambia. Tanganyika and Zanzibar unite as the Republic of Tanzania.	USA begins regular bombing raids on North Vietnam; first US Marines arrive in South Vietnam to support Vietnamese army. Cultural revolution launched in China. India and Pakistan at war over Kashmir. White minority government makes Unilateral Declaration of Independence in Rhodesia (UDI). Opposed by the west leading to trade embargoes. Singapore secedes from Malaysia to become independent state.	UN imposes economic sanctions against Rhodesia Military coup in Nigeria ends regime of Abubakar. Red Guards purge the Revisionists in the Chinese Cultural revolution. International Day of protest is held against US policy in Vietnam. Assassination of Dr Verwoerd in South Africa – succeeded by John Vorster.	Military coup in Greece brings military junta to power. Six Day War (June 5–10): Israel launches pre-emptive war and imposes crushing defeat on Arabs; occupies Sinai desert, Arab Jerusalem, the west bank of Jordan and the Golan Heights of Syria: UN arranges ceasefire. More race riots in the USA in Detroit and Newark: the *Long Hot Summer*; the emergence of Black Power. Che Ernesto Guevara the Cuban leader is killed in Bolivia: he becomes cult hero. Britain reduces its armed forces and cuts back its Far East commitments. Eastern (Ibo) region of Nigeria attempts to secede as Biafra; the beginning of the Nigerian Civil War.	Britain withdraws from East of Suez. May unrest in Paris: general strike, student demonstrations, de Gaulle flees Paris but is subsequently endorsed in elections. Alexander Dubcek introduces liberal reforms in Czechoslovakia; Soviet troops invade and Dubcek is ousted from power. Civil Rights leader Martin Luther King is assassinated. Presidential candidate Robert Kennedy is assassinated: Nixon wins US presidential election. Tet Offensive: Vietcong launch massive offensive against South Vietnam.
Religion & Learning	Universities of East Anglia, Kent, Lancaster, Stirling, Strathclyde and Malawi are established. McLuhan *Understanding Media*.	Marcuse *Culture and Society*. Universities are established at Ulster, Warwick and Zambia.	Seven new universities are created in Britain bringing to 18 the number created between 1961 and 1966. Mao Zedong *The Quotations of Mao Zedong*.	Marcuse and others *A Critique of pure tolerance*. Leakey discovers fossil remains *Kenyapithecus africanus* which are 20m years old. McLuhan *The Medium is the Message*.	Worldwide student unrest affects Paris, Rome, Copenhagen, Tokyo, London, West Germany and throughout the USA.
Cities & Social Development	*The Sun* newspaper is founded in Britain. US Race Riots result from the enforcement of Civil Rights Laws.	Post Office Tower in London is completed (189m). Britain enacts its first Race Relations Act. Race riots in Watts, USA, 34 die and 4,000 arrested.	EEC countries adopt Common Agricultural Policy. Colour television is widely adopted.	Lake Point Tower, Chicago, 70 storey (196m): the world's tallest reinforced concrete apartment building. 100 million telephones now in service in USA.	Britain passes Commonwealth Immigration Act: further restrictions upon immigrants. Completion of the Aswan High Dam in Egypt.
Discovery & Invention	US Ranger 7 reaches the Moon: sends back 4,000 photos. (Ranger 4 – first US craft to land on moon in 1962.) Britain suffers from 'brain drain' of its scientists to the USA. Beginning of drilling for oil in North Sea.	British Petroleum discovers natural gas in North Sea. Russian Cosmonaut and then an American Astronaut walk in space.	US surgeons use a plastic heart to keep a patient alive for several days. US Surveyor I makes soft landing on the moon.	Dr Christiaan Barnard, South Africa, performs the first heart transplant operation; patient dies after 18 days. Venus IV, Russian spacecraft, makes soft landing on Venus.	Ryle discovers pulsars: radio stars emitting regular pulses of energy. France tests H-Bomb. Manned US spacecraft Apollo 8 journeys 384,000 kilometres to the moon and back.
The Arts	Pinter *Homecoming*. Films: *The Red Desert, Dr Strangelove, A Fistful of Dollars*. C. P. Snow *Corridors of Power*. Pop: Beatles *Can't Buy Me Love, A Hard Day's Night, I Feel Fine*, Rolling Stones *It's All Over Now, Little Red Rooster*, Animals *House of the Rising Sun*, Chuck Berry *No Particular Place To Go*.	Films: *The Pawnbroker, Dr Zhivago, War and Peace (Russian version)*. Osborne *A Patriot for Me*. Pop: Beatles *Ticket to Ride, Help!, Day Tripper*, Rolling Stones *The Last Time*, Kinks *Tired of Waiting For You*, Byrds *Mr. Tambourine Man*.	Orton *Entertaining Mr Sloane*. Films: *The Rise to power of Louis XIV, Un Homme et une Femme, The War Game*. Greene *The Comedians*. Pop: Sinatra *Strangers in the Night*, Beach Boys *Good Vibrations*, Four Tops *Reach Out I'll be There*.	Films: *Le Weekend, The Graduate, El Dorado, Accident*. Mailer *Why are we in Vietnam?* Stoppard *Rosencrantz and Guildenstern are Dead*. Pop: Monkees *I'm a Believer*, Beatles *All You Need is Love*. Procul Harem *A Whiter Shade of Pale*.	Solzhenitsyn *The First Circle*. Joe Orton *Loot*. Films: *Les Biches, 2001, The Odd Couple*. Pop: Rolling Stones *Jumping Jack Flash*, Beatles *Hey Jude*.

	1969	1970	1971	1972	1973
Politics & Military History	Willy Brandt becomes West German Chancellor: revalues the mark; begins Ostpolitik towards USSR. Civil disturbances in Ulster; Britain sends troops to support the civil authorities. Arafat becomes leader of the Palestine Liberation Organization. Leading British conservative, Enoch Powell, proposes the repatriation of Black and Asian citizens.	Riots at Gdansk in Poland: Gomulka resigns after 14 years. Civil War in Jordan: Palestine guerrillas against government forces. Biafra surrenders: end of the Nigerian civil war. US troops invade Cambodia. National Guard in the USA fires upon student demonstrators at Kent University, killing 4.	Vietnam fighting spreads to Laos and Cambodia. Amin seizes power in Uganda. Vote is extended to all over 18 in the USA. War between East and West Pakistan: India assists Bengali-establish independent state of Bangladesh. China finally admitted to the UN; Taiwan (Formosa) is expelled. Women gain the vote in Switzerland.	Civil war breaks out in Lebanon. Nixon visits China and the USSR: pursues a policy of détente. Britain imposes direct rule in Northern Ireland. Ceylon becomes a republic and changes name to Sri Lanka. President Allende of Chile pursues policy of major nationalization.	Britain, Ireland and Denmark join the EEC. Peace of Paris: USA withdraws from Vietnam. Military coup in Chile overthrows Allende government and brings in American-backed right wing regime. Yom Kippur War: the fourth Arab-Israeli war, military honours more even than in the previous wars. Arab oil producing nations put embargo on oil to western nations which support Israel; precipitate oil crisis; OPEC quadruple oil price. East and West Germany establish diplomatic relations and acknowledge their post-war separation for the first time. Brezhnev and Nixon meet: sign treaty to limit nuclear war.
Religion & Learning	Leach *Genesis as Myth and other essays*. Britain establishes an open university: teaching is done through television and radio.	Major unrest in American universities: 448 universities and colleges are closed or on strike.			Levi-Strauss *Anthropologie Structurale*, Vol. II.
Cities & Social Development	South Africa refuses to allow an MCC cricket team to visit the country because it contains a coloured player, Basil D'Oliveira. White Paper *In Place of Strife* is an attempt by a Labour government in Britain to reform Trade Union movement.	Divorce is permitted in Italy. 231 million television sets worldwide.	USA devalues the dollar: Japan and most European currencies are revalued upwards. Rolls-Royce are declared bankrupt. Billie Jean King, the tennis star, becomes the first woman athlete to earn $100,000 a year.	Strict anti-hijack measures are introduced internationally, especially at airports. Military draft is phased out in the USA whose armed forces become all-volunteer.	Energy crisis precipitates western economic crisis. Britain on three-day working week to save energy following miner's strike. World Trade Center, New York twin towers each 411.5m high.
Discovery & Invention	BP discovers large oil deposits in Alaska. Apollo 11 lands the American Astronauts Neil Armstrong and Buzz Aldrin on the Moon. Anglo-French supersonic Concorde makes its first test flight.	British Petroleum (BP) discovers oil in North Sea. China puts her first satellite into space. Boeing 747 airliner (the Jumbo Jet) goes into service. The Russian spacecraft Soyuz 9 performs a record 18 day orbit of the earth; Luna 17 lands an 8-wheeled vehicle on the moon to explore its surface.	US Satellite Mariner 9 orbits Mars. Tanker of 378,377 tonnes is launched in Japan: the largest ship ever built. US astronomers discover two 'new' galaxies adjacent to the Earth's own Galaxy, the Milky Way.	Leakey and Isaac discover a skull in Kenya which is 2.5 million years old: ancestor of man.	US Skylab I, II and III space missions are successfully completed.
The Arts	Roth *Portnoy's Complaint*. Films: *Satyricon, Zabriskiè Point, Easy Rider, Midnight Cowboy*. Pop: Marvin Gaye *I Heard It Through the Grapevine*, Bob Dylan *Nashville Skyline*. Woodstock Music Festival in USA attracts 300,000 fans.	Films: *Tristana, MASH*; almost all the great Hollywood companies become part of conglomerates. Pop: Simon & Garfunkel *Bridge over Troubled Water*, Jimi Hendrix *Voodoo Chile*, The Doors *Morrison Hotel*.	Films: *The Decameron, A Clockwork Orange, The Ceremony, Straw Dogs*. The Kennedy Centre for the Performing Arts is opened in Washington DC. E. M. Forster *Maurice*, (post.). Pop: T Rex *Get it On*, George Harrison *My Sweet Lord*.	Films: *The Discreet Charm of the Bourgeoisie, Roma, Cabaret*. Shostakovich 15th Symphony. *Fiddler on the Roof* longest running show on Broadway closes after 3,242 performances. Pop: Alice Cooper *School's Out*, Rod Stewart *Every Picture Tells a Story*, Deep purple *Machine Head*.	Greene *The Honorary Consul*. Films: *Aguirre, Wrath of God, Mean Streets*, the beginning of a Hollywood revival. Solzhenitsyn *The Gulag Archipelago*. Pop: David Bowie *Hunky Dory*, Roxy Music *For Your Pleasure*.

bove: Edwin Aldrin on the oon. Aldrin and Neil rmstrong brought the Apollo ogramme to a triumphant imax when they landed Apollo 's lunar module on the surface the moon on 20 July 1969.

ight: The Apollo 11 lunar odule on the moon. The odule lifted off from the lunar rface after a stay of just under 4 hours, taking the two stronauts to a successful ndezvous with the command odule piloted by Michael ollins.

ar right: Apollo's Saturn V unch vehicle, first successfully red in 1967. During the 2½ inutes for which its motors are nning, the Saturn V consumes 3.6 tonnes of propellant every econd.

On 4th October 1957, a converted Soviet missile put into orbit the first artificial satellite, Sputnik 1. The event shook the government establishment in the US. It showed that the Soviet Union had the technology to shoot guided weapons laden with bombs at American shores. Furthermore, the demonstrated capability to do what scientists had promised for centuries – to inject objects away from the earth's gravitational field and out of the atmosphere – represented a huge propaganda coup. The US had to strike back.

In 1958 the government set up its National Aeronautics and Space Administration to co-ordinate space activities. The following year the administration selected its first batch of seven astronauts. But the USSR won the race to put the first man into space when, on 12th April 1961, Yuri Gagarin made his historic 108-minute orbit of the earth. The next month President Kennedy made probably his most famous speech. He committed the US to put a man on the moon by the end of the decade.

But how to do it? There were three options. In the most straightforward, a rocket blasts off from earth, detaching a lunar module near the moon, which lands directly on the surface. In the second possibility, rockets would make two separate flights into orbit around the earth the first bringing the booster hardware for the lunar voyage and the second would release the astronauts' spacecraft. While orbiting the earth the components would dock to produce the 'lunar tug' needed for the second stage of the journey.

But NASA decided, in 1962, to choose the third technique, championed by John Houbolt, a space engineer. A rocket jettisons into space a two-stage capsule, which enters orbit around the moon. It separates to leave one astronaut in orbit in the command module while two others descend in the lunar capsule to the surface. The capsule includes small boosters with which the craft propels itself back to the command module, thus enabling the astronauts' safe return to earth.

NASA practised this strategy with a series of docking experiments using its two-man Gemini spacecraft. Apollo 8, with a three man crew, made the first manned lunar flight during Christmas 1968, completing 10 orbits but stopping short of an actual landing.

Finally Apollo 11 was ready to make the historic journey and on 21st July Neil Armstrong, his pulse an incredible 150 beats a minute, stepped onto the moon with the words, 'A small step for man, a large step for mankind.'

The $25,000 million Apollo programme had reached its climax. A further five manned lunar landings were undertaken between 1969 and 1972. The Houbolt technique was clever. The strategy required a rocket with a lower power than that needed for the 'direct descent' option. This was because the payload it needed to carry was less heavy. Consequently it was much cheaper. The second, 'earth-orbit' technique was ruled out because of the logistic difficulties of refuelling a 'lunar tug' while orbiting the earth. Interestingly, this option is now being mooted for long solar-system flights that involve a refuelling stage at the low-orbit space station that the US wants to build for the 1990s.

The USSR, with its early lead in space technology, tried hard to beat the US to the moon. It sent a series of unmanned probes, including a set of Zond spacecraft which were big enough to carry people and which circumnavigated the moon as early as September 1968. But it appears that technical problems with their rockets late in 1968 dissuaded the Soviets from mounting a challenge the following year. After this, the USSR had to be content with a series of further advances in unmanned spacecraft, including a probe that in 1970 returned lunar soil to earth. *(P.W.)*

The earliest stages of industrial development had depended in part on the energy stored in water and wind as well as in the muscles of men and animals but, in the long-term, the exploitation of coal to provide steam power had been crucial to the economic development of the Western nations in the 18th and 19th centuries. The economic advances of the 20th century were to depend fundamentally on another fossil fuel: oil.

It had not seemed very likely in the beginning. When a group of local business men sponsored Edwin L. Drake to sink the first commercial oil well 21 metres deep at Titusville, Pennsylvania in 1859, they had their eyes set only on the potential market for a fuel to supply household light and heat. The oil-rush that followed in the Appalachian oil-field – 175 more wells were sunk within a year – was primarily based on the production of kerosene for the farms and small towns of the United States.

The wider applications of mineral oil were not neglected for long, though. It formed a significant element in the advances in industrial lubrication made in the later 19th century. Most important of all, an effective engine powered by the internal combustion of oil had been developed by the 1880s. Such an engine was in many ways more efficient than the coal-fired steam engine: in fuel consumption – since oil produces at least 50% more energy than the same weight of coal – in ease of fuel storage and handling and in cleanliness. By the beginning of the 20th century, oil had made substantial advances in the powering of industrial machinery and of ships, where it had clear advantages over other sources of energy.

In the first half of the 20th century, the history of oil was the history of the motor car. Up to the Second World War, well over half the world's oil was produced and consumed in the USA, and well over half the oil used in the USA drove motor vehicles. Outside the USA and transport, coal remained the dominant source of power in this period; as late as 1940, three-quarters of the world's energy was provided by coal and less than 20% by oil.

Because of its ease of extraction, oil remained a remarkably cheap fuel. The USA had a glut of oil until the 1960s and – particularly after the Second World War – other oilfields were opened up in the Middle East and South America, often producing oil at even cheaper rates than the regulated prices of the North American fields. Because oil was so plentiful and so cheap, the industrial nations increasingly substituted it for coal, notably in the production of electricity. Some of the more recently industrializing countries, notably Japan, had few power resources of their own and came to rely on imported oil for most of their energy needs. By the early 1960s, coal was supplying less than half the world's energy, while oil had come to provide a third and natural gas, closely linked to oil in its extraction, another 15%; ten years later, coal had fallen to less than a third, oil was approaching 50% and natural gas was close to 20%.

All this time, the amount of oil extracted annually in the world had been rising at a remarkably steady rate, doubling every eight or nine years. The figures produced a perfect exponential curve. But the arithmetic of exponential growth becomes frightening after a while; the continued doubling of large numbers very soon produces impossible totals. The arithmetic suggested that, by the end of the 1970s, the world would demand far more oil than it could easily produce and that, not very long afterwards, it would run out altogether.

The arithmetic was never put to the test; it merely hung over the world of the later 20th century as a grim warning and an incentive to panic. By the early 1970s, the oil market

Above: The Torrey Canyon *being pounded to pieces by the waves after going aground on the Seven Stones Reef between the Isles of Scilly and Land's End in 1967. Some 30,000 tonnes of crude oil were released by the wreck, polluting many kilometres of beach in one of the worst ecological disasters of the oil age.*

Right: The Statfiord B platform under construction. Destined for a site in the Norwegian sector of the North Sea this concrete structure was placed in position in 140 metres of water in 1981. It relies entirely on its immense weight to keep it stable.

had dramatically changed shape. The USA's oil output w slowing down, the end of its reserves within sight. Nor America's share of world production had fallen to a quarte that of the Middle East had risen to a third. When anoth 10% in South America and nearly 15% in Africa we thrown in, the Third World countries provided nearly 60 of the world's oil. And they were beginning to conclude – demand pressed relentlessly upwards – that they we getting very little benefit from the arithmetic of supply an demand.

The rest is very recent and still painful history. I 1973–4, the OPEC oil producers of the Third Wor pushed prices 500% higher than they had been in 197 while Arab boycotts after the 1973 Arab-Israeli war c supplies to unsympathetic countries. In 1979, the Irani Revolution and renewed demand combined to raise pric by another 150%. In the subsequent world depression, o prices have drifted downwards, but they still threaten rise whenever a market balanced on a knife-edge of supp and demand hears of threats to Middle East stability c senses increased economic activity.

In all this, the exponential climb has been broken. O demand levelled out over the 1970s and has fallen in th past few years. Periods of chronic industrial depression, least partially induced by the oil crisis, have had much to d with this, but the higher prices and known limits o resources have encouraged fuel conservation and a searc for alternative sources of power. But some of these, such a natural gas, are also finite; others, particularly nucle power, carry their own problems. The search continu and, meanwhile, we continue to use up what is left of the o *(R.J.)*

	1974	1975	1976	1977	1978
Politics & Military History	Greek-Turkish conflict in Cyprus escalates: Turks invade Cyprus, leads to partition. Watergate Scandal forces President Nixon to resign. Army coup in Portugal overthrows government of Caetano: leads to independence for Portugal's colonies in Africa – Angola, Mozambique and Guinea-Bissau. Revolution in Ethiopia leads to downfall of Emperor Haile Selassie: a military *Dergue* takes power.	Communist victories in Cambodia. South Vietnam surrenders to North, end of Vietnam War. Suez Canal is reopened (it had been closed since the 1967 war). Britain holds first ever referendum and votes 2–1 to remain in EEC.	Cod War between Britain and Iceland. Assassination of General M. Muhammad of Nigeria. Major riots in Soweto African Township outside Johannesburg against the compulsory learning of Afrikaans in schools. Opening of the TANZAM (Chinese built) Railway from Dar es Salaam in Tanzania to Kapiri Mposhi in Zambia. Death of Mao Zedong ends era of Chinese history.	Ethiopia-Somalia conflict in Ogaden region. South African crackdown on Black newspapers, anti-apartheid organizations and Black leaders. UN imposes mandatory arms embargo on South Africa. President Sadat of Egypt visits Israel: addresses Knesset.	UN force is sent to Lebanon because of border troubles with Israel. USA agrees to diplomatic relations with China and ends those with Taiwan. Muldergate Scandal in South Africa.
Religion & Learning	Pope Paul VI canonizes Teresa Iban.	Dr Coggan becomes the 101st Archbishop of Canterbury – the Pope is represented at the ceremony.	Continuing sectarian murders of Roman Catholics by Protestants and Protestants by Catholics in Northern Ireland.	Page written by Galileo in 1612 sells at auction for £17,500.	Historic Crown of St Stephen returned to Hungary from the USA. Temple of Augustus Caesar is recovered from the Island of Philae now under waters of Nile. Cardinal Karol Wojtyla, a Pole, becomes Pope John Paul II, the first non-Italian to hold the post in 450 years.
Cities & Social Development	Smallpox epidemic in India kills between 10,000 and 20,000. Drought in Sahel region of Africa leads to severe famine. Sears Tower, Chicago: 442m high and currently the world's tallest building.*	Massive airlift of refugees from Vietnam to USA. *Scottish Daily News* published, the first workers' co-operative national newspaper. British unemployment rises above one million for first time since before WW2.	India raises minimum ages for marriage: men 18 to 21, women 15 to 18. Queen Elizabeth II visits USA for bicentennial celebrations. Explosion at Seveso Plant in Italy leads to a 7km radius area being contaminated by poison chemicals.	President Carter pardons American draft dodgers. International Commission of Jurists reports to UN massacres in Uganda under Amin – as many as 80,000 to 90,000 victims. Biko inquest in South Africa 'absolves' police and authorities of his death in detention.	World's first test tube baby is born in Oldham, Lancashire.
Discovery & Invention	US Mariner satellite transmits detailed pictures of Venus and Mercury. India becomes the sixth nation to explode a nuclear device.	First European Nuclear Energy Conference is held in Paris. Chinese team including a woman scale Everest by the North Face. Salyut IV space station spends record 63 days in space.	Workmen discover a perfectly preserved rose in the wall of Romsey Abbey dating from 1120; thought to be oldest botanical specimen found in Europe. Viking II goes into orbit round Mars. Soviet Luna 24 makes soft landing on moon and takes soil samples with automatic scoop.	Astronomers observe rings round Uranus for the first time. Royal College of Physicians' report on smoking suggests every cigarette shortens the habitual smoker's life by $5\frac{1}{2}$ minutes. Miners in Shantung, China, unearth bird fossil of Miocene Period in beautiful state of preservation.	Russian Cosmonauts spend 84 days in space in Salyut VI. First balloon crossing of the Atlantic is achieved by three Americans. Two Russian Cosmonauts spend 140 days in orbiting space station.
The Arts	Films: *Amarcord, Chinatown, Godfather II, Alice doesn't live here anymore.* Patrick White *The Eye of the Storm*, Australian novel.	The estate of Picasso is valued at £650 million. Films: *One Flew Over the Cuckoo's Nest.* Pop: Led Zeppelin *Physical Graffiti*, Pink Floyd *Wish You Were Here.*	The Queen opens Britain's new National Theatre in London. Films: *Network, Rocky.*	BBC Symphony Orchestra appoints as principal conductor the Russian Gennadi Rozhdestvensky. Films: *Annie Hall, The Goodbye Girl.* Pop: Wings *Mull of Kintyre.* Punk era starts in Britain with bands like The Sex Pistols – aggressive music and fashion soon follow.	Executors of Lady Spencer-Churchill reveal that she destroyed the Graham Sutherland portrait of Winston Churchill. Films: *Coming Home, The Deer Hunter.* Pop: Jam *All Mod Cons*, Fleetwood Mac *Rumours.*

*discounting TV masts, the tallest of which is 645m.

	1979	1980	1981	1982	1983
Politics & Military History	After mounting pressures and riots the Shah leaves Iran; exiled religious leader, Ayatollah Khomeini, returns and an Islamic Republic is proclaimed. First direct elections to the European Parliament are held in the 9 EEC countries. Amin flees Uganda as the Ugandan opponents of his regime backed by the Tanzanian army advance on Kampala. Egypt and Israel sign a peace treaty in Washington. Commonwealth Conference in Lusaka adopts proposals to end UDI in Rhodesia: both sides join talks in London; a cease-fire and elections are agreed and Britain resumes control over Rhodesia. Soviet backed coup in Afghanistan.	Conference of Islamic States meeting in Pakistan condemns Russian invasion of Afghanistan. Mugabe's ZANU win the elections in Rhodesia which becomes independent in April as Zimbabwe. US rescue mission to Iran (sent to free Embassy hostages) fails. Death of President Tito of Yugoslavia ends era of Non-Aligned leadership. Beginning of Iraq-Iran War. China puts the widow of Mao Zedong on trial. Major labour unrest in Poland: the US, EEC and NATO warn USSR not to invade Poland.	Iran frees the US hostages after 444 days of captivity. *Gang of Four* are sentenced to death in China. Bobby Sands starves himself to death in Belfast prison; leads to riots in Roman Catholic areas of Belfast. President Sadat of Egypt assassinated. Coup in Ghana overthrows President Limaan and brings Jerry Rawlings to power.	Britain and the Vatican establish full diplomatic relations after four and a half centuries. El Salvador offensive against rebels fails: civil strife continues. OPEC cuts oil production to maintain prices against continuing world recession. Argentina seizes the Falkland Islands; Britain sends expeditionary force; Falklands War ends in Argentina forces surrendering. Spain joins NATO. Iran-Iraq war: Iranian troops enter Iraq. Israel invades southern Lebanon. Poland bans the labour movement Solidarity.	World debit crisis: growing apprehension of Western bankers at possibility of Third World countries repudiating debts. Former Gestapo official Klaus Barbie arrested in France. Beirut: bombing of US embassy and US and French military HQ; fighting in Lebanon is unabated for most of the year. Philippines opposition leader Benigno Aquino is assassinated. USSR shoots down Korean Air Lines jetliner straying into Soviet airspace; all 269 aboard are killed. US and other troops invade Grenada. End of military rule in Argentina with election of Raúl Alfonsin.
Religion & Learning	Nobel Peace Prize awarded to Mother Theresa of Calcutta.	Public execution of 63 persons who had taken part in the raid on the Grand Mosque at Mecca in 1979 in Saudi Arabia. Roman Catholic Archbishop Romero, one of El Salvador's most respected champions of human rights, assassinated. UNESCO Report shows that one third of the world's population can neither read nor write.	Islamic Summit held at Taif in Saudi Arabia. Attempt to assassinate Pope John Paul II in Vatican City; he is seriously wounded. Bitter row between *Third World* countries and West over UNESCO plan for a *new world information order.*	Archbishop of Canterbury and the Pope pray together in Canterbury Cathedral in historic meeting of two Church leaders.	US Catholic bishops aprove pastoral letter condemning nuclear war and calling for nuclear arms reduction. Gospels of Henry the Lion sold at Sotheby's for record £8.1 million.
Cities & Social Development	Britain suffers *winter of discontent* with strikes of many municipal and other services. Wave of bombs in Northern Ireland shops and hotels. Earl Mountbatten and 3 others killed by bomb explosion on boat in Sligo.	Race riots in Miami: 14 killed, 300 injured, 1,000 arrested. Polish Unions form Solidarity which is registered in Warsaw.	Los Angeles Board of Education ends mandatory school busing to achieve racial integration in schools. Brixton riots in south London. Thirty British cities and towns experience riots – poverty is the cause.	US Supreme Court rules that the children of illegal aliens must have access to schools.	Martial law formally lifted in Poland.
Discovery & Invention	American Bryan Allen makes the longest ever man-powered flight, flying across the English Channel in 2 hours 20 minutes.	France develops its own neutron bomb. US reveals it has developed a *Stealth* aircraft capable of evading radar detection. US Voyager I flies past Saturn and reveals spectacular pictures of the planet's rings.	US launches the world's first space shuttle, the *Columbia*, which makes 36 orbits of the earth.	China fires first missile from a submarine and becomes fifth nation with this capability. Success of the first permanent artificial heart for Barney B. Clark in Salt Lake City, USA.	US space probe Pioneer 10 (launched 1972) crosses the orbit of Neptune and leaves the solar system. Sally Ride, aboard the space shuttle *Challenger*, becomes the first US woman in space.
The Arts	Films: *Kramer vs Kramer, Norma Rae.* Pop: Blondie *Parallel Lines*, Police *Regatta da Blanc.*	Greene *Dr Fischer of Geneva.* Films: *The Elephant Man, Kagemusha, The Marriage of Maria Braun.* Burgess *Earthly Powers.* Pop: John Lennon assassinated in New York.	Rushdie *Midnight's Children.* Updike *Rabbit is Rich.* Films: *On Golden Pond, Chariots of Fire, The Draughtsman's Contract, Man of Iron.* Pop: Human League *Dare.*	Burgess *The End of the World News.* Keneally *Schindler's Ark.* Theroux *The Mosquito Coast.* Films: *Gandhi, Sophie's Choice, ET, Heaven's Gate.* Pop: Dire Straits *Love over Gold.*	William Kennedy *Ironweed.* Raymond Carver *Cathedral.* Tom Stoppard *The Real Thing.* Films: *Tootsie, Terms of Endearment, Under Fire.* Pop: Michael Jackson's *Thriller* becomes the bestselling album of all time.

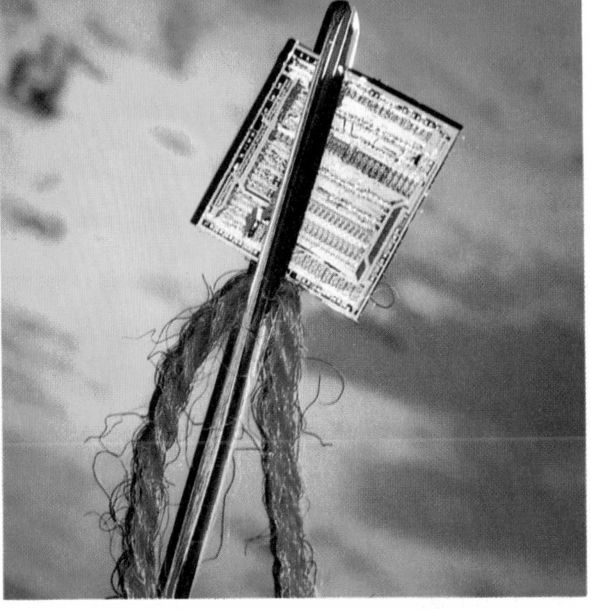

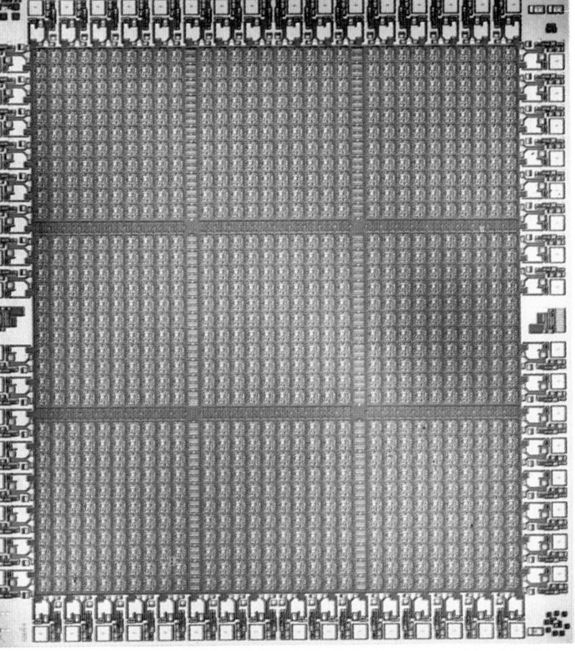

Above: Meteostat satellite. Since the first satellite was launched in 1957, satellites in geosychronous orbits – orbits that keep the satellite over the same spot on the earth's surface – have revolutionzed international communications, made worldwide TV link-ups commonplace and vastly improved weather forecasting.

Above right: Ferranti F100-L microprocessor threaded through the eye of a needle.

Left: Silicon chip under high magnification. The small size, high reliability and ever declining cost of the chip are the factors responsible for the present day revolution in information technology.

The world is awash with information. From the beginnings of civilization, that has always been the case. Any human activity – speaking, eating, playing music or working out mathematical equations – produces information that humans can store, collate and disseminate. They can do all of these things, although far more commonly they fail to take any notice of the information whatsoever.

What has changed in recent years is the technology required to handle information. What we nowadays call information technology is far from new. It began with the pieces of wood with which our caveman ancestors scratched signs in the sand, thus starting the continuous trend in which people made gradual advances in the classification and distribution of human knowledge to create wealth.

But people today have at their disposal a welter of devices and techniques to deal with information. They include computers, satellites, telephone exchanges, electronic printers, photocopiers and typesetting devices.

As a result the amount of information that is recorded and put at people's disposal is on the increase. It is estimated that more than 50 per cent of the working populations in industrialized countries have jobs that involve mainly the sifting and channelling of information of some sort or other.

In most developed countries, before long there will be at least one microprocessor for every person. A microprocessor is the tiny 'guts' of a computer, imprinted on a small sliver of silicon. About 70 communications satellites are in the geostationary ring, 36,000km above the earth, which is the most suitable orbit for such vehicles. These can channel information around the world at anything up to 500 million binary digits a second – equivalent to the transmission of the 20 million books in the British Library every two days.

Not all the information involves computers. Britain enacts new laws and statutes each year that add up to about 10,000 pages of legal text. In the US, scientists have an annual output of about half a million learned papers – and the figure is growing.

What to do with all this information? Paradoxically, the same technologies that increase the flow of data provide us with the means to make sense of it in an efficient way. Hence the drive to employ sophisticated 'message sorters', computerized hardware to analyse and sift information in many electronic information systems. Such sorters may eventually employ techniques of artificial intelligence – ways of using computers in which the machines take on something of the reasoning power of the human brain.

Ultimately, electronic mechanisms may become linked to biological materials, even the cells of the human body itself. Scientists are working on ways to transfer signals from microchips to, for example, nerve endings. With such techniques, humans would have a direct way of sending their thoughts to electronic machinery – to command the hardware, for example, to drive vehicles or translate between different languages. It would be the first step in giving mankind complete control of a new array of robot hardware: information technology would enable people and robots, for the first time, to speak the same language and understand each other. *(P.W.)*

	1984	1985	1986	1987	1988
Politics & Military History	After a bloodless coup, Maj.-Gen. Buhari becomes ruler of Nigeria. USA and Vatican resume diplomatic relations after more than 100 years. Soviet CP Chairman dies; succeeded by Chernenko. British, Italian, US, and then French peace-keeping forces withdraw from Lebanon. Duarte is elected president of El Salvador. Indian government troops storm Sikh Golden Temple at Amritsar. Indian PM Indira Gandhi is assassinated and succeeded by her son, Rajiv. Signs that recession may be ending but 36 million unemployed in OECD countries. China and Great Britain agree Hong Kong will revert to Chinese rule in 1997. British PM Margaret Thatcher narrowly escapes assassination in IRA terrorist bombing.	Ronald Reagan is sworn in for a second term as President of the United States. Britain's coal strike ends after almost a year. Soviet leader Konstantin Chernenko dies and is succeeded by Mikhail Gorbachev. President Nimeiry of the Sudan is overthrown by the army. Sudan, like neighbouring Ethiopia, is in the grip of drought and famine. Sikh extremists kill more than 70 people in terrorist attacks in India. Eduard Shevardnadze succeeds Andrei Gromyko as Soviet foreign minister. French agents sink Greenpeace vessel *Rainbow Warrior* in Auckland harbour. Coup in Uganda deposes President Milton Obote. Palestinian terrorists hijack the Italian cruise liner *Achille Lauro* in the Mediterranean. General Wojciech Jaruzelski is chosen as Poland's new head of state. Reagan–Gorbachev summit meeting in Geneva; the first US–USSR heads of state meeting in six years.	Spain and Portugal become the 11th and 12th members of the European Community. After a turbulent election, Mrs Corazon Aquino is declared President of the Philippines, replacing Ferdinand Marcos. Haiti ousts its dictator Jean-Claude Devalier who flees to France. US jets bomb Libya in retaliation for Libya's alleged support of terrorism. Kurt Waldheim, UN Secretary-General 1972–81, is barred from entering the USA because of his alleged complicity in Nazi war crimes. Commonwealth leaders meeting in London disagree over question of trade sanctions against South Africa. Mrs Thatcher opposes the general wish to see such sanctions. Javier Perez de Cuellar is re-elected for a second five-year term as UN Secretary General. Samora Machell, President of Mozambique, dies in a plane crash.	China and Portugal agree for the return of Portuguese -ruled Macao to China in 1999. Fianna Fail forms the new government after Irish elections. On 10th March Charles Haughey succeeds Garret Fitzgerald as *Taioseach* (prime minister). USS *Stark* is hit by missiles while on patrol in the Persian Gulf. Margaret Thatcher and the Conservatives win the British general election. Violence in Mecca leads to the deaths of 400 Iranian Muslim pilgrims. Iran accuses Saudi Arabian police of shooting Iranians. 11 people are killed and 60 injured by an IRA bomb attack on a Remembrance Day service at Enniskillin, Northern Ireland. Iran-*contra* report by US Senate is critical of the Reagan administration. USA and USSR sign treaty to eliminate intermediate range nuclear missiles.	Three IRA members are shot dead by security forces in Gibraltar while allegedly planning a bomb attack. President Mitterand is re-elected in France for a second seven-year term. Kim Philby, who spied for the USSR for 28 years until fleeing from Britain in 1963, dies in the USSR, aged 76. Vietnam announced its troops are to withdraw from Kampuchea. Ne Win resigns as leader of Burma after 26 years. Civil unrest follows. US Navy cruiser *Vincennes* accidentally shoots down an Iranian airliner in the Persian Gulf. All 290 people on board the plane are killed. Iran accepts ceasefire agreement to end the Iran–Iraq war. Ceasefire in Afghanistan, Soviet forces speed up their withdrawal. Chilean voters reject General Pnochet in a referendum, but he refuses to stand down. George Bush is elected President of the United States.
Religion & Learning	Nobel Peace Prize awarded to Bishop Desmond TuTu, black Anglican cleric in South Africa and campaigner against apartheid.	Tensions between Sikhs and Hindus continue in the Punjab. Pope John Paul II visits Latin America; Belgium, Luxembourg and the Netherlands; and African countries.	Pope John Paul II visits Colombia, India, Australia and the Pacific Islands. Leaders of 12 religious groups hold a World Day of Prayer for Peace at Assisi, Italy.	The New South Wales court of appeal upholds a supreme court ruling refusing to grant the British government a banning injuction on the controversial book *Spycatcher* by Peter Wright. American TV evangelist Jim Bakker resigns after a sex-related scandal. Terry Waite, the Archbishop of Canterbury's special envoy, is kidnapped in Beirut.	America's leading TV evangelist Jimmy Swaggart quits following a sex scandal. Barbara Harris elected as the first woman bishop in the US Episcopal Church.
Cities & Social Development	USSR and other Eastern block countries boycott Olympics in Los Angeles. Famine in Africa attains immense proportions. Gas leak at chemical plant in Bhopal, India, kills more than 2,000.	Israel reveals secret airlift of Ethiopian Jews to Israel. Dresden opera house reopens. English and Italian soccer fans riot in Brussels: 41 people die; English clubs banned from European matches.	The accident at the Chernobyl nuclear power plant in the USSR causes massive radiation leaks over a wide area. Local people are evacuated and the wrecked plant sealed in concrete for ever. Waldheim is elected President of Austria.	Gunman Michael Ryan runs amok in Hungerford, Berks, kills 14. Hurricane lashes south-east England, uproots 9 million trees. Wave of selling hits world stock markets.	Australia celebrates bicentennial of the arrival of the first fleet from England. World Health Organization meeting in Geneva expresses concern at the increase in reported AIDS cases. The XXIVth Olympic Games open in Seoul, South Korea.
Discovery & Invention	Top quark discovered at CERN, Switerland. Oxford U. Press announces entire OED is to be digitized and made accessible by computers.	Soviet cosmonauts reactivate space station *Salyut 7*. Halley's Comet makes its 30th recorded appearance. Remote-controlled submarine locates the wreck of the liner *Titanic*, sunk in 1912.	Seven astronauts are killed when the US space shuttle *Challenger* explodes shortly after take-off. *Voyager* aircraft, an ultra-lightweight design carrying Dick Rutan and Yeana Yeager of the USA completes a nine-day, non-stop flight around the world.	More than 70 nations agree at Montreal on measures to reduce chlorofluorocarboans and protect the ozone layer. First supernova (expoding star) visible to the naked eye for 383 years is discovered.	Scientists claim that the 'greenhouse effect' has already come to pass. Mystery virus kills thousands of seals in the North Sea.
The Arts	Films: *Amadeus, Ghostbusters, The Killing Fields, A Passage to India.* Pop: Prince *Purple Rain.*	Musicals: *Les Misérables, Big River.* Plays: *Neil Simon Biloxi Blues.* Films: *The Purple Rose of Cairo, Witness.* Pop: Live Aid concerts organized by Bob Geldorf raise £42 million for famine relief. Madonna *Like a Virgin.*	Plays: Michael Frayn *Benefactors*, Neil Simon *Broadway Bound.* Films: *Crocodile Dundee, Top Gun, A Room With a View.* Pop: Madonna *True Blue*, the Rolling Stones *Harlem Shuffle.*	Films: *Radio Days, Empire of the Sun.* Pop: Whitney Houston *Whitney*, Michael Jackson *Bad.*	Films: *Fatal Attraction, Crocodile Dundee II, Three Men and a Baby, The Last Temptation of Christ.* Pop: Yazz/Plastic Population *The Only Way is Up*, Kylie Minogue *I Should Be So Lucky*, Cliff Richard *Mistletoe and Wine.*

INDEX

Datechart entries are indicated by the date column in which they appear; main text entries are indicated in **bold** type; illustrations are shown in *italic*. A minus sign denotes BC next to a single date.

ACKNOWLEDGEMENTS

The editor thanks the following photographers, agencies, galleries, museums and other establishments for their help in supplying photographs for this book.

The editor also wishes to thank Penguin Books Ltd, 536 King's Road, London SW10 for permission to reproduce the four small maps on page 169 illustrating the Marne campaign, which were originally drawn by David Woodroffe for Colin McEvedy's *Penguin Atlas of Recent History*.

Front cover Robert Harding; Back cover British Museum; 12 bottom ZEFA; 13 left Picturepoint, right Hirmer Foto-archive; 14 top left and right Michael Holford, bottom R. Sheridan; 17 top centre Picturepoint, top right R. Sheridan, bottom right Michael Holford; 18 top and bottom Michael Holford; 21 Michael Holford; 22 British Museum; 23 bottom Michael Holford; 24 R. Sheridan; 27 top R. Sheridan, centre Scala; 28 top E.T. Archive, bottom ZEFA; 31 top Michael Holford, bottom left ZEFA, bottom right Sonia Halliday; 32 top ZEFA, bottom left and right Scala; 35 top Michael Holford, bottom left ZEFA, bottom right Scala; 36 top Scala, bottom Sonia Halliday; 39 centre Scala, bottom Mansell Collection; 40 top left Michael Holford, top right and bottom R. Sheridan; 43 top left Michael Holford, top right MEPhA; 44 top left E.T. Archive, top right ZEFA, bottom Picturepoint; 47 top right Copyright University Museum of National Antiquities, Oslo, Norway, bottom Picturepoint; 48 R. Sheridan; 49 Mansell Collection; 51 bottom left ZEFA, bottom right MEPhA; 52 top The BBC Hulton Picture Library, centre Bodleian Library, Oxford, bottom Michael Holford; 55 top right Michael Holford, bottom R. Sheridan; 56 left E.T. Archive, right Courtesy of the Smithsonian Institution, Freer Gallery of Art, Washington D.C.; 57 left SACU, right E.T. Archive; 58 Giraudon; 59 Giraudon; 60 top Collection of the National Palace Museum Taiwan, Republic of China; 62 The BBC Hulton Picture Library; 63 left ZEFA, right Mansell Collection; 64 Scala; 65 left The BBC Hulton Picture Library, right Sonia Halliday; 67 top right Picturepoint, bottom right The BBC Hulton Picture Library; 69 top left Bernisches Historisches Museum, top right R. Sheridan; 71 Scala; 73 top left Sonia Halliday, top right The BBC Hulton Picture Library, bottom right Sonia Halliday; 75 top right Mansell Collection; 76 Mary Evans Picture Library; 77 The BBC Hulton Picture Library; 78 top right National Maritime Museum, bottom The BBC Hulton Picture Library; 81 top Picturepoint, bottom left and right Michael Holford; 82 bottom Scala; 85 top British Museum, centre left Michael Holford, bottom Fotomas; 86 top right Ann Ronan Picture Library, bottom Mary Evans Picture Library; 89 top left Fotomas, top right British Museum, bottom Mansell Collection; 90 top left Fotomas, top right and bottom Mansell Collection; 92 The Trustees of the Portsmouth Estates; 94 The National Gallery, London; 95 Rijksmuseum, Amsterdam; 96 Mansell Collection; 98 The BBC Hulton Picture Library; 99 Scala; 101 Mansell Collection; 102 Mansell Collection; 103 Mansell Collection; 104 The BBC Hulton Picture Library; 105 Michael Holford; 106 The BBC Hulton Picture Library; 107 Mary Evans Picture Library; 109 Ullstein Bilderdienst; 110 top right Mansell Collection, bottom The BBC Hulton Picture Library; 113 top Wurzburg Residenz, bottom The BBC Hulton Picture Library; 114–115 Fotomas; 116 top left India Office Library, bottom E. T. Archive; 119 top Michael Holford; centre Mansell Collection; 121 top Library of Congress, bottom Courtesy of the Connecticut Historical Society; 122 Lauros-Giraudon, right The BBC Hulton Picture Library; 125 centre The BBC Hulton Picture Library; bottom Michael Holford; 129 top left and centre The BBC Hulton Picture Library, top right Giraudon, bottom Picturepoint; 130 top left and right Mansell Collection, bottom Picturepoint; 133 top The BBC Hulton Picture Library, bottom right Mansell Collection; 134 top right Mansell Collection, bottom Telarci-Giraudon; 137 Fotomas; 139 Mary Evans Picture Library; 141 top right Giraudon; 142 Mansell Collection; 145 Mansell Collection; 149 top The BBC Hulton Picture Library, bottom Mansell Collection; 150 top The BBC Hulton Picture Library, bottom Mansell Collection; 153 The BBC Hulton Picture Library; 155 The BBC Hulton Picture Library; 157 Mansell Collection; 159 The BBC Hulton Picture Library; 161 centre The BBC Hulton Picture Library, bottom Michael Holford; 162 Picturepoint; 163 Mansell Collection; 165 The BBC Hulton Picture Library; 167 The Ford Motor Company; 168 The BBC Hulton Picture Library; 169 The BBC Hulton Picture Library; 170 top The BBC Hulton Picture Library, centre Novosti, bottom Keystone; 173 top The BBC Hulton Picture Library, bottom left Picturepoint; 174 top Frank Driggs Collection, centre right and bottom Kobal Collection; 177 The BBC Hulton Picture Library; 178 top left Keystone, top centre Ullstein Bilderdienst, top right Picturepoint, bottom The BBC Hulton Picture Library; 181 top and centre left Keystone, centre right Ullstein Bilderdienst; 182 top Keystone, bottom left Picturepoint, bottom right Keystone; 185 left The BBC Hulton Picture Library, right Keystone; 186 top left Ullstein Bilderdienst, top right Keystone, bottom The BBC Hulton Picture Library; 189 Keystone; 190 left Keystone, right Mobil; 193 NASA; 194 top ZEFA, bottom left Keystone, bottom right Picturepoint; 197 top left Marconi, top right Ferranti, bottom Ferranti.